ENOCH AND THE MOSAIC T

ENOCH AND THE MOSAIC TORAH

The Evidence of Jubilees

Edited by

Gabriele Boccaccini *&* Giovanni Ibba

with the collaboration of

Jason von Ehrenkrook, James Waddell, and Jason Zurawski

WILLIAM B. EERDMANS PUBLISHING COMPANY
GRAND RAPIDS, MICHIGAN / CAMBRIDGE, U.K.

© 2009 William B. Eerdmans Publishing Company

All rights reserved

Published 2009 by

Wm. B. Eerdmans Publishing Co.

2140 Oak Industrial Drive N.E., Grand Rapids, Michigan 49505 /

P.O. Box 163, Cambridge CB3 9PU U.K.

Printed in the United States of America

14 13 12 11 10 09   7 6 5 4 3 2 1

Library of Congress Cataloging-in-Publication Data

Enoch and the mosaic Torah: the evidence of Jubilees /
   edited by Gabriele Boccaccini & Giovanni Ibba;
   with the collaboration of Jason von Ehrenkrook,
   James Waddell, and Jason Zurawski.
        p.   cm.
Includes bibliographical references and index.
ISBN 978-0-8028-6409-3 (pbk.: alk. paper)
1. Book of Jubilees — Criticism, interpretation, etc. — Congresses.
2. Enoch Seminar (2nd : 2003: Venice, Italy).   I. Boccaccini, Gabriele, 1958-
II. Ibba, Giovanni, 1962-   III. Ehrenkrook, Jason von.
IV. Waddell, James, 1938-   V. Zurawski, Jason.

BS1830.J8E56 2009
229'.911 — dc22
                                                        2009013095

www.eerdmans.com

Contents

Contents

PART TWO: THE MELTING OF MOSAIC AND
            ENOCHIC TRADITIONS

Contents

Abbreviations

AB	Anchor Bible
ABD	*Anchor Bible Dictionary*
AGJU	Arbeiten zur Geschichte des antiken Judentums und des Urchristentums
AION	*Annali dell'Istituto Orientale di Napoli*
AJEC	Ancient Judaism and Early Christianity
AJSL	*American Journal of Semitic Languages and Literatures*
ALD	Aramaic Levi Document
ANRW	*Aufstieg und Niedergang der römischen Welt*
Ant	Josephus, *Antiquities*
AOAT	Alter Orient und Altes Testament
AOS	American Oriental Series
APAT	*Die Apokryphen und Pseudepigraphen des Alten Testaments*
APOT	*The Apocrypha and Pseudepigrapha of the Old Testament.* Edited by R. H. Charles. 2 vols. Oxford, 1913
ASTI	*Annual of the Swedish Theological Institute*
ATANT	Abhandlungen zur Theologie des Alten und Neuen Testaments
AUSS	*Andrews University Seminary Studies*
b.	Babylonian Talmud
BASOR	*Bulletin of the American Schools of Oriental Research*
BASP	*Bulletin of the American Society of Papyrologists*
BBB	Bonner biblische Beiträge

BEATAJ	Beiträge zur Erforschung des Alten Testaments und des antiken Judentum
BETL	Bibliotheca ephemeridum theologicarum lovaniensium
Bib	*Biblica*
BibOr	Biblica et orientalia
BJS	Brown Judaic Studies
BN	*Biblische Notizen*
BSac	*Bibliotheca sacra*
BZAW	Beihefte zur Zeitschrift für die alttestamentliche Wissenschaft
CBQ	*Catholic Biblical Quarterly*
CBQMS	Catholic Biblical Quarterly–Monograph Series
CCWJCW	Cambridge Commentaries on Writings of the Jewish and Christian World
CEJL	Commentaries on Early Jewish Literature
ConBNT	Coniectanea biblica: New Testament Series
CSCO	Corpus scriptorum christianorum orientalium
DBSup	*Dictionnaire de la Bible: Supplément*
DJD	Discoveries in the Judaean Desert
DSD	*Dead Sea Discoveries*
EDSS	*Encyclopedia of the Dead Sea Scrolls.* Edited by L. H. Schiffman and J. C. VanderKam. Oxford, 2000
EgT	*Eglise et théologie*
EncJud	*Encyclopaedia Judaica*
ErIsr	*Eretz-Israel*
EstBib	*Estudios bíblicos*
ET	English translation
FJMB	Forschungsstelle Judentum Mitteilungen und Beiträge
GTS	Grazer theologische Studien
HAR	*Hebrew Annual Review*
Hen	*Henoch*
HeyJ	*Heythrop Journal*
HSM	Harvard Semitic Monographs
HSS	Harvard Semitic Studies
HTR	*Harvard Theological Review*
HTS	Harvard Theological Studies
HUCA	*Hebrew Union College Annual*
IDB	*The Interpreter's Dictionary of the Bible*
IEJ	*Israel Exploration Journal*

IJA	*International Journal of Apocrypha*
Int	*Interpretation*
JA	*Journal asiatique*
JAAR	*Journal of the American Academy of Religion*
JBL	*Journal of Biblical Literature*
JE	*The Jewish Encyclopedia.* Edited by I. Singer. 12 vols. New York, 1925
JJS	*Journal of Jewish Studies*
JNES	*Journal of Near Eastern Studies*
JQR	*Jewish Quarterly Review*
JSHRZ	*Jüdische Schriften aus hellenistisch-römischer Zeit*
JSJ	*Journal for the Study of Judaism*
JSJSup	Journal for the Study of Judaism Supplement Series
JSOT	*Journal for the Study of the Old Testament*
JSOTSup	Journal for the Study of the Old Testament–Supplement Series
JSP	*Journal for the Study of the Pseudepigrapha*
JSPSup	Journal for the Study of the Pseudepigrapha Supplements
JSQ	*Jewish Studies Quarterly*
JSS	*Journal of Semitic Studies*
JTS	*Journal of Theological Studies*
LCL	Loeb Classical Library
LJPSTT	Literature of the Jewish People in the Period of the Second Temple and the Talmud
LUOSMS	Leeds University Oriental Society Monograph Series
LXX	Septuagint
m.	Mishnah
MGWJ	*Monatsschrift für Geschichte und Wissenschaft des Judentums*
MT	Masoretic Text
NHS	Nag Hammadi Studies
NIDB	*New International Dictionary of the Bible*
NTL	New Testament Library
NTOA	Novum Testamentum et Orbis Antiquus
NTS	*New Testament Studies*
OBO	Orbis biblicus et orientalis
OLP	Orientalia Lovaniensia Periodica
Or	*Orientalia*
OrChr	*Oriens christianus*
OTL	Old Testament Library

OTP	*The Old Testament Pseudepigrapha.* Edited by James H. Charlesworth. 2 vols. Garden City, N.Y.: Doubleday, 1983, 1985
OtSt	Oudtestamentische Studiën
PAAJR	*Proceedings of the American Academy of Jewish Research*
PVTG	Pseudepigrapha Veteris Testamenti graece
RAC	*Reallexikon für Antike und Christentum*
RB	*Revue biblique*
REJ	*Revue des études juives*
RevQ	*Revue de Qumran*
RHPR	*Revue d'histoire et de philosophie religieuses*
RHR	*Revue de l'histoire des religions*
RivB	*Rivista biblica italiana*
RSR	*Recherches de science religieuse*
RStB	*Ricerche storico bibliche*
SAOC	Studies in Ancient Oriental Civilizations
SBLEJL	Society of Biblical Literature Early Judaism and Its Literature
SBLSBS	Society of Biblical Literature Sources for Biblical Study
SBLSP	Society of Biblical Literature Seminary Papers
SBLSymS	Society of Biblical Literature Symposium Series
SBLTT	Society of Biblical Literature Texts and Translations
SC	Sources chrétiennes
SCS	Septuagint and Cognate Studies
SEÅ	*Svensk exegetisk årsbok*
SJLA	Studies in Judaism in Late Antiquity
SJOT	*Scandinavian Journal of the Old Testament*
SNTSMS	Society for New Testament Studies Monograph Series
SP	Samaritan Pentateuch
SPB	Studia postbiblica
STAR	Studies in Theology and Religion
STDJ	Studies on the Texts of the Desert of Judah
StPB	Studia post-biblica
SVTP	Studia in Veteris Testamenti pseudepigraphica
TRu	*Theologische Rundschau*
TSAJ	Texte und Studien zum antiken Judentum
TSK	*Theologische Studien und Kritiken*
TUGAL	Texte und Untersuchungen zur Geschichte der altchristlichen Literatur

VT	*Vetus Testamentum*
VTSup	Vetus Testamentum, Supplements
WMANT	Wissenschaftliche Monographien zum Alten und Neuen Testament
WUNT	Wissenschaftliche Untersuchungen zum Neuen Testament
y.	Jerusalem Talmud
ZA	*Zeitschrift für Assyriologie*
ZABR	*Zeitschrift für altorientalische und biblische Rechtsgeschichte*
ZAW	*Zeitschrift für die alttestamentliche Wissenschaft*
ZDMG	*Zeitschrift der deutschen morgenländischen Gesellschaft*
ZDPV	*Zeitschrift des deutschen Palästina-Vereins*
ZRGG	*Zeitschrift für Religions- und Geistesgeschichte*
ZS	*Zeitschrift für Semitistik und verwandte Gebiete*
ZWT	*Zeitschrift für wissenschaftliche Theologie*

Preface: The Enigma of Jubilees and the Lesson of the Enoch Seminar

Gabriele Boccaccini

The early Enoch literature does not contain any reference to the Mosaic Torah and does not emphasize the distinctively Mosaic laws designed for Israel. At the time of the Maccabean revolt, the book of Dream Visions relates the ascent of Moses to Mount Sinai but conspicuously omits either the making of a covenant or the giving of the law. By contrast, Jubilees gives room to both Mosaic and Enochic traditions within the Sinaitic revelatory framework.

What should we make of such differences? Was the omission of any reference to the Mosaic Torah in the early Enoch tradition purely accidental, an unwanted consequence of the mystical literary genre or interests of the text? Or does it reflect the reality of an ancient form of Judaism that developed apart from, or even against, the Mosaic Torah? Does the book of Jubilees witness to the emergence of a new synthesis of Enochic and Mosaic traditions, or does it testify to the mystical interests of the very same elites that cherished the Mosaic Torah? Had the book of Jubilees anything to do with the emergence of the Essene movement and of the Qumran community? If so, then to which extent?

All these questions were at the core of the Fourth Enoch Seminar at Camaldoli (8-12 July 2007). The meeting marks the largest conference of international specialists ever gathered to study the book of Jubilees, and possibly to address any Old Testament Pseudepigrapha. With James VanderKam, Jacques van Ruiten, and George Nickelsburg were virtually all the major specialists in the document, eighty-four scholars from seventeen countries

(Australia, Canada, Denmark, Ethiopia, Finland, France, Germany, Hungary, Israel, Italy, the Netherlands, Norway, Poland, South Africa, the United Kingdom, the United States of America, and the Vatican), veterans or newcomers of the Enoch Seminar, who for the occasion were asked to contribute to our understanding of the document in its original historical and literary context.

An impressive number of twenty-eight papers (those here published) were submitted and circulated in advance. They were discussed at Camaldoli in plenary sessions and small groups, and then revised for publication. In addition, nineteen short papers were presented. Edited by Pierpaolo Bertalotto and Todd Hanneken, they have been published separately in a companion issue of the journal *Henoch* (vol. 31, no. 1, 2009).

Special thanks go to all the distinguished specialists for contributing to this volume, to Giovanni Ibba (University of Siena) for his expert support in the editing process with the precious assistance of Jason von Ehrenkrook, James Waddell, and Jason Zurawski, to J. Harold Ellens, Todd Hanneken, and Isaac Oliver for their hard and skillful work as secretaries of the Enoch Seminar, to the Department of Near Eastern Studies of the University of Michigan and to the Michigan Center for Early Christian Studies for their loyal and generous sponsorship, and last but not least, to Eerdmans for producing this third volume in collaboration with the Enoch Seminar, following *Enoch and Qumran Origins: New Light on a Forgotten Connection* (2005) and *Enoch and the Messiah Son of Man: Revisiting the Book of Parables* (2007).

As in the previous meetings of the Enoch Seminar (Florence 2001, Venice 2003, and Camaldoli 2005), the debate at Camaldoli 2007 could not avoid repeatedly returning to the very same question: "How distinctive was Enochic Judaism?" John J. Collins, one of the leaders of the Enoch Seminar, recently addressed the question in an article in *Meghillot: Studies in the Dead Sea Scrolls V-VI; A Festschrift for Devorah Dimant*, edited by M. Bar-Asher and E. Tov (Haifa: University of Haifa; Jerusalem: Bialik Institute, 2007), *17-*34. While concluding that indeed "Enochic Judaism reflects a distinctive form of Judaism in the late third/early second period" (*33), Collins highlighted the major points of controversy among second temple specialists. What was Enochic Judaism: a militant opposition party, a competing form of Judaism, or a mystical school whose frame of interest was simply something other than the Mosaic Torah? Were the authors of this literature "dissident priests" or something else? The uncertainties that surround the definition of Enochic Judaism affect and complicate its relation with Jubilees and the sectarian documents of Qumran. The latter look clearly more "Mosaic" than Enochic, even though "there is no doubt that the Enochic writings helped shape the worldview of that sect" (*33).

Since its scholarly revival in the mid–nineteenth century when August Dillmann published the first modern translation in German and the first critical edition of the Ethiopic text (Dillmann 1851, 1859), the emphasis given to its Mosaic or Enochic elements led scholars to assign Jubilees either to the Pharisees (Rönsch 1871; Charles 1899) or to the Essenes (Jellinek 1855) or to Enoch circles (Albeck 1930). The discovery and publication, in the mid–nineteenth century, of the Hebrew fragments at Qumran settled the question of the original language of the document and made much more likely the association of Jubilees with the Essenes and their calendar (Jaubert 1953, 1957), but did not solve the mystery of the origin of the document. The understanding was that Jubilees testified to an early stage in the history of the Essene movement (Testuz 1960) and represented an early example of rewritten Bible (Vermes 1961).

The contemporary study of Jubilees began in the late 1970s with the studies of James VanderKam, who, while confirming the association of the document with the Essenes, began exploring its relation with the Enoch literature (VanderKam 1977, 1978). The contribution of the Groningen Hypothesis and the Enochic-Essene Hypothesis further complicated the picture as they challenged the identification between Qumran and the rest of the Essene movement and suggested a closer relation of Jubilees with non-Qumran Essenes (Boccaccini 2005). If Enochic Judaism was "the parent of the Essene movement and the grandparent of the Qumran Community," then the presectarian book of Jubilees should be seen as evidence of the transition between Enoch and Qumran.

At Camaldoli 2007 at least four tendencies emerged. Some claimed that Jubilees was a direct product of Enochic Judaism with some Mosaic influence — Mosaic features were simply subordinated to Enoch ideology. Some suggested that Jubilees was a conscious synthesis of Enochic and Mosaic tradition, yet remaining autonomous from both. Some asserted that Jubilees was essentially a Mosaic text with some Enochic influence — in the confrontation it was Moses who prevailed. Finally, some questioned the very existence of a gulf between Enochic and Mosaic traditions as competing forms of Judaism at the time of Jubilees.

In the best tradition of the Enoch Seminars, no attempt was made to reach any agreement or compromise; the goal was to let any voice be heard and carefully considered in an open forum context. Hence, readers should not expect to find here any shared solution to the Jubilees enigma. What they will find in this volume is not a new coherent view of Jubilees sponsored by the Enoch Seminar, but rather a lively debate among the most distinguished international specialists, each struggling for a better understanding of a document whose Enochic and Mosaic elements seem to make it fit poorly in any ancient or modern categories.

Yet the Enoch Seminar is much more than a neutral forum, where problems are conveniently exposed in all their nuances and perhaps made more intriguing by the competing solutions offered by different authors. We do not share the answers but we all have come to agree that the key for understanding the mysteries of second temple Jewish thought cannot be found within the manageable boundaries of our own specialization alone, but only through a mutually enriching experience of listening and comprehending the achievements of one another.

Since its emergence in the sixteenth century, the field of Second Temple Judaism and Christian Origins has been constantly on the verge of collapsing into the plurality of its subfields. In the past it was largely religious concerns that created a clear separation between Christian and Jewish studies and relegated the noncanonical literature to a subordinate status. Now the problem seems to be primarily the high degree of specialization required to master one subject or one body of literature, and the contemporaneous process of democratization and globalization of knowledge that has multiplied the bibliography into an untamable monster. As a result, the fragmentation of second temple Jewish studies has become endemic and scholars of the field often appear reluctant to cross boundaries and venture into another's domain.

The international scholars who have joined the Enoch Seminar do not resign themselves, and restrict their dreams, to the goal of finding a comfortable niche for themselves. The experience of the Enoch Seminar has proved to us the validity of the method of analysis that tears down the misleading walls of separation that still divide our field of research, and counterbalances the current fragmentation of the field, in its many subfields of specialization, by recovering the unity and integrity of the period. In our view Enoch has become much more than the hero of "Enochic Judaism." He has become the symbol of our intercanonical and interdisciplinary effort, as he is present in each and all of the canons and subfields that anachronistically divide the sources and the scholarship of the period: Old Testament, Apocrypha, Pseudepigrapha, Dead Sea Scrolls, Jewish-Hellenistic literature, New Testament, apostolic fathers, and the like.

In this perspective the 2007 Camaldoli meeting has marked a fundamental step in the life of the Enoch Seminar with the decision by the participants to provide more structured governance and a consistent plan for the development of the field of Second Temple Judaism and Christian Origins in the years to come. Hanan Eshel (Bar-Ilan University) and Loren Stuckenbruck (Durham University) have joined the founding director Gabriele Boccaccini (University of Michigan) as the vice-directors of the Enoch Seminar. Future meetings are now planned four years in advance under the responsibility of a chair (Andrei Orlov in 2009; Matthias Henze in 2011 . . .), and a parallel series of biennial graduate conferences has been successfully launched (the Enoch Graduate Seminars — Ann Arbor 2006; Princeton 2008; Budapest 2010; Notre Dame 2012 . . .). Far from being a gathering of Enoch specialists or "believers" in Enochic Judaism, the group is now expanding its activities to the entire field of Second Temple Judaism and Christian Origins.

The best piece of evidence of the coming of age of the Enoch Seminar is the creation of the new Web site (www.enochseminar.org), beautifully designed by Pierpaolo Bertalotto (University of Michigan). As a synthesis of our past accomplishments and future plans, the Web site provides not only detailed information about the meetings of the Enoch Seminar and of the Enoch Graduate Seminar, but also a general picture of the status of studies in Second Temple Judaism and Christian Origins. The "International Scholarship" page includes a comprehensive directory of specialists who are currently working in the field, country by country. Secondly, it gives biographical and bibliographical information on the history of research in the field from the time of the invention of the press (late fifteenth century) to the present. Thirdly, it offers a selection, decade by decade, of the most influential books published in the field, with special emphasis on the latest titles. Finally, it gives a list of the major works of art (paintings, dramas, operas, novels, movies, and the like) that offer a fictionalized account of characters and events from the second temple period. All this information is not available anywhere else, yet this is the historical memory that is the foundation, the rock, on which alone a solid house can be built. The Web site has effectively opened a third "space" besides the Enoch Seminar and the Enoch Graduate Seminar — a virtual space in comparison to that offered by the meetings, yet no less real, where all specialists and students of the field can meet and share their work and learn of each other, breaking national and specialization boundaries without abandoning or betraying those boundaries.

At Camaldoli (and with this volume) we scholars of the period might not have solved all the enigmas of Jubilees, but we have found in the process a comfortable house for our investigations and a renewed sense of purpose, unity, and mutual commitment for the years to come.

List of Participants (Camaldoli 2007):

1. Luca Arcari, University of Naples, Italy
2. Daniel Assefa, Capuchin Franciscan Institute, Ethiopia
3. Christophe Batsch, University of Lille, France
4. Albert Baumgarten, Bar-Ilan University, Israel
5. Kelley Coblentz Bautch, St. Edward's University, USA
6. Andreas Bedenbender, Dortmund, Germany
7. Jonathan Ben-Dov, University of Haifa, Israel
8. John S. Bergsma, Franciscan University of Steubenville, USA
9. Christoph Berner, Georg-August-Universität Göttingen, Germany
10. Pierpaolo Bertalotto, University of Bari, Italy
11. Katell Berthelot, CNRS, France
12. Siam Bhayro, University of Cambridge, England
13. Gabriele Boccaccini, University of Michigan, USA
14. Darrell Bock, Dallas Theological Seminary, USA
15. Gianantonio Borgonovo, Catholic University of Milan, Italy
16. Daniel Boyarin, University of California at Berkeley, USA
17. James H. Charlesworth, Princeton Theological Seminary, USA
18. Calum Carmichael, Cornell University, USA
19. Esther Chazon, Hebrew University of Jerusalem, Israel
20. Michael Daise, William and Mary College, USA
21. Gene Davenport, Lambuth University, USA
22. Michael Davis, Princeton Theological Seminary, USA
23. Marcello Del Verme, University of Naples, Italy
24. Karoly Dobos, Catholic University of Budapest, Hungary
25. Lutz Doering, King's College London, England
26. Henryk Drawnel, Catholic University of Lublin, Poland
27. Torleif Elgvin, Lutheran Theological Seminary, Norway
28. John C. Endres, Jesuit School of Theology at Berkeley, USA
29. Esther Eshel, Bar-Ilan University, Israel
30. Hanan Eshel, Bar-Ilan University, Israel
31. Daniel Falk, University of Oregon, USA
32. Crispin Fletcher-Louis, St. Mary's London, England
33. Ida Fröhlich, Catholic University of Budapest, Hungary
34. Claudio Gianotto, University of Turin, Italy

35. Charles Gieschen, Concordia Theological Seminary, USA
36. William K. Gilders, Emory University, USA
37. Lester L. Grabbe, University of Hull, England
38. Maxine Grossman, University of Maryland, USA
39. Betsy Halpern-Amaru, emeritus, Vassar College, USA
40. Matthias Henze, Rice University, USA
41. Martha Himmelfarb, Princeton University, USA
42. Jamal-Dominique Hopkins, Crichton College, USA
43. Giovanni Ibba, University of Siena, Italy
44. David Jackson, University of Sydney, Australia
45. Jutta Jokiranta, University of Helsinki, Finland
46. Robert A. Kraft, University of Pennsylvania, USA
47. Helge S. Kvanvig, University of Oslo, Norway
48. Erik Larson, Florida International University, USA
49. William Loader, Murdoch University, Australia
50. Grant Macaskill, St. Andrews University, Scotland
51. Luca Mazzinghi, Central Italy Theological Seminary, Italy
52. Hindy Najman, University of Toronto, Canada
53. George W. E. Nickelsburg, emeritus, University of Iowa, USA
54. Bilhah Nitzan, emeritus, Tel-Aviv University, Israel
55. Eric Noffke, Valdensian Faculty of Theology, Italy
56. Daniel Olson, D&J Scott Publishing, USA
57. Andrei A. Orlov, Marquette University, USA
58. Dorothy Peters, Trinity Western University, Canada
59. Anders Klostergaard Petersen, University of Aarhus, Denmark
60. Claire Pfann, University of the Holy Land, Israel
61. Stephen Pfann, University of the Holy Land, Israel
62. Pierluigi Piovanelli, University of Ottawa, Canada
63. Annette Yoshiko Reed, McMaster University, Canada
64. Eyal Regev, Bar-Ilan University, Israel
65. Jacques van Ruiten, University of Groningen, Netherlands
66. Paolo Sacchi, emeritus, University of Turin, Italy
67. Stephane Saulnier, Newman Theological College, Edmonton, Canada
68. Lawrence H. Schiffman, New York University, USA
69. James M. Scott, Trinity Western University, Canada
70. Michael Segal, Hebrew University of Jerusalem, Israel
71. Aharon Shemesh, Bar-Ilan University, Israel
72. Joseph Sievers, Pontifical Biblical Institute, Vatican City
73. Daniel Stökl Ben-Ezra, CNRS, France

74. Loren T. Stuckenbruck, Durham University, England
75. David W. Suter, St. Martin's University, USA
76. Shemaryahu Talmon, emeritus, Hebrew University of Jerusalem, Israel
77. Sam Thomas, California Lutheran University, USA
78. Cristiana Tretti, Milan, Italy
79. James C. VanderKam, University of Notre Dame, USA
80. Pieter Venter, University of Pretoria, South Africa
81. Ralph Williams, University of Michigan, USA
82. Benjamin Wold, University of Tübingen, Germany
83. Benjamin Wright, Lehigh University, USA
84. Azzan Yadin, Rutgers University, USA

Secretaries

1. J. Harold Ellens, University of Michigan, USA
2. Todd Hanneken, University of Notre Dame, USA
3. Isaac W. Oliver, University of Michigan, USA

PART ONE

JUBILEES AND ITS LITERARY CONTEXT

The Manuscript Tradition of Jubilees

James C. VanderKam

The book of Jubilees began its modern life as an object of study by Western scholars when copies of the work were found in Ethiopia and brought to Europe in the 1840s. Since that time a large number of copies in Geʿez have been identified and photographed, and fragmentary evidence for the text of the book in Hebrew, Greek, Latin, and Syriac has come to light. Actually, much of the Greek evidence had been available for a long time: in the 1720s Johann Fabricius had collected citations from Jubilees in Greek and Latin in his *Codex Pseudepigraphus Veteris Testamenti.*[1] Today there are more such passages available than the ones Fabricius had assembled.

In this paper I will present a report detailing all the textual sources for the book of which I am aware and a short analysis of them. The presentation will follow a chronological order. For clarity's sake, the early history of the text and the evidence for it can be summarized briefly in these five statements:

> Jubilees was written in Hebrew (extant evidence: fourteen mss. from Qumran).
> Jubilees may have been translated from Hebrew into Syriac (excerpts, no ms. copies).
> Jubilees was translated from Hebrew into Greek (excerpts, no ms. copies).

---

1. The two-volume work appeared in 1722-23 (Hamburg: T. C. Felginer). The Jubilees citations may be found in 1:849-64; 2:120-22.

Jubilees was translated from Greek into Latin (one partially preserved copy).

Jubilees was translated from Greek into Ethiopic (nearly thirty copies).

I. Hebrew

The earliest mention of a Hebrew form of the book of Jubilees is found in CD 16:2-4, an identification that I maintain despite Devorah Dimant's recent rejection of it.[2] The text, after mentioning the Torah of Moses in which everything is precisely defined (מדוקדק), refers the reader to another work for "the interpretation of their times for the blindness of Israel regarding all these things" and cites a title for it: ספר מחלקות העתים ליובליהם ובשבועותיהם. In it too the matter in question receives precise definition (מדוקדק). The reading of CD 16:2-4 is now documented in part by 4Q270 6 ii 17 and 4Q271 4 ii 5.[3] A very similar wording of a title is found in three places at and near the beginning of Jubilees.

> Prologue: "These are the words regarding the divisions of the times of the law and of the testimony, of the events of the years, of the weeks of their jubilees"[4]
>
> 1:4 "He related to him the divisions of all the times — both of the law and of the testimony"
>
> מ[חלקות]הע[ע]תים לתור[ה] :4Q216 1.11
>
> 1:26 ". . . the divisions of time which are in the law and which are in the testimony and in the weeks of their jubilees" (4Q216 4 4 preserves a couple of letters from the expression; cf. also 4Q217 frg. 2 1)

The caves from Qumran have yielded a goodly number of copies of Jubilees, all written in Hebrew, and coming from a range of dates. These are the securely identified copies, their contents, and their suggested paleographical dates.

2. D. Dimant, "Two 'Scientific' Fictions: The So-called Book of Noah and the Alleged Quotation of Jubilees in CD 16:3-4," in *Studies in the Hebrew Bible, Qumran, and the Septuagint Presented to Eugene Ulrich*, ed. P. Flint, E. Tov, and J. VanderKam, VTSup 101 (Leiden: Brill, 2006), 242-48.

3. J. Baumgarten, *Qumran Cave 4.XIII: The Damascus Document (4Q266-273)*, DJD 18 (Oxford: Clarendon, 1996), 156, 178.

4. Translations of Jubilees are from my *The Book of Jubilees*, 2 vols., CSCO 510-11, Scriptores Aethiopici 87-88 (Louvain: Peeters, 1989), vol. 2.

Manuscript	Passage(s) Preserved	Paleographical Date
1Q17	27:19-20	early Herodian
1Q18	35:8-10	late Hasmonean[5]
2Q19	23:7-8	Herodian
2Q20	46:1-3	1st cent. C.E.
3Q5 3, 1	23:6-7, 12-13	1st cent. C.E.[6]
4Q176 19-21	23:21-23, 30-31	Herodian[7]
4Q216	Prologue, 1:1-2, 4-7, 7-15, 26-28; 2:1-4, 7-12, 13-24	125-100/ca. 50[8]
4Q218	2:26-27	early Herodian
4Q219	21:1-2, 7-10, 12-16, 18–22:1	late Hasmonean[9]
4Q220	21:5-10	early Herodian[10]
4Q221	21:22-24; 22:22, 30 (?); 23:10-13; 33:12-15; 37:11-15; 38:6-8; 39:4-9	late Hasmonean or early Herodian[11]
4Q222	25:9-12; 27:6-7; 48:5 (?)	late Hasmonean[12]

5. The Cave 1 fragments were published in D. Barthélemy and J. Milik, eds., *Qumran Cave 1*, DJD 1 (Oxford: Clarendon, 1955), 82-84 with pl. XVI.

6. The Cave 2 and 3 fragments were published in M. Baillet, J. Milik, and R. de Vaux, eds., *Les 'petites grottes' de Qumran*, DJD 3 (Oxford: Clarendon, 1962), 77-79, with pl. XV; and 96-98, with pl. XVIII. 3Q5 was originally presented in this volume as "une prophétie apocryphe" by the editor Baillet, but R. Deichgräber ("Fragmente einer Jubiläen-Handschrift aus Höhle 3 von Qumran," *RevQ* 5 [1964-66]: 415-22), A. Rofé ("Fragments from an Additional Manuscript of the Book of Jubilees in Qumran Cave 3" [in Hebrew], *Tarbiz* 34 [1965]: 333-36), and Baillet himself ("Remarques sur le manuscrit du Livre des Jubilés de la grotte 3 de Qumran," *RevQ* 5 [1964-66]: 423-33) soon recognized frgs. 1 and 3 as coming from Jub 23.

7. 4Q176 was published as "Tanḥûmîm" in J. Allegro, *Qumrân Cave 4 I (4Q158-4Q186)*, DJD 5 (Oxford: Clarendon, 1968), 60-67, with pls. XXII-XXIII. M. Kister later identified frgs. 19-21 as coming from Jubilees ("Newly-Identified Fragments of the Book of Jubilees: Jub 23:21-23, 30-31," *RevQ* 12 [1987]: 529-36).

8. For an earlier edition, see J. VanderKam and J. Milik, "The First *Jubilees* Manuscript from Qumran Cave 4: A Preliminary Publication," *JBL* 110 (1991): 243-70. Two dates are given because 4Q216 was copied by two scribes, with the outer sheet (containing the first columns) added to an older manuscript.

9. For an earlier edition, see VanderKam and Milik, "A Preliminary Publication of a Jubilees Manuscript from Qumran Cave 4: 4Qjub^d (4Q219)," *Bib* 73 (1992): 62-83.

10. For earlier editions of 4Q218 and 220, see VanderKam and Milik, "4Qjub^c (4Q218) and 4Qjub^e (4Q220): A Preliminary Edition," *Textus* 17 (1994): 43-56.

11. For an earlier edition, see VanderKam and Milik, "4Qjub^f: A Preliminary Edition," *HAR* 14 (1994): 233-61.

12. For an earlier edition, see VanderKam and Milik, "4Qjubilees^g (4Q222)," in *New*

James C. VanderKam

4Q223-24	32:18-21; 34:4-5; 35:7-22; 36:7-23;	late Hasmonean[13]
	37:17–38:13; 39:9–40:7; 41:7-10;	
	41:28 (?)	
11Q12	4:6-11, 13-14, 16-18 (?), 29-31; 5:1-2;	late Herodian
	12:15-17, 28-29[14]	(ca. 50 C.E.)

There are also some fragmentary Qumran texts that have been identified as coming from Jubilees but about which some skepticism is in order.

| 4Q217 | 1:29; 2:28-30(?) | Hasmonean (before |
| | | 50 B.C.E.) |

Joseph Milik identified 4Q217, a papyrus manuscript, as a copy of Jubilees and thought it contained the Hebrew text of Jub 1:29 (frg. 1); 1:29–2:1 (frg. 2), 2:28-30 (frg. 3), 1:24 (?; frg. 6), and 2:14 (?; frg. 7). If he were correct, we would have to posit substantial differences between the Hebrew and Ethiopic texts of Jubilees at this point. The identification is most uncertain, but it seems unlikely to me that the eleven surviving fragments from 4Q217 provide enough evidence to include it among the copies of Jubilees from Qumran.[15]

Qumran Texts and Studies — Proceedings of the First Meeting of the International Organization for Qumran Studies, Paris 1992, ed. G. Brooke and F. García Martínez, STDJ 15 (Leiden: Brill, 1994), 105-16.

13. The Cave 4 copies, other than 4Q176, were published in VanderKam and Milik, "Jubilees," in Qumran Cave 4.VIII: Parabiblical Texts, Part 1, DJD 13 (Oxford: Clarendon, 1994), 1-140, with pls. I-II, IV-IX.

14. The Cave 11 fragments were published in F. García Martínez, E. Tigchelaar, and A. van der Woude, eds., Manuscripts from Qumran Cave 11 (11Q2-18, 11Q20-30), DJD 23 (Oxford: Clarendon, 1997), 207-20, with pl. XXVI. For an earlier edition, see van der Woude, "Fragmente des Buches Jubiläen aus Qumran Höhle XI (11QJub)," in Tradition und Glaube: Das frühe Christentum in seiner Umwelt. Festgabe für Karl Georg Kuhn, ed. G. Jeremias, H. Kuhn, and H. Stegemann (Göttingen: Vandenhoeck & Ruprecht, 1972), 140-46, with pl. VIII. Milik subsequently placed some small fragments, "A propos de 11QJub," Bib 54 (1973): 77-78. See also García Martínez, "Texts from Cave 11," in The Dead Sea Scrolls: Forty Years of Research, ed. D. Dimant and U. Rappaport, STDJ 10 (Leiden: Brill, 1992), 23. Attention should be drawn to the editors' comments regarding 11Q21, published as 11Qtemple^c. They note that the physical appearance and layout are much like those of 11Q12, and the hand may be that of the scribe of 11Q12. However, they were not able to locate the fragments in the known text of Jubilees, while it does show some overlap with the Temple Scroll (411-14, with pl. XLVIII). In Textual and Historical Studies in the Book of Jubilees, HSM 14 (Missoula: Scholars Press, 1977), 18-101, I reedited the Hebrew fragments then available and compared their readings with the versional evidence.

15. For the edition, see DJD 13, 23-33, with pl. III.

4Q482   13:29 (or Gen 14:22-24); 36:9 (?)   Herodian[16]

There are eight small pieces grouped under 4Q482. Maurice Baillet debated whether frg. 1 corresponded with Jub 13:29 or with Gen 14:22-24. He was able to read twenty-four letters spread over five lines, with only one (uncertain) complete word (הם in line 3). If he has correctly read עליון in line 1, the possessive that he reconstructs partially in line 2 would not be very far distant from it, thus suggesting a rather short line, while the reference to *Mamre* that he finds in line 3 has a parallel only at a considerably greater distance in Jub 13:29. Nothing else matches the context in Jubilees. There is a similar problem with spacing in comparison with Gen 14:22-24. The piece probably has the text of neither Jub 13:29 nor Gen 14:22-24. For frg. 2 Baillet asked whether it held the text of Jub 36:9. It has ten letters distributed over three lines. It seems that the word יחרוש (which can mean "he will devise") made him think about Jub 36:9 where *yaxaššeš* (= he will seek) appears, as does "sky," which would correspond with שמים in line 2. But the verbs do not have the same meaning, and as a result there is nothing to identify the words on the fragment with Jub 36:9. Baillet was able to locate none of frgs. 3-8.

4Q483   Gen 1:28 (Jub 2:14?)   Herodian

The two tiny fragments preserve, respectively, little and nothing distinctive. The second has only one legible letter, but the first has eleven of them located on three lines. The word that made Baillet think the fragment could be from Jub 2:14 is what he reads as וכיבשוה, although he considered reading it as וכובשים. Jub 2:14 contains the assignment given to humanity to rule the earth (הארץ can be read on line 2). Yet, if a plural verbal form is properly read, it would not agree with Jub 2:14.[17]

4Q484   Mid-1st cent. C.E.

Baillet published under this number twenty fragments, the most productive of which offers five letters (frg. 1 ישׂשכר), three marked with a circlet

16. 4Q482 and 4Q483 were published by Baillet, *Qumrân Grotte 4.III*, DJD 7 (Oxford: Clarendon, 1982), 1-2, with pl. I. In neither case was he sure about the identification, as the alternative identifications and question marks that he supplied show.

17. Puech has now maintained that 4Q483 is a copy of Genesis ("Un nouveau manuscrit de la Genèse de la grotte 4: 4Q483 = pap4QGenèse°," *RevQ* 19, no. 74 [1999]: 259-60). That is, he agrees with Baillet's first suggestion for it.

and one with a dot (frg. 5 also has five letters but on two lines). So he searched for uses of "Issachar" in the literature and very tentatively suggested that 4Q484 was a Hebrew copy of the Testament of Judah. Apparently the presence of עדן in frg. 7 pointed more to the Testament of Judah (the word is used at 25:2) than to the Testament of Issachar. He also notes that the verb קום can be read on frg. 19, and it is presupposed in TJud 24:1 and perhaps v. 5.[18] Émile Puech later restudied the fragments while working on the edition of 4Q538 that Milik had identified as from a Testament of Judah. Puech revised some of Baillet's readings and determined that 4Q484 should be renamed 4Qjub[j].[19] He thought a *shin* or a *lamed* followed the name "Issachar" on frg. 1 (Baillet had indicated no additional letter) and thought it fit Jub 28:22 or 34:20. On either reading of a letter after "Issachar," the fragment would not match the Ethiopic wording in Jub 28:22 (*semo yessākor barabuʿu*), nor in 34:20 (*wa-semā la-beʾesita yessākor ḥēzaqā*). For frg. 2, where Baillet placed two midline dots on either side of אני, Puech reads ("certainement") טמאני ראובן as in Jub 33:7 (*ʾarkʷasani robēl*). The identification is possible but the reading is far from assured. The other fragments Puech must treat differently, as there is either no word or no context, but he does think Baillet's reading of עדן in frg. 7 is wrong; a better reading is מדן, a name found in Jub 19:12. As the name appears in Gen 25:2 as well, I do not think we have warrant for regarding 4Q484 as another copy of Jubilees.[20]

The Qumran fragmentary copies are not the only evidence for the Hebrew version of Jubilees, and there are also indications that Jubilees exercised a modest influence in later Hebrew literature.

As the editors and commentators have regularly noted, some midrashim embody expansions closely resembling ones in Jubilees. The following are especially noteworthy.

1. *The Book of Asaph* (or *The Book of Noah*): The first part of the text has close similarities with Jub 10:1-14, the story about the 90 percent reduction in the number of demons allowed to afflict the descendants of Noah. The text is available in A. Jellinek, *Bet ha-Midrash: Sammlung kleiner Midraschim und vermischter Abhandlungen aus der älteren jüdischen Literatur,*

---

18. DJD 7, 3, with pl. I.

19. Puech, "Une nouvelle copie du Livre des Jubilés 4Q484 = pap4QJubilés[j]," *RevQ* 19, no. 74 (1999): 261-64.

20. Puech ("Une nouvelle copie," 264 n. 7) also writes that identifying 4Q516 as a copy of Jubilees is not excluded, but the only evidence he cites is frg. 9 where Baillet read חרן, placing circlets above all three letters (DJD 7, 300). But Jubilees is only one of several works that mentions the name, and the reading is not certain.

3rd ed. (Leipzig: F. Nies, 1853; reprinted, Jerusalem: Wahrmann Books, 1967), third part, pp. 155-56. It begins: "This is the book of remedies that the first sages copied from the book of Shem, Noah's son, which was transmitted to Noah at Mt. Lubar, one of the mountains of Ararat, after the flood." While the first part of the short text looks very much like the section in Jubilees and thus can, in some places, be used in evaluating some details in the text,[21] *The Book of Asaph* does not constitute an extended quotation from Jubilees. The writer presents the story in a somewhat different order and lacks parts of it as it appears in Jubilees, for example, God's acceding to Mastema's request that he be allowed to retain one-tenth of the demons. The author of *The Book of Asaph* does not state the source for the story other than saying Noah received it.

2. *Midrash Wayyissā'û:* In the second half of the midrash, the war between Jacob and Esau is recounted in a way parallel with the story in Jub 37–38. Jellinek published this midrash as well in the third part of his *Bet ha-Midrash*, 1-5. The situation with *Midrash Wayyissā'û* is reminiscent of the one for *The Book of Asaph:* similar material is offered but the text reads far differently than the parallels in Jubilees. The first section of the midrash details Judah's wondrous military exploits against the king of Tappuach and others by his brothers and father. There are several points of contact (e.g., the names of cities) between it and Jub 34:2-9.[22]

There are traces of the influence of Jubilees elsewhere in Jewish literature. These show that, in some form, information from Jubilees continued to be of use to commentators on the text of Genesis and Exodus.[23]

In *Textual and Historical Studies in the Book of Jubilees,* I compared the readings of the Hebrew fragments that had been published at that time with the readings of the four Ethiopic manuscripts on which R. H. Charles had based his edition. I found that the best Ethiopic readings and the Hebrew

21. For examples, see VanderKam, *The Book of Jubilees,* 2:58-60. R. H. Charles reproduced the relevant part of *The Book of Noah* in his *Ethiopic Version of the Hebrew Book of Jubilees,* Anecdota oxoniensia (Oxford: Clarendon, 1895), appendix I:179. M. Himmelfarb translates the section in question and discusses it in "Some Echoes of *Jubilees* in Medieval Hebrew Literature," in *Tracing the Threads: Studies in the Vitality of Jewish Pseudepigrapha,* ed. J. Reeves, SBLEJL 6 (Atlanta: Scholars Press, 1994), 127-36.

22. Charles printed the latter half of the midrash as appendix II, 180-82, in his *Ethiopic Version of the Hebrew Book of Jubilees.* See also VanderKam, *Textual and Historical Studies,* 218-38.

23. For further information, see A. Epstein, "Le livre des Jubilés, Philon et le Midrasch Tadsché," *REJ* 21 (1890): 80-97; *REJ* 22 (1891): 1-25; Himmelfarb, "Some Echoes," 115-41.

ones corresponded very closely. Oddly enough, there are even cases where the Hebrew is defective and the Ethiopic has preserved the correct reading. Though the Hebrew base of that comparison was small, it provided evidence that the Ethiopic text of Jubilees is a careful rendering of the original text (via a Greek translation). Work with the Cave 4 copies that became available later has reinforced the conclusions drawn in that study, although there are indeed differences between the Hebrew and Ethiopic readings in a number of details. Another factor supporting the reliability of the Ethiopic version of Jubilees is the fact that the citations from Genesis and Exodus in the book have the characteristics of what Frank Cross called the Palestinian text-type of the Pentateuch or what we could call a text closely related to the type that lies at the base of the Samaritan recension.

II. Syriac

There may have been a Syriac translation of the book of Jubilees, possibly made from a Hebrew base. The evidence for a Syriac version is much like that for a Greek version: we have indirect evidence pointing toward such a conclusion but no manuscript of a Syriac translation. The surviving evidence is as follows:

1. The first text that raised the possibility that Jubilees had been translated into Syriac was BM Additional 12.154, folio 180 published by Antonio Maria Ceriani in 1861.[24] Because Jubilees' list of the names of the matriarchs seems to have been of such widespread interest, the text, which begins: "The names of the wives of the patriarchs according to the book which is called Jubilees among the Hebrews," is reproduced here:

> The name of Adam's wife was Eve;
> of the wife of Cain was 'Asawa.
> The name of Seth's wife was 'Azura, his sister,
> and of the wife of Enosh was Na'um, his sister;
> of Cainan Mahalalut, his sister;
> of Mahalala'el Dina, the daughter of his uncle;
> of Ya'ar [= Jared] Baraka, the daughter of his uncle;
> of Enoch 'Edni, the daughter of his uncle;

24. A. M. Ceriani, *Monumenta Sacra et Profana*, 2 vols. (Milan: Bibliotheca Ambrosiana, 1861), 2:ix-x.

of Methuselah 'Edna, the daughter of his uncle;
of Lamech 'Enushay, the daughter of his uncle.
The name of the wife of Noah 'Amizara, the daughter of his uncle;
of the wife of Shem Sedqatnebab;
of Ham Nahalmahuq;
of Japheth 'Adnatnashe.
The name of the wife of Arpachshad was Rusa, the daughter of
   Shushan;
of Cainan his son Malka, the daughter of Maday;
of Shelah his son Ma'aka, the daughter of his uncle;
of the wife of Eber 'Azura, the daughter of Nebrod;
of Peleg Mana, the daughter of Sana'ar. In the days of Peleg the tower
   was built; its height 5433 cubits, stadia.
The name of the wife of Ra'u was 'Arwa, the daughter of Ur;
of Serug Malka, the daughter of Keber his uncle;
of Nahor his son Isaqa, the daughter of Nastag the Chaldean;
of Terah 'Edna, the daughter of his uncle Abram. She gave birth to a
   son and named him Abram after the name of her father;
but of Abram, Isaac, and Jacob, the names of the wives are known;
but of the sons of Jacob: of Reuben 'Ada, of Simeon Ya'aka'a the
   Canaanitess; of Levi Malka from the daughters of Aram; of Judah
   Bat-shua' the Canaanitess; of Issachar 'Azaqa; of Zebulun 'Ednay;
   of Dan Tob-hagla; of Naphtali Rusha from Bet-Naharin; of Gad
   Ma'aqa; of Asher Yona; of Joseph Asnat; of Benjamin 'Asamana.
The name of the daughter of Pharaoh who was kind to Moses was
   Tarmutay.
But according to others Ra'usa.

Some Grecisms in the text (e.g., the spelling of Jubilees [*ywbly'*], *stadion*)
suggested the base might have been Greek. The possibility that Jubilees had
been translated into Syriac increased when a series of citations of the book
were isolated in a chronicle.

   2. Chronicle to the year 1234: This lengthy chronicle shows that writers in the Syriac tradition used Jubilees as did their Greek-writing col-
leagues to supplement Genesis and Exodus. In it there are citations of 137
verses in Jubilees and allusions to 8 others. E. Tisserant analyzed the citations and, basing his inference on the lack of Greek influence in them and
the fact that the author used only Syriac and Arabic sources, concluded that
they came from a Syriac translation of Jubilees made directly from the He-

brew Jubilees.[25] The inference is possible, but there are other ways of explaining the evidence.

III. Greek

There is solid reason for thinking that the book of Jubilees was translated from Hebrew into Greek, even though no copy of a Greek translation has been identified. As a result, one must use other kinds of arguments to establish the existence of the translation.

1. Ethiopic biblical literature was translated from Greek. As Jubilees is regularly included among the scriptural books of the Abyssinian church, it too would have come from a Greek model.

2. Clues in the Ethiopic text betray a Greek base for the translation. Besides transliterated Greek words and names spelled in their Greek forms, there are mistakes in the Ge'ez text that can be explained convincingly by positing a Greek *Vorlage* for the Ethiopic reading. One example recently suggested by William Gilders is in Jub 7:4: "he [Noah] put some of its blood on the meat of the altar." Since there would have been no meat on the altar for this חטאת offering, Gilders proposed that the original Hebrew here would have been, not בשר, but קרנות, so that Noah put the blood on the horns of the altar. Neither the Hebrew nor Ethiopic terms for these two words are likely candidates for confusion, but κέρατα (horns) and κρέατα (flesh, a plural form of κρέας) could easily have caused the mistaken reading in the Ge'ez manuscripts.[26]

3. A few citations of and allusions to Jubilees, made by writers of Greek who used Greek sources, have survived. These are not abundant in number but do make it reasonable to think that a translation of Jubilees into Greek (or at least a Greek rendering of parts of it) existed. While most of the evidence comes from relatively late texts, the sources of the late citations may go back to a much earlier time in history.

---

25. E. Tisserant, "Fragments syriaques du Livre des Jubilés," *RB* 30 (1921): 55-86, 206-32. For the edition of the chronicle, see J. B. Chabot, *Chronicon ad annum Christi 1234 pertinens I*, CSCO 81, Scriptores Syri 36 (Louvain: Secrétariat du CorpusSCO, 1920). I reproduced the Syriac fragments in *The Book of Jubilees*, 1.

26. W. Gilders, "Where Did Noah Place the Blood? A Textual Note on Jubilees 7:4," *JBL* 124 (2005): 745-49. For other examples of such confusions, see Charles, *The Book of Jubilees or the Little Genesis* (London: Adam and Charles Black, 1902), xxx.

Epiphanius (ca. 315-403): The bishop of Salamis (Constantia) on Cyprus wrote two major works, in both of which he made brief use of Jubilees.

The Panarion (= *The Medicine Chest; Against Heresies* is the Greek title): He composed this compilation of what he considered deviant views in a two-to-three-year period during the mid-370s. It is a "historical encyclopedia of heresy and its refutation. Epiphanius undertook the monumental task of listing all pre- and post-Christian sects — a total of eighty — from Adam till his own lifetime, sketching their history and chief doctrines as he understood them, and telling the faithful, in a few words, what answer to give them."[27] His employment of Jubilees comes in section 3 of book 1 where he treats sect #39, the Sethians. He wished to refute their ideas about Cain and Abel as sons of two men, about whom two angels quarreled, leading to the murder of Abel. The power on high, called Mother and Feminine, seems to have won the contest. She then caused the generation of Seth and placed her power in him (see 2, 1-3, 4). Against these ideas, "foolish, weak and full of nonsense," Epiphanius defends the story about the first family as presented in Genesis. In 5, 5 he introduces several quotations from Genesis that he calls scripture. The Jubilees allusions are part of his refutation of Sethian views (6, 1-5; see also 7, 1-3).

> But, as is apparent in Jubilees or "The Little Genesis" ['Ὡς δὲ τοῖς Ἰωβηλαίοις εὑρήσκεται καὶ τῇ λεπτῇ Γενέσει καλουμένη], the book even contains the names of both Cain's and Seth's wives — to the utter shame of these people who have recited their myths to the world. For after Adam had had sons and daughters it became necessary that, for the time being, his sons marry their own sisters. Such a thing was not unlawful; there was no other human stock. In a manner of speaking, in fact, Adam practically married his own daughter himself, since she was fashioned from his body and bones and had been formed in union with him by God. And this was not unlawful. And his sons were married, Cain to his older sister, whose name was Saue [τῇ ἀδελφῇ τῇ μείζονι Σαυὴ]; and a third son, Seth, who was born after Abel, to his sister named Azura [τῇ λεγομένη αὐτοῦ ἀδελφῇ Ἀζουρᾷ]. As the Little Genesis says, Adam had other sons too — nine after these three — so that he had two daughters but twelve sons, one of whom was killed while eleven survived.[28]

27. F. Williams, *The Panarion of Epiphanius of Salamis Book I (Sects 1-46)*, NHS 35 (Leiden: Brill, 1987), xvi.

28. The translation is from Williams, *The Panarion*, 259.

He draws the information about the wives' names from Jub 4:9, 11, and Jub 4:10 mentions the nine additional sons. Epiphanius, in the sequel, speaks about the necessity of marrying cousins in the next generations (7, 2), a point made repeatedly by the author of Jubilees in chap. 4 (vv. 15, 16, 27, 28, 33). Epiphanius does not introduce the material from Jubilees as scripture, and Jubilees is not among the biblical books he names in his treatise *Measures and Weights;* but the information in the book of Jubilees was reliable enough for him to use in refuting a sect that attributed a different origin and nature to Seth.

Measures and Weights (392): Though Epiphanius wrote his "Bible handbook"[29] in Greek, the full text has not survived in the original but is available in a Syriac translation. Fortunately, the section from Jubilees is among the extant Greek sections. When discussing the scriptural measure *modius,* he notes that it contains twenty-two *xestai.* "Now I speak of the 'just' *modius,* as the Law is accustomed to say, according to the sacred measure. For, O lover of good, God did twenty-two works between the beginning and the seventh day, which are these: . . ." He then lists the twenty-two works of the first week, obviously reproducing Jubilees' creation account, though he does not here name his source (21-22; see also 23-24). The extent of the citation and its precision (the twenty-two works are the same and are correctly distributed over the six days) offer grounds for thinking Epiphanius had access to a Greek translation of Jubilees, not simply a work containing extracts from it. He also reproduces Jubilees' connection between the twenty-two works of creation until the sabbath and the twenty-two generations until Jacob (see also 3-4).

Other than Epiphanius, almost all the Greek citations from Jubilees appear in Byzantine chronographies that date from several centuries later. The earliest and most important of these was authored by George Syncellus, who compiled his *Chronography* circa 808-10. According to Heinrich Gelzer, Syncellus took information deriving from Jubilees from sources such as Panadorus and Annianus who were themselves dependent on the work of Julius Africanus (ca. 180–ca. 250).[30] William Adler sees the tradition differently. As Syncellus's work with the text of Jubilees does not always agree with its employment in the Alexandrian chronographers, he seems not to have

---

29. J. E. Dean, ed., *Epiphanius' Treatise on Weights and Measures: The Syriac Version,* SAOC 11 (Chicago: University of Chicago Press, 1935), 3.

30. H. Gelzer, *Sextus Julius Africanus und die byzantinische Chronographie,* 2.1: *Die Nachfolger des Julius Africanus* (Leipzig: J. C. Hinrichs'sche, 1898).

derived the information directly from them but through other sources. Adler notes, for instance, that Syncellus regularly claimed that traditions attested in Jubilees alone were from Josephus's *Antiquities:* "But his very regular pattern of misattributing citations from *Jubilees* to Josephus' *Antiquities* makes it clear that at a prior stage in the transmission of these two works, material from the two works had become confused."[31] Adler thinks Syncellus and other Byzantine historians used a certain kind of reference work: "This was, as has been proposed, not a continuous chronological narrative, but rather a collection of source material. In a work of this sort Josephus and *Jubilees* were regularly cited together, since, in the scope and nature of the material treated, the two works were parallel."[32] Such epitomes, which included excerpts from a number of sources regarding the issues and passages under discussion, were the sorts of materials from which the chronographers drew their information that derived ultimately from works such as Jubilees; they did not use the sources themselves.

Milik argued that a series of even less well-known Byzantine historians had drawn data from Jubilees and had taken them directly from the writings of Julius Africanus. If so, this would trace the translation of Jubilees back to a time no later than the early third century C.E.[33]

Besides the Greek material that has been collected by several editors,[34] there is now additional evidence for the influence of Jubilees in Christian exegesis of Genesis. The Catena on Genesis, some of which has only recently been edited, contains some passages that either mention Jubilees as their source or reflect data from it. For example, #551 (Cain's wife was named Ἀσαούλ), #585 (it lists the names of the wives of the patriarchs recorded in Gen 5 along with their family affiliation, just as in Jub 4), #590 (on Gen 5:21-24: Ἐνὼχ πρῶτος ἔμαθε γράμματα, καὶ ἔγραψε τὰ σημεῖα τοῦ οὐρανοῦ καὶ τὰς τροπὰς καὶ τοὺς μῆνας [Jub 4:17: "He was the first of mankind who were born on the earth who learned (the art of) writing, instruction, and wisdom

---

31. W. Adler, *Time Immemorial: Archaic History and Its Sources in Christian Chronography from Julius Africanus to George Syncellus,* Dumbarton Oaks Studies 26 (Washington, D.C.: Dumbarton Oaks Research Library and Collection, 1989), 191.

32. Adler, *Time Immemorial,* 193.

33. Milik, "Recherches sur la version grecque du livre des Jubilés," *RB* 78 (1971): 545-57.

34. The largest compilation is still that of H. Rönsch, *Das Buch der Jubiläen oder die kleine Genesis* (Leipzig: Fues's Verlag [R. Reisland], 1874), 251-382, although he included more than just Greek material. See also A. Denis, *Fragmenta Pseudepigraphorum Quae Supersunt Graeca,* PVTG 3 (Leiden: Brill, 1970), 70-102; I reproduced them in *The Book of Jubilees,* 1.

and who wrote down in a book the signs of the sky in accord with the fixed pattern of their months"]), #833 (names and relations of the wives of the second Cainan, Sala, Eber, Phaleg [Jub 8:5-7; 10:18]), #839 (but see below on Didymus), #857 (the second Cainan's astronomy and divination), #861 (names and family relations of the wives of Ragau, Serouch, Nahor [Jub 11:1, 7, 9]), #1804b (Bilhah and Dinah died while mourning for Joseph, giving Jacob three reasons for grief and accounting for the day of atonement; see Jub 34:14-15, 18); cf. #1829 (regarding Tamar; another reference to the Covenant/Testament [see below]), and ##1850, 2268 (on the chronology of Joseph's life). Of special note are the following two entries.

#867: In the comment on Gen 11:28 ("Haran died before his father Terah in the land of his birth, in Ur of the Chaldeans"), the Catena entry explains: "Arran died in the fire with which Abram burned the idols of his father, when he went in to remove them. Abram was then 60 years of age when he burned the idols — (years) that are not figured in the years of his life because he was in unbelief until then, as it is written in Jubilees [καθὼς γέγραπται ἐν τῷ Ἰωβηλαίῳ]."[35] The passage is alluding to Jub 12:12-14: "In the sixtieth year of Abram's life (which was the fourth week in its fourth year [1936]), Abram got up at night and burned the temple of the idols. He burned everything in the temple but no one knew (about it). They got up at night and wanted to save their gods from the fire. Haran dashed in to save them, but the fire raged over him. He was burned in the fire and died in *Ur* of the Chaldeans before his father Terah. They buried him in *Ur* of the Chaldeans."

The passage unmistakably offers information documented in Jubilees, which is named as the source, using a traditional formula for introducing a scriptural citation. Abram's age at the time (sixty years) comes from Jub 12:12, as does his act of torching the sanctuary; it also mentions that Haran died while trying to rescue the idols. But the notion that the first sixty years of Abram's life were not counted in his true age — a note that relates to the much discussed problem of the chronology in Gen 11:26, 32 — does not come from Jubilees, or at least not from the form of the text represented in the Geʿez copies, although Jubilees is mentioned as the source in immediate connection with this remark. The passage may imply that the Greek Jubilees had a more expanded text at this point, but it is also possible that the writer confused sources for this problem.

---

35. For the text, see F. Petit, ed., *La chaîne sur la Genèse: Édition intégrale II Chapitres 4 à 11*, Traditio Exegetica Graeca 2 (Louvain: Peeters, 1993), 218. The translation is mine.

#2270: The first twenty-three lines, as the editors note, are a reproduction, with some changes, of Jub 46:6-12; 47:1.[36] This previously unedited text is, unlike so much of the remaining Greek material, a very close quotation of an extended passage from Jubilees.

For the sake of completeness, attention should be drawn to six citations in Didymus the Blind that he attributes to what he calls the Book of the Covenant (ἡ βίβλος τῆς διαθήκης). Five of these appear in his commentary on Genesis, and a sixth in his commentary on Job. In no case does he cite from it; he always speaks indirectly about it. Some editors of Didymus's works have claimed that these come from Jubilees, and one must admit that there is a similarity in content between four of the six citations and Jubilees. Closer study shows, however, that they are not likely to have been drawn from Jubilees, though the Book of the Covenant would be a good name for it.[37]

IV. Latin

There was a Latin translation of Jubilees, made from a Greek model, and one partial copy of it is available. That copy was published by Ceriani in 1861.[38] He found it in the manuscript designated Ambrosiana C 73 Inf. The manu-

---

36. *La chaîne sur la Genèse: Édition intégrale IV Chapitres 29 à 50*, 455.

37. For the texts and the views of the editors, see D. Lührmann, "Alttestamentliche Pseudepigraphen bei Didymos von Alexandrien," *ZAW* 104 (1992): 231-49, here 239-45. Lührmann denies that the Book of the Covenant in these passages is Jubilees. A. Crislip has recently published parts of a Coptic text, P.CtYBR inv. 495, which he dates to the fourth to fifth century C.E. The florilegium quotes at least six passages, four of which are from Jubilees: 8:28-30; 7:14-16; 15:3; 4:33 (an allusion). Crislip says we should not rule out the possibility there was a Coptic translation of Jubilees ("The *Book of Jubilees* in Coptic: An Early Christian *Florilegium* on the Family of Noah," *BASP* 40 [2003]: 27-44, with pls. 1-2). The Coptic material may have come from a Greek source. In addition, W. Lowndes Lipscomb has published an Armenian list of the names of, among others, the patriarchs and their wives, with the wives' names corresponding to the ones given in Jub 3:34–11:14. As he notes, there are five other texts (besides his list and the one in Jubilees) that provide these names, and he offers a chart comparing the names in all seven. The others are the Syriac list of names (see above), the scholia in the LXX minuscule 135, and three late Hebrew texts ("A Tradition from the Book of Jubilees in Armenian," *JJS* 29 [1978]: 149-63). It is possible that the Armenian list also came from a Greek intermediary, though Syriac is not excluded.

38. Ceriani, "Fragmenta Parvae Genesis et Assumptionis Mosis ex Veteri Versione Latina," in *Monumenta Sacra et Profana*, 1:9-64; for the Jubilees text see 15-54. Rönsch (*Das Buch der Jubiläen*, 10-95, with commentary on 96-196), Charles (*The Ethiopic Version of the Hebrew Book of Jubilees*), and I (*The Book of Jubilees*, 1:270-300) have reissued the text.

script is a palimpsest, and the text of Jubilees and that of the Testament of Moses occupy the lower level and are thus difficult to read. Ceriani was able to decipher a large amount of text, beginning at Jub 13:10 and running, with gaps, until 49:22. "In these sections [twenty-five of them] one finds all or parts of 439 verses (335 of the total of 1307 verses in the Ethiopic version). Much has been lost at the beginning, but once the legible Latin begins it preserves nearly half of the text. That is, if one subtracts the number of verses from 1:1–13:9 (the section of text that precedes the beginning of the first decipherable Latin passage), the percentage of the verses available in Latin is 47.5 (439 of 923). It can safely be said that both in quantity and quality, the Latin is second only to the Ethiopic version."[39] It is difficult to overemphasize the importance of this text. Ceriani dated the copy to the fifth or sixth century C.E. This means that it is approximately a millennium older than the earliest surviving copy of Jubilees in Ethiopic (see below). One hopes that with modern photographic techniques more of the manuscript could be read. The Latin and Ethiopic (see below) translations furnish independent reflections of the lost Greek version of Jubilees.

V. Ethiopic

The complete (as nearly as we can tell) book of Jubilees has survived only in manuscripts inscribed in the classical language of Ethiopia. August Dillmann was able to use two poor copies of the text when he published his edition in 1859 (38 and 51 in the list below),[40] and Charles used the readings from Dillmann's two manuscripts (taken from Dillmann's edition) and from two others (12 and 25) for his edition of 1895. When I prepared my edition of Jubilees (1989), twenty-seven copies of the book had been identified and made available in one form or another.

9*	14th century
12*	15th century
17*	15th century
20*	15th–16th century

---

39. VanderKam, *The Book of Jubilees*, 2:xviii.
40. Charles, *Mashafa Kufale sive Liber Jubilaeorum, qui idem a Graecis* Ἡ Λεπτὴ Γένεσις *inscribitur, aethiopice ad duorum librorum manuscriptorum fidem primum editit* (Kiel: C. G. L. van Maack; London: Williams and Norgate, 1859).

21*	16th century
22	16th century
23	16th century
25*	16th century
35*	17th century
38*	17th century
39*	17th–18th century
40	17th–18th century
42*	18th century
44*	18th century
45	18th century
47*	18th century
48*	18th century
50	18th–19th century
51	19th century
57	19th century
58*	19th century
59	19th century
60	19th–20th century
61	20th century
62	20th century
63*	20th century
64	20th century[41]

I collated all these manuscripts for Jub 1–2, by which time the family relations among them were very clear; for the edition, I completely collated the fifteen manuscripts asterisked in the list above. The evidence suggested to me that the copies represented several different manuscript traditions (ms. 44 is unique):

20-25-35
39-40-42-45-47-48-51-59
39-40-48-59

41. W. Baars and R. Zuurmond had collected information on the various manuscripts and had procured copies of many of them, preparatory to a new edition they were planning ("The Project for a New Edition of the Ethiopic Book of Jubilees," *JSS* 9 [1964]: 67-74). Many of the manuscripts have been microfilmed for the Ethiopian Manuscript Microfilm Library (EMML) (in Addis Ababa) and the Monastic Manuscript Microfilm Library (Collegeville, Minn.). In the above list, ##21, 39, 40, 42, 44, 47, 48, 59, 60, 62, 63 are available from EMML.

```
42-47-51
45
17-63
9-38-50
12-21-22-23
57-58-60-61-62-64
57-58-60-61
62-64
```

The EMML catalogues published since 1989 list no more copies of Jubilees. A search of all the catalogues does reveal some texts that are of interest for the study of the book in Ethiopic. Included among other items in the following numbers are:

#1276 (mid-20th century): an Amharic commentary on Jubilees (folios 196a-207b)

#1281 (1973): an Amharic commentary on Jubilees (194a-233a)

#1693 (1865-1913): notes of commentary on Jubilees (136b-142a)

#1694 (1910?): an Amharic commentary on Jubilees (92a-107b)

#1835 (15th century): among many homilies are ones in honor of St. Ura'el (Uriel, folios 166a-179b) based in part on Jubilees (174b), of St. Fanu'el (190b-200a), in which the emperor Zar'a Ya'qob's favorite quotation from Jubilees is included (Jub 2:1; folio 192a), and of St. Sadu'el (226a-237b), based on Enoch, Ezekiel, and Jubilees (229b)

#1847 (1944/1945): an Amharic commentary on Jubilees (77b-81b)

#2436 (17th century): notes concerning the book of Jubilees (118b-120ab)

#2849 (18th century): folios 3a-92b contain a Ge'ez grammar and vocabulary; apparently in a section on the meanings of words in different books, Jubilees is included (72b)

#4769 (19th century): parts of Jubilees (99a-126b)

#4493(1528): in a Horologium (44a-100a), two passages from Jubilees are included (2:4? [75b-76b] and 39:13-22 [76b-77a]).

Although many more texts are available, the last catalogue (vol. 10) from the EMML project was published in 1993, so there has been a delay. The Web site says volume 11 should be appearing soon.

My studies of the individual Ethiopic manuscripts and comparisons of their readings with the versional evidence led me to the conclusion that, despite a long history of copying and multiple translations, the Ethiopic text of Jubilees is in surprisingly good shape — in contrast to some other Jewish works such as 1 Enoch. A number of factors probably contributed to the textual stability of Jubilees.

1. Jubilees retells familiar stories from Genesis and Exodus; this fact could have hindered major deviation. A related factor is, however, also worth underscoring: the text of Jubilees does not show signs of being modified in the direction of the biblical texts in the various languages through which it passed. So, for example, when one compares all of Ethiopic Jubilees' citations from Genesis and Exodus with the ancient versions for those passages, the version with which it disagrees most frequently is the Ethiopic version of Genesis and Exodus.[42]

2. Jubilees as an entire unit was accorded high status by some Jews and Christians. The evidence for the esteem in which it was held at Qumran has been summarized a number of times, and the fact that it is regularly included in Ethiopic manuscripts that contain the books of the Old Testament shows its standing in the Abyssinian church.

3. As a reflection of that high status, writers of various kinds of literature drew upon Jubilees and its traditions to clarify passages in Genesis/Exodus or to fill in gaps that they left. This was the case for midrashists and for chronographers. The fact that they drew material from passages early and late in the book raises the likelihood that full versions of the book existed even in the languages for which we at present lack a manuscript copy (Greek, Syriac).

42. See, for example, VanderKam, *Textual and Historical Studies,* 103-205; *"Jubilees* and the Hebrew Texts of Genesis-Exodus," *Text* 14 (1988): 71-86.

The Composition of Jubilees

Michael Segal

Jubilees is almost universally considered to be the work of a single author, although some scholars have allowed for the possibility of local interpolations or additions to the text. All the many differences between Jubilees and the biblical books that it rewrites (Genesis and Exodus), including additions, omissions, and changes to the biblical text, assuming that one can determine the specific textual version upon which Jubilees is based, are attributed to a single author, the putative "author of Jubilees." This assumption forms the basis of the vast majority of studies of Jubilees, which attempt to describe the perspective of the book as a whole from many different angles.

Although scholars have recognized the generic differences between different passages in the book (rewritten stories, legal passages, chronological framework, testaments, etc.), they have not by and large viewed these differences as any indication of the diverse origins of the passages. The combination of different genres is certainly insufficient in and of itself to support the possibility of complex literary development, since an author is not limited by generic distinctions. However, as will be suggested here, such a theory can indeed be demonstrated by highlighting contradictions and tensions that are found between these different genres throughout the book.

Two scholars have previously proposed that Jubilees developed through a complex process of literary composition, but neither of their theories has been widely accepted. The first, Ernest Wiesenberg, on the basis of discrepancies within the chronology presented in the book, suggested that they are the result of redactional layers within the chronological framework itself.[1] As James VanderKam noted, most of these contradictions should be taken not as evidence of an editorial process, but rather as local inconsistencies, either errors that resulted from regular transmissional processes or inconsistencies that emerged due to the attempt to apply an extensive chronological framework to all the stories in the patriarchal period.[2]

Gene Davenport proposed an alternative theory of literary development.[3] On the basis of his analysis of the Ethiopic text of Jubilees and the eschatological ideas present in the book, he suggested that Jubilees consists of a basic layer and two subsequent redactions. This theory too has been rightly criticized for these reasons: (1) it is based upon Davenport's own perception of a consistent approach to eschatology, and (2) some of his philological analysis was based upon supposed contradictions that have subsequently been shown not to reflect the original Hebrew text of Jubilees.[4]

Thus, the scholarly consensus has remained until today that Jubilees represents a unified composition. The question of the unity of Jubilees obviously has far-reaching implications for the study of the book in many different areas. Fundamental questions, such as the date of composition of the book, need to be reexamined or redefined if the book is composed of various materials from different periods of time. It is possible that one can confidently date a specific passage in the book, but that would not necessarily reflect the date of the composition as a whole, since the dated passage might either be a source used by the composition, or alternatively, the contribution of the editor. Similarly, the worldview of the author would need to be reexamined. If one can isolate or identify competing or conflicting notions within the book, must one attempt to synthesize or harmonize them into one single worldview, or are these differences the result of the combination of materials of differing origins? Can one speak of the worldview of an entire composition if the work is the product of a complex process of literary development?

---

1. E. Wiesenberg, "The Jubilee of Jubilees," *RevQ* 3 (1961): 3-40.

2. J. C. VanderKam, "Studies in the Chronology of the Book of Jubilees," in VanderKam, *From Revelation to Canon: Studies in Hebrew Bible and Second Temple Literature*, JSJSup 62 (Leiden: Brill, 2000), 522-44 (here 532-40); trans. of "Das chronologische Konzept des Jubiläenbuches," *ZAW* 107 (1995): 80-100.

3. G. L. Davenport, *The Eschatology of the Book of Jubilees* (Leiden: Brill, 1971).

4. For a summary of the arguments against Davenport, see J. C. VanderKam, "The Origins and Purposes of the *Book of Jubilees*," in *Studies in the Book of Jubilees*, ed. M. Albani, J. Frey, and A. Lange, TSAJ 65 (Tübingen: J. C. B. Mohr [Paul Siebeck], 1997), 3-24 (here 12-13).

In recent decades some scholars have identified a few short passages in Jubilees that stand in tension with or even contradict other verses in Jubilees. These passages relate either to chronological details (Devorah Dimant — regarding 4:21) or halakic positions (Menahem Kister — regarding chaps. 7 and 32; Liora Ravid — regarding 50:6-13).[5] While their discussions were limited to individual passages, both Dimant and Kister suggested that these discrepancies are the result of the combination of traditions from different sources in the compositional process of Jubilees. The contradictions between them can thus be traced to their different provenance. In my recently published book, I have proposed and attempted to demonstrate that Jubilees is indeed the product of a process of literary development, but based upon a very different model than that previously suggested by Wiesenberg or Davenport.[6] In this paper I will attempt to briefly summarize my arguments and theory presented in that analysis.[7]

I. Chronological and Halakic Redaction

The two most prominent characteristics of Jubilees are: (1) the chronological framework by which all events in the patriarchal period are dated, and (2) the addition of legal passages to the rewritten narratives throughout the book. While there are other notable features, such as a developed angelology and the possible priestly provenance of the book, these latter areas are not unique to Jubilees. The two former characteristics are the two primary aspects emphasized in Jubilees' self-designation throughout chap. 1, "the Book of the Divisions of the Time of the Torah and the *Te'udah*."[8]

---

5. D. Dimant, "The Biography of Enoch and the Books of Enoch," *VT* 33 (1983): 14-29 (here 21, esp. n. 17); M. Kister, "Some Aspects of Qumranic Halakhah," in *The Madrid Qumran Congress: Proceedings of the International Congress on the Dead Sea Scrolls, Madrid, 18-21 March, 1991,* ed. J. Trebolle Barrera and L. Vegas Montaner, 2 vols., STDJ 11 (Leiden: Brill, 1992), 571-88; L. Ravid, "The Relationship of the Sabbath Laws in *Jubilees* 50:6-13 to the Rest of the Book" (in Hebrew), *Tarbiz* 69 (2000): 161-66.

6. M. Segal, *The Book of Jubilees: Rewritten Bible, Redaction, Ideology, and Theology* (Leiden: Brill, 2007).

7. Each of the examples mentioned here, and summarized in a few paragraphs, is given much more extensive treatment in that study.

8. It is beyond the scope of this discussion to analyze the meaning of the term *te'udah;* in Segal, *The Book of Jubilees,* chap. 14, I suggest that this term should be understood as "covenant." Whether or not this interpretation is accepted, the legal context of the term "Torah" is undisputed.

I would like to suggest that the composition is not a homogeneous book composed by one author. Rather, it is possible to identify internal contradictions, doublets, tensions, and discrepancies, both in details and in reference to the biblical stories in general. This situation attests to the variety of traditions that can be found side by side within the same book. The redactor sometimes relied upon the Pentateuch itself, but often adopted other compositions, along the lines of the examples of rewritten Bible known to us from the second temple period. Such rewritten texts were common in Jewish literature in antiquity, as exemplified by compositions such as 1 Enoch, the Testament of the Twelve Patriarchs, and the Genesis Apocryphon. The ideas embedded in these written traditions did not always agree with the views of the redactor, thus creating the internal problems to be described below. The final product, as known to us today, is not the work of one individual, but a combination of different traditions, sources, and authors. I suggest that the redactor's contribution can be found in the chronological framework throughout the book, in the legal passages juxtaposed to the rewritten stories, and in those passages that contain the unique terminology of the legal passages (such as chaps. 1, 2, 6, and 23:9-32).

To describe this process I have coined the terms "chronological redaction" and "halakic redaction." As noted above, these two themes are combined in the opening chapter of the book, and this combination is also found at its conclusion (50:13 — "as it was written in the tablets which he placed in my hands so that I could write for you the *laws of each specific time in every division of its times*"). Therefore, while I have distinguished between these two redactional processes in order to emphasize the unique elements of each aspect, both are ultimately the work of the same editor responsible for the composition of Jubilees, and therefore belong to the same redactional layer.

The following list presents ten examples of contradictions within Jubilees, which I suggest lead to the conclusion that it could not be the exclusive work of a single author. The list is divided into two sections: the first half details those differences between the rewritten narratives and the chronological framework, while the second section outlines the tensions between the rewritten narratives and the legal passages.

Michael Segal

A. Contradictions between the Rewritten Narratives and the Chronological Framework

1. *The length of a "jubilee" period.*[9] In all of Jubilees, the duration of a "jubilee" period is 49 years, as demonstrated by comparing the chronological framework in the book with the chronological data in the Pentateuch itself, and particularly in its genealogical lists.[10] Furthermore, in a few instances the book calculates a decimal number (as found in the Bible) according to the heptadic system of jubilees, weeks, and years. Thus Jub 23:8 describes the length of Abraham's life, based upon Gen 25:7: "He had lived for three jubilees and four weeks of years — 175 years" (3 x 49 = 147; 4 x 7 = 28; 147 + 28 = 175).

In contrast, Jub 4:21, which describes Enoch's sojourn with the angels following the birth of his son (when he was 65 years old according to MT, SP, and Jubilees; 165 according to LXX), is based upon a different understanding of the length of this period. According to this verse, "he was, moreover, with God's angels for six jubilees of years."[11] This period of six jubilees is parallel to the period described in Gen 5:22: "And Enoch walked with God after he begat Methuselah 300 years." A simple calculation reveals that according to Jub 4:21, a "jubilee" lasts for 50 years, in contrast to the rest of the book.[12]

9. This example was first noted by Dimant, "Biography of Enoch," 21.

10. While a complete study of the chronological data in Jubilees is beyond the scope of this article, it should be noted that it is generally closer to the dates preserved in the Samaritan Pentateuch, in contrast to the other textual witnesses.

11. The description of Enoch's sojourn with the angels for six jubilees is also reflected in a composition entitled 4QPseudo-Jubilees[c] [4Q227] 2, 1-2 (DJD 13, 171-75):

1	[			E]noch after we taught him
2	[		]o[	] six jubilees of years

While it has generally been suggested that this scroll presents a composition based upon Jubilees, it is possible that this perspective needs to be reversed, and in fact this fragment (or a similar composition) may actually represent a possible source for Jubilees itself.

12. VanderKam (*Calendars in the Dead Sea Scrolls: Measuring Time* [London: Routledge, 1998], 121 n. 18; *The Book of Jubilees*, Guides to Apocrypha and Pseudepigrapha [Sheffield: Sheffield Academic Press, 2001], 33) interpreted this verse in accordance with the general meaning of "jubilee" in Jubilees (49 years), and arrived at the conclusion that Enoch spent 294 (6 x 49 = 294) years in heaven, and returned to the earth 6 years prior to his death. However, it is difficult to accept this harmonistic interpretation that overlooks the direct usage of Gen 5:22. J. M. Scott, *On Earth as in Heaven: The Restoration of Sacred Time and Sacred Space in the Book of Jubilees*, JSJSup 91 (Leiden and Boston: Brill, 2005), 23-71, also interpreted the "six jubilees of years" as 294 years, and on this basis, suggested that this verse has

Dimant correctly concluded that "This shows that Jub. borrows from various sources, often without reconciling the contradictions."

2. *The order of the births of Jacob's sons.* The births of Jacob's sons (except for Benjamin) are listed in Gen 29–30, and organized there according to their mothers: Leah (first four children), Bilhah, Zilpah, Leah (final two children), Rachel. According to a straightforward reading of Gen 31:41, all the children were born during a 7-year period (in the second period of 7 years during which Jacob worked for Laban), and it is therefore reasonable to assume an overlap between the births.[13] According to the dates presented in the chronological framework of Jub 28 (vv. 14-15, 18), such an overlap occurred between the births of Leah's first children and the births of Bilhah's sons, as Dan (Bilhah's older son) was conceived prior to the birth of Levi (Leah's third son) and was born before Judah (Leah's fourth):

		Jubilee	Week	Year	Year from Creation
28:11	Birth of Reuben	44	3	1	2122
28:13	Birth of Simeon	44	3	3	2124
28:14	Birth of Levi	44	3	6	2127
28:15	Birth of Judah	44	4	1	2129
28:18	Birth of Dan	44	3	6	2127

In contradiction, according to 28:17, **all four** of Leah's first children were born before Bilhah was even given to Jacob: "When Rachel saw that Leah had given birth to **four sons for Jacob — Reuben, Simeon, Levi, and Judah** — she said to him: 'Go in to my servant girl Bilhah . . .'" Some scholars have attempted to resolve this contradiction by emending the dates found in the chronological framework.[14] However, it is more convincing to understand

---

fundamental significance for the chronological conception of Jubilees. This suggestion is difficult to accept, as it is highly unlikely that such a fundamental notion was left unstated, but more significantly, it is predicated on the assumption that the chronological note in Jub 4:21 refers to a 49-year period, in contradiction to Gen 5:22.

13. Contrast *S. 'Olam Rab.* 2, which posited that there was no overlap between them, and therefore each pregnancy extended only over a seven-month period. Interestingly, Jubilees extended the period of births to also include the final six years during which Jacob remained in Laban's household.

14. See H. Rönsch, *Das Buch der Jubiläen oder die kleine Genesis* (Leipzig: Fues's Verlag, 1874), 327-31. Rönsch generally relied on other compositions, primarily the Testament of the Twelve Patriarchs, to reconstruct the dates in Jubilees. These suggested emendations were accepted by R. H. Charles, *The Book of Jubilees or the Little Genesis* (London: Adam and Charles Black, 1902), 170-72.

the presence of this contradiction in the text as the result of a literary process in which the dates of the chronological framework were superimposed upon an already rewritten story.

3. *"Let the days allowed him be 120 years" (Gen 6:3).* Interpreters from antiquity until today are divided as to the meaning of the 120-year limitation that was instituted in response to the intercourse between the sons of god and the women and the subsequent birth of the giants (Gen 6:1-4). Some posit that this limitation applies to humanity in general, including the giants who were half-divine and half-human.[15] The establishment of a maximum age for human life expectancy drew a boundary between the heavenly and earthly realms.[16] Alternatively, other interpreters have suggested that the sons of god story is related to the flood story that follows, and in fact provides a justification for this cataclysmic punishment. According to this approach, 120 years is the length of time from the Watchers' descent until the flood.[17]

Within the rewritten story in Jub 5, the limitation of 120 years applies to the giants (5:7-9), the offspring of the Watchers, in accordance with the first interpretive approach to Gen 6:3:

> 5:7Regarding their children there went out from his presence an order to strike them with the sword and to remove them from beneath the sky. 5:8He said: "My spirit will not remain on people forever for they are flesh. Their lifespan is to be 120 years." 5:9He sent his sword among them so that they would kill one another. They began to kill each other until all of them fell by the sword and were obliterated from the earth.

At the same time, according to the chronological framework, the Watchers sinned in the twenty-fifth jubilee, A.M. 1177-1225 (Jub 5:1, referring to 4:33), while the flood took place in the year 1308 (5:22-23). The difference between

---

15. Cf. *LAB* (pseudo-Philo) 3.2; Josephus, *Ant* 1.75; the opinion of R. Joshua b. Nehemiah in *Genesis Rabbah* 26:6 (Theodor-Albeck, ed., 251-52).

16. Compare the story of the Garden of Eden, where there is a concern if a human is to consume from the tree of life and thus live forever (Gen 3:22).

17. Cf. 4Q252, col. 1, lines 1-3; S. *'Olam Rab.* 28; *Targum Onqelos* to Gen 6:3; *Targum Neofiti; Fragmentary Targum; Targum Pseudo-Jonathan; Mek. R. Ishmael Shirta* 5; *Genesis Rabbah* 30:7; *b. Sanhedrin* 108a; *Avot of Rabbi Nathan* A 32; Jerome, *Questions on Genesis* 6:3; Augustine, *City of God* 15.24.24; Rashi, Ibn Ezra, and Radaq to Gen 6:3. See M. J. Bernstein, "4Q252: From Re-Written Bible to Biblical Commentary," *JJS* 45 (1994): 1-27 (here 5-7); J. L. Kugel, *The Bible as It Was* (Cambridge: Harvard University Press, 1997), 112-14.

these two dates fits a period of 120 years, and reflects the second interpretive approach to Gen 6:3.

In this case, the process of literary development that led to the combination of these interpretive traditions can be identified. The rewritten narrative in Jub 5 parallels the version of events presented in 1 En 10–11. This can be demonstrated, for example, by the presence of two judgments of the angels in the Jubilees account, both before and after their offspring kill each other in internecine warfare, corresponding to the judgments of Asael and Shemihazah in the 1 Enoch version, with the punishment for the giants in between. In the latter text (which is chronologically earlier), the presence of separate judgments for each figure is due to the combination of at least two separate traditions within the Book of the Watchers.[18] However, the double judgment in Jubilees both prior to and following the death of the giants through civil war is redundant and must therefore be the result of the dependence of Jub 5 upon the 1 Enoch material. This dependence explains the inclusion of the interpretive approach to Gen 6:3 as a limitation on human life span. This same notion is found in the precisely parallel place in 1 En 10:9-10, and was included in Jubilees when the entire passage was incorporated into the later book. The dating of the story in Jubilees' chronological framework to approximately 120 years prior to the flood was then superimposed upon the rewritten version of the story that was adopted from 1 Enoch, thus leading to the juxtaposition of both interpretive approaches.

B. Contradictions between the Rewritten Narratives and the Legal Passages

4. *The date of the entry into the Garden of Eden.* According to Jub 3:17, which is part of a rewritten narrative, Adam was exiled from the Garden of Eden on the seventeenth of the second month, **exactly** seven years after he entered. Thus, one can conclude that he arrived in the Garden on that same calendar date. The legal passage embedded within this rewritten story (3:8-14) con-

18. For analyses and suggested divisions of the traditions and sources combined in 1 En 6–11, see, e.g., G. Beer, "Das Buch Henoch," in *Die Apokryphen und Pseudepigraphen des Alten Testaments*, ed. E. Kautzsch, 2 vols. (Tübingen, Freiburg, and Leipzig: J. C. B. Mohr [Paul Siebeck], 1900), 2:217-310 (here 225); D. Dimant, "'The Fallen Angels' in the Dead Sea Scrolls and in the Apocryphal and Pseudepigraphic Books Related to Them" (in Hebrew) (Ph.D. diss., Hebrew University of Jerusalem, 1974), 23-72; G. W. E. Nickelsburg, "Apocalyptic and Myth in Enoch 6–11," *JBL* 96 (1977): 383-405.

nects the dates of entry for Adam and his wife to the law of the parturient mother from Lev 12. According to this legal passage, Adam entered the Garden forty days after he was created (v. 9). On the basis of the 364-day calendar used throughout Jubilees, which begins each year on a Wednesday, the calculation of the dates reveals that forty days after Adam's creation is the thirteenth of the second month, not the seventeenth.

Month 1						
Sunday	Monday	Tuesday	Wednesday	Thursday	Friday	Sabbath
			1	2	3 Man created	4 End of the first week
5	6	7	8	9	10 Seven days after the creation of man	11 Seven days after the first week
12	13	14	15	16	17	18
19	20	21	22	23	24	25
26	27	28	29	30		

Month 2						
Sunday	Monday	Tuesday	Wednesday	Thursday	Friday	Sabbath
					1	2
3	4	5	6	7	8	9
10	11	12	13 Forty days after the creation of man	14 Forty days after the first week	15	16
17 Adam entered the Garden (*Jub.* 3:17)	18	19	20	21	22	23
24	25	26	27	28	29	30

It is impossible to ignore this discrepancy of four days between the dates, because the precedent for the law is based entirely upon these dates.[19]

In addition, one can suggest an exegetical reason for why the sin in the Garden is dated to the seventeenth of the second month, unrelated to Lev 12, as this is the same date as the beginning of the flood (MT and SP to Gen 7:11; Jub 5:23-24). The paradigmatic sin led to the paradigmatic punishment. The emphasis on exactly seven years in the Garden is presumably intended to emphasize a complete period of time.[20]

5. *Did Judah sin?* According to the rewritten story of Judah and Tamar, Judah's sons had not consummated their marriages with her, and she was therefore not legally considered Judah's daughter-in-law (Jub 41:2, 5, 27; cf. Lev 18:15; 20:12). He therefore did not sin when he had intercourse with her. In contrast, according to the legal passage (vv. 23-26), Judah indeed sinned, but repented, and was therefore forgiven. The legal passage emphasizes the process by which Judah was forgiven, and this atonement is possible only if he actually sinned.

6. *The source for the method of Tamar's punishment.* After Judah heard that his daughter-in-law Tamar was pregnant, he decided that she should be put to death by burning (Gen 38:24). The punishment of fire in cases of sexual impropriety appears only twice in the Pentateuch: "the daughter of a priest who profanes herself through harlotry" (Lev 21:9), and "a man who takes a wife and her mother" (Lev 20:14). In the rewritten story in Jub 41, Judah wished to have Tamar killed on the basis of "the law which Abraham had commanded his children" (v. 28). This apparently refers to Abraham's warning in his testament to his descendants (or a similar tradition): "If any woman or girl among you commits a sexual offence, burn her in fire" (Jub 20:4), an expansion of the prohibition and punishment of the priest's daughter from Lev 21:9 to all Israelite women.

In contrast, the legal passage in Jub 41:23-26 preferred to derive this punishment by means of exegesis according to which the punishment of burning for intercourse with a daughter-in-law (expressly prohibited in Lev 18:15; 20:12, but without the method of punishment) is the same as that of a mother-in-law ("a wife and her mother") described explicitly in Lev 20:14. These two scenarios are symmetric situations, where the men and women have interchanged roles.[21]

---

19. *Pace* J. M. Baumgarten, "Some Problems of the Jubilees Calendar in Current Research," *VT* 32 (1982): 485-89 (here 489 n. 8).

20. Cf. 12:15 — two weeks; 19:1 — two weeks, 12 — two weeks; 24:12 — three weeks; 47:9 — three weeks, 10 — three weeks.

21. As I suggested in Segal, *The Book of Jubilees*, 67-69, the legal logic behind this com-

7. *Fourth-year fruits.*[22] Lev 19:23-25 defines the halakic status of fruits during the first five years of a tree's life. During the first three years, it is prohibited to partake in these fruits (v. 23), while in the fifth year it is permitted to eat of them (v. 25). Regarding the fourth year, the Pentateuchal law (v. 24) defines the fruit as "*qodeš hillûlîm* (SP *ḥillûlîm*) to the Lord." Rabbinic exegesis interpreted this expression as an obligation to eat the fourth-year fruits in Jerusalem, or to redeem the fruits with money and to buy food with this money in Jerusalem, as is done with the second tithe.[23] In contrast, Qumran sectarian compositions posit a different meaning for this enigmatic expression: the fourth-year fruits are considered one of the priestly prerogatives.[24] Jub 7:35-37 agrees with the sectarian position: "in the fourth year its fruit will be sanctified. It will be offered as firstfruits that are acceptable before the most high Lord . . . so that they may offer in abundance the first of the wine and oil as firstfruits on the altar of the Lord who accepts (it). What is left over those who serve in the Lord's house are to eat before the altar which receives (it)" (v. 36). However, according to the story at the beginning of Jub 7, in the fourth year Noah picked grapes from which he made wine, which he then put in a container. Noah did not offer the grapes on an altar, nor did he drink from the wine until the fifth year (vv. 1-6).[25] According to the sectarian halakah, Noah and his sons should have offered the wine on the altar, and then been allowed to drink from it already in the fourth year, in light of their priestly status (compare the detailed description of his offering of sacrifices in vv. 3-6). Scholars have attempted to harmonize the laws in vv. 35-37 with the story in vv. 1-6;[26] Kister, however, concluded from this contradiction that Jubilees includes multiple traditions of different origins.

8. *The length of Abraham's journey and the Akedah as a source for which*

---

parison is similar to that expressed in Damascus Document 5:7-11, which views the incest prohibitions in Lev 18 and 20 as applying equally and symmetrically both to men and women.

22. This example was identified by Kister, "Some Aspects of Qumranic Halakhah."

23. *m. Maʿaser Sheni* 5:1; *Sifre Numbers* 6; *y. Peʾah* 7:6 (20b-c), and similarly Josephus, *Ant* 4.227. See C. Albeck, *Das Buch der Jubiläen und die Halacha*, Hochschule für die Wissenschaft des Judentums 27 (Berlin: Siegfried Scholem, 1930), 32-33; J. M. Baumgarten, "The Laws of ʿOrlah and First Fruits in Light of Jubilees, the Qumran Writings, and Targum Ps. Jonathan," *JJS* 38 (1987): 195-202 (here 196); Kister, "Some Aspects," 577-78.

24. 11QT 60:3-4; 4QMMT B 62-64; in addition to *Targum Pseudo-Jonathan* to Lev 19:24, cf. Baumgarten, "The Laws of ʿOrlah," 196; Kister, "Some Aspects," 577-78.

25. The story at the beginning of the chapter is very similar to that presented in 1QapGen 12, as Kister, "Some Aspects," 583-85, noted.

26. Albeck, *Das Buch der Jubiläen*, 33; Baumgarten, "The Laws of ʿOrlah," 198 n. 20.

festival? According to the rewritten story in Jub 17:15–18:17 (parallel to the Akedah story in Gen 22:1-19), God appeared to Abraham on the night of the twelfth of the first month (17:15), and commanded him to offer his son Isaac as a sacrifice. Abraham awoke that morning, departed on his journey, and on the third day (18:3), the fourteenth of the first month (the festival of Passover), arrived at the location where the Akedah took place, Mount Zion (18:13). Before he had the opportunity to sacrifice his "firstborn" son Isaac (vv. 11, 15), God sent an angel to prevent him from doing so, and Abraham offered a ram in Isaac's place. These four motifs — the date (fourteenth of first month), the firstborn being saved, the location in Jerusalem, and the sacrifice of a sheep — are found in only one biblical context, the Passover law. The rewritten story thus functions as a foreshadowing of the Passover law. According to the rewritten story (based upon Gen 22), Abraham and Isaac reached the land of Moriah on the third day of their journey. Following the trial, Abraham returned with his servants to Beersheba, a destination that, unless noted otherwise, should have been reached on the third day. The round-trip should not have taken any longer than six days (and perhaps only five, assuming that Abraham and Isaac set out to return to Beersheba on the day of the Akedah itself). The rewritten story does not mention the number seven at all.

In contrast, the legal passage at the end of chap. 18 (vv. 18-19) transforms the story into a precedent for the seven-day festival of *Maṣṣot* (fifteenth to twenty-first of the first month), and explicitly assumes that the journey lasted seven days. Even if one assumed that the rewritten story posited a seven-day journey, the dates of the trip (beginning on the twelfth of the first month) do not correspond to the Festival of Unleavened Bread (beginning on the fifteenth of the month).

9. *The plague of the firstborn.* In the rewritten story regarding the plagues and the exodus from Egypt (Jub 48), God and the angel of presence work *against* the will of Mastema in helping Moses return to Egypt, in the bringing of all the plagues (in particular the slaying of the firstborn), and in the salvation of Israel. There is explicit emphasis on God's active role in meting out the plagues himself (vv. 5, 8). In contrast, according to the juxtaposed legal passage in Jub 49, the Lord sent "the forces of Mastema," described two verses later as "the Lord's forces," to kill the firstborn (49:2), and refrained from being directly involved in this plague. These two descriptions thus differ in terms of God's role in this specific story, but more significantly in the place of the forces of evil (represented by Mastema) in the world, who work either at cross-purposes with God or as his agents.

33

10. *The punishments for Reuben and Bilhah.* In the brief story in Gen 35:22, which describes how Reuben slept with his father's concubine Bilhah, there is no reference to a punishment for Reuben or Bilhah. Other biblical passages criticize Reuben for his behavior (Gen 49:3-4), and describe how this led to his loss of the birthright (1 Chron 5:1-2), but do not mention an individual punishment in response to their behavior. This absence is at odds with biblical laws that prohibit intercourse with one's father's wife (Lev 18:8; 20:11; Deut 23:1; 27:20), and especially Lev 20:11, which calls for the death penalty for both the man and his father's wife. According to Pentateuchal law, both Reuben and Bilhah should have been punished by death.

The rewritten story in Jub 33:1-9a presents Bilhah as the victim of rape, thus offering a justification for her nonpunishment. There is no explicit mention of a punishment for Reuben in this section, although interestingly, in the Testament of Reuben, which preserves a partially overlapping version of the events,[27] he is indeed punished, as Reuben recounts, "he struck me with a severe wound in my loins for seven months" (TReu 1:7), a particularly apt punishment for sexual impropriety.

In contrast, the legal passage (vv. 9b-20) uses completely different legal categories to absolve Reuben and Bilhah. Instead of compulsion versus free will, the legal passage acquits both Reuben **and** Bilhah from any punishment for a different, technical reason: "for the statute, the punishment, and the law had not been completely revealed to all" (v. 16). This approach does not impart significance to the individual's intentions or motivations, but rather to the status of the laws themselves at the time of their violation.

II. The Literary Development of Jubilees

While each of these individual contradictions can be harmonized to resolve the inherent tension, as has been suggested by scholars regarding a few of the examples, I suggest that their cumulative effect is sufficient to demonstrate that the book is not the product of one author. The presence of two different, and often contradictory, interpretations or traditions side by side in each of these cases should not be viewed merely as "overkill," to use the term

27. For an analysis of the relationship between the versions of the story in Jubilees and the Testament of Reuben, see J. L. Kugel, "Reuben's Sin with Bilhah in the Testament of Reuben," in *Pomegranates and Golden Bells: Studies in Biblical, Jewish, and Near Eastern Ritual, Law, and Literature in Honor of Jacob Milgrom*, ed. D. P. Wright et al. (Winona Lake, Ind.: Eisenbrauns, 1995), 525-54 (here 550-54).

coined by Kugel, according to which multiple interpretive solutions to the same problem were combined together in one composition,[28] because there is no reason for these solutions to be consistently differentiated by their literary genre. Moreover, the chronological contradictions, and especially the case of the births of Jacob's sons (example 2), do not lend themselves to easy explanation as the result of the conscious combination of exegetical traditions, as one would expect a single author to weave together these alternate traditions to form a cohesive and coherent story.

As a final point, the Watchers story (example 3) perhaps provides us with a key to understanding this process of development. It should be noted that the borrowing of 1 En 10–11 described above is limited to Jub 5:1-12. The subsequent section, vv. 13-18, emphasizes the legal aspects of the Watchers story — each group described in that passage (Watchers, giants, people) receives an appropriate punishment, as set out for them before they behaved sinfully. This additional passage is marked by terminology similar to that found in legal passages throughout Jubilees, and one can safely assume that it is of the same provenance as the other legal passages. I suggest that Jub 5 can be taken as an empirical model for the literary development of the book as a whole, based upon the following pattern: a rewritten biblical text (1 En 10–11) was adopted, placed within a new chronological framework (the addition of the date in 5:1 — see above), and supplemented by a juxtaposed legal passage.

In the case of Jub 5, a contradiction between the chronological framework and the rewritten narrative was identified, but no such tension is present between the story and the legal passage. However, the literary evidence, and specifically the dependence upon an extant text, attests to the boundaries of the borrowed material (Jub 5:1-12) and the contributions of the redactor (vv. 13-18). In contrast to Jub 5, in most of the examples of contradictions listed above, there is no direct, literary evidence that Jubilees borrowed from a specific composition. However, using this passage as a model for the book as a whole, the notion of a redactor with halakic and chronological emphases who incorporated extant rewritten texts can be used to explain the presence of the contradictions between the rewritten narratives and the other two genres. The differences between them are the result of their different origins, and they were combined as part of the compositional process of the book of Jubilees.

---

28. J. L. Kugel, *In Potiphar's House: The Interpretive Life of Biblical Texts* (San Francisco: Harper, 1990), 256-57.

The Relationship between
Jubilees and the Early Enochic Books
(Astronomical Book and Book of the Watchers)

John S. Bergsma

The task of this paper is to investigate the relationship between the earlier Enochic books — the Astronomical Book (hereafter AB; i.e., 1 En 72–82) and the Book of the Watchers (hereafter BW; 1 En 1–36) — and the book of Jubilees. It is generally assumed that there is a literary relationship between these works, and — largely on the basis of their estimated dates of composition — that the direction of influence flows from the Enochic texts to Jubilees. First, the evidence and arguments for the dating of the three documents will be reviewed. Second, AB and BW will each be compared with Jubilees to observe similarities and differences in narrative and theology. Finally, generalizations will be made about the nature of Jubilees' relationship to the early Enochic literature.

I. The Dating of the Astronomical Book, the Book of the Watchers, and Jubilees

A. The Date of the Astronomical Book

The Astronomical Book, considered the earliest of the Enochic texts, is frequently assigned a third century B.C.E. date on the basis of the following data:[1]

---

1. For a thorough discussion see J. C. VanderKam, *Enoch and the Growth of an Apocalyptic Tradition*, CBQMS 16 (Washington, D.C.: CBA, 1984), 79-88.

1. *Manuscript Evidence. At least one apparently Enochic astronomical text from Qumran dates to circa 200* B.C.E. The most important evidence for establishing the relative antiquity of AB is the manuscript evidence from Qumran, which yielded four fragmentary Aramaic scrolls that bear a relationship to the Ethiopic version familiar to us. The nomenclature, dating, and contents of the manuscripts are detailed in the following table:[2]

Qumran Document	Paleographic Dating	Contents
4QEnastr[a] (4Q208)	ca. 220-180 B.C.E.	Table of moon phases possibly summarized in 1 En 73:4-8
4QEnastr[b] (4Q209)	ca. 10 B.C.E.- 10 C.E.	Table of moon phases, but also parts of 1 En 76:14-77; 78:10; 78:17-79:2; 82:9-13
4QEnastr[c] (4Q210)	ca. 50 B.C.E.	Parts of 1 En 76:3-10; 76:13-77:3; 78:6-8
4QEnastr[d] (4Q211)	ca. 50-1 B.C.E.	Unparalleled in 1 Enoch but apparently a completion of 82:15-20

The relationship between these Qumran manuscripts and the dating of AB is, unfortunately, not straightforward. The Qumran texts are quite fragmentary and witness to a larger document that included material that was sum-

---

2. For the source of this information and general discussion of the date of AB, see J. T. Milik, *The Books of Enoch: Aramaic Fragments of Qumran Cave 4* (Oxford: Clarendon, 1976), 7-22; also M. A. Knibb, *The Ethiopic Book of Enoch*, 2 vols. (Oxford: Clarendon, 1978), 2:11-12. The dating of any individual scroll may be debated. The paleographic dates provided here are those of Milik. Few scholars have the expertise, resources, and access necessary to reassess Milik's work. His proposed dates have been challenged by radiocarbon dating: see A. Jull, D. Donahue, M. Broshi, and E. Tov, "Radiocarbon Dating of Scrolls and Linen Fragments from the Judean Desert," *Atiqot* 28 (1996): 85-91 (here 86), and G. Doudna, "Dating the Scrolls on the Basis of Radiocarbon Analysis," in *The Dead Sea Scrolls after Fifty Years: A Comprehensive Assessment*, ed. P. Flint and J. VanderKam, 2 vols. (Leiden: Brill, 1998-99), 1:430-65. However, as Doudna points out, even carbon dating can produce erroneous results due to sample contamination, inaccurate calibration curves, laboratory error, and other factors. Doudna reports a date range for 4QEnastr[a] of 160-40 B.C.E. (*one sigma*, i.e., 68 percent confidence [462]), but also points out the possibility of contamination in the group of texts to which the sample of 4QEnastr[a] belonged (452). We have chosen, for the present, to disregard the carbon dating until greater confidence can be expressed about the certainty of the results.

marized or (by intention or accident) omitted in the later Ethiopic version. Furthermore, the oldest manuscript by far, 4QEnastr[a], consists only of a table of moon phases, which is not present in Ethiopic AB (although perhaps summarized in 1 En 73:4-8). Enoch is not mentioned within 4QEnastr[a]: it is possible, though unlikely, that it represents a free-standing astronomical work only later associated with Enoch. 4QEnastr[b] does include *both* (1) sections of text overlapping with 4QEnastr[a] *and* (2) material with an observable textual relationship to portions of Ethiopic AB. J. T. Milik, editor of the *editio princeps,* concluded from this that 4QEnastr[a] was indeed an Enochic document whose demonstrably Enochic portions were missing but partially extant in 4QEnastr[b].[3]

If one wished to contest the explicitly Enochic character of 4QEnastr[a], then the next earliest manuscript with a significant relationship to Ethiopic AB is 4QEnastr[c] from the mid–first century B.C.E. But even in this case, 4QEnastr[c] is not simply the Aramaic *Vorlage* for the Greek from which Ethiopic AB was translated. It is a considerably different text, although similar enough that a literary relationship is certain.

To summarize: the Qumran evidence demonstrates, at least, that by the mid–first century B.C.E. an Enochic astronomical book larger than, but textually related to, the Ethiopic Enoch 72–82 was in circulation. Furthermore, it is highly probable that 4QEnastr[a] was indeed an Enochic text, part of the larger Aramaic AB abbreviated in the Ethiopic, and thus the date of the composition of this document would be at the latest *(terminus ad quem)* in the late third century B.C.E. — substantially earlier than the usual date assigned to Jubilees.

2. *Internal Evidence. The simple schemes and formulas of AB appear closely related to primitive Babylonian astronomical texts dating as early as the seventh century B.C.E.* The astronomical principles of AB are simplistic and, unfortunately, inaccurate. It is striking, however, that the same linear progressions of increasing light or darkness and the same ratios expressing the relative lengths of day and night are found in texts from the infancy of Babylonian astronomical science, especially in the so-called MUL.APIN texts.[4] The earliest extant tablet of the MUL.APIN series dates from 687 B.C.E.

---

3. See VanderKam, *Enoch,* 81-82.

4. For fuller discussion of the relationship between AB and the Qumran astronomical texts, see H. Drawnel, "Some Notes on Scribal Craft and the Origins of the Enochic Literature," *Hen* 31, no. 1 (2009). Drawnel points out the similarities of 4Q208 and 4Q209 not only to the MUL.APIN texts, but especially to the Babylonian *Enuma Anu Enlil* (EAE) astrological series, which originates in the second millennium B.C.E.

(VAT 9412). Full explanations of the numerous connections between Enochic AB and the MUL.APIN texts have been made by Neugebauer and VanderKam — the details need not detain us here.[5] Suffice it to quote Neugebauer: "There is no visible trace [in the Enochic AB] of the sophisticated Babylonian astronomy of the Persian or Seleucid-Parthian period."[6]

While Neugebauer denies that this information is of any help in dating the composition of Enochic AB,[7] it seems to this author, at least, that the absence from AB of any of the advances in ancient Near Eastern astronomy from the Persian or Hellenistic periods argues for an origin of this literature in the Babylonian exile. AB may be an appropriation of the astral science of Babylon to which the Judean scribes/scholars were exposed during this time period.[8]

3. *External Evidence. Pseudo-Eupolemus seems to know AB.* Two fragments of Pseudo-Eupolemus's work on the Jewish people, cited by Alexander Polyhistor and preserved in turn by Eusebius (*Ecclesiastical History* 9.17.2-9; 18.2), make reference to Enoch's astronomical knowledge. According to Pseudo-Eupolemus, Enoch (1) was instructed in astrology by the angels, and so (2) became the first astrologer, and (3) transmitted his knowledge to Methuselah. These three elements are the basic premises of AB, leading to the conclusion that Pseudo-Eupolemus was familiar with the work. Pseudo-Eupolemus's date of writing is difficult to establish, but circa 200 B.C.E. is a reasonable hypothesis.[9] This would again place the *terminus ad quem* of AB in the late third century B.C.E.

The manuscript, internal, and external evidence suggest a date of composition of Aramaic AB at least in the third century B.C.E. and probably earlier.

B. The Date of the Book of the Watchers

The Book of the Watchers is generally dated circa 200 B.C.E. or earlier, yet after AB, based on the following data:

---

5. See discussion in O. Neugebauer and M. Black, *The "Astronomical" Chapters of the Ethiopic Book of Enoch (72 to 82)* (Copenhagen: Munksgaard, 1981), 11-12, 20; VanderKam, *Enoch*, 92-104.

6. Neugebauer, *"Astronomical" Chapters*, 4; VanderKam, *Enoch*, 102.

7. Neugebauer, *"Astronomical" Chapters*, 4.

8. Cf. VanderKam, *Enoch*, 101-2; Milik, *The Books of Enoch*, 12-18; J. Ben-Dov, "The Babylonian Lunar Three in Calendrical Scrolls from Qumran," *ZA* 95 (2005): 104-20, esp. 107-8, 112; Drawnel, "Some Notes on Scribal Craft and the Origins of the Enochic Literature."

9. VanderKam, *Enoch*, 85.

1. *Manuscript Evidence. The earliest Qumran manuscript of BW dates to circa 175 B.C.E.* The Qumran Aramaic fragments of BW are summarized in the following table:[10]

Qumran Document	Paleographic Dating	Contents
4QEn^a (4Q201)	ca. 200-150 B.C.E.	Parts of 1 En 1–12
4QEn^b (4Q202)	ca. 150 B.C.E.	Parts of 1 En 5–14
4QEn^c (4Q204)	ca. 50-1 B.C.E.	Parts of 1 En 1–36; 89; 104–107
4QEn^d (4Q205)	ca. 50-1 B.C.E.	Parts of 1 En 22–27; 89
4QEn^e (4Q206)	ca. 100-50 B.C.E.	Parts of 1 En 22; 28–34; 88–89

The most important manuscript for our purposes is the first and oldest, 4QEn^a, dating to the first half of the second century B.C.E. This probably pushes the *terminus ad quem* of the composition of the book into the late third century.

2. *Internal Evidence. BW shows the influence of Hellenistic culture, but no clear allusions to Antiochus Epiphanes and the Maccabean revolt.*[11] The most convincing example of Hellenistic influence in BW is the similarity in career profile between the angel Asael (or Azaz'el) and the Greek titan Prometheus.[12] There are also similarities, although less specific, between the description of the Watchers' offspring and the Greek legends of the giants.[13]

Some have argued that the portrayal of the Watchers' rapacious offspring — the giants — is a veiled criticism of the *diadochoi*, who claimed divine descent and whose governing policies impoverished and oppressed their subjects.[14] Bartelmus argues that BW was composed during the reign of the most notorious of the *diadochoi*, Antiochus IV Epiphanes.[15] However, there is no clear allusion to Antiochus Epiphanes in BW. Furthermore, it is not necessary to see the giants as literary reflections of the *diadochoi*, since the descrip-

10. See discussion in VanderKam, *Enoch*, 111-12; Milik, *The Books of Enoch*, 22-41; Knibb, *Ethiopic Book of Enoch*, 8-11.

11. On the Hellenistic influence on BW generally, see G. H. Van Kooten, "Enoch, the 'Watchers,' Seth's Descendants and Abraham as Astronomers: Jewish Applications of the Greek Motif of the First Inventor (300 BCE–CE 100)," in *Recycling Biblical Figures*, ed. A. Brenner and J. W. van Henten, STAR 1 (Leiden: Deo, 1999), 292-316.

12. See R. Bartelmus, *Heroentum in Israel und seinem Umwelt*, ATANT 65 (Zürich: Theologischer, 1979), 161-66; VanderKam, *Enoch*, 126-28.

13. VanderKam, *Enoch*, 127.

14. Discussed in VanderKam, *Enoch*, 128.

15. Bartelmus, *Heroentum*, 179-83.

tion of the giants in BW can be explained as a development of the story of Gen 6:1-4. The dual descent — angelic and human — of the giants is simply an exegetical conclusion from Gen 6:4. The fact that they were gigantic may be derived from interpreting Gen 6:4 in light of Num 13:3. Being of gigantic stature and the sons of wicked angels, their behavior, one would assume, was highly consumptive, oppressive, and violent. Thus, there is no reason to invoke the *diadochoi* as the specific inspiration for these characteristics.

Even though there are no clear allusions to any specific Hellenistic rulers in BW, a Hellenistic influence is present. This influence indicates a date in the very late fourth century at the earliest *(terminus a quo)*. The lack of any reflection of the crisis under Antiochus IV suggests a *terminus ad quem* in the early second century B.C.E.

3. *Internal Evidence. The latter part of the book (1 En 33–36) seems to summarize AB.* The last few chapters of BW paraphrase the content of AB: 1 En 33:2-4 summarizes 1 En 72:3 and 75:1-4; 1 En 34–36 paraphrases 1 En 75–76. One may conclude that AB was known to the author/editor of BW. It is interesting to note, however, that the larger portion of AB is taken up with the cycles of the sun and moon, and neither is mentioned in the last chapters of BW (1 En 33–36). Instead, stars and winds — which are of lesser concern to AB — are the focus of attention.

The combined data make it likely that BW was composed no later than the end of the third, and no earlier than the end of the fourth century B.C.E.

C. The Date of Jubilees

The date of composition of the book of Jubilees is estimated by VanderKam at circa 160-150 B.C.E. based on the following data:[16]

1. *Manuscript Evidence. The oldest Qumran manuscript (4Q216) dates from 125 to 100 B.C.E.* A total of fifteen manuscripts of Jubilees were discovered at Qumran. Here our only concern need be with the oldest, 4Q216, which preserves a fair amount of text from Jub 1–2 and dates from the last quarter of the second century B.C.E. Since 4Q216 is almost certainly not the autograph, the *terminus ad quem* for the composition of Jubilees probably lies in the third quarter of the second century.[17]

16. The best discussion remains J. C. VanderKam, *Textual and Historical Studies on the Book of Jubilees*, HSM 14 (Missoula: Scholars Press, 1977), 207-85.

17. See J. A. T. G. M. van Ruiten, "A Literary Dependency of Jubilees on 1 Enoch?" in

2. *Some narratives in Jubilees have been shaped to reflect events of the Maccabean period.* As VanderKam states it, "the battles of Jacob and his sons in *Jubilees* are probably literarily re-structured accounts of Judas Maccabeus' most important battles and campaigns."[18] The two examples are Jacob's war with the seven Amorite kings in Jub 34:2-9, which parallels Judas Maccabeus's victory over Nicanor and his allies in 161 B.C.E., and Jacob's war with Esau and allies in Jub 37:1–38:14, corresponding to Judas's defeat of the Idumeans and allied forces circa 163 B.C.E.[19] The evidence for the first example is especially compelling, and would establish the *terminus a quo* for the composition of Jubilees at circa 160 B.C.E.

3. *Jubilees does not reflect the schism between proponents of the solar calendar and the rest of Judaism.* Later Qumran documents do reflect this schism. VanderKam and others place the break between the forebears of the Qumran community (solar calendar advocates) and establishment (i.e., Jerusalemite) Judaism during the reign of the Maccabean high priests Jonathan (152-142 B.C.E.) or Simon (142-134 B.C.E.). Of these two, Jonathan seems the more likely. If the author of Jubilees had written as late as circa 140 B.C.E., one would expect reference to more recent events,[20] and less adulation of the priesthood in light of the corruption of the Maccabean high priests.[21]

On the basis of this data, VanderKam establishes the date of the composition of Jubilees in the rather narrow window 160-150 B.C.E.

II. The Relationship of the Astronomical Book and Jubilees

The discussion of the dating of AB and Jubilees above demonstrates that it is highly likely that Aramaic AB was in existence prior to the composition of Jubilees. One could argue to the contrary only by denying that 4QEnastr[a] ever formed a part of a larger Aramaic AB, which would lower the paleographic *terminus ad quem* to the mid–first century B.C.E. (4QEnastr[c]). But such a denial seems unwarranted. Moreover, the lack of Hellenistic in-

---

Enoch and Qumran Origins: A New Light on a Forgotten Connection, ed. G. Boccaccini (Grand Rapids: Eerdmans, 2005), 90-93.

18. VanderKam, *Textual and Historical Studies,* 217.

19. VanderKam, *Textual and Historical Studies,* 218-38.

20. Judas Maccabeus's victory over Nicanor in 161 B.C.E. is the last datable event to which Jubilees clearly alludes.

21. See VanderKam, *Textual and Historical Studies,* 284.

fluence on AB and the fairly clear presence of it in Jubilees certainly suggest that AB is the product of an earlier era.

Furthermore, many scholars have concluded from Jub 4:17-18, 21 that the author of Jubilees had knowledge of AB, the contents of which seem quite well summarized, especially in v. 17.[22] Opinion varies whether v. 21 refers to AB or the second half of BW (1 En 17–36).

J. A. T. G. van Ruiten and M. A. Knibb have pointed out, however, that although Jub 4:17-18 mentions Enoch composing a work whose description sounds like AB, there are in fact no passages in Jubilees that exhibit demonstrable literary dependency on the text of AB, in marked contrast to the literary relationship between Jubilees and Genesis.[23]

It is true that the author of Jubilees does not reproduce the text of AB in the same way he reproduces the text of Genesis. However, this need not mean that the text of AB was unavailable to him; only that he chose to handle the Enochic texts differently than that of Genesis. While he follows the biblical text fairly closely at times, he is content merely to summarize the contents of AB and other Enochic works.

The influence of AB on Jubilees is, oddly, not as significant as one might expect. Of course, the two works have several commonalities:

- The 364-day "solar" calendar is the only legitimate one.
- Astronomical and meteorological phenomena are guided by spiritual beings (cf. Jub 2:2; 1 En 82:7-20).
- The natural order is scrupulously obedient to divine laws.
- Enoch is the first astrologer, having been educated by angels.

However, all these commonalities were probably widely present in second temple Judaism. Therefore, one cannot say that Jubilees borrowed the 364-day calendar directly from AB. Rather, both works probably reflect a common calendrical tradition.

The differences between AB and Jubilees are actually more interesting than the similarities:

22. See VanderKam, "Enoch Traditions in Jubilees and Other Second-Century Sources," in *SBLSP* 13 (1978), 229-51 (here 233-34); Milik, *The Books of Enoch,* 11; P. Grelot, "Hénoch et ses Écritures," *RB* 82 (1975): 481-500 (here 484-85).

23. Van Ruiten, "Literary Dependency," 90-93; M. A. Knibb, "Which Parts of 1 *Enoch* Were Known to *Jubilees*? A Note on the Interpretation of *Jubilees 4.16-25*," in *Reading from Right to Left: Essays on the Hebrew Bible in Honour of David J. A. Clines,* ed. C. Exum and H. G. M. Williamson, JSOTSup 373 (Sheffield: Sheffield Academic Press, 2003), 254-62.

1. *Different calendrical conflicts are reflected in the two books.* AB is emphatic about the truth of the 364-day calendar; however, it never inveighs against proponents of a luni-solar or 365-day arrangement. Instead, AB's opponents are those who fail to count the four epagomenal days: "There are people who err concerning them [the four epagomenal days] by not counting them in the reckoning of the year: . . . the year is completed in 364 days" (1 En 82:5-6).[24] Apparently, then, AB reflects a conflict with advocates of a 360-day calendar.

The calendrical opponents of Jubilees are quite different. Jub 6:36-38 warns about those who "examine the moon diligently, because it [the moon] will corrupt the times." Those who consult the moon will "not make a year *only* three hundred and sixty-four days" (6:38). The modifier "only" implies that the opposing moon-consultors *lengthen* the year. So surely what is being opposed is a luni-solar calendar periodically intercalated to comply with the actual (365.25) solar cycle.

2. *From the perspective of Jubilees, AB shows disappointingly little interest in superannual calendrical units (i.e., weeks of years and jubilee cycles).* To be precise, AB does not mention them at all. Of course, this does not prevent the author of Jubilees from attributing the knowledge of weeks and jubilees to Enoch: he "recounted the weeks of the jubilees, and made known to them the days of the years, and set in order the months and recounted the Sabbaths of the years" (Jub 4:18).[25] It is possible that this is an allusion to the Apocalypse of Weeks (AW), which mentions "weeks" instead of "Sabbaths" or "jubilees." However, in AW the "weeks" are long epochs of variable length, not strict seven-year sequences as they are in Jubilees. Moreover, AW does not place its "weeks" within a jubilary cycle ("weeks of jubilees"), nor does it discuss "Sabbaths of years." Therefore, it does not seem likely that Jub 4:18 reflects the contents of AW. Instead, this may well be the author's creative and expansive redescription of the contents of Enoch's astronomical book. Although it is to be doubted that the Aramaic form of AB known to the author of Jubilees included anything about weeks of years and jubilees, nonetheless the author of Jubilees is confident that this information was revealed to Enoch and he wrote it down in texts that are no longer extant.

---

24. From Neugebauer, *"Astronomical" Chapters*, 31.
25. Translation from R. H. Charles, *The Book of Jubilees or the Little Genesis* (London: A. & C. Black, 1902).

GENERALIZATIONS

To summarize, it is almost certain that the author of Jubilees knew and endorsed AB. However, AB made only a limited impact on the theology or narrative of Jubilees. The most important elements Jubilees shares with AB are its calendar and its general perspective on the cosmos, but Jubilees is not *dependent* on AB for these concepts. Rather, both texts reflect a stream of second temple Jewish thought. Different calendrical debates are at the heart of the two texts. What the author of Jubilees would have liked to find most in AB — namely, the enumeration of divisions of weeks of years and jubilees — simply wasn't there. Nonetheless, Jubilees freely attributes this knowledge to Enoch.

A general contrast between "scientific" and "cultic-liturgical" interests may be observed. AB is fascinated with the "science" of the heavenly bodies in part, at least, for its own sake, whereas Jubilees sees no point in astronomical knowledge except as it is relevant to establishing the proper cultic calendar.

III. The Relationship of the Book of the Watchers and Jubilees

The discussion of the dating of BW and Jubilees above demonstrated that it is highly unlikely that BW postdates Jubilees. To argue such would require that one either (1) take the lowest possible date (on paleographic grounds) of the oldest manuscript of BW from Qumran (4QEn[a]), i.e., circa 150 B.C.E., and then assume that BW was composed very shortly after Jubilees; or (2) argue that Jubilees is pre-Maccabean, which is unlikely in light of Jub 38:14, which could hardly have been penned before the Maccabean conquest of Edom under John Hyrcanus (163 B.C.E.).

Therefore, one is justified in assuming that Jubilees postdates BW, and the apparent literary relationship between the two works may be interpreted in terms of Jubilees' dependence on BW.

The influence of BW on Jubilees is most apparent in four passages, described in the following table:[26]

Passage Synopsis of Contents

4:16   The Watchers descend during the days of Jared, to teach mankind and "perform judgment and righteousness" on earth.

4:21-26 Summarizes the contents of BW, with modification: The angels

---

26. The unexcelled study of the dependence of Jubilees on Enochic material remains VanderKam, "Enoch Traditions in Jubilees and Other Second-Century Sources."

showed Enoch everything in heaven and earth. He witnessed against the Watchers, was taken to Eden, and now resides there, recording and condemning the sins of humanity until the day of judgment.

5:1-11   Paraphrases 1 En 6:1–10:16, with modification. The Watchers descend to earth and take wives. Violent giants are born, who oppress and corrupt both man and beast. God punishes the Watchers by binding them under the earth, and the giants are condemned to kill one another by the sword.

7:21–8:4 Noah recaps Jub 5:1-11 (cf. 1 En 6:1–10:16), the basic Watchers story, while warning his sons about the demons who will mislead them (cf. 1 En 15:8–16:3). Cainan son of Arpachshad finds a stone engraved with the Watchers' astrological lore, and sins by copying it and (apparently) learning to practice astrological divination. This is the origin of the astrology of Cainan's descendants the Chaldeans (cf. Jub 11:8), which Abram eventually rejects (cf. Jub 12:16-18).

10:1-17   Concerning the evil spirits that came forth from the bodies of the slain giants (cf. 1 En 15:8–16:3), Noah pleads to God that they be bound in the underworld. The prince of the demons, Mastema, pleads to the contrary, that he be allowed some servants to do his will on earth. God binds nine-tenths of the demons but leaves one-tenth to carry out Mastema's will.

11:4-6   Mastema and the remnant of demons left to him are mentioned as contributing to the evil activities of Noah's descendants.

After chap. 11 the Watchers fade from view in the narrative of Jubilees, and with them the influence of BW, with the exception of a brief mention of the giants in Jub 20:5.

Jubilees accepts and endorses the basic narrative of BW. The two works can be said to agree on the following points:

- The "Sons of God" of Gen 6:1-4 are fallen angels (Watchers) who copulated with women and produced giants.
- The Watchers taught illicit mysteries to mankind.
- The giants are at least partially responsible for the violence and evil that brought God's judgment in the form of the flood.
- Enoch rebuked and issued judgment against the Watchers and their offspring.
- The Watchers were bound under the earth, the giants killed each other off, but demons came forth from the dead giants.

- These demons continue to plague mankind even after the flood.
- Enoch was eventually shown the secrets of the entire cosmos.

Despite the fact that Jubilees embraces these basic premises, its author introduces a large number of modifications to the plot of the Watchers story, several of which are theologically significant.[27] A. Reed and L. Stuckenbruck have both made insightful and thorough contributions to the analysis of the differences between BW and Jubilees.[28] Here, we must be content only to mention the most important differences:

1. *The motive for the descent of the Watchers is different.* Jub 4:15 notes that the Watchers "came down" in the days of the ancestor Jared (יָרַד, "to descend") in order "to teach the sons of man, and perform judgment and righteousness on earth." This is in stark contrast to BW, in which two hundred angels bind each other by a solemn oath *while still in heaven* to descend to the earth and take human wives (1 En 6:1-8). After taking the women, the angels begin to teach secret arts and sciences (1 En 7–8), but this was not a motivation for their initial descent.

Thus, in Jubilees the Watchers come down initially for a noble purpose (to teach and judge) and only later corrupt themselves. In BW, however, the Watchers succumb to the temptation of feminine attraction while still in heaven, swear an oath to commit a grievous sin, carry out the act, and then aggravate the situation by communicating illicit knowledge.

One can only speculate on the reason Jubilees modifies the narrative of BW.[29] Perhaps the BW account seemed theologically problematic: How could angels fall prey to sensual temptation and deliberately, self-consciously organize themselves into a rebellious body while still in heaven and presumably in or near the presence of God himself? In Jubilees it is only after the Watchers leave heaven to carry out their task on earth that — apparently after

---

27. For some discussion of the differences, see I. Fröhlich, "Enoch and Jubilees," in *Enoch and Qumran Origins,* 141-47. Unsurprisingly, VanderKam has also examined the Watcher story in both BW and Jubilees. See VanderKam, "The Angel Story in the Book of Jubilees," in *Pseudepigraphic Perspectives: The Apocrypha and Pseudepigrapha in Light of the Dead Sea Scrolls,* ed. E. G. Chazon and M. Stone, STDJ 31 (Leiden: Brill, 1999), 151-70. VanderKam's analysis proceeds in a different fashion from mine, but our conclusions are similar.

28. See A. Y. Reed, "Enochic and Mosaic Traditions in Jubilees: The Evidence of Angelology and Demonology" (paper read at Fourth Enoch Seminar, Camaldoli, Italy, 8-12 July 2007); and L. T. Stuckenbruck, "The Book of Jubilees and the Origin of Evil," in this volume.

29. VanderKam discusses the issue in "Enoch Traditions in Jubilees," 244.

the passage of some years (cf. Jub 5:1) — they succumb to temptation. Perhaps the extended time of service away from the heavenly realm makes their defection more plausible. God, too, is not implicated in their sin to the same degree. In the BW narrative one is tempted to ask, "Could God not have opposed or prevented the Watchers' pact-of-sin taking place in the heavenly realm?" In contrast, Jubilees assures its readers that God sent the Watchers to the earth for good purposes, and there on earth — far from him — they eventually defected.

2. *Enoch never appeals on behalf of the Watchers, he only witnesses against them.* The section describing Enoch's intercession on behalf of the Watchers (1 En 12–16) is elided in Jubilees, no doubt because the whole scenario presents multiple theological difficulties. First, it is inappropriate for a human being to intercede on behalf of angelic beings in general, as BW itself acknowledges (1 En 15:2). Second, since the Watchers' sin was so serious, why did Enoch agree to take up their case before the Almighty? It calls into question his good moral judgment. Jubilees avoids these difficulties by presenting Enoch only in the role of witnessing *against* the Watchers and their iniquity.

3. *Mankind bears more responsibility for evil; they are not merely passive victims of the Watchers, giants, and demons.* In 1 En 7–9 the Watchers and their giant offspring oppress the population of the earth with violence, and their innocent victims bring their case before God posthumously (1 En 9:10). God's response is, in part, to send the flood (1 En 10:2). There is a serious difficulty with this scenario: If the Watchers and their offspring are responsible for oppressing the human population of the earth, why does God respond by wiping out the human population in the flood? It would seem that God is punishing the victims. Thus, in BW the sins of the Watchers do not provide a moral justification for the flood. Indeed, BW does not stress the causal relationship between the Watchers' sins and the flood. The flood is not narrated (as it is in Jubilees), and 1 En 10:2 is the only mention of either Noah or the flood in the whole of BW.

Jubilees is more faithful to the intention of the text of Gen 6:1-4. It never directly states — even if it implies — that the Watchers misled mankind or *caused* mankind to be evil. Instead, in passages such as Jub 5:2-3 and 7:22-25, mankind (and the animals) are described as corrupting *themselves.* Therefore, the flood appears as morally justified. It wipes out all human and animal life, because both man and animals had freely given themselves over to great evil — even if enticed and assisted by the Watchers. This is one of several differences between Jubilees and BW in which Jubilees emerges with a tighter, more logically and theologically coherent narrative.[30]

4. *The postflood activity of demons is portrayed as much more limited.* In BW evil spirits emerge from the bodies of the slain giants and are free to wreak havoc in human society indefinitely (1 En 15:8-12). In Jub 10:1-14 the origin of the demons appears to be the same, but Noah petitions God to bind them, with the result that nine-tenths are bound in the place of judgment. One-tenth is left to carry out the will of the Satan-figure Mastema on earth. Thus the range of influence of the demons in Jubilees is considerably more limited than in BW.[31]

This is part of a consistent *tendenz* of Jubilees vis-à-vis BW to emphasize human rather than demonic responsibility for the iniquities of human society. A pointed example of this is Jub 11:1-6, which describes the degradation of human society after the death of Noah. Responsibility for the corruption is attributed to Noah's descendants in vv. 2-4. At the end of v. 4 it is finally mentioned that "cruel spirits *assisted* them and led them astray,"[32] and v. 5 mentions the activity of Mastema. The entire passage illustrates Jubilees' approach to the problem of human sin: human beings give themselves over to sin and so are responsible for it, although there is no doubt that evil spirits encourage the process. After Jub 11 there is very little mention of evil spirits being responsible for human sin in the rest of Jubilees.[33]

As a corollary to this discussion, it may be pointed out that Jubilees does not show the concern for the names and identities of the evil Watchers that BW does. BW enumerates their names and roles in various places (cf. 1 En 6:7; 8:1-4), and places at their head at times one Azaz'el (or Asael), and at other times a certain Semyaza (or Shemihaza). The only named demon in Jubilees, by contrast, is their leader Mastema, a Satan figure who combines the roles of Azaz'el and Semyaza. In this way Jubilees resolves the awkward confusion in 1 Enoch concerning the identity of the head demon.

---

30. For further discussion on the origin of evil in BW and Jubilees, see G. Borgonovo, "Jubilees' Rapprochement between Henochic and Mosaic Tradition," *Hen* 31, no. 1 (2009). Borgonovo agrees that Jubilees stresses human responsibility for evil, in agreement with the biblical text and in contrast to the Enochic literature.

31. See Reed, "Angelology and Demonology," 4-7.

32. Translated by O. S. Wintermute, *OTP,* 2:78.

33. Mastema is behind the testing of Abraham at the Akedah, but he is unable to lead Abraham into sin (Jub 18:9-12). He attempts to slay Moses (48:1-4) and is a motivating force behind the Egyptians' persecutions of Israel (48:9-19).

GENERALIZATIONS

Jubilees accepts the basic story of BW but adapts it rather freely, reshaping it to avoid several perceived theological problems — the origin of evil in heaven, the lack of a moral justification for the flood, Enoch's troublesome advocacy for evil angels, and others. BW shows its influence on Jubilees in the narrative extending from Jub 4 (the life of Enoch) to Jub 11 (the lives of Noah's immediate descendants). Thereafter the presence of BW is scarcely felt in Jubilees' narrative.[34]

BW is more an explanation for human evil in general than an explanation of the cause of the flood. BW traces the evils of humanity to the evil spirits of the giants and ultimately to their fathers, the Watchers, who sinned already in heaven. Thus the heavenly realm is the ultimate source of earthly evil. Jubilees, on the other hand, while accepting in principle BW's contention that some of societal evil has a supernatural origin (i.e., fallen angels), nonetheless emphasizes human responsibility to a much greater degree. Humans give themselves to evil, although evil spirits contribute to the process. In this way evil in Jubilees finds its origin in, and is limited to, the earthly realm.[35] As was noted above, in Jubilees the Watchers fall after they have already descended to the earth.

Finally, if a few broad observations may be permitted, the results of this study point to the fact that the influence of the early Enochic material in Jubilees is limited, for the most part, to the narratives of Jubilees from Enoch to Noah, roughly corresponding to Gen 5–9. Enoch's importance to Jubilees does not, in our opinion, come close to rivaling the importance of Moses.[36]

---

34. L. Arcari ("The Myth of the Watchers and the Problem of Intermarriage in Jubilees," *Hen* 31, no. 1 [2009]) understands the Watcher myth to function as a paradigmatic narrative grounding Jubilees' later condemnation of exogamous marriages. While this hypothesis is possible, I am not persuaded by it. The author of Jubilees draws no parallel between the Watchers' marriages and those between Jews and Gentiles in Jub 30:1-24 or elsewhere. Instead, he grounds his prohibitions against miscegenation in the Mosaic tradition.

35. VanderKam also makes this point, in "Enoch Traditions in Jubilees," 244.

36. In this respect I differ from H. S. Kvanvig, "Jubilees — between Enoch and Moses: A Narrative Reading," *JSJ* 35, no. 3 (2004): 243-61. In my opinion, the role of Enoch and the influence of the Enochic literature are not so great on Jubilees that the plot of the book should be characterized as "mediating" between the two figures. Moses and his tradition clearly dominate. Of course, the 364-day calendar of the Enochic tradition is important to Jubilees. But the calendar is valued because it facilitates scrupulous observance of Mosaic festivals, not because of its Enochic authority per se. On the superiority of Moses to Enoch, see D. M. Peters, "Noah Traditions in Jubilees: Evidence for the Struggle between Enochic and Mosaic Authority," *Hen* 31, no. 1 (2009).

The concerns and "theologies" of Jubilees and the early Enochic literature are actually significantly different in several respects. The differences concerning the origin of evil have been mentioned. We may add that Jubilees lacks the "scientific" interest of AB, takes a different attitude toward technology than BW, and shows a concern for the Mosaic law and cultic-liturgical observance quite lacking in either AB or BW.

Daniel and Jubilees

Matthias Henze

The purpose of this paper is to compare two Jewish writings from the second temple period, Daniel and Jubilees. The two books are linked by several affinities. First, both texts were written roughly at the same time, possibly within a decade of each other. The book of Daniel reached its final form during the years 167-164 B.C.E., the time of the persecutions under Antiochus IV. The date of composition of the book of Jubilees is more elusive, though a date in the 160s or 150s B.C.E. seems most likely.[1] Second, Daniel and Jubilees are both in their own way products of the Maccabean revolt. In Daniel the references to Antiochus are unambiguous and explicit. In Jubilees the connection with the Maccabean uprising is more tentative and has to be inferred. The prohibition of nakedness (Jub 3:30-31; cf. 1 Macc 1:14; 2 Macc 4:12) and the "prediction" of a time of apostasy during which the Israelites will no longer practice circumcision (Jub 15:33-34; cf. 1 Macc 1:15) are often quoted in this regard, though these passages may simply refer to controversial issues that arose during the advance of Hellenism in general. Third, both Daniel and Jubilees are of a considerable apocalyptic bent. Since neither Daniel nor Moses, Jubilees' protagonist, is ever taken into heaven, both texts belong, in terms of form criticism, to the group of "historical" apocalypses.

---

1. J. C. VanderKam, *The Book of Jubilees*, Guides to Apocrypha and Pseudepigrapha 9 (Sheffield: Sheffield Academic Press, 2001), 17-21; similarly G. W. E. Nickelsburg, *Jewish Literature between the Bible and the Mishnah*, 2nd ed. (Minneapolis: Fortress, 2006), opts for a date "in the early 160s" (73).

The Antiochean persecution provided the apocalyptically minded with a fresh momentum that led to the composition of a small yet diverse group of apocalypses of which Daniel and Jubilees are part. And fourth, a little over half a century after their composition, both Daniel and Jubilees found their way into the library of the Qumran community. The unusually high number of manuscripts discovered of both texts — no fewer than eight of Daniel and fifteen of Jubilees[2] — may be seen as an indication that the books were held in high esteem, and possibly even considered "authoritative" (CD 16:3-4), by the members of the community. It is easy to see how Daniel's apocalyptic outlook and Jubilees' priestly and legal concerns would have been highly popular at Qumran. Moreover, the Qumran library yielded a number of varied writings that closely resemble both books, the so-called Pseudo-Daniel (4Q243-245) and the Pseudo-Jubilees texts (4Q225-227). These hitherto unknown compositions show that there existed a very active continuous tradition of composing stories and visions associated with Daniel and Jubilees.[3]

While the two books have obvious affinities, some of which can be explained by the common Maccabean milieu from which they stem, in many other respects they diverge from one another. Their literary structures are entirely different, for example, as are their theological foci. Most strikingly, their reception history beyond Qumran took very different routes. Daniel became part of the Western biblical canons, whereas Jubilees never did.

My comparison of these two writings revolves around three aspects that also provide the structure for this essay: the authors' apocalyptic expectations, their use of biblical exegesis, and their chronological, specifically their heptadic, calculations. Any one of these topics deserves a full-length study of its own. What I hope to show in this brief comparative essay, however, is that while all three aspects are of central importance to both Daniel and Jubilees, they fulfill rather different functions in the two books. The is-

---

2. The numbers are taken from J. C. VanderKam and P. W. Flint, *The Meaning of the Dead Sea Scrolls* (New York: Harper San Francisco, 2002), 149 and 197.

3. Scholarly literature on this matter has grown exponentially in recent years; on Jubilees, see J. C. VanderKam, "The *Jubilees* Fragments from Qumran Cave 4," in *The Madrid Qumran Congress: Proceedings of the International Congress on the Dead Sea Scrolls, Madrid, 18-21 March, 1991*, ed. J. Trebolle Barrera and L. Vegas Montaner, STDJ 11 (Brill: Leiden, 1992), 635-48; C. Hempel, "The Place of the Book of *Jubilees* at Qumran and Beyond," in *The Dead Sea Scrolls in Their Historical Context*, ed. T. H. Lim (Edinburgh: T. & T. Clark, 2000), 187-96. On Daniel, see P. W. Flint, "The Daniel Tradition at Qumran," and L. T. Stuckenbruck, "Daniel and Early Enoch Traditions in the Dead Sea Scrolls," both in *The Book of Daniel: Composition and Reception*, ed. J. J. Collins and P. W. Flint, 2 vols., VTSup 83 (Leiden: Brill, 2001), 2:329-67 and 368-86; E. Ulrich, "Daniel, Book of," in *EDSS*, 170-74.

sues are fundamentally the same — apocalypticism, exegesis, and the calendar — but they are developed to different ends entirely. In other words, Daniel and Jubilees stem from closely related thought worlds whose concerns largely overlap, but as literary compositions the two books function differently. To observe that there are certain "parallels" between the two texts, then, is not merely to point to a literary phenomenon. Instead, the affinities speak to the fluidity, permeability, and exchange of thoughts in general that are characteristic of the literature of our period.[4] As we are gaining a better understanding of the contours of the Jewish communities of the second century B.C.E. and of the diverse literatures they produced, a comparative reading of the extant writings may help to cast into sharper relief the distinct strands of early Jewish thought and their evolution over time.

Apocalyptic Expectations

The apocalyptic nature of the book of Daniel hardly needs elaboration, though it may be helpful to review some of its constitutive elements. I do not wish to suggest that Daniel is the model of all apocalypses, as if the canonical writings enjoyed some privileged status and should serve as templates for the genre, nor do I claim that the apocalyptic genre can be described adequately by merely listing its prominent features. But it is useful to ask what it is that makes Daniel an apocalypse.

The book of Daniel is part of ancient Israel's revelatory literature. Its truth claims are not based on theological reasoning but derive from an appeal to revelation. What is recorded here is what Daniel received directly from God in the form of three visionary revelations (chaps. 7; 8; and 10–12). Daniel duly recorded everything he learned and kept it sealed "until the time of the end" (Dan 12:4, 9). The biblical book readily falls into two halves, the narrative frame that consists of a collection of biographical narratives *about* Daniel and his three companions in the first half (chaps. 1-6), and the visions related *by* Daniel in the latter half (chaps. 7–12).[5] There are no eschatological speculations in the first part of the book, nor do the Danielic court tales resemble in any way the testamentary genre so prominent in revelatory

4. On the issue of "para-mania," see R. Kraft, "Para-mania: Beside, Before, and Beyond Bible Studies," *JBL* 126 (2007): 5-27.

5. See the helpful collection J. J. Collins and P. W. Flint, eds., *The Book of Daniel: Composition and Reception*, 2 vols., VTSup 83 (Leiden: Brill, 2001), especially the article by R. G. Kratz, "The Visions of Daniel," 1:91-131.

literature. Rather, the purpose of the tales is to introduce Daniel and to establish his credentials as a worthy recipient of the apocalyptic lore. The revelations that form the core of the apocalyptic section of the book (chaps. 7–12) are allegorical dream visions, i.e., reviews of history in the form of *ex eventu* prophecies. It is important to note that the events portrayed here are simultaneous and not sequential. In other words, the visions do not progress chronologically from one historical event to the next, but each vision roughly covers the same events, culminating in the Antiochean desecration of the temple and the persecution of the Jews during the years 167-164 B.C.E. The Seleucid ruler Antiochus IV Epiphanes is the "little horn . . . that spoke arrogantly" (Dan 7:8) who "set up the abomination that makes desolate" in the temple in Jerusalem (Dan 11:31; 12:11).[6]

The fact that we can determine with some confidence the historical crisis that triggered the composition of Daniel's visions provides us with important clues for why the biblical book was written in the first place. Its function is twofold, to explain the current misery and to console the persecuted. To explain the current conflict the author adopts a view of the world that is found widely in apocalyptic literature. This view of reality is predicated on an elaborate construal of the heavenly world. Earthly and heavenly reality stand in stark contrast to each other, and events on earth are the direct reflection of what is happening in heaven. The angelic discourse in 10:18–11:1 illustrates this well. There Daniel learns of a cosmic conflict among the heavenly forces currently being waged in heaven. The prince of the Persian kingdom and the prince of Greece are in combat with Michael, the guardian angel of Israel, and with the anonymous interpreting angel who is speaking to Daniel, presumably Gabriel. The clash between Antiochus and the Jews is merely the *pendant* to the current heavenly confrontation.

The second function of the book of Daniel is to console. The first vision in chap. 7 is of central importance in this respect. Daniel witnesses a heavenly courtroom scene in which God strips Antiochus of his power, puts him to death, and hands dominion over to the "Son of Man" (7:13-14).[7] Similarly, 11:41-45 "predicts" the imminent death of the Seleucid villain. Such a promise of the judgment and even death of Israel's persecutor must have resonated strongly with the persecuted. The promise of judgment is ex-

6. G. W. E. Nickelsburg, "Apocalyptic Texts," in *EDSS*, 29-35.

7. J. J. Collins, *A Commentary on the Book of Daniel*, Hermeneia (Minneapolis: Fortress, 1993), 277-94; on the religio-historical background of the Son of Man, now see G. Boccaccini, ed., *Enoch and the Messiah Son of Man: Revisiting the Book of Parables* (Grand Rapids: Eerdmans, 2007).

tended even further in the second judgment scene in the book, the final section that looks to the eschatological resurrection of the dead (12:1-3). Those who are found "inscribed in the book" will be rescued. This is followed by the resurrection of the dead, for some to eternal life, and for others to everlasting abhorrence. The great day of reckoning carries a special promise for one group that is specifically singled out, "the wise" (12:3). They are not identified beyond their theological epithet. Not all of them will survive the persecutions, and so their reward is the promise of resurrection, when they will "shine like the brightness of the sky . . . like the stars for ever and ever" (12:3).[8]

The book of Jubilees shares several of the features that render Daniel an apocalypse, but these elements are less dominant, while other, non-apocalyptic elements that play only a minor role in Daniel are much more prevalent in Jubilees, most notably the book's developed interest in halakah. Since the dawn of its modern reading, scholars have discussed whether or not Jubilees can rightly be called an apocalypse.[9] The lack of an agreement regarding Jubilees' genre and the variety of different proposals that have been advanced are indicative of the composite literary character of the book. The issue is further complicated by the fact that overtly apocalyptic thought is expressed only in a handful of places in Jubilees, most prominently in chaps. 1 and 23.[10] This has led some scholars to propose that the apocalyptic passages are later additions to the book.[11] Such literary-critical decisions based on alleged "tensions" are unnecessarily speculative. It is true, however,

8. J. F. Hobbins, "Resurrection in the Daniel Tradition and Other Writings at Qumran," in *The Book of Daniel*, 2:395-420; C. Hempel, "*Maskil(im)* and *Rabim*: From Daniel to Qumran," in *Biblical Traditions in Transmission: Essays in Honour of Michael A. Knibb*, ed. C. Hempel and J. M. Lieu (Leiden: Brill, 2006), 133-56.

9. See the list of scholars in A. Lange, "Divinatorische Träume und Apokalyptik im Jubiläenbuch," in *Studies in the Book of Jubilees*, ed. M. Albani, J. Frey, and A. Lange (Tübingen: Mohr Siebeck, 1997), 25-38; Lange himself concludes that "[e]ine Klassifikation des Jubiläenbuches als apokalyptische Schrift ist . . . abzulehnen" (35). J. J. Collins, *The Apocalyptic Imagination* (Grand Rapids: Eerdmans, 1998), 83, states diplomatically that "*Jubilees* represents a borderline case for the apocalyptic genre." The discussion is a welcome reminder that genres are not absolute categories but modern abstractions that help us categorize ancient literature.

10. G. L. Davenport, *The Eschatology of the Book of Jubilees* (Leiden: Brill, 1971), distinguishes between "passages intended to teach eschatology" (1:4-29 and 23:14-31) and "non-eschatological passages that contain significant eschatological elements" (1:1-5; 5:1-19; 8:10-15; 15:1-34; 16:1-9; 22:11-23; 24:8-33; 31:1-32; and 34:1-18).

11. See, for example, C. Berner, "50 Jubilees and Beyond? Some Observations on the Chronological Structure of the Book of Jubilees," *Hen* 31, no. 1 (2009).

that apocalyptic ideas represent only one aspect of Jubilees' thought world, and so the composition as a whole should not be called an apocalypse.[12]

It may be helpful to begin by stating what Jubilees does *not* include. There is no revelatory vision in Jubilees that so often is the preferred medium in apocalypses, nor is there a heavenly journey or any other form of epiphany. Scholars who felt compelled to call Jubilees an apocalypse evidently did so not on formal grounds but rather because of the book's obvious affinity with other apocalypses. The strongest case can be made for Jubilees' similarity to, and in several instances dependence upon, 1 Enoch. The author of Jubilees was clearly familiar with the Enochian Book of the Watchers and the Astronomical Book. Affiliations with other parts of 1 Enoch, particularly with the Book of Dreams, are equally obvious.

The first chapter of Jubilees introduces the reader to some key concepts that will be foundational for the understanding of the book. One of them is the story of how Jubilees was written. There we learn that when Moses ascended Mount Sinai, he received much more than the Torah. God gave Moses a historical overview from the beginning of time to its consummation, a survey of "the divisions of all the times," and then commanded Moses to write everything down in a book (Jub 1:4). The command is repeated at the end of chap. 1 and thus forms an *inclusio* for the book's introduction. "Now you write all these words which I tell you on this mountain: what is first and what is last and what is to come during all the divisions of time which are in the law and which are in the testimony and in the weeks of their *Jubilees* until eternity — until the time when I descend and live with them throughout all the ages of eternity" (1:26).[13] The passages aptly describe the eschatological horizon within which the book wants to be read. The events Moses is commanded to record do not fall within the boundaries of biblical history, let alone can they be found in Genesis and Exodus, the two books Jubilees paraphrases, but they cover *all* of history, "the weeks of their *Jubilees* throughout all the years of eternity" (prologue). The book of Jubilees itself does not span all of history from beginning to end but gives us only an excerpt of what was revealed to Moses on Mount Sinai. But this in no way compromises the claim that the book wants to be understood in a larger eschatological context.

12. The verdict of M. Testuz, *Les idées religieuses du Livre des Jubilés* (Geneva: E. Droz, 1960), still holds true. "Ainsi, le Livre des Jubilés est un ouvrage de genre composite, qui tient à la fois du livre historique, de l'ouvrage de legislation, du livre chronologique, de l'apocalypse et du genre des testaments" (12; see also 165-77).

13. All translations are taken from J. C. VanderKam, *The Book of Jubilees*, CSCO 510-11 (Louvain: Peeters, 1989).

The passage is also telling in that it provides a fictitious account of how Jubilees was composed. In the verse following the excerpt quoted above, God tells the angel of the presence to dictate to Moses the divine lore (1:27). However, from 2:1 on it is Moses who records what the angel reads to him. In either case, the author makes the claim that the book as a whole is a revelation that Moses received on Mount Sinai. Unlike Daniel, Moses does not have any visions, but the mode of revelation that led to the composition of the two books is the same. In both cases the revelatory accounts amount to powerful claims to authority.

In the introductory chapter of Jubilees God promises Moses that God will show him all of human history. There are several eschatological passages in the book, the longest and most explicit of which is found in chap. 23. The notice of the death of Abraham (23:1-8) provides the author with an opportunity to reflect on the life spans of humans, "from now [i.e., the time of Abraham] until the great day of judgment" (23:11). The prophecy that follows the account of Abraham's death describes how the ages of individuals will initially be diminished as part of a divine punishment until they reach a certain low during a generation simply referred to as "the evil generation" (23:14).[14] Then that generation's children will repent, and after many tribulations, human life spans will increase again until they reach close to one thousand years (23:27-29). Like the eschatological outlook at the end of the book of Daniel, the chapter culminates in the promise of the resurrection of the dead, a passage immediately reminiscent of Dan 12. "Then the Lord will heal his servants. They will rise and see great peace. He will expel his enemies. The righteous will see (this), offer praise, and be very happy forever and ever. They will see all their punishments and curses on their enemies. Their bones will rest in the earth and their spirits will be very happy. They will know that the Lord is one who executes judgment but shows kindness to hundreds and thousands and to all who love him" (23:30-31). Both Dan 12:1-3 and Jub 23:30-31 describe an eschatological scene in which resurrection and judgment are closely intertwined (see also 1 En 27:1-4, which may well have served as the *Vorlage* for both). The text does not necessarily imply that the resurrection is universal and affects all who have died. It is certain, however, that not all who are resurrected will gain life eternal. Built into the account in Dan 12:1-3 is the special promise to "the wise" that they will be brought to life and shine like the stars. Similarly in Jub 23, "the righteous" — they are

---

14. J. Kugel, "The *Jubilees* Apocalypse," *DSD* 1 (1994): 322-37; some scholars have found here an allusion to the Maccabean period.

also called God's "servants" — will receive healing, and in response will offer their infinite praise to God. Their enemies, on the other hand, will be punished and cursed. Such double judgment is hardly new. The opposition of righteous and sinners is found throughout biblical literature, particularly in sapiential texts and in the psalms, yet it is here propelled to an eschatological extreme and applied to the last judgment scene.

The book of Jubilees displays several traits that are clearly apocalyptic. As the introductory chapter makes clear, the author of Jubilees writes with an eschatological context in mind, even though the book relates only a small section thereof. History is heading for an eschatological finale, marked by God's intervention, the resurrection of the dead, and judgment day. It is also clear, however, that, while these eschatological concepts delineate the imaginative frame of the book, they are not developed in any detail. They were not triggered by, nor do they focus on, a concrete percussive event such as the Antiochean persecution in the book of Daniel. In Daniel, the apocalypse is the literary response to a specific historical crisis that in turn becomes the focal point of the visions; in Jubilees apocalypticism is the mental horizon of the author's imagination, not the literary mold of the book.

Biblical Exegesis

In chap. 9 of Daniel, we find Daniel studying Scripture. "I, Daniel, perceived in the books the number of years that, according to the word of the Lord to the prophet Jeremiah, must be fulfilled for the devastation of Jerusalem, namely, seventy years" (Dan 9:2). The reference is to Jeremiah's prediction that Babylon would fall after 70 years (Jer 25:11-12; cf. Jer 29:10). The author of Daniel is writing at a time when the temple was desecrated and Judaism was under siege, and so the redemption promised by Jeremiah still seemed to lie in the future, even though the 70 years of Jeremiah had long passed. To solve the obvious problem, the angel Gabriel reinterprets the 70 years to mean seventy weeks of years, or 490 years (Dan 9:24-27).

The oft-quoted episode has become somewhat of a *locus classicus* in scholarly treatments of inner-biblical exegesis, since it is one of the few places in the Bible where a biblical author explicitly refers to an earlier book and interprets it. The use of earlier prophecies in Daniel's revelatory visions is made explicit in Dan 9 — but it is implicit throughout the latter half of the book. No other part of the canon has been as formative for the composition of Daniel's apocalyptic texts as the Prophets. The author speaks in the prophetic idiom, using language and speech forms at home in the Prophets. So pervasive is the use of prophetic pronouncements that one modern interpreter aptly described Dan 10:1–12:10 as "a catena of prophetic fragments."[15]

Three brief examples suffice to make the point.[16] Dan 11:36 predicts the downfall of the Syrian ruler Antiochus. Right after the section that describes the sacrileges in Jerusalem and the desecration of the temple (Dan 11:29-35), the author goes on to "predict" that Antiochus's offensive behavior will continue for a while until he meets his just punishment, which, it turns out, has already been ordained. "He [Antiochus] shall prosper until the period of wrath is completed, for what is determined shall be done" (רְהִצְלִיחַ עַד־כָּלָה זַעַם כִּי נֶחֱרָצָה נֶעֱשָׂתָה). The language makes clear that our author is referring to Isa 10:23-27, an oracle promising the Israelites relief from the Assyrians. The promises that "the LORD God of hosts will make a full end" (כִּי כָלָה וְנֶחֱרָצָה; Isa 10:23) and that his "indignation will come to an end" (וְכָלָה זַעַם; Isa 10:25) are here combined and transferred. The promise of relief from the Assyrians has turned into a promise of the demise of Antiochus.

Second, much has been made of "the wise" (הַמַּשְׂכִּלִים) in Daniel. Their precise identity remains obscure, though we learn that they educate others (Dan 11:33) and "lead many to righteousness" (מַצְדִּיקֵי הָרַבִּים; Dan 12:3) and hence will receive a special reward in the resurrection. Modern commentators have long observed that the wording of the passage is based on the fourth Servant Song in Isa 52:13–53:12.[17] The passages agree in several respects, but the verbal overlap is especially striking in Isa 53:11, the conclusion to the Song in which God promises that the Servant will be vindicated: "The righteous one, my servant, shall make many righteous" (יַצְדִּיק צַדִּיק עַבְדִּי לָרַבִּים).[18]

---

15. M. Fishbane, *Biblical Interpretation in Ancient Israel* (New York: Oxford University Press, 1985), 516.

16. The first two examples are taken from M. A. Knibb, "'You Are Indeed Wiser Than Daniel': Reflections on the Character of the Book of Daniel," in *The Book of Daniel in the Light of New Findings*, ed. A. S. Van Der Woude, BETL 106 (Louvain: Leuven University Press, 1993), 399-411, and Knibb, "The Book of Daniel in Its Context," in *The Book of Daniel*, 1:16-35, who follows Fishbane, *Biblical Interpretation*, 487-99.

17. H. L. Ginsberg, "The Oldest Interpretation of the Suffering Servant," *VT* 3 (1953): 400-404; G. W. E. Nickelsburg, *Resurrection, Immortality, and Eternal Life in Intertestamental Judaism and Early Christianity: Expanded Edition*, HTS 56 (Cambridge: Harvard University Press, 2006 [1972]), 38-41.

18. We are reminded that "the righteous" in Jub 23:30, a passage with obvious affinities to Dan 12:1-3, are also called God's "servants," clearly an allusion to the Servant Song.

Third, while "the wise" will receive their postmortem reward, the wicked will awaken "to shame and everlasting contempt" (לַחֲרָפוֹת לְדִרְאוֹן עוֹלָם; Dan 12:2). This text, too, harkens back to the prophet Isaiah, in this case to the final prose oracle, which describes a gruesome scene in which the priests go out and "look at the dead bodies of the people who have rebelled against me . . . they shall be an abhorrence to all flesh" (Isa 66:24). The word for "abhorrence" (דֵּרָאוֹן) occurs only in these two texts in the Hebrew Bible, and in both cases the shame is thought to be everlasting. Daniel here takes the eschatological passages in Isaiah to the next level, so that "Third Isaiah reads like a description of the time of the writing of Daniel."[19]

In a classic study on the topic of inner-biblical interpretation, Michael Fishbane has provided a thorough analysis of Daniel's reuse of earlier prophecy.[20] In his section titled "The Mantological Exegesis of Oracles" Fishbane discusses a wealth of examples taken from Dan 9–12 in which the biblical author reuses biblical prophecies. The assumption is that by the time of Daniel, the precise meaning of the ancient prophecies, much like that of oracles, visions, or omens, was no longer self-evident and hence required interpretation. It could be that a prophecy was found to have failed or that it remained unfulfilled or simply was in need of reinterpretation. Because of this oracularization of Scripture, the word of the prophet itself had become the subject of interpretation; it had to be decoded and, in a sense, translated so that it could be reapplied to the current situation. In support of his argument Fishbane produced a significant number of text examples from Daniel for which he was able to trace their linguistic origin to the prophetic corpus.

Fishbane has revealed the full extent to which the apocalyptic texts in Dan 9–12 are indebted to biblical prophecy. There is hardly a verse here that is not anchored in the prophetic discourse. Fishbane's model of "mantological exegesis" works for Dan 9 and its reinterpretation of Jeremiah. I remain unconvinced, however, that it works equally well for the numerous other prophetic texts we hear echoes of in Dan 9–12. There is nothing in Daniel to suggest that the prophetic utterances seemed obscure and unintelligible, let alone had become the subject of interpretation like an oracle or an omen. In Dan 9:2 the text stresses that Daniel "understood" (אֲנִי דָּנִיֵּאל בִּינֹתִי) the words of Jeremiah. Similarly, the examples adduced by Fishbane hardly suggest that the texts in Isaiah caught Daniel's attention because of their obscurity. True, the *angelus interpres* does assist Daniel with his understanding to

19. Nickelsburg, *Resurrection*, 34.
20. Fishbane, *Biblical Interpretation*, 474-524.

solve the "cognitive dissonance."[21] But what is obscure, dissonant, and in urgent need of interpretation are not the words of the prophets but the content of Daniel's visions.

It is my contention, then, that what prompted the author of Daniel to make such extensive use of the prophetic texts was not their dissonance but — quite to the contrary! — their consonance with the situation at hand. Daniel is firmly rooted in the prophetic tradition.[22] The wise, for example, did not use the language of Isa 53 and apply it to themselves to fill an esoteric epithet once again with meaning. The enormous reception history of the Servant Song strongly suggests that ancient interpreters found nothing obscure about it. Rather, by adopting the identity of the suffering servant, the wise make the powerful statement that their suffering has a vicarious quality and eventually will be rewarded (Isa 53:12). Even though they have to suffer under Antiochus and some of them are certain to die, in the end they will be vindicated and glorified.

The hope for resurrection as expressed in Dan 12:1-3 is another case in point. In a recent study on the history of this Jewish doctrine, Jon Levenson argues forcefully that, even though the literal expectation of the resurrection of the dead may have been a new concept first introduced in Dan 12, the language and symbolism by which it is expressed had long been present and available in ancient Israel. His comments are worth quoting in full.

> Modern historians, researching the origin of the Jewish idea of resurrection, understandably think of it as an innovation and seek a situation of keen discontinuity in which it arose. This is not necessarily wrong, but it does underestimate the verbal particularity and the textual character of its appearance — points of greater significance to the ancient Jewish culture itself. Given the rich intertextual connections and dependence in which it is enveloped, the resurrection of the dead in Dan 12:1-3 may have seemed (at least to some sectors) much less innovative than it does to those who, ignoring its linguistic embedding, think of it as an *idea*. Much is lost when the resurrection of the dead is treated as a free-floating concept whose essence remains constant no matter what the culture in which it appears or to which it migrates.[23]

---

21. Fishbane, *Biblical Interpretation*, 509 and 510.

22. Our earliest sources clearly thought of Daniel as a prophet (4QFlor ii 3; Matt 24:15; Josephus, *Ant* 10.2.4, 7); see K. Koch, "Is Daniel Also among the Prophets?" *Int* 39 (1985): 117-31.

23. J. D. Levenson, *Resurrection and the Restoration of Israel: The Ultimate Victory of the God of Life* (New Haven: Yale University Press, 2006), 185.

What Levenson describes for the doctrine of resurrection holds true for the reuse of prophetic language in Daniel in general. Reusing prophetic pronouncements and reapplying them to his own situation, the author of Daniel shows his indebtedness to Scripture and places his own work squarely in the prophetic tradition, not because he found it obscure but because he found it congenial. The language of Isaiah and of the other prophets was ideally suited to describe Daniel's revelatory experiences not least because of its rich eschatological connotations. In many respects, the book of Daniel and the apocalyptic ideas it espouses form the logical extension of biblical prophecy.

Biblical exegesis is a key factor in the book of Jubilees as well, though of a different sort altogether.[24] Two aspects in particular are relevant for our present inquiry, both of which underscore the differences in the use of the Bible in Daniel and Jubilees. First, Jubilees belongs to a sizable group of early Jewish texts that are concerned with the patriarchal period. Their purpose is to paraphrase and rework Genesis-Exodus. These compositions were particularly popular at Qumran and were found there in significant numbers. The key figure, in Jubilees as in many of the other compositions, is Moses.[25] By choosing Moses as the pseudonymous hero of the book, the author of Jubilees carefully places his work in a stream of second temple writings that are part of an ongoing "Mosaic discourse."[26] This is rather different from the book of Daniel. And second, Jubilees has a developed interest in Jewish law. Much of the rewriting of Genesis-Exodus is motivated by the author's urge to solve a specific halakic problem, having to do, inter alia, with the calendar, particularly with the Sabbath, and with several priestly and Levitical matters. The halakic portions of Jubilees can be profitably compared with other Jewish, particularly early rabbinic, texts. In short, whereas much of the exegesis in Daniel serves a larger, eschatological purpose, the author of Jubilees is more concerned with solving legal problems. Here, eschatology is conspicuous by its absence.

---

24. J. Endres, *Biblical Interpretation in the Book of Jubilees,* CBQMS 18 (Washington, D.C.: Catholic Biblical Association, 1987); G. J. Brooke, "Exegetical Strategies in Jubilees 1–2," in *Studies in the Book of Jubilees,* 179-205; J. C. VanderKam, "The Scriptural Setting of the Book of Jubilees," *DSD* 13 (2006): 61-72.

25. G. J. Brooke, "'The Canon within the Canon' at Qumran and in the New Testament," in *The Scrolls and the Scriptures: Qumran Fifty Years After,* ed. S. E. Porter and C. A. Evans (Sheffield: Sheffield Academic Press, 1997), 242-66, and his "Genesis, Commentary on," in *EDSS,* 300-302; D. K. Falk, "Moses, Texts of," in *EDSS,* 577-81.

26. H. Najman, *Seconding Sinai: The Development of Mosaic Discourse in Second Temple Judaism,* JSJSup 77 (Leiden: Brill, 2003), 41-69.

Heptadic Chronologies

The book of Daniel shows a clear awareness of things chronological. To contextualize the events of the book in terms of world history and to provide a comprehensive time frame, the author devised his own chronological scheme, the periodization of history into four kingdoms. The succession of the four world empires is the main theme of chaps. 2 and 7, but it also underlies the visions in chaps. 8 and 11. The chronological remarks found in the chapter headings, specifically in the superscriptions of the vision reports (Dan 1:1; 2:1; 7:1; 8:1; 9:1; and 10:1, 4), follow the same model and provide specific dates for specific episodes. The four-kingdom scheme is concerned exclusively with the end of history, not with its beginning, which is never considered in Daniel. Its aim, as is made very clear in 7:1-8, is not merely to divide history into four equal parts but to argue that the ruler of the fourth empire, who rules at the time of the author, is significantly worse than any previous world ruler. The promise that the ruthless tyrant will soon be stripped of his power and dominion will be handed over to Israel (Dan 7:27) gives Daniel's message an eschatological urgency. The four-kingdom model is not intended to function as a full-fledged calendar. Instead, it focuses attention on the end-time, which is thought to be imminent.

A chronological system of a different sort is found in 9:24-27, Daniel's interpretation of Jeremiah's prophecy already mentioned above. Here the author does not follow a quarter system, but a heptadic system. Similar chronologies that measure history or periods thereof in sabbatical weeks and jubilees are found in a number of texts written around the time of the Maccabean revolt, including the Enochic Apocalypse of Weeks, the Animal Apocalypse, several texts from Qumran, and of course, both Daniel and Jubilees.[27] The roots of these chronologies are biblical, reaching back to the Torah. The most explicit treatment of an ancient calendar based on units of seven years is found in Lev 25, which contains instructions for the sabbatical and the jubilee years. The chapter begins by calling for a rest for the land every seven years (the sabbatical year) and moves on to legislate that every fiftieth year (the jubilee year) all property that had changed hands had to be returned to its original owner. Also, every Hebrew who had sold himself into

---

27. J. C. VanderKam, "Sabbatical Chronologies in the Dead Sea Scrolls and Related Literature," in *The Dead Sea Scrolls in Their Historical Context*, 159-78; C. Berner, *Jahre, Jahrwochen und Jubiläen. Heptadische Geschichtskonzeptionen im Antiken Judentum*, BZAW 363 (Berlin and New York: De Gruyter, 2006).

slavery was to be released. It seems likely that Daniel's interpretation of Jeremiah was influenced by Lev 25. According to Gabriel's calculation, then, the time from the Babylonian destruction of the first temple to the demise of Antiochus IV spans seventy weeks of years, or ten jubilees, i.e., 490 years. The critical themes associated with the jubilee year in Lev 25 — release, freedom, renewal, return, and restoration — all assume new significance in their eschatological context. The significance of Daniel's rendering of Jeremiah's prophecy does not lie in its concrete calendrical use but in its symbolic value and in the powerful promise that Antiochus's rule will be overcome.[28]

The chronological system of Jubilees has often been analyzed, and there is no point in rehearsing the details again.[29] It suffices merely to highlight some of its main features and to compare them with Daniel. Already Jubilees' prologue underscores the primary importance the author places on the exact calculation of the biblical events according to a sabbatical calendar. The essential measurements of time are "years," "weeks," and "jubilees." These are mentioned throughout the book and form a chronological grid that is underlying the whole of the composition. How does this compare with the book of Daniel? In Daniel heptadic calculations are found only in chap. 9, while the book as a whole is organized along the lines of the four world empires. As a consequence, the jubilee chronology remains somewhat schematic; it is the principle that matters, not its exact calendrical applicability. In Jubilees, by contrast, the sabbatical chronology is the main organizing principle for the entire book, as the prologue already makes clear. The book seeks to demonstrate in some detail how Israel's earliest history followed the heptadic chronology. For both authors the heptadic chronology was of ultimate theological significance — but "theological" here meant different things entirely. For the author of Daniel, who looked to the future, the heptadic calculation was an ideal vehicle to make his apocalyptic promise that history is unfolding according to a preordained divine plan and that the eschatological salvation will bring freedom and restoration as it was foreshadowed already in Lev 25. For the author of Jubilees, who looked to the past, the concern was with Israel's earliest history. For him the significance of the heptadic chronology was to prove that the events of Genesis-Exodus were all in compliance with the sabbatical calendar. In fact, it is noteworthy

28. Fishbane, *Biblical Interpretation*, 482-89.

29. J. C. VanderKam, "Das chronologische Konzept des Jubiläenbuches," *ZAW* 107 (1995): 80-100; VanderKam, *The Book of Jubilees*, 94-100. On the calendar specifically, see A. Jaubert, "Le calendrier des Jubilés et de la sect de Qumrân. Ses origines bibliques," *VT* 3 (1953): 250-64.

that none of the apocalyptic sections in Jubilees makes an explicit reference to the heptadic chronology that otherwise is so important to the author. Sabbatical measurements were crucial not for their eschatological significance but as a way of calculating a precise chronology of the events narrated in Genesis-Exodus.

The Chronologies of the Apocalypse of Weeks and the Book of Jubilees

James M. Scott

Both in whole and in part the chronology in the Apocalypse of Weeks (1 En 93:1-10 + 91:11-18) is obviously different from the one in the book of Jubilees, and it would be easy therefore to assume that the two chronologies are independent of one another.[1] The main difference between the two works is clear: although they contain sabbatical chronologies with strong affinities to Dan 9, which reinterprets the 70 years of Jerusalem's desolation (Jer 29:10) as seventy "weeks" of years, the respective chronological systems are quite different in their overall scope. Whereas the Apocalypse of Weeks encompasses all of human history within its ten "weeks,"[2] Jubilees heptadically periodizes only Genesis to Exodus, looking forward to the repossession of the land 40 years hence.[3] VanderKam stresses that although Jubilees interprets the exo-

---

1. Translations of the Apocalypse of Weeks are from George W. E. Nickelsburg and J. C. VanderKam, trans., *1 Enoch: A New Translation Based on the Hermeneia Commentary* (Minneapolis: Fortress, 2004), 140-43. Translations of the book of Jubilees are from J. C. VanderKam, trans., *The Book of Jubilees*, CSCO 511, Scriptores Aethiopici 88 (Louvain: Peeters, 1989).

2. For a succinct summary of the Apocalypse of Weeks, see J. J. Collins, "From Prophecy to Apocalypticism: The Expectation of the End," in *The Encyclopedia of Apocalypticism*, vol. 1, *The Origins of Apocalypticism in Judaism and Christianity*, ed. J. J. Collins (New York and London: Continuum, 2000), 129-61 (esp. 139-40).

3. For a survey of Jubilees' chronological system, see J. C. VanderKam, *The Book of Jubilees*, Guides to Apocrypha and Pseudepigrapha 9 (Sheffield: Sheffield Academic Press, 2001), 94-96; VanderKam, "Studies in the Chronology of the Book of Jubilees," in *From Revelation to Canon: Studies in the Hebrew Bible and Second Temple Literature*, ed. J. C. VanderKam, JSJSup 62 (Leiden: Brill, 2000), 522-44.

dus and conquest as jubilean events, "[w]hether the author meant to imply more about the chronology of the post-conquest period *cannot be inferred from the text*."[4]

There are also significant differences in the constituent parts of the two chronological systems, including, for example, the heptadic units employed in each (i.e., "weeks" [= 490 years?] in the Apocalypse of Weeks[5] versus "jubilees" [= 49 years], "weeks" [= 7 years], and "years" in Jubilees) and — depending on the numerical value of the "weeks" in the Apocalypse of Weeks — the relative dating of historical events in the two writings. For example, whereas in the Apocalypse of Weeks the year 2450 A.M. (i.e., the end of the "fifth week") coincides with the building of the temple (1 En 93:7), in Jubilees, the same year corresponds to the culmination of the momentous "jubilee of jubilees," the entrance into the land that would take place 40 years after the revelation to Moses on Mount Sinai in 2410 A.M. (cf. Jub 48:1; 50:4).

Despite these difficulties, I have attempted elsewhere to argue that the chronological system of the book of Jubilees is indeed influenced by the chronology of the Apocalypse of Weeks, and that therefore the Apocalypse of Weeks can be used cautiously to help fill in some of the gaps of the postconquest era that Jubilees mentions but does not explicitly periodize in terms of its awkward system of jubilees, weeks, and years.[6] The tentative nature of my reconstruction was clear to me from the outset, but it seemed plausible in view of several factors: (1) the schematic nature of the sabbatical chronologies of which Jubilees is a prime example; (2) the stimulating suggestion of George Nickelsburg and James C. VanderKam that Jub 4:18-19, which deals with the Enochic origin of the book's chronology, actually alludes to the Apocalypse of Weeks; (3) the chronological trajectories in the book; and (4) the mirroring effect of the sequence of events in Jub 23:8-31 with earlier parts of the book. In the present paper I would like to reinforce my argument that the Apocalypse of Weeks may have influenced the chronology of the book of Jubilees.

---

4. VanderKam, *The Book of Jubilees*, 96, emphasis mine.

5. Cf. J. S. Bergsma, *The Jubilee from Leviticus to Qumran: A History of Interpretation*, VTSup 115 (Leiden: Brill, 2007), 241. Even if it is argued that the "weeks" in the Apocalypse of Weeks are of unequal length, it is still possible — and perhaps even probable — that Jubilees would have understood the Apocalypse's "weeks" as equal units of time.

6. Cf. J. M. Scott, *On Earth as in Heaven: The Restoration of Sacred Time and Sacred Space in the* Book of Jubilees, JSJSup 91 (Leiden: Brill, 2005). The following deliberations are based largely on this book, which also constituted the point of departure in my original conference paper.

I. The Apocalypse of Weeks and the
Book of Jubilees as Apocalypses

The possibility that the Apocalypse of Weeks influenced the book of Jubilees begins with the recognition that both works are apocalypses. An apocalypse is "a genre of revelatory literature with a narrative framework, in which a revelation is mediated by an otherworldly being to a human recipient, disclosing a transcendent reality which is both temporal, insofar as it envisages eschatological salvation, and spatial insofar as it involves another, supernatural world."[7] There is no doubt that the Apocalypse of Weeks is an apocalypse, but more needs to be said about Jubilees, since chaps. 1 and 23 are the only parts of the book that are generally regarded as fitting the description of an apocalypse, containing special revelations to Moses through angelic mediation from the testimony inscribed on the heavenly tablets (cf. 1:26-27; 23:32).

I have argued that these two chapters are so thoroughly integrated within the chronological structure and message of the book that it is artificial to isolate them as separate apocalypses. The apocalypse in the first chapter sets the stage for the rest of the book, and the final chapter recalls that setting, providing closure for the whole book (50:2). Hence, the whole of Jubilees should be seen as one unified apocalypse, albeit a revelation that includes, as part and parcel of its fundamental fabric, a copious amount of halakic material and quasi-historical narrative. Indeed, if one of the main purposes of the book was to teach the proper observance of halakah from reworked primeval and patriarchal narratives, then special revelation of the narrated events was absolutely essential to lend divine authority to the author's interpretive moves.

In asserting the literary unity of Jubilees, I am, of course, assuming the final form of the book more or less as we now have it. Although there have been recent attempts to reconstruct the compositional history of the book,[8]

---

7. This is the widely accepted definition of the literary genre "apocalypse" in J. J. Collins, "Introduction: Towards the Morphology of a Genre," in *Apocalypse: Morphology of a Genre,* ed. J. J. Collins, Semeia 14 (Missoula: Scholars Press, 1979), 1-20 (9). Although the definition of an "apocalypse" is admittedly modern and somewhat arbitrary, it still serves the useful purpose of grouping texts that exhibit a coherent and recurring pattern of features constituted by the interrelated elements of form, content, and function. The discussion of the literary genre "apocalypse" should not be abandoned in favor of other kinds of formal comparisons between texts (e.g., Jubilees and wisdom literature). It is not a matter of "either-or" but of "both-and."

8. Cf. C. Berner, *Jahre, Jahrwochen und Jubiläen. Heptadische Geschichtskonzeptionen*

most scholars have viewed Jubilees as a literary unity. This is not to deny that the book contains many anomalies. As VanderKam acknowledges, there are in fact a number of mistakes or inconsistencies in the book, but "all of them are explicable in simpler terms than assuming sundry editions of the book."[9]

Superficially, Jubilees is a reworking of Gen 1 to Exod 24 (or even to chap. 32),[10] and, as shown by the beginning and the end of the book, the setting of the book is portrayed as the actual revelation given to Moses on Mount Sinai. Thus, Jubilees opens (1:1-4) with the Lord summoning Moses to ascend the mountain to meet with him, referring to Moses' stay on the mountain (Exod 24:18; cf. 34:28) that took place the day after the covenantal ceremonies described in Exod 19–24. The book also ends with a direct reference to the revelation to Moses on Mount Sinai (Jub 50:2: "On Mt. Sinai I [sc. the angel of the presence] told you about the sabbaths of the land and the years of jubilees in the Sabbaths of the years"). Scattered throughout Jubilees are several reminders that the contents of this book are addressed to Moses (on Mount Sinai and through angelic mediation). Obviously, therefore, the author of Jubilees wanted the revelation and covenant at Sinai to be understood in light of the whole biblical history that preceded it (Genesis-Exodus).

Yet Jubilees is not so much a covenantal book as an apocalypse within a covenantal setting that inherently lends it authority. As a result, the Sinaitic covenant is somewhat relativized, so that, for example, the election of Israel goes back, not to the exodus from Egypt or to the making of the covenant at Sinai, but rather to the very beginning of creation (Jub 2:19-22). Moreover, many of the laws given to Israel on Sinai according to the biblical record are dated back to earlier periods (e.g., the Festival of Weeks was instituted not at Sinai [Exod 23:16; 34:22] but when Noah disembarked from the ark [Jub 6:17-19]). Since the direct authority of divine revelation was needed to achieve this relativization, we can be fairly sure that chaps. 1 and 23 belonged to Jubilees originally. I have argued that the reason for this backdating and relativization is directly linked to a central thesis of the book: the revelation on Sinai is a reiteration of the deterministic divine plan for the world, whereby all things on earth, especially the cultus in the land, will eventually correspond to the way

---

im Antiken Judentum, BZAW 363 (Berlin and New York: De Gruyter, 2006), 234-328; M. Segal, *The Book of Jubilees: Rewritten Bible, Redaction, Ideology, and Theology*, JSJSup 117 (Leiden: Brill, 2007).

9. VanderKam, "Studies in the Chronology," 540.

10. Cf. J. C. VanderKam, "The End of the Matter? Jubilees 50:6-13 and the Unity of the Book," in *Heavenly Tablets: Interpretation, Identity, and Tradition in Ancient Judaism*, ed. L. LiDonnici and A. Lieber, JSJSup 119 (Leiden: Brill, 2007), 267-84 (278-79).

things are in heaven and have been from the beginning. Thus, for instance, the Festival of Weeks reinstituted at Sinai (Jub 6:19) was originally given to Noah after the flood (vv. 16-17), although it "had been celebrated in heaven from the time of creation until the lifetime of Noah" (v. 18), in accordance with the ordinance written on the heavenly tablets (v. 17).

As apocalypses, both the Apocalypse of Weeks and the book of Jubilees share a worldview that includes a deterministic view of history. In other words, events proceed in accordance with a divine plan that is foreordained in heavenly tablets. Hence, the apocalyptic worldview of these two writings is clearly foundational to the chronological schemes contained in each.

Both the Apocalypse of Weeks and the book of Jubilees appeal to the antediluvian knowledge of Enoch to establish the validity of their chronological systems. Thus, in the Epistle of Enoch (1 En 92–105), the antediluvian Enoch introduces his ten-"week" chronology in the Apocalypse of Weeks with the words, "Concerning the sons of righteousness, and concerning the chosen of eternity, and concerning the plant of truth, these things I say to you and I make known to you, my sons, I myself, Enoch. The vision of heaven was shown to me, and from the words of the watchers and holy ones I have learned everything, and in the heavenly tablets I read everything and I have understood" (93:2). Similarly, Jubilees credits Enoch as the first who established both calendar and chronology (Jub 4:17-19). With respect to chronology, Jubilees reports:

> (18) He [sc. Enoch] was the first to write a testimony. He testified to mankind in the generations of the earth: The weeks of the jubilees he related, and made known the days of the years; the months he arranged, and related the sabbaths of the years, as we [sc. the angels of the presence] had told him. (19) While he slept he saw in a vision what has happened and what will occur — how things will happen for mankind during their history until the day of judgment. He saw everything and understood. He wrote a testimony for himself and placed it upon the earth against all mankind and for their history.

The similar wording of these passages is remarkable: the "vision" and revelation to Enoch through angelic mediation encompassed "everything." Indeed, Nickelsburg and VanderKam have suggested that Jubilees alludes to the Apocalypse of Weeks at this point,[11] although van Ruiten has countered

---

11. Cf. Scott, *On Earth*, 128 with n. 129.

that it is difficult to point to an exact parallel.[12] In answer to van Ruiten's critique, VanderKam is right to insist, however, (a) that even if we are not sure that an item is from one Enochic book or another, it may still be from one or both of them; (b) that Jub 4:17-26 in particular corresponds quite closely in theme, if not in wording, to several Enochic texts; and (c) that it seems more economical to assume dependence on these written Enochic sources than to appeal to unknown ones, especially since Jubilees underscores that Enoch left written works behind and even pictures him as continuing his scribal activity after his removal from human society to the Garden of Eden.[13]

The comprehensive nature of the revelation to Enoch in the Apocalypse of Weeks and the book of Jubilees pertains especially to their chronological systems, which are universal in scope insofar as they extend from creation to new creation.[14] The Apocalypse of Weeks begins with a reference to "the first week" (1 En 93:3), which strongly implies creation, and ends with the expectation that "the first heaven will pass away in it, and a new heaven will appear" (91:16), alluding to the new creation in Isa 65:17 ("For I am about to create new heavens . . .").[15] Between these two poles, the whole span of human history is schematically represented in this short apocalypse. Likewise, the book of Jubilees contains a universal scope in its chronological system. Thus, we read in Jub 1:29:

> The angel of the presence, who was going along in front of the Israelite camp, took the tablets (which told) of the divisions of the years from the time the law and the testimony were created — for the weeks of their jubilees, year by year in their full number, and their jubilees from [the time

12. Cf. J. van Ruiten, "A Literary Dependency of Jubilees on 1 Enoch?" in *Enoch and Qumran Origins: New Light on a Forgotten Connection*, ed. G. Boccaccini (Grand Rapids: Eerdmans, 2005), 90-93 (esp. 92-93); see also M. A. Knibb, "Which Parts of 1 Enoch Were Known to Jubilees? A Note on the Interpretation of *Jubilees* 4.16-25," in *Reading from Right to Left: Essays on the Hebrew Bible in Honour of David J. A. Clines*, ed. J. C. Exum and H. G. M. Williamson, JSOTSup 373 (Sheffield: Sheffield Academic Press, 2003), 254-62.

13. Cf. J. C. VanderKam, "Response: Jubilees and Enoch," in *Enoch and Qumran Origins*, 162-70 (esp. 163-64).

14. See further Bergsma, *The Jubilee*, 240: "Moreover, after the ten weeks, the apocalyptic author [of the Apocalypse of Weeks] expects 'many weeks without number,' somewhat similar to *Jubilees'* vision of a future in which 'jubilees will pass by until Israel is pure . . . until eternity' (*Jub.* 50:5)."

15. Cf. Jacques van Ruiten, "The Influence and Development of Is 65,17 in 1 En 91,16," in *The Book of Isaiah — Le livre d'Isaïe: les oracles et leurs reflecteurs. Unité et complexité de l'ouvrage*, ed. Jacques Vermeylen, BETL 81 (Louvain: Leuven University Press, 1989), 161-66.

of the creation until] the time of the new creation when the heavens, the earth, and all their creatures will be renewed like the powers of the sky and like all the creatures of the earth, until the time when the temple of the Lord will be created in Jerusalem on Mt. Zion. All the luminaries will be renewed for (the purposes of) healing, health, and blessing for all the elect ones of Israel and so that it may remain this way from that time throughout all the days of the earth.

The reference here to the renewal of the luminaries can be compared to Isa 65:17 ("For I am about to create new heavens . . ."), especially since Jubilees refers to "the new creation" in this context. Moreover, Jub 23, which has many similarities to chap. 1 and once again adumbrates world history from creation to new creation, clearly alludes to the new creation expected in Isa 65:17-25, with its hope of increased human longevity in the latter days.[16]

In the foregoing we have seen that there are several remarkable similarities between the Apocalypse of Weeks and the book of Jubilees as apocalypses. There is even a strong possibility that Jubilees alludes to the Apocalypse of Weeks. Now we are in a position to explore a tentative reconstruction of Jubilees' chronological system. As we shall see, Jubilees is not only beholden to the Apocalypse of Weeks for some of its fundamental chronological perspectives, especially those pertaining to the dating of the exile and its aftermath, but is also critical of the Enochic work at certain crucial points.

II. A Reconstruction of Jubilees' Chronological System

Jubilees is a polemical writing with a distinctly priestly orientation that seeks to prove the validity of its own position over against other competing perspectives with respect to two major issues — sacred space and sacred time. Like other pseudepigrapha in the second temple period, Jubilees is vying for predominance in the name of divine revelation transmitted through authoritative figures of the past. To this end, Jubilees portrays itself not only as containing the divine revelation written on heavenly tablets and given through angelic mediation to Moses on Mount Sinai, but also, and more importantly, as encapsulating the very revelation that angels had already given to Enoch in the antediluvian period.

According to Jub 4:21 (cf. Gen 5:22), Enoch was "with God's angels for

---

16. Cf. Scott, *On Earth*, 103-25, 138-39.

six jubilees of years. They showed him everything on earth and in the heavens — the dominion of the sun — and he wrote down everything." This appeal to Enoch is the book's clincher, part of a general tendency within the writing to ascribe its scriptural interpretations regarding cultic and halakic matters to the primeval and patriarchal periods. For Jubilees, Enoch, the seventh patriarch in the line from Adam, is the prototypical priest, the mediator par excellence between heaven and earth. Enoch is the model that the priestly author of the book seeks to emulate. Enoch is also the harbinger of the author's most treasured hope — the restoration of sacred space and sacred time, so that all things, especially the cultus in the restored land of Israel, eventually will be "on earth as in heaven." For as we learn in Jub 4:25-26, Enoch's priestly service in the primeval sanctuary of the Garden of Eden sets up a trajectory to the expected priestly service in the eschatological temple on Mount Zion in the new creation. By that time at the latest, all things in heaven and earth will conform to the Creator's original intention.

As a polemical writing, Jubilees engages in critical dialogue with its scriptural base text and the Enochic apocalyptic tradition within which it stands. Although the book is firmly based on Israel's scriptures, it is nevertheless also, at least in part, a radical reworking of those texts. Jubilees shapes the biblical text, particularly Genesis to Exodus, so that it conforms to the book's own theological agenda and chronological scheme. Similarly, Jubilees adapts and reinterprets Enochic apocalyptic tradition, most notably the Apocalypse of Weeks, in order to assert that its own version of the revelation to Enoch (and to Moses after him) has the greater claim to authenticity and authority. To this end, the book seeks to demonstrate the divinely ordained symmetry between the temporal and spatial axes in the space-time continuum.

Fundamental to our reconstruction of Jubilees' chronological system are two overarching trajectories in the book nestled one within the other: on the one hand, the trajectory set up by the all-inclusive revelation to Moses of the division of the years in their jubilees "from the time of creation until the time of the new creation when the heavens, the earth, and all their creatures will be renewed like the powers of the sky and like the creatures of the earth, until the time when the temple of the Lord will be created in Jerusalem on Mt. Zion" (Jub 1:29); on the other hand, the trajectory set up by the juxtaposition of Enoch's entrance into the primeval sanctuary of the Garden of Eden and the expected entrance of the eschatological priesthood in the rebuilt temple on Mount Zion, "which will be sanctified in the new creation" (4:23-26; cf. 1:29). The first trajectory provides the basic jubilean structure for the whole course of history as outlined in the book from creation to new creation. The second trajectory, which likewise extends to the new creation, focuses more particularly on the eschatological temple and its cultus, using the prototypical priest Enoch and his movements as the anchor point and *terminus a quo* for the correspondence between *Urzeit* and *Endzeit* on this trajectory.

In between these two overarching trajectories is the much smaller trajectory of Israel in the Promised Land, which comes at the end of the book, forming a kind of bookend with the opening revelation to Moses in the first chapter (note the similar reference to periodization in terms of sabbaths and jubilees in both cases). Thus, Jub 50:2-5 states:

> (2) On Mt. Sinai I told you about the sabbaths of the land and the years of jubilees in the sabbaths of the years, but its year we have not told you until the time when you enter the land which you will possess. (3) The land will observe its sabbaths when they live on it, and they are to know the year of the jubilee. (4) For this reason I have arranged for you the weeks of years and the jubilees — 49 jubilees from the time of Adam until today, and one week and two years. It is still 40 years off (for learning the Lord's commandments) until the time when he leads (them) across to the land of Canaan, after they have crossed the Jordan to the west of it. (5) The jubilees will pass by until Israel is pure of every sexual evil, impurity, contamination, sin, and error. Then they will live confidently in the entire land. They will no longer have any satan or any evil person. The land will be pure from that time until eternity.

In other words, the entrance into the land is predicted to take place forty years from the revelation at Sinai (2410 A.M.), at the culmination of the jubilee of jubilees (2450 A.M.).[17] This date is significant because the all-important synchronization between heavenly and earthly cultus, if it is to happen at all, must commence upon initial entrance into the land; otherwise, the people will again err with respect to the observance of jubilees and the sabbaths of the land.

---

17. Cf. VanderKam, "End of the Matter?" 281, referring to Jub 50:2-3: "The author names two subjects — the Sabbaths of the land and the years of jubilee — both of which derive from Leviticus 25 (understood to belong to the Jubilean setting of Moses' first forty-day sojourn atop Sinai). The legislation in Leviticus 25 is intended for the time when Israel will live in the land (v. 2), and this idea is expressed at the end of Jub 50:2. The phrase 'Sabbath of the land' occurs in Lev 25:6 (cf. vv. 4-5), and the year of jubilee (for the phrase see, e.g., Lev 25:28) is treated in vv. 8-17, while most of the remainder of the chapter deals with legal matters related to it."

The author of Jubilees knows, of course, that Israel's time in the land was doomed to failure, as the Deuteronomic pattern of sin-exile-restoration (SER) in chap. 1 makes clear. Thus, Jub 1:7 directly states: "I know their defiance and their stubbornness (even) before I bring them into the land which I promised by oath to Abraham, Isaac, and Jacob." The sins of Israel in the land will include, among other things, violations of the calendar: abandoning God's covenantal festivals, his sabbaths, and the jubilee (1:10, 14). Elaborating on Israel's life in the land and employing once again the Deuteronomic SER pattern, Jub 23 expects that the people will have "forgotten commandment, covenant, festival, month, sabbath, jubilee, and every verdict" (v. 19). The fact that chap. 23 is referring to Israel's sinful life in the land before the exile is confirmed by comparing to it 50:5, which refers to the restoration period (see above). This corresponds to 23:29, which likewise refers to the restoration: "They will complete and live their entire lifetimes peacefully and joyfully. There will be neither a satan nor any evil one who will destroy." In other words, Jubilees recognizes that Israel's entire time in the land before the exile would be characterized by sin, but that this condition would be rectified at the time of the restoration. Hence, the theme of Israel's expected sin in the land is reiterated in very similar terms in chaps. 1, 23, and 50, thus giving these mutually reinforcing chapters a framing function for the book as a whole.

If, as VanderKam has recently argued, Jub 50:1-5 coheres seamlessly with the rest of the book,[18] then all three of the interconnected framing chapters have a claim to being original. Moreover, since all three chapters look forward to the restoration period, when Israel will reenter the land and reestablish the cultus on a new basis corresponding to that in heaven from the beginning, the surface narrative of the book stops where it does, at "T minus 40 years" before entrance into the land, for two main reasons: (1) because, from the author's perspective, the original entrance into the land was already long past, and (2) because Israel's history essentially recapitulates itself at the time of the restoration: the eschatological entrance into the land corresponds chronologically to the original entrance into the land. Indeed, Jubilees is all about recapitulation. The two overarching trajectories of the book demonstrate that the new creation recapitulates the original creation, and the entrance of the eschatological priesthood into the future temple of

---

18. Cf. VanderKam, "End of the Matter?" 267-84, who shows not only that Jub 50:6-13 accords with the author's manner of introducing laws throughout the book but also that the entire chapter coheres well with the rest of the book.

the Lord on Mount Zion corresponds to Enoch's entrance into the primeval temple of the Garden of Eden. Thus, for example, by the time of the restoration at the latest, the people will recommence the celebration of the sabbath, in accordance with the originally intended divine will for everything on earth, particularly the cultus in the Promised Land, to correspond to the way things are in heaven. For from the creation of the world, the Lord separated for himself Israel as a special people to keep sabbath with him and the highest angels (Jub 2:19, 21, 31).

Another way in which Jub 1, 23, and 50 cohere chronologically is illustrated by the way the story of Abraham is framed in chap. 23. Upon mentioning Abraham's death and burial with his wife Sarah in the double cave at Machpelah (23:1-7), the author mentions Abraham's life span in terms of its number of jubilees ("three jubilees and four weeks of years — 175 years") and how human longevity in general had declined from "the time of the ancients" (vv. 8-9). In doing so, the author performs a complex interpretive move that correlates precisely with his interest in temporal and spatial symmetries. On the one hand, we see his interest in temporal symmetry in his emphasis on the decline and recovery of human longevity in Jub 23:8-31. For just as human longevity progressively declined from the creation of the world until the entrance into the land from Adam's 930 years (i.e., 70 years fewer than 1,000 years) to Moses' 120 years (Jub 4:29-30; 5:5, 8; 23:9; cf. Deut 34:7), and then further plummeted after Israel was in the land to a maximum life expectancy of 70 years (Jub 23:15; cf. Ps. 90:10), so also human longevity will incrementally increase after Israel's restoration to the land, from the meager 70-year life span to the originally intended divine ideal of 1,000 years (Jub 23:27; cf. Ps 90:4). Thus, according to Jub 23:27, after the people return to the right way, "The days will begin to become numerous and increase, and mankind as well — generation by generation and day by day until their lifetimes approach 1000 years and to more years than the number of days (had been)." The fact that human longevity started at 70 years fewer than the divine ideal, decreased from there to a maximum of 70 years, and finally will attain the divine ideal, thus besting Adam's previous high by 70 years, shows that Jub 23 still operates within the heptadic structure that otherwise characterizes the book, including the story of Abraham's death, which provides the narrative hook for the apocalyptic material.

Thus, the proof of the existence of divine providence — and therefore the correctness of Jubilees' version of things — is in its rhythmic working in history: construction, destruction, and reconstruction. All this was decreed from heaven to occur in periods that were equal in length and therefore symmetrical. In this conception of the progress of world history, Jubilees represents a major advance over the Apocalypse of Weeks, which also has periods of equal length (ostensibly 490-year "weeks"), but fails to achieve the same degree of bilateral symmetry in world history. Instead, the Apocalypse of Weeks has merely a partial and asymmetrical complement between "weeks" 1-7 and 8-10, with the center of history constituting the building of the temple at the culmination of "week" 5 (1 En 93:7).

Alongside this interest in temporal symmetry, Jub 23 demonstrates the author's interest in spatial symmetry, particularly the twofold loss and return of the Promised Land to Israel. To appreciate this point, we must recall that Jub 50:4-5 contains the chronology of Jubilees that runs throughout the entire book and ends at the expected entrance into the Promised Land. This occurs at the culmination of the jubilee of jubilees, when the nation will experience on a grand scale what an individual Israelite could have experienced in the year of jubilee — freedom from servitude and return to ancestral land (cf. Lev 25). The return of Israel to its ancestral home presupposes Jubilees' lengthy section about the original assignment of the land to Shem after the flood and the theft of the land by Canaan soon thereafter (chaps. 8–10).

Thus, from the perspective of Jubilees, when Israel conquered the land from the Canaanites it was a matter of retaking property that rightfully belonged to them in the first place. It will not go unnoticed, however, that the theft of the land by Canaan was paralleled in the author's own day by the theft of the land by the Greco-Macedonians, which likewise constituted a violation of the eternal oath made by the sons and grandsons of Noah: "All of them said: 'So be it'! So be it for them and their children until eternity during their generations until the day of judgment on which the Lord God will punish them with the sword and fire because of all the evil impurity of their errors by which they have filled the earth with wickedness, impurity, fornication, and sin" (Jub 9:15).[19]

The day of judgment is mentioned again in Jub 23:10-11. The appropriateness of the apocalyptic section of chap. 23 (and its connection with the earlier oath in chap. 9) can be seen by the fact that the narrative trigger for

19. Cf. P. S. Alexander, "Jerusalem as the Omphalos of the World: On the History of a Geographical Concept," *Judaism* 46 (1997): 147-58 (esp. 149-51); Alexander, "Jerusalem as the Omphalos of the World: On the History of a Geographical Concept," in *Jerusalem: Its Sanctity and Centrality to Judaism, Christianity, and Islam*, ed. L. I. Levine (New York: Continuum, 1999), 104-19 (esp. 105-7), who argues that Jubilees is a Hasmonean document that is politically motivated: it contrasts Jerusalem to Delphi, makes Greek influence in the East illegitimate, and justifies Hasmonean expansion.

the apocalyptic section is the story of Abraham's death and burial in the double cave of Machpelah (Jub 23:7), which was the only foothold the patriarchs had in the Promised Land (Gen 23:17-20).[20] Not only Sarah but also Abraham, Isaac and Rebekah, and Jacob and Leah were buried there (Gen 49:29-32; 50:13). Although Jub 23 obviously presupposes the story of Abraham's purchase of the cave in Gen 23, the author evidently does not want to emphasize that Abraham bought it from the Hittites, since that would undermine his thesis that the land belonged to Israel as an inheritance that was subject to the law of jubilee on a grand scale. Jub 23 anticipates the time when the Lord will expel his enemies from the land (v. 30), the ones who had caused such chaos in Israel and sin against Jacob (v. 23). This is evidently a thinly veiled allusion to conditions in the author's own time.

If the author of Jubilees believes that the original entrance into the land corresponds chronologically to the eschatological entrance into the land, then the timing of the first event at the jubilee of jubilees (2450 A.M.) very likely corresponds to a fixed date in the future from the author's own time.[21] We know from the Sin-Exile-Return pattern in chaps. 1 and 23 that the author of Jubilees reckons with a period of exile, although its length is nowhere explicitly given in the book. It could have been a known quantity traditionally, such as the 70 "weeks" = 490 years = 10 jubilees in Dan 9:24.

Hence, by using a combination of evidence from the book itself (particularly periodicity and symmetry) and from other sabbatical chronologies (especially the Apocalypse of Weeks), I have attempted to deduce when the author of Jubilees thought the restoration would begin. The Apocalypse of Weeks mentions that at the conclusion of the sixth week (2940 A.M.) the temple will be destroyed, and "the whole race of the chosen root will be dispersed" (1 En 93:8). It seems quite possible that Jubilees accepts this date for the exile, for when we postulate, in accordance with established tradition, that the exile was to last 490 years, something very interesting occurs: 3430 A.M. is the beginning of the restoration (as in the Apocalypse of Weeks) and the exact mirror of the jubilee of jubilees in 2450 A.M. across the axis of symmetry (the exile in 2940 A.M.).

In other words, for Jubilees the period from the original entrance into

---

20. Even though the author of Jubilees regards the land as Israel's inherited right because of the assignment of the land to Shem, he still thinks of it as the "promised land." Cf. Jub 1:7, which refers to "the land which I promised by oath to Abraham, Isaac, and Jacob."

21. If the original entrance into the land was to occur forty years after the revelation to Moses on Mount Sinai, does the author of Jubilees assume that the eschatological restoration to the land was to occur forty years from the time of writing?

the land until the reentry into the land at the time of the restoration would be two periods comprised of precisely 490 years, for a total of 980 years. The notion that the time in exile corresponds to the time in the land could be a reflection of the idea in 2 Chron 36:21 that the exile, which will last 70 years as Jeremiah had predicted (Jer 29:10), will befall Israel because of its neglect of the sabbatical and jubilee years (Lev 25:1-13). This presupposes that Israel failed properly to observe the sabbaths of the land from the very outset. Viewed through the lens of the interpretation of Jeremiah's prophecy in Dan 9:24, the compensatory punishment for Israel's missed sabbaths in the land could have been reckoned as 490 years (70 x 7 = 49 x 10). The sabbatical logic of this calculation would have cohered very well with Jubilees' own concern for the proper observance of the sabbath, on which in fact the book ends (Jub 50:1-13), and the other heptadic cycles of the sun.

The inherent plausibility of this reconstruction should not be missed. There can be little question that the author of Jubilees would have considered the date for the end of the exile and the beginning of the restoration every bit as important, if not more so, as the jubilee of jubilees that figures so largely in the surface narrative of the book as a whole. For the author and his community probably considered themselves as standing on the threshold of the restoration, just as the Apocalypse of Weeks — the other heptadic chronology with a universal scope from creation to new creation — most likely saw its community as standing on the threshold of the eighth "week," which commences the protracted restoration period ("weeks" 8-10).

III. Conclusion

We have argued that although in some respects the chronologies in the Apocalypse of Weeks and the book of Jubilees differ substantially from one another, in other ways they are quite similar. Their similarity suggests a literary relationship between the two writings, and the possible allusion of Jub 4:18-19 to the Apocalypse of Weeks seems to show the direction of the influence. If this is correct, Jubilees was not uncritical of its source. For the period before the exile, Jubilees goes its own chronological way, especially insofar as it evidently expects a much longer length of time from creation to the conquest.

For the period commencing with the exile, however, it can be credibly argued that Jubilees tracks the Apocalypse to a remarkable degree. Evidently, both writings expect the end of exile and the beginning of the restoration to occur on the same date (3430 A.M.). Although Jubilees does not explicitly mention this date, it leaves enough clues via its heptadic cycles and extensive symmetries to demonstrate that the culmination of the jubilee of jubilees (2450 A.M.) would correspond ideally to that blessed date across an axis of symmetry, the exile (2940 A.M. in the Apocalypse of Weeks). In that case, Jubilees appears to expect that Israel's time in the land (2940 A.M.–2450 A.M. = 490 years) would equal its time in exile (3430-2940 = 490 years), in accordance with the kind of sabbatical logic that we see reflected in 2 Chron 36:21 (cf. Dan 9:24).

The Aramaic Levi Document,
the Genesis Apocryphon, and Jubilees:
A Study of Shared Traditions

Esther Eshel

The complex interrelationships between the second temple period works that are based on, or retell, the stories of Genesis are a matter of scholarly debate. Although it is not always feasible to show direct influence, examination of linguistic and thematic parallels has the potential to indicate influence or borrowing and its possible direction. The three Jewish texts examined here — the Aramaic Levi Document (hereafter ALD), the Genesis Apocryphon, and Jubilees — share the background of Genesis. However, each elaborates on the biblical text in a different way, based on its sources, on the one hand, and its author's worldview on the other.

The underlying premise of this article is that ALD and the Genesis Apocryphon served as sources for Jubilees, as demonstrated by the examination of parallels, mostly thematic but also linguistic in nature. These parallels relate to Levi and his investiture to the priesthood, to Noah and the world division among his sons and its accompanying *mapa mundi,* and to the imagery of the two ways.

I. ALD and Jubilees: Jacob's Journey
and the List of Trees for Sacrificial Use

I consider ALD the oldest extant work in a series of writings attributed to the fathers of the priestly line. It was first discovered in the Cairo Geniza,[1] and at

1. For a detailed description of the various textual witnesses of ALD, see J. C. Green-

82

present ten pages of the Geniza manuscript of this work are known. Seven Qumran scrolls, all fragmentary, have been identified as copies of this work. The single copy from Cave 1, and the six from Cave 4, can be dated paleographically to the late Hasmonean or early Herodian period. Neither the work's beginning nor its end has survived.[2] ALD is significant for its religious ideas, which illumine the early postbiblical period, for the light it sheds on early priestly practice, for its understanding of wisdom, and for its emphasis on the transmission of ancient learning.

In the edition of ALD published by the late Jonas Greenfield, Michael Stone, and myself, we date this work to the third or the early second century B.C.E. at the latest. This dating is grounded in paleography, the centrality of the priesthood, and ALD's use of a solar calendar similar to the one promoted by 1 Enoch, Jubilees, and the Qumran sectarian writings.[3] The absence of polemic surrounding the calendar in the surviving fragments of ALD contrasts with the situation in Jubilees and supports this early dating, making ALD one of the earliest known postbiblical Jewish writings. On the basis of an examination of shared traditions found in both ALD and Jubilees, we argue that ALD served as a source for Jubilees and the Damascus Document, as well as for the Testament of Levi.

The two main examples of shared thematic traditions provided here, which are discussed in detail in our edition of ALD, demonstrate that Jubilees was familiar with, and relied on, ALD. (For additional scattered examples, see the commentary to our edition.) The first example concerns the story of the events found in ALD 4:9–5:8 and its parallel in Jub 31–32. Both recount, though not necessarily in the same order, Jacob's journey from Shechem to Bethel and Levi's visions, adding events that have no biblical background. Levi's vision in ALD 4, which combines priestly and royal functions, is followed by Levi's investiture as a priest, and his receiving tithes from Jacob and being blessed and instructed by his grandfather Isaac in chap. 5. These instructions are detailed in chap. 6. But certain incidents

---

field, M. E. Stone, and Esther Eshel, *The Aramaic Levi Document*, SVTP 19 (Leiden: Brill, 2004), 1-6.

2. Two of the copies from Qumran (4QLevi^d and 4QLevi^e) contain shorter texts than the Geniza manuscript. Moreover, ALD probably inspired two other works found at Qumran, 4QTestament of Qahat (4Q542) and 4QVisions of Amram (4Q543-549). Another work related to ALD is the Testament of Levi (= TPL, which is part of the Testaments of the Twelve Patriarchs), especially three insertions in one of its Greek manuscripts (Athos Koutloumous 39, called manuscript *e*).

3. Greenfield, Stone, and Eshel, *The Aramaic Levi Document*, 20.

found in ALD 4:9–5:8 (and TPL 8:1; 9:1-6) occur earlier in the story in Jubilees. The parallel stories are set out in the following table:[4]

ALD	Jubilees
	31:1 Start off in Shechem 31:3 Jacob goes to Bethel, invites Isaac and Rebecca to come to Bethel 31:4-5a Isaac refuses, invites Jacob, Levi, and Judah to go with Isaac to the residence of Abraham
	31:5b-29 The meeting of Jacob and Rebecca with Levi and Judah and their blessing
	31:30-32 Upon Isaac's orders, Jacob returns to Bethel with Rebecca and her nurse Deborah
4:9-12 Levi's vision of investiture	32:1 Levi's dream at Bethel, of being appointed to the eternal priesthood of the Most High
5:1a "We" go to Isaac	
5:1b Isaac's blessing of Levi	
5:2 Jacob gives a tithe to Levi Jacob invests Levi	32:2-3a Jacob giving the tithe; Birth of Benjamin; Jacob counting his sons — Levi as the tenth son 32:3b Levi as the tithe 32:3c Jacob invests Levi
	32:4-15 Jacob's celebration of the Festival of Booths
5:3-5 Levi offers sacrifices and blesses his father and brothers in Bethel	
5:6 Levi leaves Bethel and encamps at the residence of Abraham	

Jubilees' additions to the biblical narrative are inserted between the sections of the Bethel narrative in Gen 35, specifically after v. 4.[5] Their pur-

---

4. A comparison of these parallels is found in Greenfield, Stone, and Eshel, *The Aramaic Levi Document*, 151.

5. J. C. VanderKam, "Jubilees' Exegetical Creation of Levi the Priest," in *From Revelation to Canon: Studies in the Hebrew Bible and Second Temple Literature* (Leiden and Boston:

pose is to create an earlier visit by Jacob to Hebron — so that he can have Isaac meet and bless his grandsons — and to explain Deborah's presence at Bethel (Gen 35:8), as Kugel notes.[6] To this we must add VanderKam's comment: "Jacob's return to his father's house in safety meant that the Lord had now accomplished for him what Jacob had requested as a precondition for carrying out the vow he had made during his first stay at Bethel."[7] These additions are consistent with the centrality of Jacob in Jubilees, as opposed to ALD, where Levi is the hero. Accordingly, Jubilees devotes considerably less space to Levi than does ALD. This is exemplified by a comparison of the brief description of Levi's investiture in Jub 32:3: "His father put priestly clothes on him and ordained him," and the greater detail of ALD 5:4: "and he invested me in the priestly garb, and consecrated me and I became a priest of the God of eternity." Also absent from Jubilees is a parallel to ALD's detailed description of Levi blessing his father and brothers at Bethel (5:5-8). As noted, the disparity between the descriptions perhaps rests in the centrality of Levi in ALD, as in the Levi literature in general. Although aware of this tradition, Jubilees' focus is less Levi-centric and therefore its account of these events is shorter and less detailed. The different weight afforded to the Levi material in each work reflects its author's worldview.

A second example of Jubilees' use of ALD also relates to the cultic realm. Isaac's instructions to Levi, found in ALD 6–10, comprehend cultic priestly teachings, including the following lists: (a) trees for sacrificial use, (b) prescriptions for animal sacrifices, (c) sacrificial ordinances, and (d) metrological equivalents.

I focus here on the list of trees found in ALD 7:6-7, which is documented in the Geniza and the Qumran manuscripts, as well as in the Greek manuscripts from Mount Athos. As seen from the following table, Jub 21:12-15 contains a very similar list:

Brill, 2000), 545-61 (here 548); in his study of the story of Levi according to Jub 30–32, VanderKam maintained that the author of Jubilees "probably had another source, the Aramaic Levi, on which to draw, whether directly or indirectly" (551), whereas R. A. Kugler, *From Patriarch to Priest: The Levi-Priestly Tradition from Aramaic Levi to Testament of Levi,* SBLEJL 9 (Atlanta: Scholars Press, 1996), 146-55, suggested an intermediary text between ALD and Jubilees.

6. J. Kugel, "Levi's Elevation to the Priesthood in Second Temple Writings," *HTR* 86 (1993): 1-64. For his latest study on the relationship between ALD and Jubilees, see Kugel, "How Old Is the *Aramaic Levi Document?*" *DSD* 14 (2007): 291-312.

7. VanderKam, "Jubilees' Exegetical Creation," 553.

ALD	*Jubilees*
cedar	cypress
juniper (bay)	silver fir
almond (Aramaic), mastik (Greek)	almond
fir	fir
pine	pine
ash	cedar
cypress	juniper
fig	date
oleaster (Aramaic), cypress (Greek)	olive wood
laurel	myrtle
myrtle	laurel wood = cedar
	juniper bush
aspalathos	balsam

Bearing in mind the difficulty of identifying these trees, and also the indefiniteness of some of the Ethiopian terms found in this passage, the two lists may be even closer than appears at first glance.[8] In our commentary on ALD we undertook a linguistic comparison of these parallel lists, which points to the originality of ALD's list. Here I focus on what appears to be a mistake in Jubilees: where ALD has עא משחא, "oleaster," the parallel in Jubilees reads "olive wood." Since משחא means "oil," עא משחא was mistakenly understood as "olive wood," while "olive tree" is זיתא in Aramaic. The prohibition in rabbinic halakah of the use of olive wood on the altar (*m. Tamid* 2:3) implies that ALD has preserved the original reading. Supporting this supposition is the fact that Jubilees' priestly halakah is generally stricter than rabbinic halakah; it is therefore unlikely that Jubilees would permit the use of olive wood on the altar. This suggests that in the process of copying the list from ALD, the original version was corrupted.

With regard to the above-noted lists found in ALD 6–10, it should be noted that despite some points of contact with later sacrificial practice as reported in rabbinic literature, these lists are largely unique and perhaps even provide evidence for the existence of cultic handbooks during the second temple period. Because it is not related to the fixed daily, Sabbath, new moon, or festival sacrifices prescribed in the Pentateuch, the list of sacrifices is particularly interesting.

8. Here I compare only the translation. For the full details and discussion, see Greenfield, Stone, and Eshel, *The Aramaic Levi Document*, 165-68.

There is also an important contextual difference between ALD and Jubilees with respect to the transmission of these cultic instructions. According to Jubilees, these instructions were transmitted to Isaac by Abraham (Jub 21), whereas in ALD they were transmitted to Levi by Isaac. This is consistent with Jubilees' worldview of the patriarchs functioning as priests, starting with Adam and continuing through Abraham, to Isaac, to Levi. As Kugel has demonstrated, this priestly line does not include Jacob; thus Isaac is the one who delivers the directives of the priesthood to Levi.[9] Accordingly, the author of Jubilees "felt no need to add another scene in which Isaac would instruct Levi in the priesthood (as *Aramaic Levi* does)."[10]

I would like to argue that these teachings are introduced by the author of ALD in their logical setting, where Isaac prepares Levi for his priestly role (chaps. 6–9). This long section concludes in chap. 10 (preserved only in the Greek manuscript from Mount Athos) with Isaac's injunctions and blessings to Levi. This chapter also contains two references to Abraham: "For my father Abraham commanded me to do thus and to command my sons" (10:3); and "For my father Abraham commanded me for thus he found in the writing of the book of Noah concerning the blood" (10:9). Apparently these references to Abraham motivated the author of Jubilees to move these cultic instructions to earlier in the account, transposing them into Abraham's instructions to Isaac, and stressing Abraham's role in the priestly line. Thus, the shared tradition of Levi's investiture to the priesthood was altered by Jubilees to harmonize with his viewpoint of the priestly lineage as proceeding from Adam through the patriarchs to Levi (and skipping Jacob).

II. The Genesis Apocryphon and Jubilees

A. The Mapa Mundi

ALD was not the only source available to, and known by, Jubilees. Another work upon which Jubilees drew was the Genesis Apocryphon. If my first examples of parallels and possible influence concerned Levi and his investiture to the priesthood, the following one relates to a different component of the Genesis narrative: the division of the world among Noah's sons and the *mapa mundi* it reflects.

---

9. Kugel, "Levi's Elevation," 19-21, 62-63; VanderKam, "Jubilees' Exegetical Creation," 560.

10. VanderKam, "Jubilees' Exegetical Creation," 560.

The Genesis Apocryphon — an Aramaic parabiblical text — recounts, with additions, omissions, and expansions, some of the stories from Gen 5–15.[11] Although generally attributed to the second or first century B.C.E., an earlier date cannot be ruled out for the composition of this work.[12] Like the other Aramaic texts found at Qumran, the Genesis Apocryphon is not considered sectarian.[13]

In a paper I wrote in honor of my friend and colleague Betsy Halpern-Amaru,[14] I discussed the *mapa mundi* in detail, mainly comparing the descriptions found in the Genesis Apocryphon (cols. 16-17), Jubilees (8–9), and Josephus (*Ant* 1.122-47). Those sources reflect both reliance on Gen 10 and a shared cartographical basis for their construction of the world,[15] namely, an updated version of this ancient, sixth century B.C.E. Ionian world map, based on Dicaearchus's (fl. 326-296 B.C.E.) division of the world by a median running through the Pillars of Hercules, the Taurus Mountains, and the Himalayas.[16] Of these texts, the Genesis Apocryphon

11. See M. J. Bernstein, "From the Watchers to the Flood: Story and Exegesis in the Early Columns of the 'Genesis Apocryphon,'" in *Reworking the Bible: Apocryphal and Related Texts at Qumran*, ed. E. Chazon, D. Dimant, and R. A. Clements (Leiden and Boston: Brill, 2005), 39-63.

12. For the latest edition of the Genesis Apocryphon, see J. A. Fitzmyer, *The Genesis Apocryphon of Qumran Cave 1 (1Q20): A Commentary*, 3rd ed., BibOr 18/B (Rome: Pontificio Instituto Biblico, 2004). The readings and translation of the Genesis Apocryphon are based on this edition. However, some readings were arrived at in conjunction with M. Bernstein; others were formulated in the course of working on this article.

13. Note that Noah waited until the fifth year to drink the fourth-year wine (1QapGen 12:13-15; see also Jub 7:1-2), as in sectarian law, rather than in the fourth year, as in rabbinic law. See M. Kister, "Some Aspects of Qumranic Halakha," in *The Madrid Qumran Congress: Proceedings of the International Congress on the Dead Sea Scrolls, Madrid, 18-21 March, 1991*, ed. J. Trebolle Barrera and L. Vegas Montaner, STDJ XI,2 (Leiden: Brill, 1992), 2:581-86. On the other hand, a reference to Noah's endogamy in choosing his children's spouses (col. 6) may point to general, nonsectarian, second temple practice.

14. E. Eshel, "The *Imago Mundi* of the *Genesis Apocryphon*," in *Heavenly Tablets: Interpretation, Identity, and Tradition in Ancient Judaism*, ed. L. LiDonnici and A. Lieber, JSJSup 119 (Leiden and Boston: Brill, 2007), 111-31.

15. Such constructs also appear in Pseudo-Philo, *Antiquities of the Bible* 4.1-10, SibOr 1 3: 110-14; Acts 2:9-11, and later, in *Genesis Rabbah* 37:1-8. The War Scroll (1QM 2:10-14) also contains a Gen 10–based list of nations to be fought in the third phase of the thirty-three-year war. See Y. Yadin, *The Scroll of the Sons of Light against the Sons of Darkness* (Oxford: Oxford University Press, 1962), 26-33. 1QM 10:14-15 also alludes to the division of the world.

16. P. S. Alexander, "Notes on the 'Imago Mundi' of the Book of Jubilees," *JJS* 33 (1982): 204; L. H. Feldman, ed., *Judean Antiquities 1-4*, vol. 3 of *Flavius Josephus: Translation and Commentary*, ed. S. Mason (Boston: Brill, 2000), 43.

is, in my opinion, the oldest surviving second-temple-period text mapping the inhabited world.[17]

The main similarity between Jubilees and the Genesis Apocryphon relates to the immediate context in which the world division is placed. Whereas the biblical Table of Nations appears *after* the death of Noah (Gen 9:29; see also Josephus, *Ant* 1.104), in Jubilees (8:10-11) Noah takes an active role in dividing the world among his sons, and the Genesis Apocryphon documents the announcement and interpretation of the division of the world in Noah's dream vision, which precedes the actual division. Another similarity relates to the reference to reliance on a written, probably heavenly source. The Genesis Apocryphon makes reference to a written source in the angel's statement: "So it is written concerning you" (15:20); to be compared with Jubilees: "He divided the earth into the lots which his three sons would occupy. They reached out their hands and took the book from the bosom of their father Noah. In the book there emerged as Shem's lot . . ." (Jub 8:11-12). Finally, both texts provide a detailed description of each son's allotment, which includes many parallels, among them shared terminology, mainly land-related terms taken from Josh 15.

Nevertheless, there are significant differences between the Genesis Apocryphon and Jubilees, some of which enable the drawing of conclusions with regard to the interrelationship between these texts. The main differences are the following:

1. The nature of direct divine involvement in the divisionary process: if the Genesis Apocryphon attributes no immediate role to angels in the division — rather, general guidelines to the division appear in the dream vision and its interpretation — according to Jubilees there is direct angelic involvement: "they divided the earth into three parts . . . while one of us who were sent was staying with them" (8:10).

2. Jubilees' expansionist tendency, with regard to both greater geographical detail and, more particularly, the provision of ethnographic information, namely, which nations inhabit a particular area, to which Josephus gives even greater emphasis.[18]

3. Another difference relates to Shem's portion. According to the Genesis Apocryphon, invasions of Shem's portion appear in Noah's dream vision,

---

17. See J. A. Fitzmyer, "Genesis Apocryphon," in *EDSS*, 1:302. Fitzmyer argues for its literary dependence on Jubilees, therefore suggesting a possible first century b.c.e. dating. See, however, M. E. Stone, "The Book(s) Attributed to Noah," *DSD* 13 (2006): 9.

18. Thus, Alexander was able to identify each grandson's territory ("Imago Mundi," 209).

apparently a reference to future violent acts, but no violent invasion is recorded in the Genesis Apocryphon's actual account of the division of the world. A different approach is documented in Jubilees, which reports invasions conducted by Canaan, the son of Ham, and negotiations for land by Madai, the son of Japheth.

4. The most crucial difference lies in the actual lots given to each son and in the prominence Jubilees ascribes to Jerusalem. According to Jubilees, Shem received all of Asia Minor, together with Syria, Phoenicia, and Palestine, whereas according to the Genesis Apocryphon, the region of Asia Minor belonged to Japheth. Genesis Apocryphon agrees here with the map of Shem's lot according to Josephus *(Antiquities)*. Moreover, the surviving text of the Genesis Apocryphon documents no concept of Jerusalem's superiority. Indeed, on the basis of the mention of "the Sea of the East" (ים מדנחא; 17:10) in Lud's allotment, I maintain that the Genesis Apocryphon did not share this bias. The "Sea of the East" can be identified as Jubilees' Mauq Sea, the present-day Sea of Azov. This reference to the Sea of the East reflects the orientation from Greece, namely, with Delphi at the center. Thus, as opposed to Jubilees, which converts the Ionic map to a Jewish perspective, placing Jerusalem at the center of the world, the Genesis Apocryphon retains the focus of the original Ionic map. Only someone using Greece as a reference point could refer to the Sea of Azov as "the Sea of the East."

Furthermore, closer examination of the parallels between these two works enables the identification of three mistakes in Jubilees. These mistakes indicate Jubilees' knowledge of, and reliance on, the Genesis Apocryphon:

1. One mistake relates to the portion allotted to Aram, where Jubilees reads "the entire land of Mesopotamia between the Tigris and the Euphrates to the *north* of the Chaldeans"; on the basis of the Genesis Apocryphon's description, it should read "to the *east*."

2. Another obvious mistake in Jubilees results from a misreading in Lud's allotment. The Genesis Apocryphon reads, "for Lud it fell the Taurus mountains" (טור תורא, 17:10), while Jubilees has "for Lud these emerged as the fifth share the mountain range of Asshur" (9:6). The Asshur Mountains are unknown from the Bible or any other Jewish source; on the basis of the Genesis Apocryphon, I submit that this reflects a scribal misreading: טור אתור instead of טור תורא.

3. According to Jubilees, the Kamaturi Islands belong to Shem's son Arpachshad; they were, however, mistakenly appended to the portion of Japheth's sons, after Tiras's portion (9:13b). Even though the possible parallel

in the Genesis Apocryphon has not survived, the disposition of these islands was clearly not appended to Tiras's portion there.

Notwithstanding these differences, the parallels between the Genesis Apocryphon and Jubilees are significant, raising the question of the relationship between the two sources. Some scholars suggest that the author of Jubilees utilized and adapted the Genesis Apocryphon to his needs, or that both authors used a common source.[19] I argue that the distinct development of the world division in each work emerges more strongly from the differences than from the similarities between the texts. The Genesis Apocryphon is the older source, in which the original Ionic map can still be traced. This text was later used by the author of Jubilees, which he converted to fit his Jewish perspective, awarding Shem the major portion and function — as he received all of Asia Minor, together with Syria, Phoenicia, and Palestine — and placing Jerusalem at the center of the world. Thus, both the identification of mistakes and a conceptual shift in the nature of the *mapa mundi* indicate that the Genesis Apocryphon served as a source for Jubilees.

B. The Two-Ways Imagery

I conclude with a preliminary attempt to trace the motif of the two ways in the works under consideration. In this examination of different aspects of a shared tradition, it is more difficult to show direct influence. Therefore the discussion aims simply to chart the uses of the tradition of the two paths in these roughly contemporaneous texts.

The concept of walking in "the path of truth" has its roots in the biblical דרך אמת ("way of truth") mentioned in Gen 24:48. The metaphor of the two ways, of the paths of good and of evil, first appears in Deut 30:15-20, where the ways of life and of death are related to obedience or disobedience of divine commandments. This metaphor also "runs like a thread through Prov 1–8."[20] These ancient texts (as well as Jer 21:8, which interprets Deut 30:15 in an ironic exegesis)[21] "appear to employ the two ways as a construct

---

19. See J. T. van Ruiten, "The Division of the Earth," in *Primaeval History Interpreted: The Rewriting of Genesis 1–11 in the Book of Jubilees*, JSJSup 66 (Leiden, Boston, and Cologne: Brill, 2000), 307ff.

20. G. W. E. Nickelsburg, *1 Enoch 1: A Commentary on the Book of 1 Enoch, Chapters 1–36, 81–108* (Minneapolis: Fortress, 2001), 455.

21. See W. L. Holladay, *Jeremiah 1: A Commentary on the Book of the Prophet Jeremiah Chapters 1–25*, Hermeneia (Minneapolis: Fortress, 1986), 573-74.

for envisioning alternative behaviors rather than to constitute a fixed two-ways literary form."[22] In his discussion of later texts using the same image, dated to the Hellenistic period (Tobit and 1 Enoch), Nickelsburg shows the continuation of the biblical parallels, where "the two ways imagery is employed as a construct for ethical admonitions."[23] A well-known parallel is found in 1QS 3:15–4:26, as well as in some related early Christian sources, among them Barnabas 18–21 and the Didache 1–6,[24] which are outside the scope of this article. In his study of this motif in early Jewish sources, Nickelsburg came to the conclusion that "the two-ways imagery in biblical and post-biblical tradition is inextricably bound up with the notion of divine recompense for human deeds. These deeds are alluded to, or described in binary or polar fashion, and right and wrong deeds bring divine blessing and punishment respectively." He further suggests: "As Jewish theology begins to think in terms of an eschatological judgment, the 'life' and 'death' that wait at the ends of the ways are constructed as eternal life and eternal destruction."[25]

I suggest that additional, early Jewish texts be incorporated in the existing discussion, namely, the texts considered here: ALD, the Genesis Apocryphon, and Jubilees, alongside Tobit. Here I can only outline the first steps of such a study of the two-ways motif, and I view this as a work in progress.

The earliest postbiblical source for the two-ways imagery is ALD 3. Preserved partially in 4QLevi[b], this text was reconstructed by Stone and Greenfield based on the Athos Greek manuscript, which preserves the prayer in full. This prayer reads as follows:[26]

> 3:4And now my children are with me,
> and grant me all the paths of truth.
> 3:5Make far from me, my Lord,

22. G. W. E. Nickelsburg, "Seeking the Origins of the Two Ways Tradition," in *A Multiform Heritage: Studies on Early Judaism and Christianity in Honor of Robert A. Kraft* (Atlanta: Scholars Press, 1999), 98.

23. Nickelsburg, "Seeking the Origins," 98.

24. Where Kraft found what he called "basic binary" form; see R. A. Kraft, "Early Developments of the 'Two-Way Tradition(s)' in Retrospect," in *For a Later Generation: The Transformation of Tradition in Israel, Early Judaism, and Early Christianity*, ed. R. A. Argall, B. A. Bow, and R. A. Werline (Harrisburg, Pa.: Trinity, 2000), 137.

25. Nickelsburg, "Seeking the Origins," 108.

26. Greenfield, Stone, and Eshel, *The Aramaic Levi Document*, 33-34, 60-61, 125-30.

the unrighteous spirit,
and evil thought and fornication. . . .
3:6Let there be shown to me, O Lord, the holy spirit,
and grant me counsel, and wisdom and knowledge and strength,
3:7-8in order to do that which is pleasing before you. . . .
3:9And let not any satan have power over me,
to make me stray from your path.

This prayer, located before Levi's dream and investiture, opens with "My Lord, you know all hearts . . ." (3:3). The unexpected note struck by "And now my children are with me" (3:4a) will be discussed below. As it stands, this prayer includes: a petition for God to show Levi "all the paths of truth" (3:4b), to distance the evil spirit from him, to grant him the holy spirit of wisdom and knowledge, which will help him act properly before God (3:6-8); and a plea for divine protection from satan, who makes him stray from God's path (3:9). As Stone and Greenfield note: "This is certainly one of the oldest passages in which two spirits are contrasted, and if the view of a third century BCE date for *ALD* is accepted, then this concept, so characteristic of the Qumran texts, must be put back to that date. The terminology used here, however, is not typical of the sectarian writings from Qumran."[27] Furthermore, as we argue in our edition of ALD, "It is related to the idea of the two ways, one good and one bad . . . but is distinct from it in its use of the idea of the two spirits."[28] Thus, in what follows I will concentrate only on the two-ways image and its parallels.[29]

I diverge briefly to discuss Levi's mention of his children at the beginning of the prayer. In our commentary to ALD 3:4 we note how "the mention of Levi's children at this point seems out of place, and the reason for their introduction is unclear. Such a mention might have been more appropriate in the context of 3:15."[30] The beginning of this verse, preserved only in the Mount Athos Greek manuscript, has a partial parallel in the Aramaic manuscripts from the Geniza and Qumran. 4QLevi[b] reads as follows:

27. M. E. Stone and J. C. Greenfield, "The Prayer of Levi," *JBL* 112 (1993): 252.

28. Greenfield, Stone, and Eshel, *The Aramaic Levi Document*, 34.

29. Other parallels, but without the contrastive negative way, are found in various Aramaic compositions from Qumran Cave 4. Thus, 4Qpseudo-Daniel[a] reads, ". . . indeed, the children of [. . .] the ways of truth" (4Q243 7 2-3); and 4Q246 2 5 reads: "[. . .] and all his ways are truth."

30. Greenfield, Stone, and Eshel, *The Aramaic Levi Document*, 125.

Esther Eshel

[. . .]ארחת קשט ארחק 12

[. . .ב]איש^א וזנותא דחא 13

12 [. . .] paths of truth. Make far
13 [. . .] evil [. . .] and fornication turn away.[31]

A comparison of ALD 3:4 to additional parallels may explain the origin of its anachronistic call for Levi's sons. I suggest that at some point in the transmission of the text, most likely when it was already translated into Greek, the copyist, who was familiar with other two-ways motifs in testamental contexts, such as Tob 4, or even with the later Epistle of Enoch, or the Testament of Asher 1, introduced a testamental formula here. I propose on this basis that the original text may have included only a request from God to show or grant Levi the paths of truth, as found in 4QLevi[b]. To summarize, ALD includes what appears to be the earliest known reference to the two ways, as well as a general reference to pleasing God by following his guidance and walking in the right path.

Another early source in which this motif occurs is Tobit. As part of his programmatic statement, Tobit states: "I, Tobit, walked the paths of fidelity and righteousness all the days of my life" (1:3).[32] The same motif appears later in Tobit's testamentary instruction to his son Tobias:[33]

Be mindful of (God) the Lord, my boy, every day of your life.
Do not seek to sin or transgress His commandments.
Practice righteousness all the days of your life,
and tread not the paths of wickedness.
For those who act with fidelity will prosper in all they (you) do.
To all those who practice righteousness. (4:5-6)[34]

For almsgiving preserves one from death and keeps one from going off into darkness. (4:10)[35]

31. M. E. Stone and J. C. Greenfield, "213a. 4QLevi[b] ar," in G. Brooke et al., *Qumran Cave 4:XVII, Parabiblical Texts, Part 3*, DJD 22 (Oxford: Clarendon, 1996), 28-31.
32. Where G[II] = G[I]; the translation is based on J. A. Fitzmyer, *Tobit*, CEJL (Berlin and New York: De Gruyter, 2003), 98.
33. According to G[II], which, unless noted, is usually identical with G[I].
34. Fitzmyer, *Tobit*, 163, according to G[II], where G[I] reads, "For if you act in fidelity, success will attend all you do. To all those who practice righteousness."
35. Fitzmyer, *Tobit*, 164.

A third reference is found in Tobit's instructions to Tobias: "On every occasion praise God and beg Him that your ways may be made straight and all your paths [G^I + and plans] may lead to prosperity" (4:19). While the motif of the two ways in Tobit and ALD is related to its biblical imagery, both works share a new context for this motif — in a prayer to God. But they differ in their relationship to Torah. Whereas ALD does not explicitly refer to the observance of God's commandments, only to "what is pleasing to you [namely, God]" (3:7), Tobit explicates his path with reference to his observance of God's commandments, which he contrasts with the sinful behavior of the Northern Kingdom (1:4-9). This emphasis on fulfillment of the divine commandments is absent from the other works considered here. Finally, as Nickelsburg notes, "the author narrativizes the idea of walking on the path in his account of Tobias's journey from Nineveh to Ecbatan (cf. 5:21-22)."[36] Thus, while there are points of contact between ALD's use of the two-ways motif and that of Tobit, particularly the prayer context, Tobit places emphasis on and links the paths to the observance of the divine commandments.

A third ancient description of the two ways appears in the Genesis Apocryphon, column VI, as part of Noah's story, which starts with his birth, as told by his father Lamech (col. II), and continues with Noah's biography, a first-person account preceded by the title "[a copy of] the book of the words of Noah" (V:29).[37] After five missing lines, the biography starts with the following words:

> [. . .] And in the furnace of my gestation I flourished to truth; and when I left my mother's womb, I was rooted in truth and I conducted myself in truth all my days, and I walked in the paths of eternal truth, and with me was the Holy [One] on the path of the way of truth, and to warn me away from the path of falsehood which leads to everlasting darkness [. . .] I girded my loins in a vision of truth and wisdom when there entered [. . .] all the paths of violence. (VI:1-5)

36. Nickelsburg, "Seeking the Origins," 99.

37. Some argue that this part of the Genesis Apocryphon originated as an independent composition, probably from the Book of Noah. See R. C. Steiner, "The Heading of the *Book of the Words of Noah* on a Fragment of the Genesis Apocryphon: New Light on a 'Lost' Work," *DSD* 2 (1995): 66-71. For a discussion of the possible existence of a lost book (or books) of Noah, see Stone's recent study, "Book(s) Attributed to Noah," 5-9, where he also relates to earlier studies. See Fitzmyer, "Genesis Apocryphon," 302-3.

This description is unique in many ways: here we find for the first time a full Aramaic description written using a poetic structure, similar to biblical *stichoi*, with parallels and contradictions. Within these lines we find the following "ways" terminology: נתיב מסלה, שביל, אורח (two of these — מסלה and נתיב — are Hebrew words found in this Aramaic composition). We also find adjectives describing the right way, using קושט, "truth," or אמת, "truth" (again, a Hebrew word). This, in turn, is contrasted with the adjectives describing the wrong way as שפר, "falsehood", חשוך, "darkness," or חמס, "violence."[38]

Noah's testimony to walking in the path of truth in the Genesis Apocryphon has its closest parallel in Tob 1:3: "I, Tobit, walked the paths of fidelity and righteousness all the days of my life." Unlike Tobit, which, as mentioned, relates the path of righteousness to Torah, in the Genesis Apocryphon, as in ALD, no reference to the divine commandments is found.

But not only is the Genesis Apocryphon's description of the two ways more detailed, it also introduces a significant new element, the eternality of both good and evil: "I walked in the paths of *eternal* truth," which is contrasted with the "path of *everlasting* darkness." Accordingly, the Genesis Apocryphon represents the bestowing of an eschatological theology on the two-ways motif.

My final example concerns a less-known parallel from Jubilees. Because its two-ways imagery is less explicit than in the previously discussed works, I rely on the Genesis Apocryphon for its extrapolation. As we saw above, in its early biography of Noah the Genesis Apocryphon documents how he walked in the path of truth. Jubilees' initial recounting of the story of Noah's ark relies on 1 Enoch (6–16; 86–88) but also quotes Gen 6:8 (Jub 5:5: "He was pleased with Noah alone"). Jubilees returns to the Noah story in 5:19, which reads: "*To all who corrupted their ways and their plan(s)*[39] before the flood no favor was shown, except to Noah alone because favor was shown to him for the sake of his children whom he saved from the flood waters for his sake *because his mind was righteous in all his ways,* as it has been commanded concerning him. He did not transgress from anything that had

---

38. This rich imagery of the two ways, including both Hebrew and Aramaic terms, brings to mind the name-midrash of Levi's sons in ALD (chap. 11); and his grandson Amram (12:4), which includes both Hebrew and Aramaic etymologies (Greenfield, Stone, and Eshel, *The Aramaic Levi Document*, 184-93).

39. The addition of "and plans" seems to have originated in Tob 4:19, where G[II] reads: "On every occasion praise God and beg Him that your ways may be made straight and all your paths may lead to prosperity," and G[I] reads: "your paths *and plans*."

been ordained for him." I suggest that the two-ways terminology underlies this description, in which Noah's righteous way is contrasted to that of others who choose the wrong way, and furthermore, that the addition of nonbiblical elements using the two-ways terminology to explicate Noah's righteousness echoes Genesis Apocryphon, col. VI: "and I walked in the paths of eternal truth" (l. 2), as opposed to "the path of falsehood which leads to everlasting darkness [. . .]" (l. 3).[40] Having demonstrated that Jubilees used the Genesis Apocryphon as a source for its map of the world and its division, I surmise that Jubilees could also have adapted it in its portrayal of Noah. Both texts describe Noah as walking in the righteous path, but Jubilees again shifts the emphasis to what is significant to its worldview, namely, that Noah follows God's commands: "as it has been commanded concerning him. He did not transgress from anything that had been ordained for him." As we have seen, this element is also found in Tobit's biography. Another element shared with Tobit is the existence of a reward for following the right way — Jubilees "because favor was shown to him," and Tobit: "For those who act with fidelity will prosper in all they do. To all those who practice righteousness" (4:6). But, as opposed to the Genesis Apocryphon, this context contains no eschatological theology.

Briefly, this preliminary discussion of the two-ways motif in ancient postbiblical sources demonstrates that it appears in several contexts: in the biography of Noah (Genesis Apocryphon, Tobit, and Jubilees); in prayer contexts (Aramaic Levi Document and Tobit); and in an instructional context (Tobit). The addition of an element of eschatological theology to this motif is found in Genesis Apocryphon. It is not possible at this stage of my inquiry, however, to show a direct relationship between the sources, though I surmise that Jubilees may have relied on the Genesis Apocryphon in its description of Noah's righteousness.

---

40. Further, VanderKam discusses the difficult phrase "favor was shown to him" (see J. C. VanderKam, *The Book of Jubilees* [Louvain: Peeters, 1989], 34), having the "Hebrew נשא פנים underline the Ethiopic words," explaining it in "a positive sense, 'to be gracious to' (Gen 32:21)." I would like to argue that Jubilees here is probably a corrupted text. The biblical phrase is ונח מצא חן בעיני הי (Gen 6:8), translated by Jubilees as "he was pleased with Noah alone," and translated literally: "Noah alone found favor before his eyes" (5:5; VanderKam, *The Book of Jubilees*, 33). This verse is referred to in Genesis Apocryphon 6:23: ואש[כחב אנה נוח חן רבו וקושט], "And I Noah found favor, greatness and truth." We might trace the development of the Jubilees version as follows: מצא חן was understood as parallel with נשא חן, the latter also found in the phrase מצא חן לפני, e.g., Esther 2:17. This is paralleled with נשא חן לפני, where לפני = פנים, thus creating the wrong phrase נוא + פנים.

III. Conclusions

This paper traces some literary-conceptual parallels between three ancient Jewish compositions. Although these parallels do not provide conclusive evidence that both ALD and the Genesis Apocryphon are older than Jubilees, I argue that the weight of the evidence shows that Jubilees was at least familiar with the traditions in these works, and probably with these works themselves. I base this conclusion on various literary and topical parallels between these sources, both where I was able to show scribal mistakes whose original readings were found in either ALD or the Genesis Apocryphon, and ideological alterations made by Jubilees in line with its worldview. These ideological changes appear in the cultic instructions delivered to Levi by Isaac, which Jubilees shifts to Abraham delivering to Isaac, as well as in the story of Noah — in both the division of the world to his sons and in the *mapa mundi*. I also postulated that Jubilees' reference to Noah's righteousness may have been grounded in the two-ways imagery of other works, of the Genesis Apocryphon in particular.

In the discussion of the world map I argued that the Genesis Apocryphon preserves the oldest map, and that Jubilees documents its later usage. I reached the same conclusions regarding Jubilees' use of the two-ways imagery. Integral to the Genesis Apocryphon's depiction of Noah is his walking in the right way, and divine guidance keeping him away from the wrong path. Jubilees reflects a short reference, both linguistic and conceptual, to this portrayal. This reference to the two-ways imagery in connection with Noah suggests that the author of Jubilees was familiar with Noah's biography as depicted by the Genesis Apocryphon.

The Book of Jubilees and the Temple Scroll

Lawrence H. Schiffman

Various approaches have been put forth since the discovery of the Dead Sea Scrolls regarding their connection with the book of Jubilees.[1] It has been argued, for example, that Jubilees is actually a "sectarian text,"[2] that is, a composition of the Qumran community, a view that is very unlikely in light of its use of proto-Masoretic Hebrew.[3] It has also been argued that Jubilees is actually the first part of the Temple Scroll,[4] a view we attempted to disprove on the basis of a careful comparison of the sacrificial calendar of the Temple Scroll with Jubilees.[5] However, despite the ease with which these overstated

---

1. Cf. L. H. Schiffman, *Reclaiming the Dead Sea Scrolls: The History of Judaism, the Background of Christianity, the Lost Library of Qumran* (Philadelphia: Jewish Publication Society, 1994), 185-88; J. C. VanderKam, "Jubilees," in *EDSS*, 1:434-38; see the detailed study of D. Hamidovic, *Les Traditions du Jubilé à Qumrân*, Orients sémitiques (Paris: Geuthner, 2007).

2. E.g., H. Lignée, "La place du livre des Jubilés et du Rouleau du Temple dans l'histoire du mouvement Essénien: Ces deux ouvrages ont-ils été écrits par le Maître de Justice?" *RevQ* 13 (1988): 331-45.

3. See E. Schürer, *The History of the Jewish People in the Age of Jesus Christ (175 B.C.–A.D. 135)*, ed. G. Vermes, F. Millar, with P. Vermes and M. Black, rev. ed., 3 vols. in 4 (Edinburgh: T. & T. Clark, 1973-87), III.1:311-14.

4. B. Z. Wacholder, "The Relationship between 11QTorah (the Temple Scroll) and the Book of Jubilees: One Single or Two Independent Compositions?" in SBLSP 24 (1985), 205-16; cf. Wacholder, *The Dawn of Qumran: The Sectarian Torah and the Teacher of Righteousness* (Cincinnati: Hebrew Union College Press, 1983), 41-62.

5. L. H. Schiffman, "The Sacrificial System of the *Temple Scroll* and the Book of Jubilees," in *Society for Biblical Literature Seminar Papers 1985*, ed. K. H. Richards (Atlanta: Scholars Press, 1985), 217-33.

claims can be falsified, there is no question that Jubilees is related to the sect of the scrolls because it was found in the Qumran library,[6] although it is certainly to be classified as part of what we call the nonsectarian section of the collection.[7] Most interestingly, however, it does seem to follow the Zadokite/Sadducean approach to Jewish law[8] found in the Qumran sectarian texts and uses the 364-day "Qumran" calendar,[9] and we will see a variety of other affinities. Close study of these relationships will allow us to get a glimpse of the complexity of textual and perhaps socioreligious divisions in ancient Judaism. In what follows we will carefully outline the affinities and contrasts between these two works, dealing with issues of language and style, theology, early Jewish law and lore, calendar, and the role of these texts in the history of Judaism.[10]

Language, Style, and Contents

As the work was clearly composed in Hebrew, in discussing its language and style we will consider only the surviving Hebrew fragments whose language and style can be compared to that of the Temple Scroll. Jubilees survives in fifteen fragmentary manuscripts,[11] whereas the Temple Scroll exists in one more-or-less complete manuscript (with the first columns rewritten at some point as a repair)[12] and three fragmentary copies.[13] Needless to say, when we

6. J. T. Milik and J. C. VanderKam, in H. Attridge et al., *Qumran Cave 4.VIII: Parabiblical Texts, Part I*, DJD 13 (Oxford: Clarendon, 1994); J. C. VanderKam, *Textual and Historical Studies in the Book of Jubilees*, HSM 14 (Missoula: Scholars Press, 1977); Hamidovic, *Les Traditions du Jubilé à Qumrân*, 97-172.

7. Cf. D. Dimant, "The Qumran Manuscripts: Contents and Significance," in *Time to Prepare the Way in the Wilderness: Papers on the Qumran Scrolls by Fellows of the Institute for Advanced Studies of the Hebrew University, Jerusalem, 1989-90*, ed. D. Dimant and L. H. Schiffman, STDJ 16 (Leiden: Brill, 1995), 23-58.

8. See C. Albeck, *Das Buch der Jubiläen und die Halacha* (Berlin: Siebenundvierzigster Bericht der Hochschule für die Wissenschaft des Judentums in Berlin, 1930).

9. J. C. VanderKam, *Calendars in the Dead Sea Scrolls: Measuring Time* (London and New York: Routledge, 1998), 27-33.

10. Cf. J. C. VanderKam, "The Temple Scroll and the Book of Jubilees," in *Temple Scroll Studies*, ed. G. J. Brooke, JSPSup 7 (Sheffield: JSOT, 1989), 211-36; J. H. Charlesworth, "The Date of Jubilees and the Temple Scroll," in SBLSP 24 (1985), 193-204.

11. A convenient listing is in Hamidovic, *Les Traditions du Jubilé à Qumrân*, 99.

12. Y. Yadin, *The Temple Scroll*, 3 vols. (Jerusalem: Israel Exploration Society and the Shrine of the Book, 1983), 1:5-12.

13. 4Q524 in É. Puech, *Qumrân Grotte 4.XVIII: Textes hébreux (4Q521-4Q528, 4Q576-*

consider the contents of Jubilees below, we will treat the entire work, relying on the Ethiopic version and the Greek fragments. We shall also note at the outset that the book is quoted explicitly in CD 16:2-4. Some have taken this as an indication of canonicity at Qumran, because of the use of the expression *meduqdaq 'al sefer*.[14]

For the most part, the Jubilees manuscripts evidence a text written in biblical Hebrew orthography and writing practice that follows essentially the language pattern to which we have become accustomed from our printed Bibles.[15] Some orthographic points indicate phonetic changes that had taken place by the second century B.C.E., as is even the case in the Masoretic text and in proto-Masoretic manuscripts from Qumran. As can be expected, passages that are essentially rewritten Bible display the language of the passages they expand. Forms of syntax tending toward Mishnaic Hebrew are absent. 4Q219 (Jub^d) does exhibit some Qumran Hebrew forms; but the syntax remains "biblical" throughout.[16] This manuscript is therefore very similar in orthography to the Temple Scroll. Peculiar here is the form *-wh* for third singular masculine pronominal, objective, and possessive suffix. Some similar forms are also found in 4Q221 (Jub^f).[17]

The Temple Scroll manuscripts are written in what is generally termed the Qumran writing system,[18] although it almost consistently makes use of the forms *hw'* and *hy'* that seem to indicate composition in Masoretic Hebrew.[19] Here, however, there is extensive architectural and cultic vocabulary that evidences the early development of words known to us in Mishnaic Hebrew, as well as a number of uses of the verb "to be" in the future use as a helping verb for future tense. Here also, the text betrays the vocabulary and style of the biblical material that has been rewritten to create a new composition.[20]

4Q579), DJD 25 (Oxford: Clarendon, 1998), 85-114; 11Q20 in F. García Martínez, E. J. C. Tigchelaar, and A. S. van der Woude, *Qumran Cave 11.II (11Q2-18, 11Q20-31)*, DJD 23 (Oxford: Clarendon, 1998), 357-409; 11Q21 in DJD 23:411-14; cf. S. White, DJD 13:319-33, for the possibility that 4Q365a may be a manuscript of the Temple Scroll. In our view this is part of a composition that served as a source for the Temple Scroll.

14. VanderKam, in *EDSS*, 1:437. On *meduqdaq*, see L. H. Schiffman, *The Halakhah at Qumran*, SJLA 16 (Leiden: Brill, 1975), 32-33.

15. E.g., 4Q216 in DJD 13:2.

16. DJD 13:40-41.

17. DJD 13:64-65.

18. E. Tov, "The Orthography and Language of the Hebrew Scrolls Found at Qumran and the Origin of These Scrolls," *Textus* 13 (1986): 31-57.

19. Yadin, *The Temple Scroll*, 1:25-33.

20. Yadin, *The Temple Scroll*, 1:33-39, 71-88. Cf. L. H. Schiffman, "The Architectural

Closely related is the question of contents, which point strongly to the totally different purposes of the two works. In fact, it is the disparity in contents that led to the suggestion by Wacholder that Jubilees might have been the first part of the Temple Scroll or, better, that the two texts are parts one and two of a larger work.[21]

On one level we can say that the contents of the works are quite different, since Jubilees is built on the narrative of Genesis and the beginning of Exodus, up to the destruction of the Egyptians at the Red Sea. Jubilees has a very significant prologue dealing with the role of Moses in revelation (chap. 1) and appendices regarding Passover (chap. 49), Jubilees (50:1-5), and the Sabbath (50:6-13).

It is precisely here that the Temple Scroll takes up the story.[22] It rewrites and re-redacts the Torah's material starting (in the scroll as preserved) in Exod 34 with the covenant and then continuing with the command to build the tabernacle (here the gargantuan temple) and running through the middle of Deuteronomy (chap. 20) where the legal section ends.[23] So from a simple, structural point of view, these works have totally different contents.

However, in reality this is not the case. While the Temple Scroll includes only one reference to the patriarchs, Jubilees includes a fair amount of material based on the laws of Exodus, Leviticus, Numbers, and Deuteronomy that can be compared with the Temple Scroll. This is because one of the themes of Jubilees is that the patriarchs observed all the laws included in the later-to-be-given Torah. Hence, much legal material is recounted in the context of telling the biblical stories. Further, for the Sabbath and Passover there are appendices — minicodes — like the *serakhim* that make up the Zadokite Fragments (Damascus Document).[24] Some of these legal discussions represent polemics against what the author considered the illegitimate behavior of his fellow Jews in the Hellenistic period. Yet at the same time, much of this material represents simply the transposition of Jewish legal views of the

---

Vocabulary of the Copper Scroll and the Temple Scroll," in *Copper Scroll Studies*, ed. G. J. Brooke and P. R. Davies, JSPSup 40 (London: Sheffield Academic Press, 2002), 180-95.

21. See above, n. 4.

22. See the detailed survey of the contents in Yadin, *The Temple Scroll*, 1:39-70.

23. Note that the preserved Temple Scroll is not complete at the end. See L. H. Schiffman, "The Unfinished Scroll: A Reconsideration of the End of the Temple Scroll," *DSD* 15 (2008): 67-78.

24. L. H. Schiffman, "Legal Texts and Codification in the Dead Sea Scrolls," in *Discussing Cultural Influences: Text, Context, and Non-text in Rabbinic Judaism*, ed. R. Ulmer, Studies in Judaism (Lanham, Md.: University Press of America, 2007), 1-39.

Zadokite/Sadducean variety into the patriarchal narratives. In this sense, the text often follows legal views similar to those of the Temple Scroll, an issue to which we will return below.

The Theory of Revelation

Both Jubilees and the Temple Scroll have in common the general fact that they are essentially divine pseudepigraphy.[25] Both books provide an opportunity for the author to put his views into the mouth of God, effectively inserting them into his rewrite of the divine revelation embodied in the original Torah. Both authors claim that the content of the new, expanded Torah text represents a true sense of the meaning of God's initial revelation.[26] Here, however, the similarity ends. Each author develops a unique theory of revelation in order to sanctify and canonize his own added "Torah."

Jubilees contains an introductory chapter that seeks to solve a well-known problem in biblical exegesis, the fact that Genesis and the first part of Exodus are composed as a story that is not framed with indications of divine or Mosaic authority.[27] The rest of the canonical Torah is regularly labeled as God's words to Moses or Moses' own words (Deuteronomy). Often commands appear as first-person divine speech. However, the patriarchal and Exodus narratives are exceptions. Hence, Jubilees includes a prologue declaring that God revealed the Genesis stories, here in their expanded form, to Moses on Sinai. Even if one argues that the prologue is not original, this is the clear implication of the entire first chapter. In this chapter Moses is bidden to write all God's revelation into a book (vv. 1-7 and 26). Clearly, this includes a rewritten Genesis-Exodus narrative. Then the "Angel of the Presence" is commanded by God to dictate to Moses from the heavenly tablets what appears to be the author's expanded Genesis-Exodus. Then the angel takes this text and, in the beginning of chap. 2, commands Moses according

25. L. H. Schiffman, "The Temple Scroll and the Halakhic Pseudepigrapha of the Second Temple Period," and M. J. Bernstein, "Pseudepigraphy in the Qumran Scrolls: Categories and Functions," both in *Pseudepigraphic Perspectives: The Apocrypha and Pseudepigrapha in the Light of the Dead Sea Scrolls,* ed. E. G. Chazon and M. Stone, with A. Pinnick, STDJ 31 (Leiden: Brill, 1999), 121-31 and 1-26, respectively.

26. J. C. VanderKam, "The Angel of the Presence in the Book of Jubilees," *DSD* 7 (2000): 378-93.

27. Cf. M. Nahmanides, *Perush ha-Ramban 'al ha-Torah,* ed. C. B. Chavel (Jerusalem: Mossad Harav Kook, 1958/59), 1:1-3.

to God's instruction to write the story of creation and the account of the Sabbath, presumably in the expanded version. Then the narrative proceeds as if it were the text that the angel commanded Moses to write, with occasional insertion of comments by the angel. The angel's dictation to Moses reappears throughout to emphasize central commandments.

We therefore have the following process of revelation claimed for the book: (1) God revealed it to Moses at Sinai; (2) God commanded Moses to write it in a book; (3) God accomplished this by ordering the Angel of Presence to dictate the book to Moses from the tablets; (4) the angel dictated the book. Jubilees strongly argues that the revelation came through Moses, who serves as an intermediary between God and Israel. However, the text goes even further. In accord with some Hellenistic approaches,[28] the text inserts another intermediary between God and Moses, apparently to avoid anthropomorphism. Hence, revelation here goes from God to the Angel of Presence, then to Moses and to Israel. All revelation takes place at Sinai, including what is in the canonical book and what is added, but here immediacy is the name of the game. Further, the author seems to distinguish the canonical Torah from his additional material, although this depends on how you interpret the difficult terms *torah, te'udah,* and *mitzvah* (Jub 2:22-24).[29]

This complex revelatory dynamic must be sharply contrasted with the Temple Scroll. In the Temple Scroll, the guiding principle of the author was to recast the sections of the Torah where Moses appears into divine first-person discourse.[30] This is especially clear in the way Moses has been eliminated even from Deuteronomy, where he appears as the speaker/author in the canonical version. The author of the Temple Scroll wants to solve the question of why, if Deuteronomy is divine revelation, it appears as a direct speech of Moses. He solves the problem by eliminating its immediacy wholesale. God speaks directly to Israel. Only once does the author err and refer to "your brother," as if he were speaking to Moses and referring to Aaron (11QT^a 44:5). The theological implication of the removal of Moses is clear. The author/redactor views his text's scriptural interpretation and law as a direct revelation of God to the children of Israel at Sinai with no inter-

---

28. See R. H. Charles, *The Book of Jubilees or the Little Genesis* (Jerusalem: Makor, 1961/62), 8 to verse 27.

29. These terms are found in the Hebrew text of 4Q216 VIII 13-17 (Milik and VanderKam, in DJD 13:19-20).

30. Yadin, *The Temple Scroll*, 1:71-73; B. A. Levine, "The Temple Scroll: Aspects of Its Historical Provenance and Literary Character," *BASOR* 232 (1978): 5-23, and Yadin's response in *The Temple Scroll*, 1:406-7.

mediary. This view contrasts radically with that of Jubilees. Jubilees has added a new angelic intermediary between God and Moses. The Temple Scroll has removed Moses, so that there is no intermediary between God himself and Israel.

Messianic Theology

The book of Jubilees includes extensive material indicating the author's views on the End of Days. The book expects, as part of its *ex eventu* "prophecy," that Israel will fail to fulfill the words of God's covenant (23:16, 19; 15:33-34). Chaps. 1 and 23 indicate that great misfortune will come upon Israel because of its apostasy. However, both chapters also expect repentance and the onset of a new age, ushered in by study of the law and observance of God's ritual and moral commandments. People will live lives of happiness with a life span of 1,000 years. Neither a messiah nor resurrection of the dead is mentioned. Essentially, the proper observances of God's law by the people is the desired expected eschaton.[31] Jub 1:29 describes that time as follows: "the day of the [new] creation when the heavens and earth shall be renewed . . . until the sanctuary of the Lord shall be made in Jerusalem on Mount Zion."[32]

Eschatological issues are hinted at only twice in the Temple Scroll. Like Jubilees, the Temple Scroll does not mention either the messiah or resurrection of the dead. In column 29, the Temple Scroll makes brief reference to the sacrificial practices it requires and the architectural plan it puts forth for the temple as being in force "up until the day of the blessing" (so Yadin)[33] or "[new] creation" (so Qimron).[34] The verbal similarity (if one reads with Qimron against Yadin) is striking. In the Temple Scroll, it is apparently expected that the End of Days would bring with it a new temple, built by God, to replace the present imperfect, man-made temple.[35] This

---

31. J. C. VanderKam, "Jubilees, Book of," in *ABD* 3:1031-32.

32. Charles, *Jubilees*, 9-10.

33. Yadin, *The Temple Scroll*, 2:129.

34. E. Qimron, *The Temple Scroll: A Critical Edition with Extensive Reconstructions* (Beersheva and Jerusalem: Ben-Gurion University of the Negev and Israel Exploration Society, 1996), 44.

35. Cf. L. H. Schiffman, "The Theology of the Temple Scroll," *JQR* 85 (Qumran Studies, 1994): 109-23; D. R. Schwartz, "The Three Temples of 4QFlorilegium," *RevQ* 10 (1979): 83-92; M. O. Wise, "4QFlorilegium and the Temple of Man," *RevQ* 15 (1991): 103-32;

passage makes clear, contrary to some scholars,[36] that the Temple Scroll is not presenting a vision for the End of Days but, rather, for the temple and Jewish law for the present. This is indeed a common element, as Jubilees also is calling for full and correct observance of the law in the present premessianic age. In this respect, both texts call for radical change in Israel's present life in the here and now. Nonetheless, on balance, we find incongruity, since the ultimate redemption of the End of Days is not taken up at all in the Temple Scroll.

Calendar

Chapter 6 of Jubilees is essentially a polemic against the luni-solar calendar known from rabbinic Judaism.[37] It advocates the 364-day calendar of solar months and solar years that we generally term the "Qumran calendar." The author of Jubilees sees the lunar cycle as confusing the holidays and making them come out on the wrong days. He refers to Enoch (Jub 4:17-18), indicating that he based his calendar on the Enoch booklets that circulated at his time. Jubilees designates the 31st days of months 3, 6, 9, and 12 as Days of Remembrance. The calendar was designed so that Shavuoth always fell on a Sunday.

The view put forward here, according to which the Temple Scroll and the book of Jubilees share the same sectarian calendar, even if some of the festivals are not the same as you will see below, cannot be conclusively proven from the Temple Scroll alone. In putting forward this view, scholars have been guided by a calendrical fragment from Cave 4 that provided a date for the Oil Festival (6/2),[38] which was only explicable assuming the Temple Scroll to share the calendar of Jubilees and Enoch. A full review of this evidence and its ramifications, as well as the scholarly debate about it, has been presented by James VanderKam, and there is no need to review the argu-

---

G. J. Brooke, *Exegesis at Qumran: 4QFlorilegium in Its Jewish Context*, JSOTSup 29 (Sheffield: JSOT Press, 1985), 178-97.

36. Wacholder, *The Dawn of Qumran*, 21-30; M. O. Wise, "The Eschatological Vision of the Temple Scroll," *JNES* 49 (1990): 155-72.

37. J. M. Baumgarten, "The Calendars of the Book of Jubilees and the Temple Scroll," *VT* 37 (1987): 71-78; J. C. VanderKam, *Calendars in the Dead Sea Scrolls: Measuring Time*, Literature of the Dead Sea Scrolls (London and New York: Routledge, 1998), 27-33.

38. J. M. Baumgarten, "4QHalakah^a 5, the Law of îadash, and the Pentacontad Calendar," in *Studies in Qumran Law* (Leiden: Brill, 1977), 131-42; also *JJS* 27 (1976): 36-46.

ments here.[39] Rather, I should like to comment on the general scholarly ambience in which we now see such questions.

Ever since the publication of 4QMMT,[40] many of us have been involved in an ongoing discussion about the relationship of the legal traditions in that document to those of the Temple Scroll and the other sectarian legal documents. It has now become clear, as a result of the contributions of quite a number of scholars,[41] that the general theory of Abraham Geiger regarding two basic schools of Jewish law in second temple times was correct.[42] We may term one school the Pharisaic-Rabbinic and the other the Zadokite/Sadducean. While the former system was known to us, despite the chronological problems, from reports in the New Testament and rabbinic literature, the latter system was little known. While some scholars still disagree with this overall thesis, this is the only way to explain the affinities that we will observe below regarding the calendar of festivals. Despite the fact that the book of Jubilees and the Temple Scroll (and for that matter other Qumran texts) do indeed share a common calendar, the specifics of their Festival Calendar, the lists of offerings, and the regulations regarding those offerings are not the same. Nonetheless, the common calendar, common approaches to the derivation of law adhering closely to the biblical text, and certain specific halakic views unify this second trend. Hence, we should not be surprised to find that a common calendar does not guarantee an entirely common halakah, despite the existence of numerous agreements in various areas of Jewish law.[43]

---

39. See above, n. 9.

40. E. Qimron and J. Strugnell, *Qumran Cave 4.V: Miqṣat Ma'aśe ha-Torah*, DJD 10 (Oxford: Clarendon, 1994), 44-63.

41. See, for example, Y. Sussmann, "Ḥeqer Toldot ha-Halakhah u-Megillot Midbar Yehudah: Hirhurim Talmudiyim Rishonim le-'Or Megillat Miqṣat Ma'aśe ha-Torah," *Tarbiz* 59 (1989/90): 11-76; Sussmann, "The History of the Halakha and the Dead Sea Scrolls: Preliminary Talmudic Observations on *Miqṣat Ma'aśe ha-Torah* (4QMMT)," in *Qumran Cave 4.V: Miqṣat Ma'aśe ha-Torah*, ed. E. Qimron and J. Strugnell, DJD 10 (Oxford: Clarendon, 1994), 179-200; *Reading 4QMMT: New Perspectives on Qumran Law and History*, ed. M. J. Bernstein and J. Kampen, SBLSymS 2 (Atlanta: Scholars Press, 1996).

42. A. Geiger, *Ha-Miqra' ve-Targumav be-Ziqatam le-Hitpaṭḥutah ha-Penimit shel ha-Yahadut*, trans. Y. L. Baruch (Jerusalem: Bialik Foundation, 1948/49), 69-102.

43. Cf. L. H. Schiffman, "The Temple Scroll and the Systems of Jewish Law in the Second Temple Period," in *Temple Scroll Studies*, 239-55.

Halakah

Because I have previously published a detailed study comparing the sacrificial laws of the book of Jubilees and those of the Temple Scroll,[44] my intention here is to summarize that study, providing just a few of the examples that I discussed there. It must be stressed that the method of legal derivation is as important as the result. We must look at how each document interpreted Scripture. If a common exegetical tradition or method can be found in these works, it might serve to clarify the relationship of one document to another.

I will present here just a few examples in detail, to allow readers to judge the nature of the research presented there. Afterward, I will review some of the discussion of my study that has taken place since. First, however, I will present the table of correspondences on sacrificial matters between the book of Jubilees and the Temple Scroll (TS):

Daily Offering	TS 13:10-16	Jub 6:14
Sabbath Sacrifices	TS 13:17–14:2	Jub 50:10-11
New Month Sacrifice	TS 14:2-8	Jub 31:1-3
First Day of First Month	TS 14:9–15:2	Jub 6:23-29
		Jub 7:2-5
		Jub 13:8-9
Days of Ordination	TS 15:3–17:4	Jub 30:18
		Jub 31:13-15
		Jub 32:1-9
Passover Sacrifices	TS 17:6-16	Jub 49:1-23
Sacrifices on Bringing		
Omer	TS 18:1-10	
First Fruits of Wheat	TS 18:10–19:9	Jub 6:17-22
		Jub 15:1-2
		Jub 16:13
		Jub 22:1-6
		Jub 14:19-20
		Jub 32:12-14
		Jub 44:4
New Wine	TS 19:11–21:10	Jub 7:36
		Jub 32:12-14

---

44. See above, n. 5.

New Oil	TS 21:12–23:2	Jub 7:36
		Jub 32:12-14
Wood Offering	TS 23:1–25:1	Jub 21:12-14
Day of Remembrance	TS 25:2-10	Jub 6:23-29
		Jub 12:16
		Jub 31:3
Day of Atonement	TS 25:10–27:10	Jub 34:12-19
Sukkot and Shemini Atzeret		
	TS 27:10–29:1	Jub 16:19-31
		Jub 8:18
		Jub 32:27-29

Our investigation of the festival sacrificial laws of the book of Jubilees and the Temple Scroll found some cases of agreement, and some of absolute disagreement. For example, the two sources disagree about the daily sacrifice. Jub 6:14 refers to the daily sacrifice, morning and evening, in connection with the covenant that God made with Noah after the flood. The text is not explicit as to whether the offering is to be provided by the priests or paid for out of public funds, a matter of great controversy in rabbinic accounts of the Boethusians (or Sadducees in some texts).[45] Nonetheless, v. 13 indicates that the commandment of daily sacrifice has been given to the children of Israel. According to v. 14, "They shall observe it . . . that they may continue supplicating . . . that they may keep it." This emphasis on the collective obligation of Israel can only indicate that the author of Jubilees, like the Pharisees, required that the daily offerings be a communally discharged obligation provided by the people as a whole. Jubilees indicates that the sacrifices serve to "seek forgiveness on your (Noah's) behalf perpetually before the Lord," an idea for which no parallel can be found in the Bible.

Temple Scroll 13:10-16 presents the laws of the daily sacrifice, based on Exod 29:38-42 and Num 28:3-8. It is impossible to tell because of a break in the text whether the author used the plural formulation of Numbers or the singular of Exodus. Some support for the notion that the author was of the opinion that the offerings could be contributed from private funds comes from the provision that the hide of the burnt offering may be kept by the

---

45. L. Finkelstein, *The Pharisees: The Sociological Background of Their Faith*, 2 vols., 3d ed., Morris Loeb Series (Philadelphia: Jewish Publication Society of America, 1966), 710-16; V. Noam, *Megillat Ta'anit: ha-Nusaḥim, Pishram, Toledotehem, be-êeruf Mahadurah Biqqortit* (Jerusalem: Yad Ben-Zvi Press, 2003), 165-73.

priest who offers it. This prescription is based on Lev 7:8, which refers to a private burnt offering *('olat 'ish)*. If the priest is to keep the hide, then the animal must have been his personal contribution. If so, the author of the Temple Scroll agreed with the Boethusians (or Sadducees) on this question. Jubilees, as was shown above, took the opposite position, that of the Pharisees, requiring that the offering come from public funds. Our two sources, then, are in fundamental disagreement regarding the nature of the daily sacrifice.

In many areas, there is substantial incongruity between these two sources; that which is important to one source is simply not treated in the other. Such a situation obtains in the sacrifice for the new month. Jub 31:1, 3 mentions the new moon in the context of Jacob's sacrifice at Bethel on the new moon of the seventh month. Here, Jacob is depicted as telling the members of his household to purify themselves and get ready to travel to Bethel where he will repay his debt to God (cf. Gen 35:2-4). This occurs on the new moon of the seventh month, which is one of the four "new years" enumerated by the author of Jubilees. It is therefore impossible to know if the purification ritual described in v. 1 is intended for new moons or if it is connected with the New Year festival of the seventh month.

Temple Scroll 14:2-8 details the offerings for the new moon. Here the author has altered the language of the Pentateuch, rephrasing extensively the commands of Num 28:11-15 and Num 15:1-13. Yadin explains that the author used Num 15 to allow him to enumerate the cereal and drink offering for each animal in turn, as opposed to mentioning all the cereal offerings first and then all the drink offerings, as is done in Num 28.[46]

Actually, the author was attracted to Num 15 for much more important reasons. The amount of oil for the offerings is nowhere specified in Num 28, only that for the libation of wine. The author used Num 15, in which the very same animals appear with the same allocations of flour and wine, to determine the amounts of oil since these are explicitly stated there. It was not the desire to reorder the material that directed the author of the Temple Scroll to this passage but rather the specification of the exact recipe for the oil of the cereal offering. When he shifted to this passage, the author ended up with its formulation and organization as well.

In any case, there is insufficient evidence on which to base any comparison of the texts. Jubilees may refer to purification for the new moon and the offering of sacrifices. The Temple Scroll presents a completely worked-

---

46. Yadin, *The Temple Scroll*, 2:56-57.

out ritual based on Pentateuchal sources. Some of these cases no doubt result from the differing emphases of the two documents. Jubilees attempts to retell the patriarchal narratives so as to attribute to them adherence to the author's particular views on questions of Jewish law and a particular calendric system. The Temple Scroll presents a code of practice for a premessianic Temple that its author hoped to see built and that he expected would function according to his code.

At the same time, many of these incongruities probably represent differences in opinion or at least in emphasis. For example, Jub 50:10-11 indicates that the daily offering may not be set aside in favor of the Sabbath sacrifice. Rather, it serves as a means of atonement, and it must be offered each day, including on the Sabbath. Temple Scroll 13:17–14:2 is a paraphrase of Num 28:9-10. However, the Temple Scroll provides no information on the disposition of offerings other than to repeat the biblical material that itself gave rise to the problem in the first place. Perhaps the Temple Scroll agrees with the view of Jubilees on Sabbath sacrifices, although definitive evidence is lacking.[47]

The cases of complete agreement testify to common traditions in some areas, and in others result from common exegetical techniques applied to the very same biblical texts. Jub 49:1-23 contains a long discussion of the celebration of the festival of Passover.[48] Most of the material is a simple retelling of the contents of Exod 12. Jub 49:6 describes the observance of the first Passover, including the eating of the paschal lamb, drinking of wine, praising and blessing God, and giving thanks. This description certainly recalls a Passover celebration similar to that envisaged in rabbinic literature, which included the paschal sacrifice, the four cups of wine, the commandment to retell the story of the exodus, and the recitation of the Hallel Psalms. V. 10 explains the difficult *ben ha-'arbayim*, literally, "between the evenings," of Exod 12:6: the sacrifice is to be observed "from the third part of the day to the third part of the night" (cf. Jub 49:19). This ruling is explained in vv. 11-12 as follows: the paschal sacrifice should be slaughtered in the last third of the fourteenth of Nisan and is to be eaten in the first third of the night of the fifteenth. Since the festival occurs fairly close to the equinox, it would be fairly accurate to say that the sacrifice must take place between two o'clock and sunset (at six) and the paschal lamb must be eaten between sunset (six) and ten o'clock in the

---

47. Schiffman, *The Halakhah at Qumran*, 128-31.

48. Cf. B. Halpern-Amaru, "The Festivals of Pesaḥ and Massot in the Book of Jubilees," in the present volume.

evening. Thereafter it is considered *notar,* that which has been left over beyond the time before which it must be eaten, and must be burned.

According to Jubilees, the Passover sacrifice must be eaten in the sanctuary, in the "court of the house which has been sanctified" (vv. 16-20). Only those over the age of twenty are to eat of the paschal lamb, and eating is probably limited to males (v. 17). This sacrifice may not be made in any other cities, only at the tabernacle or at the temple. In v. 22 there begins the command of the Festival of Unleavened Bread (cf. Lev 23:6). It is to be a seven-day festival. Each day a sacrifice is to be brought (v. 22).[49]

Temple Scroll 17:6-16 describes the Passover celebrations.[50] The Temple Scroll requires that the paschal offering be sacrificed before the evening sacrifice *(minúat ha-ʿerev).* This is in opposition to Tannaitic halakah, which requires that the *minúah* be offered before the paschal lamb. On this matter, the Temple Scroll and Jubilees may agree since Jubilees requires the offering in the last third of the day, i.e., after 2:00 P.M., and we know that the *minúah* was normally offered at about 3:30. On the other hand, it is possible that Jubilees, like the Tannaitic tradition,[51] expected that in order to accommodate the paschal offering, the daily *tamid* sacrifice was offered early on the fourteenth of Nisan.

Like the book of Jubilees, the Temple Scroll requires that the paschal lamb be eaten only by those above twenty. Yadin suggests that this ruling is based on the interpretation of Exod 30:14, and Num 1:2-3, as well as Exod 12:6.[52] According to the (almost definite) restoration of Qimron, only males are included in the commandment.[53]

There is a major difference concerning the time of eating of the paschal lamb. Jubilees requires that the offering be eaten by 10:00 P.M., the end of a third of the night. Although the Torah allowed the paschal sacrifice to be eaten until the morning (Exod 12:10), the Tannaim required that it be eaten before midnight, "in order to separate a person from the possibility of transgression."[54] The Temple Scroll allows it to be eaten all night, or at least, no mention is made of any other ruling.

49. J. C. VanderKam, *The Book of Jubilees,* CSCO 511, Scriptores Aethiopici 88 (Louvain: Peeters, 1989), 324.

50. Yadin, *The Temple Scroll,* 1:96-99; 2:72-75.

51. *m. Pesahim* 5:1.

52. Yadin, *The Temple Scroll,* 1:96.

53. Qimron, *The Temple Scroll,* 27.

54. *m. Berakhot* 1:1, according to the reading of the Talmud Yerushalmi and Mekhilta' of R. Ishmael Bo 6. Cf. Albeck, "Hashlamot ve-Tosafot, Zeraʿim," *Shishah Sidre Mishnah,* 6 vols. (Jerusalem: Bialik Institute; Tel Aviv: Dvir, 1954), 1:326.

The Temple Scroll and the book of Jubilees agree that the paschal lamb must be eaten within the temple precincts. Yadin suggests Deut 16:7 as the source of this law and notes that the Karaites agree. The Tannaim, on the other hand, allow it to be eaten anywhere in Jerusalem.[55] Both texts echo Lev 23:6-8 in describing the ensuing festival as a seven-day feast of unleavened bread. Sacrifices are to be offered on each day according to both works. The extensive ceremony for the Omer festival mentioned in Temple Scroll 18:1-10 has no equivalent whatsoever in the book of Jubilees.

The case of the Passover celebration affords an example of an area in which some significant prescriptions of Jubilees and the Temple Scroll are in complete agreement. Nevertheless, there are still some matters upon which they offer different opinions.[56]

The Judaism of the Second Commonwealth period was one of variegated sects and ideologies. That there was indeed some relationship between these two texts is apparent from their inclusion in the library of the Qumran community. We see the halakic traditions of these two texts as derived from outside the community, perhaps from its antecedents that were followers of the common Zadokite/Sadducean approach. The sect would have read and studied these materials precisely because of the affinities they shared with its own beliefs and principles. The book of Jubilees and the sources of the Temple Scroll constitute part of the world from which the Qumran sect emerged and in which it strove to attain its own spiritual ideals. Each of these texts represents an independent view of the festival sacrificial cycle, based on exegesis of the scriptural texts and a certain shared common Zadokite/Sadducean heritage. There can be no possibility, however, of seeing the sacrificial codes of Jubilees as based on those of the Temple Scroll or vice versa.[57]

---

55. *m. Zevahim* 5:8.

56. Cf. J. Milgrom, "The Concept of Impurity in *Jubilees* and the *Temple Scroll*," *RevQ* 16, no. 62 (1993): 277-84; M. Himmelfarb, "Sexual Relations and Purity in the Temple Scroll and the Book of Jubilees," *DSD* 6, no. 1 (1999): 11-36; L. Doering, "Purity and Impurity in the Book of Jubilees," in the present volume.

57. Our study of the sacrificial law of the Aramaic Levi Document indicates that its law includes many aspects of the Zadokite/Sadducean trend that it has somehow combined with Pharisaic-rabbinic prescriptions on other issues. Cf. L. H. Schiffman, "Sacrificial Halakhah in the Fragments of the *Aramaic Levi Document* from Qumran, the Cairo Genizah, and Mt. Athos Monastery," in *Reworking the Bible: Apocryphal and Related Texts at Qumran; Proceedings of a Joint Symposium by the Orion Center for the Study of the Dead Sea Scrolls and Associated Literature and the Hebrew University Institute for Advanced Studies Research Group on Qumran, 15-17 January, 2002*, ed. E. G. Chazon, D. Dimant, and R. A. Clements, STDJ 58 (Leiden: Brill, 2005), 177-202.

At this point, we wish to take up James VanderKam's disagreement with our conclusions. He has set them forth in a careful investigation of the festival calendar of the Temple Scroll and the book of Jubilees in which he directly responds to my earlier-mentioned article.[58] VanderKam argues that the differences that I have noted may be accounted for by taking into consideration a variety of factors, most notably the concentration of Jubilees on the Genesis narrative, which lacks many of the halakic details that are discussed in the Temple Scroll. I have reread this argument and still do not agree. The very names of the festivals claimed by Jubilees to have been observed by the patriarchs are derived from elsewhere in the Torah. If these festivals could be imported into the patriarchal narratives, why could not their details have been as well? VanderKam wants to argue that despite some differences that he is willing to recognize, the festival calendars are essentially identical. This argument may boil down to whether the glass is half empty or half full, but I think on reflection that both of our earlier studies were somewhat off the mark. I think we both assumed that what was under discussion was the relationship of two disparate works to one another. Hence, we sought large numbers of differences or general agreement to indicate affinity or disagreement. Now we realize that affinity need only be among what we might call a family, a tradition, that is, to what family of ancient halakah a text belongs. Once we have placed the Temple Scroll and Jubilees in the same family, whatever specific differences we may uncover may now be understood as testimony to the diversity within such sub-corpora of ancient Jewish legal thinking. Just as the Genesis Apocryphon and the book of Jubilees need not agree in their "aggadic" understanding of Genesis, so the Temple Scroll and Jubilees need not agree in their legal rulings to be part of the same trend.

Conclusion

The relationship of Jubilees and the Temple Scroll is complex. The two texts share a common calendar, but have different theologies, contents, in some cases sacrificial laws, and express differing ideas about eschatology. This does not, however, mean that the texts are unrelated. They both belong to the common culture and tradition of a group of sectarian groups to which our Qumran sectarians, the author of the sources of the Temple Scroll, and

58. VanderKam, "The Temple Scroll," 225-31.

the author of Jubilees belonged. Common teachings and aspirations united these groups. Further, Jubilees and the Temple Scroll are both forms of re-written Torah, one rewriting what we might call (borrowing rabbinic termi-nology) the "aggadic" parts of the Torah and the other rewriting the halakic parts of the Torah. But the relationship between these documents is certainly not as close as, say, the relationship between the Temple Scroll and 4QMMT. In my view, the Temple Scroll was put together mostly from pre-Qumranian Sadducean type legal sources and the book of Jubilees emerged from similar circles. However, these are certainly not compositions of the same group, be it the Qumran sect or some predecessor.

Jubilees, Sirach, and Sapiential Tradition

Benjamin G. Wright III

At first blush Jubilees and Jewish wisdom literature would appear to have little in common. Wisdom and wisdom language do not appear in Jubilees, whose primary concern seems halakic. As a rough indicator, one need only scan the margins of Orval Wintermute's *OTP* translation of Jubilees, where he notes related passages in biblical, early Jewish, and Christian texts. Of the dozens of passages listed there, maybe three or four come from the corpus usually identified as wisdom. By contrast, 1 Enoch, which Jubilees knows, displays quite a number of similarities to Jewish wisdom.[1]

Yet content and genre might be less important considerations for thinking about Jubilees and Jewish wisdom than the strategies they adopt to solve common problems. Looking at Jubilees and Jewish wisdom together bears some potentially significant fruit. Jubilees, for example, employs some aspects of wisdom discourse, particularly in the final speeches of its major patriarchal figures to their sons, that function to convince the reader to adopt the book's values and ideology. In such contexts of passing down instruction from a father (and in Jubilees a mother in one instance) to a son, common discursive elements with wisdom do not surprise, even if the content in Jubilees does not always look very wisdom-like.

One particular complex in Jubilees, however, highlights some broader

---

1. See G. W. E. Nickelsburg, "Enochic Wisdom: An Alternative to the Mosaic Torah?" in *Hesed ve-emet: Studies in Honor of Ernest S. Frerichs,* ed. J. Magness and S. Gitin, BJS 10 (Atlanta: Scholars Press, 1998), 123-32.

issues in early Jewish literature. Oft noted has been the central role in Jubilees played by the heavenly tablets and the written transmission of what is found thereon. In addition to the specific halakic regulations enjoined in Jubilees, one important problem has been how Jubilees legitimates its own particular interpretation of the law as binding on all of Israel. One tack has been to argue that Moses took down these laws (i.e., Jubilees' interpretations) at the dictation of the angel of the presence who was transmitting what was written on the heavenly tablets. Thus, the halakic claims of Jubilees have equal status to the Torah of Moses, since both Jubilees and the Torah stem from them. That is, Jubilees' interpretations are not *really* interpretations, but their primordial origins on the heavenly tablets afford them divine authorization. If we look to one of the quintessential wisdom texts of early Judaism, one predating Jubilees by only a few decades, the Wisdom of Ben Sira, we can identify a similar strategy for legitimating the author's interpretations. Only in this case primordial Wisdom serves as the authorizing mechanism.

Finally, in Jubilees, while all the major figures write, some do more; they read and study. Besides their other roles, they play the part of the ideal scribe. In writing, reading, and studying, the heroes of Jubilees become the authoritative voices of the tradition that guard it against corruption or illegitimate use. As such they function as exemplars for contemporary scribes to emulate in their own guardianship of the tradition transmitted in Jubilees. They form a chain of transmission, ensuring that what came from the heavenly tablets has been handed down accurately, but they also act as examples to follow so as to assure those in the present that the authoritative tradition remains unsullied.[2]

I. "And Now, My Children"

Throughout Jubilees one could isolate individual passages that parallel material in wisdom texts. They are few, however, and do not characterize Jubilees in any general sense. So, to give one example, in three passages (5:16; 21:4; 33:18) Jubilees emphasizes that God does not "accept gifts," that is, take bribes, but God judges righteously. Jub 5:16 is typical: "And he is not one who accepts

---

2. For reasons of space, I use Ben Sira as my text of comparison. Others might illuminate these strategies further. 4QInstruction would make an excellent addition to this discussion.

persons (i.e. is partial), and he is not one who accepts gifts when he says that he will execute judgment on each one."[3] We find an identical sentiment in Sir 35:14 expressed in very similar language: "Do not offer him a bribe, for he will not accept it; and do not rely on a dishonest sacrifice; for the Lord is the judge, and with him there is no partiality." While we could catalogue such parallel passages, I do not think any list would reveal much of substance about Jubilees and any relation it might have to sapiential tradition.

Jubilees does employ a variant of a literary strategy often found in wisdom texts — the construction of the sage and disciple as father and son. In wisdom literature the sage's use of direct address ("My son") constructs the disciple as his child, and the sage thereby assumes the authority of the student's parent. At the same time, the "I" and "you" of the direct address function as empty signs through which the vocatives and imperatives address *the reader,* and in this way the text "recruits" its reader, who must respond.[4] The texts in which we find this father-son discourse employ various discursive tactics "to inscribe the reader's filial subjectivity and hence the authority of the author's teaching."[5] One example is the metaphor of walking a path or road, which constructs the student as a traveler traversing the acceptable path of life (and which appears in Jub 21:22).

A variation of this father-son discourse appears in some narrative texts where a father speaking to his children occupies a prominent place in the narrative. Some passages, like Tob 14 or 1 En 82:1-4, constitute parts of larger and more diverse works. In other texts, like the Testaments of the Twelve Patriarchs, the father-son speech constitutes the overarching framework. The narratives often display some of the same features and topics as the "I-you" discourse of the sapiential works in order to place the reader in the position of the author's "son," but they accomplish the aim of engaging the reader a bit differently. Rather than the second-person address of the sage that confronts the reader directly, a third-person father transmits teaching to his son(s), which he commands that they teach their children and their children and their children after them. The reader stands at the end of a long chain of

---

3. Translations from Jubilees are from Wintermute in *OTP.*

4. See my article "From Generation to Generation: The Sage as Father in Early Jewish Literature," in *Biblical Traditions in Transmission: Essays in Honour of Michael A. Knibb,* ed. C. Hempel and J. M. Lieu, JSJSup 111 (Leiden: Brill, 2006), 309-32. For much of the theoretical discussion I rely on C. Newsom, "Women and the Discourse of Patriarchal Wisdom: A Study of Proverbs 1–9," in *Gender and Difference in Ancient Israel,* ed. P. L. Day (Minneapolis: Fortress, 1989), 142-60.

5. Wright, "From Generation to Generation," 315.

transmission of teaching from fathers to sons, and the text thus constructs the reader as a descendant of the narrative father. What perhaps creates the highest degree of obligation in the reader to adopt the values of the narrative father is the father handing *writings* to his sons that must be transmitted to subsequent generations, since the reader, who is presumably reading or listening to that book, has a palpable connection to the instruction being handed down.[6]

In the testamentary speeches of fathers to their sons in Jubilees, we see something of this same device at work, although it is not foregrounded here as in 1 Enoch or the Testaments of the Twelve Patriarchs. In Jubilees these speeches contain quite a number of important halakic matters, observance of which the father-son testamentary speech reinforces. Two mechanisms operate in the Jubilees speeches. First, the context, like both second- and third-person father-son constructs, is one of instruction where the father explicitly notes that the teaching is not only for his immediate progeny but also for subsequent generations. Thus, the reader, who almost certainly identifies himself/herself as a descendant of the narrative figure, becomes one of the children of the text and is thus obligated to obey the father's teaching. Second, Jubilees notes in at least one case that a patriarch's books were intended to be transmitted to subsequent generations.

Two examples show how the context of Jubilees puts readers in the position of the patriarch's children. Noah's final speech to his children begins in 7:20 with a narrative review of the causes of the flood, which God wrought "on account of the blood that they poured out in the midst of the land" (7:25). The text then switches to Noah speaking in the first person. He tells his sons that he has observed their deeds, and he fears that when he dies "you will pour out the blood of men upon the earth. And you will be blotted out from the surface of the earth" (7:27). Jub 7:29-33 contains a series of commands in both third person ("no man who . . .") and second person ("you shall not be like . . .?"), and 7:31 continues, "Cover the blood, because I was commanded to testify to you *and to your children together with all flesh*." So, in 7:34 when Noah addresses "my children," although it is parallel to the address in 7:26, the intervening v. 31 has created ambiguity about whether Noah is addressing his narrative children only or whether his descendants, the book's readers, are also included. Noah commands that his children "do justice and righteousness so that you may be planted in righteousness on the surface of the whole earth." Laws about firstfruits, which are to be offered

6. Wright, "From Generation to Generation," 327-31.

"upon the altar of the Lord," follow, and the "servants of the house of the Lord" will eat anything left over. What looks like an anachronistic reference to priests and the temple is essentially not, since the reader, for whom priests and temple are a contemporary reality, has been included among the children addressed by the ancient figure.

Whereas Noah's speech creates ambiguity about the identification of the "children" to whom the patriarch speaks, that identification is clearer in the narrative about Abraham, and the work of constructing the reader as one who falls in Abraham's line begins early. In 12:23, employing the language of Gen 12:3, God calls Abraham and promises to bless him and all the nations. Then Jubilees adds, "And I shall be God for you and your son and for the son of your son and for all of your seed." Thereafter, mention of Abraham's "seed" must be read in the light of this statement, which the author intended to include the reader. The author further circumscribes the Jewish reader in the commandment to circumcise, which applies to "the sons of Israel," another anachronism for the "Abraham" of the narrative, but not for our author. When Abraham finally bids farewell to his children, he commands them,

> that they should guard the way of the Lord so that they might do righteousness and each might love his neighbor, and that it should be thus among all men so that one might proceed to act justly and rightly toward them upon the earth, and that they should circumcise their sons in the covenant which he made with them, and that they should not cross over either to the right or left from all of the ways which the Lord commanded *us* and that *we* should keep *ourselves* from all fornication and pollution, and that *we* should set aside from among *us* all fornication and pollution. (20:2-3, emphasis mine)

By this time the reader is well prepared for this sudden shift in person. After all, the members of Jubilees' audience are predisposed to seeing themselves as children of Abraham. The rhetorical scheme exploits that predisposition in order to make Abraham speak directly to all his children, both remote and contemporary, via an extensive list of warnings and admonitions that includes avoiding fornication, keeping away from idols, and properly worshiping God.

A second strategy for forging the parent-child bond that places the reader in the obliged position emphasizes the passing down of books from the patriarchal father. The book that the reader possesses or hears is the same one originally written by the father figure of the text. So in 1 En 82:1-3 Enoch gives books to Methuselah in which he has recorded all the wisdom he has revealed to Methuselah, "so that you may give it to the generations of the world. Wisdom I have given to you and to your children and to those who will be your children so that they may give this wisdom which is beyond their thought to their children for the generations."[7]

Unfortunately, there is nothing this explicit in Jubilees, but the importance of writing and the presence of several books, which reflect what is written in the heavenly tablets, suggest that Jubilees itself is the end product of a chain of transmission that originated with patriarchal figures. Here, though, we must distinguish between establishing the authority of Jubilees based on the preexisting heavenly tablets and constructing the reader as a descendant of the patriarchal father for the purpose of obligating him/her to acquiesce to what is in the book(s), since the written text substitutes for the father's voice. That is, the book that is passed down enables intervening generations to be skipped so that the patriarch speaks directly to his "child." In one suggestive passage (45:15), upon Jacob's death "he gave all of his books and his fathers' books to Levi, his son, so that he might preserve them and renew them for his sons *until this day.*" The exact relationship between these books and Jubilees remains unclear, except that in this instance the tradition inherited from the ancestors is preserved in a priestly context, one that presumably represents something of Jubilees' self-understanding, and thus has some relationship to Jubilees itself.[8] In fact, most of the major figures in Jubilees write books, in some cases more than one, but Jubilees does not present them as identical to itself. In fact, they must be different from Jubilees, even if they reflect the heavenly tablets in some way, since Moses acts as the amanuensis for the angel of the presence in writing the book. Indeed, Jubilees itself is never portrayed as a book that Moses has transmitted to his children.

So the two strategies that we see in some wisdom and narrative literature that construct the reader as the child of the "father" of the text appear only in a somewhat attenuated way in Jubilees. Although they do not function centrally in the book as mechanisms for authorizing its ideology, they play a supporting role.

---

7. Translation is from G. W. E. Nickelsburg and J. C. VanderKam, *I Enoch: A New Translation* (Minneapolis: Fortress, 2004).

8. J. C. VanderKam, *The Book of Jubilees* (Sheffield: Sheffield Academic Press, 2001), 81, 120.

II. "Therefore It Is Commanded in the Heavenly Tablets" (Jubilees 3:31)

In thinking about the relationship between Jubilees and Jewish wisdom, I have found the work of Hindy Najman productive. She begins her article "Interpretation as Primordial Writing: Jubilees and Its Authority Conferring Strategies" with the following observation: "Writings from the Second Temple period consistently invoked the Torah of Moses as authoritative sacred writing. Although the tradition was shared, attempts to make Scripture relevant and accessible generated diverse views about how to interpret and apply this authoritative writing. As a result distinctive interpretations and practices emerged. It became essential that writers justify their interpretations."[9] Jubilees, along with several other second temple works, pursued a strategy that created "an authorizing link to the already accepted Torah of Moses."[10] Jubilees' author presents the work as revelation given to Moses from the heavenly tablets, from which also the Torah of Moses derived. Thus, Jubilees combines claims to the authority of its interpretations with its self-presentation as sacred writing whose ultimate origins lie in the same place as the Torah of Moses — the heavenly tablets from which the angel of the presence dictates to Moses. For Najman, Jubilees' author develops four primary strategies for conferring authority on his work. Two of these are of interest here: (1) "*Jubilees* repeatedly claims that it reproduces material that had been written down long before on the 'heavenly tablets,' a great corpus of divine teachings kept in heaven"; and (2) "The entire content of the book of *Jubilees* was dictated by the angel of the presence at God's own command. Hence it is itself the product of divine revelation."[11]

Although scholars often make much of genre in second temple literature, I am struck by the way different *kinds* of texts resort to similar mechanisms for resolving common difficulties. For my purposes, I want to look at how Ben Sira approaches the problem of authorizing his interpretations of Torah, since I think his solution compares with that of Jubilees. Even though he regards the Torah of Moses as sacred and authoritative,

---

9. Hindy Najman, "Interpretation as Primordial Writing: Jubilees and Its Authority Conferring Strategies," *JSJ* 30 (1999): 379-410 (here 379).

10. Najman, "Interpretation as Primordial Writing," 379. See also, Najman, *Seconding Sinai: The Development of Mosaic Discourse in Second Temple Judaism*, JSJSup 77 (Leiden and Boston: Brill, 2003).

11. Najman, "Interpretation as Primordial Writing," 380.

Ben Sira famously does not quote from it explicitly.[12] Like the author of Jubilees, though, Ben Sira interprets this authoritative corpus, whether he is clarifying what it means to honor parents (3:1-16) or alluding to the destruction of Sodom and Gomorrah (16:8). He does not cite an authoritative text to underwrite his interpretations, but rather he appeals to primordial Wisdom as his source of authority. Whereas Jubilees' halakic prescriptions resided on the primordial heavenly tablets long before the angel of the presence dictated them to Moses (the first of Najman's strategies), Ben Sira appeals to Wisdom, which also existed primordially with God, as his source of understanding.

In a similar way that in Jubilees the angel of the presence links the heavenly realm with the earthly, assuring the accuracy of what Moses writes, so primordial Wisdom links heaven and earth, authorizing Ben Sira's teaching. Sir 24 is perhaps the *locus classicus* for understanding how Ben Sira theologizes about Wisdom — and not without good reason. Wisdom speaks on her own behalf; she begins by describing her presence throughout all the earth (vv. 1-6). She then seeks "rest" (v. 7). But where? God sends her to Israel, specifically to the Jerusalem temple where she ministers "before him" (vv. 10-12). The eternal and primordial Wisdom is established in the temple, where she flourishes (vv. 13-17).

Given her presence in the temple, one might expect Ben Sira to make explicit some priestly connection with Wisdom, but in vv. 19-22 Wisdom calls to anyone who desires her.[13] These verses form a segue to the next place that one finds Wisdom, the Mosaic Torah: "All these things are the book of the covenant of the Most High God, a law that Moses commanded us, an inheritance for the gatherings of Jacob" (v. 23). Unfortunately, the phrase "these things" is rather vague, but it must refer to what Ben Sira has just said about Wisdom. Her presence not only legitimates the temple cult, but she is also embodied in the Torah, and her access is not restricted only to priests. As in Jubilees, in Sirach the law, in a sense, exists before the Sinai event. Unlike Jubilees, however, Ben Sira does not envision another revelation to Moses, but he identifies primordial Wisdom as a heavenly, preexistent feature of the Mosaic Torah. This idea has powerful consequences, as we shall shortly

12. For problems with the word "canonical" in this context, see especially Robert A. Kraft, "5.1 Scripture and Canon in Jewish Apocrypha and Pseudepigrapha," in *Hebrew Bible/Old Testament: The History of Its Interpretation*, vol. 1, *From the Beginnings to the Middle Ages (Until 1300)*, ed. Magne Sæbø (Göttingen: Vandenhoeck & Ruprecht, 1996), 67-83.

13. The connection is made in the praise of Simon II (chap. 50), which contains similar imagery to chap. 24.

see. The grammar of the next three verses in Greek indicates that Ben Sira is referring to the law:[14]

25It (i.e. the law) fills wisdom like Phison
and like Tigris in days of new things.

26It supplies understanding like Euphrates
and like Jordan in days of harvest,

27It shines forth education like light,
like Geon in days of vintage.

The focus then returns to Woman Wisdom:

28The first man did not complete knowing her,
and so the last one did not track her out,

29for her thought was filled from the sea,
and her counsel from the great abyss.

Ben Sira continues the fluvial imagery of vv. 28-29, but this time in a self-reference:

30And I, like a canal from a river
and a water channel, issued forth into an orchard.

31I said, "I will water my garden,
and I will drench my flower bed."
And look! The canal turned into a river for me,
and my river turned into a sea.

32Still I will again make education enlighten like dawn,
and I will shine them forth to far off.

33Still I will again pour out teaching like prophecy,
and I will leave it behind for generations of eternity.

34See that I have not toiled for myself alone
but for all who seek it (or, her) out.

---

14. No Hebrew survives for chap. 24. Translations from the Greek of Sirach are mine, taken from A. Pietersma and B. G. Wright, eds., *A New English Translation of the Septuagint* (New York: Oxford, forthcoming).

Ben Sira's watery odyssey ends at the sea, the place of Wisdom's thought. Only then can he engage in the activities of the sage outlined in vv. 32-34. In this central chapter of the book Ben Sira claims to have tapped the primordial Wisdom embodied in Torah. In fact, his teaching becomes the conduit to Wisdom for anyone who would seek her (v. 34). The discourse of chap. 24 makes the adjurations to seek Wisdom found elsewhere in the book all the more meaningful.

Ben Sira's authorizing strategy in chap. 24, then, works very much like the first of the strategies that Najman discovers in Jubilees. For Ben Sira, authority is not as bound up in writtenness as is true of Jubilees, even though he does speak of the Torah of Moses as a book and he refers to his own teaching as inscribed "in this book" (50:27). But the authority for his teaching does derive, as in Jubilees, from a primordial source that existed long before the actual Torah of Moses. Unlike the heavenly tablets, which Najman calls "a great corpus of teachings kept in heaven," Wisdom is not a corpus of teachings but is the divine presence that inhabits the Torah. Find Wisdom, as Ben Sira clearly thinks he has, and one has access to what Torah is all about. Thus, whereas Jubilees authorizes its teaching by appealing to the heavenly tablets, Ben Sira legitimates the activities and teaching of all the sages, not just his own, since hypothetically anyone who single-mindedly pursues Wisdom can possess her.

The second of Jubilees' authority-conferring strategies is that Jubilees is the product of divine revelation. The angel of the presence ensures the accuracy of what is dictated to Moses, who transcribes it all faithfully. Here the angel's intermediary function reinforces the authority of the revelation as divine. James VanderKam has demonstrated that the angel of the presence not only speaks in God's name but also performs acts attributed elsewhere to God.[15] As both VanderKam and Najman argue, such intimacy with God enhances Jubilees' authority and frames it as revelation from the deity given to Israel via the scribal hand of Moses.[16]

Ben Sira does not frame his work as the product of revelatory activity, but nonetheless he does try to connect his teaching with revelation. We have seen that in the discourse of 24:30-34 he derives his teaching from Wisdom, which is embodied in Torah. As a result, he can characterize his teaching as prophecy. Later, in chap. 39, Ben Sira describes the activity of the scribe/sage.

---

15. J. C. VanderKam, "The Angel of the Presence in the Book of Jubilees," *DSD* 7 (2000): 378-93.

16. VanderKam, "Angel of the Presence," 392-93; Najman, *Seconding Sinai*, 60-63; Najman, "Interpretation as Primordial Writing," 400-403.

Two elements stand out. First, the sage studies "the wisdom of all the ancients, and he will be occupied with prophecies" (v. 1). He delves into obscure sayings and tries to uncover the meaning of riddles. But second, the sage prays to God and confesses his sins. Then,

> 6If the great Lord wants,
> he will be filled with a spirit of understanding.
> He will pour forth words of his wisdom,
> and in prayer he will acknowledge the Lord.
>
> 7He will direct counsel and knowledge,
> and on his hidden things he will think.
>
> 8He will illuminate the instruction of his teaching,
> and in the law of the Lord's covenant he will boast.[17]

Remarkably, this passage begins with God giving inspiration to the sage. He then pours forth wisdom and teaching. The short paragraph ends with the claim "in the law of the Lord's covenant he will boast." This reference to the Torah reinforces the relationship between Torah, where primordial Wisdom resides, and Ben Sira's inspired interpretations. We know that Ben Sira was not enamored of claims to heavenly journeys and visions (see for instance 3:21-24) or of knowledge claimed to come from dreams (34:1-8).[18] If primordial Wisdom is to be found in the Torah of Moses and the sayings of the sages who interpret it, then the connection between concentrated study and divine inspiration and prophecy makes sense. It is no surprise that Ben Sira might warn his disciples against pursuing speculative or revelatory experiences: "The things that have been prescribed for you, think about these" (3:22a).

III. "Write for Yourself All These Words" (Jubilees 1:7)

One cannot read Jubilees without being impressed by the importance of writing in the book. More notable is the series of people who write. Beginning

17. Translation is from the Greek. No Hebrew is extant.

18. On this issue, see my article "Putting the Puzzle Together: Some Suggestions concerning the Social Location of the Wisdom of Ben Sira," in *Conflicted Boundaries in Wisdom and Apocalypticism*, ed. B. G. Wright and L. M. Wills, SBLSymS 35 (Atlanta: Society of Biblical Literature, 2005), 89-112.

with Enoch, "the first who learned writing and knowledge and wisdom," continuing to Noah and extending up to Moses, the putative author of Jubilees, the main figures of Israelite history preserve and transmit texts, which contain many topics central to Jubilees. Thus, Enoch writes a book that contains "the signs of the heaven according to the order of their months," i.e., calendrical matters (4:17). After Moses, perhaps the most interesting writer in Jubilees is Abraham. In 12:25 God commands the angel of the presence to enable Abraham to hear and speak Hebrew, "the language of creation." Abraham takes his father's books, which are in Hebrew. He copies them; then he studies them. In the process of study the angel causes him "to know everything which he was unable to understand" (12:27). Presumably Terah's books reflect the heavenly tablets, and throughout the narrative Abraham faithfully keeps various ritual laws and observances, such as circumcision and the feasts of Sukkoth and Shavuoth, which one suspects were ordained in the books Abraham inherited. In his long farewell, Abraham enjoins first his children, then Isaac, and then Jacob to do justice and righteousness, actions that he amplifies at great length and with much halakic detail.

The figures in Jubilees who engage in writing form an authoritative and trustworthy chain of transmission of material from the heavenly tablets, which culminates in the revelation to Moses. In these instances, a synergistic relationship obtains between the characters in Jubilees and their worthiness to receive laws derived from the heavenly tablets and then to transmit them. That they are deemed worthy of the heavenly tablets and that they faithfully keep the laws contained therein makes them exemplars for anyone reading the book. They also serve as exemplars in another way. In Jubilees, the act of writing certifies faithful copying and transmission as much as it signals composition. That is, writing functions as a means of accurately preserving through the generations the contents of the heavenly tablets. So Noah can appeal to what Enoch commanded Methuselah, and Methuselah, Lamech, and Lamech, Noah (8:38-39). Abraham discovers sacrificial law "written in the books of my forefathers in the words of Enoch and in the words of Noah" (21:11). Moses takes dictation; Abraham copies Terah's books; Jacob copies down everything he reads (on the angelic seven tablets) and hears in a dream (32:26); he also gives "all of his books and his fathers' books" to Levi in order that Levi can "preserve them and renew them" (45:15). These people represent ideal scribes who accurately preserve and transmit the contents of the heavenly tablets; they are the proper guardians of the sacred authoritative texts.

The author of Jubilees makes a kind of twofold claim then. First, scribal activity as undertaken by the exemplars *in the book* has preserved unsullied the contents of the heavenly tablets, which are divine. Second, the author is at the same time presenting an authorizing case for *his* interpretations, which he has constructed as authoritative revelation faithfully passed down. By this strategy the scribal author of Jubilees can both acknowledge the sanctity of the Mosaic Torah *and* preserve the authoritative interpretation of Torah, which in Jubilees stands alongside the Torah of Moses, since their origins are both in the heavenly tablets.

It is not too much of a stretch to see a similar strategy at work in Ben Sira. In his description of the scribe/sage, Ben Sira distinguishes the ideal scribe from the laborer. The scribe's wisdom depends on leisure time (38:24). Only the scribe can sit in councils or decide legal cases; only the scribe stands among rulers expounding discipline or judgment (38:32-33). After describing those who labor, Ben Sira exclaims, "How different the one who devotes himself to the study of the law of the Most High God!" (38:34). Sir 39:1-3 suggests that the scribe preserves and penetrates what has been handed down, qualifying him to serve among rulers and nobles (39:4). As a result,

> 39:9Many will praise his understanding,
> and it will never be blotted out;
> his memorial will not depart,
> and his name will live for generations of generations.
>
> 39:10Nations will narrate his wisdom,
> and an assembly will proclaim his praise.
>
> 39:11If he abides, he will leave behind a name greater than a thousand,
> and if he rests, it will be favorable for him.

How different indeed is the scribe! As Ben Sira tells it, the scribe is best positioned and most able to learn wisdom, which, of course, connects him with proper observance of the law. Ben Sira transmits this wisdom — that is, the authoritative interpretation of the law — in his teaching.

Ben Sira also employs the concept of "fear of the Lord," so central to his book, to enhance the status of the ideal scribe. He makes clear that "fear of the Lord," a multivalent notion for him, supersedes all social status and class. While several passages suggest that anyone can cultivate proper "fear of the Lord" (cf. 10:19, 22; 25:10-11), if we look a bit more closely, we find that only the scribe is in a position to achieve it. For Ben Sira, "fear of the Lord" primarily means finding and acquiring wisdom and keeping the commandments. Sir 19:20 perhaps sums it up best: "The whole of wisdom is fear of the Lord, and in all wisdom there is the fulfillment of the Law." Who is more able to accomplish this than the scribe? Laborers cannot seek wisdom; there is not time. The rich and powerful encounter more pressing demands that prevent them from such pursuits. Claudia Camp and I have argued that the idea of "fear of the Lord" helps Ben Sira to rationalize certain social inequalities that he judges problematic, and it elevates the status of the scribe in his social world.[19] But like Jubilees, Ben Sira's scribe is the guardian of wisdom and the keeping of the law — along with its proper/authorized interpretation. He argues for this claim in a way very different from Jubilees, however. Both Jubilees and Ben Sira construct the scribe as the guardian of tradition and authorized interpretation. In Jubilees the exemplars are the ancient figures who kept the laws and received the heavenly tablets, but in Ben Sira it is the ideal scribe. I suspect, though, that even more than an ideal figure, Ben Sira is presenting himself to his disciples as the exemplar, the one who needs to be emulated.[20]

IV. Jubilees and Wisdom

While I have not exhausted here what could be said about Jubilees and sapiential tradition, particularly as we see it in Ben Sira, what I have sketched out suggests that attending primarily to genre differences might mask other significant aspects of our literature. One need only read Jubilees and Ben Sira, for example, to see that they are formally quite different. Yet, common questions and problems seem to occupy both of them. How does one legitimate and authorize interpretations of an authoritative text? How can they convince a reader to accept their positions? Who are the appropriate guardians of the tradition as it has been handed down, and who are the authorized interpreters of that tradition? To answer these questions, the author of Jubilees and Ben Sira resort to similar strategies, even if they execute them differently. In this light, then, whatever formal distinctions we recognize between these two works potentially distract us from noticing their common problems and their individual solutions to them.

19. B. G. Wright III and C. V. Camp, "'Who Has Been Tested by Gold and Found Perfect?' Ben Sira's Discourse of Riches and Poverty," *Hen* 23 (2001): 153-74.

20. Ben Sira's self-presentation raises interesting questions for Najman's connection of exemplarity with the issue of pseudepigraphy. See her chapter in this volume as well as her other work cited there.

To conclude, I want to present one short illustration of how deeply embedded the issue of form and genre is in scholarship. Cana Werman has suggested a genealogical relationship between Jubilees and wisdom literature. She writes, "I would like to suggest that the *Book of Jubilees* is also a development of wisdom literature, though from a source other than Proverbs. Wisdom is not mentioned in *Jubilees;* Torah and *Te'udah* — Torah and predestined history — replace Wisdom. Torah and *Te'udah* in *Jubilees* is [*sic*] an entity that existed before creation. . . . The history of the world, predestined and engraved on the heavenly tablets, unfolds in the created world. Torah, i.e., cultic laws, shapes this world."[21] She argues that Jubilees emphasizes the historical dimension so that "a thoughtful examination of history will provide the correct interpretation of the biblical laws and will ensure correct conduct in life." And so Jubilees "contains a sapiential message; it calls on wise men to meditate on history and to apply their conclusions to the interpretation of law."[22]

Despite the fact that Werman sees some similar aspects in the sapiential literature of Qumran, and, of course, 4QInstruction's *raz nihyeh* is a prime example, I do not see the necessity of claiming that Jubilees is somehow wisdom literature or a descendant of wisdom literature because one can identify these similarities. To say that Torah and predestined history "replace Wisdom" suggests that otherwise Jubilees and Ben Sira are quite close — a suggestion I find difficult to sustain. To conclude, as she does, "As Ben Sira emerged from Proverbs, so *Jubilees* emerged from the sapiential literature now found at Qumran," necessitates driving a wedge between Ben Sira and the Qumran wisdom texts that ignores the extensive similarities among all of them, a wedge that I think unnecessary and counterproductive. It seems more likely that Jubilees *and* the wisdom texts from Qumran *and* Ben Sira all address problems that other second temple texts have in common with them as well. I do not see any need to argue for some genetic relationship between Jubilees and wisdom in order to make sense out of what they share.[23] One of the things I find so fascinating about these texts, and that certainly deserves more study, is the creative variety of ways, both similar and dissimilar, that their authors and tradents found to address them.

21. C. Werman, "What Is the *Book of Hagu?*" in *Sapiential Perspectives: Wisdom Literature in Light of the Dead Sea Scrolls*, ed. J. J. Collins, G. E. Sterling, and R. A. Clements, STDJ 51 (Leiden and Boston: Brill, 2004), 125-40 (here 126).

22. Werman, *"Book of Hagu,"* 126-27.

23. For over a decade the Wisdom and Apocalypticism in Early Judaism and Christianity Group of the SBL has been working to deconstruct the categories "wisdom" and "apocalyptic." See Wright and Wills, *Conflicted Boundaries in Wisdom and Apocalypticism.*

The Heavenly Counterpart of Moses in the Book of Jubilees

Andrei A. Orlov

One of the enigmatic characters in the book of Jubilees is the angel of the presence who dictates to Moses heavenly revelation. The book provides neither the angel's name nor a clear picture of his celestial roles and offices. Complicating the picture is the angel's arrogation, in certain passages of the text, of what the Bible claims are God's words or deeds.[1] In Jub 6:22, for example, the angel utters the following: "For I have written (this) in the book of the first law in which I wrote for you that you should celebrate it at each of its times one day in a year. I have told you about its sacrifice so that the Israelites may continue to remember and celebrate it throughout their generations during this month — one day each year."[2] James VanderKam observes that according to these sentences "the angel of the presence wrote the first law, that is, the Pentateuch, including the section about the Festival of Weeks in the cultic calendars (Lev. 23:15-21 and Num. 28:26-31, where the sacrifices are specified)." VanderKam further notes that "these passages are represented as direct revelations by God to Moses in Leviticus and Numbers, not as statements from an angel."[3]

---

1. J. C. VanderKam, "The Angel of the Presence in the Book of Jubilees," *DSD* 7 (2000): 378-93 (here 390).

2. J. C. VanderKam, *The Book of Jubilees*, 2 vols., CSCO 510-11, Scriptores Aethiopici 87-88 (Louvain: Peeters, 1989), 2:40.

3. VanderKam, "Angel of the Presence," 391.

This essay represents the revised version of my article published in *Bib* 88 (2007): 153-73. I am thankful to the editors of *Biblica* for permission to reproduce the material in this publication.

Jub 30:12, which retells and modifies Gen 34, repeats the angel's authorial claim: "For this reason I have written for you in the words of the law everything that the Shechemites did to Dinah and how Jacob's sons said: 'We will not give our daughter to a man who has a foreskin because for us that would be a disgraceful thing.'"[4]

Even more puzzling is that in these passages the angel insists on personally *writing* the divine words, thus claiming the role of the celestial scribe in a fashion similar to Moses.[5] Also striking is that this nameless angelic scribe posits himself as the writer of the Pentateuch ("For I have written (this) in the book of the first law"), the authorship of which the tradition ascribes to the son of Amram. What are we to make of these authorial claims by the angel of the presence?

Is it possible that in this puzzling account about two protagonists, one human and the other angelic — both of whom are scribes and authors of the same "law" — we have an allusion to the idea of the heavenly counterpart of a seer in the form of the angel of the presence?[6] In Jewish apocalyptic and early mystical literature such heavenly doubles in the form of angels of the presence are often presented as celestial scribes. The purpose of this paper is to provide conceptual background for the idea of the angel of the presence as the heavenly counterpart of Moses in the book of Jubilees.

I. The Background: The Heavenly Counterpart of the Seer in the Jacob and the Enoch Traditions

Before proceeding to a close analysis of the traditions about the heavenly counterpart of Moses and its possible identification with the angel of the

---

4. VanderKam, *The Book of Jubilees*, 195.

5. The scribal office of Moses is reaffirmed throughout the text. Already in the beginning (Jub 1:5, 7, 26) he receives a chain of commands to write down the revelation dictated by the angel.

6. On the angelology of the book of Jubilees see R. H. Charles, *The Book of Jubilees or the Little Genesis* (London: Black, 1902), lvi-lviii; M. Testuz, *Les idées religieuses du livre des Jubilés* (Geneva: Droz, 1960), 75-92; K. Berger, "Das Buch der Jubiläen," in *JSHRZ* 2.3 (Gütersloh: Gütersloher Verlaghaus Gerd Nohn, 1981), 322-24; D. Dimant, "The Sons of Heaven: The Theory of the Angels in the Book of Jubilees in Light of the Writings of the Qumran Community" (in Hebrew), in *A Tribute to Sarah: Studies in Jewish Philosophy and Cabala Presented to Professor Sara A. Heller-Wilensky*, ed. M. Idel, D. Dimant, and S. Rosenberg (Jerusalem: Magnes, 1994), 97-118; VanderKam, "Angel of the Presence," 378-93; H. Najman, "Angels at Sinai: Exegesis, Theology and Interpretive Authority," *DSD* 7 (2000): 313-33.

presence, we will provide a short excursus on the background of the idea of the celestial double of a seer. One of the specimens of this tradition is found in the targumic elaborations of the story of the patriarch Jacob that depict his heavenly identity as his "image" engraved on the Throne of Glory.

The Jacob Traditions

The traditions about the heavenly "image" of Jacob are present in several targumic texts,[7] including *Targum Pseudo-Jonathan, Targum Neofiti,*[8] and *Fragmentary Targum.*[9]

For example, in *Targum Pseudo-Jonathan* for Gen 28:12, the following description can be found: "He [Jacob] had a dream, and behold, a ladder was fixed in the earth with its top reaching toward the heavens . . . and on that day they (angels) ascended to the heavens on high, and said, 'Come and see Jacob the pious, whose image is fixed (engraved) in the Throne of Glory, and whom you have desired to see.'"[10] Besides the tradition of "engraving"

---

7. The same tradition can be found in the rabbinic literature. *Genesis Rabbah* 68:12 reads: ". . . thus it says, Israel in whom I will be glorified (Isa. xlix, 3); it is thou, [said the angels,] whose features are engraved on high; they ascended on high and saw his features and they descended below and found him sleeping." *Midrash Rabbah,* 10 vols. (London: Soncino Press, 1961), 2:626. On Jacob's image on the Throne of Glory, see also *Genesis Rabbah* 78:3; 82:2; *Numbers Rabbah* 4:1; *b. Hullin* 91b; *Pirqe Rabbi Eliezer* 35. On the traditions about Jacob's image engraved on the Throne, see E. R. Wolfson, *Along the Path: Studies in Kabbalistic Myth, Symbolism, and Hermeneutics* (Albany: State University of New York Press, 1995), 1-62, 111-86.

8. "And he dreamed, and behold, a ladder was fixed on the earth and its head reached to the height of the heavens; and behold, the angels that had accompanied him from the house of his father ascended to bear good tidings to the angels on high, saying: 'Come and see the pious man whose image is engraved in the throne of Glory, whom you desired to see.' And behold, the angels from before the Lord ascended and descended and observed him." *Targum Neofiti 1: Genesis,* trans. M. McNamara, M.S.C., Aramaic Bible 1A (Collegeville, Minn.: Liturgical Press, 1992), 140.

9. "And he dreamt that there was a ladder set on the ground, whose top reached towards the heavens; and behold the angels that had accompanied him from his father's house ascended to announce to the angels of the heights: 'Come and see the pious man, whose image is fixed to the throne of glory. . . .'" M. L. Klein, *The Fragment-Targums of the Pentateuch according to Their Extant Sources,* 2 vols., AB 76 (Rome: Biblical Institute Press, 1980), 1:57 and 2:20.

10. *Targum Pseudo-Jonathan: Genesis,* trans. M. Maher, M.S.C., Aramaic Bible 1B (Collegeville, Minn.: Liturgical Press, 1992), 99-100.

on the Throne, some Jewish materials point to an even more radical identification of Jacob's image with *Kavod,* an anthropomorphic extension of the Deity, often labeled there as the Face of God. Jarl Fossum's research demonstrates that in some traditions about Jacob's image, his celestial "image" or "likeness" is depicted not simply as engraved on the heavenly throne, but as seated upon the throne of glory.[11] Fossum argues that this second tradition is original. Christopher Rowland offers a similar view in proposing to see Jacob's image as "identical with the form of God on the throne of glory (Ezek. 1.26f.)."[12]

The Enoch Traditions

Scholars have previously noted that Enochic materials were also cognizant of the traditions about the heavenly double of a seer. Thus, the idea about the heavenly counterpart of the visionary appears to be present in one of the booklets of 1 (Ethiopic) Enoch. It has been observed[13] that the Similitudes seems to entertain the idea of the heavenly twin of a visionary when it identifies Enoch with the Son of Man. Students of the Enochic traditions have been long puzzled by the idea that the Son of Man, who in the previous chapters of the Similitudes is distinguished from Enoch, suddenly becomes identified in 1 En 71 with the patriarch. James VanderKam suggests that this puzzle can be explained by the Jewish notion, attested in several ancient Jewish texts, that a creature of flesh and blood could have a heavenly double or counterpart.[14] To provide an example, VanderKam points to traditions about Jacob in which the patriarch's "features are engraved on high."[15] He

11. J. Fossum, *The Image of the Invisible God: Essays on the Influence of Jewish Mysticism on Early Christology,* NTOA 30 (Fribourg: Universitätsverlag Freiburg Schweiz; Göttingen: Vandenhoeck & Ruprecht, 1995), 140-41.

12. C. Rowland, "John 1.51, Jewish Apocalyptic and Targumic Tradition," *NTS* 30 (1984): 504.

13. See J. VanderKam, "Righteous One, Messiah, Chosen One, and Son of Man in 1 Enoch 37–71," in *The Messiah: Developments in Earliest Judaism and Christianity; The First Princeton Symposium on Judaism and Christian Origins,* ed. J. H. Charlesworth et al. (Minneapolis: Fortress, 1992), 182-83; M. Knibb, "Messianism in the Pseudepigrapha in the Light of the Scrolls," *DSD* 2 (1995): 177-80; Fossum, *The Image,* 144-45; C. H. T. Fletcher-Louis, *Luke-Acts: Angels, Christology, and Soteriology,* WUNT, ser. 2:94 (Tübingen: Mohr/Siebeck, 1997), 151.

14. VanderKam, "Righteous One," 182-83.

15. VanderKam, "Righteous One," 182-83.

emphasizes that this theme of the visionary's ignorance of his higher angelic identity is observable, for example, in the Prayer of Joseph.

I have argued that the idea of the heavenly counterpart of the visionary is also present in another second temple Enochic text — 2 (Slavonic) Apocalypse of Enoch.[16] 2 En 39:3-6 depicts the patriarch who, during his short trip to the earth, retells to his children his earlier encounter with the Face. Enoch relates:

> You, my children, you see my face, a human being created just like your-selves; I am one who has seen the face of the Lord, like iron made burn-ing hot by a fire, emitting sparks. For you gaze into my eyes, a human be-ing created just like yourselves; but I have gazed into the eyes of the Lord, like the rays of the shining sun and terrifying the eyes of a human being. You, my children, you see my right hand beckoning you, a human being created identical to yourselves; but I have seen the right hand of the Lord, beckoning me, who fills heaven. You see the extent of my body, the same as your own; but I have seen the extent of the Lord, without measure and without analogy, who has no end.[17]

Enoch's description reveals a contrast between the two identities of the visionary: the earthly Enoch ("a human being created just like yourselves") and his heavenly counterpart ("the one who has seen the Face of God"). Enoch describes himself in two different modes of existence: as a human be-ing who now stands before his children with a human face and body *and* as a celestial creature who has seen God's face in the heavenly realm. These de-scriptions of two conditions (earthly and celestial) occur repeatedly in tan-dem. It is possible that the purpose of Enoch's instruction to his children is not to stress the difference between his human body and the Lord's body, but to emphasize the distinction between *this* Enoch, a human being "created just like yourselves," and the *other* angelic Enoch who has stood before the Lord's face. Enoch's previous transformation into the glorious one and his initiation into the servant of the divine presence in 2 En 22:7 support this suggestion. It is unlikely that Enoch has somehow "completely" abandoned his supra-angelic status and his unique place before the Face of the Lord

---

16. A. Orlov, *The Enoch-Metatron Tradition*, TSAJ 107 (Tübingen: Mohr/Siebeck, 2005), 165-76; Orlov, "The Face as the Heavenly Counterpart of the Visionary in the Slavonic *Ladder of Jacob*," in *From Apocalypticism to Merkabah Mysticism: Studies in the Slavonic Pseudepigrapha*, ed. A. Orlov, JSJSup 114 (Leiden: Brill, 2007), 399-419.

17. F. Andersen, "2 (Slavonic Apocalypse of) Enoch," in *OTP*, 1:91-221 (here 163).

granted to him in the previous chapters. An account of Enoch's permanent installation can be found in chap. 36 where the Lord tells Enoch, before his short visit to the earth, that a place has been prepared for him and that he will be in front of the Lord's face "from *now* and forever."[18] What is important here is that the identification of the visionary with his heavenly double involves the installation of the seer into the office of the angel (or the prince) of the presence *(sar happanim)*. The importance of this account for the idea of the heavenly counterpart in 2 Enoch is apparent because it points to the simultaneous existence of Enoch's angelic double installed in heaven and its human counterpart, whom God sends periodically on missionary errands. Targumic and rabbinic accounts about Jacob also attest to this view of the heavenly counterpart when they depict angels beholding Jacob as one who at one and the same time is both installed in heaven and sleeping on earth. In relation to this paradoxical situation, in which the seer is able not only to be unified with his heavenly counterpart in the form of the angel of the presence but also to retain the ability to travel back into the earthly realm, Jonathan Smith observes that "the complete pattern is most apparent in the various texts that witness to the complex Enoch tradition, particularly 2 *Enoch*. Here Enoch was originally a man (ch. 1) who ascended to heaven and became an angel (22:9, cf. 3En 10:3f. and 48C), returned to earth as a man (33:11), and finally returned again to heaven to resume his angelic station (67:18)."[19]

What is also important in 2 Enoch's account for our ongoing investigation is that while the "heavenly version" of Enoch is installed in heaven, his "earthly version" is dispatched by God to another lower realm with the mission to deliver the handwritings made by the translated hero in heaven. In 2 En 33:3-10, for example, the Lord endows Enoch with the mission of distributing the heavenly writings on earth:

> And now, Enoch, whatever I have explained to you, and whatever you have seen in the heavens, and whatever you have seen on earth, and whatever *I have written in the books* — by my supreme wisdom I have contrived it all. . . . Apply your mind, Enoch, and acknowledge the One who is speaking to you. And you take *the books which I (!) have written. . . .* And you go down onto the earth and tell your sons all that I have told you. . . . And deliver to them the books in your handwritings, and they

---

18. 2 En 36:3. Andersen, "2 Enoch," 161, emphasis mine.
19. J. Z. Smith, "Prayer of Joseph," in *OTP*, 2:699-714 (here 705).

will read them and know their Creator. . . . And distribute the books in your handwritings to your children and (your) children to (their) children; and the parents will read (them) from generation to generation.[20]

This account is striking in that while commanding the adept to travel to the lower realm with the heavenly books, God himself seems to assume the seer's upper scribal identity. The Deity tells Enoch, who is previously depicted as the scribe of the books,[21] that he wrote these books. This situation is reminiscent of some developments found in Jubilees where the angel of the presence also seems to take on the celestial scribal identity of Moses. It is also noteworthy that in Jubilees, as in 2 Enoch, the boundaries between the upper scribal identity of the visionary who claims to be the writer of "the first law" and the Deity appear blurred.[22]

In 2 En 33 where the divine scribal figure commands the seventh antediluvian hero to deliver the book in his (Enoch's) handwritings, one possibly witnesses the unique, paradoxical communication between the upper and the lower scribal identities.

The fact that in 2 En 33 the patriarch is dispatched to earth to deliver the books in "his handwritings," the authorship of which the text assigns to the Deity, is also worthy of attention given that in the traditions attested in Jubilees, where Moses appears as a heavenly counterpart, the angel of the presence claims authorship of the materials that the tradition explicitly assigns to Moses. Here, as in 2 Enoch, book authorship can be seen as a process executed simultaneously by both earthly and heavenly authors, though it is the function of the earthly counterpart to deliver the books to humans.

Angels of the Presence

It is significant that in both Enoch and Jacob traditions the theme of the heavenly counterpart is conflated with the imagery of the angels of the pres-

---

20. 2 En 33:3-10 (the shorter recension). Andersen, "2 Enoch," 157, emphasis mine.

21. See 2 En 23:6: "I wrote everything accurately. And I wrote 366 books." Andersen, "2 Enoch," 140.

22. Cf. Jub 6:22 and 30:12. On the blurred boundaries between the angel of the presence and the Deity in Jubilees, see VanderKam, "Angel of the Presence," 390-92. It should be noted that the tendency to identify the seer's heavenly identity with the Deity or his anthropomorphic extent (known as his *Kavod* or the Face) is discernible in all accounts dealing with the heavenly counterpart.

ence. For our study of the tradition in Jubilees, where the angel of the presence might be serving as the heavenly counterpart of the son of Amram, it is important to note that both Jacob and Enoch traditions identify the heavenly counterparts of the seers as angelic servants of the presence.

Thus, in 2 Enoch the seventh antediluvian hero is depicted as the angelic servant of the presence permanently installed in front of God's face.[23] The Slavonic apocalypse repeats again and again that the seer is installed before the divine Face from "now and forever." The later *merkabah* developments reaffirm this prominent office of Enoch's upper identity in the form of angel Metatron, portraying him as a special servant of the divine presence, *sar happanim.*

In the Jacob traditions the heavenly counterpart of the son of Isaac is also depicted as the angel of the presence. Thus, in the Prayer of Joseph, the text that gives one of the most striking descriptions of the preexistent heavenly double of Jacob, the heavenly version of the patriarch reveals his identity as the angel of the presence: "I, Israel, the archangel of the power of the Lord and the chief captain among the sons of God . . . *the first minister before the face of God.*"[24]

The imagery of angels of the presence or the Face looms large in the traditions of the heavenly counterpart. What is striking here is not only that the heavenly double of the visionary is fashioned as the angel (or the prince) of the presence, but also that the angelic guides who acquaint the seer with his upper celestial identity and its offices are depicted as angels of the presence. In this respect the figure of the angelic servant of the divine presence is especially important. Both Jacob and Enoch materials contain numerous references to the angel of the presence under the name Uriel, who is also known in various traditions under the names of Phanuel and Sariel.

In 2 En 22–23, Uriel[25] plays an important role during Enoch's initiations near the Throne of Glory.[26] He instructs Enoch about different sub-

---

23. 2 En 21:3: "And the Lord sent one of his glorious ones, the archangel Gabriel. And he said to me, 'Be brave, Enoch! Don't be frightened! Stand up, and come with me and stand in front of the face of the Lord forever.'" 2 En 22:6: "And the Lord said to his servants, sounding them out, 'Let Enoch join in and stand in front of my face forever!'" 2 En 36:3: "Because a place has been prepared for you, and you will be in front of my face from now and forever." Andersen, "2 Enoch," 136, 138, and 161.

24. Smith, "Prayer of Joseph," 713.

25. Slav. *Vereveil.*

26. The beginning of this tradition can be found in the Astronomical Book where Enoch writes the instructions of the angel Uriel regarding the secrets of heavenly bodies and

jects of esoteric knowledge to prepare him for various celestial offices, including the office of the heavenly scribe. 1 En 71 also refers to the same angel but names him Phanuel. In the Similitudes he occupies an important place among the four principal angels, namely, the place usually assigned to Uriel. In fact, the angelic name Phanuel might be a title that emphasizes the celestial status of Uriel/Sariel as one of the servants of the divine *Panim*.[27]

The title Phanuel is reminiscent of the terminology found in various Jacob accounts. In Gen 32:31 Jacob names the place of his wrestling with God Peniel — the Face of God. Scholars believe that the angelic name Phanuel and the place Peniel are etymologically connected.[28]

This reference to Uriel/Sariel/Phanuel as the angel who instructs/wrestles with Jacob and announces to him his new angelic status and name is documented in several other sources, including *Targum Neofiti* and the Prayer of Joseph. In the Prayer of Joseph, for example, Jacob-Israel reveals that "Uriel, the angel of God, came forth and said that 'I [Jacob-Israel] had descended to earth and I had tabernacled among men and that I had been called by the name of Jacob.' He envied me and fought with me and wrestled with me."[29]

In the Slavonic Ladder of Jacob, another important text attesting to the idea of the heavenly counterpart, Jacob's identification with his heavenly counterpart, the angel Israel, again involves the initiatory encounter with the angel Sariel, the angel of the divine presence or the Face. The same state of events is observable in Enochic materials where Uriel serves as a principal heavenly guide to another prominent visionary who has also acquired knowledge about his own heavenly counterpart, namely, Enoch/Metatron. The aforementioned traditions pertaining to the angels of the presence are important for our ongoing investigation of the angelic figure in Jubilees in view of their role in accession to the upper identity of the seer.

---

their movements. M. Knibb, *The Ethiopic Book of Enoch: A New Edition in the Light of the Aramaic Dead Sea Fragments*, 2 vols. (Oxford: Clarendon, 1978), 2:173.

27. *Hekhalot Rabbati* (*Synopse* §108) refers to the angel Suria/Suriel as the Prince of the Face. On the identification of Sariel with the Prince of the presence, see H. Odeberg, *3 Enoch or the Hebrew Book of Enoch* (New York: Ktav, 1973), 99; Smith, "Prayer of Joseph," 709.

28. G. Vermes suggests that the angelic name Phanuel "is dependent on the Peniel/Penuel of Genesis 32." See G. Vermes, "The Impact of the Dead Sea Scrolls on Jewish Studies," *JJS* 26 (1975): 13.

29. Smith, "Prayer of Joseph," 713.

II. The Heavenly Counterpart of Moses

The Exagoge of Ezekiel the Tragedian

With this examination into the background of the traditions about the heavenly counterpart found in the Enoch and the Jacob materials in place, we will now proceed to some Mosaic accounts that also attest to the idea of the celestial double of the son of Amram. One such early Mosaic testimony has survived as a part of the drama *Exagoge*, a writing attributed to Ezekiel the Tragedian, which depicts the prophet's experience at Sinai as his celestial enthronement. Preserved in fragmentary form in Eusebius of Caesarea's[30] *Praeparatio evangelica*, the *Exagoge* 67-90 reads:

> Moses: I had a vision of a great throne on the top of Mount Sinai and it reached till the folds of heaven. A noble man was sitting on it, with a crown and a large scepter in his left hand. He beckoned to me with his right hand, so I approached and stood before the throne. He gave me the scepter and instructed me to sit on the great throne. Then he gave me a royal crown and got up from the throne. I beheld the whole earth all around and saw beneath the earth and above the heavens. A multitude of stars fell before my knees and I counted them all. They paraded past me like a battalion of men. Then I awoke from my sleep in fear.
>
> Raguel: My friend, this is a good sign from God. May I live to see the day when these things are fulfilled. You will establish a great throne, become a judge and leader of men. As for your vision of the whole earth, the world below and that above the heavens — this signifies that you will see what is, what has been and what shall be.[31]

Scholars argue that, given its quotation by Alexander Polyhistor (ca. 80-40 B.C.E.), this Mosaic account is a witness to traditions of the second century B.C.E.[32] Such dating puts this account in close chronological proximity to the book of Jubilees. It is also noteworthy that both texts (Jubilees

---

30. Eusebius preserves the seventeen fragments containing 269 iambic trimeter verses. Unfortunately, the limited scope of our investigation does not allow us to reflect on the broader context of Moses' dream in the *Exagoge*.

31. H. Jacobson, *The Exagoge of Ezekiel* (Cambridge: Cambridge University Press, 1983), 54-55.

32. C. R. Holladay, *Fragments from Hellenistic Jewish Authors*, vol. 2, *Poets*, SBLTT 30, Pseudepigrapha Series 12 (Atlanta: Scholars Press, 1989), 308-12.

and *Exagoge*) exhibit a common tendency to adapt some Enochic motifs and themes into the framework of the Mosaic tradition.

The *Exagoge* 67-90 depicts Moses' dream in which he sees an enthroned celestial figure who vacates his heavenly seat and hands over to the son of Amram his royal attributes. The placement of Moses on the great throne in the *Exagoge* account and his donning of the royal regalia have often been interpreted by scholars as the prophet's occupation of the seat of the Deity. Pieter van der Horst remarks that in the *Exagoge* Moses becomes "an anthropomorphic hypostasis of God himself."[33]

The uniqueness of the motif of God vacating the throne and transferring occupancy to someone else has long puzzled scholars. An attempt to deal with this enigma by bringing in the imagery of the vice-regent does not completely solve the problem; the vice-regents in Jewish traditions (for example, Metatron) do not normally occupy God's throne but instead have their own glorious chair that sometimes serves as a replica of the divine Seat. The enigmatic identification of the prophet with the divine Form can best be explained, not through the concept of a vice-regent, but rather through the notion of the heavenly twin or counterpart.

In view of the aforementioned traditions about the heavenly twins of Enoch and Jacob, it is possible that the *Exagoge* of Ezekiel the Tragedian also attests to the idea of the heavenly counterpart of the seer when it identifies Moses with the glorious anthropomorphic extension. As we recall, the text depicts Moses' vision of "a noble man" with a crown and a large scepter in the left hand installed on the great throne. In the course of the seer's initiation, the attributes of this "noble man," including the royal crown and the scepter, are transferred to Moses, who is instructed to sit on the throne formerly occupied by the noble man. The narrative thus clearly identifies the visionary with his heavenly counterpart, in the course of which the seer literally takes the place and the attributes of his upper identity. Moses' enthronement is reminiscent of Jacob's story, where Jacob's heavenly identity is depicted as being "engraved" or "enthroned" on the divine Seat. The account also emphasizes that Moses acquired his vision in a dream by reporting that he awoke from his sleep in fear. Here, as in the Jacob tradition, while the seer is sleeping on earth his counterpart in the upper realm is identified with the *Kavod*.

---

33. P. W. van der Horst, "Some Notes on the *Exagoge* of Ezekiel," *Mnemosyne* 37 (1984): 364-65 (here 364).

Conclusion

One of the important characteristics of the aforementioned visionary accounts in which adepts become identified with their heavenly doubles is the transference of prominent celestial offices to the new servants of the presence. Thus, for example, transference of the offices is discernible in the *Exagoge* where the "heavenly man" hands over to the seer his celestial regalia, scepter and crown, and then surrenders his heavenly seat, which the Enoch-Metatron tradition often identifies with the duty of the celestial scribe. Indeed, the scribal role may represent one of the most important offices that angels of the presence often surrender to the new servants of the Face. Thus, for example, 2 Enoch describes the initiation of the seer by Vereveil (Uriel) in the course of which this angel of the presence, portrayed in 2 Enoch as a "heavenly recorder," conveys to the translated patriarch knowledge and skills pertaining to the scribal duties. What is important in this account is its emphasis on the act of transference of the scribal duties from Vereveil (Uriel) to Enoch, when the angel of the presence surrenders to the hero the celestial library and even the pen from his hand.[34]

These developments are intriguing and may provide some insights into the puzzling tradition about the angel of the presence in the book of Jubilees.[35] Jubilees, like the Enochic account, has two scribal figures; one of them is the angel of the presence and the other is a human being. Yet the exact relationship between these two figures is difficult to establish in view of the scarcity and ambiguity of the relevant depictions. Does the angel of the presence in Jubilees pose, on the fashion of Uriel, as a celestial scribe who is responsible for initiation of the adept into the scribal duties? Or does he represent the heavenly counterpart of Moses who is clearly distinguished at this point from the seer? A clear distance between the seer and his celestial identity is not unlikely in the context of the traditions about the heavenly coun-

---

34. 2 En 22:10-11 (the shorter recension): "The Lord summoned Vereveil, one of his archangels, who was wise, *who records all the Lord's deeds.* And the Lord said to Vereveil, 'Bring out the books from storehouses, and give a pen to Enoch and read him the books.' And Vereveil hurried and brought me the books mottled with myrrh. And he gave me the pen from his hand." Andersen, "2 Enoch," 141.

35. When one looks more closely at the angelic imagery reflected in the book of Jubilees, it is intriguing that Moses' angelic guide is defined as an angel of the presence. As has already been demonstrated, the process of establishing twinship with the heavenly counterpart not only reflects the initiatory procedure of becoming a Servant of the Face, it also always presupposes the initiation performed by another angelic servant of the Face.

terpart. In fact, this distance between the two identities — one in the figure of the angel and the other in the figure of a hero — represents a standard feature of such accounts. Thus, for example, the already mentioned account from the Book of the Similitudes clearly distinguishes Enoch from his heavenly counterpart in the form of the angelic son of man throughout the whole narrative until the final unification in the last chapter of the book. The gap between the celestial and earthly identities of the seer is also discernible in the targumic accounts about Jacob's heavenly double where the distinction between the two identities is highlighted by a description of the angels who behold Jacob sleeping on earth and at the same time installed in heaven. A distance between the identity of the seer and his heavenly twin is also observable in the *Exagoge* where the heavenly man transfers to Moses his regalia and vacates for him his heavenly seat.

There is, moreover, another important point in the stories about the heavenly counterparts that could provide portentous insight into the nature of pseudepigraphical accounts where these stories are found. This aspect pertains to the issue of the so-called emulation of the biblical exemplars in these pseudepigraphical accounts that allows their authors to unveil new revelations in the name of some prominent authority of the past.[36] The identity of the celestial scribe in the form of the angel of the presence might further our understanding of the enigmatic process of mystical and literary emulation of the exemplary figure, the cryptic mechanics of which often remain beyond the grasp of our postmodern sensibilities.

Could the tradition of unification of the biblical hero with his angelic counterpart be part of this process of emulation of the exemplar by an adept? Could the intermediate authoritative position[37] of the angel of the presence, predestined to stand "from now and forever" between the Deity himself and the biblical hero, serve here as the safe haven of the author's identity,

---

36. On the process of the emulation of the biblical exemplars in the second temple literature, see H. Najman, *Seconding Sinai: The Development of Mosaic Discourse in Second Temple Judaism*, JSJSup 77 (Leiden: Brill, 2003); Najman, "Torah of Moses: Pseudonymous Attribution in Second Temple Writings," in *The Interpretation of Scripture in Early Judaism and Christianity: Studies in Language and Tradition*, ed. C. A. Evans, JSPSup 33 (Sheffield: Sheffield Academic, 2000), 202-16; Najman, "Authoritative Writing and Interpretation: A Study in the History of Scripture" (Ph.D. diss., Harvard University, 1998).

37. This "intermediate" authoritative stand is often further reinforced by the authority of the Deity himself through the identification of the heavenly counterparts with the divine form. On this process, see our previous discussion about the blurring of boundaries between the heavenly counterparts and the Deity.

thus representing the important locus of mystical and literary emulation? Is it possible that in Jubilees, as in other pseudepigraphical accounts, the figure of the angel of the presence serves as a transformative and literary device that allows an adept to enter the assembly of immortal beings consisting of the heroes of both the celestial and the literary world?

Is it possible that in the traditions of heavenly counterparts where the two characters of the story, one of whom is represented by a biblical exemplar, become eventually unified and acquire a single identity, we are able to draw nearer to the very heart of the pseudepigraphical enterprise? In this respect it does not appear to be coincidental that these transformational accounts dealing with the heavenly doubles of their adepts are permeated with the aesthetics of penmanship and the imagery of the literary enterprise. In the course of these mystical and literary metamorphoses, the heavenly figure surrenders his scribal seat, the library of the celestial books, and even personal writing tools to the other, earthly identity who now becomes the new guardian of the literary tradition.

Jubilees and the Samaritan Tradition

Lester L. Grabbe

One of the research delights with which many have occupied themselves in recent years is "comparative midrash," "comparative haggadah," and interpretative tradition. The most interesting focus of such work is the book of Genesis, which has so often been the basis for haggadic traditions.[1] A prime example of "rewritten Bible," the book of Jubilees cries out for comparison with other traditions relating to Genesis. Because the Samaritan tradition is still not very well known, though, little seems to have been done about comparing the Jubilees traditions with those among the Samaritans. A comprehensive, detailed comparison is beyond the scope of the present article, but my aim is to look at some main areas where parallels exist and ask whether Jubilees and the Samaritan tradition spring from common roots.

The only study of which I am aware in this area came to negative conclusions: the book of Jubilees is definitely not Samaritan.[2] It indeed seems

1. In the late 1970s I proposed a project to compile a catalogue of interpretative traditions on Genesis. The idea was presented to a meeting of Philo scholars brought together by Professor Burton Mack of the Institute for Antiquity and Christianity at Claremont, to a fair amount of skepticism as to the feasibility of such a project. I nevertheless discussed it with several specialists who agreed to take part, but my own academic situation was overtaken by events: I moved to the U.K., my time was taken up with a new academic post, and my research interests moved down new paths. I am not sure I have ever given up the idea, but the task would be a huge one, even if one stopped at 70 C.E. — if it went forward into the rabbinic and patristic periods, it would be enormous.

2. R. Pummer, "The *Book of Jubilees* and the Samaritans," *EgT* 10 (1979): 147-78. This article did not come to my attention until my research on the present paper was virtually

on the surface that Jubilees is not a Samaritan work, but my aim is somewhat different. The fact that Jubilees is probably not Samaritan does not by itself rule out that it and the Samaritans share haggadic and interpretative traditions. We know from half a century of study that even though the Qumran group was probably an isolated community and movement — at least according to the majority of scholars — they still preserved many literary and theological parallels with other Jews and Jewish groups. It would hardly be surprising if Jubilees had some common material with the Samaritans, but we cannot know until the matter is investigated.

There is a major problem in any comparison: the lack of good information on the development of many Samaritan beliefs. Most of the Samaritan literature cannot be dated earlier than the fourth century c.e., and it is not possible to trace much of Samaritan theology beyond that date to an earlier period. Thus, if one wants to know whether a particular Samaritan tradition was as early as Jubilees — or perhaps even earlier — or only developed much later, in many cases we cannot give a satisfactory answer. For this reason, in the present study I generally do not talk about developments of thought or whether the Samaritan tradition is likely to be early or not. Only in the period from the fourth century to the present can evolution and development be sketched with any confidence.

From a typological point of view, the Samaritans look like a Jewish sect — or from their point of view, Judaism is an Israelite sect while they are orthodox. Still, it is not always easy to know what the Samaritans believe or have believed in certain basic areas. A problem for a study such as this is the lack of good editions and even basic scholarship on Samaritan writings. Many of the Samaritan sources are late, even from the twentieth century. This does not mean that such sources do not contain ancient elements, but compared with much Jewish literature, the Samaritan writings are comparatively unstudied. There are not many Samaritan specialists, and analysis of much Samaritan literature has barely begun. A basic tool of research is *A Companion to Samaritan Studies,* as well as the collection of essays entitled *The Samaritans.*[3] Unfortunately, there is no critical edition of the Samaritan

---

complete; whether I would have continued with the project if I had seen Pummer's study earlier is an academic question that I cannot answer.

3. A. D. Crown, R. Pummer, and A. Tal, eds., *A Companion to Samaritan Studies* (Tübingen: Mohr Siebeck, 1993); A. D. Crown, ed., *The Samaritans* (Tübingen: Mohr Siebeck, 1989). See also the article surveying recent study: I. Hjelm, "What Do Samaritans and Jews Have in Common? Recent Trends in Samaritan Studies," *Currents in Biblical Research* 3 (2004-5): 9-59. For a translation of a number of Samaritan documents, see J. Bowman, *Sa-*

Pentateuch. The supposed critical edition by A. von Gall[4] is based on several manuscripts, but the editor made arbitrary emendations, especially in the orthography. A. Tal has produced an edition based on manuscript no. 6 of the Samaritan synagogue in Shechem, which will be the basic text used here.[5] Editions of other Samaritan writings will be noted when they are referred to. Fortunately, for Jubilees we are in a better position.[6]

Chronology

It is interesting that chronology is important both to the book of Jubilees and such Samaritan writings as the *Tulidah*[7] and the *Asatir*.[8] The *Asatir* is essentially a paraphrase of much of Genesis, and is thus a literary parallel to Jubilees. This suggests that it might provide traditions in common with Jubilees. Both put a lot of chronological detail into their text. Modern scholars can either regard this as a waste of space on inconsequential information or assume that the writers thought such data was important. It is well known

---

maritan Documents Relating to Their History, Religion, and Life, Pittsburgh Original Texts and Translations 2 (Pittsburgh: Pickwick, 1977).

4. A. F. von Gall, ed., *Der Hebräische Pentateuch der Samaritaner* (Giessen: Töpelmann, 1918; reprint, Berlin: Töpelmann, 1966).

5. A. Tal, ed., *The Samaritan Pentateuch Edited according to MS 6 (C) of the Shekhem Synagogue*, Texts and Studies in Hebrew Language and Related Subjects 8 (Tel Aviv: Tel Aviv University Press, 1994).

6. Text and translations of the Ethiopic text are cited from J. C. VanderKam, ed., *The Book of Jubilees: Text and English Translation*, 2 vols., CSCO 510-11, Scriptores Aethiopici 87-88 (Louvain: Peeters, 1989).

7. None of the editions of the *Tulidah* is satisfactory (also called Chronicle 3 in the numbering by J. Macdonald [*The Theology of the Samaritans*, NTL (London: SCM, 1964), 44-49]). The published editions include A. Neubauer, "Chronique samaritaine, suivie d'un appendice contenant de courtes notices sur quelques autres ouvrages samaritains," *JA* 14 (1869): 385-470 (text and French translation); M. Heidenheim, "Die samaritan. Chronik des Hohenpriesters Elasar," *Vierteljahrsschrift für deutsch und englisch-theologische Forschung und Kritik* 4 (1871): 347-89 (German translation only); J. Bowman, *Transcript of the Original Text of the Samaritan Chronicle Tolidah* (Leeds: University of Leeds, 1954 [text only, using a different manuscript from Neubauer; apparently a number of transcription errors]).

8. These are part of the so-called Samaritan chronicles. The *Asatir* is labeled Chronicle 1 in Macdonald's scheme of chronicle references (see previous note). A standard edition of the *Asatir* is M. Gaster, *The Asatir: The Samaritan Book of the "Secrets of Moses" Together with the Pitron or Samaritan Commentary and the Samaritan Story of the Death of Moses* (London: Royal Asiatic Society, 1927). A better edition of the text is Z. Ben-Hayyim, "סכר אסטיר," *Tarbiz* 14 (1942-43): 104-90; *Tarbiz* 15 (1943-44): 71-87.

that Jubilees is named for a chronological system based on a forty-nine-year cycle of jubilees. This might seem strange since the Pentateuch appears to envisage a fifty-year cycle (Lev 25:8-12). It also has often been commented that antediluvian patriarchs have three different chronological schemes, with each major version of Gen 1–10 having its own system of counting the ages of the patriarchs.[9] The following table shows the chronological data from Adam to Jacob in the three versions. (N.B. the dates are all A.M. [*anno mundi*, the era counting from creation]. The data in column 4 [Jubilees] has been reconstructed from the dates found in the table on pp. 150-51.)

Biblical Text	SP	LXX	MT	Jubilees
5:3: Adam begets Seth				
5:6: Seth begets Enosh	130	230	130	130
5:9: Enosh begets Kenan	105	205	105	98
5:12: Kenan begets Mahalalel	90	190	90	97
5:15: Mahalalel begets Jared	70	170	70	70
5:18: Jared begets Enoch	65	165	65	66
5:21: Enoch begets Methuselah	62	162	162	61
5:25: Methuselah begets Lamech	65	165	65	65
5:28: Lamech begets Noah	67	167	187	65
[5:32; 11:10: Noah begets Shem]	53	188	182	49-55
7:11: Noah's age when flood came	[502]	[502]	[502]	[500-506]
11:10: Shem's age at the time of the flood	600	600	600	601-7
11:10: Shem begets Arpachshad	98	98	98	101
11:12: Arpachshad begets Shelah				
[Cainan LXX, Jubilees]	100	100	100	103
[11:13: Cainan begets Shelah LXX, Jubilees]	135	[135]	35	[65]
11:14: Shelah begets Eber		[130]		[57]
11:16: Eber begets Peleg	130	130	30	71
11:18: Peleg begets Reu	134	134	34	64
11:20: Reu begets Serug	130	130	30	12 [*sic*]
11:22: Serug begets Nahor	132	132	32	108
11:24: Nahor begets Terah	130	130	30	57
	79	79*	29	62

*variant 179

9. A basic study of various chronographic systems in early Jewish writings is L. L. Grabbe, "Chronography in Hellenistic Jewish Historiography," in *Society of Biblical Literature 1979 Seminar Papers*, ed. P. J. Achtemeier, SBLSPS 17 (Missoula: Scholars Press, 1979), 2:43-68.

Biblical Text	SP	LXX	MT	Jubilees
11:26: Terah begets Abram (11:32; 12:4)		130		
17:17; 21:5: Abraham begets Isaac	70	100	130	70
25:26: Isaac begets Jacob	100	60	100	112
	60		60	58

Jubilees has figures that only occasionally agree with the Samaritan Pentateuch, the Septuagint, or the Masoretic text. In most cases, though, it is closest to the Samaritan Pentateuch up until the flood, but after the flood it seems to go its own way. This will be investigated in the next section.

One area where Jubilees contains information not found in the biblical text is that relating to the time when the sons of Jacob were born. The only other early Jewish writing providing such data is Demetrius the Chronographer, fragments of which are preserved in Eusebius's *Praeparatio evangelica:*[10]

Biblical Text	Jubilees*	Demetrius**
29:32: Reuben born (Leah)	28:11: 44.3.1:9/14 (2122 A.M.)	9.21.3: 8:10
29:33: Simeon born (Leah)	28:13: 44.3.3:10/21 (2124)	9.21.3: 9:8
29:34: Levi born (Leah)	28:14: 44.3.6:1/1 (2127)	9.21.3: 10:6
29:35: Judah born (Leah)	28:15: 44.4.1:3/15 (2129)	9.21.3: 11:4
30:6: Dan born (Bilhah)	28:18: 44.3.6:6/9 (2127)	[9.21.5: 14:8; originally 11:4?]
30:8: Naphtali born (Bilhah)	28:19: 44.4.2:7/5 (2130)	9.21.3: [12:2; see 9.21.8]
30:11: Gad born (Zilpah)	28:20: 44.4.3:8/12 (2131)	9.21.3: 12:2
30:13: Asher born (Zilpah)	28:21: 44.4.5:11/2 (2133)	9.21.3: 12:12
30:18: Issachar born (Leah)	28:22: 44.4.4:5/4 (2132)	9.21.4: 12:12
30:20: Zebulun born (Leah)	28:23: 44.4.6:7/7 (2134)	9.21.5: 13:10
30:21: Dinah born (Leah)	ditto (twins)	9.21.5: [14:8; see 9.21.8]
30:23-24: Joseph born (Rachel)	28:24: 44.4.6:4/1 (2134)	9.21.5: 14:8
35:18: Benjamin born (Rachel)	32:33: 44.6.1:8/11 (2143)	9.21.10: [30:??]

*(Order of dates: jubilee.week.year:month/day)

**Praep. ev. (year:month)

There are problems because the text of Demetrius has clearly suffered some damage in transmission and thus does not always make sense. Editors

10. On Demetrius, see C. R. Holladay, *Fragments from Hellenistic Jewish Authors*, vol. 1, *Historians*, Texts and Translations 20, Pseudepigrapha Series 10 (Atlanta: Scholars Press, 1983), 51-91; J. Hanson, "Demetrius the Chronographer," in *OTP*, 2:843-54.

tend to emend the text to a lesser or greater extent. Even though the emendations differ from editor to editor, the general understanding appears to be reasonably consistent. This is because it quickly becomes apparent that Demetrius is assuming ten months between births even though several of the children were born at the same time. When the two texts are carefully compared, though, there is no correspondence between Demetrius and Jubilees and no evidence of a connection. The two calculations seem independent of one another.

An area where both Jubilees and Samaritan sources seem to have something in common is the jubilee year. The Samaritan *Tulidah* gives the jubilee a pivotal role in its chronological scheme. The Samaritans, however, seem not to have counted the jubilee in the same way that the book of Jubilees does. According to *Tulidah* 5-6, five jubilees make 246 years. This is because the first jubilee is counted as 50 years but subsequent ones are counted as 49 years. The reason for this is not explained, but apparently the same calculation is used for every five jubilees. Thus ten jubilees are 492 years and twenty are 984 years; however, the sixtieth jubilee is inconsistently counted as 2,951 instead of 2,952, and the sixty-fifth as 3,196 instead of 3,198. Again, there is no explanation. In any event, the *Tulidah* and Jubilees are very close up to the Noachic deluge.

Jubilees and the *Asatir*

Although the *Asatir* runs parallel to Jubilees, it is surprising how little overlap there is. Both evidently have interpretative material from their respective traditions, but the traditions are different. Below is a table summarizing this detail:

Jubilees	SP	Samaritan Tradition: *Asatir*
3:15: Adam and Eve in Garden 7 years		[1:25: Adam and Eve 8 days in Garden]
4:1: Cain born in 64-70 A.M.; Abel in 71-77		
4:1: Awan daughter of Adam and Eve		1:3: Al'alah twin sister of Cain; Makeda twin sister of Abel
4:2: Cain slays Abel (99-105 A.M.)		1:24: Cain slays Abel (30 A.M.)
4:7: Seth born in 130 A.M.	130	1:26: Adam begets Seth (130 A.M.)
4:8: Azura daughter of Adam and Eve		
4:9: Cain marries his sister Awan		[1.4: Cain lives in city named Nikl]
4:9: Cain builds city called Enoch		

Jubilees	SP	Samaritan Tradition: *Asatir*
4:11: Seth marries his sister Azura		
4:11: Seth begets Enosh (228 A.M.)	235	
4:13: Enos begets Kenan (325 A.M.)	325	
4:14: Kenan begets Mahalalel (395 A.M.)	395	
4:15: Mahalalel begets Jared (461 A.M.)	460	
4:16: Jared begets Enoch (522 A.M.)	522	
4:20: Enoch begets Methuselah (587 A.M.)	587	
		2:32, 33-39: Enoch dies
4:27: Methuselah begets Lamech (652 A.M.)	654	
4:28: Lamech begets Noah (701-707 A.M.)	707	
4:30: day of testimony in heaven = 1,000 years		
4:33: Noah begets Shem (1207 A.M.)	[1209]	
5:23: Flood comes (1308 A.M.)	1307	4:21: from creation to day of visitation: 1,307 years
7:18: Shem begets Arpachshad (1310 A.M.)	1309	
8:1: Arpachshad begets Cainan (1375 A.M.)	*	4:31-32; 5:12-28: Nimrod
8:5: Cainan begets Shelah (1432 A.M.)	1444	
8:7: Shelah begets Eber (1503 A.M.)	1574	
8:8: Eber begets Peleg (1567 A.M.)	1708	
8:11–9:13: Noah divides the earth among his 3 sons		[4:13: Noah divides earth 62 years after flood]
10:18: Peleg begets Reu (1579 A.M.).	1838	[4:19: after division of earth, 4,293 years remaining of 6,000]
11:1: Reu begets Serug (1687 A.M.)	1970	
11:8: Serug begets Nahor (1744 A.M.)	2100	
11:10: Nahor begets Terah (1806 A.M.)	2179	
11:14: Terah begets Abram (1876 A.M.)	2249	
16:13-15: Abram begets Isaac (1988 A.M.) (13:16; 15:1)	2349	
19:13: Isaac begets Jacob and Esau (2046 A.M.) (19:1)	2409	
		11:20: Moses foretold what would happen in next 3,204 years

*No Cainan in SP; Arpachshad begets Shelah.

Both the *Asatir* and Jubilees contain a good deal of detail not found in the text of Genesis. Yet neither tends to have much overlap. Sometimes they both add detail to the text (e.g., the names of the wives married by the antediluvial patriarchs or the cities built by them), but the details have no relation to one another. Topics that are evidently important to one (because space is devoted to them) do not occur in the other or are mentioned only very briefly. For example, Jubilees does not seem to be interested in Nimrod. This is in contrast to the legend found in some other Jewish writings,[11] but a developed legend occurs in the *Asatir*. On the other hand, Jubilees contains expanded stories about Jacob's wars with the Amorites (34:2-9) and with Esau and his sons (37–38), which have no place in the *Asatir* nor any other Samaritan writing.

On the chronological side, the previous section noted that the Samaritans also use the jubilee, but they calculate the first jubilee as fifty years, then forty-nine years until the fifth jubilee. Whether because of this or in spite of it, the flood occurs in 1308 A.M. in Jubilees and 1307 in the *Asatir* and other Samaritan sources. The preflood genealogies of Jubilees are close to the Samaritan Pentateuch, but with little exact correspondence. From the flood on, however, the Samaritan Pentateuch tends to agree with the Septuagint, whereas Jubilees tends to use smaller figures (but still greater than those in the Masoretic text) and is quite different from the Samaritan. Jubilees does have one agreement with the Septuagint: it includes Cainan between Arpachshad and Shelah (in contrast to both the SP and the MT, which make Shelah the son of Arpachshad). A study much needed is a thorough investigation of the Jubilees chronology to determine whether internal patterns are operating. One factor that complicates any attempt to discern patterns in the figures of Jubilees is that the Jubilees chronology is not always internally consistent. We have the obvious error in the case of Peleg, who has a son at age twelve (10:18). But other problematic figures relate to Abraham's age when he begets Ishmael (14:24) and then Isaac (16:13-15).

The concept of human history encompassing 6,000 years, on the analogy of the week, ending with a 1,000-year "sabbath," is well known from later Jewish and Christian writings.[12] We find the same chronological scheme in the *Asatir* (4:19; 11:20), though this is probably a medieval writing. Was the concept found as early as the book of Jubilees? Jub 4:30 speaks of a day equaling 1,000 years in the testimony of heaven. The full scheme of 6,000

---

11. See L. Ginzberg, *Legends of the Jews, I: Bible Times and Characters from the Creation to Jacob,* trans. Henrietta Szold (Philadelphia: Jewish Publication Society of America, 1909), 177-217; Ginzberg, *Legends of the Jews, V: Notes to Volumes I and II, from the Creation to the Exodus* (Philadelphia: Jewish Publication Society of America, 1925), 198-218.

12. See Grabbe, "Chronography," 2:51-55.

years of human history before the eschaton is not spelled out in Jubilees, which means that we cannot be certain it existed for the writer of that book. But there is a possible parallel here.

Calendar

Along with chronology, both Jubilees and the *Asatir* are concerned about the calendar. Jubilees states as follows:

> 6:30All the days of the commandments will be 52 weeks of days; (they will make) the entire year complete. 6:31So it has been engraved and ordained on the heavenly tablets. One is not allowed to transgress a single year, year by year. 6:32Now you command the Israelites to keep the years in this number — 364 days. Then the year will be complete and it will not disturb its time from its days or from its festivals because everything will happen in harmony with their testimony. . . . 6:36There will be people who carefully observe the moon with lunar observations because it is corrupt (with respect to) the seasons and is early from year to year by ten days.

As is well known, Jubilees followed a solar calendar of 364 days (slightly short of the true solar year of about 365.25 days) that could conveniently be divided into 52 weeks and four quarters of 13 weeks (91 days) each. The lunar calendar was specifically rejected.

The details of the Samaritan calendar are not easily gleaned from the *Asatir* or many other Samaritan documents, but what soon becomes clear is that the Samaritans followed a luni-solar calendar, i.e., a calendar in which each month is determined by the phases of the moon but in which the lunar year is regularly adjusted to bring it into line with the solar year. What this means in practice is that a thirteenth month is intercalated every two or three years, so that over a period of almost exactly nineteen years, the lunar and solar cycles come into alignment. It is the same principle as the Jewish calendar,[13] including use of the Metonic cycle and the Julian year. Whereas the modern Jewish calendar is now calculated, the principles of the Samaritan calendar have been a carefully guarded secret; however, there is evidence

---

13. For more details, see S. Stern, *Calendar and Community: A History of the Jewish Calendar 2nd Century BCE–10th Century CE* (Oxford: Oxford University Press, 2001).

that it is now also calculated.[14] The two do not necessarily coincide because of differences in the pattern of adding an intercalary month.

Angelology

Although the "fallen angels" tradition is perhaps not as central to Jubilees as it is to 1 Enoch, it is still important, occurring in more than one passage:

> 5:1 When mankind began to multiply on the surface of the entire earth and daughters were born to them, the angels of the Lord — in a certain (year) of the jubilee — saw that they were beautiful to look at. So they married of them whomever they chose. They gave birth to children for them and they were giants. . . . 5:6 Against his angels whom he had sent to the earth he was angry enough to uproot them from all their (positions of) authority. He told us to tie them up in the depths of the earth; now they are tied within them and are alone. 5:7 Regarding their children there went out from his presence an order to strike them with the sword and to remove them from beneath the sky. . . . 5:9 He sent his sword among them so that they would kill one another. They began to kill each other until all of them fell by the sword and were obliterated from the earth. 5:10 Now their fathers were watching, but afterwards they were tied up in the depths of the earth until the great day of judgment when there will be condemnation on all who have corrupted their ways and their actions before the Lord.

A little further in the narrative another reference occurs:

> 7:21 For it was on account of these three things that the flood was on the earth, since (it was) due to fornication that the Watchers had illicit intercourse — apart from the mandate of their authority — with women. When they married of them whomever they chose they committed the first (acts) of uncleanness. 7:22 They fathered (as their) sons the Nephilim. They were all dissimilar (from one another) and would devour one another: the giant killed the Naphil; the Naphil killed the Elyo; the Elyo mankind; and people their fellows.

14. S. Powels, *Der Kalender der Samaritaner anhand des* Kitāb Ḥisāb as-Sinīn *und anderer Handschriften,* Studia Samaritana 3 (Berlin and New York: De Gruyter, 1977); Powels, "XI. The Samaritan Calendar and the Roots of Samaritan Chronology," in *The Samaritans,* 691-742.

This tradition of the fallen angels is characteristic mainly of 1 Enoch and of Jubilees. Parts of the "fallen angels" myth are found here and there, but the full myth occurs only in these two books. In Jubilees it is abbreviated, but it appears to have much the same contents as that in 1 Enoch, as far as we can tell. Although a Satan/devil tradition is widespread in Judaism and later in Christianity,[15] including the idea that Satan fell from heaven, the "fallen angels" myth in these two books takes a particular form.

When we look at the Samaritans, we certainly find angels, but Samaritan angelology as a whole remains relatively undeveloped compared to other streams of Judaism.[16] The Samaritan tradition has developed some individual personal angels with names and specific tasks. But compared to the angelic tradition of 1 Enoch, it is fairly simple. Particularly important is the discourse on angels by Abu'l Hasan.[17] There are four named angels (Phanuel, Anusa, Kabbala, and Nasi) of the good sort. The "Angel of the Presence" (also called God's *Kabod* ["Glory"]) is important in various Pentateuchal passages.[18]

What is most curious, though, is the near absence of evil angels. Although a few names occur, a Satan/devil tradition is not strongly developed in Samaritan literature. There are references to "sons of Belial," such as we find in the biblical text, and a reference to Azazel, but these are mainly confined to the Day of Atonement. Absent is a "fallen angels" tradition comparable in any way to the one in Jubilees and 1 Enoch, which led Macdonald to write, "No case can be made out for a Samaritan belief in evil angels or demons as an integral part of their system of belief."[19] This means that a core belief of Jubilees has no real parallel in the Samaritan tradition.

Afterlife

Jubilees has one well-known passage about the afterlife:

> 23:30Then the Lord will heal his servants. They will rise and see great peace. He will expel his enemies. The righteous will see (this), offer

15. Cf. L. L. Grabbe, "The Scapegoat Ritual: A Study in Early Jewish Interpretation," *JSJ* 18 (1987): 152-67.

16. Macdonald, *The Theology*, 397-404.

17. See the translation of a central passage in Bowman, *Samaritan Documents*, 248-51.

18. J. E. Fossum, *The Name of God and the Angel of the Lord: Samaritan and Jewish Concepts of Intermediation and the Origin of Gnosticism*, WUNT 36 (Tübingen: Mohr Siebeck, 1985), 220-38.

19. Macdonald, *The Theology*, 404.

praise, and be very happy forever and ever. They will see all their punishments and curses on their enemies. 23:31 Their bones will rest in the earth and their spirits will be very happy. They will know that the Lord is one who executes judgment but shows kindness to hundreds and thousands and to all who love him.

The standard interpretation has been that this represents a type of "resurrection of the spirit"; i.e., in contrast to some forms of Judaism, the body is not resurrected. It remains in the earth but the spirit continues to live, usually in a celestial realm.[20]

As with the Jews, the eschatological views of the Samaritans developed over the centuries, and there were differences between the sects.[21] There are some rabbinic statements to the effect that the Samaritans did not believe in the resurrection, and in "Samaritan sources from the fourth century to the fourteenth century the evidence for a belief in resurrection is also uncertain."[22] However, it appears that the Dositheans sect did believe in the resurrection.[23] In any event, resurrection has become a part of Samaritan thinking in recent centuries, even if it is difficult to trace it to an earlier period. One interpretation is that the original Samaritan eschatology was limited and set on the earth; a more transcendent version, with the concepts of the Day of Vengeance (a sort of day of judgment or "day of the Lord") and the resurrection, developed later, perhaps some key elements as late as medieval or later times. Whether the Samaritans had a belief like that in Jubilees is uncertain, but it is possible.

Messiah/Messianic Kingdom

One aspect of Samaritan eschatology is belief in the Taheb. This figure is often compared to the Jewish messiah. This has been denied because the Taheb is basically an eschatological prophet like Moses; however, considering the

20. G. W. E. Nickelsburg, *Resurrection, Immortality, and Eternal Life in Intertestamental Judaism,* HTS 26 (Cambridge: Harvard University Press, 1972), 31-33.

21. F. Dexinger, "V. Samaritan Eschatology," in *The Samaritans,* 266-92; M. Gaster, *The Samaritan Oral Law and Ancient Traditions,* vol. 1, *Samaritan Eschatology* (London: Search Publishing Co., 1932).

22. Dexinger, "V. Samaritan Eschatology," 283.

23. S. J. Isser, *The Dositheans: A Samaritan Sect in Late Antiquity,* SJLA 17 (Leiden: Brill, 1976), 143-50.

varieties of messianic belief in second temple Judaism, belief in the Taheb does not look out of place.[24] The term "messiah" seems to be lacking, but this is also the case with some Jewish figures who are labeled messianic. The Taheb is a prophet but also a king in some texts. He sets up a kingdom on earth and lives for 110 years, after which he dies before the eschaton.[25] One can compare this with the messianic figure in 4 Ezra 7:28-44 who also dies (after a reign of 400 years).

One can speak of a sort of "messianic kingdom" in Jubilees in such passages as 1:29 and 23:26-31. There seems to be no messiah as such, however; the closest we come is a reference to a prince from the tribe of Judah (31:18-20). The wording is rather vague, though, and it is not clearly a messiah. It could be referring to the future Israelite king in the image of David. The king was of course anointed and thus a "messiah," but only in that sense does a messiah seem to be discussed. In any case, Jubilees and the Samaritans appear to have rather different concepts.

Conclusions

No evidence suggests that Jubilees is a Samaritan work. There are too many incongruities with Samaritan beliefs. To take one small example, Jubilees clearly gives a special place to Jerusalem in 1:28-29:

> 1:28"The Lord will appear in the sight of all, and all will know that I am the God of Israel, the father of all Jacob's children, and the king on Mt. Zion for the ages of eternity. Then Zion and Jerusalem will become holy." 1:29The angel of the presence, who was going along in front of the Israelite camp, took the tablets (which told) of the divisions of the years from the time the law and the testimony were created — for the weeks of their jubilees, year by year in their full number, and their jubilees from [the time of the creation until] the time of the new creation when the heavens, the earth, and all their creatures will be renewed like the powers of the sky and like all the creatures of the earth, until the time when the temple of the Lord will be created in Jerusalem on Mt. Zion.

24. See L. L. Grabbe, *Judaic Religion in the Second Temple Period: Belief and Practice from the Exile to Yavneh* (London and New York: Routledge, 2000), 271-91, and the literature cited there.

25. Dexinger, "V. Samaritan Eschatology," 272-76.

The real question was whether Jubilees might have certain special traditions or interpretations in common with the Samaritan tradition, and this was the question investigated in the present paper. It was not an easy question to answer because many traditions in Jubilees seem to have no parallels in the Samaritan tradition, which means that no comparison could be made. Nevertheless, the two writings could be compared in several areas. The following are the general results from the areas studied here:

- Both Jubilees and the Samaritan tradition have developed haggadic material relating to the Genesis stories that add much interpretative detail. Yet much of this does not correspond because one has haggadic material where it is absent in the other. This means that comparison is not always easy.
- Where both traditions have comparable haggadic expansion, they generally do not coincide in the details. For example, daughters are born to Adam and Eve and become the wives of antediluvial patriarchs in both traditions, but the names do not match in the two traditions. Similarly, both talk of cities founded by the preflood figures, but again there is no coincidence of detail.
- Jubilees seems to have a similar reckoning of the chronology from creation to the Noachic deluge, but there is hardly any agreement on the exact figures for the antediluvian genealogies. From the flood on, Jubilees is quite different, with a much shorter chronology, differing from the Samaritan by almost 400 years by the time of Abraham. Thus, the approximate agreement up to Noah's flood does not appear at all significant, but further study of the various chronological systems is needed.
- The Jubilees reckoning of the ages of Jacob's sons is almost unique, but a parallel is found in Demetrius the Chronographer. The two systems do not agree, though.
- The jubilee year is important to both Jubilees and the Samaritan *Tulidah.* They use different ways of calculating the jubilee, however, and there seems little correspondence in detail.
- The Samaritan tradition, like the Jewish and Christian, had developed a scheme of 6,000 years of human history before the eschatological millennial "sabbath." It is not entirely clear that such a scheme can be found in Jubilees, but 4:30 might hint at this concept.
- The Samaritans use a luni-solar calendar, with much in common with the traditional Jewish calendar, in contrast to the solar calendar of Jubilees.

- Although the Samaritans had an angelology, it does not seem to have been very extensively developed. But what is especially missing is a myth of evil fallen angels such as that in Jubilees and 1 Enoch.
- The Jubilees concept of "resurrection of the spirit" resembles the Samaritan view of the afterlife but probably no more so than it resembles the Jewish view. Both sets of writing seem to be drawing on a common stock of Jewish beliefs about the afterlife.
- Jubilees does not seem to have a concept of a messianic figure (though one could argue for a "messianic kingdom"), unlike the Samaritan Taheb.

The present study has been far from exhaustive, but it has looked at some of the major areas where Jubilees and the Samaritan tradition can be compared. Some examples of coincidence in detail were found, but these mostly could be explained as accidental or arising from a common Jewish tradition. It would have been interesting if clear examples of parallels could be found, but so far they have eluded me. Many early Jewish traditions have parallels in the Samaritan tradition and vice versa; the lack of coincidence between Jubilees and the Samaritan tradition seems in part a reflection of the fact that Jubilees often has unique traditions when compared with other early Jewish literature. Thus, one should be careful about extrapolating from the situation with Jubilees to other Jewish writings. Each tradition — whether Jewish or Samaritan — must be examined individually before conclusions can be reached.

PART TWO

THE MELTING OF MOSAIC
AND ENOCHIC TRADITIONS

Enochic Judaism — a Judaism without the Torah and the Temple?

Helge S. Kvanvig

Master Narrative and Counterstory

The biblical image of history is above all created through the addition of the Pentateuch and the Deuteronomistic Work of History. By this combination there was created an image of history reaching from creation to exile with clear accents on foundational events that determined the fate of the people: election through Abraham, exodus, the Torah on Sinai, conquest, temple, apostasy, and exile. By ending in the exile, the narrative ends with a question mark provoking an answer to all subsequent readers: What is the next turn of history? What are the traces left in the narrative design of history that point toward a new future?

To present this biblical image of history in compressed form, I have chosen the covenantal renewal in Neh 8–10 as a representative text. There for the first time the basic elements of the biblical image of history are woven together in one coherent picture in order to advocate a specific religious identity where the law and the temple play a major role. Neh 8–10 is accordingly a micronarrative within the biblical macronarrative, and there is a clear interplay between the origin of the forceful macronarrative and the composing of Neh 8–10. We consider Neh 8–10 as representative for a distinct piety in Judaism. We treat the narrative in its basic configuration as exemplary; we do not claim that there is direct genetic relationship between this particular text and the Enochic writings.

In comparing narratives we need a reflection on how narratives interact. I have here chosen a terminology borrowed from H. Lindemann Nelson. She analyzes the relationship between what she designates as master narratives, counterstories, and alternative stories.[1] She uses these designations to analyze social interaction, how narrative identities could be oppressive or liberating. I use these designations purely as literary categories. A master narrative is a foundational story in a larger community. It is at interplay with other narratives of a similar kind. Together they summarize shared understandings in the community and exercise authority over moral norms. They have the capacity to present a worldview that seems self-evident.[2] A counterstory is a story that contests the worldview of the master narrative, not by trying to erase the narrative itself, but by making significant changes in its literary web. The result is that the new restored narrative communicates something entirely different. The counterstory is definitely in opposition to the master narrative, but not necessarily polemical. It works counter in a more subtle way by dissolving the communicative force of the master narrative, through displacement of plots and characters.[3] Alternative stories also deviate from master narratives, but they do not contest them. They can add, move, and remove features from the master narrative to make new accents in it, but not to dissolve its communicative force. Alternative narratives can live together and lend authority to each other.

C. A. Newsom has made a somewhat similar distinction in her book about the construction of religious identity in Qumran. She distinguishes between dominant discourse and counterdiscourse. The Qumran community created a counterdiscourse over against the dominant discourse of the Judean society.[4] Her definitions of "dominant" and "counter" are close to those found in Lindemann Nelson's approach, bearing in mind that discourse is a much broader category than narrative. It is also a more demanding one, since a dominant discourse of "normal" Judaism has to be constructed.

In the following we will apply the categories of master narrative, counterstory, and alternative story to three texts: Neh 8–10, the Book of the Watchers (1 En 1–36), and the Apocalypse of Weeks (1 En 93:1-10 + 91:11-17). The focus will be on how the Torah and the temple are contextualized in these texts.

---

1. H. L. Nelson, *Damaged Identities, Narrative Repair* (Ithaca, N.Y., and London: Cornell University Press, 2001), 6-20, 150-88.

2. Cf. Nelson, *Damaged Identities*, 6f.

3. Nelson, *Damaged Identities*, 152ff.

4. C. A. Newsom, *The Self as Symbolic Space: Constructing Identity and Community at Qumran* (Leiden: Brill, 2004), 17-21.

Nehemiah 8–10: A Master Narrative

The whole narrative starts with the reading of the Torah and the celebration of Sukkoth (7:72b–8:18). Then comes the prayer where the foundational events in history are recorded (9:1-31): creation, Abraham, exodus, Sinai, wilderness wandering, conquest, life in the land ending in a final disaster. After the revelation of the law at Sinai, the apostasy of the people starts and increases, especially after the conquest. The prayer ends in a petition for mercy and a confession (9:32-37).[5] The narrative continues in Neh 10 by telling how the people join an agreement to follow the Torah, which includes renouncement of mixed marriages, keeping the Sabbath regulations, and obligations toward the temple.

The different parts of the unit have different origins and dates.[6] The whole composition is generally held to be one of the youngest in the Hebrew Bible; both Pakkala and Blenkinsopp see it as an insertion after the Chronicler's redaction of Ezra/Nehemiah.[7] We are thus moved at least to the beginning of the Hellenistic period. The date and origin of the prayer in 9:5ff. have been intensively debated.[8] After a long discussion Boda dates the prayer to the period that preceded Ezra and Nehemiah, i.e., in the very early postexilic period.[9] An early postexilic date seems unlikely, however, because the prayer uses both the Priestly source to the Pentateuch and the Deuteronomistic Work of History — for instance, it knows the literary unit Exod 19–20.

We will first concentrate on the prayer. Already von Rad in 1971 characterized the genre of Neh 9 as *Gerichtsdoxologie,* together with especially Ezra 9:6-15 and Dan 9. The history of the community was recalled under the perspective of disobedience to the Torah and contrasted to the patience and forgiveness of God.[10] Boda follows von Rad and characterizes the prayer as a

---

5. For the structure, cf. H. G. M. Williamson, "Structure and Historiography in Nehemiah 9," in *Proceedings of the Ninth World Congress of Jewish Studies* (Jerusalem: Magnes, 1985), 117-31 (here 120ff.).

6. Cf. J. Blenkinsopp, *Ezra-Nehemiah,* OTL (Philadelphia: SCM, 1989), 284ff., 301ff., 310ff.

7. J. Pakkala, *Ezra the Scribe: The Development of Ezra 7–10 and Nehemiah 8,* BZAW 347 (Berlin: De Gruyter, 2004), 180-211; Blenkinsopp, *Ezra-Nehemiah,* 54f.

8. Cf. the discussion in M. J. Boda, *Praying the Tradition: The Origin and Use of Tradition in Nehemiah 9,* BZAW 277 (Berlin: De Gruyter, 1999), 11-16.

9. Boda, *Praying the Tradition,* 189-97.

10. G. von Rad, "Gerichtsdoxologie," in *Gesammelte Studien zum alten Testament II* (Munich: Kaiser, 1973), 245-54.

"penitential prayer."[11] The plots in these prayers consist of two equally significant elements that constitute the overall narrative. There is a story part where the history of the people is recalled under the perspective of guilt, and there is the actual confession of sin, or penitence, where the one who entreats or the people appeal to the mercy of God. The intention is to create a turning point in history where the people are freed from the guilt of the past and given a new future of grace.

Some important accents in this presentation of history link the recall of history to the present situation of ceremonial commitment. The first is the role of the Torah. The Torah is central in all parts of the narrative: in the first part in the reading of the Torah and the celebration of Sukkoth (7:72b–8:18), in the prayer (9:3, 13-14, 26, 29, 34), and in the ceremonial commitment (10:29-30). In the obligations toward the temple the Torah is referred to twice (10:35, 37). This is especially important, because here what became the two most important institutions in postexilic Judah are brought together in one unity, the Torah and the temple.

The second accent is the *berit,* the covenant. There are two important observations to be made here. First, the covenant is made with the people through Abraham, it is not linked to Sinai. Therefore the covenant is a binding promise from God (Neh 9:8). Second, the content of the covenant is the land. Even though the *berit* is mentioned only twice, about Abraham in 9:8 and in the appeal in 9:32, the promise of the land is a theme through the whole recall of history. Thus in this historical configuration two basic foundations from the past are lifted up as the conditions for the people's survival, the promise of the land, the *berit,* and the commitment to the Torah.

As a whole, Neh 8–10 is the story about the rebirth of the people of God. They were once born through the sacred history of God leading from Abraham to Sinai. Then followed a long, dark history of rebellion where they were kept alive only through the grace of God. Now the people are at the turning point of their history again. Through the commitment to the Torah they will again enter into the history of grace, freed from their present oppressors, cf. 9:34; 10:1. As a story about rebirth, this is also a story about identity. It lines out what kind of people from now on belong to the people of God, and what characterizes the people of God. These characteristics concern both the past and the present. The new identity embraces both the history and the present commitment. From now on a true Judean is a person formed through the history of *berit* and Torah; he is separated from other

11. Boda, *Praying the Tradition,* 26-32.

people living in the area through his ethnic purity, his Torah observance, and his cultic responsibilities toward the temple. These characteristics are the core characteristics in what has been labeled covenantal Judaism.[12]

The line of demarcation between the insiders and the outsiders is sharply drawn and seems absolute. Nevertheless, there is an ambiguity in this sharp distinction. It is symbolic rather than real. The law in Ezra-Nehemiah is never exactly defined; it is simply "the law of Moses," which clearly has an openness toward new interpretations.[13] The reading and reinterpretation of the Torah is thus a part of what Najman designates as the Mosaic discourse, starting with Deuteronomy. This discourse has its clear limits, because it bases its legitimacy on the authority of Moses, but it is flexible in the way this authority is carried out in the actual interpretation.[14] Thus such interpretations are alternative; they exist together within the Mosaic discourse. Stories within this master paradigm can be at tension with each other, but they derive authority from and lend authority to the Mosaic Torah.

The Book of the Watchers

The Book of the Watchers is composed of three main parts, which can be approximately dated from the last part of the fourth century to the middle of the third: the Oracle of Judgment (1 En 1–5), the Watcher Story (6–16), and the Journeys of Enoch (17–36). The Watcher Story contains two sections: the Rebellion Story (6–11) and the Enoch Story (12–16).

There is considerable agreement about the growth of the book.[15] The Rebellion Story (6–11) forms the oldest part. The next step is the inclusion of this story in the Enoch Story (12–16), creating the Watcher Story (6–16). Then comes the adding of the Journeys (17–36), and as the final step the Oracle of Judgment that introduces the whole book (1–5).

The core of the book is accordingly the Rebellion Story. This story tells how apostasy is bred into this world. There are three codes at play, forbidden

12. Cf. the discussion in Newsom, *Self as Symbolic Space*, 23-36.

13. Cf. S. Japhet, "Law and 'the Law' in Ezra-Nehemiah," in *Proceedings of the Ninth World Congress of Jewish Studies*, 99-115.

14. Cf. H. Najman, *Seconding Sinai: The Development of Mosaic Discourse in Second Temple Judaism*, JSJSup 77 (Leiden: Brill, 2003), 1-19.

15. Cf. the discussion in G. W. E. Nickelsburg, *1 Enoch 1: A Commentary on the Book of Enoch 1–36, 81–106*, Hermeneia (Minneapolis: Fortress, 2001), 25f.

sexuality, violence, and illegitimate knowledge. In structure the story follows the flood story.[16] This story is again explicated in 1 En 12–16 and 1–5.[17] We may call these two sections "alternative stories" if we concentrate on the narrative elements in 1–5. The stories are alternative in the way they both use the Rebellion Story as master narrative, but utilize the basic elements of this story in a new narrative design that does not contradict the master story.

1 En 12–16 carries the Rebellion Story further in its mythical realm. The basic plot of the story is the penitence and the question of petition for the Watchers and their offspring (13:4-5). The three basic codes from the Rebellion Story are present, but there is a clear emphasis on forbidden sexuality as transgression of the divine order (12:4; 15:3-7).[18] This transgression resulted in the origin of evil spirits on earth (15:8–16:1).[19]

Suter said the Watcher Story was formed as a polemic against the Jerusalem priesthood, because priests married women outside priestly families.[20] Nickelsburg has argued the same, but confined to the Enoch Story, which seems more likely since the code of sexuality is more focused in this section.[21] Nickelsburg has carried the argument further by pointing out several similarities between the Enoch Story and the last chapters in Ezra: both Enoch and Ezra are titled "scribe" (1 En 12:3-4; Ezra 7:6), Enoch intercedes for the Watchers using words similar to Ezra's prayer of confession (1 En 13:4-5; Ezra 9:6), the plot is similar in both, and both deal with the transgression of marriage rules.[22]

The parallels to Ezra have most bearing in relation to the temple. If the

---

16. Cf. H. S. Kvanvig, "Cosmic Laws and Cosmic Imbalance: Wisdom, Myth and Eschatology in the Early Enochic Writings," in *The Early Enoch Tradition,* ed. G. Boccaccini (Leiden: Brill, 2007).

17. Cf. D. R. Jackson, *Enochic Judaism: Three Defining Paradigm Exemplars* (London: Clark, 2004), 31ff.

18. Cf. A. Y. Reed, *Fallen Angels and the History of Judaism and Christianity* (Cambridge: Cambridge University Press, 2005), 44-49.

19. H. S. Kvanvig, "Gen 6,3 and the Watcher Story," *Hen* 25 (2003): 287-92.

20. D. W. Suter, "Fallen Angels, Fallen Priests: The Problem of Family Purity in 1 Enoch," *HUCA* 50 (1979): 115-35; Suter, "Revisiting 'Fallen Angel, Fallen Priest,'" in *The Origins of Enochic Judaism,* ed. G. Boccaccini, Henoch (Turin: Silvio Zamorani, 2002), 137-42.

21. G. W. E. Nickelsburg, "Enoch, Levi and Peter: Recipients of Revelation in Upper Galilee," *JBL* 100 (1981): 575-600 (here 584f.). Broader material to support the argument is presented by M. Himmelfarb, "Levi, Phinehas, and the Problem of Intermarriage at the Time of the Maccabean Revolt," *JSQ* 6 (1999): 1-24.

22. Nickelsburg, *1 Enoch 1,* 230f. The same argument was presented by H. S. Kvanvig, *Roots of Apocalyptic,* WMANT 61 (Neukirchen-Vluyn: Neukirchener, 1988), 101.

Watchers are cast in the role of impure priests, as a parallel to the impure people in Ezra, the Enochic text is utterly critical to the legitimacy of the cult in the second temple. If Enoch and Ezra stand parallel as intercessors in plots with similar traits, we note that the outcome of the intercession is opposite. The story of Ezra is a story of penitence like Neh 8–10, where also the purity of the people is concerned. In both stories the outcome is forgiveness. The stories create a point of demarcation in history where the positive outcome serves to legitimize the practices of the future. The story in 1 En 12–16 works in the opposite direction. There is no forgiveness for the Watchers/priests. They are still under condemnation. In this sense the Watcher Story functions as a counterstory to stories of penitence and forgiveness related to the second temple. It turns the plot in the opposite direction; the petition is denied.

This implied polemic against the temple in Jerusalem seems also to be reflected in the geographical setting of 1 En 12–16. Enoch went to the Waters of Dan, south of Mount Hermon, to receive his revelation (13:7). And from there he ascended to the heavenly temple, which is more connected to Mount Hermon than to Zion.[23] The vision itself shows that Enoch as a patron of the Enochians was not deprived access to the temple, but it was in heaven, not in Jerusalem.

Since 1 En 1–5 frequently alludes to writings in the Hebrew Bible, it is tempting to use traditions present in these texts as a key to interpret the section. Hartman claimed that the covenant constituted the referential background. He found three specific markers in the text that pointed toward the covenant: the theophany and judgment connected to Sinai (1:4, 9), the terminology of the denouncement speech, and the curses and blessings, spread all over 1 En 2–5, which both reflected the pattern of a covenantal ritual.[24] I think the markers are too vague to point to a specific covenantal ritual, if such a ritual ever existed. The closest we come in the postexilic period is the ceremony in Neh 8–10, which shows no links to 1 En 1–5.

Hoffmann follows a more general approach. He suggests that the notion of the Mosaic Torah underlies the wisdom terminology of the Enochic writings and that this notion has to be seen as the context at places where the Mosaic Torah is not directly addressed.[25] Thus he claims that "die Nennung

---

23. Cf. Nickelsburg, "Enoch, Levi and Peter," 582-87.

24. L. Hartman, *Asking for a Meaning: A Study of Enoch 1–5*, ConBNT 12 (Lund: Gleerup, 1975), 123f.

25. H. Hoffmann, *Das Gesetz in der frühjüdischen Apokalyptik* (Göttingen: Vandenhoeck, 1999), 126f.

des Berges Sinai impliziert die Gabe der Tora."[26] Likewise, he claims that 1 En 5:4 contains a reference to the Mosaic Torah revealed at Sinai.[27] I am severely in doubt that the concept of the Mosaic Torah as we know it from Neh 8–10 and the Pentateuch simply can be taken for granted in these passages.

The background of 1 En 1–5 is not to be sought outside the Enochic traditions, but inside. 1 En 1–5 is primarily formed on the basis of the Watcher Story as a master narrative: 1:2 in relation to the vision in chaps. 14–15, the Watchers in 1:5, the proud words and the curse in 1:9; 5:5-7 in relation to 6:3-5; "no peace" in 5:4-5 in relation to 12:5-6; 13:1; 16:4; the fate of the righteous in 1:7-8; 5:6-9 in relation to 10:7, 16-22; 11:1-2. The basic plot in the two sections is the same. Both the Watchers and the sinners have violated the cosmic order; cf. 2:1–5:4. What takes place in a mythical realm in 1 En 6–16 is transferred to the human realm in 1 En 1–5.

But there are some important differences. 1 En 6–16 tends to depict humans most as victims, while they are responsible for their acts in 1–5. The description of the righteous in 10:16–11:2 has a more universal outlook: "all the sons of men will become righteous," 10:21. 5:5-9 is narrower in its outlook; the chosen form a distinct group over against the sinners. And in 5:8 wisdom is promised for the chosen, a motif lacking in 10:16–11:2. It seems as if 1 En 1–5 reflects a later stage in history when the Enochians have a more distinct profile.

Three passages need special attention in regard to the Torah: 1 En 1:4, 9, and 5:4. 1 En 1:4, 9 describes a theophany where God will come with myriads of holy ones from his heavenly dwelling and tread on Mount Sinai to execute judgment. This text has two important referential backgrounds. First, the text clearly draws on motifs found in what scholars maintain is the oldest Sinai tradition.[28] God reveals himself in a theophany coming from Sinai as his dwelling to rescue his people (Judg 5:4-5; Deut 33:2; Ps 68:8-9, 18). These motifs of "the God of Sinai," theophany, and rescue are combined with the motif of judgment similar to Mic 1:3-4.

The second important background is to be found in the Journeys of Enoch, where the eschatological dwelling places of God, the righteous, and the wicked are revealed. In 1 En 25–27 two mountains are described. The first

---

26. Hoffmann, *Das Gesetz in der frühjüdischen Apokalyptik*, 129.

27. Hoffmann, *Das Gesetz in der frühjüdischen Apokalyptik*, 131.

28. F. Crüsemann, *The Torah: Theology and Social History of Old Testament Law* (Edinburgh: T. & T. Clark, 1999), 31-37; K. Koch, "Jahwäs Übersiedlung vom Wüstenberg nach Kanaan: Zum Herkunft von Israels Gottesverständnis," in *Der Gott Israels und die Götter des Orients* (Göttingen: Vandenhoeck & Ruprecht, 2007), 171-209 (here 190-92).

is "the high mountain," 25:3; the second is "the holy mountain" at the center of the earth, 26:1-2. The two mountains are clearly to be identified as Sinai and Zion.[29] Sinai seems also alluded to as the throne of God in 18:8. Both in 18:8 and 25:3 the description of Sinai has some similarities with what is said about Sinai in 1:4: it is the location of God's final theophany.[30]

The second mountain is Zion. Here the eschatological temple of God will be situated, 25:5-6, Gr[Pan]: ἐν τόπῳ ἁγίῳ, τὸν οἶκον τοῦ θεοῦ, τὸ ἅγιον, with Ethiopic equivalences. This is the eternal resting place of the righteous, 25:5-7, while the sinners after the judgment are located in the Hinnom Valley beneath, 27:2-5. The text collects from broad traditions known from the Hebrew Bible where Zion has the central role in the eschatological drama; see for instance the final section of Isaiah, 65:17–66:24.

There is accordingly no need to expect a reference to the Torah in the passage about Sinai in 1 En 1:4. The passage draws on the presumably oldest Sinai tradition where Sinai is the abode of God, who reveals himself in theophanies. There is, however, more reason to ask why only Sinai is picked up from the eschatological scenery in 1 En 25–27 and Zion left out. In a broad tradition in the Hebrew Bible it is Zion, and not Sinai, that is in the center of the eschatological drama. If there is any implied polemic in 1 En 1:4, 9, it is in the exclusion of Zion in the final judgment and salvation.

If Sinai isolated does not imply the Torah in 1 En 1:4, there is an important link from 1:4 to 1:9 and further to 5:4 that may establish a Torah reference. 1 En 1:9 concludes the theophany starting in 1:4 by underlining the wicked words and deeds of the sinners. Then the deeds of nature are listed as contrast in 2:1–5:3. In 5:4 the deeds of the sinners are picked up again, creating a bridge to 1:9.[31]

The central passage in 5:4 is commonly translated "you have not acted according to his commandments." The word "commandment" translates Ethiopic *te'zāz* and Greek ἐντολή. The Greek word is the common translation in LXX for Hebrew מצוה, the ordinary word for "commandment" that often parallels "torah" in the Hebrew Bible, frequently in Neh 8–10 (9:13, 14, 29, 34; 10:30). The terminology of 5:4 is closely connected to Sinai in 1:4. It is therefore tempting to connect Sinai and law, although one could argue that

---

29. J. J. Collins, "Before the Fall: The Earliest Interpretations of Adam and Eve," in *The Idea of Biblical Interpretation: Essays in Honor of James L. Kugel*, ed. H. Najman and J. Newman (Leiden: Brill, 2004), 293-308 (here 302-4); Nickelsburg, *1 Enoch 1*, 54f., 312ff.

30. Cf. K. C. Bautch, *A Study of the Geography of 1 Enoch 17–19*, JSJSup 81 (Leiden: Brill, 2003), 120-25.

31. Cf. Nickelsburg, *1 Enoch 1*, 157f.

the Enochic Sinaitic law had another content than the Mosaic one. Enoch would, nevertheless, have joined the Mosaic discourse.

However, enough Aramaic text survives in 4Q201, ii, 11-13 to restore a quite reasonable Aramaic wording of the passage in the transition from 1 En 5:3 to 5:4: "year [after year his works do not change], they carry out his word. However, you have changed your works [and do not carry out his word . . .]." The key words are here עובד, "work," and מאמר, "word, speech, command." There is a direct link in terminology between the word of God that nature follows in its work and the same word of God that the sinners change in their work. The concept is God's rule in nature, as it is perceived in creation hymns; cf. Pss 33:4-15 and 148:5-13. Of special interest here are two occurrences of *me'mar* in the *Targum of Job,* both related to God's rule in nature. In 11Q10, xxviii, 9 it circumscribes Hebrew קול, God's "voice" (Job 37:2); in xxxiii, 8 it translates Job's "mouth," פה, in the rhetorical question whether Job can be compared with God in power (Job 39:27). Thus *me'mar* is no technical term for law that implies a reference to the Torah on Sinai; it is a reference to the cosmic order that according to Enoch should rule both nature and human lives.

The examination of the Book of the Watchers points in two different directions concerning the temple and the law. There are enough reasons to suppose that the scribes of this book were critical toward the temple. It is no surprise that the temple is of concern since it is the basic institution of Judah that should interest scribes with priestly ambitions. The critical attitude is, however, not presented in open polemic. The critic works in a more subtle way, as we have described in the relation between master narrative and counterstory. Especially tricky here is the plot created in 1 En 12–16 where the Watchers were cast in the roles of priests who had lost their purity in the same manner as the people in stories of penitence, but were denied forgiveness and placed under condemnation.

The question of the Torah is different. As far as I can see, there is no reference to a Mosaic Torah revealed on Sinai at all. This could be seen as a deliberate denial of its legitimacy. But this would be a conclusion *ex silentio*. There is a considerable difference between the temple as the basic institution and the Torah of Moses as a literary construct, known from Neh 8–10 and the redaction activity in the formation of the Pentateuch and the Deuteronomistic Work of History. The silence about this Mosaic Torah could therefore rather be disregarded, because it had not yet gained broad authority. For the oldest part of the book it could even be ignorance, because they were not familiar with the plot created in the Deuteronomistic tradition.

I am therefore hesitant to use the relation to the Torah at this early point of the Enochic tradition as a touchstone for the relation between an Enochic group and other parts of the Judean society. I think Nickelsburg is basically right when he emphasizes that it is the special character of the Enochic revealed wisdom that makes it different from Mosaic Judaism, rather than the lack of the Torah, at least at this early point of the Enochic writings.[32] As a special kind of combination of wisdom and eschatology, the early Enochic writings belonged to a particular wisdom tradition. Only in the later development of this tradition does it meet the Mosaic Judaism, as we know it from for instance Neh 8–10, as a challenge.[33] At the beginning there was created a master narrative of the rebellion in heaven with a plot very different from the master narrative in Neh 8–10 and similar narratives in the Priestly and Deuteronomistic traditions.

The Apocalypse of Weeks

The date of the Apocalypse of Weeks (1 En 93:1-10 + 91:11-17) has been severely discussed.[34] I am inclined to think it is a separate unit incorporated into the Epistle of Enoch (1 En 92–105). Further, I think that the lack of any reference to the Maccabean revolt points to an earlier date than this revolt.[35] Accordingly, the Apocalypse is the first text known that recounts the whole history from *proton* to *eschaton*. In the narration Enoch predicts the whole of history on the basis of what is written on the heavenly tablets. The real author is to be found in the seventh of the ten weeks, thus forming the past history from the first to the seventh week as *vaticinia ex eventu* and his future

---

32. G. W. E. Nickelsburg, "Enochic Wisdom: An Alternative to the Mosaic Torah," in *Hesed Ve-Emet: Studies in Honor of Ernest S. Frerichs*, ed. J. Magness and S. Gitin (Atlanta: Scholars Press, 1998), 123-31.

33. This would be similar to the development in other wisdom traditions as they are described by Sanders, with the difference that the Enochians never adopted the Mosaic Torah in the way it was done in for instance Ben Sira; cf. J. T. Sanders, "When Sacred Canopies Collide: The Reception of the Torah of Moses in the Wisdom Literature of the Second Temple Period," *JSJ* 32 (2001): 121-36.

34. Cf. for a recent discussion, C. Berner, *Jahre, Jahrewochen und Jubiläen*, BZAW 363 (Berlin: De Gruyter, 2006), 118-25.

35. Cf. Berner, *Jahre, Jahrewochen und Jubiläen*; Nickelsburg, *1 Enoch 1*, 440f., 447-49.

"history" up to the tenth week as real predictions. This has the curious effect that the author and his circle are placed within the narrated events, and not at the end of them as is normal in narrative recalls of history.

In the recall of past history from the first to the seventh week, narrative history as we know it from the Hebrew Bible clearly forms the backbone. There are some significant parallels to the recall of history in Neh 9. First, with the distinguished place of Abraham: in both Neh 9:7-8 and in the Apocalypse, third week, 93:5, future Israel rests on the election of Abraham. Second, in the distinguished place of the Torah: in Neh 9:13-14 the revelation of the Torah on Sinai forms the center of the gracious acts of God, constituting the people. In the Apocalypse the Torah is the second founding event after the election of Abraham (fourth week, 1 En 93:6). One can discuss whether Ethiopic *šerʿat* here and in 93:4 should mean "law" or "covenant."[36] I am inclined to translate "law," since there is no reception of a covenantal terminology.[37] In any case, this is not crucial, because the Sinaitic covenant would include the Torah.

Third, in both Nehemiah and the Apocalypse there is the notion of apostasy as the people respond to the founding acts of God. In Nehemiah this starts immediately after the gift of the Torah and increases during the life in the land (Neh 9:26-29). In the Apocalypse this is concentrated in the life in the land (the sixth week, 1 En 93:8). Fourth, in both cases the apostasy led to a severe disaster as God's punishment (Neh 9:32; 1 En 93:8). Fifth, in both cases the people recounting past history are placed in a situation of transition: in Nehemiah making a vow to the Torah as the basis for a new future in the covenant with Abraham; in the Apocalypse, the seventh week, 1 En 93:10, the people reappear as the chosen through Abraham.

There are some differences between Neh 9 and the Apocalypse. Neh 9 starts with creation (9:6), which is not told in the Apocalypse. The Apocalypse recounts the flood and Noah (93:4), which is not told in Neh 9. More noteworthy, however, the Apocalypse lists the first temple as the third founding event constituting Israel (fifth week, 93:7), while the first temple is passed in silence in Neh 9 — although the cult of the second temple is rooted in the Torah in Neh 10:32-40. The structure of the story in Neh 9 is to list the founding acts of God as told in the classical credos, adding Sinai, and to contrast these acts with the apostasy of the people in the land. There they stress the negative statements known from the Deuteronomists. In this

---

36. Cf. Nickelsburg, *1 Enoch 1*, 444, 446.
37. Berner, *Jahre*, 136f.

respect the Apocalypse is more in line with the books of Kings and the Chronicler.

These differences do not disturb the unanimity of the two narrative records of history. If we regard Neh 8–10 as an example of a master narrative, the Apocalypse is an alternative narrative. Some features are included, others are neglected, but they belong to the repertoire out of which Neh 8–10 is formed. At this point the Apocalypse does not contest the communicative force of Neh 8–10. They both claim that true Israel rests on the election of Abraham and the commitment to the Torah. In this vein Hoffmann concludes that although the apocalyptics claim to be the only true interpreters of the Torah, there is no degradation of or critical attitude toward the Mosaic Torah in the Apocalypse.[38]

There are, however, some disturbing elements to be considered. The first is the communicative framework of the Apocalypse.[39] Enoch addresses his speech to his sons (4Q212, iii, 19-20 = 1 En 93:2). These sons are characterized as the "sons of righteousness, the chosen of eternity and the plant of truth"; cf. for the last נצבת יצבתא in iii, 19-20. The same wording occurs in the election of Abraham in the third week (93:5), and in the election of the chosen ones in the seventh week (93:10); cf. נצבת קשט עלמא, "plant of everlasting righteousness," in iv, 12-13. In this way the history of Israel is embedded in a speech of Enoch, drawing a line from himself and his sons to Abraham and to the chosen of the seventh week, freed from a "perverse generation."

A further complication becomes clear when we consider the structure of the whole Apocalypse. Although it is clear that the pattern of unities of seven and the number seven are of utmost importance,[40] these are not the only structuring elements. VanderKam has pointed out that besides the schemes of seven the Apocalypse is structured symmetrically in the relation between the weeks.[41] Berner has elaborated this feature.[42] The symmetrical

---

38. Hoffmann, *Das Gesetz*, 187.

39. Cf. Berner, *Jahre*, 133f.

40. Cf. K. Koch, "Sabbatstruktur der Geschichte: Die sogenannte Zehn-Wochen-Apokalypse (1Hen 93,1-10; 91,11-17) und das Ringen um die alttestamentlichen Chronologien im späten Israelitentum," in *Vor der Wende der Zeiten* (Neukirchen-Vluyn: Neukirchener, 1996), 45-76; Collins, *The Apocalyptic Imagination* (New York: Crossroad, 1987), 50f.; Collins, *Apocalypticism in the Dead Sea Scrolls* (London and New York: Routledge, 1997), 52-56; Berner, *Jahre*, 156-68; Kvanvig, "Cosmic Law and Cosmic Imbalance" (forthcoming).

41. J. C. VanderKam, "Studies in the Apocalypse of Weeks," *CBQ* 46 (1984): 511-23 (here 518-21).

42. Berner, *Jahre*, 149-55.

relationships between the weeks are, however, complex since they occur on many levels and in many details. We will here concentrate on those features we think surface in the way they make up the backbone.

In the relation between the beginning and end of the Apocalypse there is a *proton-eschaton* typology. We think this basically parallels the two first weeks with the tenth. The tenth week introduces weeks without number filled with righteousness (91:17), just as righteousness endures in the first week. The tenth week starts with the judgment of the Watchers (91:15), where the word קֵץ, "end," occurs (iv, 23). This parallels the first end in the second week (93:4).[43]

From the weeks 3-5 the founding events of the history of Israel are listed: the election of Abraham, the revelation of the Torah, and the building of the temple (93:5-7). These are foundations that are made for the future: the election of the chosen through Abraham "forever and ever" (93:5), the Torah "for all generations" (93:6), the temple "forever" (93:7). These founding events are paralleled in two ways, first negatively in the sixth week (93:8), then positively in the seventh-to-ninth weeks (93:10–91:14).

The events in the sixth week contradict what is stated about the foundational events in the three weeks before. First, all who live in this week will become blind and stray from wisdom. This contrasts the visions and the revelation of the Torah on Sinai.[44] The second contrasting element is that the temple is burnt. The third is that the whole race of the chosen plant will be dispersed. These contradictions to the everlasting election of the chosen, the Torah for all generations, and the temple forever make up the basic plot of the Apocalypse.

The tension is solved in the three following weeks, starting with the seventh week of the author and his circle. In this week the chosen will reappear (93:10); in the next week the new temple will be built (91:13). The only thing missing then is the Torah for all generations. In the ninth week *kʷennanē Ḥedeq* in Ethiopic and דִין קְשׁוֹט in Aramaic (iv, 19-20), "righteous judgment," will be revealed to all the sons of the whole earth (91:14). The same Ethiopic phrase is used about Abraham in 93:5. We do not know any places where Abraham executed judgment of any kind. What we know is

---

43. Cf. Kvanvig, "Cosmic Law and Cosmic Imbalance."

44. The blindness of the people thus relates to the Sinai events in the same manner as in the Apocalypse of Animals, 1 En 89:28-35; cf. J. C. VanderKam, "Open and Closed Eyes in the Animal Apocalypse (1 Enoch 85–90)," in *The Idea of Biblical Interpretation,* 279-92 (here 280ff.). The only difference is that the law is missing in the Apocalypse of Animals. The blindness is related to the vision of God at Sinai; cf. 89:31-33.

that he was the revealed of the books of his forefathers, including the primeval Torah in Jub 12:25-27.[45] Nickelsburg interprets the phrase in the context of Third Isaiah where all humanity will join the Torah and the covenant (Isa 56:6-7; 60; 66:18-24).[46] An allusion to the law may also be included in the phrase לארח קשט, "to the righteous way" (iv, 22), since the Hebrew equivalent דרך is often used in relation to the Torah. Accordingly, there are reasons to interpret what is revealed in the ninth week to all humanity, not only as judgment, but also as the law, which forms the basis for judgment and righteousness. But we must admit, the wording is ambiguous, since the wording from the Sinaitic Torah in 93:6 is not repeated.

It is important to notice how these reoccurrences of the chosen ones, the temple, and the righteous law are arranged. The only reoccurrence up to the time of the author is the chosen ones, to which he belongs himself. They are elected out of a perverse generation. The two other reoccurrences lie in the future. The reoccurrence of the law is especially tricky, because the terminology here is not taken from the Sinaitic Torah, but from Abraham and the chosen ones in the way these are described in the seventh and eighth week; cf. 1 En 93:10; 91:12; and iv, 12-16. The law to be revealed in the future is not any longer simply the law from Sinai, but the one rooted in the wisdom following the line from Enoch to Abraham to the chosen ones, to which the author belongs.

Election through Abraham, election through the Torah, and election through the temple are all cornerstones in the two narratives Neh 8–10 and the Apocalypse. But when we read this from the perspective of the postexilic period, we recognize that according to the Apocalypse there existed only one group of chosen ones in contrast to the rest of the people, there existed no legitimate temple, and there existed no legitimate law, at least outside the sevenfold wisdom and knowledge the chosen were provided. Thus in relation to Neh 8–10 as an example of a master narrative, the Apocalypse displays all traits of a counterstory, contesting the communicative force of the master narrative by displacing its plot. Through this displacement we must conclude that the Apocalypse did not join the Mosaic discourse in postexilic Judaism. It rather derived its authority from and lent its authority to an Enochic discourse.

45. Cf. Berner, *Jahre*, 138f.

46. Nickelsburg, *1 Enoch 1*, 449. The Aramaic דין is attested in the meaning "law"; cf. Murabb'at 20,3.8: דין משה, "law of Moses"; cf. K. Beyer, *Die aramäischen Texte vom Toten Meer* (Göttingen: Vandenhoeck & Ruprecht, 1984), 309.

The Concept of Covenant in Jubilees

William K. Gilders

I. Covenant in Jubilees: The Evidence of Jubilees 1

Covenant is a key category in the book of Jubilees.[1] Indeed, Jubilees is *fundamentally* a covenantal document.[2] In the present form of the work, the con-

---

1. This paper draws on and is in dialogue with several studies that focus in some way on covenant in Jubilees: A. Jaubert, *La Notion d'Alliance dan le Judaïsme aux abords de L'Ère Crétienne* (Paris: Éditions du Seuil, 1963), esp. 89-115; B. Halpern-Amaru, "The Metahistorical Covenant of *Jubilees*," in Halpern-Amaru, *Rewriting the Bible: Land and Covenant in Postbiblical Jewish Literature* (Valley Forge, Pa.: Trinity, 1994), 25-54; E. Juhl Christiansen, "Covenant Consciousness in the Book of Jubilees," in *The Covenant in Judaism and Paul: A Study of Ritual Boundaries as Identity Markers,* AGJU (Leiden: Brill, 1995), 67-103; J. C. VanderKam, "Covenant and Biblical Interpretation in Jubilees 6," in *The Dead Sea Scrolls Fifty Years after Their Discovery, 1947-1997: Proceedings of the Jerusalem Congress, July 20-25, 1997,* ed. L. H. Schiffman, E. Tov, and J. C. VanderKam (Jerusalem: Israel Exploration Society, 2000), 92-104; J. van Ruiten, "The Covenant of Noah in *Jubilees* 6.1-38," in *The Concept of the Covenant in the Second Temple Period,* ed. S. E. Porter and J. C. R. de Roo, JSJSup (Leiden: Brill, 2003), 167-90. See also my essay "Blood and Covenant: Interpretive Elaboration on Genesis 9.4-6 in the Book of Jubilees," *JSP* 15 (2006): 83-118.

2. *Pace* J. M. Scott, who asserts that "*Jubilees* is not so much a covenantal book as an apocalypse with a covenantal setting that inherently lends it authority" ("The Chronologies of the Apocalypse of Weeks and the Book of Jubilees," in this volume), covenant is not simply the context for the revelation to Moses but an essential element of its content. What is revealed to Moses clarifies the significance, nature, role, and place of covenant in God's dealing with the world and with Israel. As VanderKam emphasizes ("Covenant and Biblical Interpretation," 92), "Jubilees is a covenant book in its structure and in its content."

text for the revelation of the book itself is the making (or better, the remaking or the renewal) of covenant at Sinai. The date given for Moses' ascent to the top of Sinai to receive the tablets of "the law and the commandments" (prologue and 1:1),[3] the sixteenth day of the third month, is significant in this regard. That is, Moses ascended the mount the day after the covenant-making rites had been performed at the foot of Sinai on the fifteenth day of the third month, which Jubilees repeatedly identifies as the day of covenant making and for commemorating and renewing the covenant.[4]

The covenantal significance of the book is clearly expressed in Jub 1:5, where God speaks to Moses and commands him to give careful attention to all he will be told, recording it in a book for the descendants of Israel, who will, God asserts, violate the covenant God is making with them (cf. 1:7 and 1:22). Nevertheless, God makes a firm prior commitment not to break faith with them. God will not abandon the rebellious chosen people: "Write (them) in a book so that their offspring[5] may see that I have not abandoned them because of all the evil they have done in straying from the covenant[6] between me and you which I am making[7] today on Mount Sinai for their offspring."

3. Unless otherwise indicated, English translations of the Ethiopic version of Jubilees are from J. C. VanderKam, *The Book of Jubilees,* CSCO 511, Scriptores Aethiopici 88 (Louvain: Peeters, 1989). I will also refer to O. S. Wintermute's English translation ("Jubilees," in *OTP,* 2:52-142), K. Berger's German rendering (*Unterweisung in erzählender Form: Das Buch der Jubiläen, JSHRZ* 2.3 [Gütersloh: Gütersloher Verlagshaus Gerd Mohn, 1981]), and the modern Hebrew rendering by M. Goldmann ("ספר היובלים," in הספרים החיצונים, ed. Abraham Kahana, 2 vols. [Jerusalem: Makor, 1978], 1:216-313). For the Ethiopic text, I follow J. C. VanderKam, *The Book of Jubilees: A Critical Text,* CSCO 510, Scriptores Aethiopici 87 (Louvain: Peeters, 1989). For the fragmentary Hebrew manuscripts from Qumran, I have used the edition of J. C. VanderKam and J. T. Milik in *Qumran Cave 4.VIII: Parabiblical Texts, Part 1,* DJD 13 (Oxford: Clarendon, 1994).

4. On the identification and significance of the fifteenth day of the third month and of the date of Moses' ascent, see Jaubert, *Notion d'Alliance,* 103-4; VanderKam, "Covenant and Biblical Interpretation," 93; VanderKam, "Studies on the Prologue and *Jubilees* 1," in *For a Later Generation: The Transformation of Tradition in Israel, Early Judaism, and Early Christianity,* ed. Randal A. Argall, Beverly A. Bow, and Rodney A. Werline (Harrisburg, Pa.: Trinity, 2000), 266-79 (here 273-79).

5. Heb. (4Q216 I 13), דורותם, "their generations."

6. VanderKam correctly, in my view, renders the Ethiopic ሥርዐት (śer'āt) here to reflect ברית in the original Hebrew. See also Wintermute. Berger renders it "Ordnung," as if Hebrew חקה had been present. Christiansen ("Covenant Consciousness," 76 n. 35) follows Berger and makes far too much of this translation, arguing that the "covenant" referred to in Jub 1:5 is to be distinguished from what had been established at the foot of Sinai. For further discussion of "covenant" terms in Jubilees, see the appendix to this chapter.

7. Heb. (4Q216 i 14), כורת, "cutting."

The purpose of the book as a whole is to stand as a witness to the Israelites that God had remained faithful to the covenant despite their failures, that the sufferings of Israel had not been the result of divine failure, but the predicted and promised consequence of their covenant violation. Thus, when all the predicted things happen as a result of Israel's disobedience, "They will recognize that I have indeed been with them" (1:6).

The first chapter of the book is crucial for understanding Jubilees' concept of covenant. It establishes the framework of meaning. God is establishing a covenant with Israel in full knowledge that they will fail to adhere to it. But this failure has no ultimate significance, because God is committed to the relationship and knows — and makes known to Moses — that it will ultimately work: "I will neither abandon them nor become alienated from them, for I am the Lord their God" (1:18).

God's relational identity is essential to Jubilees' view of covenant; God is committed to the people, committed to being their God. Thus, in Jub 1:22-25 God responds to Moses' plea for the people begging God not to allow the predicted disasters to occur. God affirms that he knows that Israel will not obey until they have been brought to an acknowledgment of their sins. Then, when they finally turn to God, God will act to transform the people into those who are fully able to obey. This passage emphasizes the ultimate accomplishment of God's purpose and highlights the nature of the relationship God will establish. It will be a father-child bond: "I will become their father and they will become my children. All of them will be called children of the living God. Every angel and every spirit will know them. They will know that they are my children and that I am their father in a just and proper way and that I love them" (1:24b-25).

II. Relationship and Covenant

At the beginning of Jubilees God makes it clear that Israel's violation of the covenant is inevitable and fully known. God's insistence that God will not abandon the Israelites, despite their violations of the covenant, indicates that the divine commitment depends on something more fundamental than the covenant made at Sinai. It is not the covenant itself that binds God. The covenant simply expresses God's commitment. This point is reinforced and illuminated in the second chapter of the work, in a passage that relativizes the covenant, indicating that it is only the formal enactment of a divine choice made long before Israel came into existence. After establishing the Sabbath,

God announces to the angels, whom he has just commanded "to keep sabbath with him in heaven and on earth" (2:18):

> I will now separate a people for myself from among my nations. They, too, will keep sabbath. I will sanctify the people for myself and will bless them as I sanctified the sabbath day. I will sanctify them for myself; in this way I will bless them. They will become my people and I will become their God. I have chosen the descendants of Jacob among all those whom I have seen. I have recorded them as my first-born son and have sanctified them for myself throughout the ages of eternity. I will tell them about the sabbath days so that they may keep sabbath from all work on them. (2:19-20)

The culminating act of creation is God's announcement of the election of the descendants of Jacob, God's decision to establish a unique relationship with them as set apart and hallowed, like the Sabbath.[8] All that follows in the book must be read in the light of this primordial announcement, which precedes any specific enactment of a covenant and makes all such enactments dependent upon it. In short, the covenant does not create a relationship, it signals it.[9] Jubilees' adoption of the biblical father-son characterization of the covenant relationship — and its utter neglect of the marriage metaphor — is significant. Marriage is a relationship that is contractual in nature and can be dissolved. The parent-child bond, in contrast, is organic and cannot truly be broken. This view of the relationship between God and Israel is integral to its concept of covenant.

The first two chapters of the work establish that God has a master plan, which must be brought to fulfillment. The rest of the work, therefore, and what it says about covenant, must be read in the light of this key theme.

---

8. It is not accidental, therefore, that the work ends with Sabbath legislation. As the beginning of the book makes clear, the establishment of the Sabbath was the moment of God's announcement of the election of Israel, and Israel is equated with Sabbath as set apart and hallowed. While the term "covenant" is absent from the final chapter, the concept is firmly present. Observance of Sabbath marks Israel's unique relationship with God. On the Sabbath in Jubilees, and its significance for Israel's identity, see L. Doering, "The Concept of the Sabbath in the Book of Jubilees," in *Studies in the Book of Jubilees,* ed. Matthias Albani, Jörg Frey, and Armin Lange (Tübingen: J. C. B. Mohr [Paul Siebeck], 1997), 179-205 (esp. 181, 183, 201).

9. Thus, as Scott notes in his article, "the Sinaitic covenant is somewhat relativized." However, even as it is *somewhat* relativized, the covenant is made more significant by being tied to a primal, predestined relationship.

III. The Establishment of the Covenant

Following the flood, a crucial moment is reached in Jubilees. For the first time the divine plan breaks into human reality with the establishment of a covenant between God and a human being. Jubilees here follows its biblical source text very closely, for this is the first point in Genesis where a covenant is made between God and humankind. However, Jubilees significantly alters the nature of this covenant by making it the foundational iteration of the exclusive covenant with Israel.[10] God makes a covenant with Noah as the progenitor of Israel, not as the progenitor of all humankind. Again, God's foreknowledge and the primordial decision are crucial. God knows already that he will have a relationship only with Israel, and the reader of Jubilees knows this from having read the beginning of the book.

The fact that the covenant with Noah is simply the first this-worldly iteration of the covenant with Israel is emphasized by the explicit linkage made between Noah's covenant and Moses' covenant at Sinai. The angel of the presence explains to Moses that it is precisely because Noah and his sons made the covenant with an oath in the third month that Moses has done the same (Jub 6:11a). Furthermore, the blood rite of the Sinai covenant ceremony and the ongoing Israelite cultic manipulations of sacrificial blood are linked to the fundamental provision of Noah's covenant: the ban on consuming animal blood and shedding human blood (6:11b-14). Legitimate use of blood stands over against its prohibited mistreatment.[11]

In Jubilees' construction of the Noachic covenant and its connection to the Sinai covenant, the relationship between the biblical accounts of the Noachic and Sinai covenants is dialectical. It is not simply the case that the author of Jubilees interprets the Sinai covenant in the light of Noah's covenant. Rather, the Sinai covenant plays a crucial role in shaping Jubilees' conception of the covenant made immediately after the flood. Of particular significance is the representation of Noah's sacrifices as precursors to God's announcement of the covenant (Jub 6:1-4). This interpretation of the sequence of events presented in Genesis, giving them meaning, reflects the explicit juxtaposition of sacrifice and covenant-making in Exod 24:3-8. Furthermore, the assertion that Noah made his covenant with an oath depends

---

10. For Jubilees, there is really only one covenant, which reaches its complete form at Sinai. See Halpern-Amaru, "Metahistorical Covenant," 28; van Ruiten, "Covenant of Noah," 190.

11. Gilders, "Blood and Covenant," 95-96.

on the fact that in Exodus the establishment of the covenant involves several verbal declarations of commitment by the Israelites, which can be seen as oaths (see, in particular, Exod 24:7). Finally, the date of Noah's covenant depends on the dating of the Sinai covenant-making to the third month (Exod 19:1). Of course, Jubilees itself presents the influence as going entirely in the opposite direction. Everything that is described in Exodus, according to Jubilees, depends on the original covenantal event after the flood.

The common date of the two covenant events is then made by Jubilees to stem from the fact that this date had always been significant. The Festival of Shavuoth ("this entire festival") had been celebrated in heaven from the time of creation (Jub 6:18). Thus, when Noah made sacrifice in the middle of the third month to purify the earth because of its sins and to offer thanks for his deliverance, he was simply realizing on earth what had already existed in heaven. The heavenly broke into the earthly. Again, this fact must be viewed in the light of the divine intention expressed early in the book. Bringing the Festival of Shavuoth into the world and tying it to an earthly covenant is a step toward the realization of God's plan to create and maintain a unique relationship with Israel.

The narrowing of the focus of the covenant also comes out in the brief paraphrase of Gen 9:12-17 in Jub 6:15-16, where we are told that the bow in the clouds was given by God to Noah and his sons as a "sign of the eternal covenant that there would not henceforth be flood waters on the earth" (6:16). Absent from the paraphrase is the emphasis in Genesis on God's commitment to all flesh and on the bow as a means by which God would remember this commitment.

Jubilees continues by declaring, "For this reason it has been ordained and written on the heavenly tablets that they should celebrate the festival of weeks during this month — once a year — to renew the covenant each and every year" (6:17). Whereas in Genesis the covenant commitment is entirely one-sided, God promising never again to send a flood to destroy the earth, here Jubilees has the observance of a covenant-renewal festival follow as a consequence of the divine promise, precisely because God had given assurance that there would never again be a flood.

As the work continues, the relationship between the two iterations of the one covenant is further developed. Moses is made party to God's foreknowledge. Just as God knows that Israel will fail to obey the covenant, so God knew, when making the covenant with Noah, that its provisions would be abandoned and would have to be restored (6:18-19). Again, the covenant itself is no guarantee of human faithfulness, and no determinant of divine loyalty. It is simply the expression within the world of that loyalty and of the divine desire for a responding human faithfulness.

IV. The Reestablishment of the Covenant

The narrative sets out the process of human failure. Then it describes the restoration of the covenantal relationship. First, Abram shows himself to be a worthy heir to Noah. From childhood he recognizes that humanity has gone astray, and he reaches out to God in his youth (Jub 11:16-17). Finally, Abram calls out to God for guidance (Jub 12:16-21), and God responds (12:22-24). God's call to Abram begins more or less as it does in Genesis (12:1-3). But then Jubilees makes a crucial addition. God announces that he will have a special relationship with Abram and his descendants: "I will become God for you, your son, your grandson, and all your descendants. . . . From now until all the generations of the earth I am your God" (Jub 12:24). Here, crucially, God shares his primordial decision with its object and announces the relationship. The relationship now exists in human reality, and it exists apart from any formal enactment of the covenant. That formal enactment will come later.

Jub 14:1-20 is based on Gen 15:1-21 and describes the formal covenant renewal, which confirms and affirms the relationship for Abram and his descendants. The additions and modifications made to the biblical source reflect Jubilees' view of covenant. First, Jubilees gives a date for the covenant event, the middle of the third month (14:10), and makes it clear that this date is significant; the covenant is made with Abram on the same date as the covenant was made with Noah (14:20). The result is that Abram renews the lapsed covenant festival (14:20a). Indeed, Jubilees may declare that Abram's action renewed the covenant itself (14:20b).[12]

Following Noah's example, and anticipating the actions of Moses, Abram sets the stage for the renewal of the covenant by offering sacrifice, guided in this activity by God. Jubilees takes the ambiguously sacrificial ritual of Genesis and makes it unambiguously sacrificial. Abram builds an altar, and when he slaughters the specified victims he applies their blood to the altar (Jub 14:11), and at the culmination of the ritual process he offers the

---

12. The Ethiopic version, as translated by VanderKam, says that Abram "renewed the festival (በዓለ) and the ordinance (ሥርዓተ) for himself forever." Wintermute also renders ሥርዓተ as "ordinance," and Berger has "Ordnung." However, it is certainly possible to translate "covenant" here and to assume that the original Hebrew had ברית. For further discussion of this point, see the appendix to this essay.

victims up in the altar fire, along with cereal offerings and wine (14:19). Here we see again the basic pattern that is crucial for Jubilees. The enacting of covenant by God always follows from and is intimately bound up with sacrifice. In the next chapter, reflecting this pattern, Jubilees adds sacrifice where it is completely absent in the biblical source text.

V. Covenant and Circumcision

Jub 15 is based on Gen 17, a central covenantal passage in Genesis. Jubilees builds on the covenantal emphasis of the source text in some significant ways. First, as I have noted, the author adds sacrificial actions as precursors to the theophany and announcement of the covenant (Jub 15:2). Furthermore, the author provides the crucial date for Abram's sacrificial performance, the middle of the third month, in connection with the festival of firstfruits, the covenant festival (15:1). In this chapter Abram is shown as acting on his own initiative, faithfully adhering to the provisions of the renewed covenant he has inherited from Noah. He celebrates the primary festival of God's covenant (cf. 1:10) on the specified date, doing what Noah's other descendants had failed to do, thereby renewing the covenant (cf. 6:17). God's response is to renew the covenant with Abram, adding to it a provision, the sign of circumcision.

This sign, however, is not really new, as the elaboration added to the biblical source text makes clear. Circumcision, as a way to mark the elect as distinct from the rest of humankind, functions to assimilate them to the supernatural realm. The angels, according to Jubilees, were created circumcised. Circumcision of those who belong to the elect people allows them to share in this heavenly perfection (15:27).[13] Whereas in Gen 17 circumcision is a mark of membership in the chosen family of Abraham, distinguishing its members from nonmembers, in Jubilees circumcision transforms a human body to the likeness of the angelic body, effecting an ontological change. It also, even more crucially, binds the circumcised male to God: "he belongs to the Lord" (Jub 15:26b). Gen 17 makes no mention of a bond with God. Again, the covenant is not itself the relationship. It is the enactment of that relationship. God has chosen Israel to be his unique possession, to hold the sta-

---

13. Christiansen, "Covenant Consciousness," 98-99. Circumcision also protects against demonic forces. See Gianantonio Borgonovo, "Jubilees' Rapprochement of Enochic and Mosaic Traditions," *Hen* 30, no. 2 (2008).

tus of God's firstborn son. The rite of circumcision visibly marks that divine choice. It is a "rite of affirmation."[14]

Since the mark makes a divine choice effective in the world, and since the existence of the mark depends on human action, failure to obey the commandment will result in loss of the covenantal relationship. Those who are uncircumcised fail to become or remain members of the category of those who belong to God, "the sons of the covenant" (15:26a).[15] They become simply like the rest of humanity, who are doomed — by divine decree — to remain alienated from God. Moreover, those who had the potential to be "sons of the covenant" but failed to be circumcised will suffer destruction as a result of their alienation (15:26b; see also 15:34), making their fate worse than that of Gentile humanity.

Again, in giving the practice of circumcision, God knows that Israel will fail to adhere to the commandment that guarantees their covenantal identity (15:33). Dire consequences will follow for the people of Israel (15:34). But, again, this predication has to be read in the light of the guarantees expressed at the beginning of the book. God will succeed in bringing into existence an Israel capable of living in relationship with God. Then, circumcision will be faithfully observed.

VI. Jacob as the Covenantal Focus

For all his significance, Abraham is not the central focus of God's covenantal attention. Rather, it is Jacob, the eponymous ancestor of the chosen people, who is at the center of God's plan.[16] This has already been made clear in Jub 2, where God announces his election of "the descendants of Jacob" (v. 20), and it is then worked out in the parts of the book based on the Jacob narratives in Genesis.

Worthy of special note in this connection is Jub 44:1-6, which is based on Gen 46:1-4. The changes and additions made to the biblical base text reflect Jubilees' specific covenantal emphases. First, Jubilees supplies the date for the beginning of Jacob's journey to Beer Sheva — the first day of the third month — and for Jacob's sacrifices there — the seventh of the month. The text then adds

14. This is Christiansen's apt characterization ("Covenant Consciousness," 96, 101).

15. I follow Wintermute's translation here. On "sons of the covenant," see the appendix to this paper.

16. On Jacob's covenantal significance for Jubilees, see Halpern-Amaru, "Meta-historical Covenant," 36-41; Christiansen, "Covenant Consciousness," 80-82, 88-89.

the information that Jacob was hesitant to continue down to Egypt, and that he waited at Beer Sheva for some kind of divine response to his anxiety. This addition serves to explain the theophany that occurs there. In Jubilees, it comes as God's response to Jacob's hesitation. But there is more. While waiting for an answer to his concerns, Jubilees tells us, Jacob celebrated the festival of the firstfruits of wheat (using old grain, since the famine made it impossible to get new grain). Faithful to his role as the bearer of the covenantal relationship, Jacob observes the covenantal festival, which renews the covenant (Jub 6:17). Then, on the sixteenth of the month, the day after the festival, God speaks to Jacob (44:5). The pattern is familiar: the covenant festival is observed, and then God appears to enact or affirm the covenant. In this case, the connection with past covenantal theophanies is reinforced by a change the author makes to the base text. In Genesis (46:2), God speaks to Jacob in a dream. But in Jubilees (44:5), God appears to Jacob (አስተርአዮ), just as he had appeared to Abraham (cf. Jub 15:3 and Gen 17:1). Jacob experiences the same direct communication his grandfather did. While the term "covenant" does not occur in this passage, covenant is clearly its focusing concern, and this focus is affirmed by the author's reworking of the biblical source so that God's direct theophany comes, as in the past, in response to the covenantal festival.

VII. Distinctive Features of Jubilees' Concept of Covenant

The attention given to covenant in Jubilees indicates its importance to the work's author. At the same time, however, Jubilees insists that the covenant does not create God's unique relationship with Israel. Rather, it enacts that relationship, which preexists the covenant. Indeed, the relationship even preexists the people with whom the covenant is made. The offspring of Jacob are designated by God to hold the status of God's firstborn son — the heir — at the culmination of creation. Being God's son makes Israel like God. Israel's sanctification is at once a condition and result of the unique relationship. Covenant brings the relationship into temporal expression and provides the means of realizing the necessary sanctification of Israel.

The Noachic covenant is the first iteration of covenant and the *basis* of subsequent covenants, which are therefore not new covenants, but simply reiterations of that original covenant. What this means is that a covenant made — in theory — with all humankind becomes a covenant only with Israel. God's universal commitment to the whole of creation finds expression in a special commitment to one part of humanity. This commitment will never change, as Jubilees' eschatological statements make clear. The full real-ization of God's relationship with Israel will be Israel's expansion and domi-nation over the whole earth and all who are not part of Israel (see, e.g., Jub 32:18-19).

While Ps 50:5 is never directly quoted in Jubilees, the author of Jubilees would surely have affirmed its basic thrust, that covenant is made with sacri-fice.[17] Reading Gen 8:20–9:17 in the light of Exod 24:3-8, the author of Jubilees established a basic pattern: God always spoke the terms of the covenant after sacrifice had been made. This pattern shapes the retelling of several Genesis narratives. Thus, the ritual described in Gen 15 is explicitly treated as sacrifi-cial in Jubilees, and a sacrificial performance is added to the narrative of the covenant of circumcision based on Gen 17. One possible reason for this em-phasis on sacrifice is tied to the sacrificial use of blood. This legitimate use stands over against illegitimate treatment of human and animal blood, and serves as a sign and reminder of the fundamental covenantal obligation to ab-stain from shedding human blood and from consuming animal blood. It also appears that Jubilees understands sacrifice in relational terms. It is the means by which a human being expresses a desire for or a commitment to a relation-ship to God. God responds to such human overtures by affirming the desired relationship through establishing or reestablishing covenant.

Appendix: Occurrences of "Covenant" in Ethiopic and Hebrew Jubilees

By my count, the Ethiopic word ኪዳን *(kidān)* occurs a total of thirty-two times in Ethiopic Jubilees. Nineteen times it appears without a suffix (6:4, 10b, 11 [2x], 16, 17, 35; 14:18, 20 [2x]; 15:19, 26, 28, 29; 16:14; 21:11; 23:19 [2x]; 30:21); nine times with the first-person singular suffix ("my covenant"; 1:10; 15:4, 9, 11, 13, 14, 19, 21; 24:11); three times it has the third masculine singular suffix ("his covenant"; 15:34; 21:4; 22:15); and once it appears with the second masculine singular suffix ("your covenant"; 22:30).[18] In every case, it refers to a covenant between God and human beings.[19]

אספו־לי חסדי כרתי בריתי עלי־זבת .17 ("Gather to me my devoted ones, who made my covenant with sacrifice").

18. This summary of occurrences of ኪዳን corrects omissions and errors in van Ruiten's otherwise extremely helpful summary of covenantal language in Jubilees ("Cove-nant of Noah," 168-70).

19. As van Ruiten notes ("Covenant of Noah," 168), Jubilees never uses the word for a

There seems to be no dispute amongst interpreters that ኪዳን in all its occurrences in Jubilees stands for Hebrew ברית. A number of lines of evidence support this consensus. First, in the Ethiopic Pentateuch, ኪዳን frequently renders Hebrew ברית. Second, in cases where Jubilees seems to quote biblical texts directly, the Ethiopic most often has ኪዳን where the biblical source text has ברית. Third, and most decisively, a Qumran fragment of Jubilees in Hebrew reads בריתי where the Ethiopic reads ኪዳንየ.[20]

However, another Ethiopic word, ሥርዓት (śer'āt), appears several times in Jubilees where it seems reasonable to assume that the original Hebrew would have had ברית. The difficulty here is that ሥርዓት also renders Hebrew חקה, which is made clear by the fact that 4Q216 ii 8 has חקותי where the Ethiopic (Jub 1:10) has ሥርዓትየ. Thus, there are grounds for uncertainty about which word stood in the original Hebrew. As a result, scholars differ in their approach to translating ሥርዓት.

Thus, Wintermute and VanderKam both render ሥርዓት as "covenant" in Jub 1:5 and 23:16, and VanderKam retroverts the Ethiopic to הברית in his reconstruction of 4Q216 i 14, which corresponds to Jub 1:5. This move is supported by the fact that כורת appears clearly on the Hebrew fragment, and this verb commonly takes ברית as its object in the Hebrew Bible. In contrast, Berger renders ሥርዓት as "Ordnung" in Jub 1:5 and 23:16, and everywhere else it occurs in the text.

In tension with their translation of ሥርዓት in Jub 1:5 and 23:16, but in agreement with Berger's approach, Wintermute and VanderKam distinguish between ሥርዓት and ኪዳን in their translations of Jub 15. Both render ኪዳን with "covenant," but Wintermute renders ሥርዓት with "ordinance" and VanderKam uses "pact," even though the Ethiopic word stands in Jubilees where the biblical source text has ברית.

In their translation of the material added onto the biblical base text (Jub 15:25-34), they maintain this distinction, except that in 15:26 Wintermute renders ውሉደ : ሥርዓት as "the sons of the covenant" while VanderKam has "the people of the pact."

It is certainly the case that there are occurrences of ሥርዓት in Jubilees where it is unlikely or even impossible that ברית stood in the original Hebrew. However, in a number of instances it seems appropriate to conclude

---

pact or agreement between people, in contrast to Genesis, where ברית several times designates such an agreement (see Gen 14:13; 21:27, 32; 26:28; 31:44).

20. 4Q216 ii 8, as reconstructed by VanderKam, reads עזבו את [את חקותי ואת]מצותי [ואת מעד]י בריתי ואת שבתותי ואת קדשי, with בריתי in the Hebrew where the Ethiopic has ኪዳንየ.

189

that ברית did appear in the Hebrew. The Ethiopic version's use of two words to render ברית likely arose from a translator's desire for literary variation. Compare for this phenomenon Jub 6:14, where two different Ethiopic verbs are used where the Hebrew almost certainly had כפר two times (and cf. LXX Exod 29:36-37, where two different Greek verbs render כפר).[21] Note, also, that the Ethiopic version of Gen 17 uses three different words to render ברית: ኪዳን (17:2, 4, 7a, 13b, 19b, 21), ሥርዐት (17:10, 11, 13a, 14, 19a), and ሕግ (17:7b, 9).[22]

Here, I list the occurrences of ሥርዐት where I view the presence of ברית in the original Hebrew as being most likely, and indicate briefly the evidence or reasons for this conclusion.

Jub 1:5: This verse is equivalent to 4Q216 i 14, where כורת appears. The Hebrew ברית is the expected object for this verb in this context. As I noted above, Wintermute and VanderKam both render ሥርዐት here as "covenant."

Jub 14:20: This verse refers to Abram as renewing the covenantal festival in connection with God's making a covenant with him. Since the purpose of human observance of this festival, according to Jubilees, is the renewal of the covenant (6:17), it is appropriate here to see Jubilees as specifying that Abram's observance of the festival achieved this effect. Indeed, apart from using ሥርዐት instead of ኪዳን, the formulation in Jub 14:20 is identical to what appears in Jub 6:17 (see also 22:15, 30). Thus, it is appropriate to render ሥርዐት here as "covenant" and to assume that the original Hebrew had ברית.

Jub 15:6: This verse is equivalent to Gen 17:4, which has בריתי where the Ethiopic Jubilees reads ሥርዐትየ. Goldmann's Hebrew translation follows Genesis here.

Jub 15:9: This verse is equivalent to Gen 17:7, which has ברית twice. The first occurrence, בריתי, is clearly rendered by Ethiopic ኪዳንየ. The second occurrence, in the expression לברית עולם, is clearly reflected in the Ethiopic ሥርዐት ፡ ዘለዓ ለም.

Jub 15:11: This verse consists of Gen 17:9, 10b, and 11. The equivalent of Gen 17:10a is missing, almost certainly simply due to scribal error, a haplography resulting from a scribe's eye jumping from אחריך at the end of Gen 17:9 to אחריך at the beginning of Gen 17:10b, omitting everything in be-

---

21. For further detail on the different renderings of כפר in Jubilees, see Gilders, "Blood and Covenant," 98-99.

22. It should be noted that this variation cannot reflect the influence of LXX, since it is consistent in having διαθήκη throughout Gen 17.

tween. At the beginning of Jub 15:9 **ħ.ዳንየ** stands where Gen 17:9 has בריתי. The occurrence of בריתי at the beginning of Gen 17:10 is not reproduced in Jubilees due to the haplography. Gen 17:11 has לאות ברית while the Ethiopic reads **ትእምርት ፡ ሥርዓትየ ፡ ዘለዓለም**, which indicates the addition of עולם in the Hebrew text of Jubilees. Compare Jub 15:28, where we find **ትእምርታ ፡ ħ.ዳን**, which must reflect something like אות הברית הזה/הזאת.

Jub 15:13: This verse is equivalent to Gen 17:13, and there is a virtually word-for-word correspondence between the biblical Hebrew text and the Ethiopic. Thus, it is most likely that the Hebrew of Jubilees simply reproduced what appears in the biblical source, such that והיתה בריתי בבשרכם לברית עולם stands behind the Ethiopic **ወይከውን ፡ ħ.ዳንየ ፡ ውስተ ፡ ሥጋክሙ ፡ ሥርዓት ፡ ዘለዓለም**, despite the fact that the Ethiopic renders the two occurrences of ברית with two different Ethiopic terms. Compare Jub 15:19, which has **ወአቀውም ፡ ħ.ዳንየ ፡ ምስሌሁ ፡ ħ.ዳን ፡ ዘለዓለም** where Gen 17:19 reads והקמתי את-בריתי אתו לברית עולם, rendering both occurrences of ברית in this case with **ħ.ዳን**.

Jub 15:25: This is a more problematic example than those discussed above, since this verse begins the additions to the biblical base text and there is no Hebrew text with which to compare the Ethiopic. Admittedly, "ordinance" (as in both Wintermute's and VanderKam's translations) apparently makes more sense here, since the word **ሥርዓት** refers to the commanded practice (**ሕግ**) and is said to be "ordained and written on the heavenly tablets." I propose that here חקת עולם may very well have appeared in the original Hebrew.[23] However, it is worthy of note that the expression ברית עולם does appear in the Pentateuch in such a way that its meaning could be taken as "eternal covenantal ordinance" (Exod 31:16). Thus, it is possible that the author of Jubilees used it here in that sense and that the original Hebrew did read ברית [ל] עולם.

Jub 15:26: Wintermute is almost certainly correct to take **ውሉደ ፡ ሥርዓት** as standing for Hebrew בני [ה] ברית ("the sons of the covenant"), given that the term "sons" most naturally indicates membership or participation, not in the ordinance of circumcision itself, but in the covenant it serves. It is also worth noting that the Ethiopic verb used here, **ተካየደ** *(takāyada)*, usually has **ħ.ዳን** as its object.

Jub 15:28: In this verse we have **ትእምርታ ፡ ħ.ዳን**, which as I noted above must reflect something like אות הברית הזה/הזאת, followed by

23. For חקת עולם in the Pentateuch, see, e.g., Exod 12:14, 17; 27:21; 29:9; Lev 3:17; 7:36; 16:29, 31, 34; 17:7; Num 15:15; 19:10, 21.

191

ሥርዓት ፦ ዘለዓ ለም. As in 15:25, it is possible that this latter expression represents חקת עולם. However, it is also possible that the Hebrew had ברית עולם[ל], again reflecting Exod 31:16.

Jub 23:16: As I noted above, both Wintermute and VanderKam render ሥርዓት here as "covenant." This verse refers to abandoning (ኀደገ) the covenant "which God made" (ዘተካየደ ፦ እግዚአብሔር). Again, the Ethiopic uses language that refers to covenant, and this suggests that the original Hebrew read את הברית אשר כרת אלוהים.

From a Movement of Dissent to a Distinct Form of Judaism: The Heavenly Tablets in Jubilees as the Foundation of a Competing Halakah

Gabriele Boccaccini

1. Jubilees: Neither "Rewritten Torah" nor "New Torah"

In 1997 Michael Thomas Davis translated into English and made available to the international audience a 1984 Spanish article by Florentino García Martínez, which still remains the most comprehensive study on the heavenly tablets in Jubilees.[1] García Martínez pointed out that the function of the heavenly tablets in Jubilees could not be reduced to their being "the divine, preexisting archetype of the [Mosaic] Torah."[2] In most cases "the instructions contained in these tablets do not coincide with the biblical text" and introduce "new halakhot."[3] García Martínez concluded his analysis by affirming that "in more than half of the cases in Jubilees . . . the Heavenly Tablets function in the same way as the Oral Torah . . . in Rabbinic Judaism. The Heavenly Tablets constitute a hermeneutical recourse which permits the presentation of the 'correct' interpretation of the Law adapting it to the changing situations of life."[4]

---

1. F. García Martínez, "The Heavenly Tablets in the Book of Jubilees," in *Studies in the Book of Jubilees,* ed. M. Albani et al., TSAJ 65 (Tübingen: Mohr Siebeck, 1997), 243-59; in Spanish: "Las Tablas Celestes en el Libro de los Jubileos," in *Palabras y Vida,* ed. A. Vagas Machuca and G. Ruiz (Madrid: Universidad de Comillas, 1984), 333-49. For an earlier treatment of the subject, see R. Eppel, "Les tables de la Loi et les tables célestes," *RHPR* 17 (1937): 401-12.

2. García Martínez, "The Heavenly Tablets," 243.

3. García Martínez, "The Heavenly Tablets," 251 and 255.

4. García Martínez, "The Heavenly Tablets," 248.

Following García Martinez's work, in 1998 and 1999 Martha Himmelfarb, Hindy Najman, and Gabriele Boccaccini — working independently of
one another — reached strikingly similar conclusions that, while confirming
García Martínez's overall analysis of the heavenly tablets in Jubilees, pointed
to a different relationship between Jubilees and the Mosaic Torah.[5] We all
emphasized that, contrary to the rabbinic view of the oral Torah, Jubilees'
concept of the heavenly tablets was not meant to enhance the centrality of
the Mosaic Torah. In describing the attitude of the author of Jubilees, we
came to the very same conclusion, formulated even with the very same vocabulary — as a result of the introduction of the concept of the heavenly
tablets, the "uniqueness" of the Mosaic Torah was "lost," "downgraded,"
"relativized," "undermined."

Gabriele Boccaccini (1998):

> Jubilees claims that the Zadokite torah does not contain God's entire
> will; it is only one of several incomplete versions of the heavenly tab-
> lets. . . . The Zadokite torah does not even contain the entire revelation
> given to Moses; it is only "the book of the first Torah" (6:22), with Ju-
> bilees also claiming a Mosaic origin. . . . The centrality and *uniqueness*
> of the Zadokite torah are *lost* in its being only one document in a
> larger written tradition, including Enochic documents and Jubi-
> lees. . . . The heavenly tablets are the only and all-inclusive repository
> of God's revelation.[6]

Martha Himmelfarb (1999):

> The heavenly tablets serve as a source of divine authority that trumps
> the authority of the Torah. Thus they put Jubilees and the Torah on a
> similar footing. Both are subordinate to the heavenly archive that appar-
> ently contains everything that appears in either of them and more as
> well. From this angle of vision, then the existence of a heavenly proto-
> type of the Torah serves not to strengthen the authority of the Torah but

---

5. G. Boccaccini, *Beyond the Essene Hypothesis* (Grand Rapids: Eerdmans, 1998);
M. Himmelfarb, "Torah, Testimony, and Heavenly Tablets: The Claim of Authority of the
Book of Jubilees," in *A Multiform Heritage (Festschrift Robert A. Kraft)*, ed. B. G. Wright (Atlanta: Scholars Press, 1999), 19-29; H. Najman, "Interpretation as Primordial Writing: Jubilees and Its Authority Conferring Strategies," *JSJ* 30 (1999): 379-410.

6. Boccaccini, *Beyond the Essene Hypothesis*, 90, emphasis added.

to *relativize* it. . . . Jubilees suggests that even as a book of law the Torah has limitations. Not only had other books already revealed some of its contents (the same is true for Jubilees itself), but there are laws engraved on the heavenly tablets that are not to be found in the Torah. Thus Jubilees demotes the Torah by *undermining* its claims to *uniqueness* and completeness, claiming for itself a separate but equal sphere.[7]

Hindy Najman (1999):

Long before Moses ascended Mount Sinai, the calendrical and historical tradition inscribed upon the heavenly tablets was transmitted, in the form of a written tradition, to Enoch and then Noah and the patriarchs. . . . While the authority of Moses' revelation at Sinai is invoked on behalf of the solar calendar, that authority is at the same time *downgraded*. Moses was not *unique*; he was one of the many bookish heroes charged with the transcription of heavenly tablets. . . . Jubilees' insistence on the pre-Sinaitic origin of its heavenly tradition . . . *undermine[s]* the special authority that had been accorded to the Mosaic Torah.[8]

We all agreed that labeling Jubilees as "rewritten Torah" would be improper and "misleading,"[9] as the document was not "motivated by an outburst of curiosity and trust in the inexhaustible comprehensiveness of the Mosaic revelation."[10] On the other hand, Jubilees was not even the "supercanonical text" that Ben Zion Wacholder believed it to be, aimed to "replace" the Mosaic Torah as a more authoritative and reliable testimony of God's will.[11] Nothing in the text of Jubilees suggests that the Mosaic Torah should be abandoned or disregarded. "In contrast to the familiar Christian claim to supersede the Sinaitic covenant with a new covenant . . . Jubilees belongs to a family of texts that claims an equivalent or perhaps even a higher authority than that accorded to Mosaic revelation insofar as the Heavenly Tablets were

---

7. Himmelfarb, "Torah," 27-28.

8. Najman, "Interpretation as Primordial Writing," 385, 388, 410.

9. Najman, "Interpretation as Primordial Writing," 409 (*pace* J. C. Endres, *Biblical Interpretation in the Book of Jubilees,* CBQMS 18 [Washington, D.C.: Catholic Biblical Association of America, 1987]).

10. Boccaccini, *Beyond the Essene Hypothesis,* 89-90.

11. B. Z. Wacholder, "Jubilees as the Super Canon: Torah-Admonitions versus Torah Commandment," in *Legal Texts and Legal Issues,* ed. M. Bernstein et al., STDJ 23 (Leiden: Brill, 1997), 195-211.

revealed prior to Sinaitic revelation."[12] In sum: *the author of Jubilees wanted neither to strengthen the Pentateuch nor to replace it.*

At first sight the work of the author of Jubilees may appear similar to that of an exegete who "moves through the familiar texts . . . solves various problems that arise from them and at times provides longer clarifications regarding the meaning and significance of the biblical events and characters."[13] Yet, this was not the author of Jubilees' self-understanding. The document was neither a new book of Chronicles, as R. H. Charles intended,[14] nor an early midrash that makes explicit what is supposedly already implicit in the text and clarifies the unwritten, out of respect for the authority and uniqueness of the Mosaic Torah. "Unlike Chronicles, Jubilees presents itself as a revelation from an angel."[15]

Jubilees claims to contain a written tradition that predates Sinai — a tradition that started, long before the exodus, with Enoch, and was implemented by Noah, Abraham, Jacob, and Levi and his sons. This parallel written tradition was finally revealed to Moses on Mount Sinai along with the Pentateuch, or "the book of the first Torah" (Jub 6:22).

The existence of the heavenly tablets as the celestial urtext explains both the similarities and the differences between Mosaic and Enochic traditions. They are similar inasmuch as they both depend on the same source. They are different inasmuch as neither is a full copy of the celestial archetype. "Jubilees understands the Heavenly Tablets as an archive of divine knowledge. The Torah and Jubilees even in combination constitute only a limited publication of its contents."[16] The heavenly tablets, not Jubilees or the Mosaic Torah, are the only comprehensive repository of God's will.

2. Mosaic or Enochic?

What makes the book of Jubilees unique is the explicit reference to both the Mosaic Torah, the Pentateuch (a tradition that historically was handed down

12. Najman, "Interpretation as Primordial Writing," 394. See also Himmelfarb, "Torah," 28: "Wacholder's claim that Jubilees represents itself as super-canonical is inaccurate"; and J. C. Vanderkam, *The Book of Jubilees* (Sheffield: Academic, 2001), 12: "[Jubilees'] purpose was not to replace the first books of the Bible."

13. VanderKam, *The Book of Jubilees*, 12.

14. R. H. Charles, *APOT*, 2:7: "The author of Jubilees sought to do for Genesis what the Chronicler had done for Samuel and Kings."

15. VanderKam, *The Book of Jubilees*, 135.

16. Himmelfarb, "Torah," 28.

by the Zadokite priesthood), and the Enochic tradition, as preserved in the books of Enoch (a parallel pre-Maccabean tradition with strong anti-Zadokite elements).[17] In earlier texts, Mosaic and Enochic traditions show evidence of mutual influence, even competition and dissent, but as far as we know, Jubilees is the first document to mention explicitly both traditions and to address theoretically the problem of their relationship.

As with any merging of traditions, the question of which component (the Zadokite or the Enochic) prevailed in their meeting from the ideological point of view is delicate and very difficult to assess.

If we look at the *figures* of Enoch and Moses, there is no doubt that in the narrative of Jubilees the figure of Moses supersedes Enoch as the central mediator and Sinai emerges as the privileged place of revelation, as John Bergsma and Dorothy Peters correctly point out.[18] Enoch was "the first who learned writing" (Jub 4:17), but it was Moses who on Mount Sinai was the repository of both the Pentateuch and Jubilees. Moses (not Enoch) is the *trait d'union* of both traditions. The role of Enoch as revealer remains confined to progenitor of one tradition only, that of Jubilees.

On the other hand, if we look at the *ideologies* of Enoch and Moses, we have a different picture. The recognition of the primacy of Moses as the central revelatory figure does not mean uncritical acceptance of the Zadokite worldview. On the contrary, by taking up the myth of the fallen angels (Jub 7:12ff.), Jubilees shares the generative idea of Enochic Judaism, that the universe and history are under the influence of rebellious demonic forces. As a consequence, history is condemned to be a process of decline and degeneration until the time of God's final vindication — an eschatological and apocalyptic "counterstory" that is totally extraneous to the "master narrative" of the Mosaic Torah and dramatically alters its theological outlook.

In my *Beyond the Essene Hypothesis*, after stressing these many elements of continuity between the Enochic tradition and Jubilees, I concluded that Jubilees was the work of an author who, following the tradition of Enoch, succeeded "in harmonizing Mosaic revelation and Enochic revelation, and in subordinating the former to the latter."[19] In this sense I warned that the exaltation of Moses and "the acceptance of the Mosaic

---

17. G. Boccaccini, *Roots of Rabbinic Judaism* (Grand Rapids: Eerdmans, 2002).

18. John S. Bergsma, "The Relationship between Jubilees and the Early Enochic Books (Astronomical Book and Book of the Watchers)," in this volume; Dorothy Peters, "Noah Traditions in Jubilees: Evidence for the Struggle between Enochic and Mosaic Authority," *Hen* 31, no. 1 (2009).

19. Boccaccini, *Beyond the Essene Hypothesis*, 90.

Gabriele Boccaccini

revelation [i.e., the Pentateuch] must not obfuscate the real intentions of the author."[20]

Other authors have reached similar conclusions in their analyses, notably:

Andreas Bedenbender (2000)

> 1 Enoch 1–5 and the later Enoch literature testify to a process of "Mosaisierung des Wächterbuches."[21]

Helge Kvanvig (2004):

> The author mediates between two basic different attitudes toward the divine revelation, the Mosaic known from the Pentateuch, and the Enochic, known from the Enochic books. The Pentateuch is used extensively both in regard to its laws and to its narrative, that forms the backbone of the story in Jubilees, but the perspective is Enochian. . . . Jubilees mediates between the Mosaic and Enochic traditions, using Moses to emphasize the importance of Enoch.[22]

David Jackson (2004):

> Jubilees seems to be the earliest attempt to read the Mosaic Torah within the framework of the calendar and paradigm exemplars of the Books of Enoch.[23]

Paolo Sacchi (2005):

> Jubilees explicitly acknowledges the law of Moses, though considering it subordinate to the laws of the heavenly tablets which are eternal. . . . Zadokite tradition is accepted, but it is inserted into the Enochic theol-

---

20. Boccaccini, *Beyond the Essene Hypothesis*, 89.

21. A. Bedenbender, *Der Gott der Welt tritt auf den Sinai. Entstehung, Entwicklung und Funktionsweise der frühjüdischen Apokalyptik* (Berlin: Institut Kirche und Judentum, 2000), 215-30.

22. H. S. Kvanvig, "Jubilees — between Enoch and Moses: A Narrative Reading," *JSJ* 35, no. 3 (2004): 243-61 (here 260, 243).

23. D. Jackson, *Enochic Judaism: Three Defining Paradigm Exemplars* (London: T. & T. Clark, 2004), 170.

198

ogy. . . . The author's aim in Jubilees is to unify the theologies of Enochism and Zadokitism.[24]

My interest was primarily in locating Jubilees as an essential link within the chain of documents (including Enochic texts) leading more directly to the emergence of the Qumran community. What my "systemic analysis" made apparent was the growth of an intellectual movement, not the history of a single, homogeneous social group. The "Qumran chain of documents" was not intended to suggest that members of the same group wrote one after the other the entire literature. In this sense my work was an expansion and clarification of an intuition already formulated in 1958 by Frank M. Cross in the aftermath of the discovery of the Dead Sea Scrolls: "The concrete contacts in theology, terminology, calendrical peculiarities, and priestly interests, between the editions of Enoch, Jubilees, and the Testaments of Levi and Naphtali found at Qumran on the one hand, and the demonstrably sectarian works of Qumran on the other, are so systematic and detailed that we must place the composition of these works within a single line of tradition."[25]

More decidedly, David Jackson has seen in Jubilees a representative of Enochic Judaism ("It is not so much that 1 Enoch or Jubilees are works of the Qumran sect, but rather that the Qumran sectarian works are works of Enochic Judaism"),[26] a position he reiterated at the conference: "Jubilees represents a significant and groundbreaking stage of development in the early history of Enochic Judaism."

While agreeing on the existence of a very close relationship between Jubilees and Enochic Judaism, I am hesitant to follow Jackson in labeling Jubilees as one of the "works of Enochic Judaism." In spite of its anti-Zadokite attitude and its dependence on Enochic concepts, there are too many elements of discontinuity, too many things that Jubilees apparently did not like in the earlier Enochic tradition. The differences are many and profound (both John Bergsma and Annette Reed highlight them in their contributions to this volume), and all of them go in the direction of enhancing human responsibility and safeguarding the eternal validity of God's covenant with Israel.

24. P. Sacchi, "History of the Earliest Enochic Texts," in *Enoch and Qumran Origins: New Light on a Forgotten Connection,* ed. G. Boccaccini (Grand Rapids: Eerdmans, 2005), 401-7 (here 404).

25. F. M. Cross, *The Ancient Library of Qumran* (Garden City, N.Y.: Doubleday, 1958), 148.

26. Jackson, *Enochic Judaism,* 221.

Besides, while it is true that the uniqueness of the Mosaic Torah is somehow diminished in Jubilees, the same applies to the Enochic books; "no writing, Enochic or Mosaic, is the exact transcript of the Heavenly Tablets; the most that even Jubilees can do is to quote them occasionally."[27]

3. Neither Mosaic nor Enochic:
A Synthesis of Mosaic and Enochic Traditions

We then meet in Jubilees a text that merges Enochic and Mosaic traditions, a strange text in which Mosaic and Enochic elements appear side by side. If Moses is the chief revealer, Enoch can be said to be the leading theologian. If Moses is the speaker, Enoch is his ghostwriter. If Moses is the king, Enoch is his éminence grise. Jubilees is indeed a puzzling text where, as Annette Reed, in her paper presented at the conference, says, "persuasive arguments for the superiority of one [Moses] can readily be matched by persuasive arguments for the superiority of the other [Enoch]."

Maybe the problem of who prevailed (Enoch or Moses) is a false problem. Were it a game, we would say it was a tie — no clear winner, no clear loser. Is it not after all what we should expect from a well-conceived synthesis?

The Mosaic Torah is conspicuously absent in the early Enochic literature. Many scholars have tried to solve the "mystery" of this absence. In his paper presented at the conference, Helge Kvanvig is "hesitant" to infer *ex silentio* "a deliberate denial of its legitimacy," and with George Nickelsburg tends to see the lack of reference to the Mosaic Torah as a consequence of "the special character of the Enochic revealed wisdom."[28] I find these arguments persuasive and in no way contradictory to the idea that the Enochians were indeed an anti-Zadokite movement of dissent. What appears inconceivable to me is that a Zadokite priest — while offering the morning sacrifice in the temple — could preach that this world was the perfect and eternal order regulated by the Mosaic Torah and in the evening, simply to denounce priestly endogamy, contradict himself and claim that the divine order had been irremediably corrupted by the sin of fallen angels. I do not see how with Seth Schwartz we could reduce the entire apocalyptic literature to "the product of

---

27. Boccaccini, *Beyond the Essene Hypothesis*, 89; see also Himmelfarb, "Torah," 28.

28. See G. W. E. Nickelsburg, "Enochic Wisdom: An Alternative to the Mosaic Torah," in *Hesed Ve-Emet: Studies in Honor of Ernest S. Frerichs*, BJS 320 (Atlanta: Scholars Press, 1998), 123-32.

the same scribal and priestly elites and subelites who produced Jewish literature in general," and dismiss the subversive character of the Enochic literature
as a mere optical illusion, "a trick of perspective."[29] Whatever the motivations
of its promoters were, since its inception "Enochic Judaism" expressed in its
"counterstory" a paradigm of disruption that challenged the Mosaic "master
narrative" and denied the Zadokite paradigm of order.

In Collins's words,

> The idea of a movement within Judaism that is not centered on the Mo-
> saic Torah may seem anomalous in the context of the Hellenistic age, but
> it was not without precedent. The biblical wisdom literature distin-
> guished precisely by its lack of explicit reference to either the Mosaic To-
> rah or the history of Israel, and it retains this character as late as the book
> of Qoheleth, which may be roughly contemporary with the early Enoch
> literature. . . . Judaism in the early second century BCE was not uniformly
> Torah centered, even among those who were familiar with the Torah and
> respected it as one source of wisdom among others. I would agree then,
> with Boccaccini and others, that the Enoch literature reflects a distinctive
> form of Judaism in the late third/early second century BCE.[30]

While "the invocation of the pre-diluvian Enoch rather than Moses as
the revealer of essential wisdom" is one of "the distinguishing traits of this
form of Judaism,"[31] it would be incorrect, however, to talk of Enochic Judaism
as "a Judaism without the Torah." The problem was not the Mosaic Torah; "at
no point is there any polemic against the Mosaic Torah."[32] The concern of the
Enochians was rather their own victimization, which they took as a paradigm
of the victimization of all of humankind. A group of priests who felt excluded
from, or marginalized within, the Zadokite priesthood gave cosmic dimension
to their exclusion. From their self-understanding they derived the impossibil-
ity of following any laws (including the Mosaic Torah) in a universe that had

---

29. S. Schwartz, *Imperialism and Jewish Society, 200 BCE to 640 CE* (Princeton: Princeton University Press, 2001), 15, 2. E. P. Sanders also viewed Jubilees as representative of "common Judaism"; see E. P. Sanders, *Paul and Palestinian Judaism* (Philadelphia: Fortress, 1977),
362-86.

30. J. J. Collins, "How Distinctive Was Enochic Judaism?" in *Meghillot: Studies in the
Dead Sea Scrolls V-VI*, ed. M. Bar-Asher and E. Tov (Haifa: University of Haifa, 2007), 17-34
(here 32-33).

31. Collins, "How Distinctive," 33.

32. Collins, "How Distinctive," 31.

been disrupted by the presence of evil. In my opinion, this is the reason why there is no explicit anti-Mosaic polemic and, as Kvanvig says, "there is no Enochic purity code, no Enochic Torah." The wisdom the Enochians received prevented them from developing any competing halakah. Their revelation was telling them that the world was not what it should have been.

Grant Macaskill emphasizes that "Enochic Judaism and Zadokite Judaism had actually much more common ground" than generally thought.[33] I think he is correct. Yet, this does not eliminate the Enochic nonconformist attitude. Two groups that share the same priestly worldview and — ideally — the same halakah may well find themselves at odds with each other. While opposing the Zadokite leadership, *the early Enochians were not competing with Moses, they were merely complaining*. They saw an illegitimate priesthood serving in the temple and evil spreading on earth out of God's control. Contrary to what the Zadokites claimed, they concluded that the Law of Moses was not ruling on earth. As long as the Mosaic Torah was the law of the Zadokite priesthood, any rapprochement was impossible.

The Maccabean revolt marked a turning point. Ironically, the tragic events of those years helped strengthen both Enochic and Mosaic traditions.

On one hand, the collapse of the Zadokite order and the hardship of the persecution confirmed the Enochic view that the world was profoundly corrupted and evil. The legitimacy of the Zadokite priesthood relied essentially on their continuous success; their downfall proved their illegitimacy.

On the other hand, the Mosaic Torah underwent a radical transformation from being the law of the ruling priesthood to becoming the national law of Israel. "The greatness of the Maccabees was to present themselves not as the leaders of a rival priestly family, as they were, but as champions of the national tradition against the Greeks. . . . It was through the experience of the Maccabean revolt that the Zadokite torah became the Jewish torah *tout court* as the essential element of Jewish national identity."[34] It was now possible to be "pro-Mosaic" without being "pro-Zadokite."

The new situation opened the path to a process of rapprochement between Enochic and Mosaic traditions, which is evident in many sources of the period, including Enochic literature. The books of Daniel and Dream Visions offer examples of texts where Mosaic and Enochic traditions are integrated. But neither text produced a real synthesis.

33. Grant Macaskill, "Priestly Purity, Mosaic Torah, and the Emergence of Enochic Judaism," *Hen* 31, no. 1 (2009).
34. Boccaccini, *Beyond the Essene Hypothesis*, 91.

In Dream Visions the Mosaic Torah simply offers the historical framework that supports the Enochic principles of degeneration. Israel is affected by evil as much as anyone else. There is no alternative halakah. There is only the repeated message that being righteous, or doing any good, is a difficult if not impossible task because of the corruption of the universe. Evil is a sort of genetic disease that spreads generation after generation, and there is no medicine. The righteousness of the chosen people may make them better off than the rest of humankind (they are "sheep" instead of "camels" or "elephants"), but it does not absolutely spare them from evil (they have lost their original nature of "bulls" and are ruled by demonic forces).

Daniel does not present his "wisdom" as a new revelation but as a post-Sinaitic "interpretation." This interpretation includes even the full understanding of the true meaning of ancient Scriptures (in Dan 9 the seer understands Jeremiah in light of Lev 26). Daniel is in no way the recipient of an oral or written tradition that parallels Scripture. Daniel is a post-Sinaitic prophet, who lived long after Moses and the Torah. Its wisdom challenges neither the legitimacy of the Zadokite priesthood nor the centrality of the Torah. It neither replaces nor downplays the Torah; it interprets the Torah. Some key principles of Enochic Judaism (degeneration of history, demonic forces, end of times, etc.) are introduced as if they were inherent to Scripture.

4. A Sectarian-Born Movement, Eager to Become Normative

While Dream Visions and Daniel provide evidence of a merging of Enochic and Mosaic traditions, neither offers a real synthesis in which both Enoch and Moses maintain their autonomy and legitimacy. In the name of Moses only, Daniel reaffirmed the validity of the Mosaic halakah and defended the Zadokite priesthood but could only offer a perspective of suffering and martyrdom in this world. In the name of Enoch only, Dream Visions reiterated the criticism toward the Zadokite priesthood and its skepticism on the effectiveness of the Mosaic halakah but offered no alternative halakah if not the hope for God's eschatological intervention.

Not everybody was persuaded. In the aftermath of the Maccabean revolt a group of priests (influenced or inspired by Enochic principles) saw in the demise of the House of Zadok not only the confirmation of their anti-Zadokite attitudes but for the first time the concrete possibility of building a positive alternative in this world. In their understanding, the Maccabean experience proved that the world was as evil as the earlier Enochic tradition

claimed but the situation was not as hopeless. They did not deny that demons played a very important role in bringing evil to earth — who could
have denied it in the wake of the tragedy of those days? — yet they claimed
that the demons' role was limited to the outside world and to the traitors of
Israel.[35] The "true" Israelites had after all the possibility to take their destiny
in their own hands, provided they remained separated from the impurity of
the Gentiles.

The balanced synthesis of Enochic and Mosaic elements allowed them
to transform what was a tiny movement of dissent and protest of disenfran-
chised priests into a new form of Judaism, "a form occupying a space between Enochic and Zadokite Judaism,"[36] which (being both Zadokite *and*
Enochic) should no longer be labeled *either* Zadokite *or* Enochic. In the
name of Moses and Enoch, Jubilees could strengthen God's control over the
universe through a strict historical and calendrical determinism, while
maintaining the idea of corruption and decline of history. By making God's
covenant with Israel not a historical deal but one of the unchangeable and
preordained rules of the universe, Jubilees made a strong point that the sin
of the fallen angels had not destroyed the uniqueness of the chosen people
but affected only the rest of the world. As the covenant was unconditionally
offered (the Jews are born in the covenant) and no corruption had disrupted
the covenant, the problem was now how to remain blameless in the covenant
in a corrupt world.

That is the great genius of Jubilees. The covenant stands firmly not *because* the universe is uncorrupted and incorruptible (as the Zadokites
claimed) but *in spite of* the corruption of the universe. Contrary to the
Enochic tradition, Israel is not defenseless. There is a "medicine" given to the
sons of Noah and the covenant embraces and protects the circumcised Jews,
unless they expose themselves to the impurity of the outside world that is
dominated by evil forces. As the chosen people are subjected to the demons
only if they do not follow God's will, the path is opened to a discussion on
which behavior should be kept in order "to stay in" and which behavior instead causes apostasy and leads Israel "out." The "shift in focus: from the
threat of demons to the danger of associating with Gentiles," which Reed
highlighted at the conference, is a shift from a passive to a proactive attitude
toward the presence of evil that early Enochians had so dramatically de-

---

35. J. C. VanderKam, "The Demons in the 'Book of Jubilees,'" in *Die Dämonen*, ed.
Armin Lange et al. (Tübingen: Mohr Siebeck, 2003), 339-64.

36. Sacchi, "History," 404.

nounced — a shift that lays the foundations for the development of an alternative halakah (what the Enochians had never done before). Jubilees overcomes the sense of despair and hopelessness of the Enoch literature and calls people to follow alternative rules. Whoever was behind Jubilees, they were tired of only complaining and being resigned, and much more eager to compete aggressively.

The concept of the heavenly tablets is at the foundation of the entire ideological building of Jubilees. It was the cornerstone that made possible a synthesis of Enochic and Mosaic principles, where both components were given equal dignity. It was the foundation that made possible the development of a competing halakah, which was not completely separated from the Mosaic Torah, while able to "correct" and integrate many of the key elements of the Mosaic tradition (calendar, purity laws, etc.).

5. A Reform Movement, Becoming (against Its Hopes) Partisan (and Sectarian)

All interpreters recognize that the author of Jubilees addresses himself to the Jewish people as a whole (not to a minority group or a group of chosen among the chosen).[37] As Regev presented at the conference, "Jubilees represents a group which aims to change society rather than withdraw from it." In the aftermath of the Maccabean revolt, this attitude left open three outcomes:

a. If Jubilees' program were accepted by the majority of the Jewish people (as the author obviously expected), Jubilees and its halakah would become normative.

b. If Jubilees' program gained no significant acceptance (in spite of the author's confidence), the movement would disappear in total failure.

c. If Jubilees' program were embraced only by a militant minority, it would survive as the platform of a party or a sect, distinguished or separated (more or less radically) from the rest of the people.

The study of second temple Judaism tells us that Jubilees never reached an undisputed status of Scripture, comparable to that of the Pentateuch. A clear distinction must be made between what Jubilees wanted to be and what it

37. M. Himmelfarb, "Jubilees and Sectarianism," in *Enoch and Qumran Origins: New Light on a Forgotten Connection,* ed. G. Boccaccini (Grand Rapids: Eerdmans, 2005), 129-31.

was. Jackson is correct when he maintains that recognizing the "nonsectarian" or "presectarian" character of Jubilees does not mean to state that the document was normative, widespread, common to all Jewish groups of the time, or representative of the common Jewish heritage in second temple Judaism.[38] On the other hand, the popularity of Jubilees, far beyond the many copies found at Qumran and vicinity, does prove that its legacy survived in influential circles of second temple Judaism, not only in sectarian cliques. Born to be a normative text, Jubilees did not gain universal recognition. Used in sectarian milieus, Jubilees was not restricted to them. The alternative is not between being "normative" and being "sectarian." Jubilees was neither; it lived the glorious career of a "partisan" text.

Since the beginning of modern research on Jubilees, scholars have tried to identify the "party" that produced and transmitted Jubilees. The priestly character of the text made some of the earlier interpreters, such as Rudolf Leszynsky and George Herbert Box, look at Jubilees as a Sadducean text.[39] But the obvious priestly character of Jubilees does not necessarily indicate continuity with the Zadokite tradition, while the emphasis on the solar calendar and the particularities of Jubilees' halakah shows that the document was at odds with the ruling authorities of the Jerusalem temple.

As we have seen, Florentino García Martínez (who wrote his article in the early 1980s) stressed the similarities between the function of the heavenly tablets in Jubilees and that of the oral Torah in rabbinic literature (*Aboth* 1:1) and of the "teachings of the fathers" of the Pharisees (Josephus, *Ant* 13.297). There was in fact a long tradition connecting Jubilees with the Pharisees, a tradition that started with August Dillmann, the father of modern research on the document, and was consolidated by the two most distinguished interpreters and translators of Jubilees of the early twentieth century, François Martin and Robert Henry Charles.[40] The discovery of the Dead Sea Scrolls made it apparent that the written tradition of Jubilees contained halakah that in no way was compatible with that of the Pharisees.[41] But for some

---

38. Jackson, *Enochic Judaism*, 2-13.

39. R. Leszynsky, *Die Sadduzäer* (Berlin: Mayer & Müller, 1912), 179-236; G. H. Box, "Introduction to the Book of Jubilees," in R. H. Charles, *The Book of Jubilees or the Little Genesis* (London: SPCK, 1917), vii-xxxiii.

40. Charles, *APOT*, 2:1-82; F. Martin, "Le Livre des Jubilés. But et procédés de l'auteur. Ses doctrines," *RB* 8 (1911): 321-44, 502-33; A. Dillmann and H. Rönsch, *Das Buch der Jubiläen* (Leipzig: Fues, 1874).

41. E. Rivkin, "The Book of Jubilees: An Anti-Pharisaic Pseudepigraph," *ErIsr* 16 (1982): 193-98.

time Jubilees continued to be commonly presented, if not as a Pharisaic text, as the precursor of rabbinic haggadah or at least a testimony of the antiquity of the rabbinic concept of the oral Torah.[42]

However, both the "teachings of the fathers" of the Pharisees and the rabbinic concept of the oral Torah are asymmetrical terms of comparison. The "teachings of the fathers" are said to be handed down in an oral (not written) fashion by "a chain of tradition" but are not said to derive from a heavenly archetype or to be revealed on Mount Sinai. Not even the core of the Mishnah makes this claim, except for a few halakoth. It is only with *Aboth* that for the first time we have the idea that "the teachings of the fathers" are also "Torah," which will lead to the development of the rabbinic concept of the "dual Torah," as the oral and written sides of the "preexistent Torah."[43] But for Jubilees what is preexistent are the heavenly tablets, not the Mosaic Torah. On Mount Sinai Moses received "two" *written* traditions, both of them equally based on the same heavenly urtext. As Najman has effectively pointed out, the opposite metaphors of "orality" and "writtenness" highlight more than anything else the different attitudes and strategies of Jubilees and the rabbis while facing "the complex relationship between the authority of sacred writing and the authority of interpretation."[44]

To better understand the place of Jubilees in ancient Jewish thought, we have to look elsewhere. From ancient Jewish sources we know that there was a group of Jews who in the second century B.C.E. parted from the rest of the people. They were called "Essenes." The striking ideological similarities between Jubilees and the Essenes did not go unnoticed even before the 1950s by authors like Adolf Jellinek and Abraham Epstein,[45] and were only strengthened by the discovery of the Dead Sea Scrolls.[46] James VanderKam's consistent conclusion since his earliest studies in the 1970s that "the author belonged to or was an immediate forerunner of the branch of Judaism that

42. Joseph P. Schultz, "Two Views of the Patriarchs: Noachides and Pre-Sinai Israelites," in *Text and Responses: Studies Presented to N. N. Glatzer*, ed. M. A. Fishbane (Leiden: Brill, 1975), 41-59; S. Tedesche, "Jubilees, Book of," *IDB* 2 (1962), 1002-3.

43. M. S. Jaffee, *Torah in the Mouth: Writing and Oral Tradition in Palestinian Judaism, 200 BCE–400 CE* (New York: Oxford University Press, 2001); G. Boccaccini, "The Preexistence of the Torah: A Commonplace in Second Temple Judaism, or a Later Rabbinic Development?" *Hen* 17 (1995): 329-50.

44. Najman, "Interpretation as Primordial Writing," 410.

45. A. Jellinek, *Über das Buch der Jubiläen und das Noah-Buch* (Leipzig: Vollrath, 1855); A. Epstein, *Beiträge zur jüdischen Althertumskunde* (Vienna: Lippe, 1887).

46. M. Testuz, *Les idées religieuses du livre des Jubilés* (Geneva: Droz, 1960).

we know as Essene,"[47] as well as Lawrence Schiffman's statement that "the high status accorded to this work by the Qumran sect" demonstrates that it was composed by "circles the sect regarded as its spiritual forerunners,"[48] are eloquent evidence of the current consensus in contemporary scholarship. Jubilees is a key text in second temple Jewish history and literature as it testifies to the very beginning of the Essene movement.

What has changed and is changing in our understanding of these complex phenomena is a new, growing awareness of the Enochic roots of Jubilees — an element that in the past was already suggested by the seminal yet then isolated voices of Benjamin Bacon and Chanoch Albeck.[49] García Martínez's article, published in 1984 after James VanderKam's studies and Paolo Sacchi's commentary, signals the turning point in contemporary research.[50] While still honoring the then general consensus of a relationship between Jubilees and the rabbinic concept of the oral Torah, García Martínez highlighted with equal vigor "the dependency of Jubilees upon the Enochic literature, from which is derived the notion of the Heavenly Tablets as a Book of Destiny in which is not only found the inscription of human evil or good, but the complete course of history."[51] In recent years the "Enochic perspective" has become the recognized starting point of any research in the interpretation of Jubilees, receiving new strength and meaning also by a new, growing awareness of the role played by Enochic literature in Essene and Qumran origins.[52]

We can now look with different eyes also at the testimony of Josephus and Philo.[53] Not surprisingly, they say that the Essenes venerated Moses as "the lawgiver" (*Jewish War* 2.145; *Apologia pro Judaeis* 1), thus emphasizing — as in Jubilees — the primacy of the *figure* of Moses over against Enoch. Second, Josephus claims that at the center of Essene thought was the concept of historical determinism (*Ant* 13.171-172) while Philo maintains that they at-

---

47. VanderKam, *The Book of Jubilees*, 143; see already his *Textual and Historical Studies in the Book of Jubilees* (Missoula: Scholars Press, 1977).

48. Cf. also L. H. Schiffman, *Reclaiming the Dead Sea Scrolls* (New York: Doubleday, 1995), 188.

49. C. Albeck, *Das Buch der Jubiläen und die Halacha* (Berlin: Scholem, 1930); B. W. Bacon, "The Calendar of Enoch and Jubilees," *Hebraica* 8 (1892): 124-31.

50. J. C. VanderKam, "Enoch Traditions in Jubilees and Other Second-Century Sources," in SBLSP (1978), 229-51; P. Sacchi, "Libro dei Giubilei," in *Apocrifi ell'Antico Testamento* 1 (Turin, 1981), 179-411.

51. García Martínez, "The Heavenly Tablets," 258.

52. See Boccaccini, *Enoch and Qumran Origins*.

53. For a detailed analysis of Josephus's and Philo's testimony on the Essenes, see my *Beyond the Essene Hypothesis*.

tributed no evil to God (*Quod omnis probus liber sit* 84), thus emphasizing the primacy — as in Jubilees' intellectual discourse — of the *ideology* of Enoch, which is so distinctively marked by the contemporaneous stress on human responsibility and victimization. But even more significantly, Josephus adds that the Essenes were the only group to have "books of their own" (*Jewish War* 2.142), thus giving evidence to their *synthesis* of *written* traditions — a claim that in second temple literature is for the first time explicitly stated by Jubilees (and only later in 4 Ezra 14:45-48).

6. Conclusion

A new scenario is before us. Far from being a group of nostalgic Zadokites,[54] the Essenes were a group of priests that like the earlier Enochians had no appreciation whatsoever for the role of the House of Zadok in the early second temple period and no regret for their demise, but being faithful to the Torah, they did not want to give up the uniqueness and effectiveness of the Mosaic covenant with Israel and leave evil the full control of this world. At the center of their revolution was the concept of the heavenly tablets, which allowed them to take what they deemed was the best of both Moses and Enoch. By making the covenant part of God's eternal order, they gave Israel a sacred haven surrounded by strong protective walls, a niche of safety as long as they would keep themselves separated from the rest of the evil world. Unlike the Enochians, they believed the Israelites were given rules to follow that could effectively protect them from impurity and evil, as long as they would keep them. Unlike the Zadokites, they did not have to maintain against all evidence that this world was God's perfect world.

The book of Jubilees was their creed and public manifesto, their religious and political platform. In the aftermath of the Maccabean revolt, they hoped to become the new leadership in the temple and in the Judean society. They did not succeed, but they did not give up either. As Essenes they would soon learn how to live separated from the rest of the people, as a minority, self-proclaimed party of "chosen among the chosen," if not as the sect of the only "children of light." Like in a besieged city surrounded by multiple walls against powerful demonic enemies, they retreated to the citadel when they saw the outer wall breached or on the verge of collapse (a group of them

---

54. *Pace* H. Lignée, "La place du livre des Jubilés et du Rouleau du Temple dans l'histoire du mouvement essenien," *RevQ* 13 (1988): 331-45.

even fled to the wilderness of Judah). Whatever city of refuge they chose, there they kept those practices that in their opinion guaranteed the integrity of the covenant and the survival of the chosen people, patiently waiting for the time God would vindicate their righteousness and faithfulness — a time they hoped for for centuries and never saw.

Abram's Prayer: The Coherence
of the Pericopes in Jubilees 12:16-27

Jacques van Ruiten

In this contribution I will concentrate on the prayer of Abram and the surrounding events in the book of Jubilees (12:16-27).[1] To be able to address the question of coherence and tradition of this passage, I will first distinguish the smaller pericopes from each other within this passage on the basis of their use of words and theme. I will then try to show how they are interrelated. Finally, I will look into the way Jub 12:16-27 is embedded in the book and try to identify the traditions within this passage.

1. The Pericopes in Jubilees 12:16-27

The events that take place around Abram's prayer (12:16-27) can be divided into four pericopes: (a) Abram observes the stars (vv. 16-18); (b) Abram's prayer (19-22a); (c) God's answer (22b-24); and (d) Abram learns Hebrew (25-27). With the exception of the third pericope, which is a rewriting of Gen 12:1-3, these pericopes can be considered additions to the biblical text of Genesis. They are distinguished from each other by subject and the repetition of words. Because of the length of the passages as a whole, I will present first the text of the smaller pericopes, followed by a short description of the literary unity of each pericope with regard to subject and use of words. For

1. I will speak consistently about Abram, since his name is changed to Abraham only in Gen 17:5 (Jub 15:7).

12:22-24 I will also go into the rewriting of the biblical text. After this, I will deal with the coherence of the four pericopes as a whole.

Jubilees 12:16-18 (Abram observes the stars)[2]

16a   In the sixth week, during its fifth year, Abram sat at night — at the beginning of the seventh month — to observe the stars from evening until morning in order to see what would be the character of the year with respect to the rains.

b   He was sitting

c   and he was observing.

17a   A voice came in his heart

b   and he said:

c   "All the signs of the stars and signs of the moon and the sun — all are in the hand of the Lord.

d   Why am I seeking?

18a   If he wishes

b   he will make it rain in the morning and evening;

c   and if he wishes,

d   he will not make it fall.

e   Everything is in his hand."

This first small passage shows the following repetition of words and phrases: "stars" (12:16a, 17c); "to observe" (12:16a, 16c); "signs" (12:17c); "evening" and "morning" (12:16a, 18b); "rain" (12:16a, 18b); "to sit" (12:16a, 16b); "all / everything is in his hand" (12:17c, 18e); and "if he wishes" (12:18a, 18c). The direct speech (12:17c-18) can be characterized as a monologue (12:17a: "A voice came in his heart"). Unlike the narrative context, the direct speech shows a poetical structure in that there is balance between the lines. Within this structure 12:17c ("all are in the hand of the Lord") balances with 12:18e ("Everything is in his hand"). In between these lines, there are two sentences with an identical beginning (12:18a, c: "if he wishes") followed by an antithetical effect (12:18b, d). It is striking that 12:17d ("Why am I seeking?") is not balanced by another line. In this way it acquires a certain emphasis.

---

2. The translation is based on J. C. VanderKam, *The Book of Jubilees, II*, CSCO 511, Scriptores Aethiopici, 88 (Louvain: Peeters, 1989). However, I feel free to deviate from this translation to do justice to the repetition of words.

Jubilees 12:19-22a (Abram's prayer)

19a   That night he prayed

b   and he said:

c   "My God, my God, God most High,

d   You alone are my God.

e   You have created everything;

f   Everything that was and has been is the work of your hands.

g   You and your kingdom I have chosen.

20a   Save me from the hand of the evil spirits who rule the thoughts of the people's heart.

b   May they not lead me astray from following you, my God.

c   Do establish me and my seed until eternity.

d   May we not go astray from now until eternity."

21a   And he said:

b   "Shall I return to Ur of the Chaldeans who are seeking me to return to them?

c   Or am I to sit here in this place?

d   Make the path that is straight before you prosper through the hand of your servant so that he may do (it).

e   May I not proceed in the going astray of my heart, my God."

22a   He finished his speaking and his praying.

This second passage is introduced with a form of "to pray" (12:19a). It also ends with a form of "to pray" (12:22a). Abram's prayer can be subdivided into two units: 12:19-20 and 12:21, with both units introduced by "and he said" (12:19b, 21a). The prayer consists of a combination of a hymn (12:19c-f) and a supplication (12:20a-d, 21d-e). The prayer also includes a question that cannot be characterized as a supplication (12:21bc). This passage shows the following repetition of words: "to pray" (12:19a, 22a); "hand" (12:19f, 20a, 21d); "to go astray" (12:20b, 20d, 21e); "until eternity" (12:20c, 20d); "return" (12:21b [2x]); "my God" (12:19c [2x], 19d, 20b, 21e); and "heart" (12:20a, 21e). The prayer has a poetical structure in that two subsequent lines are balanced by each other with regard to the use of words and contents (12:19c and 12:19d; 12:19e and 12:19f; 12:20a and 12:20b; 12:20c and 12:20d; 12:21b and 12:21c; 12:21d and 12:21e).[3] Also in this passage is one unbalanced line (19g: "You and your kingdom I have chosen").

---

3. The passage shows *parallelismus membrorum*, which is characteristic of the prosodic structure of poetry in the Hebrew Bible.

The third pericope, in which God answers Abram's prayer, can be considered a rewriting of Gen 12:1-3, the call to go to Canaan. Therefore, I will now put both texts side by side.[4]

Genesis 12:1-3		Jubilees 12:22b-24 (God's answer)	
1a	*And the Lord said to Abram:*	22b	*And behold, the word of the Lord was sent to him through my hand, saying:*
1b	*"Go from* your land and your family and your father's house to the land that I will show you.	c	*"Now you, come* from your land, from your family, and your father's house to the land that I will show you.
2a	I will *make* of you a great [ ] people.	d	I will *establish* you into a large AND POPULOUS people.
2b	I will bless you,	23a	I will bless you,
2c	and make your name great.	b	and make your name great.
2d	You will become a blessing [ ].	c	You will become blessed IN THE LAND.
		d	<u>All the *peoples* of the land will be blessed in you.</u>
3a	I will bless those who bless you,	e	Those who bless you I will bless,
3b	and *him* who curses you I will curse;	f	and *those* who curse you I will curse.
3c	<u>and all the *families* of the land will be blessed in you."</u>		
		24a	I WILL BECOME GOD FOR YOU, YOUR SON, YOUR GRANDSON, AND ALL YOUR SEED.
		b	DO NOT BE AFRAID.
		c	FROM NOW UNTIL ALL THE FAMILIES GENERATIONS OF THE LAND I AM YOUR GOD."

4. In the following synoptic overview, I have tried to present a classification of the similarities and dissimilarities between Genesis and Jubilees. I have used small caps to highlight those elements of Genesis that do not occur in Jubilees, and vice versa, i.e., the omissions and additions. I have used "normal script" for the corresponding elements between both texts, i.e., the verbatim quotations of one or more words from the source text in Jubilees, besides additions or omissions. Sometimes there is a rearrangement of words and sentences. I have underlined those elements.

The third pericope, in which God answers Abram's prayer, can be considered a rewriting of Gen 12:1-3, the call to go to Canaan. This passage shows the following repetition of words: "to bless" (12:23a, 23c, 23d, 23e [2x]); "to curse" (12:23f); "land" (12:22c [2x], 23c, 23d, 24c); "I will become God for you" (12:24a; cf. 12:24c); and "family" (12:22c, 24c ["generations"]). The poetical structure of the passage is reflected in the balance between the two subsequent lines (12:22c and 12:22d; 12:23a and 12:23b; 12:23c and 12:23d; 12:23e and 12:23f; 12:24a and 12:24c). One line is not balanced, namely, 12:24b ("do not be afraid").

With regard to the text of Gen 12:1-3, Jub 12:22b-24 shows additions (12:22d; 12:23c; 12:24), variations (12:22b, 22d), and rearrangement (12:23d). Jub 12:22b can be considered a variation of Gen 12:1a. In fact, it also has some additions: "and behold"; "the word of"; and "saying," in addition to the variation "was sent through my hand" instead of "said," and "to him" instead of "to Abram." This rewriting results in an avoidance of a direct contact between God and Abram. It is the angel who mediates between them. This mediation occurs also in the addition 12:25-26. In Jub 13:3 (cf. Gen 12:7), just after Abram entered the land of Canaan, the Lord here speaks directly to Abram without the intermediary of an angel. From then onward God addresses himself directly to Abra(ha)m.

Jub 12:22d uses the word "to put; to establish" *(rassaya)*, where Gen 12:2a has "to make" (עשה; LXX: ποιέω). The same word is used in Abram's prayer (12:20c). Possibly the use of *rassaya* has been influenced by the blessing in Gen 13:16 ("I will establish [שׂום] your descendants like the dust of the earth") for which Jub 13:20b reads: "I will establish [*rassaya*] your descendants like the sands of the sea."[5] Also, the addition "and populous" in Jub 12:22d is possibly influenced by a parallel passage. I refer to Gen 18:18 (לגוי גדול ועצום: "a great and populous people"). Also, one textual witness of the Septuagint Gen 12:2a (*d* 458) adds "and populous" (καὶ πολύ).[6]

Jub 12:23c shows a combination of variation ("blessed" instead of "a blessing") and addition ("in the land"). This transformation stresses the fact that Abram is the one who is blessed. It does not focus on his role as being a

---

5. See also Gen 21:18 ("I will make him [אשׂימנו] a great nation," where Jub 17:7 reads: "I will make him [*rassaya*] into a great nation"). Compare Gen 46:3 ("for I will there make of you [אשׂימך] a great nation," where Jub 44:5 reads: "I will make [*sar'a*] you into a great nation there"), but the difference between the Ethiopic verbs *rassaya* and *sar'a* seems to be very small. Cf. VanderKam, *Book of Jubilees, II*, 289.

6. Cf. VanderKam, *Book of Jubilees, II*, 73.

blessing *for others,* as can be argued from Gen 12:2d.[7] Moreover, Jubilees adds that Abram is blessed *wǝsta mǝdr,* which I have translated here (and in 12:23d) as "in the land."[8] This is in conformity with the translation of *mǝdr* in 12:22c. Moreover, both in Genesis and in Jubilees the blessing of Abram is related to his entrance into the land. Both in Genesis and Jubilees the promise of an abundance of offspring is combined with the promise of the land.[9]

The rearrangement of Gen 12:3c in Jub 12:23d is possibly due to a specific view of the poetic structure of the passage. In Gen 12:1-3 one can point to a balance between 12:1b and 12:2a; 12:2b and 12:2c; 12:3a and 12:3c. In this structure both Gen 12:2d and 12:3c are not balanced by any adjacent line. By putting Gen 12:3c after Gen 12:2d (in Jub 12:23cd) and, moreover, by adding the words "in the land" to Gen 12:2d, Jubilees strengthens the balance between these lines (Gen 12:2d, 3c). The use of *"peoples"* (*'aḥzab*) instead of "families" (מִשְׁפְּחֹת; Eth. *'azmād*) is possibly influenced by the use of "peoples" in comparable contexts: Gen 18:18 ("and all the *peoples* of the land will be blessed in him") and Gen 22:18 (cf. Gen 26:4) ("and in your seed will all the *peoples* of the land bless themselves"). Note, however, that Gen 28:14 uses the word "families" ("and in you and your seed will all the *families* of the land be blessed").

The reading in Jub 12:23f (*"those* who curse you"; plural) instead of the

---

7. R. W. L. Moberly, *The Bible, Theology, and Faith: A Study of Abraham and Jesus,* Cambridge Studies in Christian Doctrine 5 (Cambridge: Cambridge University Press, 2000), 124, and Keith N. Grüneberg, *Abraham, Blessing, and the Nations: A Philological and Exegetical Study of Genesis 12:3 in Its Narrative Context,* BZAW 332 (Berlin: De Gruyter, 2003), have argued that Gen 12:2d does not make Abram a source of blessing to others, but rather promises that he will be signally blessed in such a way that others will notice.

8. So also O. S. Wintermute, *"Jubilees:* A New Translation and Introduction," in *OTP,* 2:81. However, in Jub 12:23d he translates this by "of the earth." R. H. Charles, *The Book of Jubilees or the Little Genesis: Translated from the Editor's Ethiopic Text* (London: Adam & Charles Black, 1902), 95, and VanderKam, *Book of Jubilees, II,* 73, translate *mǝdr* in both cases by "the earth." K. Berger, *Das Buch der Jubiläen,* JSHRZ, V.3 (Gütersloh: Gerd Mohn, 1981), 395, reads "auf der Erde."

9. Israel has the status of God's people from the creation onward. Israel is separated from the other peoples and lives in a sacred space. For the centrality of the land in the book of Jubilees, see J. M. Scott, *On Earth as in Heaven: The Restoration of Sacred Time and Sacred Space in the* Book of Jubilees, JSJSup 91 (Leiden: Brill, 2005), 161-209. Scott stresses that the holy land of Israel with its central sanctuary is the focal point of the concept that the goal of history is the realignment of sacred space with sacred time so that everything will become "on earth as in heaven." The universalistic strains in the book are subordinated to its particularistic emphasis on Israel and the temple in the land. The exact boundaries of the land are precisely defined.

Masoretic text of Gen 12:3b ("*him* who curses you"; singular) reflects the plural reading that is also found in the Samaritan Pentateuch, Septuagint, and the Peshitta. It is not necessary, therefore, to consider this a variation.

Finally, the most striking element in the rewriting is the addition of Jub 12:24. In Gen 12:1-3 there are no clues that could explain this addition. One could, of course, think of a possible influence from comparable passages, especially from the introduction to the concluding of the covenant in Gen 17 (Gen 17:1-8). Apart from the promise of the land and of numerous offspring, the conclusion of the covenant includes a promise that God makes to Abram and his descendants (Gen 17:7-8: "And I will establish my covenant between me and you, and your descendants after you throughout their generations, for an everlasting covenant, *to be God to you and to your seed after you*. And I will give to you, and to your descendants after you, the land of your sojournings, all the land of Canaan, for an everlasting possession, *and I will be their God*").[10] Although I would not exclude the possibility that 12:24 alludes to the covenant of Gen 17, God's answer in 12:24 is a confirmation of Abram's supplication in the first place and reflects the multiple invocation of "My God, my God, God most high. You alone are my God" (12:19cd).

In the last pericope of this passage Abram learns Hebrew:

Jubilees 12:25-27 (Abram learns Hebrew)

25a Then the Lord God said to me:

b "Open his mouth and his ears to hear

c and speak with his tongue in the revealed language."

d For from the day of the collapse it had disappeared from the mouth(s) of all mankind.

26a I opened his mouth, ears, and lips

b and began to speak Hebrew with him — in the language of the creation.

27a He took his fathers' books

b (they were written in Hebrew)

c and copied them.

d From that time he began to study them,

e while I was telling him everything that he was unable (to understand).

f He studied them throughout the six rainy months.

---

10. The rewriting of Gen 17:7-8 in Jub 15:9-10 is very literal.

In this pericope the narrative in which the actions of Abram play a part is dominant. This was also true in the first passage (12:16-18). As far as the subject is concerned (the learning of Hebrew and the studying of the books of his father), this pericope is somewhat loosely connected with the other pericopes. Within the pericope the following repetition of words and phrases occurs: "to speak in the language" (12:25c, 26b); "to open mouth and ears" (12:25b, 26a); and "Hebrew" (12:26b, 27b).

2. The Coherence of Jubilees 12:16-27

The four pericopes are distinguished from each other by subject and the use of words. However, there is coherence in the four passages as a whole. In the first place, all the pericopes are located in Haran. In the second place, one can point to a unity of time to a great extent. The events take place when Abram was seventy-five years of age (cf. 12:16: "In the sixth week, during its fifth year," which is 1951 A.M.). The destruction of the house of idols in the preceding passage took place in the sixtieth year of Abram's life (12:12), after which it is mentioned that they stayed for fourteen years in Haran (12:15). In the following passage his departure is dated two years after the prayer (cf. 12:28: "In the seventh year of the sixth week"). The aspect of time is specified in that the observation of the stars and the prayer took place during the night (cf. 12:16a, 19a) and the studying of the books during a period of six months (cf. 12:27f). Moreover, both in the beginning and at the end the text climatological circumstances are referred to, namely, the rain (cf. 12:16a, 18, 27). In the third place, one can point to the use of persons. Both in the preceding (12:12-15) and in the following passage (12:28–13:6) several members of Abram's family are mentioned,[11] whereas in 12:16-27 it is mainly Abram who is the person acting. One sees him watching the stars all alone (12:16-18), after which he addresses God in prayer (12:19-22a). God answers Abram's prayer through an angel (12:22-24, 25-26). Finally, it is Abram who copies and studies the Hebrew books (12:27).

Moreover, one can point to the repetitions of some words that occur in more than one passage: "night" (12:16a, 19a), "to sit" (12:16a, 16b, 21c), "(all /

---

11. In 12:12-15: "Haran" (14a), "his father Terah" (14d), "Terah" (15a), "he and his sons" (15a), and "his father" (15d). In 12:28–13:7: "his father" (12:28a), "his father Terah" (12:29a), "Lot the son of your brother Haran" (12:30d; 13:1b), "your brother Nahor" (12:31a), and "his wife Sarai" (13:1b).

everything in his) hand" (12:17c, 18e, 19f; cf. 12:20a, 21d, 22b), "to seek" (12:17d, 21b), "seed" (12:20c, 24a), "to establish" (12:20c, 22d), and "heart" (12:17a, 20a, 21e).

The second (Abram's prayer) and the third pericope (God's answer) are especially interrelated. Abram's questioning of whether he has to return to Ur of the Chaldeans (12:21bc) not only refers back to the burning down of the house of idols (12:12-14), but also prepares God's call to leave his land and his father's house in order to go to the land that he will show him (12:22c). The supplication in 12:20c ("Do establish me and my seed until eternity") is reflected in the promise that God will bless Abram in this land and establish him as progenitor of a large and populous people (12:22d-23). The multiple invocation of "My God, my God, God most high. You alone are my God" (12:19cd) is reflected in God's answer of "I will become God for you" (12:24a). The supplication to save him from the hand of the evil spirits (12:20ab) is not answered explicitly. However, the call to leave his father's house to go to the land that God will show him (12:22c) can be understood as a liberation from the power of the evil spirits. In the new land Abram will prosper and be blessed. He need not be afraid. Several elements in the prayer and its answer are put chiastically in the text, as is shown in the following table:

A   You alone are my God (19d)
B   Establish me and my seed (20c)
C   Shall I return to Ur of the Chaldeans or sit in this place (21bc)?

C′   Come from your country (22c)
B′   I will establish you into a large and populous people (22d-23)
A′   I will become God for you (24a, c)

3. Abram's Prayer in Relation to Other Prayers in Jubilees

The strong similarity in form and content with other prayers in the book of Jubilees confirms the unity of the passage as a whole (12:16-27). One can point specifically to Noah's prayer (10:1-14), but Moses' prayer (1:19-21) is also relevant in this respect. As far as the content is concerned, one can refer also to Abram's blessing of Jacob (19:26-29). These texts show an affinity to each other not only because the one who prays begs for God's help to hold back the influence of the evil spirits, but also because the cause for the prayer, its form, and God's reaction show similarities.

3.1. Abram's Prayer and Noah's Prayer

The following scheme shows the similar structure of Abram's prayer and that of Noah, together with the cause for the prayer and God's reaction:

Noah's prayer (Jub 10:1-14)	Abram's prayer (Jub 12:16-27)
1. *Cause for the prayer:* dominion of the evil spirits (10:1-2)	1. *Cause for the prayer:* rejection of astrology through the recognition of God's power (12:16-18); dominion of the evil spirits (12:20ab)
2. *Form of the prayer*	2. *Form of the prayer*
a. praise (10:3c-h)	a. praise (12:19c-f; cf. 12:4)
b. supplication (10:3hi, 4, 5b-6)	b. supplication (12:20, 21d-e; cf. 11:17bc).
3. *Actions after the prayer*	3. *Actions after the prayer*
a. At God's request the angels bind 90 percent of the evil spirits after intercession by Mastema (10:7-9, 11)	a. God answers Abram through an angel, and calls him to the land (12:22b-24)
b. God orders the angels to teach Noah about the medicines (10:10, 12-13)	b. God orders the angels to teach Abram the Hebrew language (12:25-26)
c. Noah writes in a book and gives it to his eldest son (10:13, 14)	c. Abram takes the books of his father and copies them (12:27)

The cause that brought about the prayer is formulated in different ways. Whereas the dominion of the evil spirits and their threatening of Noah's grandchildren (10:1-2) form the direct cause for Noah's prayer, Abram's prayer is caused by the recognition of the omnipotence of God when he practices astrology (12:16-18). However, Abram does pray to save himself "from the hand of the evil spirits who rule the thoughts of the people's heart" (12:20ab). He continues, praying that they may not lead him astray from following God. It is possible that the practice of astrology should be understood as a manifestation of the misleading of the evil spirits. Other passages in Jubilees show a clear connection between the demons and astrology. In 8:1-4 astrology is identified with the illegal teaching of the watchers. After Kainan was instructed in the art of writing (8:2b), he found an inscription on a rock that described the astrological teachings of the watchers "by which they used to observe the omens of the sun, moon, and stars, and every heavenly sign" (8:3). These signs were probably used to predict the future.[12] Kainan copied these instructions from the stone "and sinned on the basis of what was in it." The teachings of the watchers contrast with the teachings of the patriarchs, which were received from the angels.[13] As far as the astrological teachings of the watchers are concerned, the author is probably referring to an Enochic tradition. In 1 En 6–11 the watchers are not only involved in illicit sexual practices and violence, but they are also involved in astrological teachings. 1 En 8:3 says that "Barakiel taught astrologers, and Kokabel portents, and Tamiel taught astrology and Asradel taught the path of the moon."[14] It is remarkable that of all the illicit angelic instructions of the watchers mentioned in the Book of the Watchers (metalworking, cosmetics, sorcery, pharmacology, spellbinding, and celestial divination), Jubilees includes only one.[15]

In 11:8 one can read that Abram's grandfather Nahor learned from his father Serug "the studies of the Chaldeans: to practice divination and to augur by the signs of the sky." This forms the direct background for Abram's predictions of the weather for the coming year in 12:16-18.[16] Although 11:8 does not show an explicit disapproval of "the studies of the Chaldeans," it is striking that in the context of Serug's birth the threats of the evil spirits and their leader Mastema are mentioned (11:4-5). This means that the studies of the Chaldeans on the practice of divination are closely related to the influ-

---

12. M. Segal, *The Book of Jubilees: Rewritten Bible, Redaction, Ideology, and Theology,* JSJSup 117 (Leiden: Brill, 2007), 260 n. 8.

13. Although this is the first time in Jubilees that the watchers are connected with astrological teachings, it should be remembered that Enoch was born immediately after the watchers came down on earth (4:15-16). The first thing he wrote down was concerned with calendrical and astronomical affairs: "the signs of the sky in accord with the fixed pattern of their months, so that mankind would know the seasons of the years according to the fixed patterns of each of their months" (4:17). The angels showed him the dominion of the sun (4:21), after which the text continues with mention of the watchers and their illicit intercourse.

14. A. Lange points to the heavy emphasis on the rejection of astrology in 1 En 8:3, which is developed further in Jub 8:3. Cf. A. Lange, "The Essene Position on Magic and Divination," in *Legal Texts and Legal Issues: Proceedings of the Second Meeting of the International Organization for Qumran Studies; Published in Honour of Joseph M. Baumgarten,* ed. M. Bernstein, F. García Martínez, and J. Kampen, STDJ 23 (Leiden: Brill, 1997), 377-435 (here 400-402).

15. A. Y. Reed, *Fallen Angels and the History of Judaism and Christianity* (Cambridge: Cambridge University Press, 2005), 92-93. Cf. Lange, "The Essene Position," 400.

16. Segal, *The Book of Jubilees,* 260.

ence of the evil spirits. In 10:5, the only place in Jubilees that explicitly refers to a connection between the evil spirits and the watchers (the watchers are "fathers of these spirits"), the relationship between astrology and evil spirits is strengthened.[17] One can conclude that in both cases the reason that brought forth the prayer is more or less the same.

As far as the form of the prayer proper is concerned, it consists of a combination of praise and supplication. In the praise, Noah (10:3) puts emphasis on God's grace ("You have shown kindness to me, saved me and my sons from the flood waters, and did not make me perish as you did to the people meant for destruction, because your mercy for me has been large, and your kindness to me has been great"), whereas Abram (12:19c-f; 12:4) puts an emphasis on God's omnipotence ("My God, my God, God most High, you alone are my God. You have created everything; everything that was and has been is the work of your hands").[18]

In Noah's prayer the supplication contains two elements. On the one hand, Noah prays that the evil spirits may not rule over Noah's children (10:3i: "And may the evil spirits not rule them in order to destroy them from the earth"; cf. 10:5-6). On the other hand, he prays for a blessing upon him and his children (10:4: "Now you bless me and my children so that we may increase, become numerous, and fill the earth"). Both elements occur also in the supplication in Abram's prayer. The request to save him from the evil spirits plays an important part (12:20ab: "Save me from the hand of the evil spirits who rule the thoughts of the people's heart. May they not lead me astray from following you, my God"). The element of blessing has its parallel in that Abram asks to establish him and his seed for eternity (12:20c) and that he as God's servant may work on the right path (12:21d).

With regard to the actions that take place immediately after the prayer, in both cases there is a twofold action of God, followed by an action of the supplicant. In both cases God addresses himself not to the supplicant but to an angel (10:7, 10-12; 12:22b, 25-26, 27e). God's first reaction to Noah's prayer is his commandment to bind *all* the demons. After Mastema, the leader of the spirits, protests and asks for some of them to be left before him so he can

---

17. According to Segal (*The Book of Jubilees,* 179-80), it is difficult to connect the story of the watchers (a onetime event in history) with a system that sets up the world order from creation onward with God and Israel on one side and Mastema, the evil spirits, and the other nations on the other (cf. Jub 2:19-21; 15:30-32). Segal considers the connection between these two viewpoints as a secondary development. It is the result of the wish to integrate the spirit traditions from 1 Enoch into a dualistic worldview.

18. Compare also 12:4 ("He created everything by his word").

exercise his authority among mankind (10:8), God allows him a tenth of them, and gives orders to bind 90 percent of the evil spirits (10:9). God's first reaction to Abram's prayer is a direct address to Abram through an angel in which Abram is summoned to leave his land and his father's house, and to go to the land that God will show him (12:22-24). The establishment in the new land seems to have a comparable function as the binding of the evil spirits. In the land where Abram and his descendants are to be blessed abundantly, the demons will have no influence.[19]

In the case of both Noah and Abram, God's initial reaction seems not to be sufficient to save their descendants from the influence of the evil spirits. In the subsequent second action, God instructs the angels. They should teach Noah all the medicines, which could protect him and his sons against attacks from the evil spirits (10:10, 12), and teach Abram the Hebrew language (12:25-26).

Finally, there is a reaction by the one who prays, which is comparable in both texts. Noah writes down in a book everything the angels have taught him. Thereafter, he gives all his books to his oldest son Shem (10:13-14).[20] Abram, who is from the line of Shem, learns Hebrew, takes his father's books, then copies and studies them (12:27). The mention of "his father's books" in 12:27 makes the connection with 10:13-14 explicit. Neither the binding of 90 percent of the demons nor his establishment in the land will give complete protection against the threat of the spirits. Books should also

---

19. Compare this with Noah's supplication in which the request that the evil spirits might not rule over Noah's children is put next to the request for a blessing upon his children (cf. 10:3i and 4a-d).

20. According to Segal (*The Book of Jubilees*, 171-73), the "book" (singular) in 10:13 cannot be identical with the "books" (plural) in 10:14. The reason to hand over the books to Shem ("because he loved him much more than all his sons") does not match up with the medicines, which were meant for *all* Noah's offspring. The transition from singular to plural even points to separate sources. The nature of the "books" (plural), which Noah handed over to his son Shem, should be understood in the light of the chain of tradition in which knowledge is handed over from generation to generation (7:38-39; 12:27; 21:10; 39:6; 45:16). In my opinion, one should not stress too much the transition from singular to plural. The fact that Noah writes a book with regard to medicines (10:13) does not exclude the fact that he has written other books. Enoch has written a book (4:17-19, 21-23), and in the end of his testament (7:38-39) Noah refers to that tradition. It is quite plausible that the new knowledge that Noah has received is going to belong to the chain of tradition. Moreover, it is really the offspring of Shem who have to be protected against the influence of the spirits. The spirits are permitted to have influence only over other peoples (15:31-32; cp. 10:8). Nevertheless, it is true that the plural in 10:14 shows that it is not just the knowledge with regard to medicines that is handed over.

be studied, books that contain, among other things, medicines against the attacks of evil spirits.

In conclusion, the comparison of Abram's prayer with that of Noah shows the similar structure of both texts. This confirms, moreover, the formal unity and the coherence in regard to the content of 12:16-27.

3.2. Abram's Prayer and Moses' Prayer

There is also a similarity between Abram's prayer with its preceding and following events and Moses' prayer (1:19-21) in the context of 1:5–2:1. The following scheme shows the structure of Moses' prayer, together with the cause for it, and God's reaction:

Moses' prayer (Jub 1:5–2:1)
1. *Cause for the prayer* (1:5-18)
2. *Form of the prayer* — supplication (1:19-21)
3. *Actions after the prayer*
   a. God answers Moses with regard to his dealing with the people (1:22-24); Moses receives an order to write (1:25)
   b. God orders the angel of the presence to dictate the story of history to Moses (1:27–2:1)

Despite a structure comparable to Abram's prayer, the cause for Moses' prayer seems to be somewhat different. Moses is reacting to a direct speech from God to him (1:5-18) in which the Deuteronomistic scheme of sin, punishment, repentance, and restoration can be found. Because of the direct interaction between God and Moses, God addresses Moses directly through the reactions to the prayer (1:22-25) and not through an angel, as was the case with Noah's and Abram's prayers. It is remarkable, however, that God also addresses Moses indirectly through an angel, since he orders the angels to dictate the story of Jubilees to Moses. Moses' prayer (1:19-21) mainly consists of supplication, although some elements of praise are integrated (20a: "your mercy"; 21a: "whom you have rescued from Egyptian control by your great power").

The structure of the supplication shows strong parallelism between the parts of the prayer:

A   O Lord my God, do not allow your people and your inheritance to go along in the strayings of their hearts (19d)

B   and do not deliver them into the hands of the nations, with the
     result that they rule over them (19ef),
C   lest they make them sin against you (19g).

A′   May your mercy, Lord, be raised over your people (20a).
     Create for them a just spirit (20b).
B′   May the spirit of Belial not rule over them (20c′)
D   so as to bring charges against them before you (20c″)
C′   and to ensnare them away from every proper path (20d)
     so that they may be wiped away from your presence (20e).

A″   They are your people and your inheritance whom you have
     rescued from Egyptian control (hands) by your great power (21a).
     Create for them a pure heart and a holy spirit (21b).
C″   May they not be trapped in their sins from now to eternity (21c).

The prayer requests a just spirit from God for his people lest they follow the
strayings of their heart (A). The parallelism between B and B′ shows that the
nations are put parallel with the "spirit of Belial." Both can rule over Israel.
This means at the same time that both can cause Israel to sin against God
(C). Whereas the nations cannot bring charges against Israel before God, the
spirit of Belial is able to do so (D). Compare 1:19-21 in this respect with 15:30-
33, in which God lets the spirits rule over the nations. God himself chooses
Israel to be his people. Only God is Israel's ruler.

As far as the use of words and phrases is concerned, Moses' prayer has
several similarities with Noah's and Abram's prayers. I refer to 1:19d ("the
strayings of their hearts"; see 12:20ab, d, 21e; cf. 11:17); 1:20a ("May your mercy,
Lord, be lifted over your people" (cf. 10:3h); 1:20c ("May the spirit of Belial
not rule over them so as to bring charges against them before you"; see 12:20;
10:3i, 6a); 1:20d ("to ensnare them away from every proper path"; cf. 12:21d).

With regard to the actions that take place immediately after the prayer,
there is a twofold action by God followed by an action not by the supplicant,
but by the angel of the presence. God addresses himself directly to the supplicant (1:22-26) and not to an angel, as was the case after Noah's and
Abram's prayers (10:7, 10-12; 12:22b, 25-26, 27e). God's first reaction is a
speech to Moses in which he tells about the future repentance and restoration of the people. In this speech Moses is ordered to write down everything
God makes known. In the subsequent, second speech, God instructs the angel of the presence to dictate the story to Moses (1:27-28). Finally, the angel

takes the tables of the division of the years and starts to dictate to Moses the content of history (1:29–2:1).

3.3. Abram's Prayer and Abraham's Blessing for Jacob

Finally, I would like to refer to Abraham's blessing for Jacob (19:26-29). There are several similarities with Abram's prayer. Abraham begs God to protect Jacob against the evil spirits (19:28a: "May the spirits of Mastema not rule over you and your descendants to remove you from following the Lord who is your God from now and forever"). The terminology that is used resembles that of Abram's prayer (12:20).[21] Immediately after this Abraham prays that God may be Jacob's father and Jacob his firstborn son (19:29: "May the Lord God become your father and you his first-born son and people for all time"). From the point of view of Jubilees, this means that God has chosen Jacob (Israel) from the beginning of time to be his unique people and his firstborn son (cf. 2:20). The consequence of this election is God's direct dominion over Israel. In contrast to this, spirits are appointed to control the other nations (cf. Deut 32:8-9; 4:19-20; Sir 17:17; Jub 15:30-32). The spirits mislead the nations on purpose and let them sin.[22] Although a father-son relationship between God and Israel is not at stake in Abram's prayer, one could say the confirmation of "I will become God for you, your son, your grandson, and all your seed" (12:24) implies that the spirits cannot take on that role. The spirits rule only over the other nations. The confirmation in 12:24 can therefore be taken as an answer to Abram's supplication to save him from the dominion of the evil spirits.

4. Enochic Traditions

Although the text of Jubilees is guided to a large extent by the biblical books of Genesis and Exodus as far as content and sequence are concerned, one should acknowledge that other sources and traditions are also incorporated into the book. The third pericope (Jub 12:22b-24) can be considered a rewriting of Gen 12:1-3. The other pericopes are additions with regard to the biblical text. Abram's prayer is closely connected with the other prayers in

---

21. Compare also 1:20; 10:8; 11:5.
22. Cf. Segal, *The Book of Jubilees*, 257-59.

the book. The prayers are caused by the threat of evil spirits. In the Bible there is no demonology. In Genesis one can read nothing about demons. Within Jubilees, however, demons occur in several places, especially in relation to the spread of mankind on the earth after the flood. They belong to the time of Noah and the early Abram, although they continue to operate in later times. Apart from the term "demon" (1:11c; 7:27; 10:1, 2; 22:17), "(evil) spirit" is also used (10:3, 5, 8, 11, 13; 11:4, 5; 12:20; 15:31, 32; 19:28). The demons are charged with causing bloodshed and with inciting people to kill each other. In this respect Jubilees seems to be influenced by other sources. The teaching about the demons seems to be part of the wider influence of material originating from the Enochic traditions.[23] One can point especially to the influence of 1 Enoch (Book of the Watchers). Jubilees shares the fundamental pattern of the Book of the Watchers in which the angels descended from heaven, married women, and sinned with them. Their children were the giants. In 1 En 15:8–16:1 it is described how the evil spirits came out of the carcasses of the giants and how they were threatening humanity: they do violence, make desolate, attack and wrestle and hurl upon the earth.[24] Jubilees seems not to be completely consistent here in that the demons are mentioned as the emanations from the angels themselves (10:5: "your watchers, the fathers of these spirits"), whereas it also understands the giants as the sons of the watchers (5:1, 6-10).[25] Moreover, it shows some deviations from

23. For the influence of Enochic traditions in the book of Jubilees, see especially J. C. VanderKam, "Enoch Traditions in Jubilees and Other Second-Century Sources," in SBLSP 1 (1978), 229-51 (reprinted in VanderKam, *From Revelation to Canon: Studies in the Hebrew Bible and Second Temple Literature*, JSJSup 62 [Leiden: Brill, 2000], 305-31). This work influenced his *Enoch and the Growth of an Apocalyptic Tradition*, CBQMS 16 (Washington, D.C.: Catholic Bible Association of America, 1984), 179-88, and formed the basis of a chapter in *Enoch: A Man for All Generations*, Studies on Personalities of the Old Testament (Columbia: University of South Carolina Press, 1995), 110-21. See also, some of his predecessors: R. H. Charles, *The Book of Jubilees or the Little Genesis* (London, 1902), xliv, 36-39, 43-44; P. Grelot, "La légende d'Henoch dans les apocryphes et dans la Bible. Origine et signification," *RSR* 46 (1958): 5-26, 181-210; J. T. Milik, *The Book of Enoch: Aramaic Fragments of Qumran Cave 4* (Oxford: Oxford University Press, 1976). VanderKam is followed by, e.g., G. W. E. Nickelsburg, *1 Enoch 1: A Commentary on the Book of 1 Enoch, Chapters 1–36; 81–108*, Hermeneia (Minneapolis: Fortress, 2001), 71-76.

24. J. C. VanderKam, "The Demons in the Book of Jubilees," in *Demons: The Demonology of Israelite-Jewish and Early Christian Literature in Context of Their Environment*, ed. A. Lange, H. Lichtenberger, and K. F. Diethard Römheld (Tübingen: Mohr Siebeck, 2003), 339-64 (here 348-50); Nickelsburg, *1 Enoch 1*, 267-75.

25. Jubilees possibly preserves several older traditions about the watchers. See Dimant, VanderKam, Segal.

its source text, e.g., the demons are put under the authority of Mastema (10:8; 11:5; 19:28; 49:2; cf. 11:11; 17:16; 18:9, 12; 48:2, 3-4, 9, 12-18). This leader of the demons is probably no demon himself, but a sort of evil angel. He is, however, not one of the watchers, because they are tied up in the depths of the earth until the great day of judgment (5:6-11). The demons do everything Mastema tells them, so that he is able to exercise the authority of his will among mankind to punish them for their evil (cf. 10:8).

5. Conclusion

In the prayer of Abram and the surrounding events (Jub 12:16-27), I identi-fied four pericopes that are distinguished from each other by subject and the use of words. These pericopes are not disconnected, however. I pointed to the coherence of the four passages as a whole. There is unity of place (Haran), of time (the seventy-fifth year in Abram's life), and of persons (mainly Abram). A comparison of Abram's prayer with other prayers in the book of Jubilees (1:19-21; 10:1-14; 19:26-29) showed the strong connection be-tween them in structure and content. The prayers are mostly included in the book of Jubilees as additions with regard to the biblical text of Genesis and Exodus. They are caused by the threat of evil spirits. In God's answer to the prayer's supplication, several means are put into action, such as dictating from the heavenly tablets, binding 90 percent of the evil spirits, teaching about medicines, copying and studying books, and making a promise to live in the land.

Abram's and Noah's prayers, the preceding events, and their acts of writing afterward can be seen as a sort of prefiguration of Moses' prayer and the dictating and copying of the book of Jubilees itself. In all these cases, there is a relationship between the teaching of the angels and the content of the book. The books contain the information necessary in the conflict with the evil spirits and are handed down from generation to generation. Through Jacob, information is handed over to Levi (Jub 45:16), Moses' great-grandfather.[26]

---

26. An important element in the rewriting of Genesis and Exodus in the book of Jubi-lees is the struggle against foreign influences, from evil spirits to other nations. The rewrit-ing seems not to be a rewriting for no particular reason, but a means of using the biblical text in this struggle.

Reconsidering Jubilees: Prophecy and Exemplarity

Hindy Najman

What is at stake in how we characterize the book of Jubilees? Perhaps most importantly, we must be aware that the current generic labels for the book of Jubilees all stake some claim about canon in the second century.[1] The implications extend to seminal Qumran documents as well.

---

1. See recent discussion of genre distinctions by C. A. Newsom, "Spying Out the Land: A Report from Genology," in *Seeking Out the Wisdom of the Ancients: Essays Offered to Honor Michael V. Fox on the Occasion of His Sixty-fifth Birthday,* ed. R. L. Troxel, K. G. Friebel, and D. R. Magary (Winona Lake, Ind.: Eisenbrauns, 2005), 437-60. On rewritten Bible as a genre, see P. S. Alexander, "Retelling the Old Testament," in *It Is Written: Scripture Citing Scripture; Essays in Honour of Barnabas Lindars, SSF,* ed. D. A. Carson and H. G. M. Williamson (Cambridge: Cambridge University Press, 1987), 99-121. For a history of scholarship on the issue, see M. J. Bernstein, "'Rewritten Bible': A Generic Category Which Has Outlived Its Usefulness?" *Text* 22 (2005): 169-96. See also G. J. Brooke, "Rewritten Bible," in *EDSS,* 777-80; S. D. Fraade, "Rewritten Bible and Rabbinic Midrash as Commentary," in *Current Trends in the Study of Midrash,* ed. C. Bakhos (Leiden: Brill, 2006), 59-78; B. Halpern-Amaru, *Rewriting the Bible: Land and Covenant in Postbiblical Jewish Literature* (Valley Forge, Pa.: Trinity, 1994); D. J. Harrington, "The Bible Rewritten (Narratives)," in *Early Judaism and Its Modern Interpreters,* ed. R. A. Kraft and G. W. E. Nickelsburg (Atlanta: Scholars Press, 1986), 239-47; G. W. E. Nickelsburg, "The Bible Rewritten and Expanded," in *Jewish Writings of the Second Temple Period,* ed. M. Stone (Assen: Van Gorcum; Philadelphia: Fortress, 1984), 89-156; E. Tov, "Biblical Texts as Reworked in Some Qumran Manuscripts with Special Attention to 4QRP and 4QparaGen-Exod," in *The Community of the Renewed*

I thank J. Collins, P. Franks, F. García Martínez, E. Tigchelaar, R. A. Kraft, E. Mroczek, and B. G. Wright III for their helpful conversations and generous comments. — HN

Suppose we characterize Jubilees as rewritten Bible. Then we are committing ourselves to the position that there was already an authoritative or canonical Pentateuch in the second century, during which it was possible to replace the Pentateuch with a text like Jubilees. As I argued in *Seconding Sinai*, I find the position very problematic:

> Like the classification of texts as pseudepigraphic, the characterization of Second Temple texts as "Rewritten Bible" is problematic. Use of the term can suggest an *anachronistic conception of a text* — as a fixed set of claims embodied in specific language, such that tampering with that language is tantamount to interfering with an author's property. When scholars who employ such a concept encounter biblical and extra-biblical texts that recount biblical narratives with variations and insertions, they may be tempted to infer that these texts aspire to replace an older, authentic biblical tradition with a new version. Instead, we should ask whether these biblical and extra-biblical writers shared our contemporary conception of a text. Although biblicists assume the existence of a somewhat fixed biblical text as early as the Persian period, they acknowledge the fluidity of biblical traditions. Even if it is still possible to speak of rewriting, the distinction between the *transmission* and the *interpretation* of biblical traditions was not as sharp as the term *Rewritten Bible* implies.[2]

We do not have evidence that entitles us to speak of a fixed and exclusive canon at the time of Jubilees' composition. However, there is evidence for a stabilized, circulating, and authoritative text much like what is eventually called the Pentateuch. In addition, we know that Jubilees shares many tradi-

---

Covenant: The Notre Dame Symposium on the Dead Sea Scrolls, ed. E. Ulrich and J. C. VanderKam (Notre Dame, Ind.: University of Notre Dame Press, 1994), 111-34. See also earlier scholarship by G. Vermes, who coined the term "Rewritten Bible": *Scripture and Tradition in Judaism: Haggadic Studies*, 2nd rev. ed., StPB 4 (Leiden: Brill, 1973; 1st ed. 1961), 10, and by C. Perrot on the notion of "texte continué": *Pseudo-Philon: Les antiquités bibliques. Tome II: Introduction littéraire, commentaire et index*, SC 230 (Paris: Cerf, 1976). For a recent discussion see M. Segal, *The Book of Jubilees: Rewritten Bible, Redaction, Ideology, and Theology*, JSJSup 117 (Leiden: Brill, 2007).

2. H. Najman, *Seconding Sinai: The Development of Mosaic Discourse in Second Temple Judaism*, JSJSup 77 (Leiden: Brill, 2003), 7-8. See also my discussion of why this term is deeply problematic in "Interpretation as Primordial Writing: Jubilees and Its Authority Conferring Strategies," *JSJ* 30 (1999): 379-410. I prefer to jettison the term altogether because it obscures more than it illuminates in the world of ancient Judean traditions.

tions and texts that we have since come to know as Pentateuchal or prophetic.[3] Perhaps, then, we could argue that Jubilees is interpreting texts we know as Pentateuchal.

But if we claim that Jubilees reflects some of the earliest interpretation of the Pentateuch — then we are assigning a secondary status to Jubilees vis-à-vis the Pentateuch. But this flies in the face of Jubilees' self-presentation: Jubilees claims that it is itself a revelation that is already and always inscribed in the heavenly tablets, long before Sinai.

It is Jubilees' claim to be revealed that has led some to say that Jubilees intends to replace Genesis or the Pentateuch.[4] However, such a suggestion is also in tension with Jubilees' self-presentation. Jubilees knows of a first Torah and understands that it is offering a second Torah that is already prior to the first Torah from Sinai, but Jubilees never claims to replace the first Torah, which it treats as having continued authority.

Indeed, there are some passages in Jubilees where the characterization of "interpretation" seems more apt, and others where what seems called for is a characterization of "parallel traditions" or even "expanded traditions," of which we possess much shorter versions in the Pentateuch. To be sure, we can state with confidence — as has been argued most recently by Aharon Shemesh[5] — that Jubilees played a prominent role for some of the authors and

---

3. See the exemplary discussion by G. J. Brooke, "The Formation and Renewal of Scriptural Tradition," in *Biblical Traditions in Transmission: Essays in Honour of Michael A. Knibb*, ed. C. Hempel and J. Lieu (Leiden: Brill, 2005), 39-60. See also J. C. Reeves, "Exploring the Afterlife of Jewish Pseudepigrapha in Medieval Near Eastern Religious Traditions: Some Initial Soundings," *JSJ* 30 (1999): 148-77, and R. A. Kraft, "The Pseudepigrapha in Christianity," in *Tracing the Threads: Studies in the Vitality of Jewish Pseudepigrapha*, ed. J. C. Reeves, SBLEJL 6 (Atlanta: Scholars Press, 1994), 55-86.

4. See, for example, B. Z. Wacholder, "*Jubilees* as the Super Canon: Torah-Admonition versus Torah-Commandment," in *Legal Texts and Legal Issues: Proceedings of the Second Meeting of the International Organization for Qumran Studies, Cambridge 1995*, ed. M. Bernstein, F. García Martínez, and J. Kampen, STDJ 23 (Leiden: Brill, 1997), 195-211. For an incisive and critical assessment of Wacholder's argument, see M. Himmelfarb, "Torah, Testimony, and Heavenly Tablets: The Claim to Authority in the Book of Jubilees," in *A Multiform Heritage: Studies on Early Judaism and Christianity in Honor of Robert A. Kraft*, ed. B. G. Wright III, Homage Series 24 (Atlanta: Scholars Press, 1999), 19-29; see her most recent discussion of Jubilees' status in *A Kingdom of Priests: Ancestry and Merit in Ancient Judaism* (Philadelphia: University of Pennsylvania Press, 2006), 53-55. For another view of Jubilees' self-understanding vis-à-vis the Pentateuch, see C. Werman, "The '[*tôrâ*] and the [*tĕ'ûdâ*]' Engraved on the Tablets," *DSD* 9 (2002): 75-103 (esp. 93-95).

5. See A. Shemesh's essay for this volume, "4Q265 and the Authoritative Status of Jubilees at Qumran."

copyists at Qumran.[6] Along these lines, Martha Himmelfarb suggests that "the existence [at Qumran] of a work or works labeled *Pseudo-Jubilees* (4Q225-27) indicates that Jubilees was of sufficient stature to warrant imitation."[7] Beyond that, we cannot say for sure that it was *authoritative* for any second temple community, much as in the case of the earliest Enochic writings.

It is very hard to determine the reception and dissemination of texts within second temple Judaism. But how then are we to label this work we call Jubilees? Under what category should it be subsumed? Having rejected "rewritten Bible," or "new Torah," or even "interpretation," I will offer a very simple and perhaps obvious alternative. It is not that I think these labels are in *all senses* inadequate for understanding aspects of the materials or traditions found in Jubilees. Rather, I think that each is inadequate for characterizing the book as *a whole*. Moreover, each betrays, in its own way, what Robert Kraft has called "the tyranny of canonical assumptions."[8]

The alternative I want to recommend is at once both obvious and bound to be provocative. If we are to characterize Jubilees as a whole, we should pay attention to its self-presentation. The book claims to be revelatory and to have a divine, angelic, and heavenly origin. It is, by its own account, part of the larger family of works from earlier exilic and postexilic traditions that we have come to know as biblical prophecy. My claim, then, is that Jubilees should be contextualized within the traditions of biblical prophecy, especially exilic and postexilic prophecy.

One source of resistance is easily anticipated, for the well-rehearsed claims that prophecy ended are very familiar to us all. But these claims — that prophecy ceases and that apocalyptic or wisdom literature emerges instead — simply do not resonate with the texts we have from late ancient Judaism. For the texts repeatedly make claims to be prophetic, and more broadly, to be revelatory. Of course, throughout late ancient Judean traditions, claims of persistent revelation are made in many different ways. But this reflects the variety we see in earlier Israelite and contemporaneous non-Israelite and non-Judean religious traditions. Angelic revelation and mediated intervention, human access to heavenly writings, symbolic prophecy,

---

6. See J. C. VanderKam, "Authoritative Literature in the Dead Sea Scrolls," *DSD* 5, no. 3 (1998): 382-402, and E. C. Ulrich, "The Bible in the Making: The Scriptures Found at Qumran," in *The Bible at Qumran: Text, Shape, and Interpretation,* ed. P. W. Flint (Grand Rapids: Eerdmans, 2001), 51-66.

7. Himmelfarb, *A Kingdom of Priests,* 53.

8. R. A. Kraft, "Para-mania: Beside, Before, and Beyond Bible Studies," *JBL* 126 (2007): 5-27.

apocalyptic vision, and inspired interpretation are all features of both exilic and postexilic prophecy.[9] The texts do not reflect any linear development from one concept of the revelatory to another.

In addition, the dichotomy of wisdom and apocalyptic or prophecy and apocalyptic has been challenged in recent years.[10] By categorizing Jubilees as apocalyptic as opposed to wisdom, or as Mosaic as opposed to Enochic, or as rewritten Bible as opposed to new Torah, we simply compromise our ability to read the texts with the openness and clarity required to carefully chart the development of second temple Judaism along with the insight required to contextualize the book of Jubilees.

Despite all this, I want to acknowledge that there is something accurate and profound about claims to the cessation of revelation. It would be more accurate, however, to speak of the *transformation* of revelation after the first exile in the sixth century B.C.E. We need to consider that despite the building of the second temple, the destruction of the first temple was never overcome.[11] There was, thus, from 587 B.C.E. on, a sense of lost intimacy with the divine, which is reflected in textual witnesses from the second temple and the post-70 eras.[12] But it was through learning how to mourn loss that these texts gained access to the divine in a different way.

It also concerns the establishment of access to the divine. To be sure, there are prophecies that communicate a special relationship with the divine, or inaccessible information about the past. One goal of revelation in the second temple period was to recover a lost relationship between God and humanity. Thus, the desire for revelation is the aspiration to approach and perhaps even imitate divine perfection by recovering an idyllic past and imagining an inspired future.

---

9. See my new work on this topic, "Defining Prophecy," in *Prophetic Ends: Concepts of the Revelatory in Late Ancient Judaism* (forthcoming).

10. For the most recent discussion of the relations between apocalyptic and wisdom literature, see *Conflicted Boundaries in Wisdom and Apocalypticism*, ed. B. G. Wright and L. M. Wills, SBLSymS (Atlanta: Society of Biblical Literature, 2005). On the relationship between prophecy and apocalyptic, see J. C. VanderKam's two essays now reprinted in *From Revelation to Canon: Studies in the Hebrew Bible and Second Temple Literature*, JSJSup 62 (Leiden: Brill, 2000): "The Prophetic-Sapiential Origins of Apocalyptic Thought," 241-54, and "Prophecy and Apocalyptics in the Ancient Near East," 255-75.

11. See M. A. Knibb, "Exile in the Damascus Document," *JSOT* 25 (1983): 99-117, and "The Exile in the Literature of the Intertestamental Period," *HeyJ* 17 (1976): 253-72.

12. See the important discussion of persistent exile in B. Nitzan's engagement of penitential prayer in her "The Penitential Prayer of Moses in Jubilees 1 and Its Relation to the Penitential Tradition of the Post-Exilic Judaism," *Hen* 30, no. 2 (2008).

But what happens to the aspiration to perfection within a community that undergoes the destruction of its political and religious institutions, and that is exiled from its homeland? Is perfection, or progress toward perfection, to be thought of only in terms of restoration and return from exile? Or are there ways in which perfection, or progress toward perfection, is possible even in the midst of suffering — perhaps even *by means* of suffering?

In the case of Jubilees, the idea of a pre-Sinaitic context for Sinaitic revelation provides a ready instrument for the explanation both of loss and of the access of a privileged few to the requisites of salvation. Those who know only what was revealed at Sinai but who are ignorant of its pre-Sinaitic backdrop do not know how to observe the law properly. This proper observance — heavily but not exclusively focused on the solar calendar — is available only to those who know the traditions revealed first to Enoch, and then passed on through a succession of worthy individuals. The task of Jubilees is to set the story straight by putting the revelation at Sinai in its pre-Sinaitic context, thanks to privileged information about exactly what the angel of the presence said to Moses at Sinai. Loss of intimacy with the divine turns out to be part of the story itself, as does the promise of recovery, for some at least. Thus Jubilees presents itself as revelation that reveals a falling away from revelation, as well as the possibility of a return.

I anticipate another kind of resistance to my suggestion. As modern, post-Enlightenment scholars, are we ready to take any text's self-presentation at face value? Should we not rather be skeptical or suspicious?

I suggest that we treat Jubilees' self-description as revealed — as Mosaic and angelic — in just the same way that we treat the self-descriptions of the books of Jeremiah and Isaiah. In none of these cases, I think, are we in a situation where we can associate the text decisively with some historical author, and in all of them a complex history of composition and redaction appears to undermine any such attribution. But to decide that these works are therefore inauthentic is to contrast them with some set of authentic, canonical texts, which is to allow confessional presuppositions to trespass in the field of scholarship. And to decide that they are forgeries is to employ what I have argued elsewhere is an anachronistic conception of authorial attribution. In a recent essay, I wrote:

> The problems facing those of us who work on pseudepigrapha may seem insuperable. However, we should not assume that political contextualization or religious affiliation is the only way of doing history, or the most important. I want to suggest that intellectual, cultural and

spiritual practices also constitute contexts within which texts can be rendered intelligible. Instead of constituting an obstacle, authorial self-effacement should be an object of study. By considering the practices of authorial effacement and pseudepigraphic attribution, we can come to understand much about the way the unknown and unknowable authors related to their own present.[13]

In this particular case, we should try to understand how Jubilees understands itself as building upon the expansion of Exodus that occurs already in Deuteronomy, all attributed to the figure of Moses. It is an instance of what I have elsewhere called Mosaic Discourse. At the same time, however, as I have argued elsewhere, it is also angelic discourse, since it presents itself as a record of what the angel of the presence said to Moses, which Moses dutifully recorded.[14] As scholars, our task is not to judge the authenticity of Jubilees' claim to be revealed. It is rather to contextualize that claim within the practices of late ancient Judaism. In what follows I want to develop my previous work on Jubilees in two respects:

I. I want to develop the point, which I have already introduced, that the book of Jubilees belongs to the corpus of books said to be revelatory, or even prophetic.[15] Once we include Jubilees in this group, we see the claims of the book in a very different light. The angelic revelation, the Mosaic inscription, and the record of heavenly traditions resonate with the better-known biblical traditions. While scholars have emphasized that Jubilees is part of the "Qumran Bible," or the "authoritative literature" of the second temple period for some Jews, we must still explore the implications of that claim. Our conception of Jubilees is altered, along with other known prophetic works, once we consider these works to be representatives of a genre, some of whose members later came to be classified as biblical.[16]

II. In my earlier work I focused on Jubilees as an example of what I called discourse tied to a founder — in the case of Jubilees, Mosaic Discourse.

---

13. H. Najman, "How Should We Contextualize Pseudepigrapha? Imitation and Emulation in 4Ezra," in *Flores Florentino: Dead Sea Scrolls and Other Early Jewish Studies in Honour of Florentino García Martínez*, ed. A. Hilhorst, E. Puech, and E. Tigchelaar (Leiden: Brill, 2007).

14. See my essay "Interpretation as Primordial Writing."

15. In my forthcoming study of ancient Jewish revelation, I discuss features that Jubilees shares with other members of the prophetic corpus. See "Defining Prophecy," in *Prophetic Ends*.

16. Cf. Kraft, "Para-mania."

Now, I want to further develop this claim by examining the way the exemplar (the founding figure associated with this tradition) functions in this text. Of course, there are other texts in which the founding figure functions prominently as the pseudonymous author, e.g., 1, 2, and 3 Enoch and 4 Ezra and 5 Ezra, among other examples. Here, however, I want to consider the role of the exemplar in the book of Jubilees, on two levels. The first is the angel of the presence and the figure of Moses. These two figures are the ones authorizing this work. They have produced it through divine revelation and have secured the heavenly stature and status of this now earthly copy to which we have access. Of course, Moses and the angel of the presence are the two most perfect figures to which a new discourse of this sort should be attributed. The angelic figure dictates faithfully and the exemplary scribe writes as they both fulfill the divine charge with inspiration and accuracy. There is, however, a second level at which the exemplar operates. This second level returns us to the question mentioned above about the role of interpretation or expansion of texts we recognize from biblical tradition. The book of Jubilees is an assembly of narratives recounting the history of exemplarity. These figures are deserving of the gift of writing and the divine, heavenly tablets. They are figures of the past on both the first (Moses) and second (the patriarchs, Jacob, etc.) levels, they are the new prophecy for the intended audience, and they ultimately come to play important roles for imagining perfection and conceiving of revelation in second temple Judaism.

I. Jubilees as a Revelatory Text

In earlier work I have focused on Jubilees' fascination with writtenness and scribalism.[17] Here it is necessary to discuss once again the claim of a cessation of prophecy, this time from a different angle. For scholars have long claimed that prophecy was transformed from that earlier immediate divine communication called prophecy into scribalism and textual interpretation. On this view, the cessation of prophecy is explained in terms of an ending of one form of divine communication (i.e., through direct divine utterance) into a mediated form of divine access through the text. The claim presupposes that textuality and writtenness became the predominant form of accessing the divine.[18] The transformation is understood as linear and demon-

17. Najman, "Interpretation as Primordial Writing."
18. See H. Najman, "Angels at Sinai: Exegesis, Theology and Interpretive Authority," *DSD* 8 (2000): 313-33.

strable on the basis of the textual witnesses from the period of second temple Judaism. While it is true that there are many examples of written authority and scribal figures who are interpreting the earlier texts, we can find such examples of prophetic writtenness in preexilic materials as well as in ancient Near Eastern traditions. In addition, texts that exhibit the features of what is categorized as *prophetic* continue to be found in the late second temple texts.[19] Rather than thinking of interpretation of texts and the development of prophecy, we should consider it one of many forms of revelation in preexilic and postexilic texts.[20] Throughout the second temple period and beyond we have texts that continue to claim that they are able to connect with the divine via heavenly journey, conversation with angels, and inspired interpretation of older, authoritative prophetic texts and/or traditions.

But surely the idea of revelation as interpretation sounds paradoxical. For, according to well-established ways of thinking, revelation and interpretation are distinct: there is revelation, which somehow gives rise to scripture; and then there is interpretation, which aims to understand and apply scripture, and hence to grasp what is revealed in revelation. The project of writing and reworking earlier revelation is sometimes considered radically distinct from receiving prophecy. Somehow textuality itself is considered earthly (as opposed to heavenly) and bereft of the immediacy (even pristine quality) of divine vision.

The act of writing itself and a written witness to revelation can be forms of the revelatory (e.g., Esther, Josiah's discovered scroll, Mishneh Torah, among others).[21] But the act of writing itself can also bear witness to the permanence of divine presence for the community even in the face of impending or recalled destruction (e.g., Jub 1).

Jubilees can tell us a great deal about the nature of an open corpus of prophetic texts in second temple Judean tradition. The prophetic corpus is not a closed canon: new traditions are being composed as the corpus of authoritative literature grows. Scholars have challenged the dichotomy between the apocalyptic and the prophetic, and thereby opened up the path to

---

19. For a recent discussion of prophecy at Qumran, see A. P. Jassen, *Mediating the Divine: Prophecy and Revelation in the Dead Sea Scrolls and Second Temple Judaism,* STDJ (Leiden: Brill, forthcoming).

20. See my forthcoming work on this subject, "Discourse Attributed to a Heavenly Founder: Emulation and Imitation," in *Prophetic Ends.*

21. See my essay "The Symbolic Significance of Writing in Prophetic Traditions," in *The Idea of Biblical Interpretation: Essays in Honor of James L. Kugel,* ed. H. Najman and J. H. Newman, JSJSup 83 (Leiden: Brill, 2004), 139-73.

considering these texts prophetic.[22] Moreover, we have no evidence that these texts are any less than "scriptural," "authoritative," or "biblical" at Qumran (these terms, of course, have an anachronistic dimension in the third and second centuries B.C.E.).

Thus, to classify Jubilees as prophecy, in the way we might call Daniel or 4 Ezra or even Pesher Habakkuk prophecy,[23] enables us to consider these texts in their own context. The possibility of writing new interpretive and liturgical and even mystical texts was still alive in late second temple Judaism. We see time and again that the possibility of prophetic inspiration and angelic visitation is invoked. By allowing ourselves to read Jubilees in the context of the texts and traditions it appropriates, we have begun to construct a context for a text that has deliberately effaced its own origin. Jubilees is located at a time when scripture was being written and was very much in conversation with the old as it attached itself to a discourse tied to a founder, which is authoritatively old by the time of the second century B.C.E.

II. Exemplars in Jubilees: Two Levels

I will now turn to the role of the author in Jubilees. As I have argued elsewhere, the figure of Moses is invoked to authorize the work in the same manner as found in Deuteronomy.[24] In *Seconding Sinai* I argued that it is useful to bring Foucault's concept of authorship to bear on the Deuteronomic tradition:

> What is the alternative to seeing this long-term expansion of Moses' role — this long history of pseudonymous attribution and rewriting — as a

22. G. W. E. Nickelsburg, "The Nature and Function of Revelation in 1 Enoch, Jubilees, and Some Qumranic Documents," in *Pseudepigraphical Perspectives: The Apocrypha and Pseudepigrapha in Light of the Dead Sea Scrolls; Proceedings of the International Symposium of the Orion Center for the Study of the Dead Sea Scrolls and Associated Literature, 12-14 January, 1997*, ed. E. G. Chazon and M. E. Stone, STDJ 31 (Leiden: Brill, 1999), 91-119; once again, see J. C. VanderKam's two seminal articles that challenged the dichotomy between prophecy and apocalyptic and prophecy and wisdom literature: "The Prophetic-Sapiential Origins of Apocalyptic Thought" and "Prophecy and Apocalyptics in the Ancient Near East"; see n. 10 above. See also I. Grunewald's discussion of what he calls para-prophecy in *From Apocalypticism to Gnosticism* (Frankfurt am Main: Peter Lang, 1988), 17-18.

23. Cf. J. Barton, *Oracles of God: Perceptions of Ancient Prophecy in Israel after the Exile* (New York: Oxford University Press, 1988).

24. See my discussion of this in *Seconding Sinai*, chap. 1.

history of fraud and tampering? Although Foucault is not primarily concerned, in his discussion of the author function, with ancient texts, and although he does not directly address the Hebrew Bible, one of his examples provides a useful contemporary analogue to the cases I am considering. It is the example of discourses that are inextricably linked to their founders, such as Marxism or Freudianism. When someone proclaims "Back to Marx!" or "Back to Freud!" she claims to represent the authentic doctrine of Marx or Freud, although she may express it in different words. Of course, today such people make known their own names, under which they author books. But, in some ancient cultures, the way to continue or return to the founder's discourse was precisely to ascribe what one said or wrote, not to oneself, but rather to the founder.[25]

In the above passage, I consider the claim that "Moses" wrote Deuteronomy or Jubilees. If we are to take that claim seriously, what is involved? First, we must seriously consider what it could mean in general — in the exilic and postexilic periods — to attribute a tradition to a figure, to say, for example, that Isaiah wrote Second Isaiah or that Moses wrote Deuteronomy or that Jeremiah wrote the whole of Jeremiah.

Regardless of whether there is a historical Isaiah, what is important is that the earliest traditions about Isaiah seem to have generated even more traditions that would attach themselves to the earlier Isaianic traditions. Just as we speak of Pythagorean texts — which are surely not physically or historically produced by Pythagoras himself, but which participate in a discourse attached to a founder — and just as we speak of Marxist or Freudian texts that were not written by either Marx or Freud, so we should perhaps speak of Isaianic texts, participating in an Isaianic discourse. Between founding figure and discourse there is a reciprocal and dynamic relationship: ascriptions to the figure constitute the discourse, while developments of the discourse constitute the figure's evolving identity.

What I want to argue is that Jubilees presents itself as part of the larger corpus of revelatory literature insofar as it participates in an already inspired discourse associated with a founder. These figures from the remote past keep writing, or at least communicating to later writers, traditions that are said to be part of a revered and inspired past.

I want to distinguish my position here from someone who might argue that there are analogues to Greco-Roman schools of philosophy in late

---

25. *Seconding Sinai*, 12.

ancient Judaism. I do not claim that we can establish in any way that there are schools of Mosaic, Enochic, or Ezran Judaisms. Neither do I think that we have the evidence that we can clearly distinguish communities that discuss Mosaic Law and Torah from those that do not. On my reading of these texts (e.g., Jubilees, 1 Enoch, Ben Sira), none of them defines a school. Neither do Jubilees or early Enochic traditions demonstrate that there were debates between actual *schools of thought,* or even show that there was an established framework of discipleship within a school. In short, there is simply no explicit textual or material evidence of the kind in the third and second centuries that supports the existence of two distinct schools associated with Enoch and Moses.[26]

Instead, distinctive founders are linked to particular discourses. These discourses are not mutually exclusive, but are instead overlapping — sometimes even within a single text. Jubilees is an example, as is 4 Ezra. In Jubilees we can find traces of Jeremianic, Deuteronomic, Enochic, and Mosaic traditions; all these have other expressions of these discourses that function and grow beside and apart from the book of Jubilees itself. But what we can see in Jubilees is that these discourses that are linked to different founders can be absorbed within a single work without any obvious tension.[27] It seems strange to construct or to posit schools when we don't have the evidence to support them. We do have much in the way of silence — and I am not prepared to construct arguments or communities or schools out of that silence. Rather, I want to focus on what we can reconstruct from the texts.

Many texts are linked and associated with the figure of Moses, and others with Enoch, and still others with Ezra. We can trace those traditions and understand that one way in which traditions were composed and developed in the ancient world was by attaching new tradition to older figures and according that new tradition the status of the old, i.e., prophetic status. I

26. For a different view in support of Mosaic and Enochic schools, see G. Boccaccini, *Beyond the Essene Hypothesis: The Parting of the Ways between Qumran and Enochic Judaism* (Grand Rapids: Eerdmans, 1998).

27. See A. Y. Reed's contribution to this conference, "Enochic and Mosaic Traditions in Jubilees: The Evidence of Angelology and Demonology." In it she discusses the author of Jubilees: "If it is difficult to determine Jubilees' assessment of the relative worth of Enochic and Mosaic texts, this is perhaps not accidental. The task of weighing the relative worth of the constitutive elements of Israel's literary heritage does not seem particularly central for the text itself. Rather, the main function of Jubilees' epistemology — aside, of course, from asserting its own authority — may be to argue that the Jewish people actually possessed a literary heritage that predated the life of Moses." See also the earlier discussion of Enoch and Moses in Jubilees in I. Grunewald, *From Apocalypticism to Gnosticism,* 35.

think it would be very helpful to link these figures to textual traditions that we come to know as "biblical." These traditions emerged over many centuries through copying, the growth and transformation of community, and interpretation of the past in the present.

The founding figure is the exemplar — here, Moses and the angel of the presence. It is clear that both Moses and the angel confer authority, but they are *also* responsible for the accuracy of the dictation and inscription of the traditions included in the book of Jubilees. They are the ones to whom the text is attributed. They are not only characters, but they are also given revelatory roles. So, at the level of authorship the text is both angelic and Mosaic.[28] The figures of the angel and Moses are trusted as the tradents and producers as they accord a heavenly and prophetic status to the tradition that builds upon and expands an already established and authoritative Mosaic tradition.[29]

There is, however, a second level throughout the book of Jubilees, a level on which well-known biblical figures function as exemplars, without the authorship or the dictation of the book being attributed to them.[30] The book itself is comprised of narratives that are built upon the reputations of selected exemplary figures — all of whom play a significant role in the transmission of the very same tablets now being dictated to Moses by the angel of the presence. But these figures are worthy of receiving these traditions *precisely* because of their own adherence to the law, their observance of the correct calendar, and their perfect sacrifices. Finally, they will receive the tablets and copy them, or preserve them and transmit them to the next tradent.

The very first tradent, Enoch, along with later tradents, who figure prominently in Jubilees as well as in the Pentateuch and other prophetic traditions, belongs to what I want to call a second level of exemplarity. It is not that the text itself is attributed to Abraham or Enoch. Nor does the fact that they are entrusted with the heavenly tablets render them authors of the text of Jubilees. Rather, they serve as examples to the reader of how to be worthy

28. See J. C. VanderKam, "The Angel of the Presence in the Book of Jubilees," *DSD* 7 (2000): 378-93, and Najman, "Angels at Sinai." See also the discussion of the angel of the presence in A. Orlov's conference paper and a more expanded version of this paper in "Moses' Heavenly Counterpart in the Book of Jubilees and the Exagoge of Ezekiel the Tragedian," *Bib* 88, no. 2 (2007).

29. Here, see the first two chapters of *Seconding Sinai*.

30. See B. G. Wright III, "From Generation to Generation: The Sage as Father in Early Jewish Literature," in *Biblical Traditions in Transmission: Essays in Honour of Michael A. Knibb*, ed. C. Hempel and J. M. Lieu, JSJSup 111 (Leiden: Brill, 2006), 309-32.

of receiving the heavenly tablets. The narratives about them, their own personal and spiritual transformations, and the successful transmission of the tablets to their progeny enable us to understand the redemptive nature of the tablets themselves as they are preserved until the time of Moses and (as the readers of Jubilees know) beyond. The myth of context, i.e., that the text itself is written in the time of Moses, is actually a redemptive narrative of preservation and transmission of the authoritative tradition.

Each figure — be it Noah or Enoch, Abraham or Levi — shows himself to be part of the distinguished, holy, and inspired line receiving and transmitting the traditions. The book of Jubilees is a book that demonstrates what it is to be exemplary and worthy of prophecy. The stories constitute the history of the heavenly tradition and its interface with earthly transmitters.

Time does not permit me to explore the various ways in which the second level of exemplars is developed along with the framework of the first level of Mosaic and angelic exemplars in Jubilees. It is the case, however, whether it is Pentateuchal reworking or the absorption of larger traditions available both to the Pentateuchal compiler(s) and to Jubilees, that the narratives about those who are worthy of transmitting the tradition provide us with a context in which we can begin to understand both the way second temple traditions are emerging and how the authors and communities behind these "new" texts seem to understand themselves to be extending and expanding older paradigms.[31]

III. Conclusion

Jubilees participates in prophetic discourse by attaching its origin to Mosaic recording and angelic dictation. Thus the text is presented as a revelation insofar as it is the earthly copy of an already established divine and heavenly original. This is done by emphasizing the role of the exemplar in generating and sustaining new discourses in Judean traditions from second temple times. Thus, the exemplar is himself the prophet who receives and transmits inspired tradition. But in addition to this, we must consider the role of the exemplars embedded within the narrative of Jubilees itself. These are the exemplars who demonstrate in their own life a kind of perfection that merits receiving the gift of reading and writing and the tablets of the heavens.

The evidence we have points to discourses associated with particular

---

31. On this point see A. Y. Reed's contribution to this volume.

founders, such as Enoch, Moses, or Ezra. This is surely not a catchall for second temple Jewish texts or, even more broadly, traditions in antiquity. However, the consideration of the exemplar is a way of organizing specific groups of materials. By attributing this "new" discourse to a founder of old, the new texts achieve a kind of continuity with the old. And yet, many additional traditions are part of the "new" discourse and can transform the earlier traditions.

The text of Jubilees understands itself to stand in the long line of prophetic traditions associated with Moses. And, just as traditions associated with Daniel and Jeremiah continue to grow during the period of Jubilees and later, so too can traditions associated with Moses continue to be part of Mosaic prophecy — not pseudoprophecy, but texts and traditions as authentic as the very words of the prophets of old. The textual evidence shows us that when we try to classify these nonbiblical but authoritative texts from second temple times, they turn out to be almost indistinguishable from biblical traditions of that time. When we stop thinking in terms of later theological and canonical divides, what we find are texts like Jubilees — texts that easily move back and forth between the Enochic and the Mosaic, between the heavenly and the earthly, and between the esoteric and the accessible.

PART THREE

JUBILEES BETWEEN ENOCH AND QUMRAN

4Q265 and the Authoritative Status of Jubilees at Qumran

Aharon Shemesh

4Q265, now titled Miscellaneous Rules, was known earlier as Serek Damascus. The rationale behind that name was the scroll's inclusion of sections resembling both the Rule of the Community and the Damascus Document.[1] Joseph Baumgarten, the editor of this scroll for its official publication in DJD 35, found the title Serek Damascus inadequate and preferred the less defined title Miscellaneous Rules. As an example of the scroll's odd, diverse content, he points to frg. 7, which "embraces the following subjects: Shabbat rules; Prohibition of priestly sprinkling on the Shabbat; Permission to walk two thousand cubits to graze animals on the Shabbat; The eschatological Communal Council; Adam and Eve in Paradise and Purification after childbirth."[2] While Baumgarten is undoubtedly right in pointing to the difficulties with regard to the content and structure of frg. 7, it should be admitted that this is not the case for the other six fragments of the scroll. In contrast to frg. 7, each of the other fragments has a well-defined single subject. Thus, frg. 1 contains the remains of what seems to be a pesher to Isa 54:1-2, frg. 3 mentions the Passover sacrifice, and frg. 4 consists of a short version of the

---

1. L. H. Schiffman, "Serekh-Damascus," in *EDSS*, 868.

2. J. M. Baumgarten, "4Q265: 4QMiscellaneous Rules," in *Qumran Cave 4.XXV: Halakhic Texts*, ed. J. M. Baumgarten et al., DJD 35 (Oxford: Clarendon, 1999), 58. Baumgarten, "Scripture and Law in 4Q265," in *Biblical Perspectives: Early Use and Interpretation of the Bible in Light of the Dead Sea Scrolls; Proceedings of the First International Symposium of the Orion Center for the Study of the Dead Sea Scrolls and Associated Literature, 12-14 May 1996*, ed. M. E. Stone and E. G. Chazon, STDJ 28 (Leiden: Brill, 1998), 25-33.

sectarian Penal Code and a partial description of the procedure for accepting new members to the community. Only a few words survived of frg. 5,
which most probably has to do with agriculture laws, and frg. 6 contains a
series of Shabbat laws similar in content and phraseology to the Damascus
Document. The fragmentary condition of the scroll's remains is indeed an
unfortunate situation, but we should be careful not to blame its author for
our inability to grasp the overall sequence and content of the scroll. As in
many other cases, we have no way to estimate what the original length of the
composition was, how much has come to us, and how much has been lost.
Therefore, it is very difficult to speculate about the original contexts of the
survived fragments.

　　With these facts in mind, we are coming back to frg. 7, which presents
the modern scholar with a real challenge. Can we solve this conundrum:
Reveal the background behind it and explain its content and the sequence
of its details?[3] My research experience of the last years teaches me that it's
worth a try.[4]

4Q265, Fragment 7

Here is the text in his original Hebrew and an English translation based on
Baumgarten's edition, though I omitted his reconstructions and made some
necessary changes. As will be explained below, some of Baumgarten's reconstructions worsen the situation and make it even harder to grasp the passage's overall structure.

On the day of [	ל ביום ה[ ] [1
[da]y of the Shabbat and not [	יו[ם השת ולא] [2
[Le]t no man of the seed of Aaron sprinkle w[ater for purification	א[ל יז איש מזרע אהרון מ]י נדה 3
[ ] *s [ ] *m big will fast on the day [	[ ]מ*[]מ* גדול יצום[5] ביום 4
[a]n [a]nimal may walk two thousand cubits	א[ת ה]בהמה ילך אלפים אמה 5

---

3. For a preliminary suggestion to explain the collection of laws in frg. 7, see M. Kister,
"Lexical and Linguistic Gleaning from the Dead Sea Scrolls," *Leshoneneu* 67 (2007): 41, and
note 78.

4. See my article "4Q251: *Midrash Mishpatim*," *DSD* 12 (2005): 280-302.

5. Baumgarten reads וצום.

6	‏[קדש שלושים רס אל ימ]	[ ]holy thirty stadia. Let n[o]
7	‏[ב]היות בעצת היחד חמשה ע[	[W]hen there will be in the council of the Community fif[teen
8	‏[הנ]ביאים נכונה עצת היח]ד	[The p]rophets. The council of the Community is established
9	‏רצון וריח ניחוח לכפר על ה[א]רץ מ*[	Pleasing and a sweet odour to atone for the l[a]nd
10	‏יספה⁶ במשפט קצי עולה והמ]	Will perish in the judgments of the periods of iniquity.
11	‏בשבוע הראיש[ון]	On the first week
12	‏אשר לא הובא אל גן עדן ועצם	[until] he was brought to the Garden of Eden and a bone
13	‏[ה]יה לה עד אשר לא הובאה אצ]לו	did she have until she was brought to hi[m]
14	‏[כי] קדוש גן עבן וכול האב אשר בתוכו קודש	[for] the Garden of Eden is sacred and every young shoot which is in its midst is a consecrate thing
15	‏וטמאה שבעת ימים כימי נדת דותה תטמא ושל]שים	(she) will be impure for seven days as in the days of her menstruation
16	‏טהרה ואם נקבה תלד וטמאה	(the blood) of her purity. And if she will bear a female she shall be impure
17	‏[תש]ב בדם טוהרה בכול קודש ‏[לא תגע]	[shall remain]n in the blood of her purity. [No] consecrate thing [shall she touch].

The fragment may be divided into four parts. The first unit, consisting of lines 1-6, contains the remains of some halakic rulings. They are phrased in the abstract style characteristic of the Damascus Document laws. The second unit, lines 7-10, has a clear sectarian nature. It mentions the "council of the Community" twice: in line 7 and in line 8, and in line 10 there appears the phrase "periods of iniquity," which is typical of the sectarian vocabulary. The third part (ll. 11-14) is a retelling of the Genesis story of the creation of Eve from Adam's rib and God's placing them in paradise. The fourth part (ll. 15-17) is again halakic in nature, dealing with the laws of impurity after childbirth.

Now, the easiest parts to identify as to background are parts 3 and 4. Baumgarten had already pointed out that these two subjects — the story of

---

6. Baumgarten reads ‏וספה.

the Garden of Eden and the laws of purification after childbirth — are joined together in Jub 3, and that the text of these units of 4Q265 is actually a shorter version of the same tradition. According to Jubilees, Adam was created in the first week and Eve in the second. God brought Adam to the Garden of Eden forty days after his creation, and he joined Eve to him forty days later at the eightieth day of his creation. Then, in what is known to be a unique characteristic of Jubilees, the composition's editor associates the law of childbirth to this narrative: "And therefore the command was written in the heavenly tablets for one who bears, 'If she bears a male, she shall remain seven days in her impurity like the first seven days, And thirty-three days she shall remain in the blood of her purity. And she shall not touch anything holy. And she shall not enter the sanctuary until she has completed these days which are in accord with (the rule for) a male (child). And that which is in accord with (the rule for) a female is two weeks — like the two first weeks — in her impurity. And sixty-six days she shall remain in the blood of her purity. And their total will be eighty days'" (3:10-11).[7]

The second unit has, as I mentioned, clear sectarian flavor. The scroll's editor has already noted its close affinity with 1QS 8:1-10. Furthermore, I'm now convinced by Menahem Kister that this unit is actually a paraphrase or even a variant version of that paragraph in 1QS. Thus line 7 in our fragment, "[W]hen there will be in the council of the Community fif[teen men]," parallels 1QS 8:1, "In the Community council (there shall be) twelve men and three priests," and the phrase "The council of the Community is established" (l. 8) appears in 1QS 8:5. Also, line 10 in our fragment is a variant of 1QS 8:9, and similarly the words יספה במשפט קצי עולה are with most probability a paraphrase of 1QS 8:10, ולחרוץ משפט רשעה. In light of these parallels the content of unit 2 in our frg. 7 becomes clear. The council of the *yaḥad* that is מטעת עולם (an eternal plant) will grow, develop, and survive the eschatological future. The *yaḥad* is בית קודש for Israel, and its members were chosen by God. Their righteous deeds please God and are accepted like sacrifices, and thus have the power to atone for the land.[8]

Let's go back to the first unit of frg. 7. Its content, we recall, is halakah and had at least six rulings, probably seven or eight. Some of these are with no doubt concerning Shabbat law. The Shabbat is explicitly mentioned in line 2, though in this case the content of the law didn't survive. The Shabbat

---

7. All Jubilees' translations are from *OTP*, vol. 2, slightly revised when needed.

8. See J. Licht, *The Rule Scroll: A Scroll from the Wilderness of Judaea, 1QS, 1QSa, 1QSb; Text, Introduction, and Commentary* (Jerusalem: Mossad Bialik, 1965), 168-75.

is also the subject of the laws at the beginning of lines 3 and 5. The first (l. 3) rules that the priests will not sprinkle the purification water on that day. As noted by Baumgarten, the same halakah appears in 4Q274 (4QTohorot A)[9] as follows: יז בשבת כי[אמר שמור את]השבת ואם יחול עליו השביעי ביום השבת אל. The halakah in line 5 is also known from another place, that is, CD 11:5: אל ילך איש אחר הבהמה לרעותה חוץ מעירו כי אם אלפים באמה, which serves Baumgarten for its reconstruction: המתהלך[חוץ לעירו]לרעות א[ת]ה[ב]המה ילך אלפים אמה. As the subject of frg. 6 is also the laws of the Shabbat, it is most plausible that our fragment (7) is indeed its direct continuation. Apparently, 4Q265 had a substantial section dealing with Shabbat laws.

In light of the above, I find Baumgarten's suggestions for the reconstruction of lines 4 and 6 not satisfying: in my opinion, they also ought to do with Shabbat laws. Baumgarten read and reconstructed line 4 as dealing with יום הכיפורים (the Day of Atonement): [ביו]ם גדול וצום ביום]הכפורים[ ]ולא ירחצו ולא יכב[סו ("[let them not bathe nor laun]der [on the] great [d]ay and fast, on the Day [of Atonement]"). I submit that the word וצום mentioned in this law is not a noun that describes the great day; rather it should be read as a verb, יצום.[10] The law is not concerning the Day of Atonement, but rather, like the surrounding injunctions, its subject is the Shabbat. Though I don't yet have a full reconstruction to offer, there is no doubt in my mind that the law's intent is to prohibit fasting on Shabbat. Fasting on the Shabbat is explicitly prohibited by Jub 50:12-13.[11]

Similarly I decline to accept Baumgarten's reconstruction for lines 5-6: ושה קרוב למ[נקדש שלושים רס יואכל איש בשר אור ("[Let no man eat meat of an ox or lamb near the Te]mple by a distance of thirty stadia"). This reconstruction is based on Temple Scroll 52:16-17, where the distance of "thirty stadia" is mentioned in connection with eating nonsacrificial meat in the temple surroundings: הטהורה אשר יש בה מום בשעריכה תואכלנה רחוק ממקדש שלושים רס ("and every pure animal in which there is a blemish you may eat it at your gates (cities) far from my Temple at a radius of thirty stadia"). Though this quotation from the Temple Scroll is indeed the only other place in the scrolls where the term "thirty stadia" is mentioned, this is by no

9. 4Q274, 2, 1, 1 (DJD 35, 103).

10. The first letter is more likely to be י than ו, as its leg is clearly shorter than that of the third letter in the word. A possible reconstruction may be: אם קטן א[ם גדול יצום ביום]השבת[.

11. On fasting on the Shabbat in rabbinic tradition, see Y. D. Gilat, *Studies in the Development of the Halakhah* (Ramat Gan: Bar-Ilan University Press, 1992), 107-22.

251

means a good enough reason to reconstruct 4Q256 according to it. "Thirty stadia" is a well-known unit used in Roman Hellenistic culture as a standard
measurement for the outer borders of a town. Thus we read in *m. Bava
Qamma* 7:7 "They may not set snares for pigeons unless it be thirty stadia from
an inhabited place" (ליונים אלא אם כן היה רחוק מן הישוב שלושים ריס).
The Persian equivalent to thirty stadia is the *persanga,* which is mentioned a
few times in the Babylonian Talmud in similar contexts. Thus, for example,
while discussing the prayer one should say when going on a journey, the Talmud (*b. Berakhot* 30a) asks: "when should he pray it?" R. Yaakov the son of
Hisdah says: "when he is already on the road — *persanga.*"[12] Line 6, I suggest,
ought to be read in line with the previous law of line 5. The first states that one
is allowed to walk an animal 2,000 cubits, and the second decrees that in other
circumstances (which were specified in the missing texts) one is allowed "[to
walk on the Sabbath day of h]oliness thirty stadia" (ילך ביום שבת] קדש
שלושים ריס). We should not be surprised that the scroll distinguishes between different situations with regard to the allowed walking distance, as this
is exactly what we find in the Damascus Document. While CD 11:5 allows graz-
ing animals in a distance of 2,000 cubits, CD 10:21 states that a man by himself
should not proceed more than 1,000 cubits.[13]

It is clear by now that the legal section of frg. 7 is homogeneous in that
all its details are concerned with the Sabbath. This observation actually presents us with the key to understanding frg. 7's structure in general and the
meaning of its second unit (mentioning the *yaḥad*) in particular. To recall,
the last part of our passage (which deals with the story of the Garden of
Eden and the laws of impurity after childbirth) parallels Jub 3. Is it surprising that the subject of chap. 2 is the Shabbat, just like in our document?! In
what follows I hope to establish that 4Q265 is a rewritten version of Jubilees,
as evident from the structure of frg. 7. As a result, the connection between
other fragments of the scroll may also be discerned.

Jubilees tells the story of creation retrospectively from the standpoint
of the Shabbat. "And the angel of the presence spoke to Moses according to
the word of the Lord, saying: Write the complete history of the creation, how
in six days the Lord God finished all His works and all that He created, and
kept Sabbath on the seventh day and hallowed it for all ages" (2:1). This is to
emphasize the importance of the Shabbat as the ultimate goal of the creation. Then in vv. 2-15, God's deeds of the six days are described followed by

---

12. Cf. *b. Berakhot* 16a.
13. For this see L. H. Schiffman, *Halakhah at Qumran* (Leiden: Brill, 1975), 91-98.

a detailed account of the first Shabbat, to which we shall return soon (vv. 16-26). From v. 26 onward the commandment to the Israelites to keep the Shabbat is given. Vv. 31-32 sum up the issue as follows: "The creator of all blessed it, but he did not sanctify any people or nations to keep the Sabbath thereon with the sole exception of Israel. He granted to them alone that they might eat and drink and keep the Sabbath thereon upon the earth. And the creator of all, who created this day for a blessing and sanctification and glory, blessed it more than all days. This law and testimony was given to the children of Israel as an eternal law for their generations." To recall, the subject of the immediately following chap. 3 is the story of the creation of Eve from Adam's rib, the entrance of the couple into the Garden of Eden, followed by the halakic instructions concerning purification after childbirth. The sequence of the narrative in this portion of Jubilees is thus:

- the list of Shabbat prohibitions,
- the election of the children of Israel from among the nations, and
- the creation of Eve, the entrance to the Garden of Eden, and laws of impurity after childbirth.

The last sentence (vv. 31-32) stresses that the people of Israel were sanctified and elected from all the nations to keep the Sabbath. This declaration is a condensed repetition of the narrative that appears earlier in this chapter (vv. 20-22).

> And he (God) said to us (the angels), "Behold I shall separate for myself a people from among all the nations. And they will also keep the Sabbath. And I will sanctify them for myself, and I will bless them and they will be my people and I will be their God.
>
> "And I have chosen the seed of Jacob from among all that I have seen. And I have recorded him as my firstborn son, and have sanctified him for myself forever and ever. And I will make known to them the Sabbath day so that they might observe therein a Sabbath from all work, and bless the one who created all things and has chosen them from all the nations so that they might keep the Sabbath together with us (ולהיות יחד עמנו שובתים). So that their deeds (the keeping of the Sabbath) will go up as sweet odour, which is acceptable before him all the days (מצוותיו יעלה ריח ניחוח אשר ירצה לפניו כל הימים ומעשה)."[14]

14. The translation provided here reflects the Hebrew version as emerged from the Qumran fragments of Jubilees (4Q216, col. 7). The Ethiopian has a longer version.

These verses have been discussed by scholars from several different angles.[15] For our purposes I wish to concentrate on the last two verses. The angel of the presence tells Moses that God chose the seed of Jacob from all the nations so that "they might keep the Sabbath together with (עמנו ולהיות יחד) us. So that their deeds (the keeping of the Sabbath) will go up as sweet odour, which is acceptable before him all the days (ומעשה מצוותיו יעלה ריח ניחוח אשר ירצה לפניו כל הימים)." The last words of this verse correspond almost verbatim to line 9 in 4Q265 frg. 7: "Pleasing and a sweet odor to atone for the l[a]nd (רצון וריח ניחוח לכפר על ה[א]רץ מ*[)." The meaning of this phrase in both, in 4Q265 and in its origin in 1QS, is that the *yaḥad* has a special status as the chosen people, so that its members' righteous deeds have the power to atone for the land. The author of 4Q265 chose to integrate this short paragraph from 1QS (or maybe a variant of it) in this specific location at the heart of frg. 7 in order, I suggest, to emphasize and strengthen the sect's historical-religious perception of itself as the true Israel and as being the present-day "seed of Jacob." In so doing, 4Q265 presents the paragraph from 1QS as an exegetical implementation of Jubilees. Note also the appearance of the word *yaḥad* (יחד) at the beginning of the verse, just as in lines 7-8 of our fragment. It is not far-fetched to assume that this linguistic similarity stimulates him to do so. Actually in its current context at the middle of frg. 7 of 4Q265, the citation from 1QS functions as a rewriting of Jubilees. While in Jubilees the chosen people are the "seed of Jacob," in 4Q265 it is the *yaḥad* and its members.[16]

---

15. On Jacob as God's firstborn son, see J. L. Kugel, "4Q369 'Prayer of Enosh' and Ancient Biblical Interpretation," *DSD* 5 (1998): 119-48. The association of the election of Israel with the Sabbath finds its expression in some other compositions from Qumran. See, for example, 4Q503 (daily prayers), 24-25 (DJD 7 [Oxford: Clarendon, 1982], 105-36). Interestingly, this idea is also the focus of one of the relatively late versions of the Shabbat prayer, used in the traditional Jewish prayer book for the Shabbat Morning Prayer *(Shacharit)*. The text relates as follows: "And You, Lord our God, did not give it (the Shabbat) to the nations of the world, nor did You, our King, grant it as a heritage to idol-worshippers, nor can uncircumcised participate in its rest — for You have given it in love to Your people Israel, to the descendents of Jacob whom You have chosen." For the dating and history of this text, see N. Wieder, "The Controversy about the Liturgical Composition *'Yismach Moshe'* — Opposition and Defense," in *Studies in Aggadah, Targum, and Jewish Liturgy in Memory of Joseph Heinemann*, ed. E. Fleischer and Y. Patohovski (Jerusalem: Magnes, 1981), 75-99.

16. The perception of the *yaḥad* as the true elected Israel is manifested throughout the scrolls. See 1QHᵃ, 7, 26-27; 1QS, 4, 22. See also D. Dimant, "Qumran Sectarian Literature," in *Jewish Writing of the Second Temple Period*, ed. M. E. Stone (Philadelphia: Assen, 1984), 536-38.

The picture that emerges from the above analysis is that the sequence of frg. 7's content follows closely that of chaps. 2 and 3 of Jubilees. It opens with a series of laws concerning the Shabbat (in fact, this unit begins in frg. 6), it moves then to describe the election of the *yaḥad* (the new "real" Israel) for observing the Shabbat with God and the angels, and it continues with the story of Adam and Eve in the Garden of Eden and the laws of purification after childbirth.

Recognizing the heavy dependence of 4Q265 on Jubilees enables us to further suggest possible explanations for the inclusion of some of the other fragments in this scroll, though it should be admitted that these are propositions that can't be proved.

As is well known, Jubilees deals with Shabbat laws twice: first within the context of the creation in chap. 2, and a second time at the end of the book in chap. 50. At the beginning of that chapter Jubilees relates not only to the Shabbat Day but also to the Sabbath of the land — the seventh year and the Jubilee year: "And I also related to you the Sabbath of the land on Mount Sinai. And the years of Jubilee in the Sabbaths of years I related to you. . . . And the land will keep the Sabbaths when they dwell upon it" (50:1-3). The subject of the previous chapter, 49, is the celebration of the Passover centered upon the paschal sacrifice in the temple. To recall, the subject of frg. 3 is the paschal sacrifice and frg. 5 concerns some agriculture laws that may very well be the laws of the *Shmita* (the seventh year): the fragment mentions "all that is sown in the earth" (l. 1) and the word ‏והפריח‎ (makes bloom) in line 2.

If all this is not mere accident, we may assume that, similar to other rewritten compositions, the author of 4Q265 collected the material concerning the Shabbat from the entire book of Jubilees. It may well be that he started his task by reviewing the legal material at the end of the book: Passover, seventh year, and Shabbat laws. This last issue — the Shabbat law — led him from the end of the book to its beginning, where he found additional material on the same subject. While there, he continued with the election of Israel and the story of the Garden of Eden along with chap. 3 of the book.

1QS 5:13-20: "The Laws of Separatism" and Jubilees 22:16-22

In light of the above discussion, I wish to return to another example of a similar phenomenon that I dealt with in the past. This example is not as clear as the one just analyzed; consequently I didn't recognize its full meaning at that time. It is thus worthwhile to repeat it here before concluding our findings and their meanings.

The Rule of the Community requires the new member to swear that he will "separate from all the men of deceit" (1QS 5:10) and comply with the following rules (1QS 5:13-20):

> He must not enter the water in order to touch the purity of the men of holiness. . . . No one may be united with him in his work or his wealth,[17] lest he burden him (with) guilty iniquity. But he shall keep far away from him in everything, for thus it is written: "Keep far away from everything false" (Exod 23:7).[18] No man of the men of the Community shall respond to their utterance with respect to any law or judgment. No one must either eat or drink anything of their property, or accept anything whatever from their hand without payment, as it is written: "Have nothing to do with the man whose breath is in his nostrils, for wherein can he be accounted?" (Isa 2:22). For all those who are not accounted within his covenant, they and everything they have must be excluded. The man of holiness must not lean on any worthless works, for worthless are all who do not know his covenant. But all those who spurn his word he will destroy from the world, and all their works are impure before him, and all their property unclean.

The Cave 4 fragments of the Rule of the Community have a shorter (and with all probability earlier) version for this series of injunctions.[19]

> And all who enter into the Council of the Community will take upon his soul by oath [to return t]o the [T]orah of Mose[s] with all (the) heart and with all (the) soul, (to) everything revealed from [the Torah] to the [multitude of] the Council of the men [of] the Community [and to separate from all the men of] deceit. They will not approach the purity of the men of [holine]ss. One will not eat with him בחיד.[20] No man of the men of the Community shall respond to their utterance with respect to any law or judgment. And no one shall be united with him in wealth and work. And no man of the men of holiness shall eat of their property;

17. Cf. CD 20:6-8.

18. Compare the *Mekhilta de-Rabbi Ishmael* (327 in the Horowitz-Rabin edition).

19. On the relation between 1QS and 4QS, see S. Metso, *The Textual Development of the Qumran Community Rule*, STDJ (Leiden: Brill, 1997).

20. See the discussion below.

neither shall he receive anything from their hands. And they shall not lean upon any works of worthless, for worthless are all who do not know his covenant.

Comparison of this text (in its two versions) to the following passage from Jubilees (22:16-22) is illuminating. This is Abraham's testament to his grandson Jacob, which he issued on his deathbed.

16And you also, my son Jacob, remember my words,
and keep the commandments of Abraham, your father.
Separate yourself from the gentiles,
and do not eat with them,
and do not perform deeds like theirs.
And do not become associates of theirs.
Because their deeds are defiled,
and all of their ways are contaminated, and despicable, and
    abominable.
17They slaughter their sacrifices to the dead,
and to the demons they bow down.
And they eat in tombs.
And all their deeds are worthless and vain. . . .
19But (as for) you, my son, Jacob,
may God Most High help you,
and the God of heaven bless you.
And may he turn you away from their defilement,
and from their errors.
20Be careful, my son, Jacob, that you not take a wife from any of the
    seed of the daughters of Canaan,
because all of his seed is (destined) for uprooting from the earth;
21 . . . and all of his seed will be blotted out from the earth,
and all his remnant,
and there is none of his who will be saved.
22And for all of those who worship idols and for the hated ones,
there is no hope in the land of the living;
because they will go down in Sheol.
And in the place of judgment they will walk,
and they will have no memory upon the earth.
Just as the sons of Sodom were taken from the earth,
so (too) all of those who worship idols shall be taken away.

There is a remarkable similarity between this passage from Jubilees and the one quoted above from the Rule of the Community in both rhetoric and the content of the injunctions listed in them. We should first consider the list of phrases Abraham used to condemn Gentile deeds. He described their actions as "defiled," "despicable," and "abominable," which are exactly the same terms 1QS uses to depict his opponents' behavior. According to the Rule, a nonmember of the community is forbidden to touch the pure food "for (he remains) impure among all those who transgress his words," and the community's members are warned not to "lean on any worthless works (מעשי הבל), for worthless (הבל) are all who do not know his covenant." Finally, we must point out the similarity between the two in describing the fate of the enemy. The author of 1QS promises that "all those who spurn his word he will destroy from the world" while Jubilees predicts: "And for all of those who worship idols and for the hated ones, / there is no hope in the land of the living; / because they will go down in Sheol."

As for the content of the injunctions themselves: Abraham instructs Jacob to separate himself from the Gentiles, not to eat with them, not to behave as they do, and not to associate himself with them. These prohibitions are very similar to those of the Rule of the Community in both content and order. This is especially evident in the Cave 4 version where, as in Jubilees, the injunction to "separate from all the men of deceit" is immediately followed by the prohibition: "One will not eat with him ביחד." The word *be-yaḥad* in this sentence is not a reference to the sect (as translated in the Charlesworth edition: "within the community") but means "together," as in the following sentence: "No one may be united (יחד) with him in his work or his wealth." In the Cave 1 version, this interdiction is followed by the admonition "lest he burden him with guilty iniquity," which shows that the focus is not on economic cooperation as such but on the fear that such a partnership may lead the member of the sect to be influenced by an outsider and subsequently fall into error and thus parallel the injunction in Jubilees: "Do not become associates of theirs."

It seems, then, that very much as was the case for 4Q265, Jubilees is the source for this piece of legislation in the Rule of the Community. Like the author of 4Q265, the Rule of the Community adjusts the original material he drew from Jubilees to his sectarian worldview: what Jubilees prohibits as separatism from Gentiles — "do not eat with them, and do not perform deeds like theirs" — the Rule of the Community prohibits as disassociation from Jews who are not part of the sect — "No one must either eat or drink anything of their property" and "No one may be united with him in his duty or his property." This is because the sectarian author of the Rule of the Community believed that only the members of the *yaḥad* were the true Israel and therefore everyone else should be considered Gentiles.

Conclusions: The Status of Jubilees in Qumran

The importance of Jubilees for the *yaḥad* and its high status in the community's library was recognized by scholars long ago.[21] This is evident from the large number of copies (more than ten) of this book found in Qumran. Many think the book of Jubilees is explicitly mentioned in the Damascus Document. CD 16:1-4 relates: "Therefore a man shall bind himself by oath to return to the Law of Moses, for in it everything is specified. And the explication of their times when Israel turns a blind eye, behold it is specified in *the Book of the Divisions of the Times into their Jubilees and Weeks.*" According to this reading, "the Book" mentioned in CD is Jubilees, and it is being here described as the authoritative source for the true meaning of the Torah of Moses and its details.[22]

The findings of the current discussion highlight three aspects of this special status of Jubilees in Qumran. The first aspect is Jubilees' being subject to a literary activity resembling the rewriting of the Bible; 4Q265's integration of a passage from 1QS into the narrative that follows Jub 2 and 3 functions in the same way as other compositions from Qumran do in their rewriting of a portion of the Bible. One of the goals of this rewriting activity is to incorporate the new sectarian (halakic or theological) stances into the authorized holy scripture. Thus, for example, the Temple Scroll (66:16-17),

21. For a comprehensive survey of the scholarly debate with regard to Jubilees' origins and dating, see J. C. VanderKam, "The Origins and Purposes of the Book of Jubilees," in *Studies in the Book of Jubilees*, ed. M. Albani, J. Frey, and A. Lange (Tübingen: Mohr Siebeck, 1997), 3-24. Some scholars tend toward a later dating for Jubilees, and some even think it is a sectarian composition authored within the *yaḥad* community; see M. Kister, "The History of the Essenes: A Study of the 'Animals Vision,' Jubilees and Damascus Document," *Tarbiz* 56 (1987): 8-18; C. Werman, "The Attitude towards Gentiles in the Book of Jubilees and Qumran Literature Compared with Early Tanaaic Halakha and Contemporary Pseudepigrapha" (Ph.D. diss., Hebrew University, 1995), 30-35.

22. Against this reading of CD, see D. Dimant, "Two 'Scientific' Fictions: The So-called Book of Noah and the Alleged Quotation of Jubilees in CD 16:3-4," in *Studies in the Hebrew Bible, Qumran, and Septuagint, Presented to Eugene Ulrich*, ed. P. W. Flint, E. Tov, and J. C. VanderKam (Leiden: Brill, 2006), 230-49. For a survey and bibliography of earlier scholarly publications concerning this issue, see there 242-43 and notes 49-51.

while rewriting the biblical list of illicit unions, incorporates into it the sectarian prohibition against marrying the niece: "A man is not to take his brother's daughter or his sister's daughter because it is an abomination" (אחותו לא יקח איש את בת אחיו או את בת). This is exactly what 4Q265 is doing by integrating the passage from 1QS into frg. 7. The result of this integration is a new retelling version of Jubilees, which has the *yaḥad* as the chosen people instead of the "seeds of Jacob" as in the original.

The second aspect of Jubilees' status as scripture in Qumran is its use as a source for halakah. One example of this role of Jubilees in Qumran is the "laws of separatism" discussed above. In order not to repeat myself, let me here offer another example. The halakic scrolls mention a few times the prohibition not to draw water from a well on the Shabbat. Thus CD 11:1-2, ישתה על עומדו ואל ישאב אל כל כלי ("let him drink where he stands, but let him not draw [water] into any vessel"). Likewise in 4Q241, 11, 3: יד [בור יהיה חונה אל ישאב ממנו ב]שבת] ("[and if by the well he is camping let him not draw from it on t[he Shabbat]").[23] There is no reference to such a prohibition in the Torah; its origin is in Jubilees, where it is mentioned twice (2:29; 50:8).

There is yet another expression of a book's canonical status. In my article on 4Q251 I showed that the scroll's editor used Exod 21–23 (the book of the covenant) as a skeleton to hang upon it and to arrange along it the halakic material he had at his disposal. The scroll is a collection of passages of diverse genres: some of them are abstract rulings in the style of the Damascus Document; others are pieces of rewritten passages of the Torah. This fact strengthens the assumption that most of the scroll's passages weren't composed in their current context but were collected by the editor from various sources. It was the editor's close knowledge of Torah and his familiarity with the biblical text that made it a natural medium for arranging the extra material he had.

It might very well be that 4Q265 exhibits the same phenomenon, but this time with regard to the book of Jubilees. At the outset of this article I emphasized the diverse literary nature of the scroll's fragments. It includes law and narrative, pesher and admonition. If the analysis I offered in this article proves to be true, then Jubilees functions here in a very similar way to the function of Exodus's portion in 4Q251, and this testifies to the close familiarity of the scroll's editor with the text of Jubilees and to its canonical status in Qumran.

---

23. The reading is from V. Noam and E. Qimron, "A Qumran Composition on the Laws of the Sabbath and Its Contribution to Early Halakhic History," *Tarbiz* 74 (2005): 513.

Purity and Impurity in the Book of Jubilees

Lutz Doering

The issue of purity and impurity in Jubilees has provoked recent debate. While some scholars assign Jubilees and the Temple Scroll "to the same legal and exegetical tradition"[1] and place them, together with the texts from Qumran, within the ancient priestly halakah,[2] others perceive profound differences.[3] L. Ravid concludes from the absence of ritual defilement in the story of Abraham's death in Jub 23:1-7 that "it does not seem probable that the author agreed with the Pentateuchal concepts of purity and impurity, or with those represented in the Judean Desert scrolls."[4] According to Ravid, Jubilees is a polemic against the priesthood who then controlled the temple. In response, J. VanderKam suggests reading Jubilees in line with the putative setting of the book in a period without a sanctuary and indebted to the traditions this book reworks.[5] My own reading of Jubilees is closer to the latter,

---

1. Thus the classic formulation by J. C. VanderKam, "The Temple Scroll and the Book of Jubilees," in *Temple Scroll Studies*, ed. G. J. Brooke, JSPSup 7 (Sheffield: JSOT Press, 1989), 211-36, 232.

2. E.g., C. Werman, "The Rules of Consuming and Covering the Blood in Priestly and Rabbinic Law," *RevQ* 16, no. 64 (1995): 621-36.

3. E.g., J. Klawans, *Impurity and Sin in Ancient Judaism* (Oxford: Oxford University Press, 2000); M. Himmelfarb, "Sexual Relations and Purity in the Temple Scroll and the Book of Jubilees," *DSD* 6 (1999): 11-36.

4. L. Ravid, "Purity and Impurity in the Book of *Jubilees*," *JSP* 13 (2002): 61-86, 63.

5. J. VanderKam, "Viewed from Another Angle: Purity and Impurity in the Book of *Jubilees*," *JSP* 13 (2002): 209-15.

although Ravid has raised some important questions. However, we need to cast our net wide enough to be able to gauge the full range of Jubilees' take on (im)purity. In what follows I shall heuristically accept the distinction between "ritual" and "moral" impurity: "ritual" impurity, as reflected in Lev 11–15, Num 19, and related texts, is natural, contracted by contagion, and can in most cases be purged by purification rituals; it is not sinful but disqualifies from contact with *sancta* (I shall, however, include dietary laws and priestly ablutions here too). In contrast, "moral" impurity, as reflected in Lev 18, 20, and related texts, consists of certain crimes; defiles the sinner, the land, and the temple; and cannot be purged by purification rituals. However, since I think the terms "ritual" and "moral" are not unproblematic, and since I also note certain "ritual" aspects of impurities designated as "moral," the terms come in quotation marks.

I. "Ritual" Impurity, Purity, and Purification in Jubilees

1. The impurity and purification of the parturient. Jub 3:8-14[6] contains a tradition about the entry of Adam and "his wife" (not named before 3:33) into the Garden of Eden with which the periods of impurity and purification after childbirth familiar from Lev 12 are etiologically linked. Two aspects are developed. First, harmonizing the two creation narratives (cf. Gen 1:27; 2:18-22), Jub 3:8 states that although Adam and his wife were created in the first week, only in the second week was she shown to him. From this, the "commandment" is inferred that women giving birth to a son shall be kept "in their defilement" (Ge'ez *westa rek^w son*) for seven days, those giving birth to a daughter, for fourteen. Lev 12 clarifies that the parturient during this period is impure like a menstruant (v. 2: כימי נדת דותה תטמא; v. 5: כנדתה; cf. 4Q265 7 15). Apparently, the *tertium* between Lev 12:2, 5 and Jub 3:8 is that after this period of impurity a woman would be allowed to mate again with her husband. Second, a longer period of less severe impurity is linked to the entry of Adam and his wife into the Garden. Both have been created outside the Garden, and angels bring Adam in after forty days but his wife after eighty days (Jub 3:9). Again, a "commandment" is inferred, this time written on the heavenly tablets, mentioning the "defilement" of seven or twice seven days and additionally a period of thirty-three days for a male child and sixty-

---

6. Text and translation: J. C. VanderKam, *The Book of Jubilees,* 2 vols., CSCO 510-511, Scriptores Aethiopici 87-88 (Louvain: Peeters, 1989).

six days for a daughter that the woman spends "in the blood of purification" (*westa dama neṣḥ;* Jub 3:10-11). This agrees with the periods mentioned in Lev 12:4-5. The rationale for this link with Eden clearly is the notion of Eden as sanctuary.[7] Lev 12:4 states that the woman during her period of purification may not touch any *sancta* (קֹדֶשׁ) nor enter the sanctuary (הַמִּקְדָּשׁ), similarly Jub 3:13. There is a close parallel to the Jubilees passage in 4Q265 frg. 7,[8] already referred to above.

However, a few questions remain open. How does the purification relate to Adam's and his wife's entry into the Garden? It should be the *mother* who needs to wait, but there is no mother here. One might perhaps reckon with influence of a tradition extending the purification period to the male or female child.[9] However, 4Q266 (=4QDᵃ) 6 ii 11, in a similar context, mentions a wet nurse that, according to some, was intended to prevent the child's defilement, which would suggest that the child is not necessarily deemed impure like the mother; but the passage is too fragmentary to allow for a definite answer, and this explanation of the presence of a wet nurse has recently been questioned altogether.[10] Ultimately, the link between the protoplasts and later humanity is as symbolic as the one between Eden and the temple: although not born from a mother, Adam and his wife represent human beings (construed as Israelites) confronted with the sanctuary and become part of the life cycle entailing defilement (as we shall see presently, *not* merely after the fall).[11] Unlike Lev 12:6, Jub 3 does not link the end of the pe-

---

7. Jub 3:12; 8:19; cf. 4Q265 7 14; 1QHᵃ 16 (8 Suk.):10-13. Cf. B. Ego, "Heilige Zeit — heiliger Raum — heiliger Mensch: Beobachtungen zur Struktur der Gesetzesbegründung in der Schöpfungs- und Paradiesgeschichte des Jubiläenbuchs," in *Studies in the Book of Jubilees,* ed. M. Albani, J. Frey, and A. Lange, TSAJ 65 (Tübingen: Mohr Siebeck, 1997), 207-19, 214: Eden and temple "stehen in einem symbolischen Repräsentationszusammenhang." Cf. G. Anderson, "Celibacy or Consummation in the Garden? Reflections on Early Jewish and Christian Interpretations of the Garden of Eden," *HTR* 82 (1989): 121-48, 129-31.

8. Cf. J. M. Baumgarten, "Purification after Childbirth and the Sacred Garden in 4Q265 and Jubilees," in *New Qumran Texts and Studies: Proceedings of the First Meeting of the International Organization for Qumran Studies, Paris 1992,* ed. G. J. Brooke with F. García Martínez, STDJ 15 (Leiden: Brill, 1994), 3-10. A. Shemesh, in his contribution to this volume, views 4Q265 as rewritten Jubilees, but it is not impossible that it draws on a tradition similar or identical to Jubilees' source.

9. George Syncellus, *Chronographia* 9 [5 Mosshammer]; perhaps Luke 2:22 (αἱ ἡμέραι τοῦ καθαρισμοῦ αὐτῶν). Cf. Baumgarten, "Purification," 5-6; H. K. Harrington, *The Purity Texts,* Companion to the Qumran Scrolls 5 (London: T. & T. Clark, 2004), 62.

10. Cf. C. Wassen, *Women in the Damascus Document,* Academia Biblica 21 (Leiden: Brill, 2005), 56-58.

11. Ravid's own suggestion that the purification period is related to a preparation for

riods of purification with a sacrifice. However, this does not imply "that a birthing woman has no way of becoming pure"[12] but rather reflects the literary choice and perhaps the traditions of the author: before the apparent investiture of Adam to priestly service (Jub 3:26-27), there is no priest in the narrative world, let alone animal sacrifice. Purification is simply achieved by waiting for the set number of days.

2. *Awareness of ritual defilement through sexual intercourse.* In Jubilees, as G. Anderson has convincingly argued, Adam and his wife have sex before and after their sojourn in Eden, but not in the Garden itself: according to Jub 3:6, dealing with the time before they were brought to Eden, Adam *"knew her (wa-'a'marā)."* And after their departure from Eden, we learn in 3:34 that "They were childless throughout the first jubilee; afterwards *he knew her."*[13] Thus, no sex in Paradise, but there had been some before, outside Eden. It stands to reason that this is again a reflection of the notion of Eden as sanctuary, just as CD 12:1-2 and 11QTᵃ 45:11-12 ban intercourse or someone having had intercourse from the Temple City. If this is correct, Jubilees can be said to share and apply the notion of sexual intercourse as ritually defiling (cf. Lev 15:18). Additionally, this seems to stand in the background of the prohibition of intercourse on the Sabbath as well. Just as Eden is holier than any other place in the primeval world (see n. 7), so the Sabbath is "holier than all (other) days" (Jub 2:26, with extant Hebrew: 4Q218 1 2; cf. Jub 2:30, 32). According to Jub 50:8,[14] the one "who lies with a woman" on the Sabbath incurs the death penalty. Ritual defilement by intercourse on the Sabbath is to be avoided because it is incommensurate with the holiness of the Sabbath (cf. CD 11:4-5).[15]

---

a *higher degree of purity* ("Purity and Impurity," 80) is unconvincing, since it makes no sense of the specific periods of forty and eighty days.

12. Thus, however, Ravid, "Purity and Impurity," 77.

13. Cf. Anderson, "Celibacy," 128-29. Ravid's claim that pre-Eden sex would "contradict the texts as we have them" ("Purity and Impurity," 78) is misleading.

14. L. Ravid, "The Relationship of the Sabbath Laws in *Jubilees* 50:6-13 to the Rest of the Book" (in Hebrew), *Tarbiz* 69 (2000): 161-66, claims that Jub 50:6-13 is a secondary addition to Jubilees, but her arguments are unconvincing; cf. L. Doering, "*Jub.* 50:6-13 als Schlussabschnitt des *Jubiläenbuchs* — Nachtrag aus Qumran oder ursprünglicher Bestandteil des Werks?" *RevQ* 20, no. 79 (2002): 359-87; J. C. VanderKam, "The End of the Matter? Jubilees 50:6-13 and the Unity of the Book," in *Heavenly Tablets: Interpretation, Identity, and Tradition in Ancient Judaism,* ed. L. LiDonnici and A. Lieber, JSJSup 119 (Leiden: Brill, 2007), 267-84.

15. Cf. Anderson, "Celibacy," 129-30 (temple-Sabbath analogy); L. Doering, "The Concept of the Sabbath in the Book of Jubilees," in *Studies in the Book of Jubilees,* 179-205, 196 ("sanctification" analogous to Exod 19:10, 14-15).

3. Priestly ablutions with water figure in the instructions given to Isaac by Abraham in Jub 21:16 (cf. 4Q219 ii 13). The closest parallels are ALD 19-21 (= 7:1-3, Greenfield, Stone, and Eshel), 26 (8:2), 53-54 (10:6-7), as well as TLevi 9:11. Jubilees seems to refer to three acts of washing, one concerning the whole body (cf. ALD 19 [7:1]; TLevi 9:11), the other two hands and feet. What is the rationale for these ablutions? It is unlikely that they relate to the impurities covered by Lev 11–15, summarized in Lev 22:2-7 for priests wishing to consume *sancta,* since we would expect purifying priests normally to wait *until sunset* to become clean (cf. Num 19:7). Should the ablutions merely "enhance the sanctity of the 'holy seed'"?[16] This makes too little of the fact that we are dealing with specific rules for priests related to sacrifices. Bathing before priestly office or washing hands and feet before sacrificing is indeed required in some biblical texts.[17] However, washing hands and feet *after* the sacrifice goes beyond these texts, but it is reflected in ALD 53-54 (10:6-7) and TLevi 9:11. Since both ALD 26 (8:2), 53 (10:6) and 11QT^a 26:10 relate washing of hands and feet to previous contact with *blood* and this figures in Jubilees immediately after as well (21:17),[18] it is possible that Jubilees' final ablution is to remove any blood from hands and feet. At any rate, Jubilees here shares a specific tradition[19] of scrupulous priestly purity.

4. Ritual purity as prerequisite for celebrating Passover. Jubilees comments on this issue merely in passing, but it should not be overlooked. In line with Num 9:13, Jub 49:9 declares that any "man who is pure" (*be'si 'enza neṣuḥ,* reiterated later in the verse [not so Num 9:13]) and "nearby" but "does not come" to keep the Passover on its day is to be uprooted. The statement affirms the notion of "ritual" purity relative to the (narratively: future) tem-

---

16. Thus Ravid, "Purity and Impurity," 74.

17. *Bathing:* Exod 29:4; 40:12; Lev 8:6; 16:4, (24); cf. ALD 1a, v. 2 [2:5]; *washing hands and feet:* Exod 30:19-21; cf. *m. Middot* 3:6; *m. Yoma* 4:5; *m. Tamid* 1:4; 2:1. Cf. H. Drawnel, *An Aramaic Wisdom Text from Qumran: A New Interpretation of the Levi Document,* JSJSup 86 (Leiden: Brill, 2004), 270-71, 276, 298.

18. On Jubilees' concern with blood see further below and Werman, "Rules," passim. Note that blood is one of the liquids transmitting impurity in *m. Makhshirin* 6:4-5; cf. the issue of oil stains in CD 12:15-17; 11QT^a 49:11-12.

19. Contra Ravid, "Purity and Impurity," 74 n. 22, who claims that Jubilees has "emulated . . . the dual purification of the High Priest on the Day of Atonement" (cf. Lev 16:4, 24), but the second one is *bathing* rather than washing hands and feet, as well as changing vestments. Cf. further on the matter M. Himmelfarb, "Earthly Sacrifice and Heavenly Incense: The Law of the Priesthood in *Aramaic Levi* and *Jubilees,*" in *Heavenly Realms and Earthly Realities in Late Antique Religions,* ed. R. S. Boustan and A. Yoshiko Reed (Cambridge: Cambridge University Press, 2004), 103-22.

ple. One may ask, of course, why Second Passover, for those unable to purify in a timely way, is not mentioned in Jubilees,[20] but I would urge some caution here: the absence of certain issues may primarily be motivated by literary concerns; Jubilees does not cover every legal detail. Surely, we should not infer that Jubilees dispenses with "ritual" purity for Passover — the double reference in Jub 49:9 suggests otherwise.

5. *Second tithe becomes impure after one year.* According to Jub 32:10-14, second tithe is to be eaten in the temple within one year of its specific "seasons" (i.e., firstfruits) for "seed," wine, and oil. V. 13 states that anything left beyond its respective season ("grows old") is to be viewed as "contaminated" *(se'uba);* "it is to be burned up because it has become impure" *(rekusa).* This is a different type of purity rule than the ones discussed so far, but it is "ritual" in nature. We know about distinct firstfruit festivals for wheat, wine, and oil from 4Q251 frg. 9 (*olim* 5) and from 11QT[a] 43:4-10.[21] The continuation in 11QT[a] 43:11-12 also provides a parallel to Jubilees' rule on second tithe, although its unfitness is expressed by a form of קדשׁ, here: "to be forfeited."[22] In contrast to rabbinic halakah,[23] Jubilees and 11QT[a] insist on consumption of the second tithe "year by year," as specified in Deut 14:22. The "impurity" (or "forfeiture") of any leftover tithe apparently results from its missing its proper time, as well as from the mixture between old and new it implies.

6. *The problem of corpse impurity and the role of the sanctuary for "ritual" purity in Jubilees.* Somewhat perplexing is the lack of concern for corpse impurity in the story of Abraham's death and burial in Jub 23:1-7: Jacob is lying in his grandfather's bosom, unaware that he has just passed away, then realizing he is dead (vv. 2-3); even Isaac, rushing to the scene, "fell on his father's face, cried, and kissed him" (v. 4). However, we need to recall that Jubilees closely follows the perspective of the angelic discourse (i.e., at Mount Si-

20. See the paper by Stéphane Saulnier, "Jub 49:1-14 and the Second Passover: How (and Why) to Do Away with an Unwanted Festival," *Hen* 31, no. 1 (2009).

21. Cf. J. M. Baumgarten, "*4Q Halakah*[a], the Law of Hadash, and the Pentecontad Calendar," *JJS* 27 (1976): 36-46. However, whereas these texts clearly assume a pentecontad festival sequence (cf. 11QT[a] 18-23; 4Q251 9 4-6), there is no such indication in Jubilees. For Jubilees' peculiar calendrical agenda, see further the chapter in this volume by Jonathan Ben-Dov, "Tradition and Innovation in the Calendar of Jubilees."

22. J. Maier, *Die Tempelrolle vom Toten Meer und das "Neue Jerusalem,"* 3rd ed. (Munich: E. Reinhardt, 1997), 176: "als Heiliges verfallen, tabuisiert, daher auch für anderweitige Verwendung unrein," referring to Deut 22:9.

23. Allowing storage up to three years (*m. Ma'aser Sheni* 5:6) and prescribing "poor tithe" every third year instead (*m. Avot* 5:9).

nai) on the material this discourse rewrites (i.e., Genesis to mid-Exodus). Thus, VanderKam has aptly pointed out that Jubilees models Isaac's contact with his father's corpse on Joseph's demeanor in Gen 50:1, and that the patriarchs in Jubilees obey only such laws *"that would have been fitting for their times."*[24] Moreover, we need to bear in mind that the reference point of the ritual purity laws is the temple, which is yet to come in Jubilees' setting.

Conversely, when we *do* find "ritual" purity addressed in Jubilees, it normally entails a *reference to a sanctuary*, be it past, future, or temporal: the Garden of Eden (above, §1, 2); the future temple (§4, 5), which is the place where priests will observe purity in handling sacrifices (§3); and perhaps the Sabbath as a "sanctuary in time" (§2). Interestingly, Jubilees retains and reworks a reference to a purification ritual in the context of Jacob's second visit to Bethel. In Jub 31:1, after the Dinah narrative, he commands his men, "Purify yourselves and change your clothes" *(neṣḥu wa-walleṭu 'elbāsikemu).* Whereas in Gen 35:2 this follows the request to renounce the idols, in Jubilees it precedes it and is thus *not* presented as a response to the renunciation. Whatever impurity it should purge, the purification here is more closely linked with setting out and going up to Bethel than in Genesis. Now, the way Bethel is presented — "the house of the Lord" (Jub 27:25) where Jacob erects a stone "to become the house of the Lord" (v. 27) and later an altar (31:3) — clearly rings of temple terminology for readers in second temple times, and Jub 32:3-9 narrates the investiture of Levi to the priesthood, his first sacrifices, and Jacob's giving tithe precisely at Bethel. Not only this: Jacob even decides to build a temple (32:16), only stopped by an angel (v. 22).[25] The importance of Levi's ordination at Bethel is also stressed in ALD 9-10 (5:1-5); TLevi 7:4; 8; 9:3, and the link with the later temple is reflected in the reference to the "covenant I made with Jacob at Bethel" in 11QT[a] 29:9-10 (cf. 5Q13 2 6). In short, it seems that Bethel, in order to allow for Levi's investiture, takes on traits of a "temple *in nuce*," and the approach to it aptly entails a purification ritual — the only one mentioned (albeit in direct speech) within the story line of Jubilees.[26] It is interesting that ALD 19 (7:1) has a pun on

24. VanderKam, "Viewed from Another Angle," 211-13 (quotation: 213, emphasis in original).

25. On Bethel in Jub 32, cf. E. Eshel, *"Jubilees* 32 and the Bethel Cult Traditions in Second Temple Literature," in *Things Revealed: Studies in Early Jewish and Christian Literature in Honor of M. E. Stone,* ed. E. G. Chazon, D. Satran, and R. A. Clements, JSJSup 89 (Leiden: Brill, 2004), 21-36, with further literature.

26. I.e., apart from the ablutions above, §3. This qualifies James Kugel's remark that "Neither Jacob nor anyone else in *Jubilees* is ever said to undergo ritual purification": *The*

"Bethel," requiring bathing and clothing "when you arise to enter the temple of God (לבית אל)."[27]

7. *Pure and impure animals.* The dietary laws form a distinct rubric, whose relation to "ritual" and "moral" impurity is variously interpreted.[28] Despite its rather casual comment, Jubilees is unambiguous about the distinction between pure and impure animals (cf. Lev 11; Deut 14:3-21):[29] when Jacob gave his tithe at Bethel, "he tithed all the clean animals and made an offering of them. He gave his son Levi the unclean animals" (Jub 32:8). It has been suggested that the author is dependent on a particular source here,[30] but the aspect in question does not stand in tension to the rest of the book.

II. "Moral" Purity and Impurity in Jubilees

Despite the evidence for "ritual" purity, it is fair to say that Jubilees is much more concerned with "moral" purity. All three classic "moral" impurities are dealt with: bloodshed, sexual sins, and idolatry. Like more severe forms of "ritual" impurity, they defile the sanctuary from afar (cf. Lev 20:3), as in Jub 30:15 and probably also in 23:21. While the root טמא is used with such "moral" impurities, there are other terms like תועבה, "abomination."[31] In fact, the Ethiopic text may not represent the semantic field accurately, since it occasionally translates תועבה with forms deriving from *rek^w s,* "impurity," a tendency in the Ethiopic version of Leviticus as well.[32] Prior to the classic "moral" impurities, we shall discuss a remarkable conceptual shift.

Ladder of Jacob: Ancient Interpretations of the Biblical Story of Jacob and His Children (Princeton: Princeton University Press, 2006), 251. For an explanation of Jacob's side trip to Hebron after he erected an altar at Bethel and before Levi's investiture, cf. 138-41.

27. Cf. Drawnel, *Aramaic Wisdom Text,* 254.

28. Cf. the discussion in Klawans, *Impurity and Sin,* 31-32. On consumption of blood, see below.

29. Ravid, "Purity and Impurity," 65, 80, erroneously claims that Jubilees does not mention impure animals.

30. M. Kister, "Some Aspects of Qumranic Halakhah," in *The Madrid Qumran Congress: Proceedings of the International Congress on the Dead Sea Scrolls, Madrid, 18-21 March, 1991,* ed. J. Trebolle Barrera and L. Vegas Montaner, 2 vols., STDJ 11 (Leiden: Brill, 1992), 2:571-88, 586-87, because of the tension with Jub 32:15.

31. Cf. Lev 18:22, 26, 27, 29, 30; 20:13. Cf. also חנף *hif'il,* Num 35:33 (otherwise only Prophets and Writings).

32. Proof is Jub 21:23 *(rek^w somu),* for which 4Q221 1 5-6 gives תועבתם, 4Q219 ii 28 the plural תועבות יהמה. Similarly, the Latin (ed. Rönsch) has at times *abominatio* where Ge'ez

1. Conceptual extension: defilement of holy time. We have seen that *Israelites* must not become defiled "ritually" through sexual intercourse on account of the Sabbath. This spatial construction of the Sabbath occurs again, with typical differences, in the "moral" realm. In Jubilees, holy time *itself* can be defiled by improper actions. Thus, Jub 2:25-26 parallels the transgression of "doing any work" on the Sabbath with "defiling it" (root *rak*ʷ*sa*), and more generally Jub 6:37 predicts the confusion of "holy" and "impure" days *(rekusa, rek*ʷ*esta)*. Provided the translation is faithful, we thus find "defilement" (root טמא) where normally "profanation" (root חלל) would be expected. According to J. Milgrom, such conceptual instability occurs first in the book of Ezekiel and has parallels in 11QTᵃ.[33]

2. Bloodshed defiles the earth/land. Bloodshed is twice explicitly related to impurity in the book (but cf. also Jub 11:5). In Jub 7:27-29, 32-33 it figures in Noah's exhortation to his sons, alluding to Gen 9:6. Instead of Genesis's appeal to the *imago Dei*, Jubilees holds that the earth "is not pure" from the blood shed on it and can only "become pure" by the blood of the one who has shed it. But Jubilees follows Gen 9:4-6 in connecting this with the prohibition of eating blood, so that bloodshed, the failure of covering the blood, and the consumption of blood all contribute to the defilement of the earth/the land. Apparently, this notion of an effect on the earth/land is informed by Num 35:33-34, even more clearly alluded to in the second passage, Jub 21:19-20. Here, the Ethiopic verb is *yāxaṭṭe'ā*, "will spoil it," which apparently corresponds to חנף *hif'il*, Num 35:33. The violence, bloodshed, and blood drinking of the Giants have a similar effect on the earth according to 1 En 7:4-6; 9:9.

3. The impurity of sexual sins, particularly of intermarriage. Sexually encoded references to impurity abound in Jubilees. Often "impurity" *(rek*ʷ*s)* and derivates are conjoined in lengthy strings with "fornication" *(zemmut)*, "contamination" *(gemmānē)*, "sin" *(xaṭi'at* or *'abbasā)*, "corruption" *(musenā)*, "error" *(gēgāy)*, or "abomination" *(saqorār)*. Such connections appear in descriptions of committed sexual sins (Jub 9:15; 20:5), predictions of future sexual immorality (9:15; 23:14), warnings against such immorality (7:20; 20:3, 6; 33:19), and the announcement of its eschatological absence (50:5). Of central importance is the qualification of sexual transgression as *zemmut*, which translates

---

has *rek*ʷ*s/rekus*, e.g., Jub 16:5. Cf. further W. Loader, *Enoch, Levi, and Jubilees on Sexuality: Attitudes towards Sexuality in the Early Enoch Literature, the Aramaic Levi Document, and the Book of Jubilees* (Grand Rapids: Eerdmans, 2007), 216-29. For Ethiopic Leviticus, cf. the passages in n. 31.

33. Cf. J. Milgrom, "The Concept of Impurity in *Jubilees* and the *Temple Scroll*," *RevQ* 16, no. 62 (1993): 277-84, 279-80.

זנות, "fornication."[34] Inter alia, it is used of the Watchers' "fornication" with women, who thus "committed the first (acts) of uncleanness" (7:21, in retrospective; cf. 4:22; 20:5; 1 En 8:2; 9:8; 10:11; 15:4); of the inhabitants of Sodom and Gomorrah who "defiled themselves and fornicated and did what is impure on earth" (Jub 16:5; cf. 20:5-6); of Tamar's reported "fornication," qualified as "impurity in Israel" (41:16-17); and of illicit sexual unions (33:20 [mss.: *zemmunā*]; cf. 41:25-26),[35] as with Reuben's intercourse with Bilhah. Here, the rationale for Jubilees' strong criticism is stated: that Israel is a holy and priestly people, "a priestly kingdom" *(mangešta kehnat)* and God's "possession" *(ṭerit;* 33:20).

This is clearly an allusion to Exod 19:5-6, a text also referred to at Jub 16:17-18, where Abraham learns from the angel(s) that one of Isaac's sons would become a "holy seed" *(zar' qeddus),*[36] not to be reckoned amongst the nations but forming "a nation of possession (?) . . . , a priesthood, and a holy people."[37] An important qualification of this view inherited from Exod 19:5-6 is the literal understanding of both holiness and priesthood, which applies these terms to all Israel to some extent realistically. Although Jubilees is particularly interested in the priesthood of Levi, all Israel are to live up to the standards of priestly holiness. Under the influence of the Holiness Code (H), this holiness becomes a reflection of God's own holiness (Jub 16:26; cf. Lev 19:2); thus, fornication and impurity must not be found in Israel (Jub 30:8; 33:20). H further focuses on the land defiled by sexual impurity (16:5; 33:10, 14; contrast the future in 50:5; cf. 1 En 10:20, 22) as well as bloodshed (see above), from which the offenders will be uprooted (Jub 21:21-22; 30:22; 33:19; cf. Lev 18:25, 28; 20:22). Within this framework, Jubilees applies H's provision for a priest's daughter engaging in "fornication" (Lev 21:9) to all Israelite women and girls: "Burn her in fire," is what Abraham tells his sons about such a woman (Jub 20:4) and what Judah suggests to do with Tamar (41:17, 28, with reference to Abraham's rule; but cf. already Gen 38:24). In addition, Jubilees seems to link

34. Cf. C. Werman, "*Jubilees* 30: Building a Paradigm for the Ban on Intermarriage," *HTR* 90 (1997): 1-22, 14. For sexual transgression in Jubilees, cf. the paper by William Loader, "Jubilees and Sexual Transgression," *Hen* 30, no. 2 (2008), and Loader, *Enoch,* 125-235. Cf. the association of טמאה with זנות and פחז in ALD 16 (6:3).

35. Cf. Lev 18; 20; 11QTᵃ 66:11-17; 4Q251 frg. 17; CD 5:7-11. Note the use of זנות in CD 4:17, 20; 4:20-5:2 refers most probably to polygyny, but it is unclear whether 5:7-11 (marriage of nieces) still belongs to that rubric.

36. In the Hebrew Bible only Isa 6:13 and particularly Ezra 9:2; see below. In Jubilees, cf. 22:27; 25:3, 12, 18. Cf. ALD 17 [6:4].

37. Cf. further Jub 19:15; 22:9, 15 and particularly 2:19-21 (election and sanctification), although there is no consistent rendering of עם סגלה in Geʿez. For this motif, cf. also Deut 7:6; 14:2; 26:18.

this punishment with the other instance in which H prescribes burning: a man having sex with his mother-in-law (Lev 20:14); the reciprocal presentation of the involved parties in Jub 41:25-26 resembles the reasoning of CD 5:9-10.[38]

However, the main focus in matters of sexual impurity is arguably on the issue of intermarriage, where Jubilees combines the stance of Ezra 9–10; Neh 13:23-31 with H's provisions for *zenut*, a view similarly underlying ALD 16-17 (6:3-4), 4QMMT B 75-82,[39] and probably 4QTQahat, 4Q225 (= 4QpsJubᵃ), and 4Q513.[40] Judah and Tamar's transgression has its deeper cause in this problem (cf. Jub 34:20; 41:1-2, 20). Warning against intermarriage begins with Abraham. In the context of a command to separate from the nations and keep away "from their impurity and from all their error" (Jub 22:19), he exhorts Jacob not to marry one of the Canaanites because they are destined "for being uprooted from the earth" (22:20); the holiness of Jacob's seed (cf. Ezra 9:2) features abundantly in the context (Jub 22:11, 13, 15, 24). Rebecca renews this warning, accusing the Canaanites of "impurity," "fornication," "lewdness," and "evil" (25:1). Jacob, at the age of sixty-three, assures her he never considered marrying a Canaanite but would wed one of Uncle Laban's daughters in Mesopotamia (25:4-10), whereupon Rebecca praises him as "a pure son and holy offspring" (25:12; cf. Isaac, Jub 27:9-12, and his negative verdict on Esau, 35:14, who "has gone after his wives, after impurity [*rekʷs*], and after their errors").

The most paradigmatic chapter, however, is Jub 30, the story of Dinah. By sleeping with her, Shechem — and by extension the Shechemites, who had abducted her — "defiled her" (Jub 30:2-3, 5-6), a notion already present in Gen 34:5, 13, 27 (cf. 1QapGen 20:15, on Sarai). In Jubilees, however, the issue is deeper than treating Dinah like a whore (thus Gen 34:21): it is ultimately about defilement of *Israel* (Jub 30:8-9),[41] creating an impurity from which "Israel will not become clean" (30:14) unless they eradicate the perpe-

---

38. Cf. A. Shemesh, *Punishments and Sins: From Scripture to the Rabbis* (in Hebrew) (Jerusalem: Magnes, 2003), 16-17; further literature in Loader, *Enoch*, 183 n. 467.

39. With C. E. Hayes, *Gentile Impurities and Jewish Identities: Intermarriage and Conversion from the Bible to the Talmud* (Oxford: Oxford University Press, 2002), 82-91 (assuming marriage with converted Gentiles); different is E. Qimron and J. Strugnell, *Qumran Cave 4. V: Miqṣat Maʿaśe ha-Torah*, DJD 10 (Oxford: Clarendon, 1994), 55, 171 n. 178a (marriage between priests and Israelites). Note that, contrary to Jubilees, MMT applies the prohibition of כלאים (Lev 19:19; Deut 22:9).

40. Cf. esp. 4QTQahat 1 i 8-9; 4Q225 1 1; 4Q513 1-2 ii 1-6; 10 ii 3-8.

41. With forms of *ʾarkʷasa*, "defile," with Israel as implied referent; Latin in 30:8: *polluerit eum*.

trators. Again, the application of the model of priests committing *zenut* becomes relevant. Accordingly, a woman given to a foreigner is burned like a priest's daughter committing *zenut* (Jub 30:7; cf. Lev 21:9); in addition, her father is to be stoned according to the law for those giving their descendants to Molech (Jub 30:7-10; cf. Lev 18:21; 20:2-5). The possibility of circumcision is not raised; it "does not convert profane seed into holy seed, and thus miscegenation is forever and always *zenut*."[42] Although Jub 30 forbids intermarriage with *any* Gentiles, in the other references the main emphasis is on *Canaanites;* for Joseph, marrying an Egyptian woman is not problematic (Jub 40:10), and Simeon and Judah even marry Canaanite women (but see the latter's trouble, above). Jubilees is informed here by different concerns: "biblical" precedent, literary patterns, and contemporary issues.[43]

C. Hayes has labeled this type of impurity "genealogical impurity," claiming it to be a specific type of "moral" impurity because its real effect comes about in the offspring, through the "spoiling" of the purity of lineage; it is not "ritual."[44] However, although purity of lineage does play a major role, she narrows the issue too much down to this when it is in fact wider: Jub 22:16-18 is a *comprehensive* call for separation from the nations, entailing prohibitions against eating with them, behaving as they do, and becoming their companion *(biṣa)*.[45] While one of the concerns is idolatry (see below), "eating" with Gentiles may include dietary and perhaps "ritual" issues. From a different angle, Olyan has argued that already Ezra-Nehemiah deal with Gentile impurity in more than one way and that at least in Neh 13:4-9 (purification of the chamber of Tobiah the Ammonite) the issue is "ritual" in nature.[46] There are further pointers suggesting that "ritual" impurity of Gentiles was not a total innovation in Tannaitic literature.[47] The demarcation of types of impurity should not be too rigid.

42. Hayes, *Gentile Impurities,* 77.

43. See further Loader, *Enoch,* 176-86, 192-96.

44. Cf. Hayes, *Gentile Impurities,* 69-70, 73, 76-77, taking issue with Werman, "*Jubilees* 30," 14-16, who perceives a conflation of impurity through physical contact and nonphysical defilement of Israel.

45. Still useful though not exhaustive is E. Schwarz, *Identität durch Abgrenzung: Abgrenzungsprozesse in Israel im 2. vorchristlichen Jahrhundert und ihre traditionsgeschichtlichen Voraussetzungen. Zugleich ein Beitrag zur Erforschung des Jubiläenbuches,* EHS Theologie 162 (Frankfurt am Main: Peter Lang, 1982), esp. 23-30. For the last item, one might compare 1 Macc 1:11 (διαθώμεθα διαθήκην μετὰ τῶν ἐθνῶν τῶν κύκλῳ ἡμῶν).

46. S. M. Olyan, "Purity Ideology in Ezra-Nehemiah as a Tool to Reconstitute the Community," *JSJ* 35 (2004): 1-16, 10-12.

47. Most importantly, 4Q266 5 ii 4-9 (l. 6: לחללה בטמאתם); cf. Josephus, *Jewish War*

4. The impurity of idolatry. In Jub 21:3-5 Abraham warns Isaac against idolatry. The Hebrew in 4Q220 1 1 (= Jub 21:5) shows that one of the words for "idols" is גלולים, often occurring in the context of impurity, particularly in Ezekiel.[48] The translator readily uses "unclean things" *(rekusān)* here. Similarly, in "Ara" they had made "unclean things" *(rekʷsa)* and other idols, and the "spirits of the savage ones" helped to commit sins and impurity (Jub 11:4; cf. 1 En 19:1). Abandoning the covenant brings about impurity, abominations, and contamination (23:17). Before Jacob travels to Bethel to build an altar, the idols must be destroyed (31:1-2; cf. Gen 35:2-4). In Jub 22:16-18 Isaac's warning against idolatry is placed in the context of separation from the nations; it combines established anti-idol polemic[49] with qualification of the "actions" and "ways" of the nations as something impure, contaminated, and abominable. Apart from Ezekiel, H has been influential, where the prohibition of idolatry and magic reflects Israel's obligation to be holy (Lev 19:4, 31; 20:1-8, 27; 26:1); magic is viewed as *zenut* (Lev 20:6, לזנות אחריהם), and idolatry defiles the sanctuary (Lev 20:3). We find similar concerns, but more dependence on Deuteronomy, in 11QTᵃ 60:16-21 (cf. Deut 18:9-13) and 4QMMT C 6-7 (cf. Deut 7:26).

III. Summary and Evaluation

1. Jubilees acknowledges *both* "ritual" and "moral" purity and impurity. While issues of "moral" (im)purity, particularly sexual morality and intermarriage, take literary and ideological precedence, the affirmation of the laws of the parturient, the notion of sexual intercourse as ritually defiling, "ritual" purity as required for Passover, priestly ablutions, temporal limits for consumption of second tithe, and dietary laws should not be overlooked. While there is no conflation of "ritual" and "moral" impurity as claimed for Qumran by Klawans, some items seem to fall into more than one rubric (blood when shed defiles the land, priests must wash after sacrifice; Gentiles are genealogically impure but also idolatrous, one should not eat with them).

2.150: Essenes purify themselves (ἀπολούεσθαι) after contact with neophytes καθάπερ ἀλλοφύλῳ συμφυρέντας. Cf. J. M. Baumgarten, "The Disqualification of Priests in the 4Q Fragments of the 'Damascus Document,' a Specimen of the Recovery of Pre-Rabbinic Halakha," in *The Madrid Qumran Congress*, 2:503-13; Harrington, *The Purity Texts*, 117-23.

48. Cf. Ezek 18:6, 12, 15; 20:7, 18, 31; 22:3-4; 23:7, 30; 36:18, 25; 37:23. Cf. in the context of תועבות 2 Kings 21:11 (cf. 1 Kings 21:26); Ezek 14:6; 16:36.

49. Cf. Jer 2:27; Hab 2:19; Wisd 14:21; Epistle of Jeremiah. Cf. also 1 En 91:9; 99:7-9.

2. In its presentation of purity and impurity, Jubilees remains within the parameters of its setting (Mount Sinai) and the narrative it reworks (Genesis to mid-Exodus). Consequently, the temple as the main object of potential "ritual" defilement (and, regarding corpse impurity, the prerequisite for the purification ritual) is largely absent. Occasionally, though, it comes into focus, either *per analogiam* (Eden, Sabbath, perhaps Bethel) or in references to the future sanctuary. And it is precisely here that we *do* find references to "ritual" purity and impurity (as well as "moral" impurity defiling the temple). To expect ritual (im)purity generally in "pretemple" narrative contexts would be anachronistic in the perspective of Jubilees.

3. This literary preference, however, gives way to a centrifugal motion within the text, which further accounts for the disproportion between "ritual" and "moral" impurity. While in narrative perspective the temple is not yet there, priests are already at hand. In line with Levitical priestly traditions, Jubilees is interested in establishing a pre-Aaronite priesthood. At the same time, the adoption of the Ezran concept of "holy seed" and a literal take on the notion of Israel as "kingdom of priests" and "holy nation" (Exod 19:6; cf. Deut 7:6) allow for application of priestly standards to all Israel. In Jubilees' narrative world, these standards are necessarily reflected mainly in the "moral" realm.

4. In terms of traditions, Jubilees is heavily indebted to H, which already *combines* "ritual" and "moral" (im)purity. H's provisions, particularly for *zenut*, have been exacerbated by the aforementioned literal application of the notions of "holy seed," "priestly kingdom," etc. (Ezra 9:2; P, D). Jubilees here represents a common stance with ALD, 4QMMT, and most likely also 4QTQahat, 4Q225 (=4QpsJub[a]), and 4Q513; ALD and MMT are important in that they also combine "ritual" and "moral" (im)purity. Common material traditions on "ritual" purity are with 4Q265 (cf. 4QD[a]) (§I.1), the Temple Scroll (§I.5), and again ALD (§I.3; Bethel). This shows to my mind that the issue of (im)purity in Jubilees is to be located on a trajectory from H to Qumran, sharpened by the "holy seed" concept. The links with the early Enoch literature are more limited in range, relating to the field of "moral" impurity: the adoption of the Watcher myth, dealing with sexual transgression, bloodshed, and idolatry; and similarities in the expectation of an earth cleansed of impurity (Jub 50:5; 1 En 10:20, 22).

5. In line with its concern for the establishment of "Mosaic" law in the period before Sinai, Jubilees allocates purity laws, both "ritual" and "moral," to this period at appropriate points in the narrative. It claims that such laws are engraved on the heavenly tablets (cf. 1 En 81:1-2), as well as lived out and/

or commanded by primeval figures and patriarchs. The emphasis on purity, both forms taken together, is considerable. Purity is mentioned for the first time shortly after the first section on the Sabbath (Jub 3:8-14, following 2:1, 17-33). Like the Sabbath,[50] purity is about Israel's identity, functioning as a token of election ("holy seed") and a boundary marker (separation from the nations). At the same time, and again like the Sabbath, it allows Israel to represent humankind par excellence (Adam and his wife observe purity), giving Israel a firm place in the world. Israel's purity is constantly in danger; the response Jubilees offers is not built on sectarianism but keeps all Israel in view.

50. Cf. Doering, "Concept of the Sabbath," passim. And see above, n. 14.

Tradition and Innovation
in the Calendar of Jubilees

Jonathan Ben-Dov

The calendar in the book of Jubilees keeps attracting great scholarly attention. The present paper will focus on some points raised in recent studies and will try to suggest additional ideas for the assessment of the calendar of Jubilees.[1] The discussion benefits from developments in the study of the 364-day calendar tradition (364DCT), from the full publication of the calendrical scrolls from Qumran, as well as from a wider scope with regard to the Book of Astronomy in 1 Enoch (AB).[2]

The book of Jubilees is never fully explicit about the calendar employed in it. Strangely, Jubilees is more a book on chronology than a book on calendars. Although calendrical details are mentioned in the book, they are explicit only in chap. 6, while the main effort of the author in his recurrent remarks on timing concentrates on matters of chronology. Thus, quite a few elements of the calendar in Jubilees are left unsettled.

The book relates to a year of 364 days (364DY), as stated explicitly in 6:32. The same figure is attested elsewhere in Enochic and Qumranic literature: 1 En 74:12; 82:6; 4Q252 Commentary on Genesis[a] II 2-3; 4Q394 3-7 i 1-3;

---

1. A fuller discussion is included in my doctoral dissertation, now prepared for publication as: *Head of All Years: Studies in Qumran Calendars and Astronomy in Their Ancient Context.* When preparing this article, I benefited from discussions with Mrs. Atar Livneh, a graduate student at the University of Haifa working on Jubilees at Qumran.

2. U. Glessmer, "Calendars in the Qumran Scrolls," in *The Dead Sea Scrolls after Fifty Years,* ed. P. W. Flint and J. C. VanderKam (Leiden: Brill, 1999), 213-78; S. Talmon, J. Ben-Dov, and U. Glessmer, *Qumran Cave 4.VI: Calendrical Texts,* DJD 21 (Oxford: Clarendon, 2001).

11QPs[a] XXVII 4-6. It would be natural to assume that all mentions of the 364DY relate to the same annual framework. This was the insight underlying the pioneering studies of A. Jaubert and S. Talmon.[3]

However, with the publication of new material the opposite side of the dialectic prevailed, as scholars tended to emphasize various discrepancies within the 364DCT.[4] Most notably, Liora Ravid pointed out the book of Jubilees as an exception from the norm in the sectarian 364DCT.[5] The Qumranic sources are generally consistent, pointing to a more-or-less stable tradition, which originated in Enochic literature and continued into *yahad* practice. In contrast, here it is claimed that the book of Jubilees seems to represent a divergent thread of the same tradition.

Jaubert's insight on the similarity of the calendar of Jubilees to the Qumran calendars has been a crucial factor in the reconstruction of the calendrical scrolls. This is in itself proof that Jaubert's system is valid through significant parts of the calendrical tradition. However, Jubilees stands in distinction from other parts of the tradition, not only with regard to the place of the moon in the calendar reckoning, but also with regard to the general structure of the year. It would seem that, although the author of Jubilees was indebted to the Jewish 364DCT, he was at the same time strongly committed to other constitutive principles, which compelled him to produce a unique cast of calendrical concepts.

The disagreements are often explicit, but usually they are implicit in the things left unsaid. It is amazing to see the amount of calendrical details left untold in Jubilees. For this reason, prudence must be practiced when attempting to reconstruct the author's position in these matters. The discussion below reviews the constitutive principles in Jubilees' calendar in order to ascertain just how much the author was indebted to, or independent from, the Jewish 364DCT.

---

3. A. Jaubert, "Le calendrier des Jubilés et de la secte de Qumrân. Ses origines bibliques," *VT* 3 (1953): 250-64; Jaubert, "Le calendrier des Jubilés et les jours liturgiques de la semaine," *VT* 7 (1957): 35-61; S. Talmon, "The Calendar Reckoning of the Sect from the Judaean Desert," reprinted with revisions in Talmon, *The World of Qumran from Within* (Jerusalem: Magnes; Leiden: Brill, 1989), 147-85. Talmon repeated his opinion in a recent publication: S. Talmon, "Calendars and Mishmarot," in *EDSS*, 1:108-17, here 114.

4. Glessmer, "Calendars in the Qumran Scrolls."

5. L. Ravid, "The Book of Jubilees and Its Calendar — a Reexamination," *DSD* 10 (2003): 371-94.

I. The Septenary Principle and the Count of Weeks

In the book of Jubilees, the central apparatus for structuring time is its division into seven-based units. Such structuring was necessary to impose order on the endless, arbitrary stretches of time experienced by mankind. Large-scale septenary (i.e., seven-based) units are the *shemitah* (week of years) and the jubilee (week of *shemitot*), applied throughout Jubilees to outline the world's history. In Jubilees this concept dictated that each numerical figure is analyzed using septenary units. Thus, for example, in the formulaic account of the life of Noah (10:15-16), and in a more pronounced way at the death of Abraham (23:8). This latter verse serves as a trigger for the so-called apocalypse of chap. 23: "He had lived for three jubilees and four weeks of years — 175 years. . . . For the times of the ancients were 19 jubilees. . . . After the flood they started to decrease from 19 jubilees. . . . All the generations that will come into being from now until the great day of judgment will grow old quickly — before they complete two jubilees."[6] Note that while the introductory verses count the lifetimes of various personalities as nineteen jubilees, or three jubilees plus four weeks, etc., numbers are given later in the apocalypse more naturally as normal decimal figures (23:15, 27).[7] For the present purposes we note that, as 23:15 shows, it was by no means necessary to count the years by jubilees, which could in fact be quite awkward. Such a practice was required only by an author extraordinarily committed to the septenary plan.

The importance of the septenary division of time is attested in Jub 4:18, where Enoch is accredited with transmitting ancient teachings: "He testified to mankind in the generations of the earth: the *weeks of the jubilees* he related,[8] and made known the days of the years; the months he arranged, and related the *sabbaths of the years*" (emphasis mine). Numerous authors

---

6. Translations of Jubilees follow J. C. VanderKam, *The Book of Jubilees*, CSCO 510 (Louvain: Peeters, 1989).

7. This difference may suggest that the apocalypse of Jub 23 was taken from an independent source and worked into the framework of Jubilees using an editorial remark. A similar conclusion was reached by C. Berner in his contribution to the present conference. On sources and redaction in Jubilees see M. Segal, *The Book of Jubilees: Rewritten Bible, Redaction, Ideology, and Theology*, JSJSup 117 (Leiden: Brill, 2007); for a different analysis of chap. 23, see C. Werman, "The Book of Jubilees and the Qumran Scrolls," *Meghillot* 2 (2004): 37-55 (here 39-48).

8. This phrase is possibly attested in 11QJubilees frg. 4: F. García-Martínez et al., eds., *Qumran Cave 11 II. 11Q2-18, 11Q20-31*, DJD 23 (Oxford: Clarendon, 1998), 213.

searched for the content of the Enochic writings known to the author of Jubilees based on this passage.[9] It is generally accepted that AB, in some textual form, was already an established branch of Enochic wisdom at the time Jubilees was written. Accordingly, it should be noted that the septenary terminology in Jub 4:17 does not refer to the inner division of the year but rather to long-range units of years. Thus, this terminology is rightly considered a projection of ideas from the Apocalypse of Weeks (AW), since AB never uses the number seven with regard to the 364DY.[10] Only once does AB mention "a count of weeks," *śarʿata sanbat* (79:4, lit. "a law of the week"), but this is done, for some unknown reason, with regard to the *lunar* year! The reference to Enoch in Jub 4:17 is therefore loyal to the original spirit of AB and AW, while Jubilees itself carries the septenary idea further, presenting it in 6:29 as the very essence of the structure of the 364DY.

From the book of Jubilees it is apparent that the septenary principle was also active in the small-scale design of the 364-day year, which was divided very neatly into weeks. This idea is presented in Jub 6:29-30, the only explicit statement in Jubilees on the structure of the year. These two verses first relate to the year quarters and then to the entire year: "Each of them (consists of) 13 weeks; . . . All the days of the commandments will be 52 weeks of days; (they will make) the entire year complete." In this passage the number of 52 weeks in a year is not a mere circumstance, an outcome of the number 364. Rather it forms the very definition of the year and of its components. In Jubilees' eyes, a "complete" year equals a stretch of 52 weeks, or rather four periods of 13 weeks each.[11] No other place within the 364DCT makes this point so clear.[12] In fact, it is not made again in the book of Jubilees. In contrast, the year is more commonly defined using the twelve months, each quarter containing three such months. This is common in 1 En 72 but also in Qumran calendars such as 4Q320 3 ii–4 i; 4Q394 frgs. 1-2; 4Q394 frgs. 3-7 i; 6Q17.

9. See J. C. VanderKam, *From Revelation to Canon: Studies in the Hebrew Bible and Second Temple Literature*, JSJSup 62 (Leiden: Brill, 2000), 310-18; recently A. Y. Reed, *Fallen Angels and the History of Judaism and Christianity* (Cambridge: Cambridge University Press, 2005), 87-89. For updated bibliography and renewed evaluation of the matter, see the contribution of J. Bergsma in this volume.

10. M. Albani, *Astronomie und Schöpfungsglaube. Untersuchungen zum astronomischen Henochbuch*, WMANT 68 (Neukirchen-Vluyn: Neukirchener, 1994), 278-80.

11. See Ravid, "The Book of Jubilees," 383ff.

12. The closest place is 11QPs[a] XXVII, which counts 52 songs for the Sabbaths of the year alongside the 364 days, the 30 festivals, and the 12 heads of months.

The fact that in the foremost opportunity for programmatic statements on the calendar the author of Jubilees chose to ignore the numbering of months and stressed the count of weeks instead reveals his extraordinary indebtedness to the septenary scheme. One may note how this idea appears again in Synchellus and Cedrenus, who were greatly influenced by Jubilees' time reckoning. In their description of the order of times as revealed by Uriel to Enoch, they revert to septenary terminology: ". . . Uriel . . . revealed to Enoch . . . that a year has 52 weeks."[13] Surprisingly, this report reflects Jub 6:30 rather than the Enochic AB!

The importance of the septenary principle in Jubilees is further underscored by two passages on Sabbath halakah, standing at the framework of the book, in chaps. 2 and 50.[14]

Despite all of the above, some reservations arise from a close analysis of the narratives in Jubilees. First, throughout the dozens of dating formulas in Jubilees there is not one case where the days of the week are mentioned.[15] This stands in striking contrast to the practice in Qumran literature, where the days of the week are meticulously recorded in date formulas. The contrast is most evident when comparing the flood narrative of Jubilees to that of the Commentary on Genesis 4Q252. While the two versions considerably touch on chronology and date formulas, only in 4Q252 are the days of the week added to the date formulas, and very thoroughly so. The same is true with regard to dates and date formulas in 4Q317, 4Q503, and all the Qumran calendars (4Q319-4Q330, 4Q394), as well as in Jewish deeds from the second century C.E. onward.[16] It is also illuminating that Synchellus's account of the flood, despite being indebted to Jubilees, adds the record of the days of the week, an element absent from the account in Jubilees.

The absence of the days of the week from the accounts in Jubilees conspicuously distinguishes this book from other second temple literature. In

---

13. M. Black, *Apocalypsis Henochi Graece*, SVTP 3 (Leiden: Brill, 1970), 12; W. Adler and P. Tuffin, *The Chronography of George Synkellos* (Oxford: Oxford University Press, 2002), 45.

14. L. Doering, "The Concept of the Sabbath in the Book of Jubilees," in *Studies in the Book of Jubilees*, ed. M. Albani et al., TSAJ 65 (Tübingen: Mohr Siebeck, 1997), 179-205.

15. Ravid, "The Book of Jubilees," 377; see already J. M. Baumgarten, *Studies in Qumran Law* (Leiden: Brill, 1977), 106.

16. R. Katzoff and B. M. Schreiber, "Week and Sabbath in Judean Desert Documents," *Scripta Classica Israelica* 17 (1998): 102-14. A few centuries later this practice was attested in the Zoʻar inscriptions of the late talmudic period (S. Stern, *Calendar and Community: A History of the Jewish Calendar, 2nd Century BCE–10th Century CE* [Oxford: Oxford University Press, 2001], 87-97).

this respect Jubilees resembles date formulas in the Hebrew Bible, where the days of the week are not invoked.[17] The reason for the difference could either be that at the time Jubilees was composed the naming of weekdays was not yet common, or rather, the author made a deliberate choice to discard this practice, seeking to imitate the biblical norm.

Secondly, the ostensible importance of the Sabbath in the framework of the book stands in glaring contrast to its near absence from the narratives. Besides in chaps. 2 and 50, the Sabbath is mentioned in the admonitions of 1:10, 14; 6:34-38; and 23:19, always as part of a formulaic chain of Israelite religious institutions.[18] This formula of covenant keeping (in fact, more of covenant breaking) is well known from elsewhere, notably in pesher Hosea and in pseudoprophetic literature (1QDM, 4QDM?, 4Q390).[19] Important as it is, it does not attest to an outstanding status for the Sabbath in Jubilees.

It is remarkable that the Sabbath is altogether absent from the narratives. Doering has noted that "The use of the term 'the seventh day' is quite reserved . . . although the author of *Jubilees* . . . quite clearly shows a sense of numerical references, it is not the quality of the heptad which is the focus of his interest."[20] The absence of the Sabbath from the narratives was often interpreted (following Jaubert) as a sign for the abstention from travel or from any other secular task on the Sabbath.[21] However, the fruit of a lively argument on Jaubert's hypothesis in recent decades is that practically every piece of evidence brought forth by Jaubert may be contested.[22] Furthermore, Baumgarten noted several quite clear cases where the Sabbath *is* violated in Jubilees.[23]

17. Cf. A. Lemaire, "Les formules de datation en Palestine au premier millénaire avant J.-C.," in *Temps vécu. Temps pensé,* ed. F. Briquel-Chatonet (Paris: Gabalda, 1998), 53-82. A useful analogy may be the psalms designated for daily recitation in Jewish liturgy. While this function of the psalms does not appear in the MT (except for the title of Ps 92, which, however, must be understood otherwise), it is included in the titles for those psalms in the Septuagint Psalter.

18. Doering, "Concept of the Sabbath," 183.

19. Werman, "The Book of Jubilees," 49-53; E. J. C. Tigchelaar, "A Cave 4 Fragment of *Divre Mosheh* (4QDM) and the Text of 1Q22 1:7-10 and *Jubilees* 1:9, 14," *DSD* 12, no. 3 (2005): 303-12.

20. Doering, "Concept of the Sabbath," 191.

21. Jaubert, "Le calendrier des Jubilés et de la secte de Qumran"; VanderKam, *From Revelation to Canon,* 81-85; R. T. Beckwith, *Calendar, Chronology, and Worship,* AJEC 61 (Leiden: Brill, 2005), 54-55.

22. E.g., Baumgarten, *Studies in Qumran Law,* 101-14; B. Z. Wacholder and S. Wacholder, "Patterns of Biblical Dates and Qumran's Calendar," *HUCA* 66 (1995): 1-40 (here 4-8).

23. J. M. Baumgarten, "Some Problems of the Jubilees Calendar in Current Research," *VT* 32 (1982): 485-89.

If Sabbath observance was important for the author, one would expect to find it attached to one of the narratives in the distinct style of the book. My argument, one may claim, is an argument from silence, but, after all, so is Jaubert's!

Jubilees fails to refer to a central aspect of the Jewish septenary time reckoning: the "pentacontad" count of days between the two harvest festivals, endorsed in Lev 23:15-21 and Deut 16:9, and greatly expanded in the Temple Scroll (henceforth: T).[24] Although the author in chap. 6 dedicates a long digression to *hag ha-shevu'im,* and despite the great awareness of the author of numerical aspects of the calendar, it is never mentioned that the festival occurs fifty days after a previous harvest festival. Given the utter importance of the debate on the date of harvest festivals in second temple Judaism, it is difficult to understand how a disciple of the 364DCT would neglect to present his opinion in this matter. Furthermore, the "additional" harvest festivals of the wine and oil, mentioned in T (11QTᵃ XVIII-XXII), are absent from Jubilees.

To be sure, Jubilees does not completely ignore the harvest festivals. In 29:16 the four cardinal days are marked as special dates for the dispatch of agricultural goods as the seasons revolve (see further below). In 32:12-13, when dealing with the second tithe, the author refers to special harvest festivals for each type of crop, with halakoth reminiscent of T: "For the seed is to be eaten in its year until the time for harvesting the seed of the year; the wine (will be drunk) until the time for wine; and the olive (will be used) until the proper time of its season. Any of it that is left over and grows old is to be (considered) contaminated."[25] But when should these "times" be fixed? The dates were not specified in chap. 32. A clue may be found in Jub 7:1-2, although the evidence is not unproblematic. In 7:1-2 Noah collects the vine from his orchard in year 4 of this orchard's planting. As a strict follower of the Pentateuchal law (Lev 19:23-25), Noah saves this produce, which was harvested at the beginning of month VII (year 4), until the beginning of year 5 (day 1 of month I); only then does he consume it together with that day's festal sacrifices. Baumgarten deduced from this passage that the author of Jubilees marked the cardinal days of the year (1/I, 1/VII) as the festivals of wine harvest, in contrast to the dates indicated in T.[26]

---

24. J. M. Baumgarten, "The Calendars of the Book of Jubilees and the Temple Scroll," *VT* 37 (1987): 71-78; Ravid, "The Book of Jubilees," 378ff. But cf. J. C. VanderKam, "The Temple Scroll and the Book of Jubilees," in *Temple Scroll Studies,* ed. G. J. Brooke, JSPSup 7 (Sheffield: JSOT, 1989), 211-36. VanderKam's reservations are discussed below.

25. VanderKam, "The Temple Scroll," 225.

26. Baumgarten, "Calendars," 73-74. Although this passage is orientated toward the

However, the case is more difficult than meets the eye. A very similar story about Noah's vineyard appears also in the Genesis Apocryphon (col. XII), including the very same dates for the harvest and consumption of the new grapes and wine. Moreover, Menahem Kister noted how the story at the beginning of chap. 7 contradicted the sectarian halakah proclaimed at the end of chap. 7 with regard to the consumption of new fruit.[27] This matter was carried further in the framework of M. Segal's comprehensive theory on the composition of Jubilees. It seems that at the beginning of chap. 7, the author of Jubilees used an external literary source, either the Genesis Apocryphon or an earlier source common to both compositions.[28] In this source, the dates of 1/VII and 1/I were recorded because of their significance for the laws of *Reva'i* (the new orchard). However, when embedded in the book of Jubilees, this old source gained renewed significance owing to the centrality of the cardinal days in the calendrical conceptions of the author.[29]

The author of Jubilees thus did not simply ignore the harvest festivals, but rather seems to have fixed them on different times than those prescribed in T. The author was undoubtedly aware of the laws in T (or a similar source), since in his description of *hag haševu'im* (6:21; cp. 22:1) he uses a phrase quite similar to 11QT[a] XIX 9:[30]

---

laws of *reva'i* (restrictions on consuming the fruit of new trees), Baumgarten convincingly claimed that special place is given in it to the cardinal (memorial) days as harvest festivals. Baumgarten, however, was not aware of the parallel in Genesis Apocryphon.

27. M. Kister, "Some Aspects of Qumranic Halakhah," in *The Madrid Qumran Congress: Proceedings of the International Congress on the Dead Sea Scrolls, Madrid, 18-21 March, 1991*, ed. J. Trebolle Barrera and L. Vegas Montaner, STDJ 11 (Leiden: Brill, 1992), 2:571-88.

28. See further the contributions of Esther Eshel and Michael Segal in the present volume.

29. Kister ("Some Aspects," 585) implies that the author of Jubilees changed the dates in the earlier narratives in order to fit his calendrical concepts: "The author of the Book of Jubilees altered this tradition to make it conform with his own halakhic view: According to its view, Noah observed the first day of the first month (i.e., Nisan), which is a holiday according to Jubilees, with the appropriate festival sacrifices." It would seem, however, that the exact opposite is right: Jubilees uses the same dates as in the earlier source! Kister is right, however, when claiming that the cardinal days (1/I and 1/VII) carry special significance when placed in their new literary context within the book of Jubilees.

30. In addition to the identical line in Jubilees and T, Pfann read a similar line in the cryptic text 4Q324d (see Stephen Pfann, "Time and Calendar in Jubilees and Enoch," *Hen* 31, no. 1 [2009]). This reading, however, is not included in previous transcriptions of the scroll (as, for example, the transcription by M. G. Abegg in D. W. Parry and E. Tov, *The Dead Sea Scrolls Reader* [Leiden: Brill, 2004], part 4, p. 54).

Jubilees: it is the festival of weeks and it is the festival of firstfruits. This festival is twofold and of two kinds

Temple Scroll: for it is [the feast of w]eeks and a feast of first fruits, a memorial for ev[er

Was the author of Jubilees aware of the "pentacontad" day count? Baumgarten thought he was aware of this concept but chose to ignore it because he had found it incongruent with other aspects of the 364DCT.[31] Ravid, in contrast, claims the author had an altogether different conception of the feast of *ševuʿot*, deliberately avoiding the pentacontad count.[32] VanderKam suggested a way to bypass the problem: "In all cases in which *Jubilees* mentions a festival, it is named explicitly in the section of the *Torah* covered by the narrative. . . . This entails that the absence of a religious holiday from *Jubilees* means only that the writer saw no warrant in Genesis–mid-Exodus for positing that it was known and practiced by the fathers."[33] This statement by VanderKam is a worthy warning against an argument from silence, especially in a sensitive text like Jubilees. This hermeneutic principle allowed VanderKam to conclude that the calendar in Jubilees is quite similar to that of T. However, in the present case we see, *pace* VanderKam, that the author was concerned about the harvest festivals not once but twice in his book (chaps. 7 and 32). In these two points the author opted for fixing the harvest festivals on the line between the agricultural seasons (32:12) and more specifically the "memorial days" (7:1-2). We must therefore conclude that the author of Jubilees had been aware of the harvest festivals according to T, but he chose to refashion this law according to his calendrical preferences or literary restraints.

To sum up the present section, Jubilees betrays an ambiguous attitude toward the septenary aspect of the 364DCT. On the one hand, long-term time reckoning was organized in septenary units that bring to mind the biblical jubilee count. In addition, Jub 6:29-30 defines the year in terms of the count of weeks. On the other hand, Jubilees deviates from the "sabbatarian" norm in a series of matters.

Even where the author of Jubilees does commit to the septenary time count, he does so in a genuinely original way, diverging from the so-to-say "mainstream" of the 364DCT. Thus, whereas the reference to Enoch in Jub 4:17 is loyal to the original spirit of AB and AW, Jubilees carries the septenary

31. Baumgarten, "Calendars," 75.
32. Ravid, "The Book of Jubilees," 378-79.
33. VanderKam, "The Temple Scroll," 221.

idea further, presenting it in 6:29 as the structural essence of the 364DY. Although the Qumran sources acknowledge that the year consists of 4 x 13 weeks, this figure is never declared as the essence of the year, as is done in Jub 6:29-30. The impression about the nonconformist nature of Jubilees' calendrical thought thus gains further support.[34]

The idiosyncrasies of Jubilees' calendar cannot be explained as originating differently than other 364DCT texts. The circles that authored the texts belonging to that tradition are simply too small and too related to each other to arise from highly divergent *Sitze im Leben*. Generally it would seem that Jubilees crystallized on the background of Enochic texts like AB and AW, in addition to halakic texts from the milieu of T,[35] but that the author chose to differ from these traditions, often to a very pronounced extent, in cases dictated by his ideological and interpretative preferences.

II. The Year Quarters

A manifest trait of the year in Jubilees is its division into four quarters and the special importance of the cardinal days for the year's structure. This element existed already in Mesopotamian prototypes of the 364DY.[36] In AB the division is also apparent, mainly in chaps. 72 and 82. The four cardinal days form the skeleton of the Enochic year, marking the borders between the annual seasons. This key role of the cardinal days became more pronounced when the framework of 360 days — originally underlying the schemes in AB — gave place to the 364DY.[37] This change resulted in a vivid debate on the exact status of the four additional days (1 En 75 and 82).

---

34. The question whether or not Jubilees' chronological system complies with that of AW and other visions of history (past or future) in units of weeks of jubilees is pertinent here. This question is debated in the chapter by Scott in this volume and in Christof Berner, "50 Jubilees and Beyond? Some Observations on the Chronological Structure of the Book of Jubilees," *Hen* 30, no. 2 (2008), and cannot be settled here. It seems, however, that Jubilees is fairly independent from AW, if not in the overall sum of years then in the method of counting the distinct time units.

35. For the sources of Jubilees see the chapter by Segal in the present volume.

36. J. Ben-Dov and W. Horowitz, "The 364-Day Year in Mesopotamia and Qumran" (in Hebrew), *Meghillot* 1 (2003): 3-26.

37. P. Sacchi, "The Two Calendars of the Book of Astronomy," in *Jewish Apocalyptic and Its History*, JSPSup 20 (Sheffield: JSOT, 1990), 128-39; G. Boccaccini, "The Solar Calendars of Daniel and Enoch," in *The Book of Daniel: Composition and Reception*, ed. J. J. Collins and P. W. Flint, VTSup 83 (Leiden: Brill, 2001), 2:311-28.

This aspect appears occasionally in Jubilees also outside the programmatic chap. 6. In chap. 29 Jacob sends agricultural products to his parents, as described in 29:16: "to his mother Rebecca, (he sent goods) four times per year — between the seasons of the months *(mā'kala gizeyātihomu la'awrāh),* between plowing and harvest, between autumn and the rain(y season), and between winter and spring." The division of the year is here connected with the agricultural tasks, as in Gen 8:22. The four cardinal days are considered suitable for sending agricultural products as gifts. This notion may be connected with the special merit of the cardinal days for bringing tithes and firstfruits (cf. chaps. 7 and 32). The phrase *"between* the seasons of the months" in 29:16 is of special importance, since it places the cardinal days at the end of each quarter (months 3, 6, 9, 12) and *before* the beginning of the ensuing quarter. This notion is not consistent with the practice of Jub 6:23-29, where the cardinal days stand at the head of months 1, 4, 7, 10. One may infer that 29:16 reflects the original concept of the cardinal days, which are in their nature "epagomenal," i.e., additional days, standing on the border between fixed time periods.[38]

By celebrating the first day of each quarter, Jubilees maintains the modus operandi of the Aramaic Levi Document, where the times of birth of Levi's children are given in such dates: the tenth month (Gershon), the first day of the first month (Kehat), the third month (Merari), the first of the seventh month (Jocheved).[39] Clearly these four days win special importance in ALD, an ideal that continued in Jub 28, where the dates for the births of Jacob's sons are given. Alongside insignificant dates for most of the sons, three prominent figures receive portentous dates in Jub 28: 1/I (Levi), 15/III (Judah), 1/IV (Joseph). Other fortunate occurrences are dated to the beginnings of seasons (see 3:32; 7:3; 13:8; 24:21; 27:19; 30:1; 31:3; 33:1; 45:1).[40] The placement of favorable occasions at the beginning of a season makes more sense than

---

38. Talmon underscored the liminality of the cardinal days, connecting it with the notion of *pegu'im* in 11QPsª XXVII; see S. Talmon, "The Covenanters' Calendar of Holy Seasons according to the List of King David's Compositions in the Psalms Scroll from Cave 11 (11QPsª XXVII)" (in Hebrew), in *Fifty Years of Dead Sea Scrolls Research: Studies in Memory of Jacob Licht,* ed. G. Brin and B. Nitzan (Jerusalem: Yad Ben Zvi, 2001), 204-19, here 215-19.

39. Chap. 11 according to J. C. Greenfield, M. E. Stone, and E. Eshel, *The Aramaic Levi Document,* SVTP 19 (Leiden: Brill, 2004), 189ff. The above authors prefer the possibility that Merari was born in the fourth month, according to a reading in 4QLeviª. For the Aramaic Levi Document as a source for Jubilees, see further the chapter by E. Eshel in this volume.

40. To resume the criticism of Jaubert's hypothesis, this point seems to indicate that, when selecting dates for meaningful occasions, the author of Jubilees gave more attention to key points in the year than to days of the week.

placing them at the end of the season, or at a hazardous border between the seasons, as in 1 En 72 and Jub 29:16. Since Jubilees is especially keen to mark festive days, it is only natural that the cardinal days mark happy opportunities like births and festivals at the beginning of each season. Yet, other signs point to an ambiguity with regard to the status of these days in Jubilees.

A programmatic statement on the importance of the cardinal days appears in the description of the fourth day of creation in Jub 2:9: "The Lord appointed the sun as a great sign above the earth for days, sabbaths, months, festivals, years, sabbaths of years, jubilees, and *all times of the years*" (trans. VanderKam). Glessmer rightly remarked that the concluding phrase of this verse, *walakʷəllo gizē laʿāmtāt*, actually refers to the days that divide the year, with the technical term *gizē* corresponding to the Hebrew term *tequfah*, which is partly extant in 4Q216 VI 8.[41]

In Jub 5–6 the special role of the cardinal days is exemplified by their integration into the flood narrative. While two of the quarterly dates are already mentioned in the biblical account (Gen 8:5, 13), the other two are noted only in Jubilees. In 5:28-30 it is stated that important phases in the course of the flood took place at the beginning of months 1, 4, 7, 10. Jub 6:23-27 resumes this thematic line when declaring these very days "memorial days and days of the seasons." This unique trait of the flood year in Jubilees is by no means required by the 364DCT; rather it reflects the special attitude of the author.[42] Compare for example the reworked flood narrative in 4Q252, which also belongs to the 364DCT, but where it is only stressed that the flood lasted one year exactly, following more closely the timetable of the biblical account, without any outstanding role assigned to the cardinal days. The author of Jubilees takes special pains to enforce a fourfold division on the flood year. The centrality of this division in Jubilees may be due to a special status given to Gen 8:22, a verse that anchors the annual seasons in the flow of events at the flood.

Both Jubilees and 4Q252 characterize the flood year as "a full year" (Heb. *šanah temimah*, 4Q252 II 2-3; Eth. *kʷəllo ʿāmat feṣṣuma*, Jub 6:30).[43]

---

41. U. Glessmer, "Explizite Aussagen über kalendarische Konflikte im Jubiläenbuch: Jub 6,22-32.33-38," in *Studies in the Book of Jubilees*, 127-64 (here 148).

42. C. Werman, "The Story of the Flood in the Book of Jubilees" (in Hebrew), *Tarbiz* 64 (1995): 183-202, points out that Jubilees was so keen to emphasize the cardinal days that he went beyond the biblical data and even contradicted them in several places. This stands in contrast to 4Q252, which is more loyal to the biblical text (MT and/or the versions).

43. The one occasion where the phrase *šanah temimah* appears in the Bible (Lev 25:30) is understood by R. Yehuda *(ha-nasi')* to refer to a solar year of 365 days (*b. Arakhin* 31a).

Both statements are connected with 1 En 106:15: "And there will be great wrath upon the earth and a flood . . . for a year" (= 4QEn^c 5 ii 20). In a way, both Jubilees and 4Q252 supply calendrical ramifications for this statement in 1 Enoch. However, it is essential to note what qualifies in each of the compositions as a "full year." While in 4Q252 II 2-3 the sufficient condition is the number of 364 days, in Jub 6:29-30 the condition is an edifice consisting of four quarters of thirteen weeks each. Jubilees' conception of the year is thus more subtly structured than the plain 364DCT.

III. The Division of the Year into Months

While two elements of the year — quarters and weeks — are considered crucial in 6:29-30, the division of the year into 12 months is entirely ignored. Indeed, while 364 divides neatly into 4 and 7, it is not easily divided into 12 months. Better results could be achieved for the ideal year of 360 days, with 12 schematic "months" of 30 days each, but since the 4 cardinal days are now counted within the year, they render the division into months complicated. In AB (chap. 72) the problem was solved by counting the additional days as number 31 at the end of months III, VI, IX, and XII. This solution was applied to the year of the flood in 4Q252 I 20, where a record of the date 31/XII is partially extant.[44] However, the author of Jubilees is reluctant to acknowledge this reckoning, possibly because in his view a month can only be a perfect and schematic unit of 30 days.

As noted by Ravid, Jubilees often refers to "the middle of the month," most notably in month III, which should have contained 31 days according to Jaubert.[45] This phrase is inapplicable in a 31-day month, and its use reveals that Jubilees had in mind a schematic 30-day month even in month III. A similar contention may rise from Jub 5:27, where a period of 150 days is equated with 5 months, against the rules of the standard 364DY, according to which at least 1 month of 31 days must occur in the sequence.

How far can we go when interpreting this data? A cautious view would see the figures of 5:27 as an innocent recapitulation of scripture, denying any practical calendrical significance to what seems like a sequence of five 30-day

---

44. Cf. the reconstruction by G. Brooke, "4Q252: Commentary on Genesis A," in *Qumran Cave 4.XVII: Parabiblical Texts, Part 3*, ed. G. Brooke et al., DJD 22 (Oxford: Clarendon, 1996), 194.

45. Ravid, "The Book of Jubilees," 381.

months. However, due to the additional data discussed above, it may be argued with Ravid that Jubilees does not recognize the existence of a 31-day month. In a paraphrase of 1 En 75:1-2, one may claim that in Jubilees the 4 additional days are counted in the reckoning of the *year,* but they stand outside the reckoning of *months.*[46] The cardinal days stand, according to 29:16, "between the seasons of the months," in a transitory position, but never within the count of months.

Boccaccini emphasized that an ideal 360-day year stood in the background of the calendar tradition, and that in some earlier texts the year was thought to consist not of 364 days but rather of 360 + 4 days.[47] The problematic figures in 5:27 prove, according to Boccaccini, that Jubilees adheres to a year of 360 + 4 days, with the additional days not counted in the continuous reckoning, the very practice opposed in 1 En 75:3 and 82:6. However, since the septenary definition of the year in Jub 6:30-31 is so fundamental for that book's ideology, it is hard to conceive of the number 364 as a secondary synthesis of 360 + 4 days. Thus, although both Ravid and Boccaccini stress the tension between ideal 30-day months and the 364DY, the models suggested by Ravid seem to account better for the data in Jubilees.

IV. Sun and Moon

In a programmatic sermon on the calendar, Jub 6:36 solemnly declares that "There will be people who carefully observe the moon with lunar observations because it is corrupt (with respect to) the seasons and is early from year to year by ten days." This verse conveys a sharp opposition to lunar observations, probably also lunar calculations, in the calendar reckoning. An impressive piece of rhetoric, this statement was applied in research to the interpretation not only of Jubilees but also of the entire 364DCT, and was considered the ultimate proof that the 364DY is a solar year, and that it stands in

---

46. See Boccaccini, "The Solar Calendars," 317-18. Curiously enough, a thirty-one-day month is hardly attested in calendrical material. The only clear attestations appear in 1 En 72. The rosters of month-lengths in 4Q320 3 ii–4 i and 6Q17 are unfortunately broken in the crucial points. In 3Q321 II 5-6 the reconstruction of day 31 is unavoidable, since on that day a "second *dwq*" occurs (S. Talmon, DJD 21, p. 71). However, this reconstruction involves an inverted order of the number, since usually in 4Q321 the units precede the tens. Even the reference to a thirty-one-day month in 4Q252 I 20 is not entirely certain, since the crucial word *w'ḥd* is absent.

47. Boccaccini, "The Solar Calendars," 318-20.

opposition to the protorabbinic luni-solar calendar.[48] In analogy to the calendar polemics in rabbinic literature, Talmon construed the moon to be an evil sign, symbolizing the dark in opposition to the bright light of the sun.

However, the publication of further calendrical sources revealed that this notion is only partially justified. We now know that the 364DCT had a constant interest in lunar phenomena, starting from its inception in AB and lasting until the latest calendrical texts from Qumran.[49] AB is determined to present models applicable not only to the sun but also to the entire heavenly host: sun, moon, and stars. This ideology is conveyed in 1 En 74:17: "Then the year is correctly completed in accord with their eternal positions and the positions of the sun; they rise from the gate from which it rises and sets for thirty days." This verse purportedly seeks to show that sun and moon equally traverse the same gates assigned to the sun in chap. 72, and that they do so according to the same time frame, thus yielding a correct (literally ṣdq, "just") order of the universe (cf. 74:12). The interest of AB in lunar phases is therefore not a secondary development, but is rather a primary concern of the author.

Later calendrical texts, which employed the 364DY in the framework of a religious community, with fixed times for ritual acts and prayers, continued to assign a central place to lunar calculations. This is most clearly seen in *mishmarot* documents such as 4Q320 and 4Q321, where lunar phases are counted side by side with the order of service in the temple and the festival calendars for the cultic year. This commitment to the tracking of lunar phases originates in the Mesopotamian prototypes of the 364DCT, and has been sustained by the Jewish tradents of the Mesopotamian knowledge, albeit with the changes required to fit their calendrical-apocalyptic needs.[50]

A great part of the 364DCT is transmitted in religious compositions that have no interest in astronomy. Thus, when the Damascus Document or the pesherim argue against the mistaken calendar practices of their opponents, or when T appoints the sacred times for sacrifice, they use the 364DY as an arithmetically efficient device for the regulation of the cult. This device

---

48. Talmon, *The World of Qumran*, 167-71; recently Talmon, "Anti-Lunar Calendar Polemics in Covenanters' Writings," in *Das Ende der Tage und die Gegenwart des Heils. Festschrift H. W. Kuhn*, ed. M. Becker and W. Fenske (Leiden: Brill, 1999), 29-40.

49. J. Ben-Dov, "The Initial Stages of Lunar Theory at Qumran," *JJS* 54 (2003): 125-38.

50. J. Ben-Dov and W. Horowitz, "The Babylonian Lunar Three in Calendrical Scrolls from Qumran," *ZA* 95 (2005): 104-20. In contrast to what is sometimes suggested, I do not think a lunar calendar was practiced at Qumran. On the contrary, the normative time frame was always the 364DY, but it was consistently aligned with schematic models of the lunar orbit.

is neither solar nor lunar, nor stellar nor any other astronomical predicate, but rather it is a schematic 364DY.

Seen on this background, the antilunar declarations in Jubilees are highly exceptional. Further evidence comes from chap. 2, where the author rewrites the creation account of the fourth day (Gen 1:14-16). V. 8 reports on the creation of sun, moon, and stars and imbues them with the traditional roles of giving light upon the earth and distinguishing day and night. However, when reaching the calendrical role of the luminaries, an altogether new idea is employed: "The Lord appointed the sun as a great sign above the earth for days, Sabbaths, months, festivals," etc. The fact that the text of Gen 1:14, which refers to "lights" in general, is transformed to refer to the sun only, clearly proves that the author entertains a solar disposition, probably also preference for a solar calendar.[51]

Why would a Jewish (proto-)sectarian author propagate a solar calendar if the 364DCT does not compel him to do so? Several possibilities may be suggested. First, from the point of view of *Traditionsgeschichte,* one may suggest that Jubilees resumes ancient Israelite traditions of solar religion.[52] This religious tradition continued in the Hellenistic period, in accord with other trends then prevailing in the non-Jewish East.[53]

Second, the polemics of Jub 6:36 must be viewed as part of an ongoing debate about the role of the moon in calendrical calculations. I present here in brief my argument from a previous publication.[54] The old "Synchronistic Calendar" (Aramaic AB) opted clearly for the inclusion of the moon in the calendrical ephemeris. However, this attitude faced some problems when it turned out that sun and moon cannot be entirely reconciled from the spatial point of view. The response to this problem was twofold. On the one hand, the author of Jubilees, endorsing his pro-solar disposition, declared that the moon should be entirely ignored. Thus, Jub 6:36 disputes not only the protorabbinic luni-solar calendar, but also the synchronization of sun and

---

51. VanderKam, *From Revelation to Canon,* 512f.; J. van Ruiten, *Primeval History Interpreted: The Rewriting of Genesis I–II in the Book of Jubilees,* JSJSup 66 (Leiden: Brill, 2000), 37f.; contra Ravid, "The Book of Jubilees," 380.

52. E.g., B. Janowski, "JHWH und der Sonnengott. Aspekte der Solarisierung JHWHs in vorexilischer Zeit," in *Die rettende Gerechtigkeit. Beiträge zur Theologie des Alten Testaments* (Neukirchen-Vluyn: Neukirchener, 1999), 192-219; M. S. Smith, "The Near Eastern Background of Solar Language for Yahweh," *JBL* 109 (1990): 29-39.

53. J. M. Baumgarten, "The Heavenly Tribunal and the Personification of Ṣedeq in Jewish Apocalyptic," *ANRW* 9, 1 (1979): 219-39.

54. Ben-Dov, "The Initial Stages of Lunar Theory at Qumran."

moon in AB. On the other hand, a reasonable solution for this problem was reached in the scroll 4Q317, which presented for the first time a fully developed concept of the three-year cycle, thus paving the way for a regular inclusion of the moon in calendrical calculations. Carbon 14 tests show that 4Q317 was penned "in the second half of the second century BCE," i.e., not long after the composition of Jubilees.[55] At that early stage, therefore, the dispute was settled against the view of Jubilees, and the moon was accepted as a standard object for speculation in sectarian documents.

Jubilees' solar orientation is therefore partly due to a disposition toward solar religion, and partly due to an early second century B.C.E. calendrical debate. This debate was eventually resolved in a different way than the one suggested in Jubilees, leaving the author of Jubilees in glaring isolation.

V. The Provenance of Jubilees' Calendar

A possibility raised in research long ago, and recently mentioned again by Ravid, is an Egyptian origin for the calendar of Jubilees.[56] This idea will be disputed below. In fact, Egyptian lore could have been a source for the entire 364DCT, especially the famous Egyptian civil calendar of 360 + 5 days. The insistence of Jubilees on schematic months of 30 days makes it an especially favorable place for spotting Egyptian influence. However, several basic facts argue against this hypothesis. First and foremost, the Egyptian civil year is divided into *three* seasons, not four, and the months are traditionally named according to their serial number within the three seasons.[57] The fourfold division of the year is so fundamental in the 364DCT, and in Jubilees especially,

55. For the present purposes it will be assumed that Jubilees was written around the mid–second century. For the dating of 4Q317, see S. J. Pfann in P. Alexander et al., eds., *Cryptic Texts. Miscellanea, Part 1: Qumran Cave 4. XXVI*, DJD 36 (Oxford: Clarendon, 2000), 523.

56. To be precise, since Ravid denies that Jubilees' calendar is a solar one, the Egyptian connection serves her for other purposes than those suggested by earlier authors. For earlier attestations of the Egyptian connection, see M. Hengel, *Judaism and Hellenism*, trans. J. Bowden (London and Philadelphia: Fortress, 1974), 1:235; 2:158; H. Stegemann, *The Library of Qumran: On the Essenes, Qumran, John the Baptist, and Jesus* (Grand Rapids: Eerdmans; Leiden: Brill, 1998), 166-69.

57. See R. A. Parker, *The Calendars of Ancient Egypt* (Chicago: Oriental Institute, 1950), 45, with special emphasis on the persistence of this practice in the Persian period and beyond. In general the treatment of ancient Near Eastern calendars in Ravid's article is not sufficiently informed. Against the Egyptian origin of the 364DCT, see Albani, *Astronomie und Schöpfungsglaube*, 161-69; A. Loprieno, "Il modello egiziano nei testi della letteratura intertestamentaria," *RivB* 34 (1986): 205-32.

that it is hardly conceivable to trace its origin in the tripartite Egyptian calendar. Further, one wonders whatever happened to the fifth epagomenal day of the Egyptian civil year.[58] The epagomenal days are grouped according to the Egyptian calendar at the end of the year, while in the Jewish sources they are interspersed, one at the end of each season. Finally, the use of schematic 30-day months is not necessarily an Egyptian concept, since it could have equally originated from the Babylonian schematic year of 360 days, as noted by Albani, and recently also by Ben-Dov and Horowitz. More generally, the Jewish 364DCT is better understood as a branch of Mesopotamian science than of the Egyptian one, since Mesopotamian teachings appear not only in AB but also in other phases of the Jewish 364DCT, as well as in apocalyptic literature in general.[59]

Since the present chapter is dedicated to the book of Jubilees in particular, the issue of foreign influences is even less relevant than elsewhere. While this question is worth pursuing when studying scientific treatises like AB or astronomical rosters like 3Q321, nothing in the calendrical conception of Jubilees would point to a foreign influence on the author. Indeed, Jubilees reveals a long list of peculiarities in the calendrical sphere, but there is no reason to trace their origins to foreign sources. Rather, as noted above, the special traits of Jubilees' calendar can be accounted for on inner-Jewish grounds, taking into account the author's ideological and hermeneutical dispositions.

The conceptions of time in Jubilees are, on the one hand, unmistakably similar to traditional Jewish concepts from the Bible and second temple literature. Jubilees used as sources a long list of extrabiblical writings, both aggadic and halakic. On the other hand, Jubilees differs from traditional Jewish literature, creating a highly original array of concepts on time reckoning. This new conception is so intricate that it would be futile to trace this element or another from it to foreign influences. Rather it is better to explain them as stemming from unique ideology, as well as resulting from the literary constraints placed on this author in the framework of retelling the Pentateuch from Genesis to mid-Exodus.

58. In an earlier presentation Ravid opted for the existence of another epagomenal day, number 365, at the end of Jubilees' year (L. Ravid and J. Kugel, appendix to L. Ravid, "Issues in the Book of Jubilees" [Ph.D. diss., Bar-Ilan University 2001], 21). This idea is not taken up in Ravid's *DSD* article.

59. H. Kvanvig, *Roots of Apocalyptic: The Mesopotamian Background of the Enoch Figure and of the Son of Man*, WMANT 61 (Neukirchen-Vluyn: Neukirchener, 1988); J. C. VanderKam, *Enoch and the Growth of an Apocalyptic Tradition*, CBQMS 16 (Washington, D.C.: Catholic Biblical Association of America, 1984); J. J. Collins, *The Apocalyptic Imagination,* 2nd ed. (Grand Rapids: Eerdmans, 1998), 26-29.

The Book of Jubilees and the Origin of Evil

Loren T. Stuckenbruck

A consideration of "the origin of evil" in the book of Jubilees raises the question of whether this is an appropriate avenue of inquiry at all or, if so, in what ways such an inquiry should be qualified. If the topic implies that we are looking for a way the author(s) of Jubilees speculated about the origin of sin as a topic in and of itself, then the investigation is misguided. After all, in searching for references to the beginnings of evil or sin in other early Jewish literature, we find that writers were less concerned with the problem in itself than with more immediate matters. This avails, whether such origins were being traced to rebellious angels (sometimes including their giant offspring),[1] to a transgression by Adam,[2] to the disobedience of Eve,[3] to women of antediluvian times,[4] to humanity,[5] to some combination of these stories,[6]

---

1. So Book of the Watchers (esp. 1 En 6:1–8:3), Astronomical Book (80:1-8: wayward stars), Animal Apocalypse (85:3–87:4), Apocalypse of Weeks (93:3-4), Birth of Noah (106:13-17), the Book of the Giants (e.g., 4Q531 1:1-8); cf. 4QAges of Creation (4Q180-181) and SibOr 3:110-158. In a number of documents, the story — without an apparent (or extant) claim about an origin of evil — functions paradigmatically, that is, as a quintessential example of consequences to come upon those who engage in comparable activities; see 4QExhortation Based on the Flood (4Q370 i 6); 3 Macc 2:4; Ben Sira 16:7.

2. Most clearly in 4 Ezra 7:116-126 and 2 Bar 54:13-22; cf. Rom 5:12.

3. See Sir 25:13-26.

4. TReu 5:1-6.

5. See the Epistle of Enoch (1 En 98:4-8).

6. See the Book of the Parables (1 En 65:1–69:29); LAE 12:1–16:3; 3 Bar 4:7-10; 2 En 30:17–31:8; and 1 Tim 2:9-15.

294

or could even be understood as part of the way God set up the cosmos to run from the very beginning.[7] The same may be said for statements in literature from the second temple period that, without referring to "origins" per se, adopt a level of discourse that assumes sin is initiated by human beings or, at least, emphasize that humans are responsible when disobedience occurs.[8] Instead, in most — if not all — instances, writers were taking up and interpreting received traditions in ways that enabled them to address and manage the social and religious circumstances with which they were acquainted.

This is not to say, however, that the writers were not interested in the question of "origins" at all, not least the author of Jubilees, whose immediate interests may be compared with the early Enochic writings, on the one hand, and the so-called Pseudo-Eupolemos materials, on the other. Fundamental to their religious programs were appeals to the way God has established the cosmos, so that a narrative or story line — whether grand and intricate or small and simple — would readily function as a way to identify activities and ideas that depart from this order.[9] In addition, by attending to "origins" we should acknowledge more broadly that Jewish writers were participating in the larger debates of the time in which representatives of Mediterranean and Near East cultures were vying for the superiority of the traditions received by their respective ethnic groups. Against assertions by advocates of Egyptian, Babylonian, and Greek culture,[10] Jewish writers during the Hellenistic age were variously adopting ways of making a case for the preeminence of Jewish religion and culture. In particular, the discourse in 1 En 6–11 and Jubilees cannot be seen in isolation from this setting.

The following discussion will briefly sketch what might be described as several beginnings regarding wrongdoing, sin, or evil in the early chapters of the book of Jubilees. These relate to five distinguishable, yet somewhat interconnected, episodes: (1) the wrongdoing of the first woman and Adam in the Garden of Eden (Jub 3:8-31), (2) the murder of Abel by Cain (4:1-6; cf.

---

7. So the Two Spirits Treatise (1QS iii 13–iv 26) and Sir 11:14; 17:7; 33:10-15; and 42:24.

8. See, e.g., more abstract statements that regard this or that activity as lying behind all other forms of malevolence (so on desire for money in SibOr 2:135-136; 1 Tim 6:10) or those texts that identify the underlying factor for sin as a particular part of the human being (Mark 7:21 par.; Matt 15:19; James 1:13-15).

9. In addition to the examples listed in nn. 1-7 above, see Rom 1:18-32.

10. The debate is mirrored in the second century B.C.E. Pseudo-Eupolemos fragments. Moreover, for the third century B.C.E., we may note the works of Berossus *(History of Babylonia)* and Manetho *(Aegyptica).*

4:9, 31-32), (3) the fallen angels tradition (5:1-19; 7:20-39; 8:1-4; 10:1-14), (4) Noah's nakedness and the cursing of Canaan (7:7-15; cf. 8:8–9:15), and (5) the tower of Babel (10:18–11:6). Limits of space require the discussion to focus on identifying the act of wrongdoing narrated in each episode, describing the impact of this deed in the text, and, finally, reflecting on what sort of "beginning" the episode signifies. While the discussion will center on Jubilees itself, comparisons with Enochic traditions probably presupposed by the text will throw light on at least one tradition-historical context within which the ideas in Jubilees were taking shape.

A. The First Woman, Adam, and the Serpent (3:8-31)

At the outset, the arrival times of Adam and his wife at the Garden of Eden — distinguished as forty and eighty days after they were created — are explained on the basis of halakah recorded in the heavenly tablets (3:10-14). During their first seven years in the Garden, Adam and his wife's activities, guided by the instruction of angels, involved tilling the Garden and guarding it against "birds, animals, and cattle."[11] This period is one of purity that was maintained by a vegetarian diet.

The text states that exactly seven years after their arrival in the Garden, the serpent approaches the woman. As in the biblical tradition (Gen 3:1, 13-15), Jubilees does not speculate about the origin of the serpent. The serpent's success in persuading the woman to eat fruit from the forbidden tree in the middle of the Garden results immediately in her shame at being naked; unlike Genesis, in which clothing is made by Adam and Eve after their disobedience (Gen 3:7), here the woman clothes herself with fig leaves before she gives the fruit to Adam (Jub 3:21). Once Adam takes the fruit, he too clothes himself with an apron made from fig leaves (3:22).[12]

The writer of Jubilees identifies several consequences of the first couple's forbidden consumption of fruit. After narrating their exclusion from the Garden, the text notes that until this point all the animals ("the cattle, the birds, everything that walks and everything that moves about") could speak (as humans) and that their language was unified (3:28-29),[13] a detail

11. Citations of Jubilees are taken from the English translation by J. C. VanderKam, *The Book of Jubilees*, CSCO 511, Scriptores Aethiopici 88 (Louvain: Peeters, 1989).

12. Jubilees follows Genesis in later having God make clothing for the couple just before they are dismissed from the Garden; cp. Jub 3:26 and Gen 3:21.

13. The preserved text is inconsistent on whether the animals had been outside the

not found in Genesis. After the couple's departure the animals' common means of communication are dissolved; moreover, in an allusion to what Genesis describes as circumstances before the incident of disobedience (see Gen 1:25; 2:19-20), the text states that the animals are dispersed according to their kinds to separate spaces created for them (Jub 3:29).

In Jubilees the situation of Adam (and his wife) is thus distinguished from that of the animals: after Adam's dismissal from the Garden, the animals no longer share one language and remain naked while Adam is alone among living creatures in being permitted to have clothing to cover his shame (3:30). Adam's distinction is explained as a law on the tablets that enjoins "those who know the judgement of the law" to "cover their shame and not uncover themselves as the nations uncover themselves" (3:31). Thus, rather than having consequences for any human proclivity to sin again,[14] Adam's expulsion from the Garden serves as a warrant for why faithful Jews should reject the practice of nudity among Gentiles. If anything, the result of Adam and Eve's transgression is less evidenced in what they themselves do afterward than it has ramifications for the animals and, by transference, for Gentiles and those who adhere to their ways. As for Adam, he continues to till the land "as he had been taught in the Garden of Eden" (3:35). In this way, the activities attributed to the first couple before their disobedience are in Jubilees more openly paradigmatic for Jewish piety (3:8-16) than is apparent from Genesis.

B. The Murder of Abel by Cain (4:1-6, 9, 31-32)

The text of Jubilees implies that Cain killed his brother out of jealousy that the sacrifice of Abel, and not his own, was found acceptable to the angels (4:2). The immediate outcome of this act was, obviously, that "the Lord blamed Cain" (4:4) and that, for this, Cain himself was killed (4:31). In the text, however, the story is told to substantiate two regulations attributed to the heavenly tablets (4:5-6, 31-32). The first explains the curse placed upon Cain (cf. Gen 4:11) as one upon "the person who beats his companion maliciously"; in addition, anyone who sees such activity and does not testify about it is to be cursed as well (Jub 4:5). This, in turn, is taken as an explanation for

---

Garden all along (3:16) or were in fact in the Garden and had to be expelled with Adam and the woman (3:29).

14. The text does not know anything of an Adamic fall.

the function of angels who report all sins, whether they have been committed openly or not, before God (4:6; cf. 1 En 99:3; 100:10; esp. 104:7-8). The second regulation derived from the story involves the death of Cain, which is made to illustrate the principle of *lex talionis* engraved in the heavenly tablets. In 4:31 the reader learns that Cain's death occurred when his house built with stones fell on him, a fitting end for someone who had killed his brother with a stone. Thus the regulation: "By the instrument with which a man kills his fellow he is to be killed. As he wounded him so are they to do to him" (4:32).

Similar to Gen 4, nothing is said about any consequence of Cain's deed *for others.*[15]

C. The Fallen Angels Tradition (5:1-19; 7:20-39; 8:1-4; 10:1-14)

The disobedience of angels to God opens a further development in the introduction of evil to the world. While this point is not debated in itself, one may ask the question: What kind of "beginning" or "origin" does this event inaugurate? In coming to terms with the question, we note that the author of Jubilees is not simply interpreting Genesis, but shows an awareness of an interpretive tradition that regarded the "sons of God" of Gen 6:2 as rebellious angels who committed sin leading to upheaval in the created order itself. As the writer expresses an awareness of writings attributed to Enoch (4:17-26), it is likely that Enochic writings provided at least one source of his knowledge.[16] A tradition-historical link of this sort between Jubilees and the Book of the Watchers, in particular 1 En 6–16, is strengthened by the statement in Jubilees that Enoch "testified to the Watchers who had sinned with the daughters of men because these had begun to mix with earthly women so that they became defiled" (Jub 4:22).

Though admitting some dependence on the earliest Enochic tradition (the Book of the Watchers and, perhaps also, the Book of Giants), the writer

---

15. Cf. perhaps also the Animal Apocalypse at 1 En 85:4-7, though the story of Cain and Abel functions more as an underlying narrative that shapes the language of complaints raised by the righteous in the face of injustices carried out against them; compare, e.g., the Book of the Watchers, 1 En 8:4–9:3 and 22:4-7.

16. In particular, the Astronomical Book (Jub 4:17), Book of the Watchers (see discussion below), Apocalypse of Weeks (4:18), and possibly the Epistle of Enoch (4:19); on the use of the latter two in Jubilees, see J. C. VanderKam, *Enoch and the Growth of an Apocalyptic Tradition*, CBQMS 16 (Washington, D.C.: Catholic Biblical Association of America, 1984), 142-44.

of Jubilees departs from the Enochic predecessors in several ways. We may distinguish the emphases of Jubilees from the Book of the Watchers chaps. 6–16 in at least four ways: (i) the location of the rebellious angels' transgression, (ii) the means of punishment carried out on these angels and their malevolent offspring, (iii) the explanation for the origin of demons, and (iv) the motif of angelic instruction.

i. First, according to Jubilees, the angels' disobedience takes place on earth. The Hebrew pun that relates the descent of the angels during the time of Jared is picked up by the writer (cf. 1 En 6:6; 106:13; 1QapGen ar iii 3) and coordinated with the time the angels begin to carry out their mission to instruct humanity "and to do what is just and upright upon the earth" (4:15; cf. 5:6). Once on the earth, the angels are then distracted from their mission and consumed by the beauty of the daughters of humanity (5:1). In addition to the forbidden sexual union that has led to the birth of violent and unclean gargantuan offspring, they are held responsible for teaching that leads to sin (see discussion of 8:3 under point iv. below).

This story in Jubilees contrasts with that of the Book of the Watchers in that chaps. 6–16 locate the beginning of the angelic rebellion in heaven. By postponing their transgression to earth, the text of Jubilees does two things. First, it preserves "heaven" as a place of sanctity where the God of Israel reigns. While the early Enochic tradition struggles to come to terms with the fall of the angels as a breach of cosmic boundaries (1 En 15:8-11), such a breach is not even part of the story in Jubilees. The earthly setting of their sin served to keep the heavenly and earthly spheres distinct, so that the boundaries established at creation are not seen to have been violated. Second, though the paradigmatic function of the fallen angels and giants in the Book of the Watchers is far below the surface of the tradition, in Jubilees it is more explicit: the angels' reprehensible actions, both their union with women and their culpable teachings, serve as a warning to anyone who would behave in the same way. This is illustrated best in Noah's exhortations to his children that they "keep themselves from fornication, uncleanness, and from all injustice" (7:20), precisely those activities that the disobedient angels and their progeny have spread to humanity (7:22-24).

So, at this stage of the story line in Jubilees, the negative consequences of the angels' sin relate primarily to the violence their gigantic offspring bring upon the earth (7:22-25) and the reprehensible instructions they have disseminated among humans (8:3). Whereas in the Book of the Watchers it is the wayward angels and giants' activities that lead to divine punishment, in Jubilees the picture is more nuanced: it is because the sins of the angels and giants have caused humanity to do the same that the flood was sent upon the earth (7:21a, 25).[17] This additional, more transparent emphasis on human responsibility in Jubilees mirrors the culpability of the angels; just as the angels were steered away from the mission they were originally given by God, so also the people of Israel should be wary of doing the same.

ii. In relation to the fallen angel tradition, the flood in Jubilees functions in a way that negotiates conceptually between the Book of the Watchers (1 En 10), the story in Gen 6–9, and its subsequent reuse in the early Enochic tradition (1 En 1–5; 98:4-8). Unequivocally, in Gen 6 the flood comes as God's response to the violence and sin committed by human beings on earth (see Gen 6:3, 13, 17). By contrast, the Book of the Watchers and Book of the Giants treat the flood tradition as but one manifestation of divine judgment against the angels and giants (see 1 En 10:2-3; the motif is more prominent in the Book of Giants: 2Q26; 4Q530 ii 4-7; 6Q8 frg. 2). The book of Jubilees, analogous to the Book of Giants' reception of the Book of the Watchers, places greater emphasis on the flood while picking up on the motif of the giants destroying one another (1 En 7:5; 10:9, 12; Book of Giants 1Q23 9 + 14 + 15?; 4Q531 4), which is noticeably absent from Genesis. The narrative of Jubilees thus weaves together elements from received traditions to create a new account: the great flood comes as the divine retribution against antediluvian sins of human beings whose wrongdoings were fueled by the transgressing angels and giants who, in turn, have likewise been punished. It is appropriate to elaborate this story line a little further below.

As just suggested, in contrast to the Book of the Watchers, Jubilees does not clearly assign the flood itself a role in God's punishment of the angels and giants. On the one hand, in 1 En 10:1-3 a deluge is announced to "the son of Lamech" after the corrupt instructions and horrific misdeeds of the watchers and giants have been described (cf. 7:1–8:3) and after the complaints by the murdered of humanity have been mediated by angels to God (cf. 8:4–9:10). On the other hand, Jub 5:3-5 and 7:20-25 suggest that it is sinful humanity — whatever the role of the fallen angels and giants in the narrative — whose deeds, as in Gen 6, are the immediate reason for the flood.[18]

---

17. Though the Book of the Watchers implicates people who have been taught by the fallen angels, the story of punishment does not so much focus on them as on the angels and the giants.

18. As mentioned above, the watchers' fornication with the women of the earth and the violence of several generations of their progeny (7:21b-24a) contribute to conditions that make divine judgment through the flood necessary, though they themselves are not expressly punished through the flood.

While in Jubilees the flood is primarily a response to sins among humans (as in Genesis), the divine punishments against the angels and giants take different forms, respectively (as in 1 Enoch). In Jubilees the angels are punished by being bound and sent to the nether regions of the earth (5:6, 10), a scenario that according to the Book of the Watchers is carried out against ʿAsaʾel (1 En 10:4-6, 8). This motif, as in the Animal Apocalypse (1 En 88:3), may reflect the influence of the Tartarus tradition known, for example, from Hesiod's *Theogony*. As for the giants, their punishment in Jubilees is restricted to their intramural violence (5:7, 9; 7:22-24) that again may be compared with the Book of the Watchers (1 En 7:3; 10:12) where, however, in 10:12 this includes the fallen angels as well.

The form of punishment meted out to the giants in Jubilees may go back to a double interpretation of the ambiguous Hebrew verb יָדוֹן of Gen 6:3. (1) In Jubilees 5:8 the verb is understood in the sense of "to dwell" (as in the LXX) — "My spirit will not *dwell* on people forever for they are flesh. Their life span is to be 120 years." (2) Distinguishable from the Greek translation, however, Jubilees applies the term "flesh" in Gen 6:3 not to human beings, but to the giants who, though they simulate humans by having bodies, destroy one another in advance of the flood (5:9). In this way, it is made clear that the giants are in the unfolding narrative not expected to survive the flood, let alone to live long enough to be punished through it; the flood itself is not the form of punishment they receive.

If the angels and giants have introduced, or at least increased, evil in the world, their malevolent deeds do not lead to a wholesale corruption of human nature. Quite the contrary: after their punishments are recounted and their condemnation on the day of judgment confirmed (5:10-11), Jub 5:12 states that God "made a new and righteous nature for all his creatures so that they *would not sin with their whole nature* until eternity. Everyone will be righteous — each according to his kind — for all time" (emphasis mine). This re-creation or renewal of human nature may seem puzzling in the aftermath of the antediluvian upheavals. However, it is not unqualified: the writer allows for a propensity to sin within human beings while maintaining that the punishment of the watchers and their offspring addressed something within humanity that had gone irretrievably awry on account of them. Jubilees thus hints at, but does not develop, a theological anthropology that views the human race as a whole as having been affected by the angelic rebellion, a consequence that is partially dealt with through God's restorative activity.

iii. While the punishment through the flood and intramural violence has a renewal of humanity as its positive consequence, Jubilees explains the ongoing reality of human wrongdoing and suffering after the flood in terms of residual effects left by the antediluvian evils. The explanation for such suffering relates to what might conveniently be called "the origin of demons." The way Jubilees accounts for the origin of evil spirits is similar to the view in both the Book of the Watchers and Book of the Giants that identifies such spirits with the spirits or souls of the dead giants (compare Jub 10:5 with 1 En 15:8-11). Another similarity is that, ultimately, the demonic forces behind evil in the world are regarded, in effect, as powers whose judgment is assured; in other words, they are already defeated beings whose complete destruction is only a matter of time (until the day of judgment; cf. Jub 10:7, 8, 11).

Though Jubilees seems to depart from the Enoch traditions in having the giants killed through intramural violence alone, the author adapts the latter's etiology of demons based on the continued existence of giants in some form after the deluge. Both traditions share the view that the giants become disembodied spirits as a consequence of their destruction of one another (1 En 15:9; 11–16:1; inferred from Jub 5:8-9 and 10:1-6); they perhaps even imply that the giants' disembodied spirits could already have been active before the deluge.[19] But there are smaller differences. The Jubilees account differs from the Enochic traditions in that the nature of demonic evil is not articulated in anthropological terms (cf. 1 En 15:4-10),[20] that is, in Jubilees the impurity of the giants as mixtures between rebellious angels and earthly women is not expressed as an *inherent* characteristic. Though it is possible that the etiology of demons in 1 En 15 is presupposed by Jubilees — after all, the union between the watchers and human daughters is considered a form of "pollution" (4:22; cf. 7:21) — it is not clear that they are described as evil per se. In effect, this strengthens the analogy between the giants' responsibility for their deeds and the responsibility humans carry when they disobey in similar fashion. Punishment comes not because of what one is or has become by nature, but is the result of willful disobedience.

In terms of how demons contribute to the postdiluvian suffering of humans, Jubilees goes into the kind of detail of which there is no trace in the Enoch traditions. The demonic spirits that bring affliction to humanity after the flood are but a tenth of their original number. Nine-tenths are com-

19. While the Book of the Watchers is silent on this point, Noah's prayer in Jub 10:5 implies that the giants' spirits, alongside the watchers, were active before the flood.

20. Cf. also Philo, *Quaestiones et solutiones in Genesin* 1.92, in which the offspring of the angels and humans are regarded as inappropriate joining of "spiritual" and "somatic" realms that should be kept separate.

pletely destroyed[21] while one-tenth are permitted to carry on with their destructive malevolence. This permission is granted as a divine concession to the petitions of Mastema, their chief, who, after God has commanded the angels to bind all the spirits for judgment, requests that some spirits be allowed to corrupt humans, lead them astray, and cause suffering through illness (10:8, 12; cf. 7:27 — Noah's words: "For I myself see that the demons have begun to lead you and your children astray").

The writer of Jubilees thus attempts to steer a fine line between human responsibility, on the one hand, and demonic cause, on the other. While evil in its various forms is regarded as a manifestation of activities of the spirits of the giants, humanity is essentially capable of rising above such influences and, to some degree, even managing afflictions by applying the herbal remedies given to Noah by one of the angels (10:10-13). If in comparison with the Book of the Watchers the situation of disobedient humans and the giants in Jubilees is less distinct and more analogous, the fallen angels tradition serves not only to explain why humans in the author's day fall prey to wrongdoing and suffering from external influences, but also serves as a warning that Jews should stay away from engaging in the giants' "fornication," "uncleanness," and "injustice" (7:20; cf. 7:21-25).

iv. One aspect of the fallen angels tradition has been mentioned above but not developed: the reprehensible instructions traced back to the rebellious angels. Their teaching was mainly concerned with "the omens of the sun, moon, and stars and every heavenly sign," that is, with astrological lore associated with wrong calendrical reckonings and objectionable forms of divination (8:3; 11:8).[22] This instruction does not disappear when the angels are punished. After the deluge, it is discovered inscribed on a stone by Kainan, who "read what was in it, copied it, and sinned on the basis of what was in it" (8:3; cf. 1 En 80:1-8 and 82:5). This learning, which is kept secret from Noah for fear that it would incur his anger (8:4), eventually finds its way down to Noah's descendants, that is, down to the time of Nahor, Abraham's grandfather (11:8). In Jubilees, then, while the watchers are originally good when sent to instruct human beings on earth (cf. 5:6), their knowledge becomes skewed through their illicit sexual union with women. Once the

---

21. Cf. Animal Apocalypse at 1 En 89:5-6, according to which all the giants are destroyed by the flood and have no afterlife.

22. On this, see Armin Lange, "The Essene Position on Magic and Divination," in *Legal Texts and Legal Issues: Proceedings of the Second Meeting of the International Organization for Qumran Studies, Published in Honour of Joseph M. Baumgarten*, ed. M. Bernstein, F. García Martínez, and J. Kampen, STDJ 23 (Brill: Leiden, 1997), 377-435 (esp. 401-3).

watchers transgress the purpose of their mission, the author distinguishes sharply between two tracks of learning that are subsequently kept distinct: (1) the wrong astrological knowledge introduced by the wayward angels and conveyed through Kainan down to Noah's descendants and, in stark contrast, (2) the correct knowledge about the movements of heavenly bodies from which agricultural cycles and calendrical reckonings are to be derived. This latter, divinely revealed knowledge, is traced back to instruction given to Enoch by the heavenly angels (cf. 4:18, 21) and is bound up with the 364-day solar calendar uncompromisingly supported by the writer throughout the work. From Enoch, it was transmitted through Noah and his family who escaped the flood and then finally reemerged as a component of the piety attributed to Abraham (12:16) and his descendants through the line of Jacob.

The separation of diametrically opposed traditions of learning in Jubilees is best seen against the background of euhemeristic traditions such as come to us through the "Pseudo-Eupolemos" fragments cited by Eusebius in his *Praparatio evangelica* frg. 1 (9.17.1-9). In Pseudo-Eupolemos, the figure of Enoch is likewise said to have been taught by "the angels" whose instruction also centered on astrological knowledge (9.17.8-9). This knowledge is also attributed to Abraham (9.17.3), who, in turn, is said to have passed it on to the Phoenicians. As we have seen, Jubilees shares the view that the knowledge revealed to Enoch eventually comes down to Abraham. There is, however, a big difference. In Pseudo-Eupolemos, the lineage of a Noachic figure (9.17.2) and Abraham (9.18.3, if this second fragment belongs to the same work) is associated with "the giants" who escaped the destruction of the flood and built a tower (9.17.2; cf. 9.18.2, where only one "giant" called Belos is in view). Furthermore, the Pseudo-Eupolemos text makes no effort to specify whether the angels who revealed astrological knowledge to Enoch were good or bad. The resulting picture — which blends the traditions of giants, learning given to Enoch, and the figures of Abraham and Noah — is one that in Jubilees is bifurcated into the two streams of tradition referred to above (see the previous paragraph). In doing this, Jubilees is following the path already set in the Book of the Watchers and especially the Book of the Giants, where the strict distinction between Enoch and Noah, on the one hand, and the angels-giants, on the other, is maintained.[23]

23. For the similar insistence that denies Noah's identity as an offspring of the watchers, see Genesis Apocryphon (1QapGen ii-v) and Birth of Noah in 1 En 106–107. See "The 'Angels' and 'Giants' of Genesis 6:1-4 in Second and Third Century BCE Jewish Interpretation," *DSD* 7 (2000): 354-77 (here 360 n. 16), and my treatment of Birth of Noah in *1 Enoch 91–108*, CEJL (Berlin and New York: De Gruyter, 2007), general comment on 1 En 106:4-7.

Another area in which Jubilees distinguishes between good and bad instruction reflects a departure from the early Enoch tradition: knowledge about the use of herbs as medicines. Jubilees not only has the angels instruct Enoch regarding the calendar (4:17; cf. 1 En 72–82), but also has one of them instruct Noah on the medicinal properties of herbs (10:10, 13), a teaching that comes in response to Noah's petition that God deliver his offspring from the evil spirits who have been corrupting them after the flood (10:1-6).[24] The use of herbs to combat the damage caused by those spirits permitted to afflict humans (thanks to Mastema's request) contrasts markedly from the Enoch tradition. In the Book of the Watchers at 1 En 8:3, the "cutting of roots" (Greek Codex Panopolitanus) is unequivocally rejected as a practice ascribed to the fallen angels. Thus, while Jubilees takes over from Enoch tradition the attribution of good and bad knowledge to good and bad angels, respectively, the content of what is good and bad is not entirely the same. Whereas the Book of the Watchers has condemned the use of medicines by attributing them to the fallen angels who have eventually generated the giants that became oppressive evil spirits (1 En 8:3; 15:8-11), in Jubilees such knowledge is revealed by good angels in order to combat the attacks of the evil spirits that originated from the giants.[25]

We may summarize how the fallen angels tradition in Jubilees relates to the beginnings of evil as follows: In adapting the myth from received traditions, the writer of Jubilees is not actually deliberating about the origin of evil per se. Instead the tradition about rebellious angels serves to underline two main points. First, it functions to explain "why things are the way they are experienced and perceived" in the author's and his readers' world. Second, as in the Book of the Watchers, if the story line provides assurance that, to the extent they are caused by the tenth of Mastema's cohort of disembodied spirits, present afflictions and sins are temporary, the evil powers are, in effect, already defeated. Unlike the Book of the Watchers, however, the writer of Jubilees goes to greater lengths to avoid any inference that demonic causality undermines human, especially Israel's, responsibility. This is achieved

---

24. On Noah's prayer in the context of Jubilees, see Stuckenbruck, "Deliverance Prayers and Hymns in Early Jewish Documents," in *The Changing Face of Judaism and Christianity*, ed. G. S. Oegema and I. Henderson (Gütersloh: Gerd Mohn, 2005), 146-65.

25. On this contrast, see B. Kollmann, "Göttliche Offenbarung magisch-pharmakologischer Heilkunst im Buch Tobit," *ZAW* 106 (1994): 289-99 (esp. 298-99). The book of Tobit, especially the longer recension, reflects a positive attitude toward "pharmacological" means applied against demonic and physical afflictions, especially as this is revealed by God's angel (so, e.g., Codex Sinaiticus to 6:1-9; 11:7-12).

not only by analogies drawn between human misdeeds and those attributed to the watchers' offspring (7:20-21), as we have seen, but also by the degree to which the notion of the giants as primarily responsible for the antediluvian violence at the expense of humanity is diminished.[26]

D. Noah's Nakedness and the Cursing of Canaan (7:7-15; cf. 8:8–9:15)

We mention this story because it is the first episode following the deluge in which something goes wrong: Ham shows Noah disrespect by looking upon his nakedness, an act that brings Noah to curse Ham's youngest son, Canaan, while blessing Japheth and Shem who, by contrast, cover his nakedness without looking. The version in Jub 7:7-15 adheres closely to its counterpart in Gen 9:21-28, though in Jubilees the consequences of the cursing and blessing are elaborated at much greater length (Gen 9:26-27 is reiterated in Jub 7:11-12, but the elaboration occurs in 8:8–9:15). In telling this story, the writer is not concerned with an "origin of evil," but rather uses it to foreshadow the superiority of Israel, among Shem's descendants, over the descendants of Ham.

E. The Tower of Babel (10:18–11:6)

As in Gen 11:1-9, the episode involves a tower in the land of Shinar the building of which is brought to a halt by God. The text of Jubilees provides more details than Genesis about why the tower was not only not constructed further but also even destroyed (cf. Pseudo-Eupolemos in Eusebius, *Praeparatio evangelica* 9.18.2). Whereas Genesis attributes the curtailment of the building activity to God's concern that humans do not apprehend the limitations of what they can do (Gen 11:6), Jubilees prefaces the story with a pronouncement about the condition of humankind put into the mouth of Ragew, the

---

26. In 7:22 there is an element of oppression by the giants (the Elyo killed humankind), though what follows are statements that people killed one another and, in 7:23, that "When everyone sold himself to commit injustice and to shed innocent blood, the earth was filled with injustice." Whereas the Book of the Watchers holds the giants responsible for destroying humanity and spilling their innocent blood (1 En 7:3; 9:1, 9), the writer of Jubilees comes close to calumniating humans for this activity (cf. 7:23-25) and has Noah warn his children against both the shedding and the consumption of blood (7:27-33).

son of Lomna and Peleg: humanity *"has now become evil* through the per-verse plan to build themselves a city and tower in the land of Shinar" (Jub 10:18, emphasis mine). One may note here that the situation referred to has not been inherited from any prior event in the narrative; it is simply pre-sented as a consequence *of the city and tower builders' own making.*

There is something, however, more profound behind this caricature of humankind as evil. While this does not amount to a categorical statement about "the human condition" — see the discussion of Jub 5:12 above — it does describe the incident as a reflection of the nadir to which human activi-ties had descended. The outcome, the dispersion of the builders into cities, languages, and nations (10:26), ushers the situation of humanity down to what had happened to the animals when Adam and Eve were expelled from the Garden of Eden: the breaking up of one mode of communication into many in accordance with each kind and location of animal. Analogous to the Garden of Eden episode, the story thus explains the diversity of kinds and species among humanity.

Conclusion

None of the five episodes considered in this paper has anything to do with the question of "where evil originally came from" or "how the activity of sin-ning got to be." Within the unfolding narrative of Jubilees, they operate as explanations for the way things are in the world as the writer and the im-plied readers perceive it. As for the effect these episodes have on humanity, there is no real link between the stories; one story does not create the basis for a degenerating human condition picked up in the next. Instead, the sto-ries are linked as different points in the narrative in their presentation of a humanity capable of adhering to divine laws engraved on the heavenly tab-lets. In line with this, it is especially clear from the story about the wayward angels and giants that the writer has reshaped tradition associated with the figure of Enoch to reinforce the responsibility humans ultimately have be-fore God, despite the erring influences of demonic powers; human beings are accountable to God on the same terms as the disobedient angels and gi-ants. Rather than etiologically explanatory, the force of these stories — in-cluding that of the fallen angels — is exhortational and paradigmatic.

Nevertheless, if there is any explanation for "the way things are" in the author's own world in Jubilees, it is found in the rebellion of the angels. This story leaves its mark in the ongoing suffering and waywardness among humanity after the deluge. Despite their decisive punishment of evil through the flood and internecine violence, these powers have left a residue that at once explains human sin and affliction while doing so in a weakened extent that anticipates and assures their eschatological eradication.

The Festivals of Pesaḥ and Massot in the Book of Jubilees

Betsy Halpern-Amaru

The book of Jubilees assigns patriarchal origins to all biblical festivals.[1] In the case of Pesaḥ and Massot, the protofestival is particularly opaque. Presented at the close of the Jubilees narrative of the Akedah, it is described as "this festival" that Abraham "used to celebrate joyfully for seven days during all the years." He names it "the festival of the Lord" in accord with the seven days during which "he went and returned safely" to Beersheba; and its future commemoration by "Israel and his descendants" is ordained and written on the heavenly tablets (Jub 18:18-19).[2] No dates are given for the celebration; no sacrifices are prescribed; and no rituals are mentioned. The only requirement is that the festival be celebrated joyously for seven days (18:19).[3]

---

1. *Shabu'ot* (*Shebu'ot* in Jubilees) was celebrated in heaven from the time of creation. Noah institutes its earthly celebration, which is observed by each of Israel's patriarchs (Jub 6:18-22; 14:20; 15:1-2; 22:1-5; 46:1-4). Abraham is the first celebrant of Sukkot, to which Jacob adds an addition (16:20-31; 32:4-7, 27-29). An allusion to an unnamed יום תרועה (Rosh Hashanah) is evident in Abraham's observation of the stars "at the beginning of the seventh month" (12:16); and an addendum to the narrative of Jacob's grief over the presumed death of Joseph has a Day of Atonement ordained for commemoration on "the tenth of the seventh month" (34:18-19).

2. Unless otherwise indicated, all quotations of Jubilees are from J. C. VanderKam, *The Book of Jubilees: A Critical Text*, CSCO 510-511, Scriptores Aethiopici Tomus 87-88 (Louvain: Peeters, 1989).

3. The Ge'ez, *sabu'a 'elata bafesseḥā*, reflects שבעת ימים במשמחה, a phrase used in the description of the Festival of Massot celebrated by the returning exiles (Ezra 6:22) and in the account of Hezekiah's fused celebration of Pesaḥ and Massot (2 Chron 30:21). Although the

Facets of the Akedah narrative intimate that Abraham's festival is associated with Pesaḥ and Massot. The travel schedule in the narrative suggests that the binding of Isaac takes place on the fourteenth day of the first month (17:15; 18:3).[4] The restraining angel refers to the rescued Isaac as *bak^wraka* (the Geʿez equivalent of בכורך) (18:11), a designation that God repeats when he renews the covenant promises (Jub 18:15; Gen 22:16).[5] The seven-day festival that commemorates Abraham's journey is named "festival to the Lord," resonating חג לה' in Exod 12:14. However, the character of Abraham's "festival of the Lord" is fully disclosed only through a close reading of the Jubilees treatment of Pesaḥ and Massot in their historical biblical settings (Jub 49). In that chapter Jubilees connects Abraham's "festival of the Lord" to both Pesaḥ and Massot and, at the same time, provides the prescriptive commands for future commemoration that are so glaringly absent in its account of the protofestival.

Jub 49 is composed of three sections: (a) a prescriptive, narrative recollection of the Pesaḥ celebration in Egypt (vv. 1-6), (b) a statute for future commemorations of Pesaḥ (חקת הפסח) (vv. 7-21a), and (c) a prescriptive, narrative recollection of the first Israelite celebration of Massot (vv. 22b-23). In each section there is engagement with biblical material and intricate intertextual exegesis. At the same time, each also conducts an internal "conversation" with other passages in Jubilees. In the two prescriptive narrative recollections the intratextual conversation is with the account of the protofestival in Jub 18; in the Pesaḥ statute the intratextual engagement involves elaboration of the day/time legislation prescribed in Jub 49:1.

---

celebration in 2 Chron 30 takes place in the second month, not the prescribed first month (2 Chron 30:2-3), it does not constitute a celebration of *Pesaḥ Sheni*. See S. Japhet, *1 and 2 Chronicles: A Commentary* (London: SCM, 1993), 939.

4. Abraham receives the directive on the twelfth, leaves Beersheba in the morning, and arrives at the mountain "on the third day." On recent scholarly calculations of the dates of the journey, see J. C. VanderKam, "The *Aqedah, Jubilees,* and PseudoJubilees," in *The Quest for Context and Meaning: Studies in Biblical Intertextuality in Honor of James A. Sanders,* ed. C. Evans and S. Talmon, Biblical Interpretation Series 28 (Leiden: Brill, 1997), 241-61 (here 247), and B. Halpern-Amaru, "A Note on Isaac as First-Born in *Jubilees* and Only Son in 4Q225," *DSD* 13, no. 2 (2006): 127-33 (here 130-31).

5. On the readings in the parallel passages of MT, LXX, OL, EthGen, see Halpern-Amaru, "A Note," 128; on the variants in the Jubilees manuscripts, see VanderKam's notes on Jub 18:11, 15 (*The Book of Jubilees,* v. 1, 104; v. 2, 108).

Prescriptive Recollection of Pesaḥ

The greater part of Jub 49 (twenty-six and one-half of twenty-eight verses) concerns Pesaḥ, with a particular, indeed what might be considered a polemical, emphasis on its date. The chapter opens with the angel-narrator urging Moses to remember the commands he had been given regarding the Pesaḥ, "so that you may *celebrate it at its time on the fourteenth of the first month,* that you may *sacrifice it before evening* and so that they might eat it *at night* on the evening of the fifteenth from *the time of sunset*" (49:1).[6] No such instructions regarding the *pesaḥ* appear in the Exodus narrative.[7] Constructed as a pastiche,[8] a patchwork of phrases alluding to multiple biblical verses, Jubilees derives its prescription from an exegesis that harmonizes conflicting biblical passages. A paraphrase of Num 9:2-3a accesses "to celebrate/to do" (לעשׂות/ *gbr*), a verb that does not appear in the instructions for the Egypt Pesaḥ, but which is normative phrasing in prescriptions of postexodus commemorations (e.g., Exod 12:48; Num 9:2-5, 11; Deut 16:1). The basic time frame for the celebration, however, is derived not from Num 9, but from an intricate play with phrases in Deut 16:1, 4, 6. Stipulating no dates, referring only to sacrifice, and suggesting multiple time frames for the sacrifice, the murky Deuteronomy prescription permits an exegetical treatment that understands the various time points as referring to different stages in the *pesaḥ* rite.

Understanding "in the evening" of Deut 16:4 and "in the evening at sunset" of Deut 16:6 as contrasting points in time,[9] Jubilees emends the Deut 16:4 phrase to "before evening" and uses it for the time of the sacrifice. (A parallel prescription is found in the Temple Scroll [11Q19 xvii 7].)[10] For

---

6. Italics indicate adoption of a biblical phrase or allusion to a biblical verse.

7. The fourteenth is specified as the date for the sacrifice in the directives for the Egypt celebration (Exod 12:6), but only "that night" is indicated as the time for the eating (Exod 12:8). According to J. Milgrom, the phrasing of certain passages where Pesaḥ and Massot are fused (Exod 12:14, 17, 18; Deut 16:4) indicates the fifteenth, an exception to the general rule that the day begins at dawn (*Leviticus,* 3 vols., AB 3 [Doubleday: New York, 2000], 1967-68). The Jubilees argument is not related to the fusion of the two festivals, but is developed solely in relationship to the timing of the *pesaḥ* celebration.

8. On pastiche as a mode of composition, see E. Chazon, "Sacrifice and Prayer in 'The Words of the Luminaries,'" in *Scripture and Prayer,* ed. J. Kugel (Cambridge: Harvard University Press, 2006), 25-41.

9. The exegesis understands "at sunset" as an intrinsic modifier of "in the evening." In contrast, rabbinic exegesis treats the three phrases in Deut 16:6 as denoting three separate time points (*Mekilta Bo* 5; *b. Berakhot* 9a).

10. The rabbinic prescription has the offering of the *pesaḥ* precede the evening *Tamid* (*m. Pesahim* 5:1; cf. Josephus, *Jewish War* 6.423).

the time of the eating, Jubilees combines "at night" (Deut 16:1) with "in the evening at sunset" (Deut 16:6). That the combination involves the beginning of a new calendar date is developed from "the time of day when you departed from Egypt" (Deut 16:6). The phrase is not included in the pastiche, for it is troublesome in its own right. The Exodus narrative has the tenth plague striking the Egyptians "in the middle of night," Pharaoh rising "in the night," summoning Moses and Aaron "in the night" and pressing the Israelites to immediately leave, by implication, that same night (Exod 12:29-32). However, according to Num 33:3, the Israelites depart in clear sight of the Egyptians "on the fifteenth day of the first month . . . on the morrow of the paschal offering," a time frame also implied in Moses' directive that the Israelites not leave their homes until the morning after the paschal offering (Exod 12:22). Harmonizing the two possibilities, Jubilees combines the explicit "at night" of Deut 16:1 with the equally explicit date in Num 33:3 to indicate that the eating of the *pesaḥ*, like the departure from Egypt, took place on the fifteenth.

Presented as a proof case for the exegetical argument for the fifteenth, the narrative that immediately follows recollects the Israelites eating the paschal offering as the tenth plague strikes the houses of the Egyptians (Jub 49:2-6). Again there is no biblical parallel for what Moses is directed to recall. Exodus offers multiple forecasts of the plague (11:4-7; 12:12-13, 23, 27),[11] a brief report of its execution (12:29),[12] but no account of the Israelites eating the *pesaḥ*.[13] Num 33:3 presents a description of the Egyptians burying their dead, but the point of contrast is with the Israelite departure from Egypt, not their celebration of the *pesaḥ*. Responding to that lacuna, Jubilees creates a portrait of the celebration on the night of the fifteenth that both fills the lacuna in Exodus and connects the Egypt Pesaḥ to its patriarchal predecessor.

Integrating facets of the multiple forecasts in Exod 11-12, the portrait demonstrates that what had been foretold in fact came to pass. The sharp contrast between the activities of the Egyptians and Israelites on the night of the fifteenth (Jub 49:5-6) fulfills the forecast in Exod 11:7; the timing ("on this night"); the nature of the strike on the Egyptians ("from the pharaoh's first-born to the first-born of the captive slave-girl at the millstone and to the cattle

---

11. Exod 11:4-7 appears in Moses' predictions to Pharaoh's court; 12:12-13 in God's predictions to Moses and Aaron; 12:23, 27 in the directives Moses gives to the elders.

12. The report presents a variant of the forecast in Exod 11:5.

13. The narrator simply indicates that "the Israelites went and did so; just as the Lord had commanded Moses and Aaron, so they did" (Exod 12:28).

as well") (Jub 49:2) executes the prediction in Exod 11:5; and the saving of the Israelites ("the plague did not come on them to destroy . . . from cattle to mankind to dogs")[14] (Jub 49:4) occurs much as foretold in Exod 11:7 and 12:13.

The most creative exegesis is the treatment of Exod 12:23, which, in contrast to the other forecasts of the plague in Exodus, introduces a "Destroyer" as its chief executor. The unusual personification all but invites the insertion of a motif involving Mastema, provocateur of the testing of Abraham.[15] However, since Mastema himself had been bound and locked up from the fourteenth onward (Jub 48:15), "the forces of Mastema" replace "the Destroyer" and, acting strictly in accordance with God's directives (49:2-4), become "the Lord's forces" (49:4). The transformations — from "the Destroyer" to "the forces of Mastema" to "the Lord's forces" — not only resolve the tension between Exod 12:23 and passages that present God as the sole executor of the plague (Exod 11:4; 12:12-13, 27, 29), but also associate the saving of the Israelites from Mastema's forces with the rescue of Isaac in the Jubilees Akedah narrative.[16]

An even closer connection between Abraham's "festival of the Lord" (Jub 18:18) and the celebration of the *pesaḥ* on the night of the fifteenth is evident in the description of the night of celebratory eating as "the beginning of the festival and the beginning of joy" (49:2). Without biblical parallel, the Jubilees-created phrasing is artfully constructed. The direct article before "festival" suggests that the Israelites are celebrating a previously established festival on the night when they are eating the Pesaḥ, and the repeated phrase, "beginning of," implies that the festival and its joy extend beyond a single day. Clearly, the intent is to imply that the Israelites are commemorating the beginning of the seven-day patriarchal festival ordained for Jacob's descendants "to celebrate . . . joyfully for seven days" (18:19). Undated and without rituals in its patriarchal context, the first night of Abraham's "festival of the Lord" now acquires both a date — the night of the fifteenth in the first month — and rituals — "eating the paschal meat, drinking the wine, glorifying, blessing and praising the Lord God of their fathers" (49:6).

---

14. The inclusion of "the dogs" is an adaptation of "not a dog shall snarl" (Exod 11:7).

15. In contrast, the introduction of Mastema into the Akedah narrative requires the addition of a Job-like preface. See J. van Ruiten, "Abraham, Job and the Book of Jubilees: The Intertextual Relationship of Genesis 22:1-19, Job 1:1–2:13 and Jubilees 17:15–18:19," in *The Sacrifice of Isaac (Genesis 22) and Its Interpretations,* ed. E. Noort and E. Tigchelaar (Leiden: Brill, 2002), 58-85 (here 71-83).

16. In contrast to M. Segal ("The Composition of Jubilees," in this volume), I see exegetical harmonization at work in Jub 49:4.

The Date of Pesaḥ

Following the recollection are a series of commands stipulating when, how, why, and where the postexodus Pesaḥ is to be celebrated. A Jubilees חק הפסח composed from multiple biblical allusions, it selectively integrates directives for the Egypt Pesaḥ with Torah commands relating to Pesaḥ, thereby clarifying the statutes in Exod 12:14 and 13:10[17] and precluding both the *Pesaḥ Sheni* instituted in Num 9[18] and the participation of the *ger* permitted in Exod 12:43-49 and Num 9:14.[19] Within the statute the schedule of the commemoration receives the most attention. It is the principal subject of six commands — three directly involving date (49:7-9), three the time of day (49:8-10) — and a secondary theme in five other commands (49:10, 14-18). The three date-focused commands are structured to provide support for a Pesaḥ commemoration that spans two dates (the fourteenth-fifteenth) and to explicitly proscribe a delay such as the *Pesaḥ Sheni* permitted in Num 9:9-14 or a deferment such as decreed by Hezekiah in 2 Chron 30:2, 13, 15. The exclusion of *Pesaḥ Sheni* may be unique to Jubilees, for the institutionalized delay is referenced in both Qumran and rabbinic texts.[20]

---

17. Standing between God's directives for the night of the plague and a prescription for eating unleavened bread, Exod 12:14 may be understood as relating to future commemoration of either Pesaḥ or Massot. If the former, its context, like that of Exod 12:24, implies that the commemoration includes the blood rite of the Egypt Pesaḥ. Equally problematic, the statute in Exod 13:10 lacks content.

18. As the following analysis will demonstrate, the case for the exclusion of *Pesaḥ Sheni* in Jubilees is not simply an argument from silence. It is based on the Jubilees abstraction of phrases from verses that explicitly involve *Pesaḥ Sheni* in Num 9 and the placement of those phrases into contexts that expressly forbid any change whatsoever to the prescribed date for the commemoration of Pesaḥ. The tactic is employed at a number of points in the legislation (Jub 49:7, 8, 9, 14, 16-17). In his paper, S. Saulnier reaches the same conclusion ("Jub 49:1-14 and the Second Passover: How (and Why) to Do Away with an Unwanted Festival," *Hen* 31, no. 1 [2009]). On the other hand, L. Doering, who attributes no significance to the multiple Jubilees injunctions against changing the date of the commemoration, cautions against such a conclusion ("Purity and Impurity in the Book of Jubilees," in this volume).

19. Exod 12:44, 48 permits only the circumcised *ger* to eat the *pesaḥ*. Num 9:14 permits the *ger*, without qualification, to celebrate the *pesaḥ*. I do not deal directly with the issue of the *ger* in this essay.

20. *Pesaḥ Sheni* clearly appears in the Qumran *mishmarot* texts (4Q259 viii 1; 4Q320 4 iii 4, 14l iv 9; v 3, 12; vi 7l; 4Q321 2 ii 5, 9; iii 8). An injunction against advancing or delaying festivals appears in several sectarian texts (1QS 1:13-15; 4Q266 2 i 1; 4Q268 1, 4), but the prohibition does not reference *Pesaḥ Sheni*. If, as Yadin suggested, a command regarding *Pesaḥ Sheni* appeared in the missing part at the top of col. xviii of the Temple Scroll, it would be

The compositional design of the date-commands is most striking. With the exception of one command where the fourteenth is specified (Jub 49:10), no dates are mentioned. Instead date numbers are represented by terms — "on its day," "at its time," "the time of its day," "the day of its time," "its festal day" — that indicate the fourteenth, fifteenth, or both. The date (or dates) designated by each day-term is revealed through an ingenious system of allusions employed in the wording of the command. This system of allusions has three distinctive features: (a) most importantly, the timing of events as set forth in the prescriptive, narrative recollection (49:1-6) is presumed, i.e., the fourteenth is indicated by explicit reference and allusions to sacrifice of the *pesaḥ* and the fifteenth by explicit and alluded references to the tenth plague and/or eating the *pesaḥ*; (b) the allusions are triggered by the particular content of a command, by a full or partial citation, by an abstracted biblical phrase, and by one of the date-terms; (c) each date-command is deliberately composed to point to both the fourteenth and the fifteenth.

The following table illustrates how this complex system of allusions functions in the first three commands of the legislation.[21]

49:7 Now you *remember this day all the days of your lifetime.* Celebrate it *from year to year* all the days all your lifetime, once a year *on its day in accord with all of its law.* Then you will not change a day from the day or from month to month.

Allusion	Source	Content	Date(s) Indicated
(1) remember this day . . .	Exod 12:14	Memory of night of plague	15th (eating)
all the days of your lifetime	Deut 16:3-4; cf. Num 33:3	Phrase from context that relates eating of *pesaḥ* to memory of day of exodus	
(2) from year to year	Exod 13:10	"Keep this statute . . . from year to year"	15th (eating)

---

the single reference in that scroll (Y. Yadin, *The Temple Scroll,* 3 vols. [Jerusalem: Israel Exploration Society, 1977-1983], 2:76). On the rabbinic treatment of *Pesaḥ Sheni,* see *m. Pesahim* 9:1-4.

21. The analysis of the date- and time-related commands adapts and, at certain points, reconsiders material I presented in "The Use of Bible in *Jubilees* 49: The Date and Time of the Pesaḥ Celebration," *Meghillot* 6 (2007).

Allusion	Source	Content	Date(s) Indicated
	Exod 12:43	Statute of the *pesaḥ* dealing with who is to eat the *pesaḥ*	
(3) on its day (*ba'elatu*/ביומו)	Lev 23:5, 37	Offerings for sacred occasions at set times; 14th for *pesaḥ*	14th (sacrifice)
(4) in accord with all its law	Num 9:14	*Pesaḥ Sheni;* participation of resident alien in sacrifice and eating of *pesaḥ*	14th-15th (sacrifice and eating)

Comments

1. The two phrases access biblical commands that deal with remembering. One, Exod 12:14 ("this day shall be one of remembrance"), immediately follows a forecast of the events on the night of the plague. The second, Deut 16:3-4, associates the exodus with the eating of the *pesaḥ* (as well as with the prohibition of unleavened bread). Selectively drawing phrases from each passage, Jubilees connects three themes — the night of the plague, the exodus, and the eating of the *pesaḥ* — all of which occurred on the fifteenth.

2. "This statute" in Exod 13:10 is understood as referring back to the statute in Exod 12:43 that deals with who is to eat the *pesaḥ*.[22]

3. The phrase, which is drawn from the Leviticus sacrificial calendar, is frequently used in the Jubilees legislation as an indicator for the fourteenth.

4. The phrase appears in the plural in Num 9:3. Jubilees accesses the singular form in Num 9:14, a passage that involves both sacrifice and eating, hence indicating the fourteenth-fifteenth. Note that this is one of several verses where words borrowed from a passage involving *Pesaḥ Sheni* are placed within a command prohibiting any change to the date of the *pesaḥ* commemoration.

49:8 For it is an *eternal statute* and it is engraved on the heavenly tablets regarding the Israelites that they are to celebrate it each and every year *on its day*, once a year, *throughout all their generations* (lit.). There is no temporal limit because it is ordained forever.

22. R. Akiba makes the same connection between Exod 13:10 and Exod 12:43 (*b. Menahot* 36b; *b. Eruvin* 96a). The opposing position of R. Jose relates "this statute" to the command regarding phylacteries (*b. Menahot* 36b; *b. Eruvin* 96a; cf. *Mekilta Bo* 17; *Targum Pseudo-Jonathan* on Exod 13:10).

Allusion	Source	Content	Date(s) Indicated
(1) eternal statute	Exod 12:14	Statute to commemorate night of plague	15th (plague, eating)
on its day	Lev 23:5, 37	Offerings for sacred occasions at set times, 14th prescribed for the *pesaḥ* offering	14th (sacrifice)
(1) throughout all their generations	Exod 12:14	15th (plague, eating, exodus)	Night of plague a festival
	Exod 12:42	Night of plague a vigil	

Comments

1. The command is constructed to connect Pesaḥ with festival (Exod 12:14), the night of the plague (12:14), and the night of the vigil commemorating the exodus (12:42), all of which involve the fifteenth.

49:9 *The man who is pure but does not come to celebrate it — on the time of its day* (lit.) to bring a sacrifice that is pleasing before the Lord and to eat and drink before the Lord on *the day of His festival* — that man who is pure and nearby is to be uprooted because he did not bring the Lord's sacrifice *at its time*. That man will bear responsibility for his own sin.[23]

Allusion	Source	Content	Date(s) Indicated
(1) the man who is pure . . . that man who is pure . . . at its time	Num 9:13	Full, but slightly altered citation	14th-15th (sacrifice and eating)
(2) on the time of its day	None		14th (sacrifice)
(3) day of His festival	Exod 12:14	Celebrate this day "as a festival to the Lord"	15th (eating)
	Exod 23:18	Prohibition against leaving the fat of offerings of "my festival" until morning	

23. Positioning of dashes mine. The positioning in VanderKam's translation obfuscates the specification of two activities on two different dates.

Allusion	Source	Content	Date(s) Indicated
	Exod 34:25	Prohibition against leaving the *pesaḥ* offering until morning	
(1) at its time	Num 9:13	Part of citation	14th (sacrifice)

Comments

1. Displaced from its biblical *Pesaḥ Sheni* context, the cited verse is split by an insertion that specifies two times for two activities, each of which has its own day, i.e., date — "to bring a sacrifice on the time of its day" and "to eat and drink before the Lord on the day of His festival."

2. A variant of the biblical "at its time" (במועדו), this Jubilees-created term is an indicator, depending on context, for either the fourteenth or the fifteenth.

3. Interpreting Exod 23:18 in the light of Exod 34:25, "My festival" is understood as referring to Pesaḥ. The phrase "festival to the Lord" also serves as an intratextual allusion to Abraham's "festival of the Lord" in Jub 18:18.

The Times of Day for Sacrifice and Eating of the *Pesaḥ*

The system of coded date-allusions also appears in Jub 49:10-12, but the primary concern of these three verses is prescription of the time of day for the two-phased celebration. Much as the three initial date-related commands collectively interpret Exod 12:14, so these commands engage in an exegetical treatment of the phrase "between the evenings" in Exod 12:6. In that directive for the Egypt Pesaḥ, the term "between the evenings" designates the time when the paschal animal is to be slaughtered on the fourteenth. The phrase also appears in Lev 23:5 and Num 9:3, but without reference to a particular aspect of the ritual. Only in the directives for *Pesaḥ Sheni* does context suggest that the time frame encompasses both sacrifice and eating (Num 9:11). Alluding to Lev 23:5 and Num 9:3,[24] Jubilees adopts the understanding of Num 9:11, but again deconstructs its context.

---

24. The opening clause of Jub 49:10 ("The Israelites are to come and celebrate the *pesaḥ*") cites Num 9:3; Jub 49:11 ("This is what the Lord commanded you — to celebrate it between the evenings") refers to the legislation in Lev 23:5.

In a *mismarot*-like division, the Jubilees exegesis separates day and night into three parts, with the last third of the day and first third of the night both termed "evening." Hence "between the evenings" refers to the period of time between the evening of the day and the end of the evening of the day, i.e., "from the third part of the day until the third part of the night" (Jub 49:10). The offering is to be sacrificed "in the boundary of the evening" of the day (49:12), a time frame refined in 49:19 by a phrase from Deut 16:6, בערב כבוא השמש ("in the evening when the sun sets"). Notably, that same phrase is employed in the prescription of Jub 49:1 to denote the time of the eating of the *pesaḥ*. Still, the exegesis remains consistent. Understanding בערב כבוא השמש as when the sun begins its descent (the evening of the day), the command in the Pesaḥ statute combines the phrase with "in the third part of the day" (Jub 49:19) to denote the time for the sacrifice, i.e., the eighth hour of the day.[25] Conversely, treating the phrase as referring to the time when the sun completes its descent (the evening of the night), the prescription in Jub 49:1 combines it with "at night," an allusion to Deut 16:1, to denote the time for the eating. A comparable time frame for the eating is given in the Pesaḥ statute (Jub 49:12). The sacrifice is to be eaten "during the evening hour(s) until the third part of the night," i.e., the eighth hour of the night, with its end point emphasized by an emended version of Exod 12:10.[26]

Prescriptive Recollection of Massot

The Jubilees treatment of Massot is immediately appended to the Pesaḥ statute. Indeed, within the same verse, the Pesaḥ statute closes with a restatement of the command for a commemoration that spans two dates (Jub 49:22a)[27] and Massot is introduced as a commemoration of the seven re-

---

25. The argument from the plural of evening is unique to Jubilees; but the extension of time for the sacrifice is also found in Philo (*Laws* 2.145) and rabbinic literature (*Mekilta Bo* 5; *m. Pesahim* 5:1).

26. "You shall not leave any of it over until morning; if any of it is left until morning, you shall burn it" (Exod 12:10). "Any of its meat that is left over from the third part of the night and beyond is to be burned" (Jub 49:12).

27. The restatement, like all the date-related legislation in the statute, employs coded terminology — "Now you Moses order the Israelites to keep the statute of the *pesaḥ* as it was commanded to you so that you may tell them . . . the **day of the days** (lit.)," i.e., the day (date) of the sacrifice and the day (date) of the eating.

maining days of Abraham's "festival of the Lord" (49:22b). Albeit far more brief, the treatment of Massot structurally parallels that of Pesaḥ in 49:1-6. Again, legislation for future commemoration of the festival is complemented by a recollection that functions as a proof text; intertextual allusions to biblical passages are creatively interwoven with intratextual references; and identical strategies are employed to prompt the intratextual exegesis — importation of the theme of joyous celebration, utilization of a motif and subtle phrases that associate Massot with the patriarchal protofestival.

The prescription for future celebration of the festival combines biblical commands — eating unleavened bread (Exod 12:15; 13:6; 23:15; 34:18; Lev 23:6; Num 28:17; Deut 16:3) and bringing daily sacrifices (Lev 23:8; Num 28:24) — with an implied obligation to rejoice ("during those seven joyous days," *sabuʿ mawāʿela fessehā*) (Jub 49:22b) that has no counterpart in the Torah.[28] The Hebrew equivalent phrase, שבעת ימי שמחה, appears in the Chronicler's account of a fused Pesaḥ/Massot celebration that is not only delayed, but also extended an additional seven days (2 Chron 30:23), neither of which is acceptable to the author of Jubilees. So, much as he had done with *Pesaḥ Sheni* in Num 9, he abstracts the phrase from the offending context and employs it as an intratextual allusion to the requirement, expressed with another "joy" phrase (שבעת ימים בשמחה in Ezra 6:22; 2 Chron 30:21), that all Jacob's descendants joyously commemorate Abraham's "festival of the Lord" (Jub 18:19).

Again the legislation is supported by a recollection, this time of the Israelites celebrating "this festival hastily" from the time they departed Egypt until they crossed the sea (Jub 49:23). The phrase "this festival" also appears in the account of the patriarchal celebration, indeed awkwardly so, for the demonstrative pronoun has no preceding point of reference (18:18). That awkwardness suggests a deliberate setup for the intratextual allusion that now links Massot to the patriarchal festival whose celebration had begun on the night of eating the *pesaḥ*. That the celebration involves a travel motif is another evocation of Abraham's festival, instituted "in accord with the seven days during which he went and returned safely" (18:18). Like the patriarchal journey, the Israelite one entails seven days of travel and deliverance (in Abraham's case from the plotting of Mastema, in this instance from the

---

28. There is no Torah mandate for joyous celebration of Pesaḥ or Massot. Indeed, its absence is particularly glaring in Deut 16 where rejoicing is prescribed for the celebrations of both Shabu'ot (Deut 16:11) and Succot (Deut 16:14-15), but not for celebration of the fused Pesaḥ/Massot festival. On the motif of joy and rejoicing in Jubilees, see B. Halpern-Amaru, "Joy as Piety in the *Book of Jubilees*," *JJS* 66, no. 2 (2005): 185-205.

threat of the Egyptians at the Reed Sea).[29] Moreover, according to the biblical description of the route taken by the Israelites, they also "went and returned safely" — from Egypt to "the edge of the wilderness" (Exod 13:20), back toward the sea (14:2), and, after crossing the sea, safely back to the wilderness (15:22).[30]

Lastly, the Israelite celebration adds another ritual to the protofestival — the eating of unleavened bread (instead of the customary festive loaves) — because the Israelites celebrated the ancient festival "hastily" from the time they left Egypt until they crossed the sea "into the wilderness of Sur," where they "completed it on the seashore" (Jub 49:23). The explanation is a creative reworking of a motif associated with both Pesaḥ and Massot. Haste is the reason given for the unleavened bread in Exod 12:39 and Deut 16:3 (cf. Exod 12:3), but in those passages it relates to a hasty departure, not to a hurried celebration. The notion of a hasty celebration appears only in the context of Pesaḥ (Exod 12:11), and, as we have seen, it is an aspect that Jubilees excludes from both the recollection of the Egypt celebration and the Pesaḥ statute. Retaining the motif in association with Massot, but rearranging it to the context of a centuries-later celebration of the patriarchal festival, the author of Jubilees sustains his portrayal of a people "ready to leave the Egyptian yoke and evil slavery" (Jub 49:6), avoids the indignities of the harried flight from Egypt described in Exod 12:31-39,[31] and affirms the image of a bold, defiant Israelite departure depicted in Num 33:3 (cf. Exod 14:8).

Conclusion

The Jubilees treatment of Pesaḥ and Massot is foremost an interpretive reworking of Exod 12–13. Its author designs an ingenious compositional struc-

---

29. Since the author uses the Mastema motif in his recollection of the Egypt Pesaḥ, he does not repeat it with Massot. However, in his account of the exodus, Mastema does appear as the instigator of the Egyptian pursuit (Jub 48:12, 15-17).

30. The biblical account gives no date for the crossing of the sea. The Jubilees notion that it was the twenty-second of the first month (the seventh day of Massot) does have a parallel in rabbinic tradition. The calculation is based on the assumption that Pharaoh began pursuing the Israelites three days after their departure on the fifteenth (Exod 3:18; 5:3). In the course of those three days the Israelites arrived at the edge of the desert (Exod 13:20), but then retraced their steps (a second three-day journey) back to the sea (Exod 14:2), which they crossed on the twenty-second (*b. Megillah* 31a; Rashi on Exod 14:5).

31. The rejection of a hurried departure may also reflect the influence of Isa 52:12.

ture that brings order and coherence to the chaotic mixture of directives for and narratives about the Egypt Pesaḥ, ordination of a Pesaḥ statute for future commemoration, and legislation for Massot. He also develops a Pesaḥ statute that fills lacunae in its Exodus counterparts with content that references the corpus of Pesaḥ-related material in the Pentateuch through an intricate system of allusions. Lastly, in presenting Pesaḥ and Massot as separate consecutive festivals permanently merged as common celebrations of a single patriarchal protofestival, this author not only serves his own interest, but may also be responding, much like modern source critics, to the discrete and fused presentations of Pesaḥ/Massot in the biblical text.

Eschatological Impulses in Jubilees

John C. Endres, S.J.

The book of Jubilees presents itself as a "history" of Israel through the perspective of Moses. It begins at Mount Sinai (Exod 24) with the revelation to Moses by God, who tells him that Israel would stray from the covenant they had just concluded with God; they would sin and be punished until they repented and returned to God. This course of events would serve to demonstrate God's great mercy in dealing with Israel. Later in chap. 1 God tells Moses to write down this entire message, which an angel of presence would dictate to him from the (heavenly) tablets on which this entire story was already inscribed. This angel proceeds to recount Israel's life and history from the creation of the world to the first Passover of the Hebrews in Egypt (Gen 1 through Exod 24). Much of this book reads like a work of "rewritten Bible," retelling the biblical tradition with a particular focus on the lives of the patriarchs and matriarchs as the setting for Israel's self-identity. As this author retells the ancient story, his emphases inculcate a number of important motifs, including: the covenant between God and the people, the laws that allow people to remain faithful covenant partners, the significant Jewish festivals of the year, the solar calendar by which they should be calculated and observed, clear notions about the spirit world and demons, and the importance of prayer to God. One could think of it as a theological history whose ideology is clearly discerned from the way it rewrites earlier sources. Scholars have excavated this text for information on many aspects of early Jewish life in the second century B.C.E. Studies of its halakah, of course, concern correspondences with the different religious groupings of the era, but the significance of the very strict interpretations of certain halakoth most likely concerns issues that establish more secure foundations for Jewish identity. Among the chief concerns today are the solar calendar, religious festivals (especially Shavuoth), comparison of legal concerns here with other Jewish groups or sects, including the writer of the Temple Scroll. In recent decades considerable attention has focused on the apparent practice of rewriting biblical texts, bringing new interpretations to the familiar and sacred story of the people Israel. The world of the spirits, especially evil spirits, receives much more attention in Jubilees than in several other Jewish works considered contemporaneous with this book.

Although second temple and Qumran studies evince great interest in messianic tendencies, including eschatology, in the various documents, the eschatology of Jubilees has not been among the most studied items in research on Jubilees.[1] Often the discussion of Jubilees focuses on messianism,[2] or on the study of the one apocalypse in Jub 23. Gene Davenport's dissertation and subsequent monograph was devoted to this issue, i.e., *Eschatology of the Book of Jubilees;*[3] but because his interpretation of eschatological passages was tied to a redactional theory and a schema of historical development of the text that did not meet widespread reception, the issue of eschatology, which motivated his study, has not received the kind of attention and impact it deserves.

Scholars have long noted connections between this book, however, and various tendencies and beliefs in the Qumran scrolls, which are frequently linked with an array of eschatological tendencies. This congruence of theological tendencies also must be considered along with the intriguing fact that fourteen (or fifteen) manuscripts of Jubilees were discovered at Qumran.[4]

I. Defining Eschatology

Varying definitions of eschatology render this discussion complex, since agreement on its constituent elements and interpretation is seldom attained.

---

1. J. VanderKam, *The Book of Jubilees,* Guides to Apocrypha and Pseudepigrapha (Sheffield: Sheffield Academic Press, 2001), comments: "To be sure, eschatology is not a dominant concern in *Jubilees,* as it is in some of the Enoch literature" (132).

2. For example, J. Klausner, *The Messianic Idea in Israel: From Its Beginning to the Completion of the Mishnah,* trans. W. F. Stinespring (New York: Macmillan, 1955), 302-9.

3. G. L. Davenport, *The Eschatology of the Book of Jubilees,* SPB (Leiden: Brill, 1971).

4. VanderKam, *The Book of Jubilees,* 16.

Historically speaking, this term has a surprisingly brief shelf life in our field, since it was "formed artificially and introduced only in 1804 by the German dogmatic theologian K. G. Bretschneider."[5] Continental theologians always considered it connected with the "dogmatic *locus De Novissimis,* expressing the concept of the 'last things' *(eschata)* expected by Christian believers."[6] Its earliest roots can be found in prerabbinic Jewish usage, e.g., in the book of Ecclesiasticus (Ben Sira) 48:24, where he says of the prophet Isaiah: "By his dauntless spirit he saw the future, and comforted the mourners in Zion" (NRSV). Typical headings defining these "last things" are, according to the classical dogmatic teachers of Lutheranism, *De morte et statu animarum post mortem, De resurrectione mortuorum, De extremo judicio, De consummatione coeli.*[7] To begin with, eschatology points us toward the future even as we are concerned with issues of the present day.

Further refinements follow. Bousset *(Die Religion des Judentums im späthellenistischen Zeitalter)* claimed that Jewish eschatological and messianic beliefs differ, since each corresponds to different needs among the Jewish people. Messianic hope was purportedly tied to the "hope for restoration of Israel's glories," whereas eschatology responded to a need "for orientation in the *individual lives* of the believers" (particularly among the educated classes) rather than the "Utopia of the common man."[8] For Bousset, then, eschatology has a more distinctive character than does messianism, linked as it often is to nationalistic hopes. For his part, Davenport's monograph speaks more generally, seeing eschatology as "any view of the future in which there are events anticipated as having significance for the life of Israel and the world, events beyond which life will be significantly different."[9]

Today there is a movement to approach the issue of definition by describing clusters of elements or motifs typical of eschatological texts. Géza Xeravits, for example, defines the adjective "eschatological" "as 'related or pertaining to the eschatological age.' By 'eschatological age' we mean a preeminent period of the *histoire sainte,* when the actual period of history reaches its climax."[10] He then suggests characteristics that mark off such pe-

5. J. Schaper, *Eschatology in the Greek Psalter,* WUNT 2. Reihe (Tübingen: J. C. B. Mohr [Paul Siebeck], 1995), 26.

6. Schaper, *Eschatology,* 26.

7. Schaper, *Eschatology,* 26.

8. Schaper, *Eschatology,* 27-28.

9. Davenport, *Eschatology,* 8.

10. G. Xeravits, *King, Priest, Prophet: Positive Eschatological Protagonists of the Qumran Library,* STDJ 47 (Leiden and Boston: Brill, 2003), 3.

riods: "God's judgement over the created world, God's victory over evil, the complete eradication of evil, and the triumph of God's people."[11] Michael Knibb presents a larger cluster of characteristics familiar from second temple Jewish literature.[12] These include: the idea of a final judgment where the righteous will be rewarded and the wicked punished; the idea of a last great battle with forces of evil; descriptions (in the form of blessings) of the blessings of the new age; the expectation of a new Jerusalem; rules for ordering life in a new age; an explanation for the delay in expected time of the end; belief in resurrection of the dead; messianic beliefs. I will indicate the presence of several of these motifs in the Jubilees' texts to be considered.

II. Eschatological Texts Par Excellence

Scholars of Jubilees generally identify two lengthy texts with strong eschatological language and content.[13] The first is God's message to Moses on Mount Sinai, in 1:4b-29 (a narrative with clear roots in Exod 24). It follows the message in the prologue, that we have here "the words regarding the divisions of the times of the law and of the testimony, of the events of the years, of the weeks of their jubilees throughout all the years of eternity as he related (them) to Moses on Mt. Sinai when he went up to receive the stone tablets" (prologue, first part).[14] The second passage is the apocalypse in Jub 23:14-31, which follows the death of Abraham (23:1-8). I will describe and discuss each text, suggest some common themes and patterns, and indicate ways in which they offer a perspective through which one can view the entire book of Jubilees.

---

11. Xeravits, *King, Priest, Prophet*, 3.

12. M. Knibb, "Eschatology and Messianism in the Dead Sea Scrolls," in *The Dead Sea Scrolls after Fifty Years: Volume II*, ed. P. Flint and J. VanderKam (Leiden, Boston, and Cologne: Brill, 1999), 379-402 (here 381-82).

13. J. VanderKam, "The End of the Matter? Jubilees 50:6-13 and the Unity of the Book," in *Heavenly Tablets: Interpretation, Identity, and Tradition in Ancient Judaism*, ed. L. LiDonnici and A. Lieber, JSJSup (Leiden and Boston: Brill, 2007), 267-84 (esp. 267-72). VanderKam, 270, notes that "the passages which Testuz considered additions were eschatological ones," i.e., 1:7-25, 28; 23:11-32; and 24:28b-30; cf. M. Testuz, *Les idées religieuses du Livre des Jubilés* (Geneva: Librairie E. Droz; Paris: Librairie Minard, 1960), 39-40. VanderKam examines a third passage, Jub 50:6-13, also considered eschatological (VanderKam, 270). The salient point is the identification of "odd" passages as likely candidates for the presentation of an eschatological vision in this book.

14. Unless otherwise noted, all translations are from J. VanderKam, trans., *The Book of Jubilees*, CSCO 88 (Louvain: Peeters, 1989), hereafter VanderKam, *Jubilees*.

III. God's Message to Moses at Sinai (1:4b-29)

Moses' sojourn of forty days and nights at Mount Sinai forms the scene of the first eschatological passage. During this time the Lord showed to him all that had happened before, and what would happen in the future; all these events were related to the division of all the times, both of the law and of the testimony (v. 4). God ordered Moses to pay careful attention to all the words revealed to him on this holy mountain, so that he could write them all down in a book. This record can be used to educate their offspring on this fact: God has not abandoned them because of all their "straying from the covenant" between God and them. So the covenant they are making this very day on Mount Sinai (v. 5) will not be a vehicle for their destruction but will help them to see that the Lord is more faithful to them than they are to him; indeed, the Lord has remained present to them (v. 6). The message follows a typical pattern, known from Deuteronomic writings: sin, punishment, returning to God, saving acts of God.[15]

Sin (1:7-11)

God already knew the people's stubbornness before he brought them into the land of promise, a land of "milk and honey" (v. 7). But this people will still commit sin. They will turn to strange gods who cannot deliver them (v. 8) and they will forget all of God's commandments, follow the ways of Gentiles, and serve the Gentiles' gods (v. 9).[16] As a result, they will suffer greatly: many among this people will be taken captive and will perish because they forsook their covenant with God. The message returns to Israel's sins, that they forgot God's statutes, commandments, covenant festivals,

---

15. R. Werline, *Penitential Prayer in Second Temple Judaism: The Development of a Religious Institution*, SBLEJL 13 (Atlanta: Society of Biblical Literature, 1998), 110-11. In his study of these passages, J. Scott speaks of the scheme of "sin-exile-restoration (SER)"; cf. J. Scott, *On Earth as in Heaven: The Restoration of Sacred Time and Sacred Space in the Book of Jubilees*, JSJSup (Leiden and Boston: Brill, 2005), 77. This rich study of these topics in Jubilees provides a wide-ranging proposal for the chronology of the book, much of which "specifies" the eschatological perspective. For reasons that will become apparent, I prefer to retain the notion of "repentance" in the Deuteronomic scheme.

16. That these sins of the nations probably include sexual sins is argued by W. Loader, *Enoch, Levi, and Jubilees on Sexuality: Attitudes toward Sexuality in the Early Enoch Literature, the Aramaic Levi Document, and the Book of Jubilees* (Grand Rapids: Eerdmans, 2007), 117.

Sabbaths, holy things, tabernacle, and temple (v. 10). They will follow some horrendous practices: constructing "high places" and "(sacred) groves," using "carved images" for their worship, and — most shocking of all — offering in sacrifice their own children.[17] The language for sinful ways employed here recalls similar charges against Israel in Deuteronomic language (Deut 31:20-21 and 2 Kings 17:15), a fact that corresponds with the Deuteronomic theology of history: sin, oppression, outcry to God/repentance, God's saving activity.

Punishment/Suffering (1:12-14)

God tries to move Israel toward repentance by telling Moses what will happen in the future (vv. 12-18). God will send them witnesses, but Israel will not listen to them; rather they will slay them and persecute those who diligently study the Torah (v. 12). The people will attempt to change and overturn everything, thus working evil "in my presence" (v. 12); it is a pattern well known from prophetic texts and the Chronicler (e.g., Jer 25:4; 2 Chron 24:19). Then God will remove his presence from them, handing them over to their enemies, "for captivity, for *booty*, and for being devoured" (v. 13), even for dispersal among the nations. After all this, even then this people will forget all of God's law, commandments, judgments; rather they will err regarding "the beginning of the month, the sabbath, the festival, the jubilee" (matters of the Jubilees' calendar, so important to this author), and also the "decree" (v. 14).[18]

Repentance (1:15)

Then the Israelites will turn to God: "After this they will return to me from among the nations with all their minds, all their souls, and all their strength" (1:15 Ethiopic). This pattern of repeated turning to God (שוב, *shuv*) is clear, and the author uses familiar Deuteronomic language (the people search, and are found) to express this pattern of repentance (v. 15).[19]

---

17. Recall the condemnation of King Ahaz for such crimes: 2 Chron 28:3 ("made his sons pass through fire"); here they will offer them to "demons" and to other products of their own imagination and creativity.

18. Cf. Scott, *On Earth*, 86-87, for this assessment.

19. This section of Jubilees exists in the Qumran 4Q216, II (l. 17). The editor,

Repentance and return to God have followed upon sin and punishment, and God seems ever patient with those who have searched for him "with all their minds and with all their souls" and promises to "disclose to them abundant peace" in response.

Saving Acts of God (1:16-18)

The next step speaks of God transforming them into a "plant of righteousness," reminding the biblical reader of Jer 32:41 and Ps 80:9. The language for effecting this change might catch readers unawares, when God proclaims that he will act "with all *my* mind and all *my* soul" (v. 16a); here the divinity appropriates language usually associated with the people's response to God, e.g., Deut 6:5 (the *Shem'a Yisrael*). As a result, this people shall be "a blessing, not a curse" (v. 16b), echoing God's words to Judah and Israel in Zech 8:13. The shift from curse to blessing may be understood as an older covenant formulary that has undergone transformation in some second temple texts. In his study of the covenant, Klaus Baltzer suggests that the curses (seen in the historical past, or even the present of the people) are balanced by blessings that seem characterized by an eschatological language and tone.[20] Specifically, God will gather them from among the Gentiles back to their land (v. 15b), will transform them into a "righteous plant" (v. 16), will (re)build the temple among them and live with them (v. 17) and become their God, and they will become God's "true and righteous people." God will never again alienate or abandon them, for "I am the Lord their God" (v. 18). Most significant for an eschatological vision is the end of God's speech in v. 15: "I will rightly disclose to them *abundant peace*."

J. VanderKam, retrojects from the Ge'ez version a Hebrew word, citing as a good parallel for his decision a similar text in 1 Kings 8:48: "if they repent (וְשָׁבוּ) with all their heart and soul in the land of their enemies . . ." (NRSV).

20. K. Baltzer, *The Covenant Formulary in Old Testament, Jewish, and Early Christian Writings*, trans. D. Green (Philadelphia: Fortress, 1971). In several places, dealing with Jewish texts, especially 1QS, Jubilees, CD (Damascus Document), and Testaments in Jubilees and Testaments of the Twelve Patriarchs, the author notes a transformation of the blessings and curses with a fairly specific "eschatology" in the text of the blessings (104-105, 107, Manual of Discipline; 117, Damascus Document; 153-155, Testament of the Twelve Patriarchs). He does not discuss Jub 1 or 23.

Prayer of Moses (1:19-21)

After God's promise of a blessed future, Moses prays to God for his people (vv. 19-21), that God not forsake them or deliver them into the power of their enemies (v. 19). He begs God to show them *mercy*[21] and "create for them a *just spirit*" (v. 20a). Moses also prays that "the spirit of Belial not rule them" (v. 20b). As if God requires motivation to act, Moses reminds the Lord that "they are your people and your heritage whom you have rescued" from Egyptian power. Near the end of his prayer the words "Create for them a pure mind and a holy spirit" remind the hearers of Ps 51:10. The final wish is that they not be caught up in their sins forever (v. 21). In the second temple era, to ask God to grant a *spirit of holiness* may be a way of expressing the notion of a spiritual transformation of God's people "at the eschaton," since speaking of the spirit of holiness "denotes a new spiritual disposition imparted by God to individual Jews."[22] They need these gifts to guard their freedom from the spirit of Belial. Moses asks God for *mercy*, a notion that may point forward to the "kindness" of the Lord in the Jubilees Apocalypse (23:31). The mention of the (maternal) notion of "mercy" here may resonate with "kindness" in the later text.

Response of God: Recapitulates the Pattern of Sin and Return (1:22-25)

God tells Moses that he knows the sinful past and ways of this people, but later they will return to God "in a fully upright manner and with all (their) minds and all (their) souls" (v. 23a). Most important, God will "cut away the foreskins of their minds and the foreskins of their descendants' minds" (v. 23b). To circumcise "the hearts of the Israelites and their descendants" is an act intended to eliminate "all possibility of future apostasy."[23] The divine

---

21. This term appears several times in Jubilees, including three times in Rebekah's blessing prayer for Jacob, 25:2, 19, 23 (where it is translated by VanderKam as "(my) *affection*"). The word *meḥrat* has connotations of "compassion, pardon, mercy, pity, clemency," and may relate to the Heb. *rḥmym*. In the Geᶜez Bible this term *meḥrat* and also its cognate forms appear frequently, often in reference to the deity.

22. B. Smith, "'Spirit of Holiness' as Eschatological Principle of Obedience," in *Christian Beginnings and the Dead Sea Scrolls*, ed. J. Collins and C. Evans (Grand Rapids: Baker Academic, 2006), 75-99 (here 76).

23. Smith, "Spirit of Holiness," 77.

response has a public character as well, since God promises that all spirits and angels will know them and the special relationship between Israel and God. All "of them will be called children of the living God," who is here called "their father" (v. 25). Moses' prayer leads God to promise that sin will be followed by joyful "return."

God Orders the Writing Down of the Message (1:26-29)

The message constitutes a vision of the blessings of a new age and a new Jerusalem, both eschatological motifs. There appear to be two commands to write down all these words; the first, in v. 26, contains an imperative form, seemingly directed to Moses, to write down all the words God "will tell you on this mountain." In a second line, God tells the angel of presence, "*Dictate to Moses*" all this history, from the very beginning until its ending time, when God will descend and actually live with his people (v. 27). This change, a command to Moses in the first and an order to the angel to dictate in the second, has long proved a *crux interpretum*; Davenport interpreted it as evidence of redactional activity, arguing that the notion of a dictating angel corresponds to a later redactional level.[24] VanderKam suspects that the different verbs in Ethiopic could reflect imprecisions of the Greek translator, who might have failed to recognize the difference between *qal* and *hiphil* forms of the verb.[25]

Then the Lord will appear so that all can see and recognize him as "the God of Israel, the father of all Jacob's children, and the king on Mt. Zion" (v. 28). The covenant promise, originally associated with Moses as the central figure, greatly expands here as it now extends to all Jacob's family of twelve descendants, but finally to the claim that Jerusalem and Zion are holy — even more surprising in the earlier worldview. This chapter concludes (v. 29) when the angel of presence takes the tablets with all this information inscribed on them and displays them. In a foretaste of things to come in this book, the audience learns that these tablets will contain a complete picture of all the "times" important for their history, including a look ahead to the renewal of all creatures, when the Lord's temple will be created in Jerusalem. Even the luminaries will be renewed, so that they can effect "healing, health,

---

24. Davenport, *Eschatology,* 15f. This point was a key element for his reconstruction of the redactional history of this text.

25. VanderKam, *Jubilees,* 6, note to v. 27.

and blessing for all the elect ones of Israel" (v. 29). The imagery here contains significant eschatological motifs, including the glowing descriptions of the "blessings of the new age," the expectation of a "new Jerusalem," and rules for ordering life in a new age.[26] This eschatological horizon in Jub 1 should provide a helpful lens for grasping the ultimate end of the interpretive retelling of many narratives in the lives of the patriarchs and matriarchs of Israel: taken together, the eschatological and narrative elements suggest concrete ways for the people of Israel to live out their covenant responsibilities, with a focus on the reality to come.

IV. The Apocalypse in Jubilees (23:14-31)

The second eschatological passage comes at an odd place in the narrative, directly after the description of Abraham's death (vv. 1-7) but before the cycle of stories about Isaac and his family. This cycle begins with the well-known story of Esau selling his birthright to Jacob (Jub 24:2-8), leaving a gap between Abraham's death and the sale of the birthright. The book of Genesis also features a type of hiatus between these two events, but there it contains a genealogy of Ishmael (Gen 25:12-18) and the birth account of Esau and Jacob (Gen 25:19-27).

Jubilees has greatly altered the sequence of events in this part of the narrative. Since Jacob and Esau were born while Abraham was yet living (Jub 19:13-14), in this version there passed fifteen years while Abraham was living and able to see these two grandsons. The audience hears of Abraham's love for Jacob (19:15-31) and his last words to his children and grandchildren. Jubilees recalls Abraham celebrating Shavuoth with his sons Isaac and Ishmael, and also Jacob, and there follows a farewell address of Abraham to his grandson Jacob (22:10-23). This testamentary speech contains many elements of a typical covenant formulary: repeating the blessings to Jacob's forebears, a clear list of covenant stipulations, and a renewed version of the blessing prayer for Jacob.[27] Grandfather Abraham inveighed against any kind of mixing with Gentiles (22:16-17), idolatry (22:18 and 22), intermarriage (22:20), and warned that idolaters can expect "to descend to sheol and

---

26. Knibb, "Eschatology and Messianism," 381-82.

27. In Jubilees the blessing was uttered by Abraham, though in Genesis Isaac proclaimed it. For analysis of this section, cf. J. Endres, S.J., *Biblical Interpretation in the Book of Jubilees*, CBQMS 18 (Washington, D.C.: Catholic Biblical Association of America, 1987), 43-44.

go to the place of judgment" (22:22b). In this afterlife the deceased have "no hope in the land of the living and no remembrance of them after death."[28] After this speech the two of them lay down, Jacob sleeping "in the bosom of his grandfather Abraham" (22:26). Abraham blessed him again (22:27-30), and then Abraham expires, attended only by Jacob, who is not aware of his death until he awakens to find his grandfather "cold as ice" (23:3).

So Jubilees has greatly altered the flow of the story, with many family events occurring after the birth of Esau and Jacob but before Abraham's death. The author may have discovered an exegetical anomaly in the Genesis text, i.e., that the narrative flow of events does not correspond to the chronology discerned in the (priestly) text of Genesis.[29] These changes also serve to heighten the positive characterization of Abraham, which is very important for Jubilees at this point of the account. The additional stories about Abraham and his family in Jubilees almost force the author to explain why Abraham, "perfect with the Lord in everything that he did," lived a much shorter life than the ancients had. Before the flood, their lives generally extended nineteen jubilees (19 x 49 = 931 years), but Abraham dies after only 175 years ("three jubilees and four weeks of years"; 3 x 49 plus 4 x 7 years). The new eschatological section will offer a solution to this problem: the increase of evil in the world has inevitably led to a shorter life span for humans. No clearer indicator of the evil can be imagined than their shorter life span (Jub 23:11), especially as they "grow old quickly" before "the great day of *judgment*." Another and more devastating problem is that "knowledge will leave them because of their old age" (v. 11). In this literary buildup to the Apocalypse (vv. 14-31), the readers already encounter the eschatological fears and hopes of the community, especially concerning the day of judgment, a shorter life span (one and one-half jubilees), and the premature loss of knowledge. The years they live will be plagued by "difficulties, toil, and distress without peace" (v. 12) deriving from injuries and blows they will receive continually as punishments (v. 13).

One approach to this text is to attend to the rewriting and redaction of biblical traditions in this eschatological section of the text.[30] Traditions from Jer 6:23a (Jub 23:23b) and Deut 28:49-50 (Jub 23:23) and Ps 79:2 (Jub 23:23) allowed this author to meditate on the message from the angel and to reflect

---

28. Endres, *Biblical Interpretation*, 45.

29. For details, cf. Endres, *Biblical Interpretation*, 24. The author of Jubilees may have been following a priestly chronology.

30. Endres, *Biblical Interpretation*, 52-62.

it in a new text. A Deuteronomic historical pattern of covenant life with God also shapes this text, which contains the four "moments" of sin (vv. 16-21), punishment (vv. 22-25), a turning point (v. 26), and saving action of God (vv. 27-31). Commentators have noted this progression,[31] and I previously considered the section through the lens of intertextuality and rewriting.[32]

The Apocalypse begins with a statement that the many and varied sufferings of humans come as a result of the sin of making the "earth commit sin through sexual impurity, contamination, and their detestable actions" (v. 14).[33] The text again mentions that the length of days for humans has been decreasing — from as many as a thousand years in days of old to a life of seventy years, or eighty for the strong, in the present day (v. 15a). Even the days we have are evil, and "there is no peace during the days of that evil generation" (v. 15b).

Sin (23:16-21)

Hearers of this account may be wondering when and how the present evils will end, so the author pulls together a variety of notions of sin, going beyond the earlier mention of sexual impurity and contamination and similar actions. Young people struggle with their elders because of sin and injustice, while other people abandon key aspects of the covenant and forget the worship regulations and calendar given them by God. And there are many other evils. As a result, people suffer, wars increase, the entire cosmos will be degraded, as the message specifies that "the earth will indeed be destroyed because of all that they do" (v. 18). Warfare and violence result from the sins of this generation, as do also the rapaciousness of the rich against the poor, and finally, defilement of the Holy of Holies (v. 21). Sin runs the gamut of the human arena: worship, sexuality, social injustice, violence, defilement of sacred persons, times, and spaces; there is here no partial, restricted view of life.

---

31. Werline, *Penitential Prayer*, 113-16. Klausner, *Messianic Idea in Israel*, 306.

32. For a very different approach to this text, cf. J. Kugel, "The Jubilees Apocalypse," *DSD* 1, no. 3 (1994): 322-37. His reading of this apocalypse, with Ps 90 as intertext, points to a time of suffering followed by "a golden age" (337), but also provides a way of reading their past history.

33. For comment on the sexual nature of these sins, cf. Loader, *Enoch, Levi, and Jubilees*, 122-25.

Punishment (23:22-25)

Punishment will come as the people are delivered up to the violence of "sinful nations who will have no mercy or kindness for them and who will show partiality to no one" (v. 23). There are visions of bloodshed and chaos and young children whose "heads will turn white with gray hair" (v. 25). Their condition will be dire. Even their outcries to God and prayers for rescue will go unheeded (v. 24).

Turning Point/Repentance (23:26)

As usual in this pattern, there comes a turning point; here it is signaled only by the notice that "the children will begin to study the laws, to seek out the commands, and to *return* to the right way." Perhaps all three verbs function synonymously: studying laws, searching out God's commands, and returning to God's ways. The verb "return" (*myt*/*meta*, probably translating שוב) also appeared in the similar passage in Jub 1:15, in which God says, "After this they will return to me." One connotation of this verb is "to be converted (relig. sense),[34] and it fits well this context.

Salvation by God (23:27-31)

Salvation by God has a dual appearance in this text: an earthly, newly acquired longevity, and passing through death of the just.[35] God's saving acts are not explicitly political, even though the punishments in vv. 22-25 have often been interpreted in this way.[36] Eschatological signs of salvation include longer lifetimes, lived in peace and joy, without satans or evil destroyers; in short, people in the eschaton will enjoy lives of "blessing and healing" (v. 29). Especially significant is the notion that the life span of the just may again

34. T. Lambdin, *Introduction to Classical Ethiopic (Geʿez)*, HSS 24 (Missoula: Scholars Press, 1978), 417.

35. Cf. G. Aranda Pérez, "Los Mil Años en el Libro de los Jubileos y Ap 20, 1-10," *EstBib* 57 (1999): 39-60, esp. 44-47.

36. For example, R. Charles saw in vv. 22-23 a description of "the sufferings of the nation during the civil wars and internal trouble that took place down to Simon's high priesthood (142-135 B.C.)": Charles, *The Book of Jubilees or the Little Genesis* (London: Adam and Charles Black, 1902), 148.

reach a thousand years (v. 27), seemingly the perfect age for humans (which Adam did not attain because he had eaten of the fruit in the garden [Jub 4:30]). Then the message reaches its peak and terms that might be taken as eschatological impulses appear in italics:

> 30Then the Lord will *heal* his servants. They will rise and see great *peace.* He will *expel their enemies.* The *righteous* will see (this), offer praise, and be very *happy* forever and ever. They will see all the punishments and curses on their enemies. 31Their bones will rest in the earth and their *spirits will be very happy.* They will know that the Lord is one who executes *judgment* but shows *kindness* to hundreds and thousands and to all who love him.

These eschatological blessings include several of the categories identified earlier as eschatological: triumph of God's people (v. 30), descriptions of the blessings of the new age (vv. 29-30, with great peace and blessing), the notion of a final judgment with reward for the righteous (v. 30), and the triumph of the righteous.

Another sign of the eschaton comes in Jub 23:31, which considers the crisis of individuals who have proven faithful to the covenant. Jubilees addresses the issue of life after death for the righteous, but in very muted terms: their bones will rest in peace in the ground, but their "spirits will be very happy" (v. 31). VanderKam assesses the teaching of this passage thus: "the writer does not anticipate a physical resurrection of the righteous dead (the wicked do not come into consideration because they are destroyed) but a continued existence for their spirits. In that form they will participate in the new age."[37] The precise meaning of the phrase continues to elicit interpretive work.

A covenant formulary seems to stand in the background of this apocalypse, while its final stage, the blessings, is transformed into an eschatological vision of a hopeful future, with an added note that the spirits of the faithful ones of Israel will continue. The eschatological horizon, however, strongly suggests a perspective for viewing their life and relationship with God. God's friend Abraham represents the hopes of all of Jacob's descendants: when they study the laws (Torah), seek out God's commands, and return/repent, they will experience a type of life characterized by all the signs of the eschaton. The eschatological vision of this apocalypse should instill

37. VanderKam, *The Book of Jubilees,* 59.

hope for the future, for many of the descendants of Abraham: living the life of covenant with the God of mercy offers hope for the future.

V. Conclusion

In my opinion, the most important aspect of these eschatological passages is the new perspective they offer for the reading of the rest of the book of Jubilees. They assess characters in new ways, focusing on their living the appropriate halakah within the perspective of both past and future life of the people. The text clarifies many points of Jewish law, showing their significance in the overall covenant pattern of their life as a people. It particularly invites readers to fasten on notions of peace and healing as eschatological reality, and thus contributes to a notion of the God of Israel as ultimately a God whose mercy is greater than anything their actions deserve.

Amplified Roles, Idealized Depictions: Women in the Book of Jubilees

Kelley Coblentz Bautch

One contribution of contemporary scholarship to the study of Judaism and Christianity in antiquity has been a focus on matters related to gender and sexuality. This interest is reflected in several fine studies of the book of Jubilees undertaken in the last decade that have concentrated on the depiction of women and sexuality. Two of the most comprehensive works that deserve mention are Betsy Halpern-Amaru's *Empowerment of Women in the Book of Jubilees* (Brill, 1999) and most recently William Loader's *Enoch, Levi, and Jubilees on Sexuality: Attitudes towards Sexuality in the Early Enoch Literature, the Aramaic Levi Document, and the Book of Jubilees* (Eerdmans, 2007). Since Maxine Grossman has recently examined masculinity in the book of Jubilees,[1] I will direct my comments especially to the depiction of women in Jubilees and how these representations relate to those of women in the Enochic corpus. There is good reason to compare Jubilees with these texts associated with Enoch as Jubilees draws upon many Enochic traditions and perhaps texts in its rewriting of Genesis and Exodus.[2]

---

1. "Affective Masculinity: The Gender of the Patriarchs in Jubilees," *Hen* 31, no. 1 (2009).

2. On Jubilees' use of Enochic works, see, for example, J. C. VanderKam, "Enoch Traditions in Jubilees and Other Second-Century Sources," in SBLSP 18, ed. P. Achtemeier (Missoula: Scholars Press, 1978), 1:229-51; also in *From Revelation to Canon: Studies in He-*

I would like to acknowledge St. Edward's University and its Presidential Excellence Award which allowed me to undertake the research for this paper. — KCB

The book of Jubilees is indeed a meaty text to explore for the scholar interested in representations of women in second temple period texts. In this rewriting of much of Genesis and Exodus, women appear more prominently than they do in the biblical narratives.[3] Roles of women familiar from the biblical texts are developed further or nuanced, or new female characters are introduced altogether. Sometimes these metamorphoses and additions respond to exegetical concerns, sometimes to polemics; the rationales for such revisions are not always mutually exclusive. As Halpern-Amaru demonstrates, female characters are significant for the book of Jubilees because of the work's concern for endogamy and the proper lineage. In that respect one has the opportunity to learn much as well about the view of sexuality that is implicitly and explicitly presented in the text; such a study has in fact been undertaken by Loader.[4]

One might hope that Jubilees would shed light on women and their status in various religious communities of the second century B.C.E. Perhaps, on occasion, the book delivers. The interjection of halakah into the narrative and references to legislation, for example, are informative about positions taken by the author on suitable marriage partners, intermarriage, and views of purity and impurity that relate to women.[5] While one may not be able to uncover as much as one would like about the lives of real women, when we examine depictions of women against Enochic literature, we may gain new insight as to how we should view the book of Jubilees within the matrix of second temple period Judaism. I begin with an overview of how

brew Bible and Second Temple Literature, JSJSup 62 (Leiden: Brill, 2000), 305-31, and M. Knibb, "Which Parts of 1 Enoch Were Known to Jubilees? A Note on the Interpretation of Jub. 4.16-25," in *Reading from Right to Left: Essays on the Hebrew Bible in Honour of David J. A. Clines,* ed. J. C. Exum and H. G. M. Williamson, JSOTSup 373 (London: Sheffield Academic Press, 2003), 254-62. For a counterview, see J. T. A. G. M. van Ruiten, "A Literary Dependency of Jubilees on 1 Enoch: A Reassessment of a Thesis of J. C. VanderKam," *Hen* 26 (2004): 205-9.

3. I use the word "biblical" to identify those texts we associate with the Hebrew Bible today; I do not imply that such works were part of a fixed canon in the early second temple period. Texts like Genesis and Exodus clearly had great appeal to certain communities and were understood by these as authoritative. See also VanderKam, "Biblical Interpretation in 1 Enoch and Jubilees," in *From Revelation to Canon,* 276-304 (here 277-78).

4. W. Loader, *Enoch, Levi, and Jubilees on Sexuality: Attitudes towards Sexuality in the Early Enoch Literature, the Aramaic Levi Document, and the Book of Jubilees* (Grand Rapids: Eerdmans, 2007).

5. On such matters, see the contribution of L. Doering ("Purity and Impurity in the Book of Jubilees") to this volume, and that of W. Loader ("Jubilees and Sexual Transgression," *Hen* 31, no. 1 [2009]).

Jubilees represents women and then compare these depictions to representations of women in Enochic texts.

I. The Amplification of Women in Jubilees

Many of the female characters in Jubilees are presented in an idealized form, shaped to speak to the concerns of the author, while communicating too little about the lives of real women at the time of the work's composition. At the same time, women are prominent within the book of Jubilees, and when compared to Genesis and Exodus, their roles are amplified. The matriarch Rebekah provides the most striking instance of a character whose story is significantly augmented and refined in Jubilees.[6] Not only is Rebekah's visibility increased in Jubilees through the addition of material (Abraham entrusts Rebekah with the news that Jacob will continue the patriarchal line and charges her to guard him [Jub 19:16-30]; Rebekah is informed by Jacob about Abraham's death and, in turn, tells Isaac [Jub 23:4]; Rebekah instructs Jacob about marriage partners and blesses him [Jub 25:1-23; cf. Gen 26:35; 27:46; 28:1]), but also she is presented, in the words of Loader, "as an ideal woman."[7] Just as Jacob is valorized by Jubilees, so too is the mother who favors him.[8]

In recasting Rebekah, the book of Jubilees eliminates aspects of her story that might be thought unflattering or unhelpful to the larger aims of the work. There is no reference to Rebekah being barren and to Isaac entreating God on her behalf, for example (cf. Gen 25:21); perhaps this could be taken as an inauspicious introduction.[9] Likewise, Rebekah's part in the de-

---

6. See, for example, J. C. Endres, S.J., *Biblical Interpretation in the Book of Jubilees,* CBQMS 18 (Washington, D.C.: Catholic Biblical Association of America, 1987), 51-84, 173-76, 217-18; B. Halpern-Amaru, *The Empowerment of Women in the Book of Jubilees,* JSJSup 60 (Leiden: Brill, 1999), 37-42; and R. Chesnutt, "Revelatory Experiences Attributed to Biblical Women in Early Jewish Literature," in *"Women Like This": New Perspectives on Jewish Women in the Greco-Roman World,* ed. A.-J. Levine, Early Judaism and Its Literature 1 (Atlanta: Scholars Press, 1991), 107-25 (here 108-11). For a critical text of the book of Jubilees, I refer to J. C. VanderKam, *The Book of Jubilees: A Critical Text,* CSCO 510 (Louvain: Peeters, 1989), and for translation, VanderKam, *The Book of Jubilees,* CSCO 511 (Louvain: Peeters, 1989). For a survey of the scope, theology, and history of the book of Jubilees, see, for example, J. C. VanderKam, *The Book of Jubilees* (Sheffield: Sheffield Academic Press, 2001).
7. Loader, *Enoch, Levi, and Jubilees,* 260.
8. See Endres, *Biblical Interpretation,* 85-119, esp. 92.
9. Cf. Halpern-Amaru, *Empowerment of Women,* 56, and Loader, *Enoch, Levi, and Jubilees,* 255. Halpern-Amaru (34) observes that Jubilees also omits initial reference to the bar-

ception of Isaac (Jub 26:1-13; Gen 27:1-17) seems understandable within Jubilees in light of Abraham's directives concerning Jacob (Jub 19:16-30). In sum, Rebekah is the impeccable matriarch with no awkward history.

Moreover, an outstanding aspect to the story of this biblical figure is Rebekah's extensive blessing for Jacob, which, as John Endres observes, is the longest in Jubilees.[10] For Endres, Jubilees' shaping of Rebekah recalls the role of a prophetess; for Halpern-Amaru, Jubilees emphasizes Rebekah's maternal concern and promotes her as partner in an ideal marriage.[11] In any event, the portrait of Rebekah is a sympathetic one according to the Weltanschauung of Jubilees, as the matriarch even appears to outshine Isaac in this work.[12] Matriarchs like Sarah and Rebekah enjoy elevated roles in Jubilees, according to Halpern-Amaru, because they are partners with their husbands in promoting and safeguarding the covenant, in addition to being wives and mothers of patriarchs.[13]

Also, the portraits of women in Jubilees are often keyed to exegesis. Often the reworkings provide additional information about female figures when the biblical text requires clarification or when divergent biblical traditions might suggest the need for reconciliation.[14] Such dynamics seem to stand behind the developing portraits of several women in large measure. For example, how does one account for God creating the human being, male and female, in his image according to Gen 1:26-28 and then creating first Adam in Gen 2:7 and then Eve at a later time from Adam's rib (Gen 2:21-25)? The book of Jubilees clarifies the discrepancy: the man and woman were created in the first week of creation, which corresponds to the events of Gen 1 (Jub 2:14); on the sixth day of the second week, the woman is taken out of man, completed and presented to him (Jub 3:8).[15] This harmonization of creation accounts, which allows Adam's earlier appearance, also provides an etiology for the law

---

renness of Sarah (cf. Gen 11:30). Though the motif of barrenness serves well the purposes of Genesis, it does not conform to the aims or concerns of Jubilees and thus is ignored. The topic does emerge, however, with the introduction of Hagar as a surrogate wife (cf. Jub 14:21-24). Loader, 251.

10. Endres, *Biblical Interpretation*, 84.

11. Respectively, *Biblical Interpretation*, 84, and *Empowerment of Women*, 60-61, 63.

12. See, for example, Endres, *Biblical Interpretation*, 83-84, 217-18.

13. Halpern-Amaru, *Empowerment of Women*, 5, 55-64.

14. Cf., for example, Halpern-Amaru, *Empowerment of Women*, 6, 133-46.

15. Halpern-Amaru, *Empowerment of Women*, 11. Cf. also van Ruiten, *Primaeval History Interpreted: The Rewriting of Genesis 1–11 in the Book of Jubilees*, JSJSup 66 (Leiden: Brill, 2000), 75, and J. R. Levison, *Portraits of Adam in Early Judaism from Sirach to 2 Baruch*, JSPSup 1 (Sheffield: Sheffield Academic Press [JSOT], 1988), 90-91, 214-15 n. 10.

of the parturient of Lev 12:1-5: women remain impure for seven days after the birth of a male child and fourteen days for a female child (Jub 3:8).[16]

Jubilees' commitment to particular theological positions or to polemical views also affects the representations of biblical women. For example, Jubilees elaborates upon Gen 35:22 (cf. also Gen 49:4 and 1 Chron 5:1), which only briefly notes sexual relations between Reuben and Bilhah. The account in Jubilees not only clarifies the nature of the encounter, but also entirely exculpates Bilhah. Jub 33:2-8 makes clear that Bilhah does not participate in any way in the encounter; she is innocent. In fact, Jubilees defends Bilhah by presenting her as a victim of rape.[17] There may be a responsibility, however, to defend Bilhah as mother of Naphtali, a tribal chief toward whom Jubilees is sympathetic.[18]

Jubilees magnifies women especially through the addition of characters to the genealogical record, women lacking in the biblical narratives. Wives and mothers of the patriarchs are given names; similarly, paternal lineage — in this context, in fact, what amounts to their credentials, per Halpern-Amaru — is identified.[19] Whereas Genesis does not address the matter of the wives of Cain and Seth (their identity or origin; cf. Gen 4:17, 26; 5:6-7), Jubilees supplies the names of their wives (respectively, Awan [Jub 4:9] and Azura [Jub 4:11]), who are also presented as their sisters. Additionally, Jubilees includes and names the wives of the patriarchs who descend from Seth (cf. Gen 5). The concern for comprehensiveness in listing the women who are part of the Sethite line is extended throughout Jubilees (Cain's line is ignored, however, following his death [Jub 4:31-32], and subsequently the genealogy of Irad to Lamech of Gen 4:18-24 is omitted).[20]

The addition of these women addresses omissions in the biblical genealogies and also serves polemic purposes as well. Such a concern for comprehensiveness in the genealogies is tied to heralding proper unions, and marriage is no small matter in Jubilees given its emphasis on endogamy.[21] The

---

16. M. Segal, *The Book of Jubilees: Rewritten Bible, Redaction, Ideology, and Theology,* JSJSup 117 (Leiden: Brill, 2007), 52.

17. Segal, *The Book of Jubilees,* 74; cf. Halpern-Amaru, *Empowerment of Women,* 110-11.

18. Halpern-Amaru, *Empowerment of Women,* 108, 118-19.

19. Halpern-Amaru, *Empowerment of Women,* 4, and "The First Woman, Wives and Mothers in *Jubilees,*" *JBL* 113 (1994): 609-26 (here 622).

20. Van Ruiten, *Primaeval History Interpreted,* 119, 174-75.

21. See, for example, Halpern-Amaru, *Empowerment of Women,* 4-5; VanderKam, *The Book of Jubilees,* 132; Loader, *Enoch, Levi, and Jubilees,* 186-96; and also L. Arcari, "The Myth of the Watchers and the Problem of Intermarriage in *Jubilees,*" *Hen* 31, no. 1 (2009).

book of Jubilees demonstrates a keen interest in the wives and mothers of the antediluvian and patriarchal periods since women, through their role in childbearing, are critical to the maintenance of the proper lineage. Jubilees communicates this concern at numerous points in its retelling of the biblical narrative.

Where the biblical texts take up genealogy but omit reference to wives or mothers, Jubilees fills in the gap and even supplies the names of such figures to complete the genealogical record, especially that of the pure family line that is traced.[22] What's in a name? The book of Jubilees conveys a great deal of information about the women it inserts into the narrative and/or about the consequence or outcome of the unions made with the women through the names given to these characters. Wives of patriarchs in the preferred family line are given names that convey positive sentiments, and not coincidentally their marriages and offspring are sanctioned within the narrative. Thus, the name of Seth and Azurah's daughter, Noam, is related to נעם, a root that connotes "to be lovely." Noam is married to her brother Enosh (4:13), the first to call upon the Lord's name (Jub 4:12); this is an example of an auspicious union. Their son Kenan marries Mualelit, whose name suggests a form of הלל, "to praise" (maybe "she who praises God").[23]

Wives of ignoble characters have names that communicate negative traits or set the reader up for an unfavorable outcome or generation; it is no surprise that the wife of Cain is named Awan (Jub 4:9), a name that is probably related to the Hebrew word for "iniquity" and "guilt" (עֲוֹן) or for "wickedness" and "trouble" (אָוֶן).[24] As John Rook observes, immediately after noting her birth (Jub 4:1), Jubilees makes reference to the murder of Abel (4:2-4).[25] Such telltale names are also given to offspring of questionable unions (see below). It is debated whether Jubilees was dependent upon sources for these names. There is some overlap between names given to wives in Jubilees and other texts of the second temple period.[26] I think Rook is correct to state

22. Van Ruiten, *Primaeval History Interpreted*, 369.

23. See J. Rook, "The Names of the Wives from Adam to Abraham in the Book of Jubilees," *JSP* 7 (1990): 105-17 (here 108-9), who follows W. L. Lipscomb, "A Tradition from the Book of Jubilees in Armenian," *JJS* 29 (1978): 149-63 (here 153), and R. H. Charles, *The Book of Jubilees or the Little Genesis* (London: A. & C. Black, 1902), 33 n. 4.

24. Rook ("Names of the Wives," 107) favors the former translation.

25. Rook, "Names of the Wives," 108.

26. For example, the Genesis Apocryphon includes the names of Bitenos and Amzara, wives respectively of Lamech and Noah, which Jubilees supplies as Betanosh ("daughter of humankind") and Emzara (possibly "mother of offspring"; see Rook, "Names of the

that while it may be impossible to determine whether Jubilees relied on a source, it is clear that these names contribute to and function within the narrative and assist in defining unions and a family or generation.[27]

Kinship also communicates information about respective unions. As Halpern-Amaru observes, "The level of kinship relation between husband and wife . . . begins at the closest degree of consanguinity and progressively moves further out."[28] It is important for the author that endogamy is at work from the beginning of the family line. Thus, the initial marriages from Seth to Azura (Jub 4:11) and Kenan to Mualelit (4:14) are brother-sister unions. This ensures that the family need not intermarry with Cainites.[29] Thereafter, as the descendants of Seth have grown and the number of women available within the family has increased, marriages occur between first cousins.[30] Attention to close kinship wanes by the fifteenth generation, such that the line of Shem is diluted by irregular unions. To signal a return to order, the brother-sister union reappears (thus, Abram's marriage to Sarai [Jub 12:9]). Once endogamous relations are reestablished in this manner, cousin marriages, such as that of Isaac to Rebekah (Jub 19:10) and Jacob to Leah and Rachel (27:10; 28:1-10), resume.[31]

Such unions cannot afford to be casually undertaken. To give one example, Halpern-Amaru has observed that in its retelling of the story of the watchers who mate with women, Jubilees emphasizes that the sin of the watchers consists of their marriage to whomever they chose;[32] that point — that the watchers selected mates according to their preferences (Jub 7:21) —

Wives," 113-14); cf. Jub 4:28, 33. Similarly the Animal Apocalypse lists the name of Enoch's wife as Edna (1 En 85:3), not entirely dissimilar from Jubilees' Edni (Jub 4:20); see van Ruiten, *Primaeval History Interpreted*, 123; Rook, 110, and also below.

27. Rook, "Names of the Wives," 106.

28. Halpern-Amaru, *Empowerment of Women*, 149.

29. See, for example, Halpern-Amaru, *Empowerment of Women*, 19, and "The First Woman," 617.

30. The descendant would marry the daughter of their father's brother or sister (for example, Malalael marries Dinah, presented as the daughter of Barakiel, the brother of Malalael's father [Jub 4:15]).

31. Cf. Halpern-Amaru, *Empowerment of Women*, 34-37. In this instance, one might think Jubilees to be addressing the scenes of Gen 12:11-13 and 20:2 in which Abram presents Sarai as his sister. Halpern-Amaru suggests that since Jubilees does not feature a deception when Abram is in Egypt (Sarai was taken by force and there is no reference to their relationship as siblings) and omits the account of Abram in Gerar altogether, the intent does not seem to be the clarification of the biblical text. Cf. Halpern-Amaru, 36.

32. Halpern-Amaru, *Empowerment of Women*, 22, 147.

is followed immediately by reference to the birth of the giants and by a notice of the increase of wickedness on earth (Jub 5:1-2; cf. Gen 6:11). The proof
of the problem is to be observed in the offspring. As Loader suggests, the nature of the sin, for Jubilees, is that the relations (here fornication, or
zemmut) led to uncleanness *(rek^w s)*.[33] The sin, essentially, is one of mixing
with inappropriate partners, and such mixing defiles (cf. Jub 4:22). Unlike
the haphazard mixing of the angels, Jubilees stresses that marriages are to be
arranged with great care;[34] for example, the unanticipated meeting between
Isaac and Rebekah of Gen 24:64-67 is omitted in Jubilees, which prefers, instead, a brief notice that Abraham brokered the relationship ("he took a wife
for his son, Isaac"; Jub 19:10).[35] Marriages made with less care and unions
with unsuitable partners are reflected in the progeny of such unions, as
noted above in the case of the giants, offspring that can seem determinative
of the nature of an entire generation. The child of Peleg and Lomna, a
woman of uncertain lineage, for example, is named Ragew ("evil"); his birth
coincides with the building of the Tower of Babel (Jub 10:18-26).

While the retelling of Genesis and Exodus affords an opportunity for
"subtle" critique of exogamy by highlighting problematic unions and their
offspring, the prohibition of intermarriage is reinforced through the instructions of Abraham to his sons and grandson Jacob (Jub 20:3-6, esp. 20:4;
22:20), and of Rebekah to Jacob (Jub 25:1-3). Further, the account of the rape
of Dinah (Jub 30:1-26; Gen 34:1-31) proves the occasion for an explicit denouncement of intermarriage. The book of Jubilees omits entirely Hamor
and Jacob's discussion of intermarriage and the proposal of circumcision as
a condition (cf. Gen 34:6-24). Even the prospect of conversion — not simply
intermarriage — in fact, is off-limits for Jubilees.[36] Simeon and Levi are portrayed unambiguously as heroes, who mete out punishment on the
Shechemites that had been divinely preordained (Jub 30:5). The brothers'
slaughter of the Shechemites is justified by the angel of the presence who
makes clear that no Israelite is to give his daughter or sister to a foreigner,
nor is he to marry a foreign women (Jub 30:7, 11).[37]

33. Loader, *Enoch, Levi, and Jubilees*, 126-45, esp. 131.

34. Loader, *Enoch, Levi, and Jubilees*, 156-57.

35. Halpern-Amaru, *Empowerment of Women*, 38, 41-42. See also, though, Endres, *Biblical Interpretation*, 21, who understands the omission as related to Jubilees' disinterest in
Isaac.

36. See, for example, Halpern-Amaru, *Empowerment of Women*, 129-58; Loader,
Enoch, Levi, and Jubilees, 167.

37. Though endogamous unions are favored for the patriarchs and matriarchs,

While more can be (and has been) said about the depiction of women in Jubilees, we have observed through such portraits much about the values and concerns of this second-century work. Women are highly visible in the book of Jubilees, and seemingly more crucial to the events of Genesis and Exodus in some respects than are their biblical counterparts. Even so, Jubilees' recasting of women characters is along ideological lines and at times exegetically driven. The women, from their depiction to their names, tend to be very stylized constructs; in this respect, they serve well the author's concerns, as they can be ciphers especially in addressing the matter of endogamous and exogamous unions. In the context of the second temple period, the expanded or amplified roles given to women in Jubilees are comparable to what one encounters in Joseph and Aseneth and The Testament of Job.[38] Given the shared traditions we find in Enochic literature and Jubilees, it is striking then that Enochic depictions of women are so little developed. As we will see with Enochic literature, women are certainly not as visible and not nearly as utilized to underscore fundamental concerns.

II. The Depiction of Women in Enochic Traditions

There is a challenge that would accompany any comparison of Enochic literature and the book of Jubilees. First, while Jubilees may reflect the use of different sources or redaction,[39] Enochic literature would be distinguished

---

Halpern-Amaru and C. Werman ("*Jubilees* 30: Building a Paradigm for the Ban on Intermarriage," *HTR* 90 [1997]: 1-22, here 3) have argued that Jubilees tolerates marriages of the patriarchs to lower-status wives of other backgrounds, so long as they are not Canaanite. For example, Hagar poses no difficulty for Jubilees — and her presentation is not altered (Jub 14:22-23) — since the descendants of Ham, including Egyptians, are not cursed even while Canaan is (Jub 7:10 and 10:29-33). Where the backgrounds of wives are not provided in the biblical text, Jubilees supplies the genealogical data that will render a woman fit or inappropriate for marriage to a patriarch. Halpern-Amaru, *Empowerment of Women*, 104. Thus, Jubilees portrays Keturah, the third wife of Abraham, and Bilhah, concubine or wife to Jacob, as women from the households in order to remove speculation that they are women of the land (Jub 19:11; 28:6). Halpern-Amaru, *Empowerment of Women*, 103-6. See, however, Loader, *Enoch, Levi, and Jubilees*, 192-93, who argues that Jubilees is more tolerant of marriage to Egyptians than to other Gentiles in general (cf. Jub 11:9).

38. See Chesnutt, "Revelatory Experiences Attributed to Biblical Women in Early Jewish Literature."

39. See Segal, *The Book of Jubilees*, and also "The Composition of Jubilees," in this volume.

on this matter by degree, as it is more heterogeneous. Enochic literature refers to a variety of works — for example, the anthology 1 Enoch — that emerge from diverse contexts.[40] In some instances, like the Book of the Watchers, individual works betray use of several sources. To further complicate the task of comparison, while certain interests or foci — for example, eschatological concerns — are found in many of these texts associated with Enoch, the works also indicate development, as well as attempts to nuance and perhaps even to discount theological positions taken in others of the writings.[41] Given the complexity of and diverse perspectives taken within Enochic works, the portrayal of women in this literature not surprisingly also is varied.

Second, the temporal scope of Enochic literature — here I refer to the aforementioned collection of texts in 1 Enoch as well as the Book of the Giants (1Q23; 1Q24; 2Q26; 4Q203; 4Q530-533; 6Q8) — is considerably narrower than Jubilees. With the exceptions of the Animal Apocalypse (1 En 85–90) and the Apocalypse of Weeks (93:1-10; 91:11-17), both historical apocalypses, the narratives of such Enochic texts are situated in the antediluvian world of the patriarch Enoch. Though the literature frequently anticipates the time of God's visitation at the end of the current era, other chapters of Israelite history are not of interest. Thus, the women who appear prominently in these texts are Eve (32:6; 69:6; 85:3-8); the wives of the watchers (especially 6:1-2; 7:1-2; 8:1, 3; 9:8-9; 10:3, 9, 11, 15; 12:4; 15:3; 19:2; 69:4-5); the wife of Enoch, Edna (85:3); and the unnamed wives of Methuselah and Lamech (106:1). As the portraits we do encounter are limited to antediluvian women, we will not find a depiction of Rebekah, for example, to hold against that in Jubilees.

Like Jubilees, though, the women can serve as ciphers for assorted values and concerns of the respective authors of Enochic literature. The literature's concern for eschatological judgment and the antediluvian context in which its hero, Enoch, lives are related to the literature's fascination with the tradition of the fallen watchers. That tradition, even variously expressed, not only serves to illustrate the result of disobedience, but it also communicates

---

40. I am not suggesting a fixed canon of Enochic literature or that the booklets and order of our contemporary 1 Enoch reflect a collection from the second temple period; I simply refer to those texts from the second temple period in which Enoch and traditions associated with the patriarch are especially prominent.

41. Cf. my "Adamic Traditions in the Parables? A Query on 1 Enoch 69:6," in *Enoch and the Messiah Son of Man: Revisiting the Book of Parables,* ed. Gabriele Boccaccini, with J. von Ehrenkrook (Grand Rapids: Eerdmans, 2007), 352-60 (here 359-60), and "Enoch, First Book of," in *NIDB* (2007), 2:262-65 (here 264).

a concern for intermarriage or sexual misdeeds, boundary crossing, and illicit knowledge. These concerns influence as well the depiction of women in Enochic literature.

In conjunction with the story of the angels' descent, women are especially defined in Enochic literature as sexual beings, though they are not particularly condemned or demonized as such.[42] As if to underscore the point, the Book of the Watchers has God announce that women were essentially created to reproduce and perpetuate the male line (cf. 1 En 15:7).[43] It is clear from some of the strata that women are not faulted for the angels' decision to descend, as they are in one of the earliest traditions concerning the watchers' sin, a narrative that focuses on the descent of Shemihazah and his band of rebellious angels.[44] In this narrative, for example, the angels led by Shemihazah hatch a plan to choose for themselves wives and through them to beget children (1 En 6:2). As VanderKam has observed of this stratum, the guilt for the sinful union lies with the angels alone and not the women.[45]

The wives appear as rather ambivalent figures in Enochic literature, however, for two reasons. First, they become associated with forbidden knowledge and the practice of illicit crafts, a topic we address below. Second, variant readings of 1 En 8:1 (Syncellus) and 1 En 19:2 (Eth. MSS Tana 9, Berlin, and Garrett) suggest that the wives led astray or seduced the angels, and certain later traditions outside the Enochic corpus (TReu 5:5-6; *Targum Pseudo-*

---

42. As Loader demonstrates, sexuality and procreation are not deemed negative for humankind within these traditions. See his *Enoch, Levi, and Jubilees,* 80. On women as sexual beings, thusly defined through their service to husbands, see G. W. E. Nickelsburg, *1 Enoch 1: A Commentary on the Book of 1 Enoch 1–36, 81–108,* Hermeneia (Minneapolis: Fortress, 2001), 1:272, and Marie-Theres Wacker, "'Rettendes Wissen' im äthiopischen Henochbuch," in *Rettendes Wissen. Studien zum Fortgang weisheitlichen Denkens im Frühjudentum und im frühen Christentum,* ed. K. Löning, AOAT 300 (Münster: Ugarit-Verlag, 2002), 115-54 (here 150).

43. According to 1 En 15:5, men, mortal beings, are given women so that they might have children through them; angels, eternal spirits, have no need for children, and therefore women are not created for them (15:7). This latter statement implies that heavenly, spiritual beings are male. See K. Sullivan, "Sexuality and Gender of Angels," in *Paradise Now: Essays on Early Jewish and Christian Mysticism,* ed. A. DeConick (Atlanta: Society of Biblical Literature, 2006), 211-28 (here 214).

44. On this stratum within 1 En 6–11, see, for example, S. Bhayro, *The Shemihazah and Asael Narrative of 1 Enoch 6–11: Introduction, Text, Translation, and Commentary with Reference to Ancient Near Eastern and Biblical Antecedents,* AOAT 322 (Münster: Ugarit-Verlag, 2005), 29-31.

45. See J. C. VanderKam, *Enoch: A Man for All Generations* (Columbia: University of South Carolina Press, 1995), 32-33.

Jonathan; Gen 6:2) certainly make this point.[46] One observes that while the wives could have been used to make points about eschatology within the Enochic texts, as is the case with the watchers and their sons whose punishments are elaborated, there is only brief allusion to the fate of the women (1 En 19:2), which most likely points to their demise and their relative lack of importance to the Enochic authors.[47] This helps us to account for the fact that the ultimate outcome of the wives has been curiously ignored in second temple and late antique works that do offer colorful expansions of Enochic texts and traditions concerning the fate of the fallen watchers.

There is a certain anxiety, however, about miscegenation and intermarriage that is communicated through various Enochic works, and it is in that regard that wives (and not only those of the watchers!) in this literature receive much attention.[48] The Animal Apocalypse, drawing on traditions related to both Shemihazah and Asael, takes up in allegorical fashion inappropriate sexual activity that involves intermingling.[49] While calling attention to the tradition of the forbidden union of the angels and mortal women, the Animal Apocalypse seems also to hold Asael accountable for provoking intermarriage between the Sethites and Cainites.[50] Moreover, 1 En 106–107, like the Genesis Apocryphon, takes up the matter of sexual misdeeds and demonstrates some anxiety about miscegenation.[51] Given the baby Noah's otherworldly appearance (1 En 106:2-3, 5; cf. also 1QapGen 2-5), the paternity is in question; Methuselah consults with Enoch, on his son's pleading, to deter-

46. On Syncellus's reading, see S. Bhayro, "The Use of Jubilees in Medieval Chronicles to Supplement Enoch: The Case for the 'Shorter' Reading," *Hen* 31, no. 1 (2009), and my "Decoration, Destruction and Debauchery: Reflections on 1 Enoch 8 in Light of 4QEn[b]," *DSD* (2008). On text-critical matters relating to 19:2, see my "What Becomes of the Angels' 'Wives'? A Text Critical Study of 1 En. 19:2," *JBL* 125 (2006): 766-80 (here 769 n. 15).

47. Bautch, "What Becomes," 778-79.

48. Concern with intermarriage may be expressed further in the story of the watchers to the extent that the account is intended to be a parody that disparages priests who have entered into inappropriate marriages or engaged in prohibited sexual conduct. See D. W. Suter, "Fallen Angel, Fallen Priest: The Problem of Family Purity in 1 Enoch," *HUCA* 50 (1979): 115-35; G. W. E. Nickelsburg, "Enoch, Levi, and Peter: Recipients of Revelation in Upper Galilee," *JBL* 100 (1981): 575-600; and E. Tigchelaar, *Prophets of Old and the Day of the End: Zechariah, the Book of Watchers, and Apocalyptic*, OtSt 35 (Leiden: Brill, 1996), 198-203.

49. Loader, *Enoch, Levi, and Jubilees*, 61.

50. See, for example, Nickelsburg, *1 Enoch 1*, 1:373; Loader, *Enoch, Levi, and Jubilees*, 61.

51. For a comparison of the two, see G. W. E. Nickelsburg, "Patriarchs Who Worry about Their Wives: A Haggadic Tendency in the Genesis Apocryphon," in *George W. E. Nickelsburg: An Ongoing Dialogue of Learning*, ed. J. Neusner and A. J. Avery-Peck, JSJSup 80 (Leiden: Brill, 2003), 177-212.

mine whether one of the angels joined with Lamech's unnamed wife to father the unusual-looking baby (1 En 106:7-8).[52]

Even while the narratives may not indicate that the women are culpable in provoking the sexual encounters, the watchers are portrayed as defiled
through these unions (1 En 7:1).[53] Defilement, as in the book of Jubilees, is
the result of the watchers having sexual intercourse with people forbidden to
them.[54] As one sees in Jubilees, itself dependent on these or comparable traditions, forbidden unions result in troublesome offspring; in the Enochic literature the problematic progeny are giants who initiate violence and leave as
a legacy their immortal spirits as demons (1 En 6; 7:2-6; 9:7-8; 15). The illicit
nature of the sexual relationship is also reflected in how the Book of the
Watchers refers to the offspring of the union: bastards, half-breeds, and sons
of miscegenation (10:9).[55]

Women also appear in Enochic texts in association with illicit knowledge, a significant theme that runs throughout this literature.[56] In one of the
strata that make up 1 En 6–11, angels teach the wives sorcery, charms, and the
cutting of roots and plants after they have sexual relations (cf. 7:1; 8:3; 16:3).[57]

---

52. While Enoch selects a mate for his son, Methuselah, the Greek (Chester Beatty–
Michigan Papyrus) of 1 En 106:1 suggests that Lamech chooses his own wife; this detail sets
the stage for the remarkable (and troubling) appearance of Noah. One recalls that choosing
one's mate, from the perspective of Jubilees, could be seen as a careless and dangerous approach to matrimony. Cf. Jub 7:20-21; Halpern-Amaru, *Empowerment of Women*, 38, 41-42,
and above.

53. Loader observes that the Ethiopic features *dammara* ("were promiscuous with,"
"united with," or "mixed with"), whereas Panopolitanus reads μιαίνεσθαι ("to defile").
Enoch, Levi, and Jubilees, 12 n. 28. The theme of women defiling the watchers occurs also in
1 En 9:8; 10:11; and 15:4. For possible interpretations of these occurrences, see Loader, *Enoch,
Levi, and Jubilees*, 12-15, and Helge Kvanvig, "Gen 6,3 and the Watcher Story," *Hen* 25 (2003):
277-300 (here 291).

54. Loader, *Enoch, Levi, and Jubilees*, 15. See also Arcari, "The Myth of the Watchers
and the Problem of Intermarriage in *Jubilees*."

55. See Loader, *Enoch, Levi, and Jubilees*, 22.

56. On the theme of illicit knowledge, see A. Yoshiko Reed, *Fallen Angels and the History of Judaism and Christianity: The Reception of Enochic Literature* (Cambridge: Cambridge
University Press, 2005), 29-49.

57. The Book of the Watchers includes a third stratum that also takes up illicit knowledge. In this instance the angel Asael teaches the manufacturing of weapons of war, adornments, and cosmetics. These forbidden arts then lead to impiety (1 En 8:1-2). Because Asael
teaches men the arts, who, in fact, produce adornments and cosmetics for their daughters as
well as the weapons of war for themselves, I do not see the daughters given special censure in
the narrative.

Tal Ilan posits that women came to be associated with such arts because "of their experience with childbirth, healing, the preparation of potions and medicines and even lamentations at the grave."[58] This particular narrative provides an etiology for and negative evaluation of such practices that may have been uniquely associated with women in this period. Loader also associates such practices (and "dangerous knowledge") with foreign wives in particular and suggests that this tradition may be rooted in concern for endogamous relations.[59] The association of women, especially of the wives of the angels, with forbidden or illicit knowledge diminishes within the Enochic works. The Animal Apocalypse and Jubilees, even while they may know the tradition concerning Asael, for example, make no mention of the theme.[60] In general, the wives of the watchers seem less "interesting" to later Enochic works.

Eve exchanges places with the wives in these narratives as Enochic texts demonstrate an increasing uneasiness with the first woman. The earliest reference to Eve among Enochic texts occurs in the Book of the Watchers. Eve, like Adam, is associated with wisdom and the protagonist of the literature, the patriarch Enoch (1 En 32:3-6). In later traditions, such as the second century B.C.E. Animal Apocalypse and first century B.C.E. or C.E. Parables, Eve's lot worsens as she becomes distanced from Adam and associated with the Cainite line (85:3) or with being deceived by a malevolent angel (69:6).[61]

In conclusion, Enochic works do not amplify women in the same manner as the book of Jubilees. The depictions of women familiar from the antediluvian world of Genesis are not sharply drawn; the references to such women are not in great supply. In context, Enochic literature does not share in the trend to expand roles for women familiar from the Hebrew Bible, as one observes in the case of Jubilees, Joseph and Aseneth, and the Testament of Job.[62] Moreover, because of the complex nature of the various works we associate with Enochic literature, we are not able to present a single

---

58. T. Ilan, *Jewish Women in Greco-Roman Palestine: An Inquiry into Image and Status* (Tübingen: J. C. B. Mohr [Paul Siebeck], 1995), 225.

59. Loader, *Enoch, Levi, and Jubilees,* 46. Tigchelaar has also read the account of the watchers as an indictment on intermarriage between Jerusalem priests and Samaritan women. See *Prophets of Old,* 198-203.

60. See Segal, *The Book of Jubilees,* 117, who also notes that Jubilees lacks the tradition of angels teaching women crafts of a questionable nature.

61. See my "Adamic Traditions," 355-58.

62. See Chesnutt, "Revelatory Experiences Attributed to Biblical Women in Early Jewish Literature."

"Enochic view of women." The study of the depiction of women illumines key themes within both the book of Jubilees and Enochic literature; women are, however, far more prominent within and seemingly useful for the book of Jubilees.

Enochic and Mosaic Traditions in Jubilees: The Evidence of Angelology and Demonology

Annette Yoshiko Reed

For those who propose the existence of a distinctive "Enochic Judaism" in second temple times and/or who see an opposition between Enochic and Mosaic traditions, the retellings of the angelic descent myth in the Book of the Watchers and Jubilees have proved pivotal (1 En 6–16; Jub 4:15-22; 5:1-11; 7:21-25; 8:3-4; 10:5). Paolo Sacchi has drawn attention to the Book of the Watchers' claim that evil originated with the antediluvian descent of the angels (cf. Gen 6:1-4), proposing that this idea lies at the heart of a distinctive movement within second temple Judaism.[1] Building on Sacchi's work, Gabriele Boccaccini has interpreted Jubilees' version of the angelic descent myth, not only as evidence for its dependence on the Book of the Watchers, but also as an emblem of its alignment with "Enochic Judaism."[2] In his estimation, Jubilees "stems from the same priestly party that produced the

1. P. Sacchi, *Jewish Apocalyptic and Its History*, trans. W. J. Short, JSPSup 20 (Sheffield: Sheffield Academic Press, 1997), esp. 47-87; Sacchi, "History of the Earliest Enochic Texts," in *Enoch and Qumran Origins: New Light on a Forgotten Connection*, ed. G. Boccaccini (Grand Rapids: Eerdmans, 2005), 401-7.

2. G. Boccaccini, *Beyond the Essene Hypothesis: The Parting of the Ways between Qumran and Enochic Judaism* (Grand Rapids: Eerdmans, 1998), 86-98. For a survey of the evidence for Jubilees' use of Enochic literature, see, e.g., J. Bergsma in this volume.

For their comments and suggestions on earlier forms of this essay, special thanks to B. Halpern-Amaru, G. Boccaccini, D. Boyarin, G. Davenport, T. Hanneken, M. Himmelfarb, H. Kvanvig, and H. Najman; it also benefited much from the lively discussion in the Enoch Seminar session on angels and demons in Jubilees.

books of Enoch" and "shares the generative idea of Enochic Judaism, the idea that evil is superhuman and is caused by the sin of the Watchers (7:21ff.)."[3] For Boccaccini, Jubilees' interweaving of traditions from Gen 6:1-4 and the Book of the Watchers thus exemplifies its efforts to bridge two competing worldviews: (1) the "Enochic Judaism" that purportedly exalted the pre-Sinaitic sage, downplayed the significance of the Pentateuch, and saw the priesthood of the second temple as corrupt, and (2) the "Zadokite Judaism" that held authority in the temple, formed the Tanakh, and embraced Moses as central to Jewish identity.[4]

Just how central, however, is the angelic descent myth to Jubilees' theology, cosmology, and narrative?[5] Are Boccaccini and others correct to read its integration of this myth as a sign of its agreement with the Book of the Watchers' beliefs in the supernatural origins of evil? Insofar as most research on Jubilees has proceeded from the assumption of its close relationship to the Pentateuch,[6] we might also question the degree to which its use of Enochic traditions stands in tension with its overarching appeal to Mosaic authority. Is our understanding of Jubilees aided by the assumption of an early opposition between Enochic and Mosaic traditions?

Traditions about angels and demons will here serve as a focus for reflecting on these questions. I will begin with a brief survey of the angelology

---

3. Boccaccini, *Beyond the Essene Hypothesis*, 87.

4. Boccaccini, *Beyond the Essene Hypothesis*, 12-16, 68-79; see also his contribution in this volume for a more nuanced articulation of the same argument. A similar point is made in H. Kvanvig, "Jubilees — between Enoch and Moses: A Narrative Reading," *JSJ* 35, no. 3 (2004): 243-45. Kvanvig here suggests that Jubilees integrates Mosaic traditions into an Enochic worldview, pointing to the interpretation of Gen 6:3 in Jub 5 as paradigmatic; he refrains, however, from any generalizations about distinct "Judaisms."

5. Assessments of Jubilees that downplay the significance of the fallen angels within the text as a whole include J. C. VanderKam, "The Angel Story in the Book of Jubilees," in *Pseudepigraphic Perspectives: The Apocrypha and Pseudepigrapha in Light of the Dead Sea Scrolls*, ed. E. G. Chazon and M. E. Stone (Leiden: Brill, 1999), esp. 154; T. R. Hanneken, "Angels and Demons in the Book of Jubilees and Contemporary Apocalypses," *Hen* 28 (2006): 14-18. See also L. Stuckenbruck's contribution to this volume.

6. Its close relationship to the corresponding portions of Genesis and Exodus has been established by a number of studies on Jubilees as exegesis; this approach and its value are exemplified by J. van Ruiten, *Primaeval History Interpreted: The Rewriting of Genesis 1–11 in the Book of Jubilees* (Leiden: Brill, 2000). In addition, its resonance with the rest of Exodus (esp. 19; 23:10-33; 24) has been recently established by J. C. VanderKam, "The Scriptural Setting of the Book of Jubilees," *DSD* 13 (2006): 61-72. Its discursive and epistemological continuities with Deuteronomy are richly explored in H. Najman, *Seconding Sinai: The Development of Mosaic Discourse in Second Temple Judaism*, JSJSup 77 (Leiden: Brill, 2003), 16-69.

and demonology of Jubilees. Then, I will ask how fallen angels fit within its schema. Lastly, I will consider what these traditions may tell us about its author's attitudes toward the Pentateuch and early Enochic literature.[7]

1. Angels, Knowledge, and the Exaltation of Israel

Depictions of angels in Jubilees revolve around two main themes: (1) the transmission of knowledge and (2) the elevation of Israel.

The first is exemplified by the angel of the presence.[8] In 1:27-29, God orders this angel to "dictate for Moses from the beginning of the creation until the time when My temple is built among them throughout the ages of eternity" (1:27).[9] The rest of Jubilees is presented as the words of this angel, who is thus placed in an authorial and authorizing position in relation to Jubilees itself, with Moses as his scribe.[10]

Throughout Jubilees' narrative portions, angels also serve a mediatory function closely connected with revelation and writing. Not only do they deliver divine messages to humankind (12:22-24), but they make truths in heaven known on earth by revealing the contents of heavenly writings to humans, who inscribe their revelations in earthly books (4:18-9; 8:11; 10:13; 12:25-27; 21:10; 32:21-26; 45:16).[11] For this, angels are depicted as specially qualified, inasmuch as they are also said to serve as witnesses to the words and deeds of God (3:4; 10:22-24) and to watch humankind, see everything, and report everything to God (4:6).

For Jubilees' association of angels and knowledge, there is some prece-

---

7. In this article, I thus limit myself to exploring parallels with the Pentateuch and early Enochic literature. Points of contact with other early Jewish traditions about angels and demons are further explored, e.g., by G. Ibba and I. Fröhlich in their Enoch Seminar contributions. It is indeed important to remember that, even as the authors/redactors of Jubilees convey a relatively systematic and rationalizing account of the place of otherworldly spirits in the divinely ruled cosmos, they seem to weave this orderly account from the threads of apotropaic prayers, folklore, and popular "magic," no less than from Pentateuchal and Enochic precedents.

8. J. C. VanderKam, "The Angel of the Presence in the Book of Jubilees," *DSD* 7 (2000): 382-84.

9. J. C. VanderKam, "The Putative Author of *Jubilees*," *JSS* 26 (1981): 209-17.

10. H. Najman, "Interpretation as Primordial Writing: Jubilees and Its Authority Conferring Strategies," *JSJ* 30 (1999): 400-406.

11. H. Najman, "Angels at Sinai: Exegesis, Theology and Interpretive Authority," *DSD* 7 (2000): 315-17.

dent in the Pentateuch's presentation of angels as messengers (e.g., Gen 16:7-11; 19:1; 21:17; 22:11, 15; Exod 3:2). Enochic parallels, however, are far more extensive. Both the Astronomical Book and the Book of the Watchers depict angels as revealing heavenly truths to humankind (1 En 33:3-4; 81:1; 82:2; 82:7). In addition, the Epistle of Enoch stresses that angels witness all human deeds (1 En 98:6-8; 99:3; 100:10-11; 104:1).

The second major role of angels in Jubilees is as foils for the exaltation of Israel and its priests. Angels are paralleled to Israel inasmuch as they are circumcised, observe Sabbath, and celebrated Shavuoth prior to Noah (Jub 2:17-21; 15:27). They also serve as the heavenly parallels to Israel's earthly priesthood (30:18). Yet angels are subordinated to Israel inasmuch as they do not serve God by choice (cf. 12:19) and insofar as they have no path to atonement if they sin (cf. 5:17). Accordingly, in Jubilees' patriarchal narratives, the angelic tasks of teaching are increasingly taken over by Israel's ancestors. Moreover, in the end, angels stand outside of God's special relationship to Israel, as evident both in his direct rule of the chosen nation (15:32) and in his sole involvement in their eschatological punishment and redemption (23:30-31).[12]

For the relationship between angels and Israel in Jubilees, we may also find some precedent in Enochic literature. In the Book of the Watchers, angels are likened to priests in the heavenly temple,[13] and Enoch's own angel-like status is suggested by his actions of mediating the petition of the Watchers (1 En 13:4-6; cf. 15:2), entering the heavenly temple (chap. 14), and rebuking the Watchers (12:4-6; 13:8; 15:2). Yet the Book of the Watchers depicts the human sage Enoch as granted direct access to God, in a manner not available even to angels (14:21). In effect, Jubilees extends Enoch's prerogatives to all of Israel, proposing that this nation's status as the children of God ultimately surpasses the status of God's angels.[14]

---

12. Hanneken, "Angels," 13-14, 22-23.

13. M. Himmelfarb, *Ascent to Heaven in Jewish and Christian Apocalypses* (Oxford: Oxford University Press, 1993), 20-23.

14. This pattern mirrors Jubilees' extension of the priestly prerogatives in the Pentateuch to all of Israel, as discussed in M. Himmelfarb, *A Kingdom of Priests: Ancestry and Merit in Ancient Judaism* (Philadelphia: University of Pennsylvania Press, 2006), 53-84. On the significance of the depiction of *all* Israel as angels, see also Himmelfarb's contribution to this volume.

2. Demons, Gentiles, and the Testing of Israel

Although Jubilees' angelology owes much to Enochic traditions, its demonology may be more indebted to Pentateuchal and other biblical models. In Jubilees demons serve two main roles. First and foremost is their role as agents of divine justice. Under the leadership of Mastema, demons are charged with testing humankind, bringing human sins to God's attention, and destroying the wicked at God's behest (Jub 1:20; 10:11; 48:15; 49:2). Second is their role as the overseers of Gentiles. Not only do they rule Gentile nations (15:31; 48), but they also are objects of non-Jewish worship (1:11; 11:4) and the forces behind the efficacy of foreign "magic" (48:9-11). Accordingly, in Jubilees demonic influence is first felt when the nations take form, with the separation of the earth between Noah's sons (11:2-6).[15] When Israel and its ancestors live under foreign rule (1:20; 11:18-22; 48), they too are affected by the strife, bloodshed, famine, and disease caused by demons. Conversely, demonic influence is absent when Jacob rules Egypt and when Israel's enemies are finally destroyed from the earth (23:29; 40:9; 46:2; 50:5).

In depicting demons as agents of divine justice, Jubilees appears to develop biblical tropes of the *satan* (esp. Job 1), as is particularly evident in its characterization of Mastema (e.g., Jub 10:11). Likewise, its association of demons with Gentiles may be rooted in Deut 32:8-9 and Ps 106:35-37.[16] We may also see traces of Enochic influence in Jubilees' demonology. For instance, the image of demons as objects of sacrificial worship finds precedent in the Book of the Watchers (1 En 19:1), as does the understanding of demons as deriving from the spirits of the slain sons of the fallen angels (15:8-9).[17]

Nevertheless, Jubilees' demonology departs from Enochic literature in significant ways. In the Book of the Watchers, the demonic terrorization of humankind is definitive of postdiluvian history; after the flood, the wicked spirits of the Giants rise up against humankind (1 En 15:11), and it is proclaimed that they will continue to do so until the last judgment (16:1; 19:1). In Jubilees the spirits of the Watchers' sons cause sin, bloodshed, pollution, illness, and famine after the flood (esp. Jub 11:2-6). It is made explicit, however,

15. Hanneken, "Angels," 18.

16. J. C. VanderKam, "The Demons in the Book of Jubilees," in *Die Dämonen*, ed. A. Lange, H. Lichtenberger, and K. F. Diethard Römheld (Tübingen: Mohr Siebeck, 2003), 353-54.

17. See Giovanni Ibba, "The Evil Spirits in Jubilees and the Spirits of the Bastards in 4Q510, with Some Remarks on Other Qumran Manuscripts," *Hen* 31, no. 1 (2009).

that they do so as part of God's plan. During the lifetime of Noah, demons are diminished in number and subordinated to Mastema to help him in his divinely appointed task of destroying and misleading the wicked (10:8-9). Lest the reader imagine Mastema and his hosts as the dark side of a cosmic dualism and/or as evil forces in active conflict with God, Jubilees stresses that their existence on the earth is the result of God's acknowledgment of humankind's chronic wickedness (10:8-9). Demons may cause suffering, but the reader is assured that their actions are part of an unerringly fair system of divine justice (cf. 5:13-14).

Moreover, demonic influence diminishes as the narrative progresses. Demons have no control over Israel (15:32). And, just as Israel takes on the functions of God's angels, so Gentiles come to replace demons as the main enemy against whom Israel struggles. Even though foreign nations are ruled by demons (15:31), they are not forces of independent evil any more than the spirits they serve; Jubilees stresses, in fact, that all nations belong to God (15:31). Consistent with Deuteronomistic principle and its expansion in biblical prophecy, Gentiles can overtake Israel only when God commands (1:13; 23:23). Just as the *satan* is an agent of divine justice, testing and accusing humankind, so foreign nations have their place in the system of divine justice as a means for punishing Israel's disobedience (e.g., 1:13; 23:23).

In one sense, then, Jubilees' demonology may be best understood as a development of Deuteronomistic understandings of divine justice, expanded by means of the typological equation of Gentiles with demons. Gentiles and demons share the same function in sacred history, namely, to test Israel's faithfulness and to mediate God's punishment of their unfaithfulness. Much like the nations in the Deuteronomistic history and biblical prophecy, demons in Jubilees pose a threat to Israel only when members of the chosen nation stray from God and his commandments.

3. Fallen Angels and the Temptations of Apostasy

What, then, of fallen angels? Jubilees' version of the angelic descent myth has garnered so much scholarly attention that we might be tempted to take their inclusion for granted. When we consider the rest of its angelology and demonology, however, their presence stands in need of some explanation. As we have seen, Jubilees' depiction of angels and demons serves to evoke an orderly cosmos in which both good and bad spirits serve his will and in which the earth is clearly divided between God-ruled Jews and demon-ruled

Gentiles. Why would the author(s) choose to include sinful angels who blur these boundaries?

In early Enochic literature, chaos and earthly evils are consistently associated with angels who transgress their proper roles. The Astronomical Book describes angels who deviate from their celestial duties and thus frustrate human adherence to the correct calendar (1 En 80:6-8; cf. 18:15).[18] The first vision in the Book of Dreams blames both angels and humans for angering God (84:4). Likewise, the Animal Apocalypse alludes both to fallen angels who came to earth before the flood (86:1-6) and to the angelic leaders who were placed over all human nations, only to stray and commit violence against their charges (89:59–90:25).

Even more striking is the function of angelic disobedience in the Book of the Watchers. Whereas the Astronomical Book and Epistle of Enoch stress human responsibility for sin (1 En 80:1; 98:4),[19] the Book of the Watchers proposes that human sinfulness was precipitated by a breach in heavenly harmony. The Watchers abandoned heaven, their appointed home (15:3, 7, 10). When they took on the human prerogatives of living on earth, marrying women, and having children (15:4-5), their acts inverted the divinely set roles in the cosmic order. The problem originated in heaven, and the results were disastrous for earth: their teachings corrupted humankind, and their sons slaughtered earthly creatures.

By contrast, Jubilees integrates Enochic traditions about fallen angels into a cosmological and theodical framework that diffuses their power as cosmic forces of chaos and rebellion. The reader is assured that no breach in heavenly harmony brought evil to the earth. Here, human beings are far from being unwitting victims of evils wrought by otherworldly forces. Sin remains a strictly earthly phenomenon — even for the angels (Jub 4:15; 5:1). Moreover, in place of the Book of the Watchers' emphasis on the corrupting force of the fallen angels' teachings (1 En 7:1; 8:1-3; 9:6), we here find a stress on the positive influence of angelic instruction throughout human history.[20]

---

18. Whereas the Book of the Watchers presents angelic rebellion as a cause of sin and suffering on earth, the Astronomical Book depicts the corruption as spreading upward — from earthly sinners (80:1) to the earth (80:2-3) to the luminaries (80:4-5) to the angels who rule them (80:6).

19. On the departure from the Book of the Watchers' understanding of the fallen angels in the Book of Dreams and the Epistle of Enoch, see A. Y. Reed, *Fallen Angels and the History of Judaism and Christianity: The Reception of Enochic Literature* (Cambridge: Cambridge University Press, 2005), 71-80.

20. Reed, *Fallen Angels,* 87-95.

According to Jubilees, heavenly angels even instructed humans in gardening (Jub 3:15), medicine (10:10-14), and the Hebrew language (12:26-27); fallen angels taught only divination (8:3-4).

If their influence is so diminished, why are fallen angels even included in Jubilees? What part do they play in its angelology, demonology, cosmology, and covenantal theology? To answer these questions, it might prove helpful to look to the literary function of these figures. In the Book of the Watchers, for instance, fallen angels function as foils for the elevation of Enoch.[21] Whereas they abandon heaven for earth and catalyze earthly corruption through their teachings, he is taken from earth to heaven and, as a result, can teach salvific knowledge that inspires righteous deeds among his sons. In the Book of the Watchers, Enoch is thus presented as a paradigm for the proper epistemological process, whereas the fallen angels emblematize knowledge falsely gained and improperly transmitted. Inasmuch as Jubilees downplays the teachings of the fallen angels, this particular dichotomy is here not operant. In its place, however, we may find a related function, rooted instead in the Israel-angels/Gentiles-demons typology so central to the rest of Jubilees.

Fallen angels are atypical of Jubilees' overarching angelology and demonology: they are the only spirits depicted as transgressing the boundaries of their divinely ordained role in the cosmos. This, however, may be precisely the reason for their significance. Betsy Halpern-Amaru has demonstrated that Jubilees uses the Watchers both as narrative exemplars of the dangers of exogamy and as literary markers that draw the reader's attention to human genealogies marred by improper marriages.[22] We might take her insight even further, suggesting that the fallen angels serve both as precedents for intermarriage and as paradigms for the Jewish adoption of Gentile practices more broadly.

Intermarriage is a central concern of Jubilees (20:4; 22:20-22; 30:7-17). The practice is here presented as defiling, not just for the individual and descendants, but also for the whole nation, the divine name, and the sanctuary (30:10, 15-16).[23] Like incest and the abandonment of circumcision (15:33-34;

---

21. A. Y. Reed, "Heavenly Ascent, Angelic Descent, and the Transmission of Knowledge in 1 Enoch 6–16," in *Heavenly Realms and Earthly Realities in Late Antique Religions*, ed. R. S. Abusch and A. Y. Reed (Cambridge: Cambridge University Press, 2004), 47-66.

22. B. Halpern-Amaru, *The Empowerment of Women in the Book of Jubilees*, JSJSup 60 (Leiden: Brill, 1999), 20-28; see also Kvanvig, "Jubilees," 249-50, and Luca Arcari, "The Myth of the Watchers and the Problem of Intermarriage in *Jubilees*," *Hen* 31, no. 1 (2009).

23. C. Werman, "Jubilees 30: Building a Paradigm for the Ban on Intermarriage," *HTR* 90 (1997): 12-15; Himmelfarb, *A Kingdom of Priests*, 69-72.

33:13-14; 41:25-26), this act is presented as a sin for which no atonement is possible (30:13-16). Hence, it is perhaps telling that Jubilees stresses the fallen angels' sexual sins and describes them as acts of fornication and impurity (4:22; 7:21; 20:5-6) — two categories also paired in the description of inter-marriage in 30:7-17. In Noah's testimony, their sin is called the "beginning of impurity" (7:21); together with the bloodshed caused by the Giants, their acts are said to defile the earth and necessitate the flood. Abraham's speech similarly cites the destruction of the Giants to warn against fornication and impurity: just as the fallen angels saw the Giants slain by God's sword in 5:9, so the human children of fornication and impurity will be doomed to de-struction by the sword (20:5-6; cf. 30:5).

In light of Jubilees' association of Israel with the angels, the possibility arises that the sins of the fallen angels are meant to be paradigmatic of the broader phenomenon of Jewish apostasy. Notably, the text's preoccupation with intermarriage is just one expression of its recurrent concern with Jews who abandon the covenant to follow Gentile practices (e.g., 1:8-11; 3:31; 6:35; 15:33-34; 21:22-23; 22:16-22). Here, moreover, Jews can be defiled, not just through marriage to Gentiles, but also through contact with them and through adoption of their practices (1:9; 21:23; 22:16). In this regard, it is in-teresting to note the Watchers' punishment for their sins: they are "up-root(ed) from (positions of) authority" and bound in prisons beneath the earth (5:6-7), just as Jews who do not circumcise their sons make "them-selves like the nations so as to be uprooted from the earth" (10:33) and just as those who walk in the ways of the nations are "uproot(ed) from the earth" (21:21).

One of the effects of Jubilees' Israel-angels/Gentiles-demons typology is to depict the act of adopting Gentile practices as contrary to the cosmic order that governs heaven as well as earth. When Jews adopt foreign worship and festivals, marry non-Jews, and refrain from circumcising their sons, they are committing sins with dire consequences: they align themselves with Gentiles, thereby placing themselves under the rule of demons, dooming their children to destruction, and exempting themselves and their children from the special angel-like status granted to Israel.

The temptation to transgress, moreover, is poignantly expressed by Ju-bilees' distinctive approach to the Watchers' earthly sojourn. Angelic sin is here imagined, not as a breach of heavenly harmony (cf. Gen 6:1-2; 1 En 6:1-3; 15:3), but as a corruption that occurred during the prolonged earthly sojourn of certain angels from heaven. They descended with good intentions (Jub 4:15), and they did not sin until after they had already spent fourteen jubilees on earth. Just as Israel is likened to the angels, so the description of the earthly corruption of the fallen angels resonates with its repeated warnings to Jews about Gentile temptations to apostasy (1:19-20; 21:22-23; 22:16-23; 30:7-15). Their punishment (5:6-7) thus serves as an apt warning for Jews who are tempted — particularly during periods of foreign rule (1:19) — to follow the "ways of the nations" and/or to take foreign wives.

If I am correct to draw this connection, then the redeployment of Enochic traditions may serve the important purpose of extending Jubilees' angelological and demonological schema to speak to the problems of its own time. Within its cosmology and theodicy, angel-like Jews will eventually be saved, and demon-ruled Gentiles destroyed. Those who pose a problem are the ones in between. Following the logic of Jubilees' purity regulations,[24] the acts of these Jews threaten all of Israel and defile the sanctuary. When even a single Jewish man or woman intermarries, the whole people suffer "blow upon blow, curse upon curse" (30:14-15).

From Jubilees' zealous warnings against the abandonment of Sabbath observance (2:25-27; 50:8-9, 12-13), circumcision (15:14, 25-26, 33-34), and endogamy (22:20-21; 30:10-16, 22), we might infer that the text is particularly concerned with Jews who are tempted to abandon the practices that differentiate them from non-Jews. As with the repeated warning against following "the ways of the nations," this concern fits well with what we know about the tumultuous decades surrounding the Maccabean revolt. In this regard, it is perhaps not surprising that Jubilees describes "the evil generation" as addicted to the sins of fornication and pollution (23:14; cf. 23:17; 50:5); before the eschatological redemption and purification, the text warns that the earth and the sanctuary will be defiled (23:18, 21) and that Israel will suffer "blow upon blow, wound upon wound, distress upon distress, bad news upon bad news, disease upon disease" (23:13).

If we follow this reading of the angelic descent myth, the fallen angels emerge as an important element in Jubilees' sacred history. They are not paradigms for human sin in any universal sense. Neither does their inclusion in Jubilees suffice to signal its embrace of a cosmology in which supernatural forces cause evil on earth. Rather, they serve as precursors, more specifically, for an "in-between" category of special interest to the author, namely, members of the chosen nation who sin — or are tempted to sin — by embracing non-Jewish ways and wives.

This interpretation also raises the possibility that Jubilees owes yet an-

---

24. Himmelfarb, *A Kingdom of Priests*, 61-72.

other debt to the Book of the Watchers. David Suter and George Nickelsburg have shown how the Book of the Watchers' depiction of fallen angels (esp. 1 En 12–16) resonates with polemics against the impure marriage practices of priests of their own times.[25] Jubilees may expand this polemic in a manner consistent with its extension of priestly prerogatives to all of Israel.[26] Rather than symbolizing fallen priests, Jubilees' fallen angels may provide proto-logical precedents for Jews who defile nation, earth, and sanctuary by choosing to align themselves with Gentiles. Inasmuch as they sin in the twenty-fifth jubilee, it is fitting that Moses learns of them in the fiftieth, just prior to the rebellious generation of the wilderness. It is also fitting that the author(s) may write of them in years surrounding the Maccabean revolt, when some Jews were engaging Hellenistic culture and dismissing the need for separation from other nations (1 Macc 1:11).[27]

4. Angelology, Epistemology, and the Status of the Pentateuch and Enochic Literature

What, then, might Jubilees' angelology and demonology tell us about its attitudes toward Enochic and Mosaic traditions? In my view, its representation of angelic teaching may prove especially telling, allowing us to consider the relative value of different earthly books from the perspective of Jubilees' own epistemology.[28]

Jubilees' epistemology centers on a view of heaven as the ultimate source for all true knowledge. Angelic teachings are here cited to explain human access to a rather dazzling array of information, including agricultural, astronomical, and medicinal skills as well as laws, records of all human deeds, predictions of the future, and information about astronomical, festal, and eschatological cycles. According to Jubilees, selections from this knowl-

---

25. D. W. Suter, "Fallen Angel, Fallen Priest: The Problem of Family Purity in 1 Enoch 6–16," *HUCA* 50 (1979): 115-35; G. W. E. Nickelsburg, "Enoch, Levi, and Peter: Recipients of Revelation in Upper Galilee," *JBL* 100 (1981): 575-600.

26. Himmelfarb, *A Kingdom of Priests*, 51-84.

27. In dating Jubilees, recent scholarship has generally followed J. C. VanderKam, *Textual and Historical Studies in the Book of Jubilees*, HSM 14 (Missoula: Scholars Press, 1977), 207-85. For a new approach to dating this text and explaining its preoccupation with intermarriage, however, see Himmelfarb, *A Kingdom of Priests*, 77-78.

28. On Jubilees' epistemology in relation to sapiential and prophetic approaches to knowledge, see the contributions of B. Wright and H. Najman in this volume.

edge have been revealed to certain human scribes, such that heavenly knowledge — including information from the heavenly tablets[29] — now circulates on earth in written forms.

Inasmuch as angels mediate access to such knowledge, its transmission from heaven to earth is limited to the chosen line of Israel. Once on earth, the books containing heavenly knowledge seem to be transmitted in a single line: Enoch's books pass to Noah, and Noah's library passes to Shem, just as Abraham, Jacob, and Levi inherit the library, as expanded by additional writings, each upon the death of its previous guardian. The assurance of the angel of the presence to Moses that Levi's descendants possess and renew this trove of writings "until this day" (45:16) serves to trace the line of transmission to Moses' own time.[30]

Insofar as this model of textual transmission grants heavenly pedigrees to all books in this line, Jubilees' epistemology appears to presuppose the widespread practice of biblical pseudepigraphy. Interestingly, it also explains and defends it. Lest anyone doubt the antiquity and authenticity of Enochic literature, for instance, Jubilees purports to record evidence for Enoch's acts of authorship as well as evidence for the trustworthy transmission of his books. This evidence, moreover, is attributed to no less a figure than the angel of the presence, who has seen everything that happened on earth from the beginning of history! Enochic books are additionally verified and vouchsafed by descriptions of their use by righteous men of the past, such as Noah and Abraham.

Furthermore, the books of Enoch, Noah, Abraham, Jacob, and Moses are presented as harmonious insofar as they stand in the same tradition of transmission (patriarchal and priestly) and inasmuch as they derive from the same ultimate source (angelic revelation and/or heavenly tablets). In effect, Jubilees takes the self-authorizing claims of earlier books like the Astronomical Book and the Book of the Watchers and situates them within the history of Israel up to the time of Moses.

Just as Jubilees accepts and extends Enochic models of textual author-

---

29. On the heavenly tablets, see, e.g., M. Himmelfarb, "Torah, Testimony, and Heavenly Tablets: The Claim to Authority of the Book of Jubilees," in *A Multiform Heritage: Studies on Early Judaism and Early Christianity in Honor of Robert A. Kraft*, ed. B. G. Wright (Atlanta: Scholars Press, 1999), 19-29, here 27; F. García Martínez, "The Heavenly Tablets in the Book of Jubilees," in *Studies in the Book of Jubilees*, ed. M. Albani et al., TSAJ 65 (Tübingen: Mohr Siebeck, 1997), 243-60; Najman, "Interpretation as Primordial Writing," 389-400; Boccaccini in this volume.

30. Cf. E. Tigchelaar, "Jubilees and 1 Enoch and the Issue of Transmission," in *Enoch and Qumran Origins*, 100.

ity, so it utilizes Pentateuchal models. As Najman has shown, the text adopts a stance akin to Deuteronomy, authorizing its own contribution with appeal to the Sinaitic setting, Mosaic mediation, and divine revelation of covenantal and priestly Law as described in Exodus, Leviticus, and Numbers.[31] In the process, Jubilees also defends the authority of the Pentateuch against anyone who might assume that this anonymous writing is merely an earthly creation: it begins by emphasizing the Sinaitic revelation as a privileged occasion for the transmission of heavenly knowledge to earth and, throughout the narrative, reminds the reader of its angelic narrator. And, lest anyone wonder why Israel's purportedly eternal and immutable laws were revealed at such a suspiciously late date in human history,[32] it traces some laws back to the distant past, reveals some as written on heavenly tablets, and parallels some to angelic practices in heaven. By describing Enoch as penning multiple books on different topics during his sojourn with the angels (4:17-19), the text also grounds the plausibility for its own claim that multiple books on different matters came down to us from Moses and Mount Sinai — not just the Pentateuch but also Jubilees itself.

Following Jubilees' own model of "authorship" and transmission, the authority of the Pentateuch and Enochic literature is subordinated to the heavenly writings from which Jubilees also draws its authority.[33] Does this subordination imply a challenge to Mosaic authority and/or Jubilees' affiliation with a "Judaism" in which the Pentateuch was not always accepted as authoritative? To make such an argument, one would need to assume that the text of the Pentateuch was already accepted by other Jews, not just as an authoritative source for law, wisdom, and history, but as revealed and authoritative in a unique sense not granted to any other books. Personally, I am not sure whether our data can bear the weight of such an assumption. In light of our evidence for the continued production and circulation of other revealed literature — in the second century and well beyond — we may not be able to assume that any book held a status akin to that of "the Bible" in the later Jewish and Christian sense of that term (i.e., an exclusively privileged site for interpretation, the very *text* of which is sacred, immutable, and omni-significant); for, indeed, the boundaries of scriptural authority re-

---

31. Najman, *Seconding Sinai*, 16-69.

32. On the broader cultural context of the impulse to "back-date" Pentateuchal law, see J. C. VanderKam, "The Origins and Purpose of Jubilees," in his *Textual and Historical Studies in the Book of Jubilees*, 19-22; Kvanvig, "Jubilees," 257-58.

33. Najman, "Angels at Sinai," 317-18; Himmelfarb, "Torah," 27.

mained fluid for quite some time, and even authoritative books circulated in different text-traditions.[34]

It may be more apt to approach the mid–second century B.C.E. as a moment in the prehistory of the biblical canon, marked by diversity and dynamism.[35] Even if all Jews accepted the authority of the Pentateuch by then, it is likely that they — like Jews and Christians long after them — held a broad range of different opinions about the precise nature of its authority, the scope of knowledge that could be gained from it, its status in relation to other Israelite/Jewish books, and its status in relationship to non-Jewish books.

In my view, the contrast between "Zadokite Judaism" and "Enochic Judaism" proves helpful insofar as it forces us to take seriously the full range of our extant evidence, as now expanded by the Dead Sea Scrolls. There is no doubt that the scholarly model proposed by Boccaccini also pushes us to seek a new understanding of texts traditionally dismissed as "Old Testament Pseudepigrapha" and what they might tell us about the religious landscape of second temple Judaism. His theories expose the methodological problems involved in assuming, even after the Qumran discoveries, that there was a single "normative" or "mainstream" Judaism in second temple times from which rabbinic Judaism developed and from which Christianity broke. In addition, the very idea of "Enochic Judaism" represents a bold — and necessary — challenge to the often unquestioned assumption that the Pentateuch held an exclusive or central position for all Jews in second temple times.

Nevertheless, it may be telling that Jubilees itself — as our most explicit early evidence for the acceptance of Enochic books — presents the Book of the Watchers as consonant with the Pentateuch and reads the two as supplementary accounts of earthly events as interpreted from a heavenly perspective. In the narrative portions of Jubilees, we see some hints that the *text* of the Pentateuch is granted a level of authority not granted the text of the Book of the Watchers.[36] Yet Enochic models are arguably more central for the text's overarching depiction of textual authority, its angelic mediators, and its human agents.[37] Jubilees' depiction of angels and fallen angels draws heavily on Enochic models. Yet it transforms these models by subor-

---

34. Himmelfarb, "Torah," 28-29.

35. J. C. VanderKam, *From Revelation to Canon: Studies in Hebrew Bible and Second Temple Literature,* JSJSup 62 (Leiden: Brill, 2000), 1-30.

36. J. van Ruiten, "A Literary Dependency of Jubilees on 1 Enoch?" in *Enoch and Qumran Origins,* 90-93.

37. Kvanvig, "Jubilees," esp. 260.

dinating them to a theodicy more in line with the Deuteronomistic principle, and its depiction of demons falls closer to Job's image of the *satan* and to Deuteronomistic and prophetic views of the role of "the nations" in the history of Israel. Arguments for the superiority of one can readily be matched by arguments for the superiority of the other.

If it is difficult to determine Jubilees' assessment of the relative worth of Enochic and Mosaic texts, this is perhaps not accidental. The task of weighing the relative worth of the constitutive elements of Israel's literary heritage does not seem particularly central for the text itself. Rather, the main function of Jubilees' epistemology — aside, of course, from asserting its own authority[38] — may be to argue that the Jewish people actually possessed a literary heritage that predated the life of Moses.

Indeed, perhaps the most striking element of Jubilees' presentation of earthly knowledge is the categorical exclusion of all non-Jews from any claim to wisdom. True knowledge is here presented, always and everywhere, as a prerogative of the chosen people.[39] The trope of angelic revealers and narrators serves to render the human practice of composing true writings inseparable from the heavenly practice of selecting worthy scribes. Likewise, the transmission of books on earth is shaped by decisions about the righteousness of potential tradents. Noah, for instance, chooses to give the books that protect humankind from demons to Shem alone, thereby dooming Japheth and Ham to demonic destruction (10:14). Later, Jacob selects the righteous Levi (45:16).

Jubilees thus asserts that Israel's ancestors were privy to angelic revelations, which were regularly renewed and faithfully transmitted by the most worthy among them. By contrast, the closest thing that Gentiles have to revealed wisdom is the corrupting knowledge about divination spread by fallen angels (8:3-4; 11:9).[40] Within Jubilees, knowledge and chosenness are coterminous categories, and Gentiles are excluded from both. Tacit is the suggestion that Jews have no need for the books or learning of Gentiles, whether philosophical, religious, or "scientific"; their own literary heritage includes information — directly from heaven — about astronomy, medi-

---

38. Najman, "Interpretation as Primordial Writing," 379-410.

39. For an elegant assessment of the broader cultural context of this concern, see Stuckenbruck in this volume.

40. This raises another possible reason that the teachings of the Watchers are here limited to divination — perhaps it was important for Jubilees to associate illicit angelic instruction with something that good Jews *do not* practice; contrast, e.g., the association of the Watchers with metalworking in the Book of the Watchers (1 En 8:1).

cine, calendar, laws, human history, the beginning of time, and the end of the world.

As with its concerns for Jewish temptations to apostasy, this concern may well resonate with the temptations posed by Hellenistic culture in particular. In light of its calendar and its status at Qumran, Jubilees has often been culled for hints of inner-Jewish schisms and debates. Yet, far from exalting a righteous remnant, Jubilees depicts Israel as a unified whole — so much so, in fact, that the sins of individuals threaten to defile the entire people.[41] Perhaps tellingly, the only Jews actively excluded from the bounds of Israel are those who exclude themselves, by choosing to abandon the marks of Jewish separateness (e.g., circumcision, Sabbath, endogamy). Like the angels who lingered too long on earth in the days before the flood, some of the author's contemporaries may have found themselves tempted to join Gentiles in meals, marriage, festivals, and friendship. To them, Jubilees reveals the cosmic ramifications of such seemingly mundane acts: to follow "the ways of the nations" is to trade away the status of angels for the rule of demons.

---

41. Himmelfarb, *A Kingdom of Priests*, 51-84.

Worship in Jubilees and Enoch

Erik Larson

Worship in Genesis was simple, direct, and personal. People sacrifice, set up a pillar and pour oil on it, pray, worship, prostrate themselves, and bless. There is only one priest of the true God mentioned in Genesis, Melchizedek. There is no one place where God is worshiped. Instead, there are many sites where altars are built and many places where worship takes place such as Mount Ararat, Bethel, Beersheba, Mamre, Mount Moriah, and Shechem. There are many acts of sacrifice, but never is there an act of atonement in Genesis.[1]

The question this paper seeks to address is how the book of Jubilees responds to this situation. What aspects of the worship of God does its author play up and what aspects does he minimize? And not only that, but whose worship does he play up and whose does he minimize? We will then compare the results with how worship is described in the works that make up 1 Enoch.

Worship in Jubilees

The sole act of worship attributed to Adam in Jubilees is the burning of incense. According to Jub 3:27, "On that day, as he was leaving the Garden of

---

1. The word *kippēr* does occur in Gen 6:14 and 32:20. But in the first instance it refers to covering the ark with pitch, and in the second to Jacob's attempt at appeasing Esau when he goes back to the land of Canaan.

369

Eden, he burned incense as a pleasing fragrance — frankincense, galbanum, stacte, and aromatic spices — in the early morning when the sun rose at the time when he covered his shame."[2] One could have hoped for more. As Adam was the first to bear the divine image and likeness, to see the pristine splendor of God's creation, and to communicate directly with the Creator with no sense of guilt or shame, his worship before the fall could have been very useful to the author of Jubilees as a pattern for all his posterity. But instead we catch only a glimpse of the worship of Paradise as Adam is on his way out. It is more than we learn from Genesis. A curious beginning, but a beginning nonetheless. Adam is a priest.[3]

The earliest rite of worship, for the author of Jubilees, is the burning of incense. What is the reason for this? One possible answer is that at the time of Adam humans were not allowed to eat animals and so it was not fitting for Adam to offer up animal sacrifice. Full use of animals would come in the days of Noah, and for the author of Jubilees he would be the first to offer them. The problem with this solution is the sacrifice of Cain and Abel, which is pre-Noachic. One could persist by noting that while the word "sacrifice" is used in the Jubilees account of Cain and Abel, it is nowhere explicitly stated what those sacrifices were. But several passages in Jubilees seem to presuppose that the reader has knowledge of Genesis, and the Cain and Abel story is likely one of them. Alternatively, another reason for incense might be that the worship of the first human should come closest to that of heaven, and in heaven no animal sacrifices are made. Perhaps.

That Adam burns the incense on his way out of Eden is significant since according to Jub 4:26, this is one of the four places on earth that belongs to the Lord. It is where Enoch offers his sacrifice as well. Adam performs his act of worship at the rising of the sun, as would later be commanded in Exod 30:7.

As noted, the first sacrifice according to Genesis is offered by Cain and Abel. In Gen 4:3-5 the Hebrew *minchah* is used to describe the offerings of both brothers. This word can mean either a sacrifice or a nonsacral gift. In the LXX this distinction is recognized so that *minchah* is translated either by *thusia* (140 times) or *dōron* (30 times). Interestingly, the LXX refers to Cain's offering as *thusia* and Abel's as *dōron*, likely to emphasize that there was a

---

2. All quotations of Jubilees are from J. C. VanderKam, *The Book of Jubilees,* CSCO 511 (Louvain: Peeters, 1989).

3. This becomes clear by comparison with the author's description in Jub 4:25 of Enoch as a priest who offered incense, on which see the discussion below.

distinction between what the two brothers presented to God. But no attempt at differentiation is found in Jub 4:2 where Abel's offering is referred to as a sacrifice. This agrees with Josephus, who likewise refers to the actions of both brothers using the words *thuein* and *thusia* (*Ant* 1.54). More importantly, however, the author of Jubilees has passed over an opportunity to explain how the practice of sacrifice came into being and what it is that makes a sacrifice acceptable or unacceptable.[4]

In the generation after Cain and Abel, in the days of Enosh, a practice to call upon the name of the Lord was begun (Gen 4:26).[5] So begins communication with God by means of speech, or worship of the word. Jubilees notes the fact without further comment, merely changing the indefinite "was begun" to specify Enosh himself: "He was the first one to call on the Lord's name on the earth" (Jub 4:12). Interestingly, in all the other passages in Genesis where "calling on the name of the Lord" is mentioned, it is in connection with the building of an altar (Gen 12:8; 13:4; 26:25). The author of Jubilees includes all three of these passages in his retelling and adds in changes of his own. In the first two, which mention Abraham's worship, the writer gives the actual words of Abraham's address to God and explicitly states that sacrifice was offered. The third regards Isaac, and one can see the changes below:

Gen 26:25	Jub 24:23
"So he built an altar there, called on the name of the LORD, and pitched his tent there."	"There he built the altar which his father Abraham had first built. He called on the Lord's name and offered a sacrifice to the God of his father Abraham."

---

4. Gary Herion, in considering Genesis, has suggested the very simple and appealing answer that Cain's sacrifice was unacceptable because it was an offering from the ground that until the time of Noah lay under a curse. The curse lasted from the time of Gen 3:17 until Noah's sacrifice, which elicited God's promise never again to curse the ground. If this solution works for Genesis, it works even better for Jubilees where the atoning significance of Noah's sacrificing is stressed. Cf. G. Herion, "Why God Rejected Cain's Offering: The Obvious Answer," in *Fortunate the Eyes That See: Essays in Honor of David Noel Freedman in Celebration of His Seventieth Birthday*, ed. Astrid B. Beck, Andrew H. Bartelt, Paul R. Raabe, and Chris A. Franke (Grand Rapids: Eerdmans, 1995), 52-65.

5. So MT, though the text is somewhat ambiguous. Cf. the discussion in S. Fraade, "Enosh and His Generation Revisited," in *Biblical Figures outside the Bible*, ed. M. E. Stone and T. Bergren (Harrisburg, Pa.: Trinity, 1998), 60-61.

In this instance, the words of the prayer are not given, but sacrifice is specified once again. More importantly, the author twice mentions Abraham to emphasize the continuation between the practices of Isaac and his father. The fact that no such connections are made between the calling of Enosh and that of Abraham/Isaac invites speculation. It could be that he was aware of the tradition found in the later rabbinic writings that Gen 4:26 actually describes the beginning of idolatry.[6] But the fact that he acknowledges that Enosh called on the Lord would mean that he did not agree with that interpretation. This is further supported by the fact that in Jub 19:24-25, a passage not paraphrasing Genesis, Abraham describes his lineage as running through Shem, Noah, Enoch, Malaleel, Enos, Seth, and Adam.

Enoch plays a significant role in Jubilees, as is well known. About his worship Jub 4:25 states, "He [Enoch] burned the evening incense of the sanctuary which is acceptable before the Lord on the mountain *of incense*."[7] The context indicates that this mountain is in or near Eden. Jub 4:26 goes on to say that there are four places on earth where the Lord will accept sacrifice: the Garden of Eden, the mountain of the east (probably Mount Lubar, where the ark comes to rest in Jub 5:28 and where Noah will sacrifice),[8] Mount Sinai, and Mount Zion. Clearly Enoch is a priest. The offering up of incense connects his activity with that of Adam. The complementary nature of their worship is shown by the fact that Adam burned his incense in the morning (Exod 30:7) while Enoch offers incense in the evening (Exod 30:8).[9]

The author of Jubilees certainly knew about several of the texts that

6. Cf. Fraade, "Enosh," 74-80 and 81 n. 71.

7. R. H. Charles (*The Book of Jubilees or the Little Genesis* [London: Adam & Charles Black, 1902], 39) suggested, and O. Wintermute ("Jubilees," in *OTP* 2:63 n. n) attempted to demonstrate, that Enoch offered incense on the mount of the east. Charles further proposed as one possibility that this mount was close to Eden. Wintermute on the other hand leaned toward Taima/Teiman in Arabia due to its connections with the spice trade. But since Jub 3:27 already has Adam burning precisely incense in Eden, we should not rule out Eden since 4:23-24 clearly locates him there. If Enoch is in Eden, then we can see the mount of the east as another place, and I prefer Ararat since it is where Jubilees has Noah offer his sacrifice. This is another of Charles's alternatives. For a full discussion of the view that Enoch is in Eden, cf. J. C. VanderKam, *Enoch and the Growth of an Apocalyptic Tradition*, CBQMS 16 (Washington, D.C.: Catholic Biblical Association, 1984), 184-88.

8. That the mountain of the east is not near the other three places mentioned here is also indicated from Jub 8:19, which says that Eden, Mount Sinai, and Mount Zion all face each other. The only one not mentioned is the mountain of the east, which is most likely Mount Ararat referred to in 8:21.

9. For the textual problem regarding the phrase "evening incense of the sanctuary," cf. the discussion in VanderKam, *The Book of Jubilees*, 28.

presently make up the work we refer to as 1 Enoch.[10] But the idea of Enoch as priest did not come from 1 Enoch. And there is no mention in any of the individual Enochic documents that he offered incense or sacrifice of any kind. However, they do state many times that Enoch blessed and praised God, either as a result of his beholding the order and glory of creation (1 En 36:4; 81:3; 83:11–84:3) or because of the revelation of God's justice in judging the wicked and rewarding the righteous (22:14; 25:7; 27:5; 81:3; 90:40). The author of Jubilees passes over in silence this aspect of Enoch's worship.

Genesis gives more attention to Noah than to anyone previous. Jubilees follows suit. The first and only act of worship performed by Noah in Genesis is sacrifice. Here is a comparison between what we find in Genesis and what is in Jubilees:

Gen 8:20-21	Jub 6:1-4
"Then Noah built an altar to the LORD, and took of every clean animal and of every clean bird, and offered burnt offerings on the altar. And when the LORD smelled the pleasing odor, the LORD said in his heart, 'I will never again curse the ground because of humankind, for the inclination of the human heart is evil from youth. . . .'"	"On the first of the third month he left the ark and built an altar on this mountain. He appeared on the earth, took a kid, and atoned with its blood for all the sins of the earth because everything that was on it had been obliterated except for those who were in the ark with Noah. He placed the fat on the altar. Then he took a bull, a ram, a sheep, goats, salt, a turtledove, and a dove and offered (them as) a burnt offering on the altar. He poured on them an offering mixed with oil, sprinkled with wine, and put frankincense on everything. He sent up a pleasant fragrance that was pleasing before the Lord. The Lord smelled the pleasant fragrance and made a covenant with him that there would be no flood waters which would destroy the earth. . . ."

10. Cf. J. C. VanderKam, *Enoch: A Man for All Generations* (Columbia: University of South Carolina Press, 1995), 110-21.

Noah's actions in Jubilees are much more explicit than what we find in Genesis. He makes atonement for the sins of the earth.[11] He offers sacrifices of only the animals that are later prescribed by the Torah. And the details about the wine, oil, and frankincense are likewise in accord with what is found in the Torah (cf. Exod 29:40). Clearly Noah joins the ranks of the pre-Mosaic priests along with Adam and Enoch.[12]

The connection between Noah and Enoch is particularly stressed by the author of Jubilees. In Jub 7:38-39 Noah says the agricultural laws he gave to his sons in the preceding verses came originally from Enoch. And in Jub 21:10, where Abraham instructs Isaac about the proper way to sacrifice, he says, "All who eat it [a peace offering left until the third day] will bring guilt on themselves because this is the way I found (it) written in the book of my ancestors, in the words of Enoch and the words of Noah." Priestly knowledge comes to the chosen people via Enoch and Noah.

The sacrifice of Noah is followed by the well-known prohibition of eating meat with blood in it. In Jubilees, not only is Noah given this command, but he and his sons swear that they will keep it as a covenant forever (Jub 6:10), a detail not found in Genesis. This covenant with Noah, as those with Abraham (14:20) and Moses (1:1), is placed in the third month. As a yearly renewal of it, Noah and his sons kept the Feast of Weeks (6:17-18). But when Noah died, his sons both left off observing the feast and violated the prohibition of eating meat with blood. The Feast of Weeks would be observed again only when Abraham, Isaac, and Jacob revived it (6:19). The implication seems to be that now only the Israelites have the right to celebrate this festival (as already indicated in 6:14). This is similar to the sentiment expressed earlier in Jubilees about the Sabbath. Jub 2:30-33 begins by saying that the Sabbath has been given to all humanity, but quickly changes to say that God "did not sanctify any people(s) and nations to keep Sabbath on it except Israel alone."

So does this mean that the author of Jubilees saw no worship of God fitting for Gentiles? Were they completely shut out? Apparently not. Jub 7:20 states: "During the twenty-eighth jubilee Noah began to prescribe for his grandsons the ordinances and the commandments — every statute which he knew. He testified to his sons that they should do what is right, cover the shame of their bodies, bless the one who had created them, honor father and

---

11. 1QapGen 10:13 also refers to Noah atoning for the earth.

12. D. Dimant, "Noah in Early Jewish Literature," in *Biblical Figures outside the Bible*, 142, notes the association of Noah with proper calendar and calendrical calculation in Jubilees and concludes, "Noah was, then, the one best qualified for celebrating festivals, namely, for functioning as a priest."

mother, love one another, and keep themselves from fornication, uncleanness, and from all injustice." This passage indicates that blessing God was as
incumbent on humanity after the flood as covering one's body and honoring
father and mother. A universal responsibility.

Genesis reveals more of Abraham's worship than of any other character. The activity most commonly attributed to him is sacrifice. There are six
instances where Abraham offers sacrifice in Genesis and seven in Jubilees:

Genesis	Jubilees	Location
12:7	13:4	Shechem
12:8	13:7-9	Bethel
13:3-4	13:15-16	Bethel
13:18		Hebron
15:7-21	14:7-20	Hebron
	15:1-2 Weeks	Hebron
	16:20-31 Tabernacles	Beersheba
22:13	18:12 Passover	Mountain in Moriah

Just as was the case with Noah, Abraham too keeps the Feast of Weeks. But
with Noah the text of Genesis provided a nice lead-in regarding the date
with its statement that the flood had subsided and the earth was dry at the
end of the second month. The covenant of Gen 8:20 could therefore be
placed at the beginning of the third month and understood as the Feast of
Weeks. For Abraham, Jubilees manufactures an entirely new occasion,
though coming close on the heels of the covenant ceremony described in
Gen 15:7-21 (= Jub 14:7-20).

A new feast instituted by Abraham is the Feast of Tabernacles. The
event is given only the slightest connection to the text of Genesis in that it
takes place when Abraham and Sarah are rejoicing at the imminent birth of
Isaac. The feast is celebrated in Beersheba, and Jubilees tells us that Abraham
built an altar there, though no mention of this is found in Genesis. But for
the feast to be observed properly the author needs an altar, and since Isaac
was known to have built one there later (Gen 26:25), it was easy enough to
assume that Abraham built one too (cf. Jub 24:23).[13] Beersheba was also the

---

13. Also Gen 21:33, a verse not used in Jubilees, does associate Abraham with worship
in Beersheba in that he planted a tamarisk tree and called upon the name of the Lord there.
Since the latter activity is often connected with building an altar, it would be easy enough to
imagine that an altar was built in this instance as well.

place where Abraham was the first to celebrate the Feast of Unleavened Bread (Jub 18:18-19) just after the sacrifice of Isaac on Mount Zion, which the author of Jubilees connects with Passover (Jub 18:1-13).[14]

In connection with two of the sacrificial occasions in the table above, Abraham is also said to call upon the name of the Lord (Gen 12:8; 13:4). But in neither of these does Genesis tell what Abraham said. Jubilees fills in the lacunae. In the first he says, "You, my God, are the eternal God," and in the second, "You, Lord, most high God, are my God forever and ever" (Jub 13:8, 16). In fact, in Jubilees Abraham's very first reaching out to God is through prayer. As he realized the errors of paganism, "he began to pray to the creator of all that he would save him from the errors of mankind" (Jub 11:17). Some years later, as he looked up and observed the stars: "That night he prayed and said: My God, my God, God most High, You alone are my God. You have created everything; everything that was and has been is the product of your hands. You and your lordship I have chosen. Save me from the power of the evil spirits who rule the thoughts of people's minds. May they not mislead me from following you, my God. Do establish me and my posterity forever. May we not go astray from now until eternity" (Jub 12:19-20). In response to this prayer, God calls Abraham to leave Ur and promises to make of him a great people.

Not only is Abraham a man of prayer, but he is a man of blessing as well. Six times Jubilees says that Abraham "blessed the Lord" (13:7; 13:15; 16:26-27; 17:2-3; 22:4-6; 23:1), whereas the verb is never used with Abraham as subject in Genesis. Moreover, as is fitting in connection with the joyous Feast of Tabernacles, each morning during the festival "he would give praise and joyfully offer humble thanks to his God for everything" (Jub 16:31). If, therefore, Jubilees enhances the portrayal of Abraham's worship through sacrifice, it does so even more with regard to Abraham's spoken acts of worship.

In contrast, however, the remarkable prayers of the unnamed servant who goes to Haran to get a wife for Isaac in Gen 24 are totally omitted from the account in Jubilees. And while other explanations are possible, one wonders if some of the lack of interest is due to the fact that the servant was not from the chosen line.[15]

---

14. Cf. B. Halpern-Amaru, "The Festivals of Pesaḥ and Massot in the Book of Jubilees," in this volume.

15. Betsy Halpern-Amaru suggests that the main cause of the author's disapproval was the irregularity of the way the marriage arrangements were made, though apparently Josephus did not share this feeling since he includes the servant's prayers in his account in *Ant* 1.242-255.

Of all the Gentiles mentioned in connection with Abraham, the most interesting and important is Melchizedek. Genesis clearly acknowledges him as a true priest of God and records that he blessed God (Gen 14:20). If Melchizedek's role is lessened and his blessing of God passed over in silence, one could argue that there was an intentional effort to minimize mention of Gentiles offering acceptable worship to God. Unfortunately, there is a lacuna in all known manuscripts of Jubilees here that keeps us from knowing whether Melchizedek was described as a true priest of God and whether the words of his blessing were recounted. The only thing we know for sure is that Abraham gave Melchizedek the tithe from his spoils. Still, there is no mention of Melchizedek elsewhere in Jubilees,[16] as there is of Enoch and Noah. And unlike Enoch and Noah, Melchizedek is not said to have passed down writings, or regulations about sacrificial procedure and worship, or predictions about future events. These facts justify the conclusion that the figure of Melchizedek was not of special significance for the author of Jubilees in establishing true religion, either among the Gentiles or among the children of Abraham.

So the question remains whether with the advent of Abraham and the concept of the chosen people, there is any role left for the Gentiles in the worship of the true and living God. The answer is difficult to discern. At the end of his life, Abraham keeps the Feast of Weeks one last time with his sons Isaac and Ishmael. After he ate of the feast prepared by Isaac, "he blessed the most high God who created the heavens and the earth, who made all the fat things of the earth, and gave them to mankind to eat, drink, and bless their Creator" (Jub 22:6). We might think from this that the principle of blessing God holds for all mankind, but this is countered by the fact that Abraham's blessing is connected to a feast that would later serve to mark Israel as God's covenant people. This point is strengthened when we note that eating, drinking, and blessing the Creator are activities connected with the Sabbath in Jub 2:21, which is given only to Israel. Moreover, just a little later Abraham on his deathbed addresses Jacob and warns him to separate from the nations, "for all their actions are something that is impure, and all their ways are defiled and something abominable and detestable" (22:16). Then follows a denunciation of their sacrifices made to the dead and their worship offered

16. There is no indication that the author of Jubilees equated Melchizedek with Shem, as later the rabbis would do, in order to explain that his priesthood passed to Levi. Cf. F. L. Horton, *The Melchizedek Tradition,* SNTSMS 30 (Cambridge: Cambridge University Press, 1976), 114-24.

to demons (22:17-22). It is difficult to see how the worship of people who are described in these terms could ever be acceptable to God.[17]

Far less space is devoted to Isaac than to either Abraham or Jacob in Genesis. The same is true in Jubilees. One addition Jubilees does make in its account of Isaac is his celebration of the Feast of Weeks with Abraham just before his death, as mentioned in the previous paragraph. Although both Ishmael and Isaac come to Hebron, it is Isaac who slaughters the sacrifice on his father's altar there. And it is Isaac who prepares "a joyful feast in front of his brother Ishmael" (Jub 22:3-4). The passive involvement of Ishmael shows the future course of his descendants away from the service of God. This may also explain why in Jub 20:1-9 Abraham commands both Ishmael and Isaac to circumcise their children and worship the Most High God rather than idols, although in Jub 15:30, in the midst of another passage dealing with circumcision, the revealing angel says God did not choose to give the covenant to Ishmael or Esau, but chose Israel instead.

This writing out of the Gentiles by the author of Jubilees continues in the narrative about Jacob. This may be seen when Jacob leaves Haran and is pursued by his father-in-law Laban. In Gen 31:53 Laban and Jacob swear an oath by "the God of Abraham and the God of Nahor." But Jubilees simply says, "Jacob swore to Laban and Laban to Jacob" (Jub 29:7). Also, in Jubilees Jacob does not ask his kinsfolk to help build the heap of stones that is to stand as a witness between himself and Laban (Jub 29:8). Jacob is thus cleared of involvement in any act that might connect him with the religion of his father-in-law, who after all was a pagan.[18]

Most significant is the retelling of the story of Dinah's rape by Shechem and the revenge taken by Levi and Simeon. Two points stand out. First, in Jubilees, immediately after the basic story has been told, the angel of the presence, who is relating it to Moses, breaks in to give a discourse about the evil of intermarriage. He warns: "If one does this or shuts his eyes to those who do impure things and who defile the Lord's sanctuary and to those who profane his holy name, then the entire nation will be condemned together because of all this impurity and this contamination. There will be no favoritism nor par-

---

17. Cf. also Jub 15:26-34 where, although it is stated that all nations belong to God (v. 31), circumcision is given to Israel in order to make them like the angels who were created circumcised (v. 27). All those not part of this human-angelic assembly, i.e., the Gentiles, are destined for destruction. If true worship is to imitate or join with the angels, then it would seem the Gentiles are excluded from it.

18. Cf. also Jub 31:2, which explicitly says the idols Rachel stole from her father were destroyed later on.

tiality; there will be no receiving from him of fruit, sacrifices, offerings, fat, or the aroma of pleasing fragrance so that he should accept it. (So) is any man or woman in Israel to be who defiles his sanctuary" (Jub 30:15-16). Clearly, for the author of Jubilees the entire sacrificial system is threatened by intermarriage. Second, the angel announces that Levi and his descendants are destined for the priesthood because of his desire to see justice done (Jub 30:18).

The prediction made is fulfilled in Jub 32, though for a different reason. Rachel is pregnant with Benjamin and Jacob is giving his tithe of all he had to the Lord, including people. Counting his sons in order from Benjamin up, the tenth was Levi and so Levi becomes priest (32:3). Jacob gives the tithe to him, and he acts as priest in the presence of his father (32:8-9). All this happens during the seventh month, the time of the Feast of Tabernacles, at Bethel. Jacob has it in mind to build a permanent sanctuary in Bethel, but is told by God in a dream not to do it. As readers, we know why: it is not one of the four places on earth that belong to the Lord, according to Jub 4:26.

While Jacob keeps the Feast of Tabernacles just as Abraham did, there is a new observance attributed to him as well. And it too occurs in the seventh month. On the tenth of this month, Jacob's sons falsely tell him of the death of Joseph, when they had really sold him into slavery. The guilt they incurred by causing their father such grief would be removed by an act of sacrificial atonement, being remembered by their descendants in an annual Day of Atonement. In the words of the angel: "This day has been ordained so that they may be saddened on it for their sins, all their transgressions, and all their errors; so that they may purify themselves on this day once a year" (Jub 34:19; cf. also 5:17-18).

Still, Joseph was not dead, and a joyful reunion with his father eventually results. Gen 46:30 reports the words of Jacob upon their meeting as follows, "Now I can die, having seen for myself that you are still alive." But Jubilees expands this greatly: "Israel said to Joseph, 'Now let me die after I have seen you. Now may the Lord, the God of Israel, the God of Abraham, and the God of Isaac — who has not withheld his kindness and his mercy from his servant Jacob — be blessed. . . . May the Lord my God be blessed forever and ever and may his name be blessed.' . . . He blessed the creator of all who had preserved him and preserved his twelve sons for him" (Jub 45:3-5). As with Abraham, the portrait of Jacob in Jubilees is richer than what we find in Genesis with regard to his worship of God through speech (cf. also 29:4; 31:31; 32:7).[19]

---

19. It is interesting in Jub 29:1-4 that while overall the text shortens the account found in Genesis, the statement about Jacob's blessing God is added.

Summary of Conclusions

In Genesis, sacrifice is mentioned twelve times (Gen 4:4-5; 8:20-21; 12:7, 8; 13:4, 18; 22:13; 26:25; 31:54; 33:20; 35:1-7; 46:1). In Jubilees this is almost doubled to twenty-three times (Jub 4:2; 6:1-4, 14, 22; 7:3-5, 30; 13:4, 9, 16; 14:9-19; 15:2; 16:20-23; 18:12; 21:7-19; 22:3-5; 24:23; 30:16; 32:4-6; 32:27; 34:18; 44:1; 49:22; 50:10). The references tend to emphasize the place, procedure, and people that make sacrificial worship proper and acceptable.

The author of Jubilees could not get around the fact that in Genesis there is no one place where sacrifice was offered. As we saw above, therefore, Jubilees follows the Genesis account in having Abraham offering sacrifice in Shechem, Bethel, and Hebron. In fact, rather surprisingly, Jubilees adds a new site to the list by referring to an altar that Abraham built in Beersheba that is not mentioned in Genesis (Jub 16:20). In spite of this, however, the author manages to indicate that the true intent of God is to limit the places that are acceptable to God for ritual worship. We see this early on with the statement in Jub 4:26 that there are four places that belong to the Lord: the Garden of Eden, the mountain of the east, Mount Sinai, and Mount Zion.[20]

A special prominence is given to Mount Zion, as one might expect. According to 4:26, it was to have a special role in the renewal of the earth since from there "the earth will be sanctified from all its sins and from its uncleanness into the history of eternity." Jub 8:19 refers to Zion as the "middle of the earth."[21] And according to Jub 8:13, Abraham offers up Isaac on Mount Zion. Then, finally, in Jub 32 Jacob desires to build a permanent sanctuary in Bethel, but God forbids it. After allowing Jacob to read the heavenly tablets in which future events are inscribed, God tells him, "Do not build up this place, and do not make it an eternal temple. Do not live here because this is not the place" (32:22). The implication is clear: the future lies with Mount Zion.

Approaching God in the proper way is also very important to the author of Jubilees. Of course, this usually means following the prescriptions that would later be laid down in the Torah. Books were written with the pre-Mosaic Torah regulations. They were authored by Enoch and Noah (Jub 21:10). Noah passed his books on to his son Shem, and from him they were passed to Abraham (10:14; 12:27). On one occasion Jacob was allowed to read

---

20. Later on in Jub 8:19 only three sites are identified as places holy to the Lord.

21. Cf. J. Scott, *Geography in Early Judaism and Christianity: The Book of Jubilees*, SNTSMS 113 (Cambridge: Cambridge University Press, 2002), 34.

in the heavenly tablets about celebrating the Feast of Tabernacles an additional day (32:28). Information was also passed on by word of mouth. Abraham gives detailed instruction to Isaac before he dies about how to worship God (21:5-20).

This leads us to consider the people who are fit to offer up worship. In Jubilees a shift takes place with the giving of the covenant to Abraham. Up until that time, the sacrifice of Abel is acceptable and Enosh can call upon the name of the Lord. But the lack of enthusiasm that the author has for these figures is clear when seen in comparison with his descriptions of the worship of Adam, Enoch, and especially Noah.

With the appearance of Abraham, a special effort is made to separate and distinguish the religious practice of Abraham, Isaac, and Jacob from that of all others. As mentioned, when Abraham gives his farewell address to Isaac, it is full of instruction about sacrificial ritual. But it is noteworthy that when he similarly addresses for the last time Ishmael and Keturah's sons, he gives them commands about avoiding immorality and idolatry, but nothing about sacrifice (21:1-10). They don't need to know. When Ishmael and Isaac celebrate the Feast of Tabernacles with their father, Jubilees is very careful to say that Isaac offered the sacrifice and prepared the meal. The story of the rape of Dinah is used as an opportunity for the angel of the presence to break in and warn against intermarriage, which will defile the sanctuary and invalidate its sacrifices.

With this determined writing out of the Gentiles beginning in the time of Abraham, it would be of greatest interest to know what the author of Jubilees made of the enigmatic Melchizedek. Unfortunately, textual corruption has robbed us of the ability to know as much as we would like. Immediately after a lacuna of uncertain length, Abraham gives Melchizedek the tithe. But the terms and conditions under which Abraham does this are unknown. The fact that the patriarchs never refer to Melchizedek as one of their sources of priestly knowledge is telling.

So far we have limited our review to sacrifice and related matters. But what about the less formal approach to God through prayer, praise, and blessing? Here too there is a significant difference between the stories told in Genesis and those told in Jubilees. In Genesis, the blessing of God occurs only two times, and both are done by the same person — the unnamed servant of Abraham who finds Isaac a bride (Gen 24:27, 48). While all mention of this servant is omitted from Jubilees, God is still blessed eighteen times. Only now it is by Noah (Jub 7:20), Abraham (13:7; 13:15; 16:26-27; 17:2-3; 22:4-6; 23:1), Rebekah (25:11-15), Jacob (29:4; 31:31; 32:7; 45:3-5), Levi (32:1), and the people of Israel (2:21; 49:6; 50:9). Often this blessing is connected with praise and thanksgiving.

An important question is whether, for the author of Jubilees, this noncultic worship is possible for Gentiles. In Jub 7:20 Noah includes a command to "bless the one who had created them" as he prescribes for his grandsons what is required of them. But succeeding events make it clear that they do not live up to their responsibilities. Is the right then forfeited? Especially after the covenant with Abraham when cultic worship becomes the prerogative of the descendants of Abraham alone? The one passage that might help answer this is Jub 22:6. After Abraham eats a feast prepared by Isaac, "he blessed the most high God who created the heavens and the earth, who made all the fat things of the earth, and gave them to mankind to eat, drink, and bless their Creator." This would seem to indicate that the Noachic ordinance still stands. But the rest of Jubilees is so negative about the Gentiles that one could well imagine that its author never seriously entertained the idea that a Gentile would or could offer sincere praise to God (cf. Jub 22:16-22).

Jubilees and Enoch

Examination of all the passages dealing with worship in the works that make up 1 Enoch shows that blessing is by far the most common. It appears eight times in the Book of the Watchers (10:21; 22:14; 25:7; 27:3-5 [3x]; 36:4 [2x]), sixteen times in the Book of the Parables (39:7, 9 [2x], 10, 12 [2x], 13; 40:4, 5; 47:2; 48:5, 10; 61:7, 9; 71:11, 12), three times in the Astronomical Book (81:3 [2x], 10), twice in the Book of Dream Visions (83:11; 84:1), and once in the Epistle of Enoch (90:40). As we have seen, blessing is also characteristic in descriptions of worship in Jubilees, suggesting an immediate connection. In Jubilees the only activity mentioned more frequently than blessing is sacrifice. In stark contrast to Jubilees, however, none of the Enochic works mentions sacrifice as a way to approach God.[22] It is true that the temple is referred to often in the Animal Apocalypse,[23] and the temple implies sacrifice. But it is still remarkable that among all the references to worship throughout the entire corpus, no direct reference to sacrifice occurs. For me this raises

22. The sole occurrence of the word is in 1 En 19:1, which speaks about the spirits of the angels leading men astray to sacrifice to demons.

23. Cf. 1 En 89:36, 40, 50, 54, 56, 66-67, 72-73, 76 (?); 90:28-29, 33-34, 36; 91:13 (?); 93:7-8.

the question of the extent to which priestly issues were truly a concern to the authors or communities behind these works.

I want to look briefly at one passage that further demonstrates the difference of thought between the works of Enoch and Jubilees. The passage is 1 En 10:20-22:

> And you [Michael], cleanse the earth from all wrong, and from all iniquity, and from all sin, and from all impiety, and from all the uncleanness which is brought about on the earth; remove them from the earth. And all the sons of men shall be righteous, and all the nations shall serve and bless me, and all shall worship me. And the earth will be cleansed from all corruption, and from all sin, and from all wrath, and from all torment; and I will not again send a flood upon it for all generations for ever.[24]

This passage expresses an ideal of universal worship that is elsewhere found in the Book of the Watchers, at 36:4. In the Book of the Parables it occurs at 48:5 and 57:3. A hint of it may appear in the Book of Dream Visions, at 84:1. While not connected with the idea of worship, a universal hope for the Gentiles appears in the Epistle of Enoch at 90:37-38 and 91:14. Thus, intriguingly, the idea occurs throughout the corpus.[25]

Where does this viewpoint come from? The concept of universal blessing is closest to sentiments found in Pss 67:3-5 and 145:5. The idea of a future for the nations after a time of judgment is perhaps most clearly expressed in Isa 24–27. But the verbal parallels are not clear enough to be certain that these passages provided the inspiration. There may be a reference to Deut 28:12 in 1 En 11:1,[26] though in my opinion the egalitarian nature of 10:21 rules out reading Enoch in the light of Deut 28. In any event, the universalistic worship envisioned in the Enochic works certainly marks a great divide with the view expressed in Jubilees.

---

24. Translation of M. Knibb, *The Ethiopic Book of Enoch* (Oxford: Oxford University Press, 1978), 2:91.

25. A slightly different view is expressed in 1 En 90:30 where the Gentiles signify their recognition of God by reverencing Israel. This idea has clear connections with Deut 28:12-13; Isa 60:11; 61:6; 66:12; Zech 8:20-23; and Hag 2:6-9.

26. But the "opening of the storehouses of blessing" might be read against Gen 7:11 "the windows of the heavens were opened."

The Book of Jubilees and Early Jewish Mysticism

Martha Himmelfarb

Does the book of Jubilees belong to the history of Jewish mysticism? Jubilees contains neither a vision of the *merkabah,* the chariot throne of God from the book of Ezekiel, nor ascent to heaven, the features central to the Jewish mysticism of antiquity as delineated by Gershom Scholem in his pioneering work, *Major Trends in Jewish Mysticism.*[1] Yet Jubilees shares other significant features with other texts of the second temple period that are often associated with early Jewish mysticism such as the Book of the Watchers (1 En 1–36) and the Songs of the Sabbath Sacrifice, as well as with the *hekhalot* texts, the literature of the fully developed *merkabah* mysticism of late antiquity. And while scholarly literature on early Jewish mysticism has in general paid little attention to Jubilees, it figures prominently in Rachel Elior's recent book on early Jewish mysticism, *The Three Temples: On the Emergence of Jewish Mysticism,* which I discuss below.[2]

As my discussion already suggests, scholars have tended to treat early Jewish mysticism as a textual tradition defined by the presence of several interrelated motifs and ideas, most prominent among them the vision of the *merkabah* and ascent to heaven noted in the previous paragraph. In this they

---

1. G. Scholem, *Major Trends in Jewish Mysticism* (New York: Schocken, 1961; 1st ed. 1941), 1-39; on early Jewish mysticism, 5.

2. R. Elior, *The Three Temples: On the Emergence of Jewish Mysticism,* trans. David Louvish (Oxford and Portland, Oreg.: Littman Library of Jewish Civilization, 2004). The Hebrew original is entitled *Temple and Chariot, Priests and Angels, Sanctuary and Heavenly Sanctuaries in Early Jewish Mysticism* (Jerusalem: Hebrew University Magnes Press, 2002).

are following Scholem's lead. While the comments on the religious character of *merkabah* mysticism scattered through the second chapter of *Major Trends* are still of interest despite advances in the more than sixty-five years since he wrote, Scholem did not spend much time on a theoretical discussion of the nature of early Jewish mysticism; the discussion of the nature of mysticism in the first chapter of *Major Trends* is concerned primarily with kabbalah, the classical form of Jewish mysticism that emerged in the Middle Ages.[3] Scholars since Scholem have given rather little attention to defining the mysticism of the early Jewish mystical tradition as a religious phenomenon in terms that could be used for comparative purposes.[4] A recent exception to this generalization is Philip S. Alexander's *Mystical Texts,* in the Companion to the Qumran Scrolls series, which treats the Songs of the Sabbath Sacrifice and other texts from among the Dead Sea Scrolls.[5] Two features of Alexander's discussion are particularly noteworthy, his claim that praxis is central to the definition of mysticism, and his challenge to Scholem's view that the *merkabah* tradition did not involve *unio mystica*.[6] This is not the place for an evaluation of Alexander's valuable but problematic work; in my view, many aspects of Alexander's readings of the texts are quite persuasive, but I am skeptical about the claim that the scrolls reflect a mystical practice and *unio mystica*.

Further, while the benefits of a clear definition of mysticism are evident for the purposes of cross-cultural comparison or even for exploration of the problem of continuity from early Jewish mysticism to kabbalah, in this paper I make use of a motif-based description of a tradition instead. The question of interest for this paper is not whether Jubilees truly belongs to the phenomenon of "mysticism" — if mysticism demands praxis, much less *unio mystica,* then surely it does not — but rather how Jubilees relates to a body of texts that share a constellation of motifs. The history of scholarly discussion of these texts makes "early Jewish mysticism" a convenient way to refer to them. While the results may not tell us much about the phenomenon

---

3. Scholem, *Major Trends,* 1-39 (chap. 1, "General Characteristics of Jewish Mysticism"), 40-79 (chap. 2, "Merkabah Mysticism and Jewish Gnosticism").

4. On this point, see E. R. Wolfson, "Mysticism and the Poetic-Liturgical Compositions from Qumran: A Response to Bilhah Nitzan," *JQR* 85 (1994): 184-202; Michael D. Swartz, "The Dead Sea Scrolls and Later Jewish Magic and Mysticism," *DSD* 8 (2001): 182-90.

5. Philip S. Alexander, *Mystical Texts,* Companion to the Qumran Scrolls 7, Library of Second Temple Studies 61 (London: T. & T. Clark, 2006).

6. Alexander, *Mystical Texts,* 7-10, 93-120, 136-38. Scholem asserts reservations, very briefly, about the centrality of *unio mystica* in mysticism, Jewish and other; *Major Trends,* 5.

of mysticism, Jubilees' relationship to these texts is nonetheless of considerable interest, with important implications for the understanding of Jubilees.

In *Major Trends,* Scholem delineated three stages of *merkabah* mysticism: traditions found in the apocalyptic literature of the second temple period; the speculation of the Tannaim, the rabbis of the first and second centuries of this era; and finally the *hekhalot* texts, which Scholem dated to the period of the *amoraim,* the rabbis of the third through fifth centuries.[7] The scholarship of the last decades of the twentieth century developed and refined Scholem's understanding of *merkabah* mysticism, but it also raised important questions about his representation of each of the three stages.[8] For the third stage, the *hekhalot* texts, in which Scholem saw ascent to heaven as the defining interest, recent scholarship has pointed out that the adjuration of angels is also a central concern;[9] there have also been strong arguments for moving the date of the *hekhalot* texts forward into the Islamic period.[10] For the second stage, the *merkabah* mysticism attested in early rabbinic literature, scholarship since Scholem has questioned the existence of a tradition of mystical practice and has emphasized the exegetical aspect of the Tannaitic traditions and even of later material in classical rabbinic sources,[11] thus demonstrating that the relationship of these *merkabah* materials to the *hekhalot* literature is less direct and more complex than Scholem suggested.[12]

7. Scholem, *Major Trends,* 43.

8. To the best of my knowledge, there is no article or book chapter devoted to a critical discussion of scholarship on the *hekhalot* literature since Scholem. For recent listings of publications that supplement each other, see Rebecca Macy Lesses, *Ritual Practices to Gain Power: Angels, Incantations, and Revelation in Early Jewish Mysticism,* HTS 44 (Harrisburg, Pa.: Trinity, 1998), 3 n. 8; and James R. Davila, *Descenders to the Chariot: The People behind the Hekhalot Literature,* JSJSup 70 (Leiden: Brill, 2001), 316-17.

9. Peter Schäfer, "The Aim and Purpose of Early Jewish Mysticism," in *Hekhalot-Studien,* TSAJ 19 (Tübingen: Mohr [Siebeck], 1988), 277-95, and *The Hidden and Manifest God: Some Major Themes in Early Jewish Mysticism,* trans. Aubrey Pomerance (Albany: State University of New York Press, 1992), esp. 142-46, 151-57; David J. Halperin, *The Faces of the Chariot: Early Jewish Responses to Ezekiel's Vision,* TSAJ 16 (Tübingen: Mohr [Siebeck], 1988), esp. 376-87.

10. Most recently, Ra'anan S. Boustan, "The Emergence of Pseudonymous Attribution in Heikhalot Literature: Empirical Evidence from the Jewish 'Magical' Corpora," *JSQ* 14 (2007): 18-38.

11. David J. Halperin, *The Merkabah in Rabbinic Literature,* AOS 62 (New Haven: American Oriental Society, 1980), esp. 179-85.

12. For a range of views on the nature of the relationship, all at some distance from Scholem's, see P. S. Alexander, "The Historical Setting of the Hebrew Book of Enoch," *JJS* 28 (1977): 156-80; Halperin, *Faces of the Chariot,* esp. 427-46; Schäfer, "Aim and Purpose," 289-95, and *Hidden and Manifest God,* 157-61; Michael D. Swartz, *Scholastic Magic: Ritual*

The first stage of *merkabah* mysticism, the traditions found in the apocalyptic literature of the second temple period, is the least developed stage in Scholem's discussion. Scholem touched briefly on apocalyptic literature in *Major Trends* and had only a little more to say in his one book on early Jewish mysticism, *Jewish Gnosticism, Merkabah Mysticism, and Talmudic Tradition*.[13] The last third of the twentieth century saw dramatic growth in scholarly interest in apocalyptic literature, and several scholars took up the challenge posed by Scholem's work, offering more detailed discussions of the themes and motifs of *merkabah* mysticism as they appeared in the apocalypses.[14]

The last decades of the twentieth century also saw the ongoing publication of the Dead Sea Scrolls, a corpus of major significance for our understanding of the apocalypses and early Jewish mysticism. Scholem was clearly aware of the potential significance of the scrolls for early Jewish mysticism, and in *Jewish Gnosticism* he noted some parallels between the poetry of the *hekhalot* texts and that of the Hodayot and the "Angelic Liturgy," as the early publication of a portion of the Songs of the Sabbath Sacrifice was called. But the slow pace of publication meant that he was not in a position to offer an overall evaluation of their significance for early Jewish mysticism before his death in 1982. By the end of the twentieth century, however, the relationship of the scrolls to *merkabah* mysticism had become a topic of considerable scholarly interest.[15] Alexander's *Mystical Texts* is the first book-length study

and Revelation in Early Jewish Mysticism (Princeton: Princeton University Press, 1996), esp. 209-29.

13. Gershom G. Scholem, *Jewish Gnosticism, Merkabah Mysticism, and Talmudic Tradition* (New York: Jewish Theological Seminary of America, 1960).

14. See, e.g., Ithamar Gruenwald, *Apocalyptic and Merkavah Mysticism*, AGJU 14 (Leiden: Brill, 1980); Halperin, *Faces of the Chariot*, 63-114; Martha Himmelfarb, "Heavenly Ascent and the Relationship of the Apocalypses and the *Hekhalot* Literature," HUCA 59 (1988): 73-100; Himmelfarb, "The Practice of Ascent in the Ancient Mediterranean World," in *Death, Ecstasy, and Other Worldly Journeys*, ed. John J. Collins and Michael Fishbane (Albany: State University of New York Press, 1995), 121-37; James R. Davila, "The Hekhalot Literature and the Ancient Jewish Apocalypses," in *Paradise Now: Essays on Early Jewish and Christian Mysticism*, ed. April DeConick, SBLSymS 11 (Atlanta: Society of Biblical Literature, 2006), 105-25.

15. See the review article of Elisabeth Hamacher, "Die Sabbatopferlieder im Streit um Ursprung und Anfänge der jüdischen Mystik," *JJS* 27 (1996): 119-54. Since 1996, see, e.g., James R. Davila, "The Dead Sea Scrolls and Merkavah Mysticism," in *The Dead Sea Scrolls in Their Historical Context*, ed. Timothy H. Lim (Edinburgh: T. & T. Clark, 2000), 249-64; Swartz, "The Dead Sea Scrolls and Later Jewish Magic and Mysticism"; and Ra'anan Abusch, "Sevenfold Hymns in the *Songs of the Sabbath Sacrifice* and the Hekhalot Literature: Formal-

of the scrolls and *merkabah* mysticism, as far as I know; as I have noted, it focuses particularly on the Songs of the Sabbath Sacrifice, but it also finds evidence for this mysticism in other texts among the scrolls, especially liturgical texts and the so-called Self-Glorification Hymn. Following Johann Maier, Alexander understands *merkabah* mysticism to have originated among Jerusalem priests; eventually some of their heirs brought the tradition to Qumran, where it underwent a reworking with the concerns of a sect alienated from the Jerusalem temple in view.[16] With the destruction of the temple, the tradition was maintained by priests who became members of the rabbinic movement, though it stood in considerable tension with the dominant ideology of the rabbis; the *hekhalot* literature that appears toward the end of the rabbinic period is, in Alexander's view, a somewhat rabbinized version of the *merkabah* tradition. Although he catalogues a body of parallels between the Qumran texts and the *hekhalot* literature, Alexander emphasizes the "oblique" character of the relationship between the two forms of *merkabah* mysticism: the former is a "sectarian reworking of a priestly doctrine," while the latter is a reworking of that original doctrine "more in keeping with the rabbinic ethos."[17]

But what is most important in Alexander's book for our purposes is the very brief consideration of Jubilees in its discussion of the larger context of the relevant scrolls in the literature of the second temple period. Alexander points out that Jubilees shares with the Book of the Watchers and other works of the second temple period two important and interrelated features that appear elsewhere in the tradition of *merkabah* mysticism: an understanding of heaven as temple and of a group of human beings as the earthly counterpart of the angels.[18] I shall return to their significance for Jubilees' relationship to the early Jewish mystical tradition shortly.

While Alexander's book focuses primarily on the scrolls, Rachel Elior's *Three Temples,* which appeared a few years before Alexander's book, undertakes to sketch the entire early history of Jewish mysticism from the Bible through the *hekhalot* texts. I have offered my views on Elior's work at some

---

ism, Hierarchy and the Limits of Human Participation," in *The Dead Sea Scrolls as Background to Postbiblical Judaism and Early Christianity: Papers from an International Conference at St. Andrews in 2001,* ed. James R. Davila, STDJ 46 (Leiden and Boston: Brill, 2003), 220-47.

16. Alexander, *Mystical Texts,* 128-31; Johann Maier, *Vom Kultus zur Gnosis,* Kairos Religionswissenschaftliche Studien 1 (Salzburg: Otto Mueller, 1964).

17. Alexander, *Mystical Texts,* 122-38; quotations, 135.

18. Alexander, *Mystical Texts,* 55-56, 139.

length elsewhere.[19] Here I will focus only on the aspects of her discussion of early Jewish mysticism in which Jubilees plays a central role.

Like Maier and Alexander, Elior finds the origins of early Jewish mysticism in priestly circles, and like Alexander, she emphasizes the contribution to its development of priests alienated from the priestly establishment of the second temple period. In her view the scrolls and other works of the period, especially the apocalypses, are the work of these alienated priests. More than Alexander, Elior sees the *hekhalot* texts as standing in direct continuity with what she calls the "heavenly corpus" of these priests, though she notes the "neutralization" of their critique of the Jerusalem temple establishment in the *hekhalot* literature, which was composed long after the destruction of that temple.[20]

Jubilees figures prominently in Elior's picture of early Jewish mysticism. Though Elior has little to say about the heavenly temple in Jubilees, like Alexander, she notes the importance of the correspondence of heaven and earth for it. But Elior also focuses considerable attention on an aspect of that correspondence that does not figure at all in Alexander's discussion, calendar:[21]

> According to the authors of Jubilees and the Apocalypse of Weeks, not only does cyclic time, as represented by the calendar, flow in an eternal sevenfold rhythm through the sabbaths of the year — but the whole of history, from beginning to end, marches forward in recurrent cycles of sabbaths, years, sabbaticals, jubilees, and ages. . . . Heaven and earth have thereby been linked together since the seven days of Creation, through signs, covenants, and oaths that constitute bonds between God and man, through the sacrifices that man offers God, in a fixed, sevenfold progression governed by the solar calendar and observed by the angels.[22]

The picture of that calendar that Elior constructs draws on the contents of a number of texts; the conflation of sources is characteristic of Elior's approach to what she takes to be a common body of mystical tradition. It

19. Martha Himmelfarb, "Merkavah Mysticism since Scholem: Rachel Elior's *The Three Temples*," in *Wege mystischer Gotteserfahrung/Mystical Approaches to God*, ed. Peter Schäfer, Schriften des Historischen Kollegs Kolloquien 65 (Munich: Oldenbourg, 2006), 19-36.

20. Elior, *Three Temples*, 232-33.

21. She devotes chaps. 3–6 of *Three Temples* to the calendar, 82-152.

22. Elior, *Three Temples*, 135.

would be difficult to deduce most of what Elior claims about the mystical calendar from the Apocalypse of Weeks, while the idea of a succession of ages is by no means obvious in Jubilees. Further, it is clearly Jubilees that provides the key to understanding the calendar's significance. But the problems in the assumption that Jubilees and the Apocalypse of Weeks share the same understanding of calendar need not detain us here. What is most important for us is that Elior calls attention to the connection between heaven and earth built into creation through the institution of the Sabbath with its ongoing implications that is central to Jubilees: "[Jubilees'] aim is to recount the mythical, mystical, and angelic nature of the oaths and the covenants, to demonstrate their cultic nature and the eternal validity of the commandments associated with them, to indicate their relationship with the sevenfold structure of the solar calendar, which links the heavens with the earth, the angels ministering in heaven with the priests ministering on earth, through the succession of weeks and sabbaths, sabbaticals and jubilees."[23]

Despite my reservations about her harmonizing approach and her use of terms such as "mythical" and "mystical" in the passage just quoted, I agree wholeheartedly with Elior's understanding of the calendar of Jubilees as reflecting the correspondence between heaven and earth. Yet Jubilees uses the idea of the correspondence between heaven and earth, heavenly temple and earthly temple, angelic service and human service, to very different ends from other works in which these correspondences play a role.

The idea of heaven as a temple is widespread in literature of the second temple period, but it has its roots in the Bible and the ancient Near East, where the temples in which human beings worship are understood as replicas of the true house of the god, located on a distant mountain or, in the case of the God of Israel, in heaven.[24] In the apocalypses of the second temple period, heaven is understood either as God's palace, as in the book of Daniel, or as a temple, as in the Book of the Watchers; the two images are complementary, two different ways of characterizing God's abode. In the Book of the Watchers the picture of heaven as temple is important for the narrative and crucial to the message of the work. In some later apocalypses, in which heaven is represented as a temple, this fact is of little consequence for the narrative or the message of the work; it is simply taken for granted.

While Jubilees never makes the idea of heaven as temple explicit, it is

23. Elior, *Three Temples*, 135.
24. See the discussion of Torleif Elgvin, "Biblical Roots of Early Mystical Traditions on the Heavenly Temple," *Hen* 31, no. 1 (2009).

implicit in Jubilees' claim that the Sabbath (Jub 2:30) and the Feast of Weeks (6:18) were observed in heaven before they were observed on earth. It is possible that Jubilees also means to claim that the Feast of Booths was observed in heaven before Abraham established it on earth since it describes Abraham as the "first man on earth" to celebrate it (16:21).[25] Jubilees explicitly requires sacrifices for these festivals as they are observed on earth;[26] this suggests that their heavenly observance would also have required use of a sanctuary, though Jubilees offers no hint of how it understands the heavenly equivalent of sacrifice, a topic on which some texts are more forthcoming.[27]

The only point related to the heavenly temple on which Jubilees is explicit is the correspondence between earthly priests and angels. Thus Isaac blesses Levi, "May the Lord give you and your descendants greatness and glory, and set you and your descendants apart from all mankind to minister to him and to serve *him* in his sanctuary like the angels of the presence and the holy ones" (Jub 31:14). This is a correspondence with a long history. It goes back at least as far as Ezekiel, who describes angels as dressed in linen (Ezek 9:2, 3, 11; 10:2, 6, 7), the fabric of priests' garments (Exod 28:42), a description picked up in the book of Daniel (Dan 10:5; 12:6-7). Once heaven is understood as a temple, the comparison is perhaps inevitable. In Jubilees priests are compared not to angels in general, but to specific classes of angels, the angels of the presence and the holy ones, the two highest classes of angels (Jub 2:18). The comparison flatters priests, but it can also be used to hold priests to account when they fail to live up to the high standards appropriate to their duties, as in the Book of the Watchers.

But for Jubilees the correlation between angels in heaven and priests on earth is only one aspect of a larger and more important correlation. As the heavenly observance of the Sabbath and the Feast of Weeks indicates, Jubilees understands not only priests but also the entire people of Israel to be the earthly counterpart of the angels; indeed, all Jews are the counterparts of the angels of the presence and the holy ones, the very classes of angels to which Levi's descendants are compared, since these are the angels who observe the Sabbath with God from its creation. This point is crucial. Jubilees is one of

25. All quotations from Jubilees are taken from the translation of R. H. Charles, rev. C. Rabin, in *The Apocryphal Old Testament*, ed. H. F. D. Sparks (Oxford: Clarendon, 1984).

26. Sabbath: "to burn frankincense and present offerings and sacrifices in the Lord's presence every day and every sabbath" (Jub 50:10); Feast of Weeks: "I have written in the book of the first law . . . *the details* of its sacrifices" (Jub 6:21).

27. See Martha Himmelfarb, *Ascent to Heaven in Jewish and Christian Apocalypses* (New York: Oxford University Press, 1993), 33-36.

many texts to extend the idea of the correspondence between angels in heaven and priests on earth to suggest that a select group of nonpriestly human beings are also the counterparts of the angels. But Jubilees stands apart from other texts of the second temple period in a very important way. In contrast to the Book of the Watchers, which depicts one exemplary human being as the equal of the angels, or to the sectarian scrolls, which understand all members of the sectarian community as the earthly counterparts of the angels, Jubilees claims that it is not extraordinarily righteous heroes of the past or members of a sectarian elite but the entire Jewish people that is like the angels.[28]

Even more striking is the contrast between Jubilees and the sectarian scrolls. For the sectarians the true Israel, the children of light, were defined by piety. For Jubilees, on the other hand, Israel is a people defined by genealogy without regard to piety; Jubilees has no place for conversion to Judaism.[29] Both the good and the wicked are Israel, or, as the rabbis, who are surprisingly close to Jubilees on this point, would later put it, "Even if he sins, an Israelite remains an Israelite" (*b. Sanhedrin* 44a).[30] Thus Israel is a kingdom of priests in part because one becomes an Israelite by birth rather than merit, just as Jewish priests attained their status through descent from Aaron rather than by any claim to piety or learning.[31]

I take Jubilees' insistence on genealogy as the way to define membership in the people of Israel as a sign of active opposition to the sectarian impulse that emerged in the Hasmonean era.[32] In his contribution to this volume, Aharon Shemesh suggests that frg. 7 of 4Q265 provides further evidence for Jubilees' Torah-like status at Qumran because it consists of three instances of reworking of Jubilees, including revision of Jubilees' Sabbath laws and the laws governing relations with Gentiles, both in light of the *yahad*'s view of itself as Israel and all other Jews as Gentiles.[33] Though Shemesh appears to ac-

---

28. I make this point in greater detail in my book, *A Kingdom of Priests: Ancestry and Merit in Ancient Judaism* (Philadelphia: University of Pennsylvania Press, 2006), 53-84.

29. Himmelfarb, *A Kingdom of Priests*, 72-78.

30. For the rabbis' view on the genealogical character of Jewish identity, see Himmelfarb, *A Kingdom of Priests*, 160-85, esp. 177-81.

31. For the significance of Jubilees' insistence on genealogy for defining the Jewish people as well as the priesthood, see Betsy Halpern-Amaru, *The Empowerment of Women in the* Book of Jubilees (Leiden: Brill, 1999), 154-55.

32. I prefer a date for Jubilees during the last third of the second century B.C.E. (Himmelfarb, *A Kingdom of Priests*, 77), but this dating is not crucial for my argument.

33. Aharon Shemesh, "4Q265 and the Authoritative Status of Jubilees at Qumran." On authoritative status at Qumran, see also Jamal-Dominique Hopkins, "The Authoritative Status of Jubilees at Qumran," *Hen* 31, no. 2 (2008).

cept sectarian provenance of Jubilees,[34] the two examples just noted serve to highlight the distance between Jubilees and the *yahad* on precisely the point most crucial to sectarian identity, the definition of the people of Israel.

Jubilees' insistence that all Jews are the earthly counterparts of the angels brings into relief an important difference between Jubilees and the other texts of the early Jewish mystical tradition in the function of the heavenly temple. There is no necessary tension between heavenly temple and earthly, as can be seen in texts of the ancient Near East or the first temple period; indeed, the heavenly temple understood as prototype of the earthly serves to guarantee the status of the earthly temple. Yet the idea of a heavenly temple is not prominent in literature of the first temple. In the period of the second temple, however, the idea becomes more prominent and the heavenly temple takes on a different role. Those dissatisfied with the Jerusalem temple saw the heavenly temple in its perfection as a reproach to those responsible for the corruption of the earthly. I do not believe that the heavenly temple of the Book of the Watchers reflects rejection of the Jerusalem temple; indeed, it is striking that the Book of the Watchers does not present the heavenly priesthood as perfect in order to rebuke its earthly counterpart. Rather, it projects the failings of some Jerusalem priests onto the angelic priesthood — but it is important to note that in heaven as on earth not all priests have gone astray.[35] The Songs of the Sabbath Sacrifice, in contrast, was used by a community that rejected the temple in Jerusalem; the recitation of its detailed depiction of the heavenly temple and its elaborate liturgy must have served at least in a very limited way as a substitute for the rejected temple. The heavenly temple of the *hekhalot* texts seems unrelated to criticism of the earthly temple, but since the texts were written centuries after the disappearance of the earthly temple, this is not surprising.

In contrast, Jubilees, written at a time when many of the pious were deeply dissatisfied with the Jerusalem temple, uses the heavenly temple neither as a substitute for a rejected temple on earth nor as the ideal against which to measure the earthly institution and the behavior of its priests. One aspect of Jubilees' insistence that many of the laws of the Torah were in force even before the Torah itself was given to Israel is its picture of the observance of the Sabbath and the Feast of Weeks in heaven before they were observed

---

34. Shemesh, "4Q265," where he considers the implications for sectarian authorship of the time that would have had to elapse for Jubilees to achieve its authoritative status.

35. Himmelfarb, *A Kingdom of Priests*, 19-21. Nor do I believe that the Book of the Watchers rejects or ignores the Torah of Moses (39-41).

on earth. Its brief allusions to the heavenly temple make explicit an aspect of the idea of the heavenly temple implicit in its function of prototype for the earthly temple that other texts of the second temple period fail to exploit: it has been there since the beginning. Jubilees' emphasis on the heavenly temple as a venue for observances that take place on earth only after the emergence of the people of Israel and the giving of the Torah has a great deal in common with the original understanding of the heavenly temple as a prototype of the earthly: it serves to valorize the rituals of the earthly temple rather than to criticize them.

PART FOUR

WHERE DOES JUBILEES BELONG?

Jubilees, the Temple, and the Aaronite Priesthood

David W. Suter

Now the author of Jubilees sought to do for Genesis what the Chronicler had done for Samuel and Kings, and so he rewrote it in such a way as to show that the law was rigorously observed even by the Patriarchs. . . . Our author's procedure is of course in direct antagonism with the presuppositions of the Priests' Code in Genesis, for according to this code "Noah may build no altar, Abraham offer no sacrifice, Jacob erect no sacred pillar. No offering is recorded till Aaron and his sons are ready" (Carpenter, *The Hexateuch*, 1. 124). This fact seems to emphasize in the strongest manner how freely our author reinterpreted his authorities for the past.

R. H. CHARLES[1]

The above epigram is the seed of my argument in a recent article examining the place of the temple in the early Enoch tradition.[2] Specifically, I argued

---

1. From R. H. Charles, *Apocrypha and Pseudepigrapha of the Old Testament*, vol. 2, *Pseudepigrapha* (Oxford: Clarendon, 1913), 7. The reference to Carpenter, *The Hexateuch*, would appear to be to J. E. Carpenter and G. Harford-Battersby, *The Hexateuch according to the Revised Version* (London and New York: Longmans, Green, 1900).

2. D. W. Suter, "Temples and the Temple in the Early Enoch Tradition: Memory, Vision, and Expectation," in *The Early Enoch Literature*, ed. Gabriele Boccaccini and John J. Collins (Leiden: Brill, 2007), 195-218.

that the portrait of Enoch as a priest offering incense in a sanctuary in Jub 4:25-26 reflects the redactional interests of the author of Jubilees and should therefore be treated separately from the early material in 1 Enoch in establishing the role of temple, priesthood, and cult in that tradition. As R. H. Charles suggests, Jubilees shows a concern for having the patriarchs sacrifice following Levitical procedure, leading the writer to expand significantly the role of the patriarchs in building altars and offering sacrifices. The absence of such an impulse in 1 Enoch, however, makes it apparent that the early Enoch tradition as a whole is singularly uninterested in the matter of priestly function in a sacrificial cultus, although in other respects it reflects a priestly perspective and has a deep and abiding interest in the temple, including the celestial temple and the eschatological temple to be built by God at the end of days. For that reason, in the previous article I set aside the portrait of Enoch as priest in Jub 4 and chose to deal exclusively with the early Enoch tradition in 1 Enoch. This essay is intended to pick up where the previous article leaves off by exploring the relation of Enoch to temple and priesthood from the perspective of his inclusion in the larger enterprise of Jubilees.[3]

While Charles's quotation provides food for thought, it is not without problems, since it assumes that the author of Jubilees would have been able to distinguish the Priestly Code from the other strands present in Genesis, which do involve the patriarchs in the offering of a sacrifice or the building of an altar. What becomes apparent as the study proceeds, however, is that the author of Jubilees systematically reads later priestly practice characteristic of the Priestly document back into the cultic activity of Abraham, Isaac, and Jacob. While the Yahwist and the Elohist do represent the patriarchs as sacrificing (see Gen 8:20-22; 12:7-8; 13:4, 18; 22:9; 26:25; 33:20; and 35:1-7), and while the author of Jubilees draws upon those accounts in his narrative (Jub 6:4; 13:4; 14:11-12; 15:2; 18:8; 24:23; and 31:3), it is apparent that his contribution to these narratives presupposes an understanding of priestly practice as reflected in the Priestly Code and not simply an adaptation of the Yahwistic

---

3. In his response to the second group of papers at the Fourth Enoch Seminar, G. Nickelsburg commented, "I was struck by the observations of David Suter in his paper for the last session. Perhaps the first to champion the anti-temple polemics in the Book of the Watchers, he is cautious about reading the Jubilees material about Enoch the priest back into the Book of the Watchers." Also note that in his contribution to the present volume, "Worship in Jubilees and Enoch," from the Fourth Enoch Seminar, E. Larson likewise concludes that the portrait of Enoch as a priest does not come from 1 Enoch. Larson also notices the lack of interest of the early Enoch literature in sacrifice, a feature I noted in contrast to Jubilees in "Temples and the Temple in the Early Enoch Tradition."

and Elohistic narratives. Although it is unlikely that the author of Jubilees is aware of the Priestly Code per se and its presuppositions concerning sacrifice, Charles is correct in drawing a sharp contrast between that strand and Jubilees.

What seems obvious in reading Jubilees is that the book engages in a kind of selective anachronism[4] in its treatment of the antediluvians and the patriarchs in light of the "subsequent" history of the Israelite cultus, and while it might be a mistake to conclude too quickly that the purpose of the cultic portrait of the patriarchs involves a polemic directed toward the party responsible for the Priestly Code per se, the treatment of cultic issues in Jubilees is too distinctive to assume that it is simply the result of considerations resulting from the narrative adaptation of Genesis.

The priestly activity of Adam and Enoch, for example, suggests a progressive unfolding of cultic practice leading up to the roles of Noah, Abraham, Isaac, and Jacob.[5] Adam offers incense in the morning and Enoch in the evening, corresponding to later priestly practice. Adam offers his sacrifice on the morning of the day on which the couple is expelled from the garden (Jub 3:27), and it is difficult to determine whether the sacrifice is offered within the garden or outside of it. The sacrifices of Abel and Cain follow in Jub 4:2, but the author seems only to mention them in passing rather than as a part of his account of the development of sacrifice. Enoch institutes the evening sacrifice of incense by offering it in the sanctuary on Mount Qater, apparently the mountain of the east, one of the four sanctuaries to be sanctified in the new creation (Jub 4:25-26).[6] Elsewhere Jubilees cites Enoch as the source of commandments regarding ritual (see 7:39 and 21:10), giving the role of Enoch in Jubilees a decidedly priestly cast.

Noah's sacrifice upon disembarking from the ark in 6:1-4 reflects further development of cultic practice in that Jubilees pictures him following what would appear to be Levitical practice in making a sin offering, including the use of frankincense to make a sweet savor before God. Gen 8:20-21 merely tells us that upon leaving the ark Noah builds an altar and makes a burnt offering. God smells the pleasing odor and resolves never again to de-

---

4. Here compare W. Loader, "Jubilees and Sexual Transgression," *Hen* 31, no. 1 (2009).

5. In "Worship in Jubilees and Enoch," Larson describes in similar terms the presentation of worship in Jubilees as a process that unfolds, reaching some conclusions about the balance of interests in Jubilees but stopping short of offering a system behind the way that the process unfolds.

6. Following the translation and notes of O. S. Wintermute, "Jubilees," in *OTP,* 2:35-142.

stroy all creatures. Jubilees, however, adds material suggestive of passages like Exod 29:40 and Lev 2:2-5 to specify the animals included in the offering and the flour, oil, frankincense, and wine that accompany it. Martha Himmelfarb notes that interest in the sweet savor created by the inclusion of incense in the offering of a sacrifice is a significant aspect of the priestly sacrificial cultus and that Jubilees is systematic in mentioning the inclusion of frankincense in the sacrifices of the patriarchs.[7] The short account of Noah's planting a vineyard in Gen 9:20 becomes in Jub 7:1-6 the occasion for the initiation of the rules regarding the treatment of the firstfruits of a vineyard (compare Lev 19:23 and Jub 7:34-39). The observance also becomes the occasion for a sacrifice with details of the sacrifice suggestive of Num 29:2-3,[8] and including frankincense and a sweet odor pleasing to God.

In Jubilees the practice of building altars and offering sacrifices is most characteristic of the story of Abraham, to the extent that we might suggest that Jubilees represents an Abrahamic more so than an Enochic or Mosaic form of Judaism. At times in Jubilees' telling of the story of Abraham, all we find is a passing reference to an altar and a burnt offering. More extensive, however, is the narrative of Abraham's dream, sacrifice, and covenant in Jub 14:1-20, which, aside from mentioning the building of an altar, seems to follow the Yahwist's seemingly primitive details of the sacrifice as described in Gen 15:7-11 without updating them in light of the details of sacrificial practice taken from Leviticus. This narrative is also notable in that it is a fairly extensive account of sacrifice that omits a mention of frankincense and a sweet odor pleasing to God. Jub 21:1-20 represents an extensive adaptation of a biblical narrative about Abraham involving the account of his last will and testament to Isaac. In Gen 25:5-7 the narrative is a straightforward will in which the patriarch leaves all his property to Isaac and makes gifts to other sons by other wives. In Jubilees the testament includes lengthy instruction to Isaac on peace offerings suggestive of Lev 3:7-10, with the authority for the instructions attributed to Enoch and Noah.

In addition to the extensive detailing of the patriarchal sacrificial practice, Jubilees traces to the patriarchal period the institution of various festi-

7. M. Himmelfarb, "Earthly Sacrifice and Heavenly Incense: The Law of the Priesthood in *Aramaic Levi* and *Jubilees*," in *Heavenly Realms and Earthly Realities in Late Antique Religions*, ed. R. S. Boustan and A. Yoshiko Reed (Cambridge: Cambridge University Press, 2004), 103-22.

8. In this paper, suggestions for the sources in the Torah used in Jubilees to amplify the narratives of the patriarchs are derived from the marginal notes supplied in Wintermute, *OTP*, 2:35-142.

vals and observances included in the Mosaic legislation. In addition to the firstfruits (Jub 7:34-39; 15:1-4), Abraham's celebration of the Feast of Booths at Beersheba is mentioned in Jub 16:20-31, with the inclusion of significant detail regarding the sacrifices offered. The Feast of Weeks or Oaths (depending upon the vocalization of *šbʿwt*) is introduced as a covenant-renewal festival in 6:17-22, where it is said to be written in the heavenly tablets. It is observed in conjunction with the covenant with Noah in 6:4-16, suggesting that the meaning "oaths" may underlie the understanding of the feast in Jubilees.[9] The covenant with Abraham in Jub 15 also seems to be associated with this festival, and it should be noted that in this case we also have the institution of the practice of circumcision. The law of the tithe is introduced to Abraham in 13:25-27. It is also observed by Jacob in 32:1-15, where Jacob fulfills the original vow that he made upon departing from Canaan. This narrative comes subsequent to the blessing of Levi as priest and features Levi's investiture and his service as Jacob's priest in the account of the sacrifice associated with the tithe. The institution of the tithe in the heavenly tablets is mentioned in 32:10-15, along with the notation that it is to belong to the priests, who are to eat it before God year after year. This last detail is interesting in that in its use in Jubilees it antedates the reason given for its institution in the Mosaic legislation where it serves to provide for the priests, who are given no territory in the division of the land of Canaan among the tribes. However, it should also be noted that Genesis shares this anachronism in that Jacob's vow in Gen 28:20-22 involves a tithe. Jubilees seizes upon the detail to build its presentation of the installation of Levi as a priest.[10]

Jubilees concludes with the institution of Passover in chap. 49 and the Sabbath in chap. 50, giving us two significant festivals associated in one way or another with the temple that appear not to be observed by the patriarchs. The placement of these last two festivals suggests that we should look for some sort of a system involved in the introduction of sacrifice, festivals, and other observances, but so far the only consideration I can discover is narrative appropriateness.[11] This seems to be the case, for example, both in the use of the Festival of Weeks/Oaths in the context of covenant making and in

---

9. See the note in Wintermute, *OTP, loc. cit.*

10. For a study of Levi in Jubilees, see J. C. VanderKam, "*Jubilees'* Exegetical Creation of Levi the Priest," *RevQ* 17 (1996): 359-73.

11. In a paper entitled "Ritual in Jubilees" presented at the Fourth Enoch Seminar, M. A. Daise made an interesting contribution to the issue of system in the presentation of sacrifice in Jubilees, although his approach does not necessarily deal with the question of progression that interests me.

the use of the tithe in the context of Levi's investiture as priest. The introduction of Passover at the end of the narrative probably reflects the fact that
this festival has such a strong historic context that it would be difficult to exercise creative anachronism in including it in the practice of the patriarchs.[12]

On the other hand, the presentation of the Sabbath in Jubilees is a puzzle. The celebration of the festival is first mentioned in conjunction with the
Garden of Eden, where we are told that the Sabbath is a festival intended for
Israel alone, and where the angels of the presence and the angels of sanctification, the two highest angelic orders, are depicted as observing the Sabbath
in heaven from the beginning. The connection of Israel with the two highest
orders of angels is significant. The angelic observance of the Sabbath suggests the much more elaborate Songs of the Sabbath Sacrifice from the Dead
Sea Scrolls, and this may be the only point in Jubilees where the celestial
temple comes into play. There is no indication, however, that Adam and Eve
observe the Sabbath, in spite of Adam's role in initiating the priestly cultus
with the morning offering of incense, and there is no indication of the observance of the Sabbath by the patriarchs[13] — although there is apparently
an attempt in 2:24 to link the blessing of the Sabbath to the blessing of the
seed of Jacob.[14] It could be noted also that Adam and Eve reside in Eden for a
Sabbath of years (3:15-16). However, while the passage dealing with creation
and the observance of the Sabbath by the angels includes the Sabbath law
(2:17-33), the introduction of the Sabbath to Israel comes at the very end of
the book, when the festival becomes the final thing revealed to Moses in
chap. 50 following the institution of Passover in chap. 49. Such an arrangement is particularly curious given the prominence of sabbaths of years in the
calendrical system utilized in Jubilees. The selective anachronism of Jubilees,
which reads the sacrificial cultus of the temple back into the practice of the
patriarch, does not seem to include the observance of the Sabbath at the hu-

---

12. However, see the essay in the present volume by B. Halpern-Amaru, "The Festivals
of Pesaḥ and Massot in the Book of Jubilees," which convincingly relates Passover in Jub 49
to the seven-day festival in Jub 18:17-19 resulting from the narrative of the Akedah, leaving us
only with the Sabbath without patriarchal roots.

13. In her study of the calendar at Qumran, A. Jaubert argues that in Jubilees there is
one day upon which the patriarchs do not travel, which must therefore be the Sabbath (*The
Date of the Last Supper* [Staten Island, N.Y.: Alba House, 1965], 27). Her argument would give
us an *implicit* rather than an explicit observance in Jubilees of the Sabbath by the patriarchs;
however, after detailed analysis in "A Reexamination of the Calendar in the *Book of Jubilees*"
(a paper supplied to the author by A. Baumgarten), J. Kugel and L. Ravid conclude that the
calendar used in Jubilees cannot be interpreted in that way.

14. Wintermute, *OTP,* 2:37 n. z.

man level. The introduction of Sabbath to the two highest classes of angels at the beginning and to Israel at the end has a certain dramatic appropriateness, but the only rationale I can determine for its placement in the narrative is in the nationalistic perspective of Jubilees — the Sabbath is reserved for the practice of Israel alone among all the nations, in conjunction with the angels of the presence and the angels of sanctification — and that it is introduced at the point at which Israel is about to move from its status as the family of the patriarch Abraham to its status as a nation.

In spite of the presupposition of priestly practice in the accounts of sacrifice by the patriarchs, the role of the temple is unusual. The sanctity of Mount Zion is presupposed from the beginning of Jubilees. In the Enoch narrative in Jub 4, it is one of the four sacred places on the face of the earth, and the narrative appears to anticipate the building of Solomon's temple and the significance of the practice of the Levitical priesthood in it. However, the status of the second temple in Jubilees is not clear. The replacement for Solomon's temple in the scheme of the book appears to be the eschatological temple, built by God himself at the end of days, and served by a priesthood tracing its lineage back to Levi, making Jubilees one of the pieces of literature from the period for which, as Michael Knibb has described it, the exile has yet to end.[15] Knibb's argument is based on the history of interpretation of the prophecy in Jeremiah that the exile will last for seventy years. In Dan 9, the seventy years become seventy generations, which represent a time of sin, while in the Animal Apocalypse in 1 En 85–90 the seventy generations become seventy shepherds, representing seventy angelic rulers of the nations. The seventy shepherds of the Animal Apocalypse are divided into four groups, Knibb argues, reflecting the four empires of Dan 2 and 7. The Animal Apocalypse treats the offerings of the second temple as polluted and the temple itself as inadequate for the glory of God, leading to the assertion that God does not dwell in it. The text anticipates the replacement of the second temple by a "house" adequate to the glory of God, built by God, in which God will dwell and at which the righteous will assemble in the last times. The passage is ambiguous about whether this "house" represents the New Jerusalem without a temple or whether the presence of a temple is implied in the city, but clearly the passage is akin to the idea of the eschatological tem-

---

15. M. A. Knibb, "The Exile in the Literature of the Intertestamental Period," *HeyJ* 17 (1976): 253-72. See also Knibb, "Temple and Cult in Apocryphal and Pseudepigraphal Writings from before the Common Era," in *Temple and Worship in Biblical Israel*, ed. J. Day (London and New York: T. & T. Clark, 2005), 401-16.

ple to be built on Mount Zion by God's hands at the end of days. The Apocalypse of Weeks in 1 Enoch is similar to the Animal Apocalypse. It treats the generation of the restoration as an apostate generation, does not mention the second temple at all, and anticipates God's building the eschatological temple at the end of days.

Although there is no direct reference to Jeremiah's prophecy in Jubilees, the book reflects the same understanding of the second temple and the eschatological temple that appears in the Animal Apocalypse and the Apocalypse of Weeks in 1 Enoch. In Jub 1, the restoration of the temple on Mount Zion is treated as an eschatological rather than a "historical" event. The present of the writer is one of the sons of Israel going astray among the Gentiles. He anticipates the time when Israel, among the Gentiles, will repent and be restored to the land, and when God will create a clean heart within them for all eternity. Twice it is said that God will build his sanctuary on Mount Zion for all eternity. With the rebuilding of the temple, God will be king on Mount Zion for all eternity. The heavenly bodies will be renewed for peace and blessing, and God will defend his people from the Gentiles. While it is possible to read the passage as referring to the restoration of the second temple, its general tenor is eschatological, written during the time of the second temple with the implication that the restoration is yet to happen.

Beyond chap. 1, Knibb finds this treatment of the second temple and the eschatological temple implied elsewhere in Jubilees. In Rebecca's blessing of Jacob in 25:14-22, the matriarch prays that God will dwell with his people and that his sanctuary will be built in their midst for all ages (see 25:21b). The eschatological passage in Jub 23:8-32 asserts that the "evil generation" of v. 14 will "defile the holy of holies through the impure corruption of their contamination" (v. 21).[16] The reference to defiling the Holy of Holies Knibb takes as implicating the high priest in the corruption. He interprets the corruption as involving illegitimate marriages, implied by the allusion to sexual impurity (reflecting the Hebrew *zenuth*) and contamination in vv. 14 and 21 (cf. Jub 30:15, where the author warns that marriages with foreigners will defile the Lord's sanctuary). Knibb relates the polemic to the one in the Book of the Watchers in 1 Enoch[17] and observes that Jubilees reflects the perspective of dissident priests opposed to the Jerusalemite priestly establishment.[18]

---

16. Knibb, "Temple and Cult," 410.

17. See my study of the polemic in D. W. Suter, "Fallen Angel, Fallen Priest: The Problem of Family Purity in 1 Enoch 6–16," *HUCA* 50 (1979): 115-35.

18. Knibb, "Temple and Cult," 409-10.

Jubilees thus affirms the sanctity of Mount Zion, which it sees as primordially established and eschatologically predestined. However, it questions the legitimacy of its current priesthood and consequently of the current temple occupying that site.

In sorting out the role of Mount Zion in the book, one must take account of the fact that Jubilees seems to recognize a multiplicity of sanctuaries.[19] In the passage that pictures Enoch offering the evening incense, there are four: Mount Sinai, Mount Zion, Eden, and the mountain of the east, which will be places where God dwells at the end of days — an eschatological idea. Jub 8:19, on the other hand, mentions the existence of three sanctuaries from creation, which will become part of the territory of Shem in the division of land among the sons of Noah. They are the Garden of Eden, Mount Sinai, and Mount Zion. Eden is treated as the Holy of Holies, the dwelling place of God; Sinai as the center of the desert; and Zion as the navel of the earth. The three places face each another, and the concept may be that the three are the *debir*, the *hekhal*, and the *'ulam* of one temple. Clearly Jubilees reflects a certain degree of creativeness in working with the Deuteronomistic one-sanctuary rule. The passage in chap. 49 dealing with the Passover as a temple festival emphasizes the role of the tabernacle located at various places in the land as an anticipation of the temple on Mount Zion in Jerusalem. Perhaps the intent is to reconcile the multiplicity of places mentioned in the Torah as dwelling places of God with the centrality of Zion.

It is also possible that the creativity reflected here needs to be coupled with the roles of the antediluvians and the patriarchs in the evolution of priestly sacrifice as an indication that Jubilees is seeking to make a statement not about the priestly role of the laity who are contemporaries of the writer[20] but about the role of priesthood, temple, and sacrifice as fundamental to the order of creation. Here we can note George Brooke's discussion of the ten temples of the Qumran literature, which would appear to support a cosmological significance of the idea of temple in Jubilees by treating Eden in that work as "the primordial temple."[21] For Brooke, the fact that Adam and Eve are brought into the Garden of Eden forty and eighty days after their

---

19. It also appears to reject one location, Bethel, as a sanctuary. See J. Schwartz, "Jubilees, Bethel, and the Temple of Jacob," *HUCA* 56 (1985): 63-85.

20. See M. Himmelfarb, "'A Kingdom of Priests': The Democratization of the Priesthood in the Literature of Second Temple Judaism," *Journal of Jewish Thought and Philosophy* 6 (1997): 89-104.

21. G. J. Brooke, "The Ten Temples in the Dead Sea Scrolls," in *Temple and Worship in Biblical Israel*, ed. J. Day (London and New York: T. & T. Clark, 2005), 417-32 (here 419-21).

creation seems to be not so much an anticipation of the rules in Lev 12:2-5 regarding the periods of purification after childbirth to be observed by a woman before entering the sanctuary, as it is the establishment of those rules. Citing C. T. R. Hayward, he observes that "this indicates that a sanctuary was an integral part of creation itself from the outset and that it 'has a good deal to do with the continuing stability and order of creation.'"[22] In addition to a cosmological and cultic ideal, however, Brooke suggests that the role of Eden as a primordial temple has a political significance in the early Maccabean period: "The author of *Jubilees* may . . . have had a sense of the political agenda of the Maccabees after the defeat of the Seleucids. . . . The sanctification of Eden is a divine guarantee of the political division of the world into three sections with the descendants of Shem, not the Greeks, clearly the rightful heirs of the land of Israel (*Jub.* 8:10-21)."[23] James Scott also gives a geopolitical twist to the role of the sanctuaries in Jubilees in his study of the appropriation in Jub 8–9 of the table of nations in Gen 10, although he makes Zion rather than Eden the focal point of the four sanctuaries and suggests that Jubilees anticipates that one day Zion, the "navel of the earth" (Jub 8:19), rather than Greece, will rule the earth (see Jub 22:11-14).[24] Unlike the Book of the Watchers in 1 Enoch, which plays upon the antagonism of Jerusalem and Dan,[25] Jubilees creates a harmonization of sacred space to present a view of the earth that is at once sacerdotal and political in character. In contrast to the one-sanctuary rule of the Deuteronomistic tradition, which limits sacred space to one geographical location, Jubilees imagines the earth as suffused with sanctity.[26]

One final twist in the sacerdotal perspective of Jubilees is the role of the practice of ritual purity in the book. Given the significance of ritual purity in the sectarian literature of the period, its relative absence from Jubilees is remarkable. Liora Ravid has argued that the absence of a concern for ritual purity in the book is indicative of a polemic in the work against the Zadokite

---

22. Brooke, "The Ten Temples," 419. See C. T. R. Hayward, *The Jewish Temple: A Non-Biblical Sourcebook* (London and New York: Routledge, 1996), 86.

23. Brooke, "The Ten Temples," 420.

24. J. M. Scott, *Geography in Early Judaism and Christianity: The Book of Jubilees*, ed. R. Bauckham, SNTSMS (Cambridge: Cambridge University Press, 2002), 32-35.

25. See D. W. Suter, "Why Galilee? Galilean Regionalism in the Interpretation of 1 Enoch 6–16," *Hen* 25 (2003): 167-212 (here 178-79 and 201-5).

26. Here contrast the conclusion reached by Larson in "Worship in Jubilees and Enoch," that "the author manages to indicate that the true intent of God is to limit the places that are acceptable to God for ritual worship."

priesthood,[27] while James VanderKam responds that Jubilees is a retelling of Genesis, so that the narrative antedates the revelation of such rules to Moses at Mount Sinai and the establishment of the tabernacle.[28] Its absence from the concerns of Jubilees thus is no indication of the importance of the concern for the maintenance of purity for the author of the book but rather is the consequence of the lack of a temple in that period to which the rules of purity might refer.

However, while it may be correct to argue that the author of Jubilees has simply chosen to omit the purity regulations of Leviticus from his selective anachronism, it is probably better not to tie that omission to the lack of a sanctuary in the patriarchal period to which the regulations might apply. In effect, the author's selective anachronism has included elements of the temple — its sacrificial cultus and its system of festivals — in the patriarchal period, and it seems necessary to ask why the purity regulations would not apply by extension to the temple service as to the sanctuary itself. At the same time, it is worth noting that the concept of sanctuary in Jubilees is not spatially and temporally defined in quite the same way it is in the Torah or the Temple Scroll, where, particularly in the latter case, the temple seems to be intended to be isolated from the world around it. In Jubilees, sanctuaries — Eden, Sinai, Zion, and the mountain of the east — are rooted in the beginning and the end. They are part of the order of creation as well as the order of the new creation at the end of days. Their purpose is the sanctification of the entire earth. The ritual practice of the patriarchs should be seen as a part of that order in that it adapts elements of the temple service to a period in which no temple actually exists. The implication may be that sanctuaries do not require temples to sanctify the earth; the service itself will suffice.

Actually, it would be a mistake to argue that purity concerns are absent from Jubilees. The book does not for the most part read the rules of ritual purity back into the world of the patriarchs in the same way that it does the priestly sacrificial practice. As we have observed, however, it does treat the Garden of Eden as a sanctuary, using it to connect the purification period for a mother after childbirth to enter the sanctuary to the periods after their creation when Adam and Eve are introduced to the garden. It might be better to suggest that Jubilees simply is not obsessed with ritual impurity, or rather that the kind of impurity with which it is obsessed is that which comes from

27. L. Ravid, "Purity and Impurity in the Book of *Jubilees,*" *JSP* 13 (2002): 61-86.

28. J. C. VanderKam, "Viewed from Another Angle: Purity and Impurity in the Book of *Jubilees,*" *JSP* 13 (2002): 209-15.

marriages to Gentiles. The book takes several occasions to warn against such marriages, and at one point marriage to a non-Israelite is described as having the potential to pollute the sanctuary (Jub 30:15-16). Levi is approved as priest in Jubilees because of his zeal and violence in acting to prevent the marriage of his sister Dinah to the Canaanite Shechem (Jub 30:18-20), a development in sharp contrast to Genesis, which has no such ordination scene, and which condemns Levi and Simeon for their violent act (see Gen 34:30 and 49:5-7). While there are differences between Jubilees and the early Enoch literature over interest in the sacrificial cultus of the temple and in approach to the concept of sanctuaries, the two bodies of literature seem to share a concern with improper marriages if the myth of the fallen angels in the Book of the Watchers is seen as a polemic directed toward priestly marriages.

In this context we should note that Lutz Doering's contribution to the present volume deals in significant detail with the complexity of the issue of purity and impurity in Jubilees, emphasizing the ascendancy of what he terms "moral" purity over "ritual" purity in that book.[29] He concludes quite correctly (judging by my conclusion that the priestly portrait of Enoch in Jub 4 is not derived from the Enoch tradition) that "The links with Enochic tradition are more limited in range, relating to the field of 'moral' impurity: the adoption of Watcher myth, dealing with sexual transgression, bloodshed, and idolatry; and similarities in the expectation of an earth cleansed of impurity (Jub 50:5; 1 En 10:20, 22)."[30]

In the final analysis, Ravid's argument regarding the laws of purity in Jubilees is not so easily dismissed. What she demonstrates is not the *absence* of the laws of impurity but the *presence* of a fairly robust system of sanctification based upon the laws written in the heavenly tablets. Key to this system is the concept of metaphysical impurity in Jubilees, which involves not just the mixture of Jew and Gentile through intermarriage but the confusion of Jewish and Greek civilization, a sin of which the author seems to hold the Zadokites guilty. Instead of rituals of purification by bathing, Ravid finds in Jubilees processes of sanctification involved in approaching and leaving an altar or holy place (cf. Jub 21:16). This system and these laws hold sway as much for the patriarchs as for later generations. The absence of certain classifications of purity laws and her argument for a critique in Jubilees not of

---

29. Doering's categories are based upon J. Klawans, *Impurity and Sin in Ancient Judaism* (Oxford: Oxford University Press, 2000).

30. Doering, "Purity and Impurity in the Book of Jubilees." Compare Loader, "Jubilees and Sexual Transgression."

the priesthood per se but of the Zadokites in particular based upon this system of sanctification thus raise a serious problem that deserves further discussion. The critiques of her work by VanderKam and Doering should go further in recognizing the conceptual difference in understanding the issue of purity and impurity implied by her argument for a system of sanctification in Jubilees. They also need to explore further the conundrum posed by the *selective* use of anachronism in Jubilees, which reads the sacrificial practice and festivals of the temple back into the world of the patriarchs more so than its system of ritual purity.[31] With the extensive use of anachronism on the part of the author, it is not enough to argue, as Doering does, that "To expect ritual (im)purity generally in 'pre-Temple' narrative contexts would be anachronistic in the perspective of Jubilees."

Conclusions

This study confirms my conclusion in "Temples and the Temple in the Early Enoch Tradition" that the role of Enoch in Jubilees as a priest offering incense in a sanctuary reflects a redactional concern of the author of Jubilees and should therefore be left out of a consideration of temple, cult, and priesthood in the early Enoch tradition. The study, however, allows me to refine to some degree my understanding of the role of Enoch in the redactional concerns of Jubilees. The sage and scribe makes more than a cameo appearance in Jubilees as a priest offering incense in the evening. He is also cited twice at crucial points in the narrative as the author of a book that represents a key source of authority on sacrificial practice. Although his role is small in terms of the lines assigned to him, so to speak, it is central to the process of selective and creative anachronism that the author of Jubilees uses to read the sacrifices and the festivals of the temple back into the narrative of the patriarchs. This difference between the early Enoch literature included in 1 Enoch and Jubilees needs to be taken as a starting point in any effort to develop an understanding of the portrait of Enoch in Jubilees. In Jubilees, Enoch is part of a system of signification involving a restatement of the roles of priest, temple, and cultus in Israel. That system must be understood first of all on the basis of clues found within the text of Jubilees itself rather than on the basis of systems imported from other literature of the pe-

31. Note here Loader, "Jubilees and Sexual Transgression," who seems to recognize the limits of anachronism.

riod. The problem is that the writer's clever use of selective anachronism makes it difficult to reconstruct that system.

In Jubilees, Enoch is presented for the first time as an authority on sacrifice, and the book presents sanctuaries and temple service as essential to the stability of the created order. The selective anachronism of the narrative portrays Israel as a nation of priests[32] whose presence and rule in the navel of the earth, the land of Israel, are essential to universal order. At the same time, this nation of priests will be served by a Levitical priesthood of ritual specialists whose role is reflected in the blessing and investiture of Levi as priest. The ultimate vision of the book sees this order inherent in creation with the inclusion of sanctuaries of Eden, Zion, and Sinai in the created order, and it anticipates the restoration of that order with the appearance of the eschatological temple on Mount Zion, built by the hand of God.

32. Himmelfarb, "A Kingdom of Priests," 89-104.

Jubilees and Enochic Judaism

David R. Jackson

Jubilees (ca. 160-150 B.C.E.) refers to and uses writings attributed to Enoch (including BW, AB, BD, and EE)[1] as authentic and authoritative divine revelations.[2] The Damascus Document (CD-A 16:1-6), in turn, refers to and uses Jubilees as a work having divine authority and authenticity.[3] These two documents create a direct chain of authority and declare their allegiances to these Enoch texts, which gives us, at least in skeletal form, an observable historical entity to which the label of Enochic Judaism has been applied. The data that identifies the Damascus Document as belonging to the Qumran sectarian texts gives us in turn a prima facie basis on which to attempt to "connect the dots."

Immediately we face the difficulty that in this chain of texts we are also dealing with significant diversity within second temple Judaism. Nickles-

1. Respectively, the Book of the Watchers; the Astronomical Book, being 1 En 72–82, noting that the Aramaic texts (4Q208-211) represent a more extensive body of work; the Book of Dreams; and the Epistle of Enoch.

2. J. C. VanderKam, "Enoch Traditions in Jubilees and Other Second-Century Sources," in SBLSP 1 (Atlanta: Scholars Press, 1978), 229-51, found that Jubilees used elements of BW (including 1 En 1–5), the AB, the BD, and the EE as well as other sources. G. W. E. Nickelsburg, *1 Enoch 1: A Commentary on the Book of 1 Enoch, Chapters 1–36; 81–108* (Minneapolis: Fortress, 2001), 72-73, concluded that Jubilees used BW, BD (at least the Animal Apocalypse [AA]), AW (Apocalypse of Weeks), and AB, including particularly 81:1–82:4.

3. See Shemesh's discussion of the significance of 4Q265 for Jubilees' canonical status at Qumran. Aharon Shemesh, "4Q265 and the Authoritative Status of Jubilees at Qumran," in this volume.

burg has observed that Jubilees "may be the earliest attestation of the Enoch traditions apart from the Enochic corpus itself."[4] As such, it offers a significant starting point from which to begin to investigate the development of this tradition.

The Enochic Paradigm and Exemplars

1 En 1–5 functions as an introduction to the BW. From the opening chapter, the author presents a parenesis making the exclusive claim that only those who follow the teaching of this book, out of all humanity, will be saved on "the day of tribulation" (1:1-2, 8-9).[5] The rest are deemed to have "gone astray" (5:4-9) and thus to incur destruction.[6]

The paradigm[7] enunciated in 1 En 2–5 presents an extreme understanding of the character of God as essentially and necessarily regular, orderly, and consistent involving absolute reliability, predictability, and symmetry in all his works and requirements. Scott makes the observation that this tradition assumes something of "a rudimentary 'unified field theory,' the ancient equivalent of the quest of modern physics to find an underlying beauty of mathematical symmetry and harmony in the order of the universe."[8] The writer of Jubilees may fairly be said to have applied this paradigm with obsessive rigor in an attempt to integrate it with the narrative of the Torah.[9] In doing so, he made a substantial contribution to an exponential agenda addressing other works that came to constitute the Tanakh, producing Testaments, halakic studies (e.g., 11QT), pesherim, and other works that, like Jubilees, attempted to integrate this perspective with narrative sections of the Tanakh.[10]

---

4. Nickelsburg, *1 Enoch 1*, 72.

5. All citations of 1 Enoch are taken from G. W. E. Nickelsburg and J. C. VanderKam, *1 Enoch: A New Translation Based on the Hermeneia Commentary* (Minneapolis: Fortress, 2004).

6. Cf. also 22:9-14; 80:4-10; 82:4-8; 83:8-10; 84:4-6; 90:26-27, 30-37; 91:4, 18-19; 92:1; 93:1-2, 9-10, 12; 94:1-5, 11; 95:2-3; 95:7–96:4; 96:8–97:6; 98:1–99:3, 10, 14; 100:5, 9; 102:10-11; 103:14-15; 104:6, 10-13; 107:1; 108:6.

7. See discussion in D. R. Jackson, *Enochic Judaism: Three Defining Paradigm Exemplars* (London: T. & T. Clark, 2004), 15-28.

8. J. M. Scott, *On Earth as in Heaven: The Restoration of Sacred Time and Sacred Space in the Book of Jubilees* (Leiden: Brill, 2005), 222.

9. Cf. the discussion in Karoly Dobos, "The Consolation of History," *Hen* 31, no. 1 (2009).

10. He was not alone in doing so (cf. Genesis Apocryphon; Aramaic Levi; Cairo

Out of this paradigm we observe the development of a special vocabulary that expressed an absolute level of approval or disapproval. These terms (e.g., "going astray"), in another system, might be passed over as incidental conventional labels. Within the Enochic paradigm, they expressed the ultimate level of categorization.

In the fictive scenario of 1 En 1–5, Enoch is given a vision and told what will happen in the future. God's created order would be violated, establishing the need for God to come down to Mount Sinai and restore it. The blame for this deviation here falls upon humanity. It is significant that the phenomena cited have relevance for the calendar. Enoch's tours of the heavens as stated in 12:1-2, 33:3-4 involved having access to the blueprints of God's design for cosmic order and regularity. This constituted a significant body of Enoch's teachings when he returned to his family (1 En 81:6ff.; Jub 4:21-23).

Nevertheless, the Enochic paradigm was never constructed on the basis of observed reality. Rather, it was an a priori logical construct based upon an intensified understanding of God's character. As such, to be both defensible and useful, the Enochic paradigm had to resolve the connection between God's character, his commitments to his chosen people, and the realities of the Jewish experience up to and including the author's generation, and so predict and interpret the resolution of these experiences. This was accomplished by means of the formulation of three paradigm exemplars[11] based on the events described in Gen 6:1-4, which I have termed, respectively, the Shemikhazah, 'Aza'el, and cosmic exemplars.

Identifying Gen 6:1-4 as the point in history where the created order (not just humanity) went astray, these three exemplars served to view and interpret that event (and its initial resolution climaxing in the Noachic flood) from three interlocking perspectives. Herein lies the benefit of seeing these as paradigm exemplars rather than in terms of the etiology of evil or as typologies. Reed notes the lack of etiology between pre- and postdiluvian events in Jubilees but terms it a "reconceptualizing" of the angelic descent. Understood within the Enochic paradigm, they would be entirely predictable *replications* demonstrating the validity of the para-

---

Genizah Testament of Levi). See E. Eshel's discussion in this volume, "The Aramaic Levi Document, the Genesis Apocryphon, and Jubilees: A Study of Shared Traditions."

11. Paradigm exemplars are ways of demonstrating that the paradigm works. They serve both to establish the theory and to suggest applications in which the theory might be replicated or applied. See Thomas S. Kuhn, *The Structure of Scientific Revolutions*, 2nd ed. (Chicago: University of Chicago Press, 1970), 186-91.

digm exemplars.[12] Etiologies define causes but don't necessarily produce solutions. Typologies predict outcomes resulting in proclamation. Exemplars demonstrate how a paradigmatic understanding of events can produce a replicable solution to a problem, and so produce pareness. As such, the Enochic paradigm created a methodology rather than just a myth.

We can illustrate this by noting the way in which the prediluvian deviation (Jub 5:2) ended, on the other side of the flood, with a complete restoration of purity and order (Jub 5:12; cf. 1 En 10:20–11:2) on earth, extending even to the biological purification of the animals. This in turn is promissory of a final eschatological purification that will last for all generations (Jub 4:16). In the same way Jubilees' recounting of postdiluvian history brings God's people into another new Eden where they will become another plantation of righteousness as they occupy the Promised Land in the Jubilee of Jubilees. Each new beginning, followed by another "going astray" and another rescued remnant, forms a pattern that can be understood from the perspectives of these replicating exemplars, rather than merely a chain of causation that can be traced back to a myth. Here we note one difference between the Deuteronomic and Enochic paradigms in that the former did not include the revelation or re-revelation of texts based on the heavenly tablets and connected with the revelation given to Enoch. Authors working with this methodology could then map all of Israel's history up to their own time in different ways that still demonstrated this replication, e.g., Apocalypse of Weeks and Animal Apocalypse. The pattern of replication could also be read at different levels within that system, such that Enoch's role as the seventh of his epoch of ten generations correlated with the seventh of the ten epochs of world history, identifying the fictive author's community as constituting an "Enoch" on the macroscale of a looming eschatology.[13] The solution then would always be to return to the original divine order, Enoch being the first man to have received the revelation of this way of salvation. This paradigm would fail only at the point where it could no longer credibly account for a growing body of contradictory data or anomalous experiences. Such may have been the point reached with the outcome of the war with Rome in 74 C.E.

Jubilees worked out in great detail how each exemplar was replicated after the flood.

---

12. A. Yoshiko Reed, *Fallen Angels and the History of Judaism and Christianity: The Reception of Enochic Literature* (Cambridge: Cambridge University Press, 2005), 87-95.

13. Cf. Kvanvig's paper in this volume, "Enochic Judaism — a Judaism without the Torah and the Temple?"

The Shemikhazah Exemplar

The Shemikhazah exemplar used the account of the sin of Shemikhazah and the Watchers, their human wives and offspring, to address the issue of ethnic impurity. As Halpern-Amaru[14] has demonstrated so effectively, the writer of Jubilees "fenced" the Torah narrative in order to make clear that only the pure may stand within the boundary of the elect. There is here an absolute distinction between the pure and the defiled. The only candidates for salvation are those who find themselves much in the same situation as Enoch and Noah — a chosen people (= pure Israelites) living in a violent and defiled world where all boundaries are being violated around them. In the books of Enoch there is no salvation possible for the women who intermarried with the Watchers, for the Watchers, nor for their offspring. Humans who participated in sexual promiscuity, violence, eating of blood, and other deceptions of the Watchers had no way back. This point is stressed as Enoch is asked to petition on behalf of the Watchers and his mission is cut off (1 En 12–16). Here the role of the priest as mediator of any restoration is stressed and linked directly to the proper function of the angels (15:2; 30:18). As the priests are to the people of Israel, so those within the boundary of the elect must be to those within the horizon of the author's parenesis.

Jubilees identified the demons as the offspring of the Watchers who sinned (Jub 10:5). Noah and his family come through the flood to face a world cleansed and purified. They have the option of a new beginning (Jub 5:12; cf. 1 En 10:20–11:2). They are the exemplar of a restored Eden, a plantation of righteousness (Jub 7:34-38; 16:26; 36:1-17; cf. 1 En 10:16; 84:6; 93:2, 5), as are the target audience of Jubilees (Jub 1:15; 5:17-19; 15:27; cf. 1 En 93:9-10). Those who violated the boundary of this plantation replicated the violation that occurred before the flood and so are "uprooted" and place themselves beyond the horizon of possible forgiveness (Jub 2:26-28; 5:3-11; 6:12; 10:30; 15:14; 15:34; 16:9; 16:16, 25; 21:22; 22:20; 24:29-33; 26:9-11; 30:7-11; 31:17, 20; 33:18-20; 35:14). The only people outside the boundary who had the option to return were those Israelites who lived as exiles and who searched for the Lord "with all their minds and with all their souls" (1:15; cf. 4:23-28).

In integrating the Shemikhazah exemplar with the Torah narrative, the writer of Jubilees drew upon wider conceptions found in the Tanakh, and in so doing constructed a figure to lead the demons. This figure is a composite.

---

14. B. Halpern-Amaru, *The Empowerment of Women in the Book of Jubilees* (Leiden: Brill, 1999).

He resembles the *satan* of Job 1–2 and Zech 3:1-6 in that he is the accuser and opponent of God's elect. He also conforms to the "evil spirits" of 1 Sam 16:14, 18:10-11, 19:9 (cf. 1 Kings 22:22-23; 2 Chron 18:21-22) who are "sent by God" (Jub 49:2-4). Like the scene in Dan 10:20–11:1, he faces off against the angelic defenders of God's elect (Jub 17:16–18:12; 48:2) and must be bound and restrained by the Lord and his angels to protect the elect (48:15, 18). His work is destruction akin to the violence and bloodshed of the prediluvian giants. But he is also, like Shemikhazah and 'Aza'el, a leader stepping forth from the number of these half-angel demons and an enemy of God. As the Watchers who sinned had a leader, so now the demons have a leader — also with two names, Belial (1:20; 15:33) and Mastema (10:7-8), which seem to be interchangeable labels of abhorrence.

The ongoing work of the demons after the flood is understood to be the prime cause of Gentile idolatry, associated with the three sins of "fornication," "impurity," and "injustice/violence" (Jub 7:20-24, 27-28; 9:14-15; 20:1-6; 23:14-17; 33:18-20; 50:4-5).

In Noah's generation the exemplar is replicated as his sons separate from each other, which is a prelude to violence (Jub 7:26-27). Noah reminds them of Enoch's warnings (vv. 38-39). Kainan reads the inscription left by the Watchers and proceeds to cross the boundary of endogamy, marrying a Japhethite (8:5). The boys then need the intervention of Noah and the angels to rightly divide the earth, but the demons move in (chap. 10). Consequently we find Noah's offspring replicating the violence of the prediluvian giants (11:2-6).

Jubilees made it clear that the demons have power over the Gentiles but not over Israel (15:28-32). If an Israelite crossed the boundary of ethnic purity, the Israelite crossed into the demonic domain and could not return. For those pious, God-seeking Israelites who found themselves in exile, the homeless patriarchs and Israel's experience in Egypt set hopeful precedents. They rightly belong within the boundary. They have the option to "come home." If they do, they place themselves beyond the reach of the demons, but that return involves placing themselves within the boundaries defined by the Enochic paradigm as interpreted by Jubilees. Any Israelite who chose to remain outside that boundary would be lost.

When Jubilees explicitly states that 'Aza'el was sent by God to teach helpful things to humans (Jub 4:15), and that the crossing of boundaries occurred subsequently, he may not (at least not substantively) have changed the original account in the Enoch books he had to hand.[15] This may not be a

---

15. See discussion in Reed, *Fallen Angels*, 35-36, noting the tension already present in

"minimizing" of the connection between the prediluvian giants and the postdiluvian demons, as Reed has suggested.[16] It was in marrying women that the Watchers crossed the boundary of spirit and flesh and so abandoned their right to return to heaven, not their initial descent (cf. 1 En 6:6; 12:4; 14:5; 15:3, 7, 10; 16:2; 84:4; 86:1). So it was also for the author's target audience. Living in a land ruled by Gentiles would not constitute "going astray." Intermarrying with them would. Jubilees did not set aside a concept of an origin of evil that occurred without a free choice. In the BW the women are not raped but marry — "they are co-perpetrators, not victims."[17]

Jubilees took the opportunity to identify within the Torah narrative other minor exemplars that conform to the pattern, in particular the experience of Lot in Sodom (Jub 20:2-7). Joseph demonstrates how an Israelite can survive under Gentile rule. Because of his rigorous moral purity, Joseph was not only protected and blessed by God, but no demon or satan could bring destruction to any who came under his leadership (40:9; 46:2). It is interesting then that in Joseph's case Jubilees seems to have made an exception. Whereas the writer avoids noticing Moses' marriage to a Midianite or Amram's marriage to his aunt, no such attempt is made to avoid Joseph's marriage to an Egyptian (30:17). His culpability is bypassed perhaps as a union imposed by Pharaoh but perhaps also because the author may have seen in the future history of Ephraim and Manasseh reason not to omit their Gentile roots. The concern for purity focuses on the female line.

The 'Aza'el Exemplar

The 'Aza'el exemplar viewed the same event from the perspective of cultural purity. 'Aza'el (1 En 10:8) was deemed responsible for revealing to humans heavenly secrets that were forbidden to them and, in so doing, empowering them to develop deviant and rebellious cultural practices. The 'Aza'el exemplar demonized the scholarship, philosophies, education, and therefore the culture of the Gentiles.[18] It also presented the elect righteous with a body of

---

1 En 9:6-10 and perhaps 86:1-2, and the juxtaposition of human and Watcher culpability in chaps. 7 and 8; and Bergsma's paper in this volume, "The Relationship between Jubilees and the Early Enochic Books (Astronomical Book and Book of the Watchers)," section III.

16. Reed, *Fallen Angels*, 77-78.

17. See discussion in Jackson, *Enochic Judaism*, 35-36.

18. See D. R. Jackson, "Demonising Gilgamesh," in *Gilgamesh and the World of Assyria*, ed. J. Azize and N. Weeks, Ancient Near East Studies Supplement 21 (Louvain: Peeters,

revelation designed to counter these influences and so maintain the distinctive lifestyle of the elect.

In the books of Enoch that Jubilees used, possession of and adherence to the revelations given to Enoch defined the elect (1 En 1:1-3).[19] This body of revelation was first given to Enoch (Jub 4:17-18a, 21, 23b; 7:38-39) and then passed down, supplemented, and renewed through the elect line of Noah (8:10-12, 18; 10:13), Shem (10:14), Abraham (11:16; 12:25-27; 21:10; 41:28), Jacob (19:14; 32:24-26; 39:6), and Levi (45:16). After Amram taught Moses to write (47:9), it came to Moses on Mount Sinai (1:1-18) as an addition to "the first law" (2:24; 6:22). At this location we are presented with the reality that Israel then possessed two canons.

Reading Jubilees within the context of the 'Aza'el exemplar, we have a framework for the relationship between this revelation and "the first law" or Torah also revealed to Moses.[20] We might best describe this relationship as a "two-canon" system. This concept labels a body of texts deemed to be authentic revelations by God, and thus authoritative, without precluding the reception of further additions over time. It does not then justify the claim that the canon was, at this time, "open."[21] Probably at no time in history has there ever been "one canon" on which all Jews or all Christians agreed. "Canon" has always been a marker of divisions. That does not mean that these canons were "open." Nor does it assume that a canon had to be defined by a top-down decree. Rather, it recognizes a bottom-up process of persuasion rather than coercion.[22]

2007), 107-14. See also Henryk Drawnel, "Some Notes on Scribal Craft and the Origins of the Enochic Literature," *Hen* 31, no. 1 (2009).

19. See also 1 En 79:1; 81:1-2, 6; 82:1-10; 83:1-2; 91:1; 92:1; 94:2; 97:1-6; 98:3; 106:19–107:1, and George W. E. Nickelsburg, "The Nature and Function of Revelation in 1 Enoch, Jubilees, and Some Qumranic Documents," in *Pseudepigraphic Perspectives: The Apocrypha and Pseudepigrapha in Light of the Dead Sea Scrolls*, ed. Esther Chazon and Michael Stone, STDJ 31 (Leiden: Brill, 1999), 92-120.

20. See the concise and helpful discussion in VanderKam, *The Book of Jubilees*, Guides to Apocrypha and Pseudepigrapha 9 (Sheffield: Sheffield Academic Press, 2001), 136-41, of Jubilees' use of not only the Torah but also other parts of the Tanakh, noting in particular that Jub 30:12 refers to the Genesis narrative (Gen 34) as "the words of the Law."

21. See James C. VanderKam, "Revealed Literature in the Second Temple Period," in *From Revelation to Canon: Studies in the Hebrew Bible and Second Temple Literature*, ed. James C. VanderKam (Leiden: Brill, 2000), 1-30.

22. Ulrich's distinction between "a collection of authoritative books of scripture" and a canon breaks down where that "collection" could be identified by its adherents — whether or not a copy of that list is extant. See Eugene Ulrich, "The Notion and Definition of Canon," in *The Canon Debate*, ed. Lee Martin McDonald and James A. Sanders (Peabody, Mass.:

We cannot be certain as to the limits of "first canon" within any part of the Jewish community at this time. It is clear that there were canons governing the faith of various communities and that the Torah[23] was widely recognized as canonical in this sense. The Enochic paradigm appears to have established its own two-canon system. Modern analogies would be the Mormons and the Seventh-Day Adventists.[24] Where a two-canon system is in place, it is the second canon that is seen as dominant by outsiders while insiders usually affirm the equal authority of both. The second canon defines the group's elect identity and governs its interpretation of the first.[25]

This second canon (and Jubilees in particular) seems to identify the first canon as a work that Israel ignored and by which Israel will be judged, giving the second canon a more prominent role in pointing to the way of salvation for the elect remnant of Israel in the last days. Himmelfarb notes that "For the Damascus Covenant, the Torah of Moses contains commandments, while *Jubilees* contains the history of Israel's failure to fulfill those commandments [CD 16:1-4]."[26]

In Jubilees Abram becomes a particular model of how one born into a world dominated by demonic idolatry could be saved. Abram goes through a process of realization, separation, seeking, and revelation. This pattern corresponds closely with the Damascus Document's recounting of the origins of the Yakhad (CD-A 1:8-13, noting "they realized their iniquity . . . they were like those who grope for a path . . . they sought him with an undivided heart . . . raised up for them a Teacher of Righteousness. . . . And he made known to the last generations what he had done for the last generation"). Nitzan has independently observed this pattern in the sequence of events leading up to God's revelation of Jubilees to Moses on Sinai.[27]

Hendrickson, 2002), 21-35. Where a "collection" of such texts constituted the basis for parenesis and the subject of polemic, as did the Enochic second canon, it had to have been identifiable.

23. Cf. the use of "in the Law" in 1 Cor 14:21 to cite Isa 28:11-12, and also John 10:34, a use that renders "the Law" somewhat synonymous with the later concept of a canon.

24. See, for example, the statement from the Seventh-Day Adventist Church (http://www.adventist.org/beliefs/fundamental/index.html) and the Mormon statement at http://www.mormon.org/learn/0,8672,1275-1,00.html.

25. See Grant Macaskill, "Priestly Purity, Mosaic Torah, and the Emergence of Enochic Judaism," *Hen* 31, no. 1 (2009).

26. Martha Himmelfarb, "Torah, Testimony, and Heavenly Tablets: The Claim to Authority of the Book of Jubilees," in *Multiform Heritage* (Atlanta: Scholars Press, 1999), 23, cited in James M. Scott, *On Earth*, 81-82. See also Calum Carmichael, "The Integration of Law and Narrative in Jubilees: The Biblical Perspective," *Hen* 31, no. 1 (2009).

27. See also discussion in Endres, "Eschatological Impulses in Jubilees," in this volume.

As Jubilees developed this concept, the author perceived this exemplar replicated even before the Watchers' sin. Adam and Eve violated the boundaries established by God in accepting the deceptive advice of the serpent in order to learn a forbidden secret (Jub 3:19). The result was sexual shame, followed by violence as the next generation turned to murder, requiring mandatory separation and a new beginning with Seth. Once again, to conform to the exemplar, only the elect remnant could be saved. Adam and Eve therefore were permitted to cover their shame, but the animals were not (3:30).

Jubilees also extended paradigm consistency (Jub 13:26) by having the languages of heaven and earth brought back into regularity (12:25-27). These texts traced back to Enoch were in Hebrew (21:10; cf. 19:27). This presents us with an obvious difficulty given that the Enoch texts in our possession are in Aramaic, as are several other works purporting to reflect prediluvian or patriarchal narratives of this tradition.[28] A Hebrew original is nevertheless a logical necessity if the Enochic agenda was the restoration and defense of a distinctive Israeli identity under Gentile domination. It is also notable that the vast bulk of the non-Tanakh texts found in the Qumran library were written in Hebrew and written after Jubilees. Abegg notes that comments in $1QH^a$ 10:19, 12:16, 15:10, and CD 5:11-12 indicate that the sect used Hebrew as a matter of principle.[29] The close association of Jubilees with Aramaic texts such as the Genesis Apocryphon, and the Aramaic Levi Document, taken with its dependence on what we have of the books of Enoch, might indicate that Jubilees effected a language shift in future adaptations of the paradigm. Whatever the case, we are left to wonder why, unlike Tobit, we have no translation of these works into Hebrew and why they were still being copied in Aramaic over a century later.

The fact that the second canon claimed to be the product of angelic dictation did not prevent later writers (e.g., 4Q252) from adapting it or even correcting internal irregularities, just as the author of Jubilees treated "the first law." This is consistent with the apparent lack of concern for a consistent textual tradition among the Qumran Tanakh manuscripts. Over time one would expect two developments to arise from this process. Firstly, the first canon would be dominated by the second. Secondly, works dealing more directly with the particulars of the target audience's day would dominate those

28. See Nickelsburg, *1 Enoch 1*, 177, on the reference to Jared as a Hebrew pun in 1 En 6:5.

29. Martin G. Abegg, Jr., "Hebrew Language," in *Dictionary of New Testament Background*, ed. Craig A. Evans and Stanley E. Porter (Downers Grove, Ill.: InterVarsity, 2000), 459-63.

establishing the methodology. We see both developments over the next two centuries.

There was probably an element of secrecy inherent in the ʾAzaʾel exemplar that would account for the use of antilanguage[30] and cryptic scripts[31] in this tradition. The association of the second canon with the concept of "mystery" and the appearance of rules of initiation restricting access to these texts (cf. 1QS 9:15-19) may reflect an adaptive response to the totalitarian decree of Simon Maccabeus requiring submission of all Jewish communities to his rulings, and banning any "meeting in our country without his permission" on pain of death (1 Macc 14:44-45).

It is the function of this second canon specifically to maintain purity, to equip the elect not to be deceived by the wisdom and teachings of the demons/ Gentiles, and to learn and observe the correct calendar so as to realign their lives with the order of heaven. As such, the ʾAzaʾel exemplar facilitated the solutions to the concerns of the other two exemplars, and tied these solutions exclusively to the revelations passed down in this tradition as "testimony"[32] or parenesis.

The Cosmic Exemplar

The cosmic exemplar viewed the same event from the perspective of liturgical purity. The angels who were thought to govern the cosmic phenomena relevant to the calendar were understood to have rebelled and thus thrown the cosmos out of synchronization with the divinely appointed order and calendar (which was perfect in symmetry) and in so doing broke the bond between the worship of God that must take place on earth and that which takes place in heaven.

The cosmic exemplar was located in heaven and so would not be replicated in the course of human history. The elect on earth needed the Enochic "second canon" revelations to learn to ignore the observable and worship according to the original design, as first revealed to Enoch during his heavenly tour.

In BW we discern a connection between the now-deviant cosmologi-

30. See Jackson, *Enochic Judaism*, 19-21.
31. See discussion in Scott, *On Earth*, 69 n. 119.
32. VanderKam, *The Book of Jubilees*, 26, notes that this appears to be the author's title for his work (Jub 1:8) and that the term is used to identify the content of angelic revelation and his central exhortations to obedience to this revelation.

cal phenomena governing the calendar and the Watchers who transgressed, firstly in the names that are given to them (1 En 6), and also in the correlation between their names and the specific secrets they have wrongfully revealed. A similar correlation can be found with the responsibilities accredited to Uriel (20:2) and Reuel, who is given the responsibility for taking "vengeance upon the world of the luminaries" (20:4). In the understanding of these texts, observable cosmic phenomena are operated by spiritual beings alternately called "spirits/winds" (1 En 18:1-5) or angels (cf. Jub 2:2-3; 1QH^a 9:10-13; cf. also 1 En 69:13-24). We are then introduced to the fact that the "stars of heaven" "transgressed the command of the Lord" (21:5-6).

This concept appears also in the AB. Throughout the AB we learn that the astronomical and meteorological phenomena are "led" by spiritual beings having a hierarchical chain of command (e.g., 1 En 72:1-3; 74:2; 75:1, 3, 5; 79:6). Some of these winds/spirits are winds/spirits of punishment (76:4). In 80:1 "leading" involves "turning" the sun, moon, and stars, but "many heads of the stars will stray from the command and will change their ways and actions and will not appear at the times prescribed for them" (80:6-7). As a result, sinners will err, because "the entire law of the stars will be closed to the sinners" and so they will "take them to be gods" and then evil will multiply and punishments will follow.

This reflects what we find in 1 En 18:15, where Enoch hears about "the stars and the host of heaven . . . that transgressed the command of the Lord in the beginning of their rising, for they did not come out in their appointed time." Like the cohorts of Shemikhazah and 'Aza'el, these are "bound . . . until the time of the consummation of their sins." These leaders are those who "keep watch so they enter at their times" (82:10). They are "watchers."

Enoch briefs Methuselah (1 En 82:5) on the subject. The specific error of the human sinners concerns their failure to observe the four days that divide the year into equal quarters (82:3-4). The problem here is the failure to conform to the symmetry of the year. The fact that observable reality doesn't line up with any known calendar at the time is not resolved by more accurate observations. We are told that as a result of this event, "in the days of the sinners" (80:2) the year is shortened and so the seasons are late. The moon does not appear at the right time (80:4). This Enochic calendar is not a construct based on observation. It is a theoretical construct based on an a priori understanding of the character of God expressed in the paradigm of rigorous order and regularity.[33] Glessmer comments: "These considerations indicate

33. See James M. Scott, "The Chronologies of the Apocalypse of Weeks and the Book of Jubilees," in this volume.

that if a comprehensive heading for the concept of calendar at Qumran is to be chosen, the oft-used term 'solar calendar' is certainly inappropriate and should be avoided. For those using this type of calendar the constitutive element was the number of 364 days, which allows the schematic assignment of weeks or Sabbaths."[34] Ben-Dov notes, "This device is neither solar nor lunar, nor stellar nor any other astronomical predicate, but rather it is a schematic 364 [day year]."[35] The God of the Enochic paradigm could not possibly stand behind or authorize a calendar as confused and irregular as one based on the observations of deviant cosmic phenomena. Where one could point out a failure of the Enochic construct to correlate with observed reality, the Enochic response was to deny the validity of that reality. There had been a cosmic departure from God's order, and that departure is correlated with the events and the names involved in the actions of Shemikhazah, 'Aza'el, and their cohort. This correlation may be reflected in the use of stars as allegorical representations of these deviant Watchers in AA at 1 En 86:1-3 (cf. also 88:1).

Drawnel[36] demonstrates persuasively that the manner in which AB developed its calculations involving the progression of the moon and the sun would have had polemical significance in favor of the 364-day calendar as against the deviance of the Babylonian scribal tradition. The specifically antilunar polemic of Jubilees may therefore simply reflect the different social challenges faced by the author.

It is noteworthy that this cosmic rebellion/deviation directly affected Israel's observation of the liturgical year, in particular, the feasts in 1 En 82:7.

Conclusion

Within the Enochic tradition each of the three exemplars is connected to the other two. Only the ethnically pure line of the elect could stand outside the dominion of the demons. To them was given by revelation the skills needed

34. Uwe Glessmer, "Calendars in the Qumran Scrolls," in *The Dead Sea Scrolls after Fifty Years: A Comprehensive Assessment,* ed. Peter W. Flint and James C. VanderKam (Leiden: Brill, 1999), 2:213-78 (here 231). See also section II of Bergsma's chapter in this volume.

35. Jonathan Ben-Dov, "Tradition and Innovation in the Calendar of Jubilees," in this volume.

36. Drawnel, "Some Notes on Scribal Craft and the Origins of the Enochic Literature"; cf. Ben-Dov, "Tradition and Innovation in the Calendar of Jubilees."

to counter demonic power and to live a lifestyle of purity without idolatry, fornication, or self-destructive violence. This Enochic self-understanding constituted a holy priesthood facilitating the return of all the descendants of this chosen line to a right standing before God on judgment day. To them alone was given the revelation needed to live that lifestyle and to maintain that distinction. It was grounded in the perfection of the heavenly tablets, communicated through a pure line of righteous elect living exemplary lives[37] under alien and deviant regimes. Enoch saw these things firsthand in the heavens. Holy angels dictated this information to him and to those who came after him down to the time of the actual authors. This revelation included the correct calendar and restored the ability of the elect to synchronize the worship of the saints on earth with the holy ones in heaven. Departure from ethnic, cultural, or liturgical purity, as defined by these exemplars, placed one beyond redemption. The result was a passionate parenesis directed to second temple Jews based on the self-validating claim of the various tradents of this body of revelation that they were marked out as the "Enoch" of their time before an impending judgment of greater proportion than Noah's day. These claims may have been disputed by a variety of attempts to domesticate the paradigm, much as various disputes arose as to the rightful identity of "the elect remnant" or "the Israel of God," all of which, taken together, attest to the power of the construct to make sense of the experience of the Jewish people in this period.

Jubilees represents a significant and groundbreaking stage of development in the early history of the use and adaptation of the Enochic paradigm. In company with the Genesis Apocryphon and Aramaic Levi, it marks the point at which the Enochic paradigm and exemplars were being applied to the postdiluvian world. It traced and analyzed replications of the exemplars up to the end of the Torah narrative and even back to the sin of Adam and Eve. It provided a model for integrating the Enochic system and revelations with those works variously accepted as first canon. These were not the arbitrary impositions of an alien structure upon the Torah but a sincere and pedantic attempt to correlate the two texts exegetically.[38] In so doing, Jubilees stimulated an exponential agenda that produced many of the works found in the Qumran library and more. For scholars today it provides a direct and

---

37. See Dorothy Peters, "Noah Traditions in Jubilees: Evidence for the Struggle between Enochic and Mosaic Authority," *Hen* 31, no. 1 (2009).

38. See Carmichael, "The Integration of Law and Narrative in Jubilees," *Hen* 31, no. 1 (2009).

overt link between those texts. It also enables us to form some idea of an internal context within which to attempt to understand the variations, tensions, and anomalies that we find in them.

This system involved an ongoing ability to self-correct. The goal of perfect internal consistency combined with the flexibility of replicating exemplars made the Enochic paradigm a most resilient system as a basis upon which to understand and deal with the complexities, confusions, powers, and often the horror of a wide range of Jewish experience over a period of around three centuries. It is well then to remember that behind and consequent upon the various texts that claimed this tradition were real people. As Kvanvig observed in the course of our discussions, "We see their fingerprints, but not their footprints." This paradigm constitutes those fingerprints.

Jubilees, Qumran, and the Essenes

Eyal Regev

I. The Act of Comparison

Comparison is one of the theoretical tools of the study of history, and particularly *Religionsgeschichte*. In the current stage of Qumran scholarship, many scholars are engaged in comparing different documents, and in certain cases, also comparing social phenomena, such as the Essenes, the *yaḥad*, and the Damascus Covenant. To compare two entities a certain degree of similarity is necessary, but comparison is provocative and insightful only when one is able to point to significant differences.[1]

II. Similarities

What, then, are the general similarities that enable us to compare Jubilees, Qumran, and the Essenes? Jubilees and the Qumran sects (or rather, the Community Rule and the Damascus Document) share a belief in predestination[2]

---

1. F. J. P. Poole, "Metaphors and Maps: Towards Comparison in the Anthropology of Religion," *JAAR* 54 (1986): 411-57; R. A. Segal, "In Defense of the Comparative Method," *Numen* 48 (2001): 339-74; J. Z. Smith, *Drudgery Divine: On the Comparison of Early Christianities and the Religion of Late Antiquity* (Chicago: University of Chicago Press; London: School of Oriental and African Studies, 1990).

2. The belief in predestination in the Instruction of the Two Spirits corresponds to Jubilees' conception that the future is written on the heavenly tablets (e.g., Jub 1:29; 23:32).

and the immortality of the soul,[3] the concept of holy and evil angels and spirits and the struggle between them,[4] a 364-day calendar,[5] the association of sin with moral impurity in the pursuit of atonement, holiness, and eternal bliss.[6] One may also add Sabbath interdictions common to Jubilees and the Damascus Document 10–11,[7] as well as specific sacrificial laws common to Jubilees, the Temple Scroll, and MMT.[8]

The Qumran sects are usually identified with the Essenes, who were described by Philo, Josephus, and Pliny the Elder: they share tension in relation to the temple, an emphasis on moral behavior, self-restraint, purity, and prayer. The Essenes and the *yaḥad* share common property, companionship, gradual admission, and according to most scholars, celibacy. The avoidance of oil (since it is thought to defile) and restrictions on the Sabbath, and the role of overseers or officials, are common to the Essenes and the Damascus Covenant.[9]

3. Jub 23:30-31. For Qumran, see 1QH[a] 9[Sukenik 3]:21-23; J. Licht, *The Thanksgiving Scroll* (in Hebrew) (Jerusalem: Bialik Institute, 1957), 83-84; E. Puech, *La Croyance des Esséniens en la Vie Future: Immortalité, Résurrection, Vie Éternelle?* (Paris: Gabalda, 1993), 366-75.

4. Jub 10:11; 18:9; 48:2-3, 12-19; 1QS 3:18-26; 4:1-2. Cf. CD 5:17-19. Similarities between angelology in Jubilees and Qumran, e.g., the War Rule, the Hodayot, were noted by D. Dimant, "bnei shanyim — torat ha-mal'akhim beseferer ha-yovlim le'or kitvei a'dat qumran," in *Tribute to Sara: Studies in Jewish Philosophy and Kabbala*, ed. M. Idel, D. Dimant, and S. Rosenberg (Jerusalem: Magnes, 1994), 110-18. For these general theological similarities, see also J. C. VanderKam, *Textual and Historical Studies in the Book of Jubilees*, HSM 14 (Missoula: Scholars Press, 1977), 260-80.

5. For the general resemblance between the two calendars, see, e.g., J. C. VanderKam, "The Temple Scroll and the Book of Jubilees," in *Temple Scroll Studies*, ed. G. J. Brooke, JSPSup 7 (Sheffield: JSOT Press, 1989), 211-36. This consensus was first disputed by L. Ravid, "The Book of Jubilees and Its Calendar — a Reexamination," *DSD* 10 (2003): 371-94. Ravid has shown that many of the liturgical characteristics of the Qumranic calendar are unattested in Jubilees, but he did not prove that there were actual contradictions between the two.

6. Cf. also G. Boccaccini, *Beyond the Essene Hypothesis: The Parting of the Ways between Qumran and Enochic Judaism* (Grand Rapids and Cambridge: Eerdmans, 1998), 93-98.

7. L. H. Schiffman, *Law, Custom, and Messianism in the Dead Sea Scrolls* (in Hebrew) (Jerusalem: Zalman Shazar, 1993), 90-135.

8. VanderKam, "The Temple Scroll and the Book of Jubilees." Cf. the articles of Shemesh in this volume and J. Hopkins, "The Authoritative Status of Jubilees at Qumran," *Hen* 31, no. 1 (2009).

9. Todd S. Beall, *Josephus' Description of the Essenes Illustrated by the Dead Sea Scrolls*, SNTSMS 58 (Cambridge: Cambridge University Press, 1988); J. M. Baumgarten, "The Disqualifications of Priests in 4Q Fragments of the 'Damascus Document,' a Specimen of the

But what do Jubilees and the Essenes have in common? Following Boccaccini's comparison of the Essenes with the entire Enochic literature, including Jubilees, one may mention the belief in predestination and immortality of the soul, as well as the belief in angels and the sensitivity to the pitfalls of sexuality.[10] Nonetheless, it seems to me that the association of Jubilees with the Essenes is indirect and dependent on their strong relationship with the Qumran sects.

III. Differences

Jubilees differs from both the *yaḥad* and the Damascus Covenant in its basic social stance. Jubilees is addressed to the people of Israel, attempting to convince them to follow the path of the eternal convent in Sinai. It emphasizes the holiness of the Jewish nation as a whole,[11] contrasting the Israelites to the immoral Gentiles and condemning contacts with Gentiles.[12] Admittedly, Jubilees is critical of the Jews who transgress the laws pertaining to the calendar, circumcision, and nudity, and perhaps also the Sabbath.[13] In one instance (30:16) Jubilees even seeks to prevent someone whose daughter married a Gentile from entering the temple. On the whole, however, Jubilees does not want certain Jews to separate themselves from the rest of the nation due to their religious or halakic scrupulousness.

In contrast, the *yaḥad* and the Damascus Covenant are sects by definition. They are strongly characterized by the three major ideological compo-

---

Recovery of Pre-Rabbinic Halakha," in *The Madrid Qumran Congress,* ed. J. Trebolle Barrera and L. Vegas Montaner, STDJ 11 (Leiden: Brill, 1992), 2:503-13 (here 503-5). One may also add the limitation on the discharge of excretions, mentioned by Philo and in the Temple Scroll and the War Rule (see below).

10. Boccaccini, *Beyond the Essene Hypothesis,* 165-96. Cf. Josephus, *Jewish War* 1.171-173; *Ant* 2.154.

11. Jub 2:19, 23, 31-33; 15:27, 32; 16:17-18; 18:19; 19:16-19, 21-24; 21:24-25; 22:12-24; 24:10; 25; 27:23; 31:14; 33:20.

12. For the Gentiles' immorality and impurity, see Jub 1:8-11; 3:31; 11:16; 12:1-8, 12-14; 19; 20:7-8; 21:3, 5; 22:16; 25:1; 30:13-15; 31:1-2; 35:14; 36:5; 48:5. For the call for separation from the Gentiles, see Jub 6:35; 9:14-15; 15:34; 22:16; 25:1; 30. For Gentile impurity in Jubilees, see C. Hayes, *Gentile Impurities and Jewish Identities: Intermarriage and Conversion from the Bible to the Talmud* (Oxford: Oxford University Press, 2002), 47, 53, 54, 55. For the prohibition on intermarriage in Jubilees, see Hayes, 73-81. See also the article by Doering in this volume.

13. Calendar: 6:23-32; 23:19; circumcision: 15:25-26, 33-34; nudity: 3:31; 7:20; Sabbath: 2:29-30; 50:8-9; 23:19.

nents of a sectarian worldview: antagonism in relation to the outside world; social separation from outsiders; and a developed sense of "difference" in their self-identity and practices or rituals.[14] The belief system of the Qumran sects, especially the *yaḥad*, is based on condemning Jews outside the sect and social separation from the surrounding society.[15] Contacts such as those created by commerce are limited or inspected by the sect rules or by the overseers.[16] The rest of the Jews are doomed as long as they persist in rejecting the sect's doctrine.[17] Simply stated, Jubilees does not correspond to the definition of a sectarian ideology. The Qumran sectarians do not adopt Jubilees' prohibition on the use of the moon in calculations, and instead follow Enoch's Astronomical Book harmonizing solar and lunar sequences with each other.[18]

The social position of Jubilees is somewhat clarified in chap. 23 (the so-called Jubilees apocalypse), where the author juxtaposes the "elders" with the "young ones." The two parties debate "the law and the covenant" (23:16), especially the calendar. The author associates the elders with impurity, contamination, detestation, and corruption and accuses them of "defiling the holy of holies with the impure corruption of their contamination" (23:21b). The author of Jubilees views his movement as the true Israel, but surprisingly, unlike the Community Rule or the Damascus Covenant, he does not seem to claim that the elders will be cut off from the nation. At the age of punishment, it seems that all Jews will suffer (23:21-25). No matter how sinful the elders may be, the author does not regard them as doomed. He also implies that the elders will ultimately accept the teachings of the young ones (23:26-31). Thus, according to the author, the unity of the Jewish people will be preserved.

The elders in Jub 23 represent the traditional and conservative elite, while the young ones are a radical party that challenges the degenerated con-

---

14. For the definition of sectarianism see R. Stark and W. S. Bainbridge, *The Future of Religion: Secularization, Revival, and Cult Formation* (Berkeley and Los Angeles: University of California Press, 1985), 49-60.

15. E. Regev, "Abominated Temple and a Holy Community: The Formation of the Concepts of Purity and Impurity in Qumran," *DSD* 10, no. 2 (2003): 243-78 (here 256-75).

16. Cf. CD 13:14-17; 20:6-8; 1QS 5:15-16; 8:20; 9:7-9.

17. CD 7:9-13; 8:2-3; 19:5-11; 1QS 4:18-20; 9:23; Licht, *The Thanksgiving Scroll*, 32-33.

18. U. Glessmer, "Calendars in the Qumran Scrolls," in *The Dead Sea Scrolls after Fifty Years*, ed. J. C. VanderKam and P. W. Flint (Leiden: Brill, 1999), 2:213-78 (here 244-55). 4Q252 1 i 8-10 also rectifies the Jub 5:27 error in claiming that the 150 days in Gen 8:3 constituted five months (Glessmer, 258-59).

Eyal Regev

sensus. I therefore believe that the elders cannot be identified with the Hellenized Jews of the Seleucid period.[19] The author's portrayal of the two parties in terms of age differences, namely, separate generations, corresponds with what the sociologist Karl Manheim called "the problem of generations." The categories of generations mark two social classes of separate "historical space," namely, distinct social units.[20] All this leads me to the conclusion that the general characteristics of Jubilees and particularly chap. 23 do not reflect a sect but rather a reform movement.[21] Jubilees represents a group that aims to change society rather than withdraw from it. It challenges the prevailing elite, wishing to lead the people in a different path.

This general social difference between Jubilees and the Qumran sects also applies to the comparison of Jubilees with the Essenes. Apart from strictness pertaining to avoidance of work on the Sabbath, the Essene social restrictions and taboos are unattested in Jubilees. One interesting contrast between the two is that whereas most Essenes lived in celibacy without women, Jubilees presents an idealized characterization of biblical matriarchs.[22]

Those who identify the "Qumran community," the "Qumran sectarians," or the "Dead Sea Scrolls sect" with the Essenes tend to overlook the fact that at least two distinct sects are reflected in the scrolls. Although the *yaḥad* of the Community Rule and the Damascus Covenant of the Damascus Document share much terminology and many general ideas, they differ in social organization, hierarchal or egalitarian structure, the stringency of social boundaries, and in other ideological aspects.[23] This fact complicates the comparison of the Essene practices and way of life with those in the scrolls, since in several cases one point of similarity between the Essenes and the *yaḥad* actually serves as a discrepancy between the Essenes and the Damascus Covenant, or vice versa. The most significant example is communal

19. In contrast to scholars such as G. L. Davenport, *The Eschatology of the Book of Jubilees* (Leiden: Brill, 1971), 41-43, following Charles.

20. K. Manheim, *Essays on the Sociology of Knowledge* (London: Routledge and Kegan Paul, 1952), 276-320.

21. Cf. already K. Berger, *Das Buch der Jubiläen*, Jüdische Schriften aus hellenistisch-römanischer Zeit, II.3 (Gütersloh: Güterloher Verlagshaus Gerd Mohn, 1981), 298.

22. B. Halpern-Amaru, *The Empowerment of Women in the Book of Jubilees*, JSJSup 60 (Leiden: Brill, 1999).

23. P. R. Davies, "The Judaism(s) of the Damascus Document," in *The Damascus Document: A Centennial of Discovery*, ed. J. M. Baumgarten et al., STDJ 34 (Leiden: Brill, 2000), 27-43; E. Regev, "The *Yaḥad* and the Damascus Covenant: Structure, Organization and Relationship," *RevQ* 21, no. 2 (2004): 233-62.

ownership of property, common to the Essenes and the *yaḥad*, whereas members of the Damascus Covenant maintained private property.[24]

There are two significant discrepancies between the Essenes, on the one hand, and the *yaḥad* and the Damascus Covenant, on the other hand. Essene abstinence from taking oaths is not attested in the scrolls, which specify regulations for taking oaths before judges to affirm lost property and mention vows as a normative and even frequent practice.[25] Essene rejection of slavery is inconsistent with evidence from the Damascus Covenant, since CD 11:12 prohibits "pressing" one's servant or maidservant (to work) on the Sabbath. However, there is no mention of servants in the Community Rule. Presumably, neither the *yaḥad* nor the Essenes used servants, since they both maintained common property and aimed at socioeconomic equality. Interestingly, recently discovered ostraca from kh. Qumran mention the delivery of a slave named Ḥisdai from Ḥolon, and may attest to the dwellers' readiness to accept slaves as property.[26]

Several relatively minor differences are also notable, since they pertain to social order, rituals, and taboos, on which sects put great emphasis. Josephus's Essenes differ from both the *yaḥad* and the Damascus Covenant in their social structure and types of leadership. The Essene overseers *(epimelētai)* care for the needs of the entire community. They have complete authority in directing the members' work.[27] Josephus also refers to Elders, who are the leaders of the Essene group.[28] The role of the Essene Elders resembles the total authority of overseers and certain priests in the Damascus

24. CD 13:15-16; 14:12-18. For the Essene communal ownership of property, see Philo, *Hypothetica* 10.11; Philo, *Quod omnis probus liber sit* 86; Josephus, *Jewish War* 2.122; Josephus, *Ant* 18.20; Pliny the Elder, *Natural History* 5.73. For the *yaḥad* see, e.g., 1QS 6:19-23; for the Damascus Covenant, see CD 13:14-16; 14:12-17.

25. CD 9:8-12; 16:1-7. For the Essenes, see Philo, *Quod omnis probus liber sit* 84; Josephus, *Jewish War* 2.135; cf. *Ant* 15.371. On oaths in the Damascus Document, see Schiffman, *Law, Custom,* 204-11, 220-27. Beall, *Josephus' Description,* 69-70, draws upon the silence of the Community Rule in relation to oaths other than those of joining converts, for creating a false parallelism with Philo and Josephus, while resolving the evidence from the Damascus Document's different stages of development.

26. For the Essenes, see Philo, *Hypothetica* 11.4; *Quod omnis probus liber sit* 79; Josephus, *Ant* 18.21. For CD 11:12, see Schiffman *Law, Custom,* 125-26. For the ostraca, see F. M. Cross and E. Eshel, "Ostraca from Khirbet Qumran," *IEJ* 47 (1997): 17-28. The conclusion that the dwellers in kh. Qumran accepted slaves as property is reasonable even if one rejects the reading of *yaḥad* in line 5, a reading according to which the ostraca attest to the admission of a new member and his property into the *yaḥad*.

27. Josephus, *Jewish War* 2.123, 129, 134.

28. Josephus, *Jewish War* 2.146.

Document.[29] Nonetheless, there is only a single and quite insignificant occurrence of "Elders" in the Damascus Document.[30] Elders are mentioned only once in the Community Rule,[31] where they are lower in hierarchy than priests, and have no special authority within the *yaḥad,* which, unlike the Essenes, has a democratic and semi-egalitarian social structure with no governing individual leader. Josephus's assertion that the Essenes "obey their elders and the majority"[32] appears to reflect a combination of CD's governing overseers and priests and the *yaḥad's* assembly of the *rabbim* ("many").

In two cases, what appears to be a parallel between Josephus's Essenes and the scrolls actually conceals a discrepancy. In their gradual admission of novices into the sect, the Essenes exclude novices from the "purer water for purification" (which obviously refers to ritual baths) for one year before the novices prove their temperance in a probation period. During the subsequent two years, novices are excluded from partaking in the common meals.[33] This parallels 1QS 6:13-23, where converts into the *yaḥad* are excluded from "the purity of the many" in the first year, and from "the drink/liquids of the many" (which probably also means purification rituals and common meals) in the second. The Essene probation period is longer, and furthermore, their inclusion in communal practices progresses in an inverse order: new Essene converts are first permitted to participate in ritual baths, and only at a later stage in communal meals, in contrast to the order of inclusion in the *yaḥad.*[34] More generally, the Community Rule and the Damascus Document also mention a much more lenient admission process compared to the Essenes, which merely requires an oath, with no probation period.[35]

---

29. CD 9:13-15; 13:15-16; 14:12-17.

30. CD 9:4.

31. 1QS 6:8. Beall, *Josephus' Description,* 47, with bibliography, argued that this is a point of resemblance.

32. Josephus, *Jewish War* 2.146.

33. Josephus, *Jewish War* 2.137-138. Beall, *Josephus' Description,* 73-74, translates *sumbiōsis* "common meals," whereas Thackeray (LCL edition, 377) translates "the meeting of the community."

34. Beall, *Josephus' Description,* 74-75, emphasized the general parallelism of gradual acceptance but understated the differences.

35. 1QS 5:7-10; CD 15:6-10. The vow of the Essene novice is part of the lengthy admission process. J. Licht, *The Rule Scroll: A Scroll from the Wilderness of Judaea, 1QS 1QSa 1QSb; Text, Introduction, and Commentary* (in Hebrew) (Jerusalem: Bialik Institute, 1965), 146-47, noted that the Essene novice takes an oath at the completion of the admission into the group, whereas converts to the *yaḥad* do so in the first stage of their admission process. Cf. *War* 2:139-142; 1QS 6:14-15; Beall, *Josephus' Description,* 77.

The Essenes dig a hole with their personal shovels to bury excretions,[36] whereas the Temple Scroll and the War Rule order the building of permanent latrines. There is no evidence in the scrolls of an implement similar to the shovel that every Essene receives when he enters the sect and carries with him wherever he goes.[37] As A. Baumgarten noted, the different practices represent different perceptions of the body.

Each of these differences in practices and taboos may be explained by the incomplete information of Josephus or Philo, as outsiders, by their individual biases, their Gentile audience, or the differences between individual local communities in different places and different periods of time.[38] However, it is difficult to explain away such a series of discrepancies concerning different issues related to taboos and social structure, which are extremely sensitive and meaningful in sectarian organizations.

One interesting Essene phenomenon that is at odds with the Qumran scrolls is Essene public prophecies and political involvement. Judas the Essene predicts that Antigonus the Hasmonean will be killed at Strato's Tower.[39] When Herod is young, Menahem predicts that he will be king of the Jews, and when Herod rules, Menahem predicts that he will reign for twenty or thirty more years but refuses to specify the precise length of his reign.[40] Simon interprets Archelaus's dream correctly, and predicts that his reign will soon come to an end.[41] In these instances, I suggest, the Essenes use their competence to foresee the future in order to attain social power and perhaps also to draw the attention of potential converts.

While several documents from Qumran attest to the belief that members (and particularly the Teacher of Righteousness) are able to reveal future events through divine revelation and interpretation of the words of the prophets,[42] the Qumranic predictions are general and refer to the End of

36. Josephus, *Jewish War* 2.148-149. Cf. 5.145.

37. A. I. Baumgarten, "The Temple Scroll, Toilet Practice, and the Essenes," *Jewish History* 10 (1996): 9-20. Note that the Temple Scroll and the War Rule rules are utopian documents. One may question whether the *yaḥad* and the Damascus Covenant actually followed them.

38. A. Dupont-Sommer, *The Essene Writings from Qumran*, trans. G. Vermes (Cleveland and New York: World Publishing Company, 1962), 66-67; J. Strugnell, "Flavius Josephus and the Essenes: *Antiquities* XVIII.18-22," *JBL* 77 (1958): 106-15; G. Vermes, *The Dead Sea Scrolls, Qumran in Perspective*, rev. ed. (London: SCM, 1994), 115-17.

39. Josephus, *Jewish War* 1.78-80.

40. Josephus, *Ant* 15.371-379.

41. Josephus, *Jewish War* 2.312-313; *Ant* 17.345-348.

42. For the general identification of these prophecies with the pesherim, see Beall, *Josephus' Description*, 110-11.

Days, whereas the Essene prophecies focus on a specific historical occasion in the nearest future.[43] Even more surprising is the fact that Menahem and Simon interact both politically and personally with Herod and Archelaus. One can hardly imagine distinguished members of the *yaḥad*, who shun all outsiders as "people of Belial," discussing their divine messages with these rulers, whom even many commoners despise.

Finally, I maintain that the most significant difference between the Essenes and both the *yaḥad* and the Damascus Covenant pertains to celibacy. It is a common assertion that the *yaḥad* were celibates, just like the Essenes, based on the argument of silence: women, children, and families are not mentioned in the Community Rule. This is convincing as long as one is blinded by the sweeping identification of the *yaḥad* as Essenes. In a forthcoming article in *Dead Sea Discoveries*[44] I maintain that when the evidence is reexamined, several intriguing questions arise: Is it possible that a celibate sect would totally ignore the interdiction to marry and procreate? Is celibacy a marginal taboo to be taken for granted in a legal codex such as the Community Rule? Is it reasonable to believe that the *yaḥad* were celibate while no single document in Qumran hints at the ideas of celibacy, virginity, etc.? If the *yaḥad* are indeed celibates, their gender taboos should have taken a prominent place in the Community Rule.

I suggest that one neglected document, 4Q502, the so-called *ritual of marriage*,[45] may demonstrate the place of women, children, marriage, and procreation in the *yaḥad*. Joseph Baumgarten interpreted 4Q502 as a ritual in which married couples declare their commitment to a celibate life since both male and female members participate in a certain ceremony.[46] But 4Q502 opens with references to "man and his wife," "to reproduce offspring," "a daughter of truth," and "his wife" (frgs. 1-3). I cannot see any reason why these expressions should be taken as merely symbolic. Furthermore, 4Q502 alludes to reproduction, marriage, and young children: "to reproduce" (frg. 1), "toddlers" (frgs. 28 and 311), "the girl's father" (frg. 108), "his wife in fruit of the womb" (frg. 309). The text also mentions "lads and virgins, young men and young women" (frg. 19); "sons and daughters" (frg. 14); "young men" (frg. 9); "to sisters" (frg. 96). They seem to be too young

---

43. R. Gray, *Prophetic Figures in Late Second Temple Jewish Palestine: The Evidence from Josephus* (New York and Oxford: Oxford University Press, 1993), 105-7.

44. E. Regev, "Chercher les femmes: Were the *Yaḥad* Celibates?" *DSD*, forthcoming.

45. M. Baillet, *Qumrân Grotte 4.III*, DJD 7 (Oxford: Clarendon, 1982), 81-105.

46. J. M. Baumgarten, "4Q502, Marriage or Golden Age Ritual," *JJS* 34 (1983): 125-35. Cf. 4Q502, frgs. 19, 24, and 34.

to be new converts. These are probably the sons and daughters of the community members.

There are several indications that 4Q502 is related to the *yaḥad*. The adverb *yaḥad* is mentioned at least four times in this very fragmented text. Furthermore, several terms are particularly characteristic of other documents of the *yaḥad*, namely, the Community Rule, the pesherim, and the Hodayot: "holy of holies," "the law of God," "daughter of truth" (or "son/men of truth" in other texts), and *teu'dah* (testimony, appointed times, stipulation). While none of these points suffices to conclude that 4Q502 originated in the *yaḥad*, taken together I think they demonstrate that this is more than probable. This may serve as a further argument against the supposed celibacy of the *yaḥad*.

Due to all these discrepancies I find it impossible to argue that the Qumran sects and the Essenes are the same or that the *yaḥad* and the Damascus Covenant are groups within the larger (and ultimately, celibate) Essene movement. But as I shall argue below, it is hard to deny that there is a certain, more complex relationship between them.

IV. Social and Historical Relationship

Jubilees' ideology is not sectarian but rather aims to take the lead and reform Judaism rather than withdraw from the rest of society. Its group therefore cannot be identified with the Qumran sects. Nonetheless, Jubilees has close affinities with several Qumranic texts, mainly the Temple Scroll and MMT.

Jubilees shares with the Temple Scroll and MMT several sacrificial laws,[47] and laws pertaining to priestly offerings. Similar to the Temple Scroll, Jubilees orders that a he-goat *(s'eir)* for atonement should be sacrificed first, in contrast to the plain text of Num 28–29 and rabbinic halakah.[48] Jubilees seems to share the Temple Scroll's celebration of the Festival of Weeks (firstfruits of wheat) on the fifteenth of the third month,[49] as well as the festivals of the firstfruits of new wine and oil.[50] Both Jubilees and MMT order

---

47. VanderKam, "The Temple Scroll and the Book of Jubilees."

48. Jub 7:4; Temple Scroll 14:10-12; 23:11; 26:5–27:4; Y. Yadin, *The Temple Scroll* (Jerusalem: Israel Exploration Society and the Shrine of the Book, 1977), 1:103, 116-17.

49. Jub 15:1; 16:13; Temple Scroll 18:10-16 (the rabbis celebrated it on the sixth of that month).

50. Temple Scroll 19:11-14; 21:12-16. Admittedly, Jub 7:36 mentions only the offerings of the first wine and oil. Both the Temple Scroll and Jubilees interpret these offerings as per-

that the animal tithe should be given to the priests, whereas according to the rabbis the owners are the recipients.[51] Jubilees, the Temple Scroll, and MMT order that the fruits of the fourth year should be given to God's servants (namely, the priests), whereas the rabbis argued that they should be eaten by their owners.[52] Both Jubilees and the Temple Scroll call for eating the Passover sacrifice in the temple, whereas according to the rabbis it may be eaten anywhere in the city of Jerusalem.[53] Both Jubilees and the Temple Scroll command that the second tithe be brought to the temple every year.[54]

Furthermore, Jubilees' stress on the impurity of the Gentiles should be associated with specific cultic laws in MMT: the refusal to accept sacrifices from Gentiles, the exclusion of Ammonites and Moabites from the temple, and perhaps also the prohibitions on bringing Gentiles' offering/tithe of wheat and grain to the temple (since they are defiled).[55]

One interesting point of correspondence between Jubilees and the Temple Scroll is related to the eschatological temple that will replace the monumental temple described in the scroll. In Temple Scroll 29:8-10, God promises: "I shall sanctify my [Te]mple with my glory, for I shall make my glory reside over it until the day of creation, when I shall create my Temple, establishing it for myself for all days, according to the covenant which I made with Jacob in Bethel." The concept of the new ideal temple at the time of the new creation is also mentioned in Jub 4:26, and the eschatological temple and the new creation are mentioned separately in several places.[56] The relevance of the covenant in Bethel in relation to the eternal temple of the Temple Scroll is puzzling. Interestingly, this point is elucidated by Jub 32, where Bethel is the site of Levi's inauguration to the priesthood by Jacob.[57]

---

mission to eat the new crop (a view not followed by the rabbis; cf. also Jub 32:11-14; Temple Scroll 43:3-11; Yadin, *The Temple Scroll*, 1:92-93). However, note that Jubilees also fails to mention the harvest of the Omer, and therefore its treatment of the festivals is not systematic. VanderKam, "The Temple Scroll," 225, believes that the Jubilees author is aware of these firstfruits holidays.

51. Jub 32:15; MMT B 63-64; *m. Zevahim* 5:8.

52. Jub 7:36; MMT B 62-63; Temple Scroll 60:3-4; 4QD^a 2 ii 6; *m. Ma'aser Sheni* 5:1-5; Sifrei Numbers *ba-midbar* 6 (ed. Horovits 6); *y. Pe'ah* 7:6 (20b-20c). Jubilees, however, adds further restrictions concerning sacrificing of the fruit and refraining from eating the plant in the fifth year.

53. Jub 49:16, 20; Temple Scroll 17:8-9; *m. Zevahim* 5:8.

54. Jub 32:10-11; Temple Scroll 43:1-17; Yadin, *The Temple Scroll*, 1:92-94.

55. MMT B 8-9, 39-40, 3-5, respectively.

56. Eschatological temple: Jub 1:17; new creation: Jub 1:27, 29; 5:12.

57. In his vision, Jacob is handed seven tablets (Jub 32:31), presumably containing sac-

Hence, this tradition is much clearer and more developed in Jubilees than the abridged account in the Temple Scroll, and it seems that here the Temple Scroll is dependent on Jubilees.

Jubilees and the homiletic section (C) of MMT share the association of sin with impurity. In MMT the authors argue, "we have separated ourselves from the multitude of the people [and from all their impurity]."[58] This impurity is probably moral, since the fragmentary continuation of this passage relates to moral sins: "and concerning . . . [the malice] and the treachery . . . and fornication [some] places were destroyed." . . . "[no] treachery or deceit or evil can be found in our hand."[59] Similar accusations are ascribed to the "evil generation" in Jub 23:14: (moral) impurity and contamination, sexual impurity (which parallels MMT's fornication) and detestable actions (which parallel MMT's malice, treachery, and deceit). Further on, similar accusations are attributed to "the elders" in Jubilees: "they have acted wickedly . . . everything they do is impure . . . all their ways are contamination," "cheating through wealth . . . they will defile the holy of holies with the impure corruption of their contamination."[60]

I am not arguing here that the MMT's Multitude of the People is identical with Jubilees' "evil generation." Rather, the fact that both are described in the same manner shows that both documents share the belief that sin defiles and use it as a fundamental conceptualization of their own social position in comparison to their adversaries.

Jubilees and MMT col. C also share the belief that the messianic age is at hand. The authors of MMT declare: "And we are aware that part of the blessings and curses have occurred that are written in the b[ook of Mos]es. And this is the End of Days, when they will return in Israel to the L[aw . . .] and not turn bac[k] and the wicked will act wickedly. . . ."[61] Jub 23:26-31 envisions that the "children" will take over after the punishment from the nations, return to the right way of the laws and commands, and an age of great

---

rificial laws that may be identified with the Temple Scroll's reference to Jacob's covenant. Jacob was commanded not to build an eternal temple in Bethel (Jub 32). This implies that, although the priestly cult officially originated in Bethel, Jerusalem is holier. Note that there was a major sanctuary in Bethel during the first and early second temple period; see J. Schwartz, "Jubilees, Bethel, and the Temple of Jacob," *HUCA* 56 (1985): 63-85.

58. MMT C 7-8.

59. MMT C 4-6, 8-9. See Regev, "Abominated Temple," 249-51.

60. Jub 23:17, 21 respectively. For further examples of moral impurity in Jubilees, see Doering's article in this volume.

61. MMT C 20-22.

peace, praise, and happiness will arrive. In both cases there is hope for religious reform that will lead to salvation. Admittedly, the sense of salvation in MMT is more imminent. The "end of days" is not merely a matter of expectation; it is a fact. This difference can be explained, not only in light of MMT's special rhetorical aim to persuade the addressee to act according to the authors' beliefs, but also by the assumption that several years elapsed between the composition of Jubilees and MMT. During these years the messianic tension may have increased.

I have pointed to halakic and ideological connections of Jubilees with the Temple Scroll and MMT, which are also not sectarian documents, at least not in the strict sociological sense of this term. If MMT and the Temple Scroll are usually regarded as preceding the formation of the *yahad* and the Damascus Covenant, Jubilees can certainly be placed in the same category. Moreover, there are several indications that Jubilees represents the events of the Hellenistic reform in Jerusalem and the Maccabean wars against the Seleucids, that is, before the Hasmonean period (a period that is certainly reflected in the pesherim).[62] I therefore believe that Jubilees preceded the formation of the Qumran sects, and should be related to (although probably not identical with) the group behind the Temple Scroll and (slightly later) MMT.

The relationship between the Essenes and the Qumran sects is difficult to reconstruct. In contrast to the Groningen Hypothesis or the Enochic Hypothesis,[63] I do not think the Essenes were the parent group of the Qumranites. First, the Essene practices on which the identification with Qumran is based are described by first century c.e. sources, two centuries after the emergence of the *yahad* and the Damascus Covenant. Second, as was shown above, the similarities between the Essenes and the Qumran sects are quite general. The only specific points of absolute similarity in the Damascus Document are prohibitions on moving vessels on the Sabbath, preparations in the course of the Sabbath, and intercourse with a pregnant woman.[64] In the Community Rule the similarities relate to the role of the priests in the

---

62. VanderKam, *Textual and Historical Studies,* 217-38. The polemics against nudity and neglecting of circumcision, as well as the hatred against the Gentiles, seem to be the strongest signs for this date. For the pesherim, see H. Eshel, *The Dead Sea Scroll and the Hasmonean State* (in Hebrew) (Jerusalem: Yad ben-Zvi Press, 2004).

63. See their evaluation in *Enoch and Qumran Origins,* ed. G. Boccaccini (Grand Rapids and Cambridge: Eerdmans, 2005), 249-454.

64. All these are found in the Damascus Document. See Baumgarten, "Disqualifications," 504-5, for references and bibliography.

preparation of bread and the priestly prayer/blessing before the meal.[65] They do not justify the conclusion that the *yaḥad* and the Damascus Covenant were part of the Essene movement or emerged from it. Nevertheless, it is impossible to deny that there is a certain relationship between them.

In contrast to the *yaḥad* and the Damascus Covenant, the Essenes pose three major taboos and boundaries on marriage, oaths, and slaves. Moreover, it seems that the Essenes have much in common with both the *yaḥad* and the Damascus Covenant: the communal ownership of property, gradual admission to the sect, and communal meals of the *yaḥad*, on the one hand, and the Sabbath prohibitions and social hierarchy of the Damascus Covenant on the other. In their attitude toward the temple, the Essenes "serve God not with sacrifices of animal, but by resolving to the sanctity of their minds," which is quite similar to the *yaḥad*'s conception of prayer and morality as (temporal) substitutes for the sacrificial rites.[66] But the Essenes also send donations to the temple, as in the Damascus Document.[67] It therefore seems that the Essenes adopt practices from both the *yaḥad* and the Damascus Covenant.

The Essenes also have a more complex, one may even say dialectic, ideology, combining strict segregation with attempts to gain public power through prophecies that concern the politics of the late Hasmonean and Herodian dynasties.

The strict boundaries, the dual dependence on practices of both the *yaḥad* and the Damascus Covenant, and the use of public predictions for political reasons indicate that the Essenes were a more complex movement than either of the Qumran sects. I think the most plausible explanation for this complexity is that the Essenes were a later development of the *yaḥad and the Damascus Covenant*.[68] Such social or religious complexity seems to be a result of a process of evolution over several generations, and the adoption of new modes of behavior that are incorporated into older practices.

---

65. Josephus, *Jewish War* 2.131; 1QS 6:4-5.

66. Philo, *Quod omnis probus liber sit* 75; 1QS 9:4-5; Regev, "Abominated Temple," 269-71.

67. Josephus, *Ant* 18.19; CD 11:18-20.

68. This conclusion holds as long as we follow Josephus and Philo and regard the Essenes as one more or less unified movement, rather than a conglomerate of different groups that differ in various practices.

V. Conclusions

The Jubilees movement can certainly be regarded as the bedrock of the Qumranic ideology, where ideas of angelology, dualism, predestination, moral impurity, atonement, and strict cultic halakah were first weaved together. But Jubilees is not a sect in any sense, but rather a reform movement. The Essenes, on the other hand, are not identical with the *yaḥad* and the Damascus Covenant, but seem to reflect later developments, especially the practice of celibacy. The groups represented in the scrolls and the other related movements differed in many respects. These differences conceal the special characteristics and uniqueness of each sect or group. Insiders must have seen many other differences and nuances that are still hidden from us. We will keep on looking for them.[69]

---

69. For a detailed analysis of the subjects discussed here, see E. Regev, *Sectarianism in Qumran: A Cross-Cultural Perspective*, Religion and Society Series 45 (Berlin and New York: De Gruyter, 2007), 219-66.

The Book of Jubilees: A Bibliography, 1850-Present

Veronika Bachmann and Isaac W. Oliver

The present bibliography includes scholarly works on the book of Jubilees from its first German translation in 1850 by August Dillmann up to the present (one may also consult previous bibliographies, including Delling 1975, Charlesworth 1976 and 1981, Berger 1981, Rosso Ubigli 1990, Lehnardt 1999, and DiTommaso 2001 — see main bibliography below). The discoveries of the Hebrew fragments of Jubilees at Qumran represented a major step for the understanding of the Book of Jubilees, and the following entries have been divided accordingly into two main sections: before and after Qumran. Each section is further divided into two parts, the first containing a list of text editions and translations, the other scholarly articles, monographs and books discussing various issues related to Jubilees.

A companion, annotated bibliographical essay, which summarizes the contents of most scholarly works written on Jubilees, and highlights the different approaches and questions raised over the last 150 years of research by scholars, has been published in the journal *Henoch* (I. W. Oliver and V. Bachmann, "The Book of Jubilees: An Annotated Bibliography from the First German Translation of 1850 to the Enoch Seminar of 2007," *Hen* 31, no. 1 [2009]). Readers are also invited to consult the contributions on the history of research of Jubilees offered by VanderKam ("The Origins and Purposes of the Book of Jubilees," in *Studies in the Book of Jubilees,* ed. Matthias Albani, Jörg Frey, and Armin Lange, Texte und Studien zum antiken Judentum 65 [Tübingen: Mohr Siebeck, 1997], 4-16; "Recent Scholarship on the Book of Jubilees," *Currents in Biblical Research* 6, no. 3 [2008]: 405-31) and by Segal

(*The Book of Jubilees: Rewritten Bible, Redaction, Ideology, and Theology*, JSJSup 62 [Leiden: Brill, 2007], 11-21).

Part 1: The Scholarly Works on Jubilees before the Discoveries of Qumran

1. Text Editions, Translations, and Commentaries

Ceriani, Antonio Maria. "Parva Genesis." In *Monumenta sacra et prophana 1.1*, 9-54, 63-64. Milan, 1861.

―――. "Nomina uxorum patriarcharum priorum iuxta librum Hebraeum Jobelia nuncupatum." In *Monumenta sacra et prophana 2.1*, ix-x. Milan, 1863.

Charles, Robert Henry. "The Book of Jubilees Translated from a Text Based on Two Hitherto Uncollated Ethiopic MSS." *JQR* 5 (1893): 703-8; 6 (1894): 184-217, 710-45; 7 (1895): 297-328.

―――. *The Ethiopic Version of the Hebrew Book of Jubilees*. Oxford: Clarendon, 1895.

―――. *The Book of Jubilees or the Little Genesis, Translated from the Editor's Ethiopic Text, and Edited with Introduction, Notes, and Indices*. London: Adam and Charles Black, 1902.

―――. "The Book of Jubilees." In *Apocrypha and Pseudepigrapha of the Old Testament*, 2:1-82. Oxford: Clarendon, 1913.

―――. *The Book of Jubilees or the Little Genesis* [with an introduction by G. H. Box, Translations of Early Documents. Series 1, Palestinian-Jewish Texts (pre-rabbinic) 4. London: SPCK; New York: Macmillan, 1917].

Dillmann, August. "Das Buch der Jubiläen oder die kleine Genesis, aus dem äthiopischen übersetzt." *Jahrbücher der biblischen Wissenschaft* 2 (1850): 230-56; 3 (1851): 1-96.

―――. *Mashafa Kufale sive Liber Jubilaeorum, qui idem a Graecis Ἡ Λεπτὴ Γένεσις inscribitur, aethiopice ad duorum librorum manuscriptorum fidem primum edidit*. Kiel: C. G. L. van Maack; London: Williams and Norgate, 1859.

Langen, Joseph. *Das Judenthum in Palästina zur Zeit Christi. Ein Beitrag zur Offenbarungs- und Religions-Geschichte als Einleitung in die Theologie des Neuen Testaments*, 84-102. Freiburg im Breisgau: Herdersche Verlagshandlung, 1866.

Littmann, Enno. "Das Buch der Jubiläen." In *Die Apokryphen und Pseudepigraphen des Alten Testaments*, edited by Emil Kautzsch, 2:31-119. Tübingen: Mohr, 1900; reprint, 1975.

Martin, François. "Le Livre des Jubilés. But et procédés de l'auteur. Ses doctrines." *RB* 8 (1911): 321-44, 502-33.

Rahmani, Ignatius Ephraem. *Chronicon civile et ecclesiasticum anonymi auctoris*. Monte Libano: Typis Patriarchalibus Syrorum, 1904.

Riessler, Paul. "Jubiläenbuch oder Kleine Genesis." *Altjüdisches Schrifttum außerhalb der Bibel* (Augsburg: B. Filser, 1928; repr. 1966; 1988): 539-666, 1304-11.

Rönsch, Hermann. "Die Leptogenesis und das Ambrosianische altlateinische Fragment derselben." *ZWT* 14 (1871): 60-98.

———. *Das Buch der Jubiläen oder Die kleine Genesis*. Leipzig: Fues, 1874; reprint, Amsterdam: Rodopi, 1970.

Rubin, Salomon. *Sefer ha-Yovlim: ha-mekhuneh Midrash Bereshit Zutrata*. Vienna: Holtsvarte, 1870.

Schodde, George H. "The Book of Jubilees Translated from the Ethiopic." *BSac* 42 (1885): 629-45; 43 (1886): 56-72, 356-71, 455-86; 44 (1887): 426-59, 602-11, 727-45 [= *The Book of Jubilees* (Oberlin, Ohio: Goodrich, 1988; reprint, Columbus, Ohio: Lazarus Ministry Press, 1999)].

Tisserant, Eugène. "Fragments syriaques du Livre des Jubilés." *RB* 30 (1921): 55-86, 206-32. Reprinted in *Recueil Cardinal Eugène Tisserant: "Ab Oriente et Occidente,"* 2 vols. (Louvain: Centre international de dialectologie générale, 1955), 1:25-87.

2. Books, Monographs, and Articles

Albeck, Chanoch. *Das Buch der Jubiläen und die Halacha*. Berlin: Scholem, 1930.

Albright, William Foxwell. *From the Stone Age to Christianity*, 266-69. Baltimore: Johns Hopkins University Press, 1940.

Bacon, Benjamin Wisner. "The Calendar of Enoch and Jubilees." *Hebraica* 8 (1892): 124-31.

Beer, Bernhard. *Das Buch der Jubiläen und sein Verhältniss zu den Midraschim. Ein Beitrag zur orientalischen Sagen- und Alterthumskunde*. Leipzig: Gerhard, 1856.

———. *Noch ein Wort über das Buch der Jubiläen*. Leipzig: Hunger, 1857.

Bohn, F. "Die Bedeutung des Buches der Jubiläen. Zum 50jährigen Jubiläum der ersten, deutschen Übersetzung." *TSK* 73 (1900): 167-84.

Borchardt, Paul. "Das Erdbild der Juden nach dem Buche der Jubiläen — ein Handelsstrassenproblem." In *Dr. A. Petermanns Mitteilungen aus Justus Perthes' geographischer Anstalt*, edited by P. Langhans, vol. 71, pp. 244-50. Gotha: Justus Perthes, 1925.

Bousset, Wilhelm. "Neueste Forschungen auf dem Gebiet der religiösen Litteratur des Spätjudentums II: Zur Litteratur der Makkabäerzeit (Fortsetzung)." *TRu* 3 (1900): 369-81.

Box, George Herbert. "Introduction to the Book of Jubilees." In *The Book of Jubilees or the Little Genesis*, vii-xxxiii. London: SPCK; New York: Macmillan, 1917.

Büchler, Adolphe. "Studies in the Book of Jubilees." *REJ* 82 (1926): 253-74.

———. "Traces des idées et des coutumes hellénistiques dans le Livre des Jubilés." *REJ* 89 (1930): 321-48.

Veronika Bachmann and Isaac W. Oliver

Charles, Robert Henry. *A Critical History of the Doctrine of Future Life in Israel, in Judaism, and in Christianity; or, Hebrew, Jewish, and Christian Eschatology from Pre-Prophetic Times Till the Close of the New Testament Canon; Being the Jowett Lectures for 1898-1899*, 245-49. London: Adam and Charles Black, 1899.

Dillmann, August. "Das Buch der Jubiläen und sein Verhältniss zu den Midraschim." *ZDMG* 11 (1857): 161-63.

————. "Beiträge aus dem Buch der Jubiläen zur Kritik des Pentateuch-Textes." *Sitzungsberichte der Königlich-Preussischen Akademie der Wissenschaften zu Berlin* 15 (1883): 323-40.

Eppel, Robert. "Les tables de la loi et les tables célestes." *RHPR* 17 (1937): 401-12.

Epstein, Abraham. *Beiträge zur jüdischen Althertumskunde* (in Hebrew). Vienna: Lippe, 1887.

————. "Le livre des Jubilés, Philon et le Midrash Tadshe." *REJ* 21 (1890): 80-97; 22 (1891): 1-25.

Finkelstein, Louis. "The Book of Jubilees and the Rabbinic Halaka." *HTR* 16 (1923): 39-61. Reprinted in *Pharisaism in the Making: Selected Essays* (New York: Ktav, 1972), 199-221.

————. "The Date of the Book of Jubilees." *HTR* 36 (1943): 19-24.

Fox, Gresham George. "Ethical Elements in the First Book of Enoch, the Book of Jubilees, and the Testaments of the Twelve Patriarchs." Ph.D. diss., University of Chicago, 1914.

Frankel, Zacharias. "Das Buch der Jubiläen." *MGWJ* 5 (1856): 311-16, 380-400.

Frenkel, Éliás (Ernö). *A Jubileumok könyve, Adalékok az ókori zsidóság egyik kronológiai m†uvéhez* (The book of Jubilees, additional materials to an ancient Jewish chronological writing). Bölcsécsdoktori értekezés. Budapest: Sárkány nyomda, 1930.

Frey, J.-B. "Apocryphes de l'Ancien Testament. 2. Le Livre des Jubilés." *DBSup* 1 (1928): 371-80.

Gelzer, Heinrich. *Sextus Julius Africanus und die byzantinische Chronographie*, 2:251-62. Leipzig: Hinrich, 1898; reprint, New York: Burt Franklin, 1967.

Ginzberg, Louis. "Libro dei Giubilei 16,30." *Rivista Israelitica* 5 (1908): 74.

Hadas, Moses. "Jub. 16:30." *AJSL* 49 (1933): 338.

Hölscher, Gustav. "Die Karte des Jubiläenbuches." In *Drei Erdkarten. Ein Beitrag zur Erdkenntnis des hebräischen Altertums*, 57-73. Heidelberg: C. Winter, 1949.

Jellinek, Adolph. *Über das Buch der Jubiläen und das Noah-Buch*. Leipzig: Vollrath, 1855.

Klein, S. "Palästinisches im Jubiläenbuch." *ZDPV* 57 (1934): 7-27.

Kohler, Kaufmann. "The Pre-Talmudic Haggada I." *JQR* 5 (1893): 399-419.

————. "Jubilees, Book of." *JE* 7 (1904): 301-4.

Krüger, M. J. "Die Chronologie im Buch der Jubiläen, auf ihre biblische Grundlage zurückgeführt und berichtigt." *ZDMG* 12 (1858): 279-99.

Kuenen, Abraham. "Der Stammbaum des masoretischen Textes des Alten Testaments." In *Gesammelte Abhandlungen zur biblischen Wissenschaft. Aus dem Hol-*

ländischen übersetzt von K. Budde, 82-124. Freiburg im Breisgau and Leipzig: Mohr, 1894.

Leszynsky, Rudolf. *Die Sadduzäer*, 179-236. Berlin: Mayer & Müller, 1912.

Levi Della Vida, Giorgio. "Una traccia del Libro die Giubilei nella letteratura araba musulmana." *Or* 1 (1932): 205-12.

Montgomery, James Alan. "An Assyrian Illustration to the Book of Jubilees." *JBL* 33 (1914): 157-58.

Pfeiffer, Robert Henry. "Jubilees." In *History of New Testament Times, with an Introduction to the Apocrypha: Part I; Judaism from 200 BCE to 200 CE*, 68-70, 538. New York: Harper and Brothers, 1949.

Rowley, Harold Henry. *The Relevance of the Apocalyptic*, 81-85. London: Lutterworth, 1944. 2nd ed. (New York: Harper and Brothers, 1946), 84-90; 3rd ed. (New York: Association Press, 1964), 99-105.

———. "Criteria for the Dating of Jubilees." *JQR* 36 (1945-46): 183-87.

Schürer, Emil. *Geschichte des jüdischen Volkes im Zeitalter Jesu Christi*, 3:371-84. 4th ed. Leipzig: Hinrichs'sche Buchhandlung, 1909.

Singer, Wilhelm. *Das Buch der Jubiläen oder Die Leptogenesis 1: Tendenz und Ursprung zugleich ein Beitrag zur Religionsgeschichte*. Stuhlweissenburg: Singer, 1898.

Torrey, Charles Cutler. "Jubilees." In *The Apocryphal Literature: A Brief Introduction*, 126-29. New Haven: Yale University Press, 1945.

Uhden, Richard. "Die Erdkreisgliederung der Hebräer nach dem Buche der Jubiläen." *ZS* 9 (1934): 210-33.

Wells, L. S. A. "The Book of Jubilees: The Earliest Commentary on Genesis." *IJA* 28 (1912): 13-17.

Zeitlin, Solomon. "The Book of Jubilees: Its Character and Its Significance." *JQR* 30 (1939-40): 1-32. Reprinted in *Studies in the Early History of Judaism* (New York: Ktav, 1974), 2:116-46.

———. "The Book of Jubilees." *JQR* 35 (1944-45): 12-16.

———. "Criteria for the Dating of Jubilees." *JQR* 36 (1945-46): 187-89.

———. "The Apocrypha." *JQR* 37 (1947): 219-48.

Part 2: The Scholarly Works on Jubilees after the Discoveries of Qumran

1. Text Editions, Translations, Commentaries, and Concordances

Agourides, Savas. "ΙΩBHΛAIA" (in modern Greek). *Theologia* 43 (1972): 550-83; 44 (1973): 34-118.

Artom, Elia Samuele. "Sefer ha-yovelot." In *Sipure agadah* 2. 6 vols. in 2. Tel Aviv: Yavneh Publishing House, 1969.

Baillet, Maurice. "Livre des Jubilés." In DJD 3, pp. 77-79. Oxford: Clarendon, 1962.

————. "Remarques sur le manuscrit du livre des Jubilés de la grotte 3 de Qumran." *RevQ* 5 (1965): 423-33.

————. "Livre des Jubilés." In DJD 7, pp. 1-2. Oxford: Clarendon, 1982.

Bauer, Johannes B. *Clavis apocryphorum supplementum. Complectens voces versionis germanicae libri Henoch Slavici, libri Jubilaeorum, Odarum Salomonis.* GTS 4, pp. 9-119. Graz: Institut für Ökumenische Theologie und Patrologie, 1980.

Berger, Klaus. "Das Buch der Jubiläen." In *JSHRZ* 2.3 (1981), 275-575.

Bonsirven, Joseph. "Le livre des Jubilés ou Petite Genèse." In *La Bible Apocryphe en marge de l'Ancien Testament*, 78-115. Paris: A. Fayard, 1953.

Caquot, André. "Jubilés." In *La Bible, Ecrits Intertestamentaires III*, 629-810. Paris: Gallimard, 1987.

Corriente, Federico, and Antonio Piñero. "Jubileos." In *Los apócrifos del Antiguo Testamento*, 2:65-193. Madrid: Ediciones Cristianidad, 1983.

Deichgräber, Reinhard. "Fragmente einer Jubiläen-Handschrift aus Höhle 3 von Qumran." *RevQ* 5 (1965): 415-22.

Denis, Albert Marie. "Les fragments grecs du Livre des Jubilés." In *Introduction aux pseudépigraphes grecs d'Ancient Testament*, 150-62. Leiden: Brill, 1970.

————. "Liber Jubilaeorum." in *Fragmenta Pseudepigraphorum quae supersunt Graeca*, 70-102. PVTG 3. Leiden: Brill, 1970.

————. *Concordance latine du Liber Jubilaeorum sive parva Genesis.* Informatique et étude de textes 4. Louvain: CETEDOC, 1973.

Fusella, Luigi, and Paolo Sacchi. "Giubilei." In *Apocrifi ell'Antico Testamento*, 1:179-411. Turin, 1981.

García Martínez, Florentino. "Book of Jubilees." In *The Dead Sea Scrolls Translated*, 238-45. Leiden: Brill, 1994.

————. "Qumran Cave 11 II: 11Q2-18, 11Q20-31." In DJD 23, pp. 207-21. Oxford: Clarendon, 1998.

García Martínez, Florentino, and Eibert J. C. Tigchelaar. *The Dead Sea Scrolls Study Edition.* 2 vols. Leiden: Brill, 1998. See 1:22-25; 1:214-15; 1:226-27; 1:360-63; 1:458-83; 2:964-65; 2:1204-7.

Goldmann, M. "The Book of Jubilees" (in Hebrew). In *The Apocryphal Books*, edited by Abraham Kahana, 1:216-313. Tel Aviv: Masada, 1956.

Kondracki, Andrzej. "Księga Jubileuszow." In *Apokryfy Starego Testamentu*, edited by Ryszard Rubinkiewicz, 271-351. Warsaw: Vocatio, 1999.

Lipscomb, W. Lowndes. "A Tradition from the Book of Jubilees in Armenian." *JJS* 29 (1978): 149-63.

Milik, Józef Tadeusz. "Livre des Jubilés." In DJD 1, pp. 82-84. Oxford: Clarendon, 1955.

————. "Fragment d'une source du psautier (4QPs89) et fragments des Jubilés, du Document de Damas et d'un phylactère dans la grotte 4 de Qumran." *RB* 73 (1966): 104, pl. II.

Noack, Bent. "Jubilaeerbogen." In *GamPseud* 3, pp. 175-301. Copenhagen: Gad, 1958.

Parry, Donald W., and Emanuel Tov, eds. *The Dead Sea Scrolls Reader III: Parabiblical Texts*. 6 vols. Leiden: Brill, 2004-2005.

Rabin, C. "Jubilees." In *The Apocryphal Old Testament*, edited by Hedley F. D. Sparks, 1-139. Oxford: Clarendon, 1984.

Rofé, Alexander. "Further Manuscript Fragments of Jubilees in Qumran Cave 3" (in Hebrew). *Tarbiz* 34 (1965): 333-36.

Stökl, Jonathan. "A List of the Extant Hebrew Text of the Book of Jubilees: Their Relation to the Hebrew Bible and Some Preliminary Comments." *Hen* 28, no. 1 (2006): 97-124.

Torrey, Charles Cutler. "A Hebrew Fragment of Jubilees." *JBL* 71 (1952): 39-41.

Tov, Emanuel, ed. *The Dead Sea Scrolls Electronic Reference Library 3*. New York: Brill, 2006.

VanderKam, James C. *The Book of Jubilees*. 2 vols. CSCO 510-511. Scriptores Aethiopici 87-88. Louvain: Peeters, 1989.

————. "The Jubilees Fragments from Qumran Cave 4." In *The Madrid Qumran Congress 2*, edited by J. Trebolla Barrera and L. Vegas Montaner, 635-48. STDJ 11. Leiden, New York, and Cologne: Brill, 1992.

VanderKam, James C., and Józef Tadeusz Milik. "A Preliminary Publication of a Jubilees Manuscript from Qumran Cave 4: 4QJub (4Q219)." *Bib* 73, no. 1 (1992): 62-83.

————. "Jubilees." In DJD 13, pp. 1-140. Oxford: Clarendon, 1994.

Vaux, Roland de. "La grotte des manuscrits hébreux." *RB* 56 (1949): 602-5.

Vermes, Geza. "Jubilees." In *The Complete Dead Sea Scrolls in English*, 507-10. New York: Penguin Press, 1997.

Wintermute, Orval S. "Jubilees: A New Translation and Introduction." In *The Old Testament Pseudepigrapha*, edited by James H. Charlesworth, 2:35-142. 2 vols. New York: Doubleday, 1983, 1985.

Wise, Michael Owen, Martin G. Abegg, Jr., and Edward M. Cook. "The Book of Jubilees." In *The Dead Sea Scrolls: A New Translation*, 316-35. Rev. ed. San Francisco: HarperSanFrancisco, 2005.

Woude, Adam S. van der. "Fragmente des Buches Jubiläen aus Qumran Höhle XI." In *Tradition und Glaube. Festgabe für K. G. Kuhn*, edited by Gert Jeremias et al., 140-46. Göttingen: Vandenhoeck & Ruprecht, 1971.

2. Books, Monographs, and Articles

Adler, William. "Abraham and the Burning of the Temple of Idols: Jubilees' Traditions in Christian Chronography." *JQR* 77 (1986-87): 95-117.

————. "The Origins of the Proto-Heresies: Fragments from a Chronicle in the First Book of Epiphanius' 'Panarion.'" *JTS* 41, no. 2 (1990): 472-501.

Albani, Matthias. "Zur Rekonstruktion eines verdrängten Konzepts: Der 364-Tage-

Kalender in der gegenwärtigen Forschung." In *Studies in the Book of Jubilees*, edited by Matthias Albani, Jörg Frey and Armin Lange, 79-126. TSAJ 65. Tübingen: Mohr Siebeck, 1997.

Alexander, Philip S. "Retelling the Old Testament." In *It Is Written: Scripture Citing Scripture; Essays in Honour of Barnabas Lindars*, edited by D. A. Carson and H. G. M. Williamson, 99-121. New York: Cambridge University Press, 1988.

Allen, Joel Stevens. "Notes on the Imago Mundi of the Book of Jubilees." *JJS* 33 (1982): 197-213.

―――. *The Despoliation of Egypt in Pre-Rabbinic, Rabbinic, and Patristic Traditions.* Supplements to Vigiliae Christianae, vol. 92. Leiden: Brill, 2008.

Anderson, Gary A. "The Status of the Torah before Sinai: The Retelling of the Bible in the Damascus Covenant and the Book of Jubilees." *DSD* 1, no. 1 (1994): 1-29.

Anderson, Jeff S. "Denouncement Speech in Jubilees and Other Enochic Literature." In *Enoch and Qumran Origins: New Light on a Forgotten Connection*, edited by Gabriele Boccaccini, 132-36. Grand Rapids: Eerdmans, 2005.

Aranda Pérez, Gonzalo. "Los mil años en el libro de los Jubileos y Ap 20,1-10." *EstBib* 57 (1999): 39-60.

Arbel, Daphna. "'Scribal Divination' in *Jubilees* and *3 Enoch*." *Hen* 31, no. 1 (2009).

Arcari, Luca. "The Myth of the Watchers and the Problem of Intermarriage in *Jubilees*." *Hen* 31, no. 1 (2009).

Baars, W., and Rochus Zuurmond. "The Project of a New Edition of the Ethiopic Book of Jubilees." *JSS* 9 (1964): 67-74.

Barthélemy, Dominique. "Notes en marge de publications récentes sur les manuscrits de Qumran." *RB* 59 (1952): 199-203.

Baumgarten, Joseph M. "The Beginning of the Day in the Calendar of Jubilees." *JBL* 77 (1958): 355-60.

―――. "The Calendar of the Book of Jubilees and the Bible" (in Hebrew). *Tarbiz* 32 (1963): 317-28.

―――. "Some Problems of the Jubilees Calendar in Current Research." *VT* 32 (1982): 485-89.

―――. "4Q503 (Daily Prayers) and the Lunar Calendar." *RevQ* 12 (1986): 399-407.

―――. "The Calendars of the Book of Jubilees and the Temple Scroll." *VT* 37 (1987): 71-78.

―――. "The Laws of Orlah and First Fruits in the Light of Jubilees, the Qumran Writings, and Targum Ps. Jonathan." *JJS* 38 (1987): 195-202.

―――. "Purification after Childbirth and the Sacred Garden in 4Q265 and Jubilees." In *New Qumran Texts and Studies: Proceedings of the First Meeting of the International Organization for Qumran Studies, Paris 1992*, edited by George J. Brook and Florentino García Martínez, 3-10. STDJ 15. Leiden: Brill, 1994.

Bedenbender, Andreas. "The Book of Jubilees — an Example of 'Rewritten Torah'?" *Hen* 31, no. 1 (2009).

Begg, Christopher T. "Rereading of the 'Animal Rite' of Genesis 15 in Early Jewish Narratives." *CBQ* 50, no. 1 (1988): 36-46.

Ben-Dov, Jonathan. "Jubilean Chronology and the 364-Day Year" (in Hebrew). In *Meghillot: Studies in the Dead Sea Scrolls V-VI; A Festschrift for Devorah Dimant*, edited by Moshe Bar-Asher and Emanuel Tov, 49-59. Jerusalem: Bialik Institute and Haifa University Press, 2007.

———. "Qumran Calendars: A Survey of Scholarship 1980-2007." *Currents in Biblical Research* 7, no. 1 (2008): 124-68.

Ben-Dov, Jonathan, and Wayne Horowitz. "The 364-Day Year in Mesopotamia and Qumran" (in Hebrew). In *Meghillot: Studies in the Dead Sea Scrolls I*, edited by Moshe Bar-Asher and Devorah Dimant, 3-26. Jerusalem: Haifa University Press and Bialik Institute, 2003.

Berger, Klaus. "Jubiläenbuch." In *RAC* 19 (1998), 31-38.

Bergsma, John Sietze. *The Jubilee from Leviticus to Qumran: A History of Interpretation*. VTSup 115. Leiden: Brill, 2007. See especially 233-50.

Berner, Christoph. *Jahre, Jahrwochen, und Jubiläen: Heptadische Geschichtskonzeptionen im Antiken Judentum*, 234-324, 509-12. Berlin and New York: De Gruyter, 2006.

———. "50 Jubilees and Beyond? Some Observations on the Chronological Structure of the Book of Jubilees." *Hen* 31, no. 1 (2009).

Bernstein, Moshe J. "Walking in the Festivals of the Gentiles: 4QpHosea[a] 2.15-17 and Jubilees 6.34-38." *JSP* 9 (1991): 21-34.

Berrin, Shani L. "'Heavenly Tablets' in the Book of Jubilees." In *Anafim: Proceedings of the Australian Jewish Studies Forum Held at Mandelbaum House, University of Sydney, 8-9 February 2004*, edited by Suzanne Faigan, 29-47. Sydney: Mandelbaum Publishing, 2006.

Beyerle, Stefan. "Angelic Revelation in Jewish Apocalyptic Literature." In *Angels: The Concept of Celestial Beings — Origins, Development, and Reception*, edited by Friedrich V. Reiterer, Tobias Nicklas, and Karin Schöpflin, 205-23. Deuterocanonical and Cognate Literature Yearbook. Berlin and New York: De Gruyter, 2007.

Bhayro, Siam. "The Use of Jubilees in Medieval Chronicles to Supplement Enoch: The Case for the 'Shorter' Reading." *Hen* 31, no. 1 (2009).

Boccaccini, Gabriele. *Beyond the Essene Hypothesis: The Partings of the Ways between Qumran and Enochic Judaism*, 86-98. Grand Rapids: Eerdmans, 1998.

———, ed. *Enoch and Qumran Origins: New Light on a Forgotten Connection*. Grand Rapids: Eerdmans, 2005.

Bonneau, Guy, and Jean Duhaime. "Angélologie et légitimation socio-religieuse dans le livre des Jubilés." *EgT* 27 (1996): 335-49.

Borgonovo, Gianantonio. "Jubilees' Rapprochement of Enochic and Mosaic Traditions." *Hen* 31, no. 1 (2009).

Böttrich, Christfried. "Gottesprädikationen im Jubiläenbuch." In *Studies in the Book of Jubilees*, edited by Matthias Albani, Jörg Frey, and Armin Lange, 221-42. TSAJ 65. Tübingen: Mohr Siebeck, 1997.

Brin, Gershon. "Regarding the Connection between the Temple Scroll and the Book of Jubilees." *JBL* 112 (1993): 108-9.

———. "The Idea and Sources of Esau's Speech in Jubilees 37 according to 4QpapJubilees[h], Unit 2, Col. IV" (in Hebrew). In *Studies in Bible and Exegesis, Vol. VI: Yehuda Otto Komlosh — In Memoriam,* edited by Rimon Kasher and Moshe A. Zipor, 17-24. Ramat-Gan: Bar-Ilan University Press, 2002.

Brock, Sebastian P. "Abraham and the Ravens: A Syriac Counterpart to Jubilees 11–12 and Its Implications." *JSJ* 9 (1978): 135-52.

Brooke, George J. "Exegetical Strategies in Jubilees 1–2: New Light from 4QJubilees[a]." In *Studies in the Book of Jubilees,* edited by Matthias Albani, Jörg Frey, and Armin Lange, 39-58. TSAJ 65. Tübingen: Mohr Siebeck, 1997.

Brownlee, W. "Light on the Manual of Discipline (DSD) from the Book of Jubilees." *BASOR* 123 (1951): 30-32.

Camponovo, Odo. *Königtum, Königsherrschaft und Reich Gottes in den frühjüdischen Schriften,* 230-37. OBO 58. Freiburg, Switzerland: Universitätsverlag, 1983.

Capelli, Piero. "Il problema del male: risposte ebraiche dal Secondo Tempio alla Quabbalah." *RStB* 19, no. 1 (2007): 135-56.

Caquot, André. "Les enfants aux cheveux blancs (Remarques sur Jubilés 23,25)." *RHR* 177 (1970): 131-32.

———. "Deux notes sur la géographie des Jubilés." In *Hommage à Georges Vajda. Etudes d'histoire et de pensée juives,* edited by Gérard Nahon and Charles Touati, 37-42. Louvain: Peeters, 1980.

———. "Les Anges inférieurs et les Anges supérieurs d'après le livre des Jubilés." *Bulletin de la Société Ernest Renan* 29 (1980) = *RHR* 198 (1981): 114-15.

———. "Explication du livre des Jubilés." *Annuaire du Collège de France* 82 (1981-82): 541-50.

———. "Le livre des Jubilés, Melkisedeq et les dîmes." *JJS* 33 (1982): 257-64.

———. "'Loi' et 'Témoignage' dans le Livre des Jubilés." In *Mélanges linguistiques offerts à Maxime Rodinson,* edited by C. Robin, 137-45. Paris: P. Geuthner, 1985.

———. "Eléments aggadiques dans le livre des Jubilés." In *Littérature intertestamentaire,* 57-68. Paris: Presses universitaires de France, 1985.

Carmichael, Calum M. "The Story of Joseph and the Book of Jubilees." In *The Dead Sea Scrolls in Their Historical Context,* edited by Timothy H. Lim, 143-58. Edinburgh: T. & T. Clark, 2000.

———. "The Integration of Law and Narrative in Jubilees: The Biblical Perspective." *Hen* 31, no. 1 (2009).

Caubet Iturbe, Javier. "El calendario de Enoc-Jubileos y el antiguo calendario hebreo." *Salmanticensis* 6 (1959): 131-42.

Cazelles, Henri. "Sur les origines du calendrier des Jubilés." *Bib* 43 (1962): 202-12.

Charlesworth, James H. "Jubilees." In *The Pseudepigrapha and Modern Research,* 143-47. SCS 7. Missoula: Scholars Press for the Society of Biblical Literature, 1976.

———. "Jubilees." In *The Pseudepigrapha and Modern Research, with a Supplement,*

143-47, 293-95. Chico, Calif.: Scholars Press for the Society of Biblical Literature, 1981.

———. "The Date of Jubilees and the Temple Scroll." In SBLSP 24 (1985), 193-204.

Chestnutt, Randall D. "Revelatory Experiences Attributed to Biblical Women in Early Jewish Literature." In *"Women Like This": New Perspectives on Jewish Women in the Greco-Roman World*, edited by Amy-Jill Levine, 107-25. SBLEJL 1. Atlanta: Scholars Press, 1991.

Choi, P. Richard. "Abraham Our Father: Paul's Voice in the Covenantal Debate of the Second Temple Period," 76-79, 91-94, 104-8. Ph.D. diss., Fuller Theological Seminary, 1996.

Christiansen, Ellen Juhl. *The Covenant in Judaism and Paul: A Study of Ritual Boundaries as Identity Markers*, 67-103. AGJU 27. Leiden: Brill, 1995.

Clark, E. Douglas. "A Prologue to Genesis: Moses 1 in Light of Jewish Traditions." *Brigham Young University Studies* 45, no. 1 (2006): 129-42.

Corinaldi, Michael. "The Relationship between the 'Beta Israel' Tradition and the Book of Jubilees." In *Jews of Ethiopia: The Birth of an Elite*, edited by Tudor Parfitt and Emanuela Trevisan Semi, 193-204. New York: Routledge, 2005.

Cothenet, Edouard. "Jubilés (Le livre des)." In *Catholicisme, hier, aujourd'hui, demain* 6 (1965), 1123-28.

———. "Pureté et impureté . . . Le livre des Jubilés." In *DBSup* 49 (1973), 509-11.

Crawford, Cory D. "On the Exegetical Function of the Abraham/Ravens Tradition in Jubilees." *HTR* 97, no. 1 (2004): 91-97.

Crawford, Sidnie White. *Rewriting Scripture in Second Temple Times*. Grand Rapids: Eerdmans, 2008.

Daise, Michael. "Ritual in Jubilees." *Hen* 31, no. 1 (2009).

Davenport, Gene L. *The Eschatology of the Book of Jubilees*. SPB 20. Leiden: Brill, 1971.

Day, John. "The Pharaoh of the Exodus, Josephus and Jubilees." *VT* 45, no. 3 (1995): 377-78.

Deichgräber, Reinhard. "Fragmente einer Jubiläen-Handschrift aus Höhle 3 von Qumran." *RevQ* 5 (1965): 415-22.

Delcor, Mathias. "Jubileos, Libro de los." In *Enciclopedia de la Biblia*, 4:711-12. Barcelona: Garriga, 1963.

———. "La fête des Huttes dans le Rouleau du Temple et dans le Livre des Jubilés." *RevQ* 15, no. 1-2 (1991): 181-98.

Delling, Gerhard. *Bibliographie zur jüdisch-hellenistischen und intertestamentarischen Literatur, 1900-1970*, 172-74. 2nd. ed. TUGAL 106². Berlin: Akademie Verlag, 1975.

Denis, Albert-Marie, and Jean-Claude Haelewyck. "Le Livre des Jubilés ou Leptogenèse: le calendrier et les tablettes célestes." In *Introduction à la littérature religieuse judéo-hellénistique*, 1:349-403. Pseudépigraphes de l'Ancien Testament. Turnhout: Brepols, 2000.

Derrett, J. Duncan M. "A Problem in the Book of Jubilees and an Indian Doctrine." *ZRGG* 14 (1962): 247-62.

Dimant, Devorah. "*The Fallen Angels* in the Dead Sea Scrolls and in the Apocryphal and Pseudepigraphic Books Related to Them" (in Hebrew). Ph.D. diss., Hebrew University, 1974.

————. "Sons of Heaven: Angelology in the Book of Jubilees in Light of the Qumran Sectarian Writings" (in Hebrew). In *Tribute to Sara: Studies in Jewish Philosophy and Kabbala Presented to Prof. Sara Heller Wilensky*, edited by Moshe Idel, Devorah Dimant, and Shalom Rosenberg, 97-118. Jerusalem: Magnes, 1994.

————. "Two 'Scientific' Fictions: The So-called Book of Noah and the Alleged Quotation of Jubilees in CD 16:3-4." In *Studies in the Hebrew Bible, Qumran, and the Septuagint Presented to Eugene Ulrich*, edited by Peter W. Flint, Emanuel Tov, and James C. VanderKam, 230-49. VTSup 101. Leiden: Brill, 2006.

DiTommaso, Lorenzo. "Jubilees (or the Little Genesis)." In *A Bibliography of Pseudepigrapha Research, 1850-1999*, 617-72. JSPSup 39. Sheffield: Sheffield Academic Press, 2001.

Dobos, Karoly. "The Consolation of History." *Hen* 31, no. 1 (2009).

Doering, Lutz. "Jub 2,24 nach 4QJub(a) VII,17 und der Aufbau von Jub 2,17-33." *BN* 84 (1996): 22-28.

————. "The Concept of the Sabbath in the Book of Jubilees." In *Studies in the Book of Jubilees*, edited by Matthias Albani, Jörg Frey, and Armin Lange, 179-206. TSAJ 65. Tübingen: Mohr Siebeck, 1997.

————. *Schabbat: Sabbathalacha und -praxis im antiken Judentum und Urchristentum*. TSAJ 78. Tübingen: Mohr Siebeck, 1999. See especially 43-118.

————. "Jub 50:6-13 als Schlussabschnitt des 'Jubiläenbuchs' — Nachtrag aus Qumran oder ursprünglicher Bestandteil des Werks?" *RevQ* 20, no. 3 (2002): 359-87.

Doran, Robert. "The Non-Dating of Jubilees: Jub 34-8; 23:14-32 in Narrative Context." *JSJ* 20 (1989): 1-11.

Drawnel, Henryk. "Some Notes on Scribal Craft and the Origins of the Enochic Literature." *Hen* 31, no. 1 (2009).

Ego, Beate. "Heilige Zeit — heiliger Raum — heiliger Mensch. Beobachtungen zur Struktur der Gesetzesbegründung in Schöpfungs- und Paradiesgeschichte des Jubiläenbuchs." In *Studies in the Book of Jubilees*, edited by Matthias Albani, Jörg Frey, and Armin Lange, 207-20. TSAJ 65. Tübingen: Mohr Siebeck, 1997.

Eiss, Werner. "Das Wochenfest im Jubiläenbuch und im antiken Judentum." In *Studies in the Book of Jubilees*, edited by Matthias Albani, Jörg Frey, and Armin Lange, 165-78. TSAJ 65. Tübingen: Mohr Siebeck, 1997.

Elgvin, Torleif. "Biblical Roots of Early Mystical Traditions on the Heavenly Temple." *Hen* 31, no. 1 (2009).

Endres, John C. *Biblical Interpretation in the Book of Jubilees*. CBQMS 18. Washington, D.C.: Catholic Biblical Association of America, 1987.

————. "Prayer of Noah: Jubilees 10:3-6." In *Prayer from Alexander to Constantine: A Critical Anthology*, edited by M. Kiley et al., 53-58. London: Routledge, 1997.

————. "Prayers in Jubilees." In *Heavenly Tablets: Interpretation, Identity, and Tradi-*

tion in Ancient Judaism, edited by Lynn LiDonnici and Andrea Lieber, 31-47. JSJSup 119. Leiden: Brill, 2007.

Eshel, Esther. "Jubilees 32 and the Bethel Cult Traditions in Second Temple Literature." In *Things Revealed: Studies in Early Jewish and Christian Literature in Honor of Michael E. Stone,* edited by Esther G. Chazon, David Satran, and Ruth A. Clements, 21-36. JSJSup 89. Boston: Brill, 2004.

―――. "The 'Imago Mundi' of the 'Genesis Apocryphon.'" In *Heavenly Tablets: Interpretation, Identity, and Tradition in Ancient Judaism,* edited by Lynn LiDonnici and Andrea Lieber, 111-31. Leiden: Brill, 2007.

Evans, Craig A. "Jubilees." In *Noncanonical Writings and New Testament Interpretation,* 31-32. Peabody, Mass.: Hendrickson, 1992.

Fabry, Heinz-Josef. "Isaak in den Handschriften von Qumran." In *From 4QMMT to Resurrection: Mélanges qumraniens en hommage à Émile Puech,* edited by Florentino García Martínez, Annette Steudel, and Eibert Tigchelaar, 87-103. Leiden: Brill, 2006.

Falk, Daniel. "Dating the Watchers: What's at Stake?" *Hen* 31, no. 1 (2009).

Fitzmyer, Joseph A. "Zu Jub 13,10-16." *BibOr* 18 (1966): 14.

Fletcher-Louis, Crispin. "The Book of Watchers, Jubilees, and the Cycle of New Year Festivals." *Hen* 31, no. 1 (2009).

Frey, Jörg. "Zum Weltbild im Jubiläenbuch." In *Studies in the Book of Jubilees,* edited by Matthias Albani, Jörg Frey, and Armin Lange, 261-94. TSAJ 65. Tübingen: Mohr Siebeck, 1997.

Fröhlich, Ida. "Enoch and Jubilees." In *Enoch and Qumran Origins: New Light on a Forgotten Connection,* edited by Gabriele Boccaccini, 141-47. Grand Rapids: Eerdmans, 2005.

―――. "'Invoke at Any Time . . .': Apotropaic Texts and Belief in Demons in the Literature of the Qumran Community." *BibN* 137 (2008): 41-74.

―――. "Theology and Demonology in Jubilees and Enoch." *Hen* 31, no. 1 (2009).

García Martínez, Florentino. "Las Tablas Celestes en el Libro de los Jubileos." In *Palabra y Vida: Homenaje a José Alonso Díaz en su 70 cumpleaños,* edited by A. Vargas Machuca and G. Ruiz, 333-49. Publicaciones de la Universidad Pontificia Comillas Madrid, Series I. Estudios 58. Madrid: Ediciones Universidad de Comillas, 1984.

―――. "4QMess Ar and the Book of Noah." In *Qumran and Apocalyptic: Studies on the Aramaic Texts from Qumran,* 1-44. Leiden: Brill, 1992.

―――. "The Heavenly Tablets in the Book of Jubilees." In *Studies in the Book of Jubilees,* edited by Matthias Albani, Jörg Frey, and Armin Lange, 243-60. TSAJ 65. Tübingen: Mohr Siebeck, 1997.

Gilders, William K. "Where Did Noah Place the Blood? A Textual Note on Jubilees." *JBL* 124, no. 4 (2005): 745-49.

―――. "Blood and Covenant: Interpretive Elaboration on Genesis 9.4-6 in the Book of Jubilees." *JSP* 15, no. 2 (2006): 83-118.

Glessmer, Uwe. "Explizite Aussagen über kalendarische Konflikte im Jubiläenbuch:

Jub 6,22-32.33-38." In *Studies in the Book of Jubilees*, edited by Matthias Albani, Jörg Frey, and Armin Lange, 127-64. TSAJ 65. Tübingen: Mohr Siebeck, 1997.

Gregory, Bradley C. "The Death and Legacy of Leah in 'Jubilees.'" *JSP* 17, no. 2 (2008): 99-120.

Goldstein, Jonathan A. "The Date of the Book of Jubilees." *PAAJR* 50 (1983): 63-86.

Görtz-Wrisberg, Irene von. "No Second Temple — No Shavuot? 'The Book of Jubilees' as a Case Study." In *The Ancient Synagogue from Its Origins until 200 C.E.*, edited by Birger Olsson and Magnus Zetterholm, 376-403. Stockholm: Almqvist & Wiksell International, 2003.

Goudoever, Jan van. "The Book of Jubilees." In *Biblical Calendars*, 62-70. Leiden: Brill, 1959; 2nd ed., 1961.

Grelot, Pierre. "Le livre des Jubilés et le Testament de Levi." In *Mélanges Dominique Barthélemy*, edited by Pierre Casetti et al., 109-33. OBO 38. Fribourg: Ed. Universitaires; Göttingen: Vandenhoeck & Ruprecht, 1981.

———. "Jean 8,56 et Jubilés 16,16-29." *RevQ* 13 (1988): 621-28.

Grintz, Jehoshua M. "Jubilees, Book of." In *EncJud* 10 (1971), 324-26.

Grossman, Maxine. "Affective Masculinity: The Gender of the Patriarchs in Jubilees." *Hen* 31, no. 1 (2009).

Halpern-Amaru, Betsy. "The First Woman, Wives, and Mothers in Jubilees." *JBL* 113 (1994): 609-26.

———. "The Metahistorical Covenant of Jubilees." In *Rewriting the Bible: Land and Covenant in Post-Biblical Literature*, 25-54. Valley Forge, Pa.: Trinity, 1994.

———. "Exile and Return in Jubilees." In *Exile: Old Testament, Jewish, and Christian Conceptions*, edited by James M. Scott, 127-44. JSJSup 56. Leiden: Brill, 1997.

———. "The Portrait of Sarah in Jubilees." In *Jewish Studies in a New Europe: Proceedings of the Fifth Congress of Jewish Studies in Copenhagen 1994 Under the Auspices of the European Association for Jewish Studies*, edited by U. Haxen, Hanne Trautner-Kromann, and Karen L. G. Salamon, 336-48. Copenhagen: C. A. Reitzel A/S International Publishers, 1998.

———. "Bilhah and Naphtali in Jubilees: A Note on 4QTNaphtali." *DSD* 6, no. 1 (1999): 1-10.

———. *The Empowerment of Women in the Book of Jubilees*. Boston: Brill, 1999.

———. "The Naming of Levi in the Book of Jubilees." In *Pseudepigraphic Perspectives: The Apocrypha and Pseudepigrapha in Light of the Dead Sea Scrolls; Proceedings of the International Symposium of the Orion Center for the Study of the Dead Sea Scrolls and Associated Literature, 12-14 January, 1997*, edited by Esther G. Chazon, Michael E. Stone, and Avital Pinnick, 59-69. STDJ 31. Leiden: Brill, 1999.

———. "Flavius Josephus and the Book of Jubilees: A Question of Source." *HUCA* 72 (2001): 15-44.

———. "Burying the Fathers: Exegetical Strategies and Source Traditions in Jubilees." In *Reworking the Bible: Apocryphal and Related Texts at Qumran; Proceedings of a Joint Symposium by the Orion Center for the Study of the Dead Sea*

Scrolls and Associated Literature and the Hebrew University Institute for Advanced Studies Research Group on Qumran, 15-17 January, 2002, edited by Esther G. Chazon, Devorah Dimant, and Ruth Clements, 135-52. STDJ 58. Leiden: Brill, 2005.

————. "Joy as Piety in the Book of Jubilees." *JJS* 56, no. 2 (2005): 185-205.

————. "Midrash in Jubilees." In *Encyclopedia of Midrash,* edited by J. Neusner and A. Avery-Peck, 1:333-50. Leiden: Brill, 2005.

————. "A Note on Isaac as First-born in 'Jubilees' and Only Son in 4Q225." *DSD* 13, no. 2 (2006): 127-33.

Hamidović, David. "Les répartitions des temps, titre du 'Livre des Jubilés', dans les manuscrits de Qoumrân." In *Le temps et les temps dans les littératures juives et chrétiennes au tournant de notre ère,* edited by Christian Grappe and Jean-Claude Ingelaere, 137-45. JSJSup 113. Leiden: Brill, 2006.

————. *Les traditions du jubilé à Qumrân.* Orients sémitiques. Paris: Geuthner, 2007.

Hanneken, Todd Russell. "Angels and Demons in the Book of Jubilees and Contemporary Apocalypses." *Hen* 28, no. 2 (2006): 11-25.

Hempel, Charlotte. "The Place of the Book of Jubilees at Qumran and Beyond." In *The Dead Sea Scrolls in Their Historical Context,* edited by Timothy H. Lim, 187-96. Edinburgh: T. & T. Clark, 2000.

Hengel, Martin. *Judentum und Hellenismus. Studien zu ihrer Begegnung unter besonderer Berücksichtigung Palästinas bis zur Mitte des 2.Jh. v. Chr.* WUNT 10. Tübingen: J. C. B. Mohr, 1969; 2nd ed. 1973; 3rd ed. 1988. ET, *Judaism and Hellenism: Studies in Their Encounter in Palestine during the Early Hellenistic Period,* 2 vols. (London: SCM; Philadelphia: Fortress, 1974).

Henshke, David. "'The Day after the Sabbath' (Lev 23:15): Traces and Origin of an Inter-Sectarian Polemic." *DSD* 15, no. 2 (2008): 225-47.

Hilgert, Earle. "The Jubilees Calendar and the Origin of Sunday Observance." *AUSS* 1 (1963): 44-51.

Himmelfarb, Martha. "Some Echoes of Jubilees in Medieval Hebrew Literature." In *Tracing the Threads: Studies in the Vitality of the Jewish Pseudepigrapha,* edited by John Reeves, 115-41. SBLEJL 6. Atlanta: Scholars Press, 1994.

————. "Sexual Relations and Purity in the Temple Scroll and the Book of Jubilees." *DSD* 6, no. 1 (1999): 11-13.

————. "Torah, Testimony, and Heavenly Tablets: The Claim to Authority of the Book of Jubilees." In *A Multiform Heritage: Studies on Early Judaism and Christianity in Honor of Robert A. Kraft,* edited by Benjamin G. Wright, 19-29. Scholars Press Homage Series 24. Atlanta: Scholars Press, 1999.

————. "Jubilees and Sectarianism." In *Enoch and Qumran Origins: New Light on a Forgotten Connection,* edited by Gabriele Boccaccini, 129-31. Grand Rapids: Eerdmans, 2005.

————. "Jubilees' Kingdom of Priests." In *A Kingdom of Priests: Ancestry and Merit in Ancient Judaism,* 53-84. Philadelphia: University of Pennsylvania Press, 2006.

Hoenig, Sidney B. "The Jubilees Calendar and the Days of Assembly." In *Essays on the*

Occasion of the 70th Anniversary of the Dropsie University, edited by A. I. Katsh and L. Nemoy, 189-207. Philadelphia: Dropsie University, 1979.

Hoffmann, Heinrich. *Das Gesetz in der frühjüdischen Apokalyptik,* 298-320. Göttingen: Vandenhoeck & Ruprecht, 1999.

Hopkins, Jamal-Dominique. "The Authoritative Status of Jubilees at Qumran." *Hen* 31, no. 1 (2009).

Horst, Pieter Willem van der. "Moses' Father Speaks Out." In *Flores Florentino: Dead Sea Scrolls and Other Early Jewish Studies in Honour of Florentino García Martínez,* edited by Anthony Hilhorst, Émile Puech, and Eibert Tigchelaar, 491-98. JSJSup 122. Leiden: Brill, 2007.

Huizenga, Leroy Andrew. "The Battle for Isaac: Exploring the Composition and Function of the 'Aqedah' in the Book of 'Jubilees.'" *JSP* 13, no. 1 (2002): 33-59.

Hultgren, Stephen. "Covenant Renewal in the Dead Sea Scrolls and Jubilees and Its Biblical Origins." In *From the Damascus Covenant to the Covenant of the Community: Literary, Historical, and Theological Studies in the Dead Sea Scrolls,* 461-92. STDJ 66. Leiden: Brill, 2007.

Ibba, Giovanni. "The Evil Spirits in Jubilees and the Spirits of the Bastards in 4Q510, with Some Remarks on Other Qumran Manuscripts." *Hen* 31, no. 1 (2009).

Jaubert, Annie. "Le calendrier des Jubilés et de la secte de Qumran. Ses origines bibliques." *VT* 3 (1953): 250-64.

———. "Le calendrier des Jubilés et les jours liturgiques de la semaine." *VT* 7 (1957): 35-61.

———. *La date de la Cène. Calendrier biblique et liturgie chrétienne.* Paris: Gabalda, 1957. ET, *The Date of the Last Supper* (Staten Island, N.Y.: Alba House, 1965).

Kister, Menahem. "Towards the History of the Essene Sect: Studies in the Animal Apocalypse, the Book of Jubilees, and the Damascus Document" (in Hebrew). *Tarbiz* 56 (1986-87): 1-18.

———. "Newly-Identified Fragments of the Book of Jubilees: Jub 23:21-23, 30-31." *RevQ* 12 (1987): 529-36.

———. "Two Formulae in the Book of Jubilees" (in Hebrew). *Tarbiz* 70 (2001): 289-300.

———. "Syncellus and the Sources of Jubilees 3: A Note on M. Segal's Article" (in Hebrew). *Meghillot* 1 (2003): 127-33.

Klausner, Joseph. "The Book of Jubilees." In *The Messianic Idea in Israel: From Its Beginning to the Completion of the Mishnah,* 302-9. New York: Macmillan, 1955.

Knibb, Michael Anthony. *Jubilees and the Origins of the Qumran Community: An Inaugural Lecture.* London: King's College, 1989.

———. "Which Parts of 1 Enoch Were Known to Jubilees? A Note on the Interpretation of Jubilees 4.16-25." In *Reading from Right to Left: Essays on the Hebrew Bible in Honour of David J. A. Clines,* edited by J. Cheryl Exum and H. G. M. Williamson, 254-62. JSOTSup 373. Sheffield: Sheffield Academic Press, 2003.

Knowles, Michael P. "Abram and the Birds in Jubilees 11: A Subtext for the Parable of the Sower?" *NTS* 41, no. 1 (1995): 145-51.

Koskenniemi, Erkki. "Moses — a Well-Educated Man: A Look at the Educational Idea in Early Judaism." *JSP* 17, no. 4 (2008): 281-96.

Küchler, Max. *Schweigen, Schmuck und Schleier. Drei neutestamentliche Vorschriften zur Verdrängung der Frauen auf dem Hintergrund einer frauenfeindlichen Exegese des Alten Testaments im antiken Judentum,* 400-438. NTOA 1. Freiburg, Switzerland: Universitätsverlag; Göttingen: Vandenhoeck & Ruprecht, 1986.

Kugel, James. "Levi's Election to the Priesthood in Second Temple Writings." *HTR* 86 (1993): 1-64.

————. "The Jubilees Apocalypse." *DSD* 1 (1994): 322-37.

————. "How Old Is the 'Aramaic Levi Document'?" *DSD* 14, no. 3 (2007): 291-312.

————. "Exegetical Notes on 4Q225 'Pseudo-Jubilees.'" *DSD* 13, no. 1 (2006): 73-98.

Kugler, Robert A. "4Q225 2 i 1-2: A Possible Reconstruction and Explanation." *JBL* 126, no. 1 (2007): 172-81.

Kundert, Lukas. "Isaak im Jubiläenbuch." In *Die Opferung/Bindung Isaaks 1: Gen 22,1-19 im Alten Testament, im Frühjudentum und im Neuen Testament,* 83-90. WMANT 78. Neukirchen-Vluyn: Neukirchener Verlag, 1998.

Kutsch, Ernst. "Der Kalender des Jubiläenbuches und das Alte und das Neue Testament." *VT* 11 (1961): 39-47.

————. "Die Solstitien im Kalender des Jubiläenbuches und im äthiopischen Henoch 72." *VT* 12 (1962): 205-7.

Kvanvig, Helge S. "Jubilees — between Enoch and Moses: A Narrative Reading." *JSJ* 35, no. 3 (2004): 243-61.

————. "Jubilees — Read as a Narrative." In *Enoch and Qumran Origins: New Light on a Forgotten Connection,* edited by Gabriele Boccaccini, 75-83. Grand Rapids: Eerdmans, 2005.

Lach, Jan. "The Liturgical Calendar of the Book of Jubilees in the Light of the Latest Discussions" (in Polish). *Ruch Biblijny i Liturgiczny* 16 (1963): 98-105.

Lambert, David. "Last Testaments in the Book of Jubilees." *DSD* 11, no. 1 (2004): 82-107.

————. "Did Israel Believe That Redemption Awaited Its Repentance? The Case of 'Jubilees' 1." *CBQ* 68, no. 4 (2006): 631-50.

Landau, David. "The Montanists and the Jubilees Calendar." *OrChr* 89 (2005): 103-12.

Lange, Armin. "Divinatorische Träume und Apokalyptik im Jubiläenbuch." In *Studies in the Book of Jubilees,* edited by Matthias Albani, Jörg Frey, and Armin Lange, 25-38. TSAJ 65. Tübingen: Mohr Siebeck, 1997.

Leach, Edmund R. "A Possible Method of Intercalation for the Calendar of the Book of Jubilees." *VT* 7 (1957): 392-97.

Lehnardt, Andreas. "Das Buch der Jubiläen (JSHRZ II / 3)." In *Bibliographie zu den Jüdischen Schriften aus hellenistisch-römischer Zeit,* 189-204. JSHRZ 6.2. Gütersloh: Gütersloher Verlagshaus, 1999.

Lichtenberger, Hermann. "Zu Vorkommen und Bedeutung von יצר im Jubiläenbuch." *JSJ* 14 (1983): 1-10.

Liebreich, Leon J. "Jubilees 50.9." *JQR* 44, no. 2 (1953): 169.

Lignée, Hubert. "La place du livre des Jubilés et du Rouleau du Temple dans l'histoire du mouvement Essénien. Ces deux ouvrages ont-ils été écrits par le Maître de Justice?" *RevQ* 13 (1988): 331-45.

Lipscomb, W. Lowndes. "A Tradition from the Book of Jubilees in Armenian." *JJS* 29 (1978): 149-63.

Loader, William. *Enoch, Levi, and Jubilees on Sexuality: Attitudes towards Sexuality in the Early Enoch Literature, the Aramaic Levi Document, and the Book of Jubilees.* Grand Rapids: Eerdmans, 2007.

―――. "Jubilees and Sexual Transgression." *Hen* 31, no. 1 (2009).

Macaskill, Grant. "Priestly Purity, Mosaic Torah, and the Emergence of Enochic Judaism." *Hen* 31, no. 1 (2009).

Machiela, Daniel A. "The Genesis Apocryphon (1Q20): A Reevaluation of Its Text, Interpretive Character, and Relationship to the Book of Jubilees." Ph.D. diss., University of Notre Dame, 2007.

―――. "'Each to His Own Inheritance': Geography as an Evaluative Tool in the Genesis Apocryphon." *DJD* 15, no. 1 (2008): 50-66.

Mendels, Doron. "The Twenties: The Book of Jubilees — the Territories and Peoples of the Land." In *The Land as a Political Concept in Hasmonean Literature: Recourse to History in Second Century B.C. Claims to the Holy Land,* 57-88. TSAJ 15. Tübingen: Mohr, 1987.

Milgrom, Jacob. "The Concept of Impurity in 'Jubilees' and the 'Temple Scroll.'" *RevQ* 16, no. 2 (1993): 277-84.

Milik, Józef Tadeusz. "Recherches sur la version grecque du livre des Jubilés." *RB* 78 (1971): 545-57.

―――. "A propos de 11Qjub." *Bib* 54 (1973): 77-78.

Morgenstern, Julian. "The Calendar of the Jubilees, Its Origin and Its Character." *VT* 5 (1955): 34-76.

Müller, Karlheinz. "Die hebräische Sprache der Halacha als Textur der Schöpfung: Beobachtungen zum Verhältnis von Tora und Halacha im Buch der Jubiläen." In *Bibel in jüdischer und christlicher Tradition: Festschrift für Johann Maier zum 60. Geburtstag,* edited by Helmut Herklien, Karlheinz Müller, and Günter Stemberger, 157-76. BBB 88. Frankfurt am Main: Anton Hain, 1993.

―――. "Die Halacha der Väter und das Gesetz des Mose: Beobachtungen zur Autorisierung der Halacha im Buch der Jubiläen." *BN* 116 (2003): 56-68.

Müller, Mogens. "Die Abraham-Gestalt im Jubiläenbuch: Versuch einer Interpretation." *SJOT* 10, no. 2 (1996): 238-57.

Muñoz León, Domingo. "Palabra y Gloria en Jubileos, Henoc Etiópico y Testamentos de los doce Patriarcias." In *Excursus en la Biblia y en la literatura intertestamentaria,* 165-95. Verbum gloriae 4. Madrid: Instituto "Francisco Suarez," 1983.

―――. "Derás en el Libro de los Jubileos." In *Plenitudo temporis: Miscelánea homenaje al Prof. Dr. Ramón Trevijano Etcheverriá,* edited by Jorge Juan Fernández Sangrador and Santiago Guijarro Oporto, 67-79. Bibliotheca Salmanticensis 249. Salamanca: Publicaciones Universidad Pontifica, 2002.

Najm, S., and Philippe Guillaume. "Jubilee Calendar Rescued from the Flood Narrative." *Journal of Hebrew Scriptures* 5 (2004-5).

Najman, Hindy. "Interpretation as Primordial Writing: Jubilees and Its Authority Conferring Strategies." *JSJ* 30, no. 4 (1999): 379-410.

Nebe, Gerhard Wilhelm. "Ergänzende Bemerkung zu 4Q176, Jubiläen 23,21." *RevQ* 14 (1989): 129-30.

———. "4Q174, 1-2, I, 6f im Lichte von 'Sektenschrift' und Jub 2,2." *RevQ* 18, no. 4 (1998): 581-87.

Newsome, James D. "Jubilees." In *Greeks, Romans, Jews: Currents of Culture and Belief in the New Testament World*, 91-93, 244-45. Philadelphia: Trinity, 1992.

Nickelsburg, George W. E. "The Book of Jubilees." In *Jewish Literature between the Bible and the Mishnah*, 73-80, 98-99. Philadelphia: Fortress, 1981.

———. "The Bible Rewritten and Expanded." In *Jewish Writings of the Second Temple Period: Apocrypha, Pseudepigrapha, Qumran Sectarian Writings, Philo, Josephus*, edited by Michael E. Stone, 97-104. LJPSTT 2. Philadelphia: Fortress, 1984.

———. "The Nature and Function of Revelation in 1 Enoch, Jubilees, and Some Qumranic Documents." In *Pseudepigraphic Perspectives: The Apocrypha and Pseudepigrapha in Light of the Dead Sea Scrolls; Proceedings of the International Symposium of the Orion Center for the Study of the Dead Sea Scrolls and Associated Literature, 12-14 January, 1997*, edited by Esther G. Chazon, Michael E. Stone, and Avital Pinnick, 91-119. STDJ 31. Leiden: Brill, 1999.

———. "The Book of Jubilees." In *Jewish Literature between the Bible and the Mishnah*, 69-74. Minneapolis: Fortress, 2005.

Nitzan, Bilhah. "The Penitential Prayer of Moses in Jubilees 1 and Its Relation to the Penitential Tradition of the Post-Exilic Judaism." *Hen* 30, no. 2 (2008).

Noack, Bent. "Qumran and the Book of Jubilees." *SEÅ* 22-23 (1957-58): 191-207.

———. "The Day of Pentecost in Jubilees, Qumran, and Acts." *ASTI* 1 (1962): 73-95.

Obermann, Julian. *Calendaric Elements in the Dead Sea Scrolls*, 285-97. Philadelphia: M. Jacobs, 1956.

Oegema, Gerbern S. "*Das Buch der Jubiläen.*" In *JSHRZ* 6.1 (2005), 78-96.

———. "Israel and the Nations in Jubilees." *Hen* 31, no. 1 (2009).

Oliver, Isaac W., and Veronika Bachmann. "The Book of Jubilees: An Annotated Bibliography from the First German Translation of 1850 to the Enoch Seminar of 2007." *Hen* 31, no. 1 (2009).

Orlov, Andrei. "Moses' Heavenly Counterpart in the Book of Jubilees and the Exagoge of Ezekiel the Tragedian." *Bib* 88, no. 2 (2007): 153-73.

Park, Sejin. *Pentecost and Sinai: The Festival of Weeks as a Celebration of the Sinai Event.* New York: T. & T. Clark, 2008.

Pascale, Ronald A. "The Demonic Cosmic Powers of Destruction in 1 Enoch 15:3–16:1 and Jubilees 10:5 and the Demonizing of the Avenging Angels." Ph.D. diss., Harvard University, 1980.

Pérez Fernández, M. "La apertura a los gentiles en el judaísmo intertestamentario:

Estudio sobre 'el Libro de los Jubileos' y 'Jose y Asenté,' tradiciones tanaíticas y Targúmicas." *EstBib* 41 (1983): 83-106.

Peters, Dorothy. "Noah Traditions in Jubilees: Evidence for the Struggle between Enochic and Mosaic Authority." *Hen* 31, no. 1 (2009).

Pfann, Stephen. "Time and Calendar in Jubilees and Enoch." *Hen* 30, no. 2 (2008).

Philonenko, Marc. "La sixième demande du 'Notre Père' et le livre des 'Jubilés.'" *RHPR* 78, no. 2 (1998): 27-37.

Pinkerton, James Isaac. "A Comparison of the Samaritan Pentateuch with the Hebrew Text of the Pentateuch behind the Apocrypha." Ph.D. diss., Dallas Theological Seminary, 1964.

Piovanelli, Pierluigi. "Les aventures des apocryphes en Ethiopie." *Apoc* 4 (1993): 197-224.

———. "The Social and Political Setting of the Book of Jubilees." *Hen* 30, no. 2 (2008).

Puech, Emile. "Une nouvelle copie du Livre des Jubilés: 4Q484 = pap4Qjubilés^j." *RevQ* 19 (1999): 216-24.

Pummer, Reinhard. "The Book of Jubilees and the Samaritans." *EgT* 10 (1979): 147-78.

Ramelli, Ilaria. "La 'colpa antecedente' come ermeneutica del male in sede storico-religiosa e nei testi biblici." *RStB* 19, no. 1 (2007): 11-64.

Rapp, Hans A. *Jakob in Bet-El: Gen 35,1-15 und die jüdische Literatur des 3. und 2. Jahrhunderts.* Herders Biblische Studien 29. Freiburg: Herder, 2001. See especially 165-254, 293-96.

Ravid, Liora. "The Special Terminology of the Heavenly Tablets in the Book of Jubilees" (in Hebrew). *Tarbiz* 68 (1999): 463-71.

———. "The Relationship of the Sabbath Laws in Jubilees 50:6-13 to the Rest of the Book" (in Hebrew). *Tarbiz* 69 (2000): 161-66.

———. "Issues in the Book of Jubilees" (in Hebrew). Ph.D. diss., Bar Ilan University, 2001.

———. "Purity and Impurity in the Book of Jubilees." *JSP* 13, no. 1 (2002): 61-86.

———. "The Book of Jubilees and Its Calendar — a Reexamination." *DSD* 10, no. 3 (2003): 371-94.

Reed, Annette Yoshiko. "'Revealed Literature' in the Second Century B.C.E.: Jubilees, 1 Enoch, Qumran, and the Prehistory of the Biblical Canon." In *Enoch and Qumran Origins: New Light on a Forgotten Connection*, edited by Gabriele Boccaccini, 94-98. Grand Rapids: Eerdmans, 2005.

Reeth, J. M. F. van. "Le Prophète musulman en tant que Nâsir Allâh et ses antécédents: le 'nazôraios' évangélique et le livre des Jubilés." *OLP* 23 (1992): 251-74.

Rietz, Henry W. Morisada. "Synchronizing Worship: Jubilees as a Tradition for the Qumran Community." In *Enoch and Qumran Origins: New Light on a Forgotten Connection*, edited by Gabriele Boccaccini, 111-18. Grand Rapids: Eerdmans, 2005.

Rivkin, Ellis. "The Book of Jubilees: An Anti-Pharisaic Pseudepigraph." *ErIsr* 16 (1982): 193-98.

Rofé, Alexander. "Further Manuscript Fragments of Jubilees in Qumran Cave 3" (in Hebrew). *Tarbiz* 34 (1965): 333-36.

Rook, John T. "A Twenty-Eight-Day Month Tradition in the Book of Jubilees." *VT* 31 (1981): 83-87.

————. "The Names of the Wives from Adam to Abraham in the Book of Jubilees." *JSP* 7 (1990): 105-17.

Rosso Ubigli, Liliana. "Gli Apocrifi (o Pseudepigrafi) dell'Antico Testamento. Bibliografia 1979-1989." *Hen* 12 (1990): 259-321, especially 295-99.

————. "The Historical-Cultural Background of the Book of Jubilees." In *Enoch and Qumran Origins: New Light on a Forgotten Connection,* edited by Gabriele Boccaccini, 137-40. Grand Rapids: Eerdmans, 2005.

Rost, Leonhard. "Das Jubiläenbuch." In *EATAP,* 98-101. Heidelberg: Quelle & Meyer, 1971.

Rothstein, David. "Sexual Union and Sexual Offences in Jubilees." *JSJ* 35, no. 4 (2004): 363-84.

————. "Jubilees' Formulation of Gen 2:23: A Literary Motif Viewed against the Legal Matrices of the Hebrew Bible and the Ancient Near East." *ZABR* 11 (2005): 4-11.

————. "Same-Day Testimony and Same-Day Punishment in the Damascus Document and Jubilees." *ZABR* 11 (2005): 12-26.

————. "Why Was Shelah Not Given to Tamar? Jubilees 41:20." *Hen* 27, no. 1-2 (2005): 115-26.

————. "Laws Regulating Relations with Outsiders in 1QS and Jubilees: Biblical Antecedents." *ZABR* 12 (2006): 107-30.

————. "'And Jacob came (in)to [אל+בוא].' Spousal Relationships and the Use of a Recurring Syntagm in Genesis and Jubilees." *Hen* 29, no. 1 (2007): 91-103.

————. "Text and Context: Domestic Harmony and the Depiction of Hagar in 'Jubilees.'" *JSP* 17 (2008): 243-64.

Ruiten, Jacques T. A. G. M. van. "The Rewriting of Exodus 24:12-18 in Jubilees 1:1-4." *BN* 79 (1995): 25-29.

————. "The Garden of Eden and Jubilees 3:1-31." *Bijdragen* 57, no. 3 (1996): 305-17.

————. "The Relationship between Exod 31,12-17 and Jubilees 2,1.17-33." In *Studies in the Book of Exodus: Redaction, Reception, Interpretation,* edited by Marc Vervenne, 567-75. BETL 126. Leuven: Leuven University Press, 1996.

————. "The Interpretation of Genesis 6:1-12 in Jubilees 5:1-19." In *Studies in the Book of Jubilees,* edited by Matthias Albani, Jörg Frey, and Armin Lange, 59-78. TSAJ 65. Tübingen: Mohr Siebeck, 1997.

————. "Biblical Interpretation in Jubilees 3:1-31." In *Lasset uns Brücken bauen: Collected Communications to the XVth Congress of the International Organization for the Study of the Old Testament, Cambridge 1995,* edited by Klaus-Dietrich Schunk and Matthias Augustin, 315-19. BEATAJ 42. Frankfurt am Main: P. Lang, 1998.

————. "Eden and the Temple: The Rewriting of Genesis 2:4–3:24 in 'The Book of

Jubilees.'" In *Paradise Interpreted: Representations of Biblical Paradise in Judaism and Christianity*, edited by Gerard P. Luttikhuizen, 63-94. Themes in Biblical Narrative 2. Leiden: Brill, 1999.

————. "The Interpretation of the Flood Story in the Book of Jubilees." In *Interpretations of the Flood*, edited by Florentino García Martínez and Gerard P. Luttikhuizen, 66-85. Themes in Biblical Narrative 1. Leiden: Brill, 1999.

————. "Visions of the Temple in the Book of Jubilees." In *Gemeinde ohne Tempel: Zur Substituierung und Transformation des Jerusalemer Tempels und seines Kults im Alten Testament, antiken Judentum und frühen Christentum*, edited by Beate Ego, Armin Lange, et al., 215-27. WUNT 118. Tübingen: Mohr Siebeck, 1999.

————. *Primaeval History Interpreted: The Rewriting of Genesis 1–11 in the Book of Jubilees*. Leiden: Brill, 2000.

————. "Abraham, Job and the Book of 'Jubilees': The Intertextual Relationship of Genesis 22:1-19, Job 1:1–2:13 and 'Jubilees' 17:15–18:19." In *The Sacrifice of Isaac: The Aqedah (Genesis 22) and Its Interpretations*, edited by Edward Noort and J. C. Tigchelaar, 58-85. Themes in Biblical Narrative 4. Leiden: Brill, 2002.

————. "The Covenant of Noah in 'Jubilees' 6.1-38." In *The Concept of the Covenant in the Second Temple Period*, edited by Stanley E. Porter and Jacqueline C. R. De Roo, 167-90. Boston: Brill, 2003.

————. "A Literary Dependency of 'Jubilees' on '1 Enoch'? A Reassessment of a Thesis of J. C. VanderKam." *Hen* 26, no. 2 (2004): 205-9.

————. "Lot versus Abraham: The Interpretation of Genesis 18:1–19:38 in 'Jubilees' 16:1-9." In *Sodom's Sin: Genesis 18–19 and Its Interpretation*, edited by Ed Noort and Eibert Tigchelaar, 29-46. Themes in Biblical Narrative 7. Boston: Brill, 2004.

————. "A Literary Dependency of Jubilees on 1 Enoch." In *Enoch and Qumran Origins: New Light on a Forgotten Connection*, edited by Gabriele Boccaccini, 90-93. Grand Rapids: Eerdmans, 2005.

————. "The Birth of Moses in Egypt according to the Book of Jubilees (Jub 47.1-9)." In *The Wisdom of Egypt: Jewish, Early Christian, and Gnostic Essays in Honour of Gerard P. Luttikhuizen*, edited by Anthony Hilhorst and George H. van Kooten, 43-65. AGJU 59. Leiden: Brill, 2005.

————. "A Miraculous Birth of Isaac in the Book of Jubilees?" In *Wonders Never Cease: The Purpose of Narrating Miracle Stories in the New Testament and Its Religious Environment*, edited by Michael Labahn and B. J. Lietaert Peerbolte, 1-19. Library of New Testament Studies 288. New York: T. & T. Clark, 2006.

————. "Angels and Demons in the Book of 'Jubilees.'" In *Angels: The Concept of Celestial Beings — Origins, Development and Reception*, edited by Friedrich V. Reiterer, Tobias Nicklas, and Karin Schöpflin, 585-609. Deuterocanonical and Cognate Literature Yearbook. Berlin and New York: De Gruyter, 2007.

————. "Between Jacob's Death and Moses' Birth: The Intertextual Relationship between Genesis 50:15–Exodus 1:14 and Jubilees 46:1-16." In *Dead Sea Scrolls and Other Early Jewish Studies in Honour of Florentino García Martínez*, edited by

Anthony Hilhorst, Émile Puech, and Eibert Tigchelaar, 467-89. JSJSup 122. Leiden: Brill, 2007.

Sanders, E. P. *Paul and Palestinian Judaism*, 362-86. Philadelphia: Fortress, 1977.

Sandmel, Samuel. *Philo's Place in Judaism: A Study of the Conceptions of Abraham in Jewish Literature*, 38-49. Cincinnati: Hebrew Union College Press, 1956; 2nd ed. 1971.

Saulnier, Stephane. "Jub 49:1-14 and the Second Passover: How (and Why) to Do Away with an Unwanted Festival." *Hen* 31, no. 1 (2009).

Schenker, Adrian. "Isaïe 63:9, le Livre des Jubilés et l'Ange de la face: est-ce-que le 'Livre des Jubilés' peut contribuer à la solution du problème textuel d'Is 63:9?" In *Studien zu Propheten und Religionsgeschichte*, 12-26. Stuttgart: Verlag Katholisches Bibelwerk, 2003.

Schiffman, Lawrence H. "The Sacrificial System of the Temple Scroll and the Book of Jubilees." In SBLSP 24 (1985), 217-33.

Schlund, Christine. *"Kein Knochen soll gebrochen werden": Studien zu Bedeutung und Funktion des Pesachfests in Texten des frühen Judentums und im Johannesevangelium*, 98-111. WMANT 107. Neukirchen-Vluyn: Neukirchener Verlag, 2005.

Schmidt, Francis. "Chronologies et périodisations chez Flavius Josèphe et dans l'apocalyptique juive." In *Aspetti della storiografia ebraica: atti del IV Congresso internazionale dell'AISG, S. Miniato, 7-10 novembre 1983*, edited by Fausto Parente, 125-38. Rome: Carucci editore, 1987.

———. "Naissance d'une géographie juive." In *Moïse géographe: Recherches sur les représentations juives et chrétiennes de l'espace*, edited by Alain Desreumaux and Francis Schmidt, 13-30. Etudes de psychologie et de philosophie 24. Paris: J. Vrin, 1988.

———. "Jewish Representations of the Inhabited Earth during the Hellenistic and Roman Periods." In *Greece and Rome in Eretz Israel: Collected Essays*, edited by Aryeh Kasher, Uriel Rappaport, and Gideon Fuks, 119-34. Jerusalem: Yad Izhak Ben-Zvi, 1990.

Schubert, Friedemann. "'El 'Aeljôn' als Gottesname im Jubiläenbuch.'" *FJMB* 8 (1994): 3-18.

———. *Tradition und Erneuerung: Studien zum Jubiläenbuch und seinem Trägerkreis*. Frankfurt am Main: Lang, 1998.

Schultz, Joseph P. "Two Views of the Patriarchs: Noachides and Pre-Sinai Israelites." In *Text and Responses: Studies Presented to N. N. Glatzer*, edited by M. A. Fishbane, 41-59. Leiden: Brill, 1975.

Schürer, Emile, and Geza Vermes. "The Book of Jubilees." In *The History of the Jewish People in the Age of Jesus Christ*, vol. 3, no. 1, pp. 308-18. Edinburgh: T. & T. Clark, 1986.

Schwartz, Joshua. "Jubilees, Bethel and the Temple of Jacob." *HUCA* 56 (1985): 63-85.

Schwarz, Eberhard. *Abgrenzungsprozesse in Israel im 2. vorchristlichen Jahrhundert und ihre traditionsgeschichtlichen Voraussetzungen. Zugleich ein Beitrag zur Er-*

forschung des Jubiläenbuches. European University Studies, Series XXIII, Theology 162. Frankfurt am Main: Peter Lang, 1982.

Scott, James M. "The Division of the Earth in Jubilees 8:11–9:15 and Early Christian Chronography." In *Studies in the Book of Jubilees,* edited by Matthias Albani, Jörg Frey, and Armin Lange, 295-323. TSAJ 65. Tübingen: Mohr Siebeck, 1997.

———. *Geography in Early Judaism and Christianity: The Book of Jubilees.* SNTSMS 113. Cambridge: Cambridge University, 2001.

———. *On Earth as in Heaven: The Restoration of Sacred Time and Sacred Space in the Book of Jubilees.* Leiden: Brill, 2005.

Segal, Michael. "Law and Narrative in *Jubilees:* The Story of the Entrance into the Garden of Eden Revisited" (in Hebrew). *Meghillot* 1 (2003): 111-25.

———. "The Book of Jubilees: Rewritten Bible, Redaction, Ideology and Theology" (in Hebrew). Ph.D diss., Hebrew University of Jerusalem, 2004.

———. "The Relationship between the Legal and Narrative Passages in Jubilees." In *Reworking the Bible: Apocryphal and Related Texts at Qumran; Proceedings of a Joint Symposium by the Orion Center for the Study of the Dead Sea Scrolls and Associated Literature and the Hebrew University Institute for Advanced Studies Research Group on Qumran, 15-17 January, 2002,* edited by Esther G. Chazon, Devorah Dimant, and Ruth A. Clemens, 203-28. STDJ 58. Boston: Brill, 2005.

———. "Between Bible and Rewritten Bible." In *Biblical Interpretation at Qumran,* edited by Matthias Henze, 10-28. Studies in the Dead Sea Scrolls and Related Literature. Grand Rapids: Eerdmans, 2005.

———. *The Book of Jubilees: Rewritten Bible, Redaction, Ideology, and Theology* (in Hebrew). Jerusalem: Magnes, 2007.

———. *The Book of Jubilees: Rewritten Bible, Redaction, Ideology, and Theology.* JSJSup 62. Leiden: Brill, 2007.

———. "The Chronological Redaction of the Book of Jubilees" (in Hebrew). In *Shai le-Sara Japhet: Studies in the Bible, Its Exegesis and Its Language,* edited by Moshe Bar-Asher, Dalit Rom-Shiloni, Emanuel Tov, and Nili Wazana, 369-87. Jerusalem: Bialik Institute, 2007.

Shatzman, Israel. "Jews and Gentiles from Judas Maccabaeus to John Hyrcanus according to Contemporary Jewish Sources." In *Studies in Josephus and the Varieties of Ancient Judaism: Louis H. Feldman Jubilee Volume,* edited by Shaye J. D. Cohen and Joshua J. Schwartz, 237-70. AGJU 67. Leiden: Brill, 2007.

Shemesh, Aharon. "4Q265 and the Book of Jubilees" (in Hebrew). *Zion* 73, no. 1 (2008): 5-20.

Skehan, Patrick W. "Jubilees and the Qumran Psalter." *CBQ* 37 (1975): 343-47.

Sollamo, Raija. "The Creation of Angels and Natural Phenomena Intertwined in the Book of Jubilees (4Qjub^a)." In *Biblical Traditions in Transmission: Essays in Honour of Michael A. Knibb,* edited by Charlotte Hempel and Judith M. Lieu, 273-90. JSJSup 111. Boston: Brill, 2006.

Steck, Odil Hannes. "Die getöteten 'Zeugen' und die verfolgten 'Tora-Sucher' in Jub

1,12: Ein Beitrag zur Zeugnis-Terminologie des Jubiläenbuches." *ZAW* 107, no. 3 (1995): 445-65; 108, no. 1 (1996): 70-86.

Stökl, Jonathan. "The Book Formerly Known as Genesis: A Study of the Use of Biblical Language in the Hebrew Fragments of the 'Book of Jubilees.'" *RevQ* 22, no. 3 (2006): 431-49.

Stone, Michael Edward. "The Book(s) Attributed to Noah." *DSD* 13 (2006): 4-23.

Stoyanov, Yuri. "Die Aufnahme von Genesis 1 in Jubiläen 2 und 4 Esra 6." *JSJ* 8 (1977): 154-82.

———. "The Treatment of the Element of Fire in Jubilees and 2 Enoch and Its Afterlife in Christian Pseudepigraphy." *Hen* 30, no. 2 (2008).

Sulzbach, Carla. "The Function of the Sacred Geography in the Book of Jubilees." *Journal for Semitics* 14, no. 2 (2005): 283-305.

Syrén, Roger. "Ishmael and Esau in the Book of Jubilees and Targum Pseudo-Jonathan." In *The Aramaic Bible: Targums in Their Historical Context,* edited by D. R. G. Beattie and M. J. McNamara, 310-15. Sheffield: JSOT Press, 1994.

Talmon, Shemaryahu. "The Calendar Reckoning of the Sect from the Judaean Desert." In *Aspects of the Dead Sea Scrolls,* edited by Chaim Rabin and Yigael Yadin, 162-99. Scripta Hierosolymitana 4. Jerusalem: Hebrew University, 1958.

Tedesche, Sidney. "Jubilees, Book of." In *IDB* 2 (1962), 1002-3.

Testuz, Michel. *Les idées religieuses du livre des Jubilés.* Geneva: Droz, 1960.

Thomas, Sam. "Enoch, Elijah, and the (Eschatological) Torah." *Hen* 31, no. 1 (2009).

Tigchelaar, Eibert J. C. "Jubilees and 1 Enoch and the Issue of Transmission of Knowledge." In *Enoch and Qumran Origins: New Light on a Forgotten Connection,* edited by Gabriele Boccaccini, 99-101. Grand Rapids: Eerdmans, 2005.

Tretti, Cristiana. "The Treasury of Heavenly Wisdom: Differing Modulations of the Concept From '1Enoch' and 'Jubilees' to Medieval Jewish Mysticism." *Hen* 31, no. 1 (2009).

Tyloch, Witold. "Quelques remarques sur la provenance essénienne du Livre des Jubilés." *RevQ* 13 (1988): 347-52.

Ulrich, Eugene Charles. *The Dead Sea Scrolls and the Origins of the Bible.* Studies in the Dead Sea Scrolls and Related Literature. Grand Rapids: Eerdmans, 1999.

Vallone, G. "Norme matrimoniali e Giubilei IV,15-33." *AION* 43 (1983): 201-15.

VanderKam, James C. *Textual and Historical Studies in the Book of Jubilees.* Missoula: Scholars Press, 1977.

———. "Enoch Traditions in Jubilees and Other Second-Century Sources." In *SBLSP* 13 (1978), 229-51.

———. "The Origin, Character, and Early History of the 364-Day Calendar: A Reassessment of Jaubert's Hypothesis." *CBQ* 41 (1979): 390-411.

———. "The Putative Author of the Book of Jubilees." *JSS* 26 (1981): 209-17.

———. "A Twenty-Eight-Day Month Tradition in the Book of Jubilees?" *VT* 32 (1982): 504-6.

———. "The Book of Jubilees." In *Outside the Old Testament,* edited by Marinus de

Jonge, 111-44. CCWJCW 4. Cambridge and New York: Cambridge University Press, 1985.

———. "Jubilees and Hebrew Texts of Genesis-Exodus." *Textus* 14 (1988): 71-85.

———. "Jubilees and the Priestly Messiah of Qumran." *RevQ* 13 (1988): 353-65.

———. "The Temple Scroll and the Book of Jubilees." In *Temple Scroll Studies: Papers Presented at the International Symposium on the Temple Scroll, Manchester, December 1987,* edited by G. J. Brooke, 211-36. JSPSup 7. Sheffield: JSOT Press, 1989.

———. "The Book of Jubilees." *Missouri Review* 15 (1992): 57-82. Reprinted in abridged form as "Jubilees: How It Rewrote the Bible," *Bible Review* 8, no. 6 (1992): 32-39, 60-62.

———. "Biblical Interpretation in 1 Enoch and Jubilees." In *The Pseudepigrapha and Early Biblical Interpretation,* edited by James H. Charlesworth and Craig A. Evans. JSPSup 14 = Studies in Scripture in Early Judaism and Christianity 2. Sheffield: JSOT Press, 1993.

———. "Genesis 1 in Jubilees 2." *DSD* 1 (1994): 300-321.

———. "Putting Them in Their Place: Geography as an Evaluative Tool." In *Pursuing the Text: Studies in Honor of Ben Zion Wacholder on the Occasion of His Seventieth Birthday,* edited by John C. Reeves, John Kampen, and Ben Zion Wacholder, 46-69. Sheffield: Sheffield Academic Press, 1994.

———. "Jubilees' Exegetical Creation of Levi the Priest." *RevQ* 17, no. 1-4 (1996): 359-73.

———. "The Aqedah, Jubilees, and PseudoJubilees." In *The Quest for Context and Meaning: Studies in Biblical Intertextuality in Honor of James A. Sanders,* edited by Craig A. Evans, Shemaryahu Talmon, and James A. Sanders, 241-61. Biblical Interpretation Series 38. Leiden: Brill, 1997.

———. "The Origins and Purposes of the Book of Jubilees." In *Studies in the Book of Jubilees,* edited by Matthias Albani, Jörg Frey, and Armin Lange, 3-24. TSAJ 65. Tübingen: Mohr Siebeck, 1997.

———. *Calendars in the Dead Sea Scrolls: Measuring Time.* Literature of the Dead Sea Scrolls. London: Routledge, 1998.

———. "Isaac's Blessing of Levi and His Descendants in Jubilees 31." In *The Provo International Conference on the Dead Sea Scrolls,* edited by Donald W. Parry and Eugene Ulrich, 497-519. Boston: Brill, 1999.

———. "The Angel Story in the Book of Jubilees." In *Pseudepigraphic Perspectives: The Apocrypha and Pseudepigrapha in Light of the Dead Sea Scrolls: Proceedings of the International Symposium of the Orion Center for the Study of the Dead Sea Scrolls and Associated Literature, 12-14 January, 1997,* edited by Esther G. Chazon, Michael E. Stone, and Avital Pinnick, 151-70. STDJ 31. Leiden: Brill, 1999.

———. "Covenant and Biblical Interpretation in Jubilees 6." In *The Dead Sea Scrolls Fifty Years After Their Discovery: Proceedings of the Jerusalem Congress, July 20-*

25, 1997, edited by Lawrence H. Schiffman, Emanuel Tov, and James C. VanderKam, 92-104. Jerusalem: Israel Exploration Society, 2000.

―――. "Studies in the Chronology of the Book of Jubilees." In *From Revelation to Canon: Studies in the Hebrew Bible and Second Temple Literature*, 522-44. JSJSup 62. Leiden: Brill, 2000.

―――. "Studies on the Prologue and Jubilees 1." In *For a Later Generation: The Transformation of Tradition in Israel, Early Judaism, and Early Christianity*, edited by Randal A. Argall et al., 266-79. Harrisburg, Pa.: Trinity, 2000.

―――. *The Book of Jubilees.* Guides to Apocrypha and Pseudepigrapha 9. Sheffield: Sheffield Academic Press, 2001.

―――. "The Demons in the 'Book of Jubilees.'" In *Die Dämonen: Die Dämonologie der israelitisch-jüdischen und frühchristlichen Literatur im Kontext ihrer Umwelt*, edited by Armin Lange, Hermann Lichtenberger, and K. F. Diethard Römheld, 339-64. Tübingen: Mohr Siebeck, 2003.

―――. "Response: Jubilees and Enoch." In *Enoch and Qumran Origins: New Light on a Forgotten Connection*, edited by Gabriele Boccaccini, 162-70. Grand Rapids: Eerdmans, 2005.

―――. "The Scriptural Setting of the Book of Jubilees." *DSD* 13, no. 1 (2006): 61-72.

―――. "The End of the Matter? Jubilees 50:6-13 and the Unity of the Book." In *Heavenly Tablets: Interpretation, Identity, and Tradition in Ancient Judaism*, edited by Lynn LiDonnici and Andrea Lieber, 267-84. JSJSup 119. Leiden: Brill, 2007.

―――. "Recent Scholarship on the Book of Jubilees." *Currents in Biblical Research* 6, no. 3 (2008): 405-31.

Vania Proverbio, Delio. "Gen. XV,19-21 = Jub. XIV,18: note miscellanee." *Hen* 14, no. 3 (1992): 261-72.

Venter, Pieter M. "Intertextuality in the Book of Jubilees." *HTS* 63, no. 2 (2007): 463-80.

Vermes, Geza. *Scripture and Tradition in Judaism: Haggadic Studies.* SPB 4. Leiden: Brill, 1961; reprint, 1973, 1983.

Vogt, Ernest. "Antiquum calendarium sacerdotale." *Bib* 36 (1955): 403-8.

Wacholder, Ben Zion. "How Long Did Abram Stay in Egypt?" *HUCA* 35 (1964): 43-56.

―――. "The Date of the Eschaton in the Book of Jubilees: A Commentary on Jub. 49:22-50:5, CD 1:1-10, and 16:2-3." *HUCA* 56 (1985): 87-101.

―――. "The Relationship between 11QTorah (the Temple Scroll) and the Book of Jubilees: One Single or Two Independent Compositions." In SBLSP 24 (1985), 205-16.

―――. "Jubilees as the Super Canon: Torah-Admonition versus Torah-Commandment." In *Legal Texts and Legal Issues: Proceedings of the Second Meeting of the International Organization for Qumran Studies, Cambridge 1995; Published in Honour of Joseph M. Baumgarten*, edited by Moshe Bernstein, Florentino García Martínez, and John Kampen, 195-211. STDJ 23. Leiden: Brill, 1997.

Weltner, Charles Longstreet. "A Textual Analysis and Comparative Study of the Joseph Narrative in the Ethiopic Book of Jubilees." Ph.D. diss., University of Dublin, 1988.

Werman, Cana. "Attitude towards Gentiles in the Book of Jubilees and Qumran Literature Compared with Early Tanaaic Halakha and Contemporary Pseudepigrapha" (in Hebrew). Ph.D. diss., Hebrew University of Jerusalem, 1995.

———. "Jubilees 30: Building a Paradigm for the Ban on Intermarriage." *HTR* 90, no. 1 (1997): 1-22.

———. "The 'Torah' and the 'Teudah' on the Tablets" (in Hebrew). *Tarbiz* 68, no. 4 (1999): 473-92.

———. "The Book of Jubilees in Hellenistic Context" (in Hebrew). *Zion* 66 (2001): 275-96.

———. "Teʿudah: On the Meaning of the Term." In *Fifty Years of Dead Sea Scrolls Research: Studies in Memory of Jacob Licht*, edited by Gershon Brin and Bilhah Nitzan, 231-43. Jerusalem: Izhak Ben Zvi, 2001.

———. "'The תורה and the תעודה' Engraved on the Tablets." *DSD* 9 (2002): 75-103.

———. "The *Book of Jubilees* and the Qumran Community" (in Hebrew). *Meghillot* 2 (2004): 37-55.

———. "Jubilees in the Hellenistic Context." In *Heavenly Tablets: Interpretation, Identity, and Tradition in Ancient Judaism*, edited by Lynn LiDonnici and Andrea Lieber, 133-58. JSJSup 119. Leiden: Brill, 2007.

Wiesenberg, Ernest. "The Jubilee of Jubilees." *RevQ* 3 (1961): 3-40.

Wirgin, Wolf. *The Book of Jubilees and the Maccabean Era of Shmittah Cycles.* LUOSMS, no. 7. Leeds: Leeds University Oriental Society, 1965.

Zeitlin, Solomon. "The Book of Jubilees and the Pentateuch." *JQR* 48 (1957-58): 218-35.

———. "The Beginning of the Day in the Calendar of Jubilees." *JBL* 78 (1959): 153-56.

———. "The Judaean Calendar during the Second Commonwealth and the Scrolls." *JQR* 57 (1966): 28-45. Reprinted in *Studies in the Early History of Judaism* 1 (New York: Ktav, 1973), 194-211.

Zuurmond, Rochus. "De misdaad van Ruben volgens Jubileeën 33:1-9." *Amsterdamse Cahiers* 8 (1987): 108-16.

———. "Asshur in Jubilees 13.1?" *JSP* 4 (1989): 87-89.

Index

Index

Index